MEDIEVAL EPICS

MEDIEVAL EPICS

BEOWULF
Translated by William Alfred

THE SONG OF ROLAND
Translated by W. S. Merwin

THE NIBELUNGENLIED
Translated by Helen M. Mustard

THE POEM OF THE CID
Translated by W. S. Merwin

THE MODERN LIBRARY · NEW YORK

THE MODERN LIBRARY

is published by

RANDOM HOUSE, INC.

Manufactured in the United States of America

Contents

BEOWULF

Translated, and with an introduction by,
William Alfred

Introduction

I

Beowulf is the only early Germanic epic left us. Like all epics, it celebrates the fidelity of a great man to an ideal of excellence. The classical description of that ideal, the principle of the *comitatus*, is set down by Tacitus in the thirteenth and fourteenth chapters of *Germania*, his treatise on the Germanic peoples of the first century, among whom were the forbears of the Anglo-Saxons:

They single out even boys for princely rank when there is special distinction in their families, or actions achieved by their fathers worthy of reward. These are gathered in bands around other men who are more solid and have stood up to tests over some period of time; and there is no cause for shame in appearing among such retainers. Quite the contrary, each band of retainers (Latin: *comitatus*) has ranks within it assigned by command of the man they follow; and a great source of rivalry among the retainers is whom the first place with the prince will fall to, and among the princes, whose band is the most numerous and the bravest of all. That is their idea of grandeur and power, always to be surrounded by a huge gathering of choice young followers, to lend them dignity in peace and protection in war. If a man's band of retainers is outstanding for numbers and valor, glory and reputation are his not only among his own people, but also among neighboring nations. Indeed such men are sought out in special missions, paid homage in gifts, and quite often all but decide wars by their great renown alone.

Once entered on the field of battle, it is disgraceful for a prince to be surpassed in bravery by his retainers, and disgraceful for the band of retainers not to match that bravery on their prince's part. It is infamy for one's whole life, and an everlasting source of reproach, to have left the field where one's prince has fallen. The first duty of their allegiance is to defend and keep their prince safe, and to lay their gallant actions to the glory of his name. The princes fight for victory, the retainers for their prince.

Fidelity to that proud and violent ideal brought glory, *dōm* as the Anglo-Saxons called it, the judgment of men on the deeds of their lifetime. In that glory, Beowulf lives and dies.

But, tempering the expression of that ideal in *Beowulf*, is the Christian coloring of the poem, the point of view of the Christian poet who composed it. The best embodiment of that point of view is the epitaph of the Abbot Alcuin (735-804), a friend and advisor of Charlemagne, and a near contemporary of the Beowulf-poet:[1]

Busy as you are, do not go yet. Please. Stay with me a moment.
Study these lines I wrote you when my blood beat.
Learn what life holds for men in these words set in order.
Looks go. They go. Yours will go as mine did.
What you are now, hurrying past this gravestone,
I was; and my name was known in every country.
And what I am now, you yourself must come to.
I looked for the world to be sweet with my heart like a spoiled child's.
Now frail as paper ash and spotted with wet dust

[1] The poem is freely translated from the Latin.

My blind skull hangs from the spine which is all that the
worms left
Of the nerves my imagination made such demands on.
Worry about your soul, not about your body,
For the will to love remains when the starved nerves stiffen.
Why clear yourself new fields? You can see as I do
How I must rest content with this pocket of clay here.
Why do you long, moist-eyed, for the day when your body
Will cuddle in silks died by snails' guts the color of sunset
When vermin mangles tough skin as moths do soft damask?
Flowers blacken with cold when the wind turns ugly;
And the flesh on your bones will bruise when death blows the
will out.
Will you do me a good turn for this song I have made you?
Will you please say, "Christ, be good to your dead servant"?
No man break into this tomb God cedes me to lie in,
Waiting for it to explode, that bugle beyond where the stars
end,
Reveille rousing the dead, and that shout from the mustering
angels:
"No matter how deep you may lie, get up from the dirt now;
Your great Judge is at hand amidst troops without number."
Alcuin was my name. I was always in love with wisdom.
Say a prayer for me that you mean when you read this writing.

The story upon which the Christian view of life is brought to
bear is as simple as the folktale of the Bear's Son (Beowulf means
"bee-wolf" or bear) which seems to have been its source. A young
Swedish prince rescues the fabled mead-hall of a great Danish king
from the depredations of an ogre-like creature descended from
Cain. When the creature's mother visits the hall in turn, seeking
vengeance, the Swedish champion tracks her to her den beneath
a lake and kills her. Fifty years or so later, now king of the Swedish
nation called the Götar, he himself is killed in slaying a fire-dragon
which has laid his country waste to avenge the violation of its
treasure-hoard. In his final battle, only one of his chosen companions stands by him in his need.
    The stark details of this fabulous biography are humanized by a
sensibility which understands how suffering and triumph work upon

men, and dignified by an imagination deeply versed in Germanic history and literature. The Beowulf-poet's grasp of his own literature is the chief source of difficulty in the poem: he merely alludes to complicated stories which are all but lost to us.

In the Finn-episode (pages 36 to 38), for instance, painstaking deductions of generations of scholars have yielded us but the barest working sense of the tale. The Frisian king, Finn, has married the Danish princess, Hildeburg. Hildeburg's brother, Hnaef, visits Finn's court with a company of retainers. There has apparently been bad blood between certain retainers of Finn, Jutish in nation, and the Danes. A battle between them flares up in which Hnaef is killed as well as the son of Hildeburg and Finn. Because of the imminence of winter, when the seas are impassable, an uneasy truce is made between the Danes and the Frisians, between Hengest, Hnaef's successor, and Finn. When the stormy weather breaks, two Danes, Guthlaf and Oslaf, sail home, and return to Frisia with reinforcements. Led by Hengest, they avenge Hnaef by killing Finn in his stronghold. They return home, taking Hildeburg with them.

Almost immediately succeeding that puzzling epitome of the tale of Finn, several lines follow in the augmented meter generally used by Old English poets to signal pathetic detail: "Then Wealhtheow made her progress, moving beneath her golden circlet, to where the two great men sat, the uncle and the nephew. Peace was as yet between them, each in good faith with the other." We know from Scandinavian sources that the Anglo-Saxon audience would have recognized in the last sentence quoted a reference to the story of Hrothulf's treachery to the survivors of Hrothgar, his uncle.

Again, the prophetic telling of the tale of Ingeld put into Beowulf's mouth (pages 57 to 59) is perplexingly oblique. All that it tells us is that the marital alliance between the Danish princess, Freawaru, and Ingeld, prince of the Heathobards, could not stand up beneath the burden of remembered bitterness between the two peoples.

That these three tales are accounts of blood-feuds which involve destructive conflicts between members of the same family would suggest that the brevity and indirection of the references to them is deliberate. That suggestion is confirmed when we consider that in every use of the narrative of the blood-feud, it is the tragic aspect of the tales that is emphasized and not the heroic. That emphasis on the pathetic taken together with the elegiac cast of the narrative structure of the poem would lead us to believe that one of the poet's main preoccupations is to reconstitute the heroic ideal held by himself and his audience.

The Beowulf-poet tells his story with a kind of structural irony which constantly alternates tragic with prosperous events. In his initial account of Hrothgar (see page 13), for example, Hrothgar is authoritatively set up as the heroic lord of a heroic *comitatus*. Such success as a soldier is his that he draws to himself a great band of young retainers eager for glory; and the size of that following dictates the construction of the "grandest of hall-buildings" to house them in. In his description of the construction of Heorot, the poet inobtrusively makes us aware of Hrothgar's domestic and foreign power: his word is law; and the task of adorning the hall is laid on many a people. And like his forbear, Beowa, his generosity matches his wealth. Thus far in his narration, the poet has been stressing the efficacy of fidelity to the ideal of the *comitatus*. But suddenly, what begins as a description of the lofty impressiveness of Heorot breaks down into an account of its destruction by fire in the feud with Ingeld. In that aposiopesis of viewpoint, that quick change of attitude, the poet betrays the moral cast of his imagination. Violence directed toward warfare for the preservation of order made Heorot possible; perverted toward feud, it will raze it to the ground.

Hard upon the poet's reference to the mere human feud which will destroy Heorot follows the first appearance of Grendel. Hrothgar, the heroic lord without peer, is about to enter upon a feud with the descendant of the father of the feud, Cain; and that feud will bring him, and with him the poet's audience, face to face, again and again, with the possible invalidity of his conviction of the full efficacy of the *comitatus*-ideal by which he lives.

It is Hrothgar's conviction of the *full* efficacy of the ideal, it must be emphasized, which the Beowulf-poet arranges his story to put to the test. The political actuality which governed the members of the poem's audience was some workable system or other based upon that ideal. And the drift of the poem is not revolutionary. The poet does not mean to undermine the *comitatus* by the mode and method of his narrative, merely to dramatize the vulnerability of any social ideal under mortal administration and the assaults of evil change and time.

Hrothgar best expresses that vulnerability in his sermon on pride (pages 51 to 52), which is not the least of the gifts offered Beowulf in gratitude for the defeat of Grendel's mother. He wishes to spare Beowulf the pain of such moments as he has lived through, moments in which the principles by which he ordered his life seemed meaningless. He is aware how hard it is for a man in the prime of youth, just returned, victorious and unscathed from a superhuman combat, to understand that all earthly victory is temporary and no man is forever safe. That is why he couches his address in delicately indirect terms. The "man of noble stock" whom he speaks of is, as we know from the end of the speech, himself; but it is also Beowulf, what Beowulf might become, what Beowulf in part does become. The relationship between Beowulf's pride of victory and the pride of life which characterized his own first fifty years as a king is what Hrothgar sees. And it is against that pride that he directs his moral song, because he knows from experience that a man must not fight to maintain himself, his dignity or self-esteem, his standing or his wealth, without first fighting against the true enemies of all men, nature inconsciently cruel, and the powers beyond nature which can infect the heart of man to make it nature's cruelest force. No matter how faithful one is to the material principles of the *comitatus,* no matter how daring one is in fulfilling the dictates of that ideal, hero or not, a man is still but a man, subject to wickedness, sickness, age and death. To realize that is to deepen one's heroism, for then one knows oneself to be standing up against savage odds, in a struggle in which physical defeat is swallowed up in moral victory.

The full burden of Hrothgar's meaning does not impress itself on Beowulf's mind until, mangled and dying, having, like the old lord, ruled fifty years, he speaks his last words to Wiglaf: "You are the last of our family left, of the Waegmundings. Fate has lured all my kinsmen to their death, great soldiers in their daring. I must go after them." His words are charged with bewilderment. The lines are incrementally arranged to emphasize that it is only at the instant of death that Beowulf understands that he must die. Incredulously, he faces fact after stark fact. Wiglaf is the only one of his family left. Fate has lured all his other kinsmen to their doom, though they were sterling men-at-arms. And he who did so many deeds of daring, who ruled his kingdom well for fifty years, and won great treasure for his people in this last mortal combat, he also must die. The just pagan hero dies dissatisfied with the sufficiency of the ideal by which he lived, dissatisfied but heroically resigned. Yet even in the depiction of Beowulf's death, the poet is not deprecating the *comitatus*-ideal. He is dramatizing what he believes to be a truth of experience: no secular ideal is sufficient to satisfy the hunger for conclusions of a heroic spirit faced with death. But though that hunger goes unsatisfied, the glory of its persistence in men remains. In the words of the Old English elegy, *The Wanderer,* "Good is the man who keeps faith to the end."

II

Beowulf is a national monument as well as poem. It was composed in the Anglian dialect of Old English some time in the second quarter of the eighth century, and has come down to us in a unique manuscript which is the work of two tenth-century West-Saxon scribes.[1] Its verse is the alliterative meter common to all old English poetry. Meaning is conveyed phrase by phrase, rather than word by word, and each phrase makes up a half line which is linked to a second half line by matching consonants or matching vowels (∠equals stressed; × equals unstressed; x́ lightly stressed):

Swa fela fyrena   fēond moncynnes,

atol āngengea,   oft gefremede

Thus, many felonies,   that foe to mankind,
that stalker all alone   often committed.

---

[1] The manuscript is one in a codex of five by the same two hands, three prose pieces: a fragmentary *Life of St. Christopher, The Wonders of the East,* the *Letter of Alexander the Great to Aristotle;* and two poems, *Beowulf* and a piece of *Judith.* In the sixteenth century, that codex was bound in with one containing four prose works in two scribal hands of the twelfth century. The volume is called Cotton Vitellius A XV, after its shelf-number in the collection of Sir Robert Bruce Cotton (1571-1631), who decorated the bays of his library with busts of Roman Emperors and Empresses. After Cotton's grandson bequeathed the collection to the nation in 1701, it was first housed in Essex House, and then in Ashburnham House, where it was damaged in a disastrous fire in 1731. It was transferred to the British Museum with the rest of the Cotton Collection in 1753.

Each half line contains two chief stresses. In accordance with the pattern into which the stresses fall, the German scholar Edouard Sievers catalogued these half lines into five chief types which he designated by the letters A through E.

Certain half lines are put to repeated use in *Beowulf* and in other poems. *Fēond moncynnes,* for example, appears three times, meaning "devil," in the metrical saint's life, *Juliana.* Struck by the high incidence of such repetitions, Albert Bates Lord applied certain tests to Old English poetry which Milman Parry had brought to bear on Homeric epic. He concluded that, like the *Iliad* and the *Odyssey* and the popular heroic verse of Jugoslavia, Old English poetry was, at least in its origins, oral-formulaic in nature, that is, that it was composed by unlettered singers from a memorized thesaurus of fixed phrases. These fixed phrases, following the terminology of Parry, Lord calls "formulas." A formula, in Parry's definition, is "a group of words which is regularly employed under the same metrical conditions to express a given essential idea." Despite strong evidence gathered by F. P. Magoun, Jr., and scholars working under him, in support of Lord's conclusion, its validity is still a disputed question.

WILLIAM ALFRED

Useful Works on Beowulf

R. W. Chambers, *Beowulf, An Introduction,* Cambridge, 1932.
John Collins Pope, *The Rhythm of Beowulf,* New Haven, 1942.
J. R. R. Tolkien, "Beowulf: the Monsters and the Critics," *Proceedings of the British Academy,* London, 1936.

This edition of *Beowulf* is made from two editions of the poem, that of F. Klaeber (New York: D. C. Heath & Co., 1941), and that of C. L. Wrenn (New York: D. C. Heath & Co., 1953).

BEOWULF

Listen. We have learned the song of the glory of the great kings of the Danes, how those princes did what was daring:

More than once, Scyld of the Sheaf pulled seats in the mead-hall out from beneath troops of his foes, tribe after tribe, struck fear into the Heruli themselves, after that time in the very beginning he was found in a bad plight. He lived to take comfort for that. He grew strong under the clouds, grew rich in men's esteem, until each of those settled around him across the whale's road had to obey him, had to pay him tribute. That was a good king.

A son was born to him, succeeding him young in the courts, whom God sent as a comfort to that people. God understood the wicked hardship which they had lived through before, for a long time without a lord. Because of that, the Lord of Life, the Governor of Glory, gave them honor in this world. Beowa was famous, Scyld's son. His splendor flowered far and wide, even to the lands where the Swedes lived.

By his goodness, by making brave and solid gifts, while he is in his father's charge, a young man will bring it about that in his old age comrades to his liking stay on with him, stand by their prince to the end when war comes. By deeds
25 worth praise, a man will make out really well among any kind of people.

Then at the time laid down by fate, Scyld, still very much a man to be reckoned with, went on the long voyage into the Lord's keeping. They bore him, then, to the beach, his own dear comrades, as he himself had bid them, when lord and friend of the Scyldings, he still had words in his power. Beloved prince of that land, he had held it long. There in harbor lay a prow that swirled up in a ring, their prince's vessel, plated with ice and pulling out towards sea. Then they laid the lord they loved in the lap of that ship, his back against the mast. Many treasures were brought there, jewels from far parts. I have heard of none fitting out a ship more handsomely with weapons of battle and clothing of war, with swords and with chain-mail. In his lap there lay a mass of treasures, which were fated to pass with him far out to the flood's possession. They appointed him gifts of no less price—national treasures—than those had done who at the outset, when he was but a child, had sent him traveling on alone across the waves. They set, besides, high over his head, a standard of gold. They let the sea-swell bear him off, gave him to the ocean. Theirs was a heart that
50 cried out, an anxious mind. No men, counselors in royal halls, heroes under heaven, can tell for a fact who hauled in that cargo.

Then Beowa of the Scyldings, that king loved by his people in their strongholds, was for a long time the talk of nations—his father had moved on elsewhere, that lord, away from his home—until, in turn, the noble Healfdene carried on his line. Grizzled and savage in war, he kept the Scyldings happy as long as he lived. Through him four children all told were brought into the world: those leaders of armies, Heorogar and Hrothgar, and Halga the Good; I have heard that one child was Onela's queen, the consort of the Swede who was good at war.

Then, luck in battle was granted Hrothgar, such esteem for his skill in war that the men in his command obeyed him promptly, until the force of young cadets grew at last into a great band of comrades. It came to his mind that he would have men build a hall building—that great mead-house which the children of men have always told tales about—and within it would deal out, to cadets as well as to veterans, shares of all things whatsoever God had granted him, except for the land which belonged to the whole people and the lives of his men. Then, I have heard the story that he laid the task of making that place of national assembly a thing of beauty on many a tribe scattered far and wide across this earth. In due time—quickly, for men—it came about that it was all ready, that grandest of hall-buildings. He who by his word alone held wide sway gave it the name of Heorot. Nor did he fall short of his boast. He dealt out golden armbands, treasure at the feasting. The hall soared upwards, noble and broad of gables. It stood waiting the battle surges of enemy fire. Still this was not yet the time when, because of the murderous attack, the feud between son-in-law and father-in-law was fated to break out.

This was the time when the demon of daring who loitered in shadows found it hard to put up with the noise of good cheer he heard loud in the hall day after day after day.

The crowding swell of the harp was there, lucid song by a master-singer. He had his say who knew how to tell the tale of the creation of men in time far off. He said that the Almighty made this earth a field so bright with beauty that the water embraces it. Rejoicing in mastery, He set sun and moon as lights to temper darkness for dwellers in this land, and filled the corners of earth with a fair tracery of branches and leaves. He also put life into every kind of creature which moves about alive.

Thus the men of that band of comrades lived happily in the noise of good cheer, until a certain fiend out of hell began to do wicked things. That furious demon was called Grendel, a famous stalker through waste places, who held the rolling marshes in his sway, his fen and his stronghold. A man cut off from joy, he had ruled the domain of his huge misshapen kind a long time, since God had condemned him in condemning the race of Cain. For the murder in which he struck down Abel, the Everlasting Lord took full vengeance on Cain: he felt no glow of satisfaction in his feuding. Instead, the Umpire of Fate drove him far from the race of man for that crime. Thence sprang into being all misbegotten things, ogres and malign elementals, and ghouls who prowl the night in stolen corpses; those giant creatures, also, who for a long time waged war against God. He paid them full pay for that.

After night came down, he went then to take stock of that lofty house, to see how the Danes in their golden armbands had settled into it after the noble toasts they had drunk in beer. He came upon a full complement of princes there, sleeping after the feast. They knew nothing of sorrow, the lame fate of men. That creature beyond salvation, furious and ravening, was ready at once; and, wild and relentless, swept thirty noble retainers away in their sleep. From there he went marching back to his domain, gloating over the kill, scouting out the way to his haunts with that full feed of corpses.

Then, in the half-light towards the break of day, Grendel's skill in warfare was no secret to men. Then, after the feasting, the weeping arose, a crowding swell of tears in the morning. That famous lord, that prince who had always been good in trouble, sat with the joy drained out of him. Majestic in strength though he was, he brooked it, put up with the sorrow he felt for his murdered noble retainers, after they had had a good look at the track left by that foe, the track of a demon with God's curse upon him. That conflict was too hard, too loathsome, and too relentless. There was no very long respite. But after a single night, he returned to wreak greater malice, atrocity and wickedness. And he never felt a moment's pang about it; he was too far gone in those things.

Then it was easy to find a man who sought rest in some other place a little more out of the way, a bed somewhere off towards the married men's quarters, when the malignity of the new retainer in their hall was driven home to them, was proven the solid truth by evidence clear as day. The man who had escaped that devil kept himself at a greater distance and with more care after that.

Thus he lorded it over them, and fought in the teeth of all justice, one against them all, until that best of houses stood empty. It was a long time. The space of twelve years, the lord of the Scyldings put up with that bitter provocation, one kind of calamity on another, sorrows that touched almost everyone. No secret, therefore, it came to be known, in songs sadly sung, to the children of men that Grendel had been waging war against Hrothgar for some time, had, one half of a year after another, been making attacks filled with hate, wickedness and atrocity, a campaign without respite. And he had no intention of holding back his fatal malice from any man in the Danish force as an offer of peace, of coming to terms by paying his fine. And no man who was truly wise there felt any call to expect a noble settlement from the hands of that murderer. Instead, the terrible creature, that shadow of death, was bent on hunting down hardened veterans and young cadets alike. He lay in wait and ambushed them. He ruled the misty rolling marshes in their unbroken night. Men do not know where Hell's strange creatures stalk on their rounds.

Thus that devil to mankind, that hateful stalker alone, often wrought outrages hard to bear. He made Heorot his haunt in the black nights, that hall bright with treasure. Not that he might approach the throne where the gifts were given. No award of treasure or show of Hrothgar's love might he know, because of the Umpire of Fate.

That was a great torment to the lord and friend of the Scyldings, a thing which was breaking his spirit. Many a mighty man sat down with him in many a private meeting. They thought hard about some course of action: what it might be best for men of noble souls to do against these sudden and ghastly forays. From time to time, at heathen sanctuaries, they came right out and promised blood-sacrifices, put into words the prayer that the Demon-Slayer should be of help to them in the face of this disaster striking at the whole people. Such was their religion, such was hope among the heathens. They had hell in their hearts. They knew nothing of the Umpire of Fate, the Judge of Deeds;

150

175

they had no knowledge of the Lord God. In any case, they were incapable of worshiping the Protector in Heaven, the Governor of Glory.

It will go ill with him who must, driven to it by some cruel assault, thrust his soul into the embrace of the fire, not fixing his hope on comfort, on things changing. It will go well with him who, after the day of his death, is allowed to make his way to the Lord, and move by desire towards refuge in the embrace of the Father.

Thus the son of Healfdene fed his mind without pause with the bitter trouble of that time. Nor could that hero, with his gift of foresight, turn those troubles aside. The conflict was too hard, loathsome and relentless which had befallen that people, a torment laid on them like fate, cruel as hate itself, the worst atrocity night can bring.

Far off in his domain, a noble retainer of Hygelac, a man of some repute among the Götar, heard that tale of Grendel's deeds. As to his gifts, he was the strongest of mankind in that day of this life, a man of nobility and of more than ordinary powers. He had them build him a stout boat to cross the waves in. He said that he meant to make his way across the swan's road to that king of battles, that famous lord, at this time when his need for men was great. People of foresight did not for a second dissuade him from that expedition, even though he did happen to be dear to them. They urged on that man bent on bravery; they looked at it as a piece of luck. The gallant man had picked champions, the bravest he could find in the whole nation of the Götar. Not the least of fifteen, he made his way to the sea-worthy timbers. That warrior, a man very knowledgeable about currents, laid their course with an eye to the shores they would coast.

The time allotted passed day by day. The vessel was launched on the waves, that boat, in the lee of the bluff. Fully equipped, the men boarded her by the prow. The tides turned, the sea churned against the sand. Fighting men were carrying their bright, handsome trappings into the hull of the ship, their splendid war-gear; soldiers were shoving off, men on a voyage to their liking, shoving the lashed timbers off. Then, across the wave's swell, very like a bird,

sped by the wind, the boat went sailing, collared with foam,
till on schedule, on the second day, its well-lashed prow
had reached the point where those sailors caught sight of
land, sea-cliffs shimmering, towering bluffs, spits nosing far
out to sea. The sea had been crossed, then, right on course
to their destination. The men from the Weders, accordingly,   225
leaped ashore fast, moored the sea-worthy timbers—their
chain-mail rang, their fighting-clothes. They gave thanks to
God that this crossing of the waves had turned out easy for
them.

Then from the embankment, the Scylding Coast-Guard,
whose duty it was to guard the cliffs by the sea, caught
sight of them carrying their glittering shields down the gang-
plank, war-equipment ready for use. Worry pressed him
hard with deep concern what kind of men these might be.
He then took off for the shore, riding his steed, Hrothgar's
noble retainer. With gestures of dignity, he shook the spear
of his authority above his head; in words of formal parley,
he put his question:

"What kind of men are you, carrying arms, dressed in
chain-mail, who have come here this way, along the road
the currents lay, bringing that towering keel in across the
swells of the sea? I have been the border-lookout for some
time, have kept watch by the sea in such a way that no
enemy has ever been able to do damage in the land of the
Danes with a force off a ship. No armed men have ever undertaken to land here in a more public way. And you certainly could not have had any knowledge of permission
from our wagers of war, of consent from our kinsmen. I
have never on earth laid eyes on a noble fighting man of
greater stature than one of you is, that warrior in the armor.
That is no hall-soldier, made to look of some account by   250
weapons, unless his looks lie, his noble build. Now rather
than that you should proceed any further from here into the
land of the Danes, and turn out to be spies, I really must
know the nation of your birth. Now hear my frank opinion,
you men who live far off, you crossers of the sea: speed is
best in making known the places that you come from."

The senior man answered him, the leader of the band
unlocked his store of words:

"As to our people, we are men of the Götar, and the
household troops of Hygelac. My father was renowned
among nations, the noble leader of armies called Ecgtheow.
He lived a great many years out before he went on his way
from his courts, an old man. Almost anyone who knows
anything anywhere on earth certainly remembers him. We
have come seeking out your lord, the son of Healfdene,
protector of his people, with an honorable end in view. Be
so good as to tell us the things we need to know. The mission
we have to the famous lord of the Danes is an important
one. And there need be no great secret about it, so far as I
can see. You will know, if it is as we have heard it told as
fact, that among the Scyldings, some enemy, what kind I do
275 not know, a mysterious creature who turns his hatred into
deeds, is, in a reign of terror on dark nights, making a great
show of malignity hard to fathom, outrageousness, and
downright murder. Because my mind is undistracted, I can
give Hrothgar good advice about that, how he, wise and
good man that he is, will overcome his enemy, how the hot
waves of trouble will slacken—if any turn in fortune has
ever been fated, any remedy been fated to follow. Otherwise forever after that, through a bad time of hardship, he
will put up with a disastrous fate as long as that best of
houses remains there on that noble place."

The Guard addressed him, from the steed he sat on
there, an officer now relieved of worry:

"A sharp soldier on guard who thinks straight has to recognize any gap between words and actions. I know from
what I have heard that this is a band friendly to the lord of
the Scyldings. Pass on, wearing your arms and your armor.
I will show you the way. I will also have these noble retainers, my comrades, guard your boat against any kind of
foe, with strict attention to duty; guard that freshly caulked
vessel in the shallows until its timbers with their lashed
prow carry this dear man back along the currents of the sea
to the Weder shore. It is always granted to men like him
300 bent on doing good to come through the clash of battle unscathed."

They went on their way then. Safe, the vessel lay to, rode

on its mooring, broad-beamed ship that it was, fast to its anchor. Boar-crests glittered above their face-guards. Encrusted with gold, bright and forged in the fire, the crests kept watch over their lives. Bent on battle, their hearts were high. The men hurried, went inland together, until they were able to make out the timbered hall, stately and worked with gold. To dwellers on earth, it was the most famous of all the buildings under heaven. In it, that great man dwelt. The splendor of it cast light across many countries.

The man brave in battle had, then, showed them the way to the bright manor-house of great spirits to the point where they might go straight to it. Not the least of soldiers in a fight, he turned his steed, and spoke these words over his shoulder: "It is time for me to go. May the Father Almighty with a show of favor keep you safe in your exploits. I will go back to the sea, keep watch for an enemy force."

The road was handsomely paved with stones; the path pointed the way to those men in formation. Their war-shirts shone; tough and locked in place by hand, the bright iron of the rings sang in their chain-mail. Then they went marching right up to the hall in their terrible outfits. Tired by their crossing, they set their wide shields with the war-proof rims against the building's wall. When they sank down to the bench, their chain-mail rang, battle-gear fit for soldiers. The spears remained, pirates' weapons, ashwood gray from the shaft on. That troop dressed in iron was turned into something to be reckoned with by its weapons.

Then a proud hero questioned those who were not the kind to back down as a man should question heroes: "Where have you brought those plated shields from, those gray mail-shirts, those cruel-looking helmets, that mass of spears? I am Hrothgar's herald and officer. I have never seen so many men from foreign parts of such great spirit. I think you have sought Hrothgar out from self-respect; not because of exile for some crime, but out of the greatness of your hearts."

Bent on daring, the proud prince of the Weders answered; stern beneath his helmet, he spoke these words in reply: "We are Hygelac's personal retainers. Beowulf is my

325

name. I want to tell the son of Healfdene, that famous lord
your prince, my mission, if he will grant us permission to
meet with him, so great a man as he is."

Wulfgar addressed them, a man with Wendel blood in
him he was, his character had been brought home to many
350 a man, his showing in war and his wisdom:

"I will ask the lord and friend of the Danes, the Scylding
prince, giver of golden armbands, our famous lord, exactly
what you petition with regard to your journey here; and I
will promptly let you know the answer which that great man
deems fit to give you." He moved off quickly, then, to
where Hrothgar sat, old and very gray, among his company
of noble fighting men.

Distinguished for his daring, he went and took his stand
before the shoulders of the prince of the Danes. He was
fully aware of good usage among real soldiers. Wulfgar addressed his lord and friend: "Men of the Götar have made
it here, come from far across the circling stretch of the sea.
Not the kind to back down, they call their senior man,
Beowulf. They are making this petition, that they be allowed, my lord, to exchange words with you. Do not refuse
them the right of an audience with you, gracious Hrothgar.
In their battle-trappings, they look worthy to be highly
thought of by noble fighting men. At any rate, the lord who
led those soldiers here is worth something."

Hrothgar made his address, protector of the Scyldings: "I
knew him when he was a boy. His father was called Ecgtheow, to whose dominion Hrethel of the Götar gave his
375 only daughter. Now his son has come here for a serious
purpose; he has found a lord and friend who will be devoted to him. Besides, sailors who brought gifts of money
from the Götar to this place as a show of thanks, have said
that when bent on war, he has the gift of the strength of
thirty men in the grip of his hand. So far as I can judge,
Holy God has sent him to us Danes as a show of mercy
against the horror of Grendel. I shall offer him treasures for
the bravery in his heart. Be quick about it; have them come
in and see this band of sworn comrades in its full complement. Make it plain to them in your words that they are
welcome among the Danish people."

Wulfgar then went to the doors of the hall; he proclaimed the message from within: "My glorious lord, the prince of the Danes, has bid me tell you that he knows your noble family, and that you all are welcome, having come here to him across the swells of the sea with a serious purpose in your minds. You are given leave to march in in your battle gear, your war-masks on your heads, to have audience with Hrothgar. Leave your shields, your wood, your murderous shafts here, abiding the outcome of your interview."

That great man arose then, many a hero around him, a majestic troop of noble retainers. Some remained there,   400
guarded the armor, as the stern man commanded. When the man had shown them the way, they hastened in formation under the roof of Heorot. That man brave in battle moved in, stern beneath his helmet, till he stood in the hall. Beowulf made his address—his chain-mail glittered on him, that net of battle meshed through the smith's skill:

"Hail, Hrothgar. I am Hygelac's kinsman and close retainer. I have undertaken many things which brought me fame in my youth. This business with Grendel came to be known to me with nothing left out, on my native soil. Sailors are saying that this hall, this finest of buildings, stands empty and useless to any man once the brightness of heaven goes under, the glow of the twilight is quenched. My men have been advising me—very fine men, wise people, my lord Hrothgar—that I should seek you out, because they know the power of a certain gift of mine. They themselves looked on when, blood-stained from my foes, I came out of several ambushes. On that occasion, I took five captive; I destroyed a whole family of ogres; and at night I killed water-monsters in the waves. I came through that hard time with no quarter given. I was taking vengeance for their attack on the Weders. They were asking for trouble. I pounded those wild foes to dust. And now with Grendel, this terrible creature, this giant, I feel the need to hold a   425
meeting on my own. Now then, king of the glorious Danes, bulwark of the Scyldings, I want to beg this one favor of you: that, protector of soldiers that you are, lord and friend of whole nations, now that I have got this far, you do not

refuse me, and this company of noble fighting men of mine, this stern troop, permission that I alone cleanse Heorot. I have also discovered that this terrible creature, because of some recklessness in him, has never bothered himself about weapons. Therefore, I think it contemptible—may my liege-lord, Hygelac, be glad for me on that account—that I should wear a sword, or broad shield with yellow border to this fight. Instead, by the strength of my grasp, I will come to grips with the enemy, and, foe facing foe, fight for life. On that occasion, he whom death takes must hope for justice from God. I think it likely that, if he is allowed to win out, he will devour the men of the Götar without flinching, as he has more than once done the best strength of your glorious men. You will have no need to cover my face. On the contrary, if death takes me, he will have me, covered with blood. He will act as bearer to my bleeding corpse. He will make the plans for burying it. Stalking alone, he will 450 devour it without a second thought; he will foul the pools of the rolling marsh with my blood. You will have no need at all to worry at any great length about the feast to be held over my remains. If battle should take me, send on to Hygelac this best of war-shirts which protects my breast, this finest of garments. It was left me by Hrethel; it is Weland's work. Fate always goes as it must."

Hrothgar made his address, protector of the Scyldings: "You have sought us out, my honored friend, Beowulf, for the sake of fighting in our defense, and as a show of God's mercy. Your father struck the last blow in one of the greatest of feuds: in a hand-to-hand fight among the Wylfings, he was the death of Heatholaf. At that time, the nation of the Weders could not keep him, because of their horror of invasion. From there, he made it across the roll of the waves to the nation of the Danes, the Scyldings with their sense of honor. I was then first ruling the Danish people. And in my youth I kept this jewel of a kingdom well, this stronghold of heroes. Heorogar was dead then. My older brother. The life gone out of him. Healfdene's son—he was better than I. After that I settled the feud by paying the fine; I sent old things of great value to the Wylfings on the water's back. He swore oaths to me. It is an affliction to my heart to

tell any man what outrages, what vicious raids Grendel has   475
visited upon Heorot. My household troops, my band of
good soldiers, has been sapped of its strength. Fate swept
them away in this horror with Grendel. God could with
ease cut that crazy killer off in his deeds! Over and over
again, men, not the kind to back down, having drunk noble
toasts in beer, have vowed over the ale-cup that they would
wait out their time to fight Grendel with the blades of their
terrible swords. Yet, in the morning, when the dawn glistened, this mead-hall, this meeting place of a brave company, was dripping with gore, every board of the floor beneath these benches spattered with blood, the hall bleeding
as if from the sword. That is why I have fewer devoted men
in this dear force of true soldiers, because death has taken
those off. Sit down now at the feast, and fix your mind on
victory won by glorious fighters, that your heart may move
you that way."

A bench was then cleared in that hall of noble toasts for
all the Götar together. There those strong-souled men,
proud in their strength, went to sit. A noble retainer who
bore a well-worked ale-cup in his hands looked to his duty:
he poured out the bright liquor. At times, a singer broke
into song, clear as light in Heorot. A noise of good cheer
among heroes was there, no small band of true soldiers,
both Danes and Weders.

Unferth made an address, Ecglaf's son, who was sitting   500
at the feet of the lord of the Scyldings. He let loose his
hidden rancor. This expedition of the great-spirited seafarer
Beowulf was a great source of insult to him, because he
could not grant that any other man on earth had ever done
more deeds worthy of fame than himself.

"Are you the Beowulf who had the contest with Breca,
who challenged him to a swimming match on the open sea,
in which the both of you, out of pride, put the swells to the
test, and for a crazy boast risked your lives in deep water?
Not a single man, friend or foe, could talk you two out of
that wretched business. You paddled out to sea, then, both
of you. There you embraced the rushing current in your
arms, did laps over courses, the sea lays, thrashed around
with your hands. You shot through the ocean. The sea

welled up in big waves, with the winter surges. Both of you struggled seven nights in the water's possession. He won out over you in swimming—he had the greater gift of strength —when in the morning, a breaker bore him to the land of the Heathoraemas. From there, dear as he was to his men, he made his way to his own beloved country, the land of the Brondings, a handsome place of refuge, where he had power over a people, a stronghold, and riches. The son of Beanstan did, as a matter of fact, completely carry out the
525 boast he had made regarding you. I therefore expect worse results from you, if you dare wait for Grendel at close quarters one whole night long, even though you have proven yourself so strong on every occasion in the on-slaughts of battle, in grim warfare."

Beowulf made an address, Ecgtheow's son: "Well, my distinguished friend Unferth, having drunk noble toasts in beer, you have had a very great deal to say about Breca. You have told us all about his exploit. I hold that the real truth is that I had greater strength at sea, had more hard-ships than any other man. As children, the two of us did resolve, and we made solemn vows—we were still in our boyhood—that we would risk our lives out on the ocean. And we did just that. We held our unsheathed swords sternly in our hands when we paddled out to sea: we planned to defend ourselves against the whales. He was not able even driven by the waves of the current to swim ahead of me, much less in the heavy sea. And I simply would not swim away from him. At that time, we were both together in the sea five whole nights until the current drove us apart, and the wind veered north, as cruel as war, the water breaking in waves, the coldest of gales, the night growing pitch-black. The waves were rough. The temper of the
550 deep-sea fish was roused. On that occasion, my tough hand-meshed shirt was a help to me against foes. This woven battle-garment, worked with gold, rested on my breast. A furious demon of a foe dragged me to the bottom. Savage in his grip, he held me fast. However, it was granted me that I should get to him with the point of my blade, my war-sword. By my hand, that attack was the death of a mighty sea-beast.

"Again and again, enraged assailants pressed me hard in the same way. I served them with my good sword as was fitting. By no means, had they the pleasure of feasting on me to the fill, those voracious monsters. They never sat down to their feast towards the depths of the sea. Instead, in the morning, wounded by the blade, they lay in the flotsam sworded asleep so that never afterwards might they put a stop to the voyaging of sailors here and there across the deep ford of the sea. Light broke from the east, God's bright beacon. The waves let up, so that I could make out land nosing out to sea, windy embankments. Fate often protects a noble fighting man whose time has not run out, when his daring proves strong. At any rate, it was granted me that I should strike down nine sea-monsters with my sword. I have never heard a song about harder fighting by night under the vault of heaven, nor of a man in worse plight in the currents of the sea. Yet I did get through the grip of those foes with my life, tired out though I was with that exploit. Then the sea, the current along the shore, the water breaking in waves, bore me in to the land of the Lapps.   575

"I have never heard a thing said about such tricky battles on your part, such horrible bouts with the sword. In the give and take of battle, Breca has never yet, nor has either of you, ever, with your pretty swords, done so bold a deed —not that I am boasting of that—even though you did happen to prove the death of your own brother, your closest kin. For that you will suffer banishment in hell, no matter how strong your wit may be.

"I tell you, in all honesty, Ecglaf's son, that Grendel, that cruel, terrible creature, would never have visited so many horrors upon your lord, so many outrages on Heorot, if your purpose, your character, were so grim in a tricky fight as you yourself think it. But he has discovered that he need have no serious fear of retaliation, of any cruel show of armed violence on the part of your men, the victorious Scyldings. He takes his toll of the Danish people. He spares none. Instead, he works his own sweet will, kills and dispatches, and expects no resistance from the Danes, those good spearmen. But now, before very long, I will bring   600 home to him in battle the strength and the daring of the Götar. He who may will go in high spirits to his mead, when, tomorrow, the full light of morning, the sun robed in brilliance, shines from the south above the children of men."

Then the giver of treasure, gray-haired and distinguished in war, was in a state of joy. The prince of the glorious Danes counted on his help: the shepherd of his people knew from what he heard the steadfast purpose in Beowulf. At that point, there was laughter among the heroes; the sound of it rang sweet; joyous were the words spoken. Wealhtheow, Hrothgar's queen, moved forth. Crowned with gold, she greeted the men in the hall, fully acquainted as she was with their families. And then the noble lady first gave the cup to the keeper of the domain of the Danes, bade him be joyful at the noble drinking of the beer, dear as he was to people. He partook of the feast and the hall-cup with pleasure, that king famed for victory. The lady of the Helmings then went around to every group of the veterans and cadets, gave them the precious flagon, until the time came when she, that queen, perfect of spirit, crowned with a circlet of gold, bore the mead-cup to Beowulf. She greeted the prince of the Götar. Proven wise in her words, she gave thanks to God because that desire of hers that she might count on some one noble fighting man for comfort from these black crimes had come to pass. He partook of the cup at Wealhtheow's hands, that soldier fierce as death; and then, inspired by the spirit of battle, broke into speech.

Beowulf made an address, Ecgtheow's son: "I made up my mind when I set out on the heavy sea, when I took my place among this band of my men, that I should either carry out the will of your people, or, fast in the demon's grasp, crumple in death. I shall do daring worthy of a noble soldier, or live my last day out in this mead-hall." Those words pleased the lady well, those remarks made for glory by the man of the Götar. Crowned with gold, the noble queen of that people went to sit by her lord.

Then after that words of self-respect were spoken within that hall as before. The people were in a state of joy. There was a rising sound of merriment from both victorious nations till presently the son of Healfdene made known his will to go to his night's rest. He had been aware of the attack by that terrible creature ordained for the noble hall ever since they last could see the light of the sun, and, night deepening above all things, shapes like shadowy helmets 650 had come stalking, lightless, under the clouds. All the company rose. There one man took leave of the other, Hrothgar, of Beowulf, and wished him luck, power over the wine-hall, and made this speech: "From the time when I could raise my hand and my shield, I have never before entrusted this hall of Danish majesty to any man except now to you. Have and hold this finest of houses now. Fix your mind on action worthy of fame. Make plain the daring that is your gift. Be on strict guard against your foe. You will not lack pleasing things, if you come through this deed of daring with your life."

Then among his company of heroes, Hrothgar, the bulwark of the Scyldings, departed the hall. He has minded to seek out as his bed-fellow Wealhtheow the queen.

Thus as men have heard had God, the Glory of Kings, opposing Grendel, appointed a keeper for that hall. He was standing his special tour of duty for the lord of the Danes. He had offered himself as a guard against the ogre! Deeply indeed did the prince of the Götar believe in his brave gift of strength, that grace granted him by the Umpire of Fate.

Then he took off his shirt of iron mail, took the helmet off his head, yielded his ornamented sword to the noble retainer, his orderly, and bade him guard that battle gear. Then before he climbed on to his bed, that great man, 675 Beowulf of the Götar, uttered a sacred boast of no mean account: "As to spoils of battle and works of war, I hold myself no cheaper than Grendel does himself. Therefore not by the sword will I put him to sleep, cancel his life, though I have that all in my power. He has no sense of the good ways that he might strike at me, cut my shield through, no matter how stout he may be in acts of wicked assault. But on this night we two will forgo the sword, if he dares look for this fight without weapons. And then may God in His wisdom, our holy Lord, award fame on whatever hand seems right to Him." Bold in a battle, he laid him down. The pillow received the face of that noble fighting man. And around him many a vigorous sailor curled up on his bed in the hall. Not one of them thought that it would be his lot ever to make his way again to the native land he loved, the nation or noble stronghold where he was reared, for they had heard that before death by massacre had taken far too many Danish men in that wine-hall. Yet the Lord gave the lot of success in warfare to them, comfort and help to the men of Weders, so that through the strength of one man,

700 through his own power, they all vanquished their foe. It is the revealed truth that Almighty God has always ruled the race of man.

In the lightless night he came stalking, that strider in shadows. The archers slept whose duty it was to guard that gabled hall; all slept but one. It was known to men that when the Umpire of Fate had not willed it, that ghastly assailant might not drag them beneath the shadows. But that man standing watch, in a rage with the foe, waited with his temper up the outcome of the battle.

Then off the rolling marsh under banks of mist Grendel came marching. He bore the anger of God. That wicked assailant had it in mind to get some man in that noble hall in his toils. He made his way under the clouds to where he knew for certain that golden hall of men was, with its plating glistening. That was not the first time that he had made it to Hrothgar's home. In all the days of his life, before or since, he never came upon noble retainers in a hall with worse luck. Then he went moving in on the mansion, a man cut off from the noise of good cheer. Held fast by forged clasps, the door flew in the moment he touched it with his hands. With murder on his mind—his blood was up then— he rushed through the mansion's entrance. After that, he

725 quickly stepped on to the beautiful floor. He moved in, with an angry heart. From his eyes, very like flame there shot a light not pretty to see. He took a good look at the many men in that mansion, that band of soldiers all sleeping together in fellowship, that troop of fighting comrades. Then his heart laughed. When the hope for a feed to the fill struck him, he made up his mind, that cruel terrible creature, that before dawn came, he would have the life out of

the body of every single one of them. It was not Fate, however, that he be allowed to make the race of men his meat
beyond that night. Hygelac's kinsman, that man of proven
power, was studying how the wicked assailant would behave in the course of sudden attacks. Nor did the terrible
creature mean to delay, but, for his first exploit, quickly
seized a sleeping man, resistlessly tore him open, bit through
what cased his bones, and swallowed him one lump after
another. In an instant, he had fully fed on the lifeless man,
even the feet and the hands.

Nearer and nearer he kept advancing. He made a grab
at the stout-hearted man on his bed. The demon reached
for him with his hand. He quickly received him with damage in mind, and brought his full weight to bear against the
monster's arm. All at once, that master of wickedness dis-   750
covered that he had never come on a stronger hand-grasp
on this planet, in any other man in the regions of earth. In
his heart, he was afraid for his life. For all that, he could not
get away from there any the sooner. His mind was eager to
be off; he wanted to flee to cover, find company among
devils. His experience there was not such as he had ever
before come up against in all the days of his life. The great
kinsman of Hygelac then remembered his speech that evening. He stood up to his full height and got a firm hold upon
him. The ogre's fingers burst. He was bent on getting away:
the noble warrior followed him step by step. The famous
creature was minded to get as far out of his grasp as he
could, and flee that place into the pools of the fen. He was
well aware that the control of his fingers was in the grasp of
a savage foe. It was a sorry expedition that the heinous assailant had made to Heorot. As to all those Danes, those
who dwelt in that stronghold, every bold, noble warrior,
theirs was a full cup of ale. The mansion shook with noise.
It was a great wonder that the wine-hall held up under
those wildly fighting men, that it did not fall to earth; but it
was braced within and without with iron hasps made by   775
smiths with careful planning. In my version of the story, at
that point many a mead-bench, studded with gold, re-
bounded from the floor where the furious men were strug-
gling. The Scylding-counselors had never before thought

that any man could ever by any means break up that splendid bone-decked mansion, by any stratagem wrench it apart, unless the embrace of flame should have swallowed it in fire. Time and time again, a strange uproar rose. A frightful terror pierced the Danes, those who were listening to the outcry from the rampart, to God's adversary bellowing his hideous song, singing a song that rang with no triumph, Hell's prisoner weeping for pain. He who by reason of his gift was the strongest of men in that day of this life had a fast hold upon him.

The protector of noble warriors would not have let that murderous visitor off alive for any payment of amends; nor did he feel that the days of his life were of use to people of any kind. Then one noble warrior of Beowulf's after another drew old swords that had been handed down to them. Each was bent on defending the life of the prince their lord, their famous captain, at whatever point they could. They did not know when they were putting up that fight, those 800 tough-minded veterans, and meaning to hack at him from every side, to flush out his soul, that not one single choice iron on earth, no war-sword at all, could ever touch him, for he had laid a spell on glorious weapons, on everything with an edge.

The running out of his time in that day of this life was fated to be wretched, and the dying demon fated to journey far, into the fiends' dominion. Then he who but a little before had in joy of heart done so much wickedness to the race of men, feuding with God, realized that his body would not stand by him, for the brave kinsman of Hygelac had him by the hand. Each hated the other to the death. The cruel, terrible creature was suffering bodily agony: it was clear that the wound in his shoulder was mortal. The sinews had sprung apart; the joints had snapped. It was to Beowulf that the victory in this battle had been granted; Grendel's fate was to flee from there, fatally wounded, seeking his haunts in the cover of the fens with the joy gone out of him. Ever more surely he knew that the end of his time had been reached, of all his days, the day of reckoning. As to the Danes, the desire of their hearts had come to pass as a result of that murderous charge.

He had cleansed it, then; he who before had come from   825
far parts, gifted with foresight and stout of heart, had saved
the hall of Hrothgar in the face of attack. He took joy in his
work that night, in that deed worthy of fame. The prince of
the fighting Götar had stood by his sacred boast, had given
them, to boot, amends for the outrage done them all, the
grief over insult which they had earlier been suffering, and,
out of some calamitous necessity, would have had to suffer,
no small cause for repining. Plain evidence of that was
when the wild fighter set the hand, arm and shoulder—
there it was all together, what Grendel grabbed with—under the gabled roof.

Then in the morning, in my version of the story, there
was many a soldier around the gift-hall. Chiefs of various
tribes had traveled from near and far to study the miracle,
the vestiges of their foe. Nor did his parting from life seem
matter for sorrow to a single man of those who were studying his path of retreat with the joy gone out of him, studying
how, his spirit gone, vanquished in his assaults, doomed
and forced to run, he had left tracks of blood on his way
from there to the monsters' lake. In that place, the face of
the water was welling with blood, a dreadful working up of
the waves. All charged with steaming gore, it pulsed with
carnage. Doomed to death, he had hidden. Then, cut off   850
from the noise of cheer, in the fen, his fortress, he laid down
his life, his heathen soul. There, Hell took him in charge.

From there veteran comrades returned, as many a young
man did from that pleasant excursion, riding their steeds
from the lake in high spirits, soldiers on horses. At that
point, Beowulf's fame was proclaimed. Again and again,
many a man said that south or north through the whole region of earth between the seas there could be no finer soldier under the circuit of heaven, no man more worthy of
rule. And they were certainly not finding fault with Hrothgar, for that was a good king.

At times, men distinguished in battle, famous for their
accomplishments, let their bay horses out in a gallop, riding
races where the lanes through uncleared ground seemed
fair. At times, the noble retainer of the king who, heaped
with honors, had a number of all kinds of old stories by

heart, calling his songs to mind, came up with a new telling
of a tale. After a while, the man, with his gift for thinking
ahead, began to play a song about this exploit of Beowulf's
and to tell his story expertly and with good success, varying
875 the phrases. He told almost everything he had heard tell of
Sigemund, of his deeds of daring, much that was unknown
—the Waelsing's great fight, his exploits in far places, his
feuds and his audacities—which the children of men had
had no certain knowledge of, save for Fitela, who was with
him when he would tell him something of that sort, uncle to
nephew, such comrades in tight places had they always
been in every kind of assault. With their swords, they had
laid low every branch of the race of ogres. After the day of
his death, no small renown sprang up for Sigemund, since,
a hard man in war, he had killed the dragon, the keeper of
treasure. On his own, the prince's son had ventured the
breakneck deed beneath the hoary stone. Fitela was not
with him. Still it was granted him that his sword should so
pierce the glittering dragon that it stuck in the rock-face,
noble iron that it was. The dragon died in agony. By his daring, that terrible creature had brought it about that he might
enjoy the use of that treasure of golden armbands at his
own will and judgment. He loaded down his sea-worthy
boat; the son of Waels bore bright jewels into the hull of his
ship. The dragon melted away in its own heat.

Through all the nations of men, he was far and away the
most famous of adventurers, was a lord of warriors because
900 of his deeds of daring—he soon prospered to that extent—
after Heremod's prowess in warfare dwindled, his strength
and his daring. Once Heremod had been betrayed into the
power of his enemies among the Jutes, he was quickly dispatched. The ebb and flow of sorrow had crippled him for
too long. He had become to his people, to all his nobles, a
lifelong affliction. Even in earlier times, many a man of
foresight who had been counting on him for help in times of
disaster, who had believed that the prince's son would succeed to his father's nobility, would keep the people well,
their treasure and their stronghold, the Scyldings' domain,
was often deeply worried about the way the stout-hearted
man was taking. Because of all these things, the kinsman of

Hygelac had, at that point, come to be the greater source
of joy to his friends, to the race of men. Wickedness had
corrupted Heremod.

At times, racing on their horses, they ran laps on the
sandy paths. The light of morning was well advanced then
and was driving on. Many a brave-hearted man went to the
noble hall to study that strange wonder. Likewise, the king,
keeper of treasuries of golden armbands, was making his
way in triumph from the women's quarters among a great
troop; and the queen was crossing the path to the mead-hall
with him in her retinue of maidens.

Hrothgar made an address. He had reached the hall,   925
had taken his stand on the landing, and was looking at the
towering roof, shingled with gold, and at Grendel's hand:

"For this good sight, let thanksgiving be promptly made
to the Almighty. I have lived through much that was hateful, many disasters at Grendel's hands. God always can
work miracle upon miracle, Lord of Glory that He is. It was
but a little while ago that I had no hope of ever living to see
any cure for my troubles. Then this finest of houses stood,
soaked with blood, spattered with carnage, an affliction
deeply affecting every one of my counselors, who had no
hope that they might defend this great fortress of my people
from devils and malignant specters. Now by the might of
the Lord this warrior has carried out the action which all of
us, with all our foresight, could not encompass. Indeed,
whatever lady bore this son into the race of men can, if she
still lives, truly say that the Ancient Umpire of Fate was
gracious to her in allotting her children. Now, Beowulf, best
of soldiers, I will cherish you in my heart as my son. Always
make full demands on this new tie. You will never lack any   950
pleasant thing in this world which I have at my disposal. I
have quite often bestowed reward for less, ennoblement by
treasure to a man below you, a man not your equal in fighting. Of yourself, you have brought it about by these actions
that your fame will live forever and ever. May the Almighty
repay you for your goodness as He has done just now."

Beowulf made an address, Ecgtheow's son: "We did this
fighting, this deed of daring, made our dangerous venture
against the strength of that uncanny creature, with great

pleasure. I did rather wish that you might have seen the demon himself in all his glory breathing his last. I thought to throw him to his death-bed with holds hard to get out of, so that through the grip of my hand he would have to lie fighting for his life, but his body escaped. I could not stop his going since the Umpire of Fate had not willed it. I never got a certain enough hold on him, deadly marauder that he was. The demon was far too strong in the legs. Yet he did leave his hand behind to save his life, his arm and his shoulder. The poor soldier got no comfort that way, however. He will live no longer for having done that, loathsome op-

975 ponent that he was, tormented by sins. For pain with a grip like Fate has strictly bound him in the bonds of death in a place where, condemned for his wickedness, he must await the Last Judgment to see how the radiant Umpire of Fate will pass final sentence on him."

Then Ecglaf's son was a quieter man in his boastful talk about his great deeds in battle when the nobles had taken a good look at the hand upon the roof, the demon's fingers. At the tip, each of the beds of the nails was the next thing to steel. Each and every one. The taloned hand of the heathen soldier was a monstrous claw. Every man said that no hard thing, not even tried-and-true iron, would ever have been able to give the wound that took off that terrible creature's bloody fighting-arm.

Then it was commanded of all hands that the inside of Heorot be furbished at once. On that occasion, the men and women were many who were setting the wine-mansion, the guest-hall to rights. Shot with gold, tapestries glittered along the walls, many wonderful sights for any man who lets his eyes linger on such things. That bright building had been badly shattered, its whole interior braced with iron clamps,

1000 its hinges sprung apart. The roof alone had come through completely unscathed, when the terrible creature, banished for his wicked deeds, had turned away in flight, despairing of his life. It is never easy to escape—let him do it who will —but, driven by fate, a man must seek out the place that lies ready for every creature with a soul, every one of the children of men dwelling on earth, where the body laid close in its last bed will sleep after feasting.

That was the time and occasion when the son of Healfdene went to the hall. The king himself wished to partake of
the feast. I have never heard of people in a larger company
bearing themselves so well around their giver of treasure.
Men enjoying glory, they sat down on the bench, took
pleasure in the plenty. In high spirits, Hrothgar and Hrothwulf, kinsmen among them, gracefully drank of many a
mead-cup in the noble hall. Heorot was filled with friends.
The great Scyldings had as yet made no shows of treachery.

The sword-hand of Healfdene then gave Beowulf a
golden standard as a reward for his victory, an embroidered war-banner, a helmet and a shirt of chain-mail. Many
saw a famous sword, a crown-jewel, brought before the hero.
Beowulf drank of the cup on the hall floor. He felt no need   1025
to be ashamed of that rich gift in front of his soldiers. I have
not heard of many men presenting four crown-jewels encrusted with gold to another on the mead-bench in so
friendly a way. Around the helmet's crown, a rim twisted
with wire held the face-guard on, so that file-honed swords
could do that battle-hardened man no serious harm when,
as a foot-soldier, it was his duty to advance on foot against
his foes.

The protector of good soldiers then had eight horses with
plated bridles led right into the hall beneath the roof-trees.
On one of them a saddle rested, worked with designs, studded with treasure. That had been the high-king's throne in
battle when it was the will of Healfdene's son to indulge in
sword-play. Never did the prowess in war of that world-
famous man fail him at the head of his troops when the slain
were falling. And then the bulwark of the friends of Ing bestowed ownership of both horses and weapons on Beowulf.
He bade him make good use of them. So nobly did the famous lord, keeper of the treasury of heroes, pay for those
battle-charges in horses and crown-jewels, that no man who
is willing to tell the truth in all fairness will ever find fault
with them.

Further, the lord of good soldiers gave a crown-jewel, an   1050
heirloom, to each of those on the mead-bench who had
made the crossing with Beowulf, and ordered that man
paid for in gold whom Grendel had killed before in his

wickedness, as he would have killed even more of them, had not God in His wisdom, and one man's great heart, withstood that fate. The Umpire of Fate was ruling the race of men as He still does now. Therefore understanding is in every way best, foresight of spirit. The man who takes joy in the world for any length of time in these present days of struggle must live through much that he loves and much that he hates.

Then in the royal presence of Healfdene's marshal of war, song was mingled with the crowding swell of music. The joyous harp was plucked, many a tale recited, when along the mead-bench it was the turn of Hrothgar's singer to play for the hall's entertainment:

"At the hands of Finn's men, when the raid struck, the Danish hero, Hnaef of the Scyldings, was fated to fall in the Frisian slaughter. Indeed, Hildeburg had no call to praise the good faith of the Jutes: without provocation, she was 1075 bereft of son and brother. Struck by the spear, they fell as Fate would have it. That was a sad princess. Not without cause did the daughter of Hoc grieve at what Fate had wrought, when morning came and she could make out kinsmen savagely killed where lately she counted her own the highest joy in the world. War had taken all Finn's noble retainers, save only a few, so that he could in no way fight out the battle with Hengest, or drive the survivors from the hall by an attack on that retainer of the murdered prince. Instead, they offered them terms: that they would make room in a whole other building, vacate a hall and a throne; that they might have half of it at their disposal together with the Jutes; and that Finn, son of Folcwalda, would at the giving of treasure each day honor the Danes, would make the stay of Hengest's troop pleasant with golden armbands just as often as he meant to lift the hearts of the Frisian people with treasures of plated gold in that hall of noble toasts.

"Then on both sides they gave their solemn word to this firm treaty of peace. Manfully and without dispute, Finn swore oaths to Hengest that he would govern the survivors with honor in accordance with the decree of his counselors; 1100 that no man there would break the treaty by word or deed, or through some plotted malice would ever demean them, even though, having lost their lord, they were following that lord's murderer, since such had been forced upon them by necessity; if, then, any Frisian should remind them of that disastrous feud by insolent talk, the edge of the sword would thereupon settle it.

"A fire was then built, and pure gold from the treasury heaved up upon it. The best of the soldiers of the fighting Scyldings was laid out on that pyre. From the fire's edge it was easy to see his blood-stained mail-shirt, the swine on his helmet, the boar hard as iron, many a prince, mangled with wounds. Great men had fallen in that slaughter. From the edge of Hnaef's fire, Hildeburg ordered her own son to be delivered to the blaze, his body to be burned, and burned at his uncle's side. The princess was stricken with grief; she lamented in songs for the dead. The war-hero was lifted to the pyre. The largest of funeral fires rolled towards the clouds; it roared before the burial mound. The skulls melted. The scars broke open; blood shot out of the cruel flesh-wounds. Flame, the greediest of spirits, swallowed all whom war had taken from both peoples. Their beauty was scattered.

"With their friends taken from them, the warriors then 1125 left to inspect their quarters, to take stock of the land of Frisia, its estates and chief stronghold. Yet Hengest did live out one blood-stained year with Finn in full wretchedness. He kept thinking of home, though he could not push his curved prow out to sea. The deep water thrashed with storm; it wrestled the wind. Winter bound the breakers along shore in a chain of ice, until a second year entered the courts, as the windy weather, bright with glory, does even now, always keeping its term. When winter was scattered, and the lap of earth lovely, the exile longed to be out of those courts he was a guest in. He would much rather have made plans for avenging his grief than for crossing the sea, if he could possibly have carried off the angry meeting which he had in mind for the sons of the Jutes. Thus he did not reject the way of the world when Hunlaf's son laid the Torch of Battle, that finest of swords, on his lap. Its edges were famous among the Jutes. In that way, cruel death by the sword befell the great-spirited Finn in turn on his own estate, when Guthlaf and Oslaf mentioned with grief the 1150 savage attack that followed their voyage there, and laid the blame on him for most of their troubles. The divided heart could not keep silent within the breast. Then the hall was crusted with the blood of their foes, as well as King Finn slain in the midst of his troop, and the queen taken. The Scylding archers carried all the furnishings of the king of that country aboard ship, and whatever they could find around Finn's estate of jewels and precious stones. In that crossing, they brought the noble woman to the Danes, led her to her people."

The song had been sung through, the singer's tale. The revelry mounted again. The noise of good cheer rang bright on the benches. Cupboys were serving wine from rare flagons. Then Wealhtheow made her progress, moving beneath her golden circlet to where the two great men sat, the uncle and the nephew. Peace was as yet between them, each in good faith with the other. Unferth the spokesman, as well, was sitting at the feet of the lord of the Scyldings. Everyone had faith in his spirit, that he had a great heart, even though he may not have been strictly honorable with his kinsmen in sword-play. Then the lady of the Scyldings spoke:

"Drink of this cup, my noble lord, my giver of treasure. Be of high heart, golden lord and friend of soldiers, and speak to the Götar in benign words as one ought to do. Be gracious to the Götar, remembering the things from far and 1175 near you now have in your gift. I am told that it was your will to hold this war-hero your son. Heorot is really cleansed! This hall of riches is radiant!

"Give these many rewards as long as you may; and leave your people and your kingdom to your sons whenever your time may come to fix your eyes on what Fate has decreed. I know my Hrothwulf to be so gracious that he will raise these young men honorably, if, lord and friend of the Scyldings, you leave the world earlier than he. I am confident that out of his goodness he will repay our sons, if he keeps in mind all that we two did before, when he was a child, for his delight and honor."

She moved along the bench then to where her children

were, Hrethric and Hrothmund, and the sons of heroes, all
cadets together. There the great man, Beowulf of the Götar,
sat between the two brothers.

The cup was borne to him, and an affectionate invitation
conveyed in words, and to his delight twisted gold was displayed, two armbands, a garment and chain-mail, and the
greatest necklace which I have ever heard tell of on earth.
I have heard of no finer crown-jewel in a treasury of heroes,
since Hama bore the Brosings' necklace off to the bright
stronghold, that jewel and its gem-studded casket. He was   1200
fleeing raids plotted by Eormenric; he had chosen the everlasting way. Hygelac of the Götar, nephew of Swerting, had
that necklace on his last expedition, when, beneath his
standard, he was defending his treasure, protecting the
slain from pillage. Fate took him after he had asked for
trouble in that raid on the Frisians: a mighty lord, he had
worn the jewel, those precious stones, across the flagon of
salt-waves; he had crumpled beneath his shield. Into the
hands of the Franks had passed the life of the king, the
clothes on his breast, and the necklace with them: soldiers
not his equal had rifled his corpse in the wake of the scythe
of war. The men of the Götar had first rights to the field of
the slain.— The hall took the roar of applause.

Wealhtheow made an address; she spoke before all the
company: "Wear this necklace with luck, Beowulf, my dear
young man, and put this garment to use, these great treasures, and make out completely well in life. Out of your
strength, be bold; and be so good as to teach these boys
what they should know. I am keeping a reward in mind for
you for that. You have brought it about that men will esteem you forever and ever, far and near, as far as the sea,
the court of the winds, rings sea-cliffs around. Prince, be   1225
happy as long as you live. I will treat you well when it
comes to treasures. Holding yourself a member of this company, do right by my sons in your actions. For every good
soldier here is faithful to the other, gentle of heart, loyal to
his liege-lord. All these noble retainers are in accord: people prepared for anything, having drunk noble toasts, the
soldiers of this company do as I ask."

She moved to her throne then. The choicest of feasts had

been laid there; the men were drinking wine. They were not aware of their fate, the cruel decree given of old which had gone forth against many a good soldier once evening had come and royal Hrothgar had departed for his chamber, for his bed. Good soldiers without number lodged in the mansion as they often had done in the past. They cleared the benches away; the floor was scattered with bedding and pillows. One of those noble feasters curled up in his bed on the floor with time running out and his doom upon him. They set their braced shields at their heads, their beautiful shields. There on the bench above each prince were displayed the helmet that towers in battle, the shirt of meshed rings and the majestic spear. That was their custom, so that they were usually ready for battle both at home and in the field, and in either case, whatever time the need of them be-

1250 fell their liege-lord. That was a good company.

They then fell into a deep sleep. One came to grief on this bed that night, as so often happened when Grendel was haunting the golden hall, doing wrong, till his end had come about, death for his sins. It came to be plain to see, a fact known to men in many places, that as a result of the sad business of making war, an avenger still lived to avenge their long-time foe. Grendel's mother, a terrible monster-princess, was brooding over her heartbreak, she whose lot it was to make the haunted water her home, the cold streams, since Cain had been the death of his only brother, of his father's son. Branded for life by his crime, he had then departed an outcast. Fleeing the noise of good cheer among men, he haunted the wasteland. From him many creatures were born demons by a decree given of old. Not the least of these had been Grendel, that savage devil full of hatred who had come upon the man on watch in Heorot, waiting for his attack. There Beowulf, a terrible creature himself, came into his clutches. However, he remembered the force of his gift of strength, the ample blessing which God had given him, and trusted to the Almighty for honor, comfort and help. On that account, he overcame his foe,

1275 brought that demon from Hell to the ground. Cast down, cut off from the noise of good cheer, that enemy of the race of man had gone off to look for a place to die. And despite

all that, here was the mother, ravening and with a grievance on her mind, bent on carrying out a course of action
full of grief to avenge the death of her son.

She had reached Heorot then, where the Danes in their
golden armbands were sleeping all around the hall. A turn
for the worse fell to the lot of the good soldiers there the
moment the mother of Grendel got in. The horror she inspired was only less to the point that the strength of women
is less, the horror inspired by a woman in a fight, compared
to that of armed men when the blade with lashed hilt,
forged by the hammer, the blood-stained sword with rugged
edges shears through the boar atop the helmet. Then in the
hall the hard-edged sword was drawn above the benches,
many a broad-rimmed shield lifted firm in the hand. No man
remembered his helmet or ample shirt of mail when a sense
of the terror struck him.

She was in haste when she was discovered; she meant to
get out of there, to save her life. She quickly got one of
the nobles fast in her clutches, as she was on her way to the
marsh. The man she murdered on his bed was the man of
the rank of comrade-to-the-king dearest to Hrothgar of all
the heroes between the seas, a princely soldier, a fighting-
man of proven glory. Beowulf was not there, for another   1300
lodging had been assigned the famous man of the Götar
after the giving of treasure.

A scream rose in Heorot. She was taking down the hand
caked with blood which she knew.

Trouble had struck afresh, come into being again in their
quarters. It was no good bargain that on both sides they
should have had to pay with the lives of those dear to them.
The old king, the grizzled war-hero, was sick at heart when
he knew that his chief-retainer was murdered, the man
dearest to him dead.

Beowulf, that fighter blessed with victory, was quickly
summoned to the royal chamber. Not the least of good soldiers, a noble champion, he made his way a little before
dawn in the company of his comrades to where the wise old
man was waiting to see whether the Almighty would ever
bring about a turn for the better after this time of trouble.
That man who would have done honor to any army

marched across the floor with his squad—the wood of the hall resounded—that he might pay his respects in a few words to the leader, the lord of the friends of Ing. He asked if the night had been pleasant for him, to his desire.

Hrothgar made an address, the protector of the Scyldings: "Do not pass the time of day. Sorrow has struck afresh at the Danish people. Dead. Aeschere is dead. Yrmenlaf's older brother. My confidant and my chancellor. The friend at my shoulder when in the thick of battle we fended blows from our heads, as the troops of infantry clashed, as the boars on the helmets slammed against each other. Whatever a good soldier should be, a tried and true prince, that Aeschere was. Some restless murdering demon has been the death of him. In Heorot! I do not know where that savage thing beat her retreat, gloating over his corpse, her heart lifted by thoughts of a feast. She was taking vengeance for that skirmish last night in which by your rugged holds you killed Grendel with violent dispatch because he had been draining and destroying my people for far too long. He fell in that fight, condemned to death for his own guilt. And now this second mighty evildoer has come, bent on avenging her son, and has pushed the feud far as it well may seem to many a noble retainer who cries out for the lord who gave him treasure in his heart, cries out at this blow to the heart so hard to bear.—Now the hand lies strengthless which satisfied your every desire!

"I have heard counselors in this hall, my subjects who live in that region, say that they have seen two such huge stalkers through the wilderness holding sway over the rolling marshes, demons from another world. One of them had been, as far as they could make out for certain, in the likeness of a woman of high degree; the second ill-fated creature had trudged the paths of exile in the shape of a man. Except that he was bigger than any other man. The people who live in that part of the country called him Grendel. They do not know his father, or whether any of these mysterious demons had been born to him before. They haunt uncharted country, wolf-caves, windy ravines, the dangerous trail through the marsh where beneath the shadows of chasm walls water from the mountains disappears in full flood deep beneath the earth. It is not far from here in miles that the pool stands. Groves glazed with frost hang over it; a thickly wooded forest overshadows its water. There every night a deadly wonder can be seen, the fire on the flood. There is no man living among the sons of men so wise that he knows the depth of it. Though the heath-striding stag with strong antlers, harried by hounds, on the run from far off, may seek the cover of that wood, he will give up the ghost, yield his life on its bank, before he will go into it to save his head. That is no holy place. From there, when the wind stirs up bad weather, a spasm in the waves rises to the 1375 clouds, till the sky gasps, and the heavens burst into rain. Our best chance now lies with you alone. You do not yet know where she dwells, the dangerous place in which you may come upon that creature with so many crimes on its head. Seek her out if you dare. I will reward you with wealth, with old treasures, twisted gold, as I did before, if you get away."

Beowulf made an address, Ecgtheow's son: "Do not grieve. You are a wise man. It is nobler for one to avenge his friend than to give way to sorrow. Each of us must live to see the end of his life in this world. Let him who may labor for glory before his death. For when all is said and done, that is best when the soul is out of a good soldier. Guardian of this kingdom, stand up. Let us quickly go and scout the trail of the mother of Grendel. I promise you this: go where she will, in the folds of the earth or the woods of the mountain or depth of the sea, she will not escape to cover. Have the kind of fortitude this day, facing one trouble on another, that I expect of a man like you."

The old man came to life. He thanked God, the Lord Almighty, for what the man had said. Then Hrothgar's horse was bridled, his mount with braided mane. The wise 1400 prince rode in majesty; a guard of foot-troops marched with him. Following her track through the wood, her footprints were plain in many places, her trail through the clearings. She had made her way straight across the dim marsh. She was carrying the lifeless body of the best of the noble retainers who governed the domain with Hrothgar. By that time, that son of princes was clambering up steep rock-faces, an exacting trail, narrow stretches of path one must take single-file, the footing unknown, ravines shooting straight down, many a water-monsters' pool. With a few expert men he was riding on ahead to scout the ground, until suddenly he came on mountain trees growing crookedly over gray stone, a wood with no joy in it. Water lay beneath, bloody and troubled. To all the Danes, to the friends of the Danes, one noble retainer after another, every good soldier, it was an agony and a torment for the heart to bear when on that cliff by the lake they came upon Aeschere's head.

The tide was rising charged with blood. The men stared at it. With steaming carnage! The horn sounded time after time, the call to the ready. The foot-troops all took their positions. Then they saw many sorts of serpents swimming about the water, uncanny sea-dragons making trial of the pool, water-monsters, besides, lying on the shelves of the ravine, the kind that in the forenoon often carry out some course full of grief on the sail-road, serpents and wild beasts. They sank out of sight, sullenly and with their blood up. They had heard the clamor, the war-horn blaring. With a shaft from his bow, the prince of the Götar knocked the spirit out of one, its power to battle in the waves, so well that it was in the vitals the hard war-arrow struck. It grew weaker and weaker in its swimming in the lake till death was getting it. In a flash, in the waves near the shore, it was hard at bay among boar-spears with their barbed heads, and was brought down by their assaults, and dragged on to the cliff, that strange piece of flotsam. The men looked hard at their ghastly visitor.

Beowulf dressed himself in his heroic armor. He was not anxious about his life. The chain-mail he fought in, hand-meshed, ample and elaborately designed, would stand the test of the pool. It could shield his body well enough that no grip in battle, no wicked hold by an angry foe could do his heart, his vitals, mortal harm. Moreover the glittering helmet protected his head: It would make a stir in the depths of the lake seeking the broil in the waves, studded with treasure, as it was, with chains fit for a prince riveted around it, as the armorer had fashioned it in days long past.

1425

1450

He had planned it with rare skill, had set boars all about it so that no blade or blades could ever cut through it. Nor was that which Unferth, the king's spokesman, had lent him the least important help to his gift of strength. Hrunting was the name of the blade entrusted to his keeping. Its hilt was a priceless treasure of great age; its blade was iron, etched with acid, hardened by blood shed in battle. In a fight it had never failed any man who swung it in his hands and dared go through exploits full of horror, pitched battle with foes. That was not the first time that it was to bring off a deed of daring.

When he made the loan of that weapon to the finer swordsman, having gained some sense of Beowulf's strength, Ecglaf's son was certainly no longer of the opinion which he had voiced earlier, drunk on wine. He himself had not dared risk his life beneath that ferment in the waves, dared do the heroic thing. There he lost his chance of glory, of repute for daring. It was not so with the other once he had armed himself for war.

Beowulf made an address, Ecgtheow's son: "O great son of Healfdene, prince among wise men, generous lord and friend of soldiers, now that I am ready for this expedition, keep in mind what we two agreed some time ago, that if I should lose my life serving your needs, you would always stand in the place of a father upon my passing away. Be a protector to my noble retainers, these right-hand men of mine, if battle should take me. Likewise, those great treasures which you gave me, dear Hrothgar, send them to Hygelac. When he fixes his eyes on that treasure, Hrethel's son, the lord of the Götar, will be able to perceive from the gold, to see for sure, that I found a giver of treasure prompted to be generous by his virtues as a man, and took joy in him while I might. And let Unferth have the blade that is mine by inheritance, my beautiful damascened sword. Let the famous man have my tough-edged weapon. I will win glory for myself with Hrunting, or death will take me."

After those words, the prince of the storm-weathering Götar made haste in his daring. He would wait for no answer. A ground-swell received the war-hero. It was well on

1475

in the day before he could grasp the lay of the land at the bottom.

Starving for a fight, wild and ravenous, she who had had the district among the floods in her charge fifty years, summer and winter, discovered at once that some mortal from 1500 above was reconnoitering the monsters' domain. She then made a lunge at him and got the war-hero in her savage clutches. None the sooner did she deal his safe body a mortal wound. Outside the rings screened him around so that she could not get through his war-coat, the meshed shirt on his limbs, with her vicious fingers. When she had reached the very bottom, the she-wolf of the lake bore the prince of the rings to her chamber by such a route that no matter how spirited he was, he could not get to use his weapons. For too many strange things made it hard for him on that swim. One sea-beast after another tried to split his war-shirt with its battling tusks. Terrible creatures were hounding him.

Then the good soldier saw that he was in some kind of enemy hall, what kind he did not know, where the water could not do him the least harm, and where because of the hall-roof no sudden attack from the flood could touch him. He saw fire-light, a white blaze brilliantly shining.

It was then that the great man saw that creature condemned to the depths, the mighty woman of the lake. He gave his war-sword so powerful a swing—his arm did not hold back in the blow—that the rings on its hilt screamed a bloodthirsty battle-cry. Then the invader discovered that his Torch of Battle would not wound, would not kill, for 1525 its edge played the prince false in his need. It had stood up before in many close fights. It had often cut the helmet and battle-clothes of a doomed man through. That was the first time for that treasure of great price that its glory failed.

Hygelac's kinsman, his mind fixed on glorious deeds, was resolute even after that, not at all holding back in his daring. Furious, not the kind of man to back down, he then let the damascened blade fly, jewel-lashed hilt and all, so that it landed on the ground, stout and steel-edged. He put his faith in his strength, in the hand-grip that was his gift. Thus a man must do when he is bent on winning lasting praise. He will not give his life a moment's thought.

The prince of the fighting Götar then seized the mother of Grendel by the shoulder. He had no regrets at all about that fight. The battle-hardened man spun her—then his blood was up—till she fell in a heap on the floor. She in turn quickly paid him back in wicked holds. She pulled him towards her. His spirit worn out, the strongest of soldiers, the champion of the army, was thrown off balance, so that he was given a fall. Then she sat on the man who had invaded her hall, and drew her short-sword, broad-bladed and with its edges glittering. She was about to avenge her child, her only son. On his shoulder rested the meshed corslet. That saved his life. It prevented the entrance of point or edge of blade. Ecgtheow's son, the champion of the Götar, would   1550 have come to the end of his exploits deep under ground, had not the battle-mail, the tough war-corslet been a help to him, and had not Holy God, the Lord in His wisdom, the Governor of Heaven, decreed victory in battle. With ease and in accordance with His justice, He had ordained it the moment Beowulf got on his feet again.

It was then that he saw in her gear a blade blessed with victory, an ancient sword of more than human make, with rugged edges, one that had done soldiers proud. It was the choicest of weapons, except that, noble and majestic as it was, a masterpiece by giants, it was larger than any other man could have carried into battle. The champion of the Scyldings, stern and savage in a fight, then grasped the ringed hilt and drew the damascened blade, and, despairing of life, struck so furiously that hard thing bit into her neck. It split the neck-bones; the blade went all the way through the doomed flesh. She crumpled to the floor. The sword was dripping blood; the soldier gloried in his deed.

The fire blazed. As surely as the candle of heaven shines in its brilliance from the sky, light shot into those depths. He looked about the hall. He moved along the rock-face. He held the hard weapon high by the hilt, Hygelac's noble retainer, angry and single-minded. The blade had not outlived its use for the war-hero. In fact, he had quickly formed the desire to pay Grendel back for the many attacks he had made upon the Danes, much more often than that one time he had struck down members of Hrothgar's household-

troop in their sleep, devoured fifteen sleeping men of the
Danish force, and carried off the same number as his vicious spoils. The furious champion had paid him such full
payment for that, that he saw Grendel lying there, worn out
by war, the soul out of him, so badly had the battle in
Heorot hurt him. The carcase bounded some distance when
it took the blow, the stout swing of the sword after its death,
and Beowulf had cut the head off it.

The sages who were watching the lake with Hrothgar
suddenly saw that the breakers were in deep convulsion,
the face of the water mottled with blood. Those grizzled
old men around the great leader agreed that they had no
hope for the prince: he would never come back to their
famous lord glorying in victory. For it seemed to most of
them that the she-wolf of the lake had murdered him. It
1600 was then three in the afternoon. The brave Scyldings left
the ledge. The golden lord and friend of men departed from
there for home. Sick at heart, his visitors remained and
stared at the pool. They wished, yet had lost all hope that
they might see their lord in the flesh.

By that time because of the blood shed in that fight, the
sword, the battle-blade, had begun to dissolve drop by
bloody drop. It was no small matter for wonder: all of it
melted much like ice when the Father who holds sway over
seasons and times loosens the knot of the frost and unwinds
the ropes that kill. He is the true Umpire of Fate. Though
he saw many things there, the prince of the storm-
weathering Götar took nothing more from the priceless goods
in those halls than the head and the treasure-encrusted hilt.
The sword had melted then. Its engraved blade had burned
away, so hot was the blood, so venomous the demon from
beyond who had died in that place. He who but a while before in hard battle had seen through the overthrow of his
foes was in the pool at once. He dove up through the water.
Those breakers, those regions filled with more than human
power, were fully purged, when the outcast demon had surrendered her days of life and this lot which is lent us.

There came the lord of those seafarers, swimming stoutly
1625 to shore. He gloried in his booty from the lake, the mighty
burden which he had with him. They went out to meet him.

They thanked God, that majestic troop of noble retainers.
For their lord's sake, they gave way to joy. They had been
permitted to see him again safe and sound. Then the helmet
and mail-shirt on the rugged man were promptly loosened.
The lake was ebbing; beneath the clouds the water was
mottled with blood shed in battle. Rejoicing in their hearts,
they made their way from there on the march. They· covered the stages of the trail, a path now familiar to them.
With difficulty for every spirited man concerned, soldiers
of royal bravery were carrying the head from the ledge at
the lake. To bring Grendel's head to the golden hall on a
spear-shaft, and that with great labor, four of them were
needed, until suddenly there they came, fourteen stout
Götar, brave in battle, marching to the mansion. Across the
cleared fields before the mead-building, the spirited lord of
men strode in their midst. A lord among noble retainers, a
man of brave deeds, of celebrated glory, he went marching
in to greet Hrothgar. Then on to the floor where the men
were drinking, Grendel's head was carried by the hair. Full
of terror though it was for those good soldiers and the lady
with them, the men looked upon it as a rare and beautiful   1650
sight.

Beowulf made an address, Ecgtheow's son: "O son of
Healfdene, prince of the Scyldings, it is with great delight
we have brought you as evidence of victory this booty from
the lake which you are looking at. I did not come through
that battle under water easily. I brought my courage to bear
upon that task with difficulty. The contest was almost
broken off, except that God proved my shield. Though the
weapon may be a good one, I could not do a thing in the
fight with Hrunting. But the Ruler of men granted it to me
that I should see hanging on the wall a beautiful sword of
great age and more than human power—He has shown the
way to friendless men so often!—which weapon I drew.
When the chance was given me, I then hacked down the
keepers of that dwelling. It was then that the war-sword
with the engraved blade burned away, as the blood, the
hottest blood ever shed in battle, spurted. I have taken that
hilt from our enemies down there. I have avenged their
vicious deeds, their massacre of Danes, as was right. Fur-

thermore, I promise you this: You and this company of
your soldiers, and every noble retainer among your subjects, both veterans and young men in training, may sleep
1675 free from worry, lord of the Scyldings, since you have no
need to dread the butchery of your good soldiers at their
hands, as you did before."

Then the golden hilt, the masterpiece of giants of old,
was given into the hands of the aged hero, the gray prince
of battles. After the downfall of those devils, when that
creature of enraged heart, a fighter against God, guilty of
murder, and his mother, too, had surrendered this world,
that work of rare smiths passed into the possession of the
lord of the Danes. It passed into the possession of the finest
of the lords of earth who dealt out treasures in the land of
the Swedes between the two seas.

Hrothgar made an address. He had studied the hilt, that
heirloom of great age. On it was written the source of the
struggle of old, when the flood, the ocean breaking its
bounds, struck down the race of giants. They had borne
themselves insolently; that was a people estranged from the
Lord Everlasting. In the water's surge, the Ruler paid them
a final reward for that. On the sword-guards, it was also
rightly engraved, set down and declared in runic letters of
pure gold for whom that sword had first been made, that
choicest of irons with its twisted hilt and damascened blade.
Then the wise son of Healfdene spoke—they all fell silent:
1700 "He who advances truth and justice in this nation, and,
as the keeper of this realm for a long time, remembers all
of its past, can well say that this great soldier was born the
better man! My noble friend, Beowulf, glory is assured for
you through the far reaches of earth, among every kind of
people. In patience and prudence of heart, you keep your
great gift of strength fully within bounds. I will stand by
that promise of my friendship made you when we two spoke
a little while ago. For a good long time, you will be the comfort of your nation, the support of your soldiers. Not the
kind of man Heremod was to the sons of Ecgwela, the
Scyldings of strict honor. He did not grow great to the delight of the Danish people, but to their slaughter and destruction. With his blood up, he murdered his comrades at

table, men who stood by him in battle, until, famous lord though he was, he died all alone with no sound of company near. Although Almighty God had in His full power exalted and advanced him in the joys which come from the gift of strength, still some hidden thing in his heart grew thirsty for blood. Cut off from the noise of good cheer, he lived to see the time when he would suffer torment for the tribulation, the lasting affliction he had been to his people. Learn by that. Understand what virtue is in a man. Taught by years of experience, I have made this song for your benefit:

"There is wonder in telling how Almighty God, in the 1725 largeness of His heart, deals wisdom, land, and rank out to the race of men. Over all these things, He has the power. Sometimes in His Charity He lets the character of a man of noble stock have full play, grants him earthly joy in his own country, a great fortress filled with men to hold as his own, puts whole parts of the world, a broad empire, so much in his sway that he cannot in his lack of foresight conceive of its ever ending for him. He passes his life in feasting. Neither disease or age gives him a moment's pause. And no grief over insult rankles in his heart, and no trouble anywhere leads to war; but the whole world turns at his will. He has no sense of anything worse, until a store of proud thoughts within him puts out shoots and grows rank while the keeper, the guardian of his soul, lies dreaming. Hemmed in as he is with things which cause trouble, that sleep is too heavy. The killer who shoots malignly from his bow is grievously near. Then he is struck to the heart beneath the armor by the bitter shaft, by the wicked, bewildering commands of the outcast demon. He cannot protect himself. What he held too long seems too little to him. Turned vicious, he grows greedy. Never for the glory of it does he award armbands encrusted with gold. And he for- 1750 gets and ignores the world to come, because God, the Governor of Glory, gave him that large share of honors early. In the end it finally happens that the body lent him breaks down. Doomed, he falls dead. Another succeeds him who recklessly deals out the rich goods, the treasure once that good soldier's, and has no sense of the terror of it all. Dear Beowulf, soldier without peer, protect yourself from that

murderous onslaught, and choose the better part, the everlasting ways. Pay no heed to proud thoughts, famous champion. Now the flowering of your strength is but for a while.
After a while, the time will suddenly come that disease or
the sword's edge will cut off your power. Either fire's grasp
or flood's surge or blade's bite or spear's flight. Or vicious
age, or the flash of your eyes will gutter and burn out! It
will be all at once, great campaigner, that death will overpower you.

    "Thus I ruled these Danes in their golden armbands fifty
years under heaven, and in war so walled them around with
spears and swords against tribe after tribe throughout this
earth that I held no man my enemy beneath the course of
the clouds. What a change from that came about, what grief
after joy, when my old enemy Grendel turned invader! Because of that strife, I bore without respite a great burden of
care on my heart. Thanks be to the Umpire of Fate, the
Lord Everlasting, that I have lived to see the time in my
life when I may gaze with my own eyes on this blood-
stained head after that struggle of such long standing. Go
to your seat now. Having proven your worth in war, give
yourself to the joy of the feast. A very great store of treasures will pass between us when it is morning."

    The prince of the Götar was in high spirits. He went at
once to seek out his bench as the wise king commanded
him. Again as before a fresh feast was beautifully served to
the valiant men sitting in the hall. The dark cover of night
deepened above the great campaigners. It was the will of
the old Scylding with the grizzled hair to seek his bed. A
desire to rest beyond restraining rose in that bold fighting-
man, the prince of the Götar. The chamberlain, the man
who in courtesy looked after all such needs of that noble retainer as travelers would have had in that day, showed the
way at once to the hero from far parts, worn out from his
adventure.

    That great heart then took its rest. The mansion towered,
gabled and shingled with gold. Its guest slept deep within it
until the black raven with high heart heralded the joyous
light of heaven. Then the bright shimmer of morning came
breaking in rays through the shadows. The visiting troops

1775

1800

were in haste: the nobles were eager to travel back to their people; the guest with the mighty soul wanted to set foot on his ship and be far from there. The stern hero had Hrunting borne to Ecglaf's son, and bade him take his sword, his cherished iron. He thanked him for the loan of it, and told him he held it a good friend in battle, of great use in war. In none of his words at all did he lay blame on the sword's edge. That was a great-hearted soldier. When bold for the voyage the warriors were ready in their armor, that prince honored by the Danes went to the dais where the other was. The hero fierce in battle had his last meeting with Hrothgar.

Beowulf made an address, Ecgtheow's son: "Now we sea-farers wish to tell you that, come as we have from afar, we long to make our way back to Hygelac. We have been royally entertained here to our hearts' content. You have been very good to us. Therefore if I can do anything on earth in the way of deeds of battle to gain a larger share of   1825
your love than I have yet done, I will be ready at once to do so. If across the circuit of the seas I learn that neighbors are oppressing you with a reign of terror, as foes have done in the past, I will bring a thousand noble retainers, heroes, to your aid. Of Hygelac, I know that, young though he may be for a prince, he will so further me by his commands and acts that I may fully pay my debt of honor to you, and in your support bear this spear, the staff of my strength, wher-ever the need for men befalls you. Furthermore, if Hreth-ric, the crown-prince, decides to visit the Götar court, he has it in him to find many friends there. Far countries are best visited by one who is himself of some account."

Hrothgar made an address in answer to him: "The Lord in His Wisdom put those sentences into your heart. I have never heard a man as young as you make a wiser speech. You are both mighty in strength and prudent in mind, wise about putting things into words. If it comes about that the spear takes Hrethel's son, if savage and bloody battle, dis-ease, or the sword takes your lord, the prince of your nation, and you still have your life, I feel it certain that the Götar   1850
cannot possibly have a better man than you to elect king, keeper of that treasury of heroes, should you be willing to rule your kinsmen's realm. So well on longer acquaintance,

dear Beowulf, does your character please me. You have brought it about that there will be mutual peace between our nations, the people of the Götar and the Danes, and that strife will cease, those wicked raids which they suffered before. As long as I rule this broad realm, there will be treasures of great price passing between them. With precious things, many a man will send greetings to another across the gannet's bath. The ring-prowed ship will always be carrying some gift or token of fondness across the heaving sea. I know that these people are by nature immovable both towards foe and towards friend, beyond reproach in every respect, in the old way."

Within the hall, the protector of good soldiers, Healfdene's son, then gave him twelve more treasures of great price. He bade him seek out his own dear people in safety with those gifts, and quickly to return. Then the lord-king of the Scyldings, great of lineage, kissed the noble retainer without peer, and took him by the neck. Tears were falling from the eyes of the gray-haired man. Of the two things within the expectation of that old and very seasoned man, he was surer of the second, that they would never afterwards be permitted to lay eyes on each other again, great-hearted men in proud meeting. That man was so dear to him that he could not hold back the sobbing in his breast, for in his heart straining against the bonds of reason, a hidden longing for this man he loved was burning in his blood. Beowulf was striding the grassy earth away from him there, proud in his gold, a hero glorying in his treasure. The vessel waited the lord its owner, where it rode at anchor. Hrothgar's bounty was often praised on the way. That was a rare king, faultless in every respect, until age, which has done harm to many, took the joys of strength away from him.

Then that troop of very spirited young warriors reached the ocean. They were wearing the mesh of rings, their hand-locked mail-shirts. As he had done before, the coast-guard caught sight of the good soldiers on their march back. By no means did he insultingly greet his visitors from the ledge of the cliff, but rode to meet them. He said that these foreign soldiers in their shining coats were making that voyage as men who would be a welcome sight to the Weders. Then

1875

in the shallows, the broad-beamed vessel was loaded with
war-gear, the curved prow with horses and treasures of
great price. The mast towered over those precious goods
from the treasury of Hrothgar.

He gave the guard on the boat a sword bound with gold;   1900
for the sake of that treasure, an heirloom, that man was
ever after held in higher honor on the mead-bench. The
ship then went on, plowing the deep water. It had left the
Danish shore behind. Then the sail, a noble sea-shroud,
was secured to the mast with rope. The timbers creaked. No
cross-wind hampered the vessel on its way. The boat traveled; collared with foam, it sailed right over the waves, its
lashed prow riding the currents of the sea, until they were
able to make out the Götar cliffs, the headlands they knew.
Driven by the wind, the keel pressed towards land, and
struck shore.

The man on harbor-watch, who had for a long time before been eagerly looking far out to sea for those valued
men, was at the breakers at once, ready for them. He
moored the broad-beamed ship securely to shore on an-
chor-ropes, lest the force of the waves prove strong enough
to drive its handsome timbers adrift. He then ordered the
treasure of those nobles carried ashore, their jewels and
golden plate. He had not far to go from there to reach his
treasure-giver, Hygelac, the son of Hrethel, in the place
near the sea-cliff where he usually stays with the officers
who are closest to him.

The building was magnificent, the king a valiant leader,   1925
noble in his hall. Hygd was very young, but discreet, a
woman of deep breeding. Though Haereth's daughter had
dwelt but a few years in the royal citadel, she was nevertheless no person of small account, and was not too sparing
with her gifts to her Götar subjects, even when it came to
great family treasures.

The brazen queen of one nation had borne herself with
an arrogance that was a dreadful sin. No brave man among
her close attendants, no one except her father, dared make
so bold as to fix his eyes upon her openly, for if he did,
he could count on having passed on him the sentence of
being bound for execution with tightened thongs. Then

immediately following the arrest, a sword was arranged for, the engraved blade of which was allowed to clear the matter up, and make a show of wicked murder. It is not behavior fitting a queen for a princess, a woman meant to be a pledge of peace, to act in such a way that she strives against the life of a man to be cherished from some mistaken sense of insult, no matter how rare a creature she may be. Hemming's kinsman put an end to that, however. Men at their ale have told the other side of the story, that she caused less trouble with her bad-tempered actions from the very moment when, noble by blood as she was, she was given as a bride decked in gold to the young champion, the moment she had made her way to Offa's hall across the tawny sea on her father's advice. There on the throne, famed for her goodness, she ever afterwards made good use all of her days of the things Fate allotted her in life. She held true to her noble love for that lord of heroes, who was, as my story has it, the finest of all the race of men, of humankind, between the seas. On that account, Offa, a man bold with his spear, was held in honor far and wide both for his acts of goodness and his acts of war. In wisdom he ruled his domain. From him sprang Eomer as a help to heroes, the nephew of Garmund, skilled in making raids.

The stern hero had by then set out among his picked squad, striding along the foreshore through the sand, over broad stretches of beach. The world's candle shone, the sun hurrying southward. They had come to the end of their voyage. With speed, they reached the place where they had learned that the protector of good soldiers, the man who killed Ongentheow, that great young king of battles was dealing out armbands within his citadel. Beowulf's coming was quickly announced to Hygelac; it was announced that that bulwark among warriors, his comrade in arms, had come into the compound alive, marching unscathed by battle to the royal chamber. Space for that troop of new arrivals was cleared within the hall at once, as the mighty man commanded.

After his liege-lord had greeted him with remarks couched in words of deep sincerity, the man who had come through that hard fight sat down face to face with him, kinsman to kinsman. Haereth's daughter moved through the hall with draughts of mead. She showed her regard for the men; she bore the flagon right up to the warriors and put it into their hands. Hygelac began courteously questioning his companions in that noble hall. A curiosity to know what the adventures of the Götar seafarers had been like would not let him rest.

"After you made the sudden decision to take part in that feud, the battle for Heorot far across the salt tides, how did it go for all of you on the voyage, dear Beowulf? Did you manage to put that notorious wretchedness to rights for the famous lord Hrothgar? With sorrow welling up in me, I was distracted with worry about that. I had no confidence in a valuable man's making that expedition. For a long time, I prayed that you would have nothing at all to do with that murdering demon, that you would let the Danes fight out their battle with Grendel themselves. I give thanks to God that I have been allowed to see you safe and sound."

Beowulf made an address, Ecgtheow's son: "The kind of battle which took place between the two of us, Grendel and me, on that field where he had visited so many causes for grief, so many ceaseless hardships, upon the victorious Scyldings, is known to quite a few men as a great encounter, my lord Hygelac. I took such vengeance for all that, that any kinsman of Grendel's who is the longest lived of that hateful family ensnared in sin will never have any call to boast about that uproar in the half-light. I went right to the Hall of Rings to pay my respects to Hrothgar. The moment he knew my purpose, he directed me at once to a seat with his own sons. His troop was delighted. Under the vault of heaven, I have never in my life seen a greater fellowship of men at their places in the mead-hall. At times, the famous queen, that pledge of peace between two nations, moved across the whole length of the floor and encouraged the young men to fall to. She would often give a twisted armband to a fighting man. At other times, Hrothgar's daughter bore the ale-flagon to the veterans from one end of the hall to the other. I heard the men who dwelt in the hall call her Freawaru, when she was passing the treasure-studded cup to the heroes. She is promised, young and

2000

2025

decked with gold, to the gracious son of Froda. The lord
and friend of the Scyldings, the keeper of the realm, has
agreed to that, and he believes it the best course, believes
that through this woman he will settle a great many murderous feuds and attacks. Usually the deadly spear rests but a
little while after the murder of a prince, no matter how
virtuous the bride may be.

"When he walks into the hall with that woman, the sight
of the men of the Danish company being feasted among
his veteran troop is likely, then, to give offense to the lord
of the Heathobards and every noble retainer of that people.
On the Danes will glisten the heritage left by their elders,
the tough and damascened prized possession of Heathobards for as long as they were permitted to make use of the
weapon until they brought their own dear comrades and
their own lives to ruin in that passage of arms. Then some
old spearman who has caught sight of an armband, and
who remembers every detail about the putting of those
soldiers to the spear, will break into speech over his beer.
His purpose will be aroused. With the heart in him grieving,
by expressing the thought within their breasts, he will begin
to put their manhood to the test, to light the fires of ruinous
war, and make this speech:

" 'My lord, can you recognize the sword, the favorite
sword, which your father was wearing to battle on his last
2050   exploit in his helmet, when the Danes murdered him, when,
after Withergild lay dead following the overthrow of his
heroic soldiers, the valiant Scyldings took charge of the
battle-field? The son of one of those murderers or another
is now walking up and down the hall here, gloating over his
finery, and is boasting about the murder, and wearing the
treasure which by rights it is your duty to make your own.'
Time after time he will incite them and keep the memory
alive with painful speeches, until the hour comes when
that retainer of the lady sleeps spattered with blood from
the slice of the sword, his life forfeit for his father's deeds.
The other will escape from there alive; he knows the country well. Then the treaty confirmed by oath will be broken
on both sides; and after that fits of murderous rage will
break in waves upon Ingeld, and his love for the woman

will grow cooler because of the torment welling up in him. I therefore do not believe that this show of favor by the Heathobards, this offer of peace to the Danes, is an act of friendship with no treachery in it.

"I will go on to speak further about Grendel, my treasure-giver, that you may have certain knowledge of the pass to which that hand to hand combat between champions came. After the jewel of heaven glided beyond the clearings, the raging demon, the rabid thing in the night, came to attack us where, as yet untouched, we were guarding the hall. The 2075 brunt of battle fell on Hondscioh that time, vicious death on that doomed man. Girded champion though he was, he was the first to die. It was with his jaws that Grendel proved the death of our splendid comrade: he gorged down the whole body of that man we loved. Still that bloody-toothed killer had no mind to stalk away from the golden hall empty-handed any the sooner because of that. Instead, secure in his power, he made a try at me. My ready hand seized him. A thing like a glove was hanging off him, large and uncanny-looking, fastened by curious clasps. It was ingeniously worked all over with devilish designs and dragon-skins. Into that he meant to put me who had done him no harm, me and many others, that brazen creature who had started the trouble in the first place. The moment I stood up, that could not be. It is too long to tell, how I paid that mighty foe retribution for his every evil when, by my deeds, my lord, I did your people credit. He got away. For a little while, he enjoyed the pleasures of life. But his right hand remained in his wake in Heorot; and from there, defeated, his heart grieving, he plunged to the bottom of 2100 the pool.

"After the next day came, and we had sat down to the feast, the lord and friend of the Scyldings gave me great rewards, golden plate, many treasures. Then there was song and story. An old Scylding who knew many tales told of things far back. Once the bold soldier struck delight from the harp, sounded its joyous wood to the depths. Once he told a tale true and sad to hear. Once the great-hearted king unfolded a story full of wonder; once, again, the old soldier hobbled with age cried out for his youth, for his strength in battle. The heart heaved within when, far gone in years as he was, he brought so much to mind.

"There we took our pleasure that way the whole day through until the second night came down upon men. That moment Grendel's mother was suddenly at hand to avenge the wrong done her. Full of grief, she had made the journey. Death had taken her son, a feud with the Weders. The unholy woman avenged her child in full: she brazenly killed a man. It was Aeschere life fled from that time, the wise old councilor. And when the morning came, the Danish people might neither put his death-spent flesh to the torch, nor even load that dear man on to the pyre. In her fiend's embrace, she had borne his body away beneath the mountain stream. Of all the agonies which had for so long been befalling Hrothgar, the prince of that nation, that was the most grievous. It was then that the broken-hearted lord begged me on your life to do the heroic thing, to risk my life and win fame. He promised me reward. As is known far and wide, I found the keeper of that surging pool savage and gruesome. There was hand-to-hand-fighting between us for a while—the lake welled with blood—and I cut the head off Grendel's mother with a blade of more than ordinary power that was in that war-hall. I did not get out of there alive easily. But I was not yet doomed. Rather the son of Healfdene, that patron of good soldiers, gave me a great mass of treasures afterwards.

"So strictly has that great king always lived by the good old ways. I lost nothing by those gifts, by that reward for my strength, for the son of Healfdene gave me great treasures of my own choosing. These it is my desire to bring and present to you with deep affection. For everything that gives me pleasure depends on you. Other than you, Hygelac, I have few close kin."

He bade them bring in the boar-crowned standard, the helmet that towered in battle, the gray mail-shirt, the majestic war-sword, and afterwards made this speech:

"O prince among wise men, Hrothgar gave me this armor, and gave me orders that I should, in a word or two, tell you about this token of his affection. He said that King Heorogar, lord of the Scyldings, had owned it a long time.

None the sooner because of that did he intend to give the war-gear to Heoroward, his brave son, no matter how well disposed he might be towards him."

I have heard that four matched bay horses followed hard upon those precious gifts. He bestowed his affection on him in horses and treasures. So a kinsman ought to do, and not weave a wicked snare for another with secret cunning, set a death-trap for the comrade at his side. His nephew was deeply loyal to Hygelac, that man stern in battle, and each was always thinking of things to give pleasure to the other.

I have heard that he gave the necklace to Hygd, that rare jeweled treasure which Wealhtheow, the prince's daughter, had given him, together with three steeds, nimble and in glittering saddles. Because of that gift of the necklace, her breast was ever afterwards resplendent.

2175

Thus Ecgtheow's son, that man famous for deeds of war, bore himself bravely in acts of goodness, and led his life by the dictates of honor. He never killed members of his household-troop when they had been drinking; there was no bad temper in him. Rather, bold in battle, he kept the ample powers which God had given him within bounds. For a long time he had been looked down on, for the men of the Götar thought him no good, and the lord of the Weders would never give him a place of much worth on the mead-bench. They were firmly convinced that he was slack, a prince with no spine in him. To that man blessed with victory, a change for the better had come about in his every affliction.

Then the king brave in battle, patron of warriors, had them bring in an heirloom of Hrethel's worked with gold. Among the Götar at that time there was no finer treasure in the way of a sword. He laid that on Beowulf's lap, and gave him seven thousand hides of land, a hall, and a princely throne. The land in that kingdom belonged by inheritance to both of them together, the country and the rights to the property, but more especially to the one who was of higher rank.

It afterwards came to pass through clashes of battle in later days that Hygelac then lay dead, and war-swords

2200

proved the death of Heardred behind his shield when those rugged champions in war, the Swedes, good at war, sought him out in his glorious nation, and attacked that nephew of Hereric in a series of raids. After that, the broad realm passed into Beowulf's hands. He ruled it well fifty years— by then the king was aged, the keeper of the kingdom old —until in the dark nights a certain creature began to lord it over him, a dragon which was guarding a hoard in a high-roofed chamber, guarding a towering barrow of stone. A path lay beneath it, unknown to men. [Upon that some nameless man made his way in there, who, having got near the heathen hoard, tampered with it. His hand bore away a large flagon studded with treasure. The dragon made no secret of the theft, even though it had been cheated by the thief's cunning while it was asleep. The people, the men of that nation living near, discovered that its blood was up.]*

He who had done the dragon that injury had not broken into the hoard deliberately and of his own free will; but the slave of some man or other, under the threat of punishment, a man always in trouble, he had been running away
2225 from a bad beating, and in need of shelter, had got in there. He quickly looked around inside [The manuscript is damaged here; and four badly defective lines follow, which it would be pointless to translate.]

There in that house of earth there were many such old treasures, since some nameless soldier had in days long past hidden there the mighty heritage of a noble race, cherished goods of great price. Death had taken them all in earlier times; and the one veteran of that force who had been walking his post there the longest also expected the same fate, expected that he might but for a little while enjoy the treasure. In a field near the waves of the sea, the barrow stood all in readiness, newly built out along the headland, secured with devices to keep it sealed. Into it the keeper of the rings bore a mass of soldiers' treasure, of golden plate worth keeping safe. He spoke these few words:

"Earth, keep this wealth that true soldiers owned, since heroes might not keep it. Those great men got it from you

* This portion of the manuscript is badly damaged, and has been heavily amended by scholars.

in the first place. Death in war, stunning disaster, has taken   2250
every member of my companies of men who surrendered
this life. We have seen the last of fellowship in the hall.

"I have none to my name who might wear a sword, or
polish the plated flagon, our drinking cup of great price. The
seasoned soldiers are scattered elsewhere.

"The hard helmet blazoned with gold will be stripped of
its plates: the burnishers sleep whose duty it was to keep
masks of battle in trim. And the war-shirt, besides, which
stood up to the bite of the blades in the clash when the wall
of shields had been broken, rusts away left behind by its
hero. When the leader in war is gone, no ringed coat of
mail can go far on the sides of his soldiers.

"No joy in the harp at all, no delight in the singing wood.
No good hawk swoops through the hall; no more does the
swift horse pound the citadel-yard with its hooves. Death
like a plague has sent family on family on its everlasting
mission."

Thus with burning mind, the one man left of them all
gave vent to his grief. Day and night he walked his cheer-
less post until the wave of death broke on his heart.

An old invader of the half-light found the hoard standing
open in all its beauty, the kind of stark and savage dragon
which all ablaze seeks out barrows, the kind that flies at
night wrapped around with fire. Those who dwelt in that
region were badly afraid of it. It must find a hoard in the   2275
earth where, aging, it will guard the heathen gold, and not
in the least be better off for that.

Thus for three hundred years the mighty invader held
sway over that noble strongly built treasure-house in the
earth until that particular man enraged it in its heart. He
bore the plated flagon to his liege-lord and begged for am-
nesty. The hoard was then ransacked, a treasure of golden
armbands borne off, and his petition was granted the
wretched man. That was the first time the lord had got a
close look at that building of the men of old.

When the serpent awoke, fresh strife arose. There was a
scent upon the stone. The remorseless-hearted creature had
come upon a footprint left by its foe: in his stealthy cunning,
he had stepped right near the dragon's head. Thus a man

who is not doomed and who has the Lord's favor can come through trouble and exile safe. The keeper of the hoard searched eagerly along the ground. It was bent on finding the man who had done it harm in its sleep. Impatient and in a savage mood, it went around the whole outside of the mound over and over. There was no man in that wilderness. Yet it was relishing the contest, the work of battle. Once it 2300 went back into the barrow. It looked for the precious flagon. It discovered at once that some man had got at its gold, its noble treasures. With difficulty, the keeper of the hoard waited until evening came. By then the barrow-guard was infuriated: their foe meant to pay them back in fire for the loss of that precious drinking-cup. Then to the serpent's delight, the day broke up. It would stay on its rock-face no more, but speeded by fire, made its way in a blaze. The beginning was as terrible for those settled in that country as the end quickly and sadly proved to be for their treasure-giver.

It was then that the demon began to spit coals of fire, to burn down the splendid domains. In its anger with men, a blinding glare of flames shot up. That horrible flier through air meant to leave nothing alive. The serpent's skill in war was plain to see in many places; the rancor of their dogged foe, how he was hounding and humbling the men of the Götar, was evident far and near. Before the break of day, it sped back to the hoard, its hidden noble hall. With fire it had ringed the men in that country around, with bale and with pyre. It put its trust in the barrow, in its skill at war and its rampart. That trust played it false.

2325 Then a terrible thing was quickly and faithfully announced to Beowulf: his own estate, the finest of halls, the Gift-throne of the Götar, had fallen to dust in the burning waves. That was a blow to the heart for the great man, the greatest of afflictions to his mind. The wise man thought that he had bitterly angered the Ruler, the Lord Everlasting, by going against ancient law. His breast welled with dark thoughts in a way that had never been his.

With its flames the fire-dragon had reduced the citadel of that people to ashes, the well-watered land outside of it and the stronghold itself. The king of battles, lord of the Weders.

studied a way to take vengeance for that. That bulwark of
warriors, lord of good soldiers, then had them build a splendid war-shield all of iron. He was well aware that no wood
in the forest would serve him as a shield against flame.
That prince tried and true was fated to see the end of these
days which are lent us, the end of his life in this world,
and the serpent with him, though he had long kept safe the
wealth of that hoard.

The lord of the rings thought it matter for scorn that he
should seek out that flier afar with a company, with any
large force. He had no fear at all of that battle, nor did he
count the serpent's skill at war, its strength and its daring,
something to reckon with, because, taking risks in close   2350
quarters, he had come through many attacks, clashes of
battle before, ever since the time he had cleansed Hrothgar's hall, soldier blessed with victory that he was, and had
crushed in battle the kin of Grendel sprung of hateful stock.

Nor was that the least of pitched battles in which they
killed Hygelac. After the king of the Götar, lord and friend
of whole peoples, Hrethel's heir, beaten down by the blade,
died from the drinks the sword took in that raid on the land
of the Frisians, Beowulf got away from there under his own
power. He made use of his gift for swimming. He had
thirty sets of armor on his arm when, all by himself, he
struck out to sea. The Hetware who had borne their shields
against him had no call at all to be proud of their skill as
foot-soldiers. Few got away from that champion of battles
to reach home again. Ecgtheow's son swam back to his nation, poor wanderer, across the circuit of the sea. There
Hygd offered him the treasury and the kingdom, the armbands and the princely throne. She felt no confidence in her
son, that he would be able to keep the family-seats against
foreign forces, now that Hygelac was dead. But the people
in their bad plight could not bring it about by any terms
with that prince that he would any the sooner be lord over   2375
Heardred and accept the rank of king. Yet he did take care
of him with fond advice, with affection sprung from a sense
of honor, until he grew older, and ruled the Götar.

Men in exile, Ohthere's sons, made their way to him
across the sea. They had withheld allegiance from the prince

of the Swedes, the finest of the sea-kings who dealt out treasures in the realm of the Swedes, a famous lord. That was the end of him. For taking them in that time, Hygelac's son got a fatal wound from blows of the sword. And when Heardred lay dead, Ongentheow's son left to visit his home, and let Beowulf keep the throne, rule the Götar. That was a good king.

In later days he put his mind on retribution for the death of his prince. He befriended Eadgils when he was in a bad plight. He advanced the cause of that son of Ohthere across the wide sea with his army, with men and with weapons. After that he took full vengeance in a fatal series of raids full of grief for the Swedes. He had the life of King Onela.

Thus Ecgtheow's son had come through every kind of raid and counterraid, every kind of daring action, till that
2400 day alone in which it was his Fate to move against the serpent. That day the lord of the Götar, one of twelve men, his blood roused by outrage, went to scout the trail of the dragon. By then they had learned what the feud had sprung from, that disastrous hatred towards men. The famous treasure-studded cup had come into his possession through the man who had given the information. He who was the author of the cause of that strife was the thirteenth man in the troop. A heart-broken prisoner, treated with scorn, he had to show them the way to that place. Against his will he went to where he alone knew the hall in the earth to be, the crypt beneath the ground near the surge of the sea, near the wrestling of the waves. The whole inside of it was filled with jewels and hammered strips of gold. Its unholy keeper, a fierce and alert fighter, beneath the earth for years and years, was keeping the golden treasures safe. It was no easy bargain for any man to win them.

The king, stern in war, the golden lord of the Götar, then took his seat on the headland. All the while he was holding audience with the men of his household-troop, the heart in him was troubled, restless and driving towards death; near beyond measure the fate which was to strike the old man, seek the treasure of his soul, and divide his life from his body. The prince's spirit was not embraced by flesh long

after that. Beowulf made an address, Ecgtheow's son: "In   2425
my youth I came through many raids, many times of war. I
remember it all. I was seven years old when my lord of
treasures, the lord and friend of whole peoples, took me
from my father. King Hrethel kept me and took me in his
charge, gave me treasure and good food, bore our kinship
always in mind. In that stronghold throughout his life, I
was a man held no less worthy of love than any one of his
sons, Herebeald and Haethcyn and my Hygelac. By certain deeds of his brother, a bed of death not of his deserving
was laid for the eldest, when Haethcyn brought torture to
his lord and friend with an arrow from his horn-tipped bow.
He missed the target, and one brother shot down the other,
his own kinsman, with the bloody shaft. That was a fight
beyond reconcilement, wrong outrageously done, tiring the
heart out in the breast. Still and all, the prince was fated to
lose his life unavenged, so mournful a thing it is for an old
man to live to see the time when his child swings young from
the gallows.

"Well may he then tell the tale in a song full of sorrow,
when his son hangs, a joy to the raven; and old and wise
though he is, he can give him no help. Morning upon morn-   2450
ing he is always bringing to mind the death of his son. He
cares nothing about living to see another heir in his strongholds, since that one came to the end of his deeds by the
hard fate of death. Shaken with grief, he looks at the place
where his son slept, the wine-hall laid waste, a couch for
the winds, pillaged of joy. In shadows they lie asleep, the
horsemen, the heroes. No sound of the harp swells there,
no show of delight in those courts as there was in days past.
He takes to his bed then; lonely for his lonely son, he sings
the song of his grief.

"It all did seem too big to him, the fields and the place
where the men lived, such restless sorrow of heart did the
lord of the Weders bear for Herebeald. He could by no
means put the cost of the feud on the killer, nor could he
any the sooner hound that man with vengeful acts, although he had lost favor with him. He whom that grief befell then surrendered the noise of cheer among men;

driven by sorrow, he chose God's light. He left his heirs a nation and a citadel, as a happy man does, when he departed from life.

"Then there was wrong done and conflict between the Swedes and the Götar, after Hrethel died, strife on both 2475 sides across the wide water, unbending hostility. And the sons of Ongentheow were strong and brave with their army. They had no intention of keeping peace across the sea, but carried out many a terrible and cruel massacre at Hreosnabeorh. My loving kinsmen took full vengeance for that raiding and outrage, as has come to be common knowledge, although one of them paid for it with his life, a hard bargain. The brunt of war fell on Haethcyn, the lord of the Götar. Then I have heard that the next morning one brother avenged the other on his murderer with the sword's edge. When Ongentheow attacked Eofor, his war-helmet split, and the old Swede fell, white from the wound. Eofor's hand remembered enough about feuding: it did not withhold the fatal blow.

"In time of war I paid him back with my shining sword for the treasures which he gave me, as it was granted me to do. He gave me land, a place to live, an estate that was a joy. No hardship ever befell him in which he had to look to the Gifthas or the Danes, or in the kingdom of the Swedes, for a soldier not my equal, and buy him with pay. I was always bent on standing before him in the first line of the troop; and that is the way I will always do battle as long 2500 as this sword holds out which has stood by me time after time early and late, ever since the day when with it I proved the death of Daeghrefn, the champion of the Hugas, before all those seasoned troops. He might never bring this beautiful set of armor, this ornament on my breast, to the king of the Frisians, for that keeper of the standard fell, a prince in daring. No sword edge was his death, but my battle-grasp; that broke up the poundings of his heart and shattered the flesh he was housed in. Now the blade's edge, this hand and this hard sword, must fight for the hoard."

Beowulf made an address; he spoke in words of solemn boasting for the last time: "I have taken risks in many battles in my youth. Old protector of my people that I am, I mean to follow yet one more feud through, and do a deed worthy of fame, if this vicious ravager rushes at me from its hall in the earth."

Then for the last time, he addressed his soldiers, his brave, helmeted men, his own dear comrades: "I would not wear a sword or any weapon against the serpent, if I knew how else I could come to grips with the terrible creature to my credit, as I did years back with Grendel. But I expect hot, rushing fire, steam and venom; that is why I have this shield and mail-shirt on. I will not back away the space of a foot from the guard of this barrow; but at this rampart will come to pass what Fate, Umpire over every man, ordains for us both. Dressed in your mail-shirts, soldiers in armor, wait on the barrow to see which of us will best come through the damage after the murderous clash. This exploit is not for you: it is not in any man's grasp but mine alone to give a taste of his strength to this terrible creature and achieve this heroic deed. I will get the gold by my daring; or battle, some stunning disaster, will take your lord." 2525

The bold challenger then rose with his shield at his side, stern beneath his helmet, and wore his battle-shirt under the ledge of stone. He trusted in his strength. That was no coward's exploit.

Great in those virtues which become a man, he who had come through many bad hours, many times of war, clashes of battle when foot-troops crashed together, caught sight of a stone arch along the rampart, and a stream bursting from it out of the barrow. The troubled water of that torrent was hot with rushing fire. Because of the dragon-flame, he could not get through to the recess near the hoard at any time without being burned. Enraged as he was, the prince of the storm-weathering Götar let a cry break from his breast. The stout-hearted man roared. His voice, bright with menace, went echoing deep beneath the gray stone. Hatred was stirred up: the keeper of the hoard recognized it for a man's voice. No longer was there time to seek peace. From the very beginning, the breath of the terrible creature, its hot battle-steam, was coming out of the stone. The earth thundered. Soldier-like beneath the barrow, the lord of the 2550

Götar swung his shield against its gruesome tenant; by then
the heart of the coiled thing was driven to go looking for
battle. The great king of battles had earlier drawn his
sword; it was a legacy of great age with very sharp edges.
In each of those creatures with murder in their hearts, there
was terror of the other. Firm in his mind, that lord among
lords took his stand with his tall shield before him. While
the serpent was coiling, he waited in his armor. Once coiled,
it went at him in a blazing glide, rushing to its fate. For the
famous lord, that shield proved good cover for life and limb
a shorter time than his heart sought of it; there and then, the
first day in his life he might make a full show of power, since
2575 Fate had not ordained victory in battle for him. The lord of
the Götar swung his hand up and struck that horrible scaly
thing with the mighty sword of his forbears. Its burnished
edge grew blunt at the bone, and cut less deeply than the
great king, hounded by misfortunes, had need. After that
blow in the battle, the barrow-guard was in a wicked mood.
It hurled its murderous fire. The fighting flames were spring-
ing up everywhere. The golden lord of the Götar boasted
no more of glorious victories: his unsheathed war-sword
had failed him in the attack, as it never should have, tried
and true iron that it was. That was no easy passing in which
the famous son of Ecgtheow was about to give up the surface of earth: against his will, he must make his dwelling
elsewhere, as every man must relinquish these days which
are lent us.

And there was no long pause then till the terrible creatures clashed again. The keeper of the hoard took heart
afresh—its breast swelled with breath. He who before had
ruled a nation suffered agony, hemmed around by fire. The
picked comrades, the sons of princes in his troop, in no
way stood by him; instead, they fled into the wood and
2600 saved their lives. In but one of them, the heart welled with
sorrow. Nothing can ever set aside the ties of the blood for
a man who thinks right.

Wiglaf was his name, Weohstan's son, a warrior well
beloved, a prince of the Scylfings and a kinsman of
Aelfhere. He saw his liege-lord enduring that heat in his
helmet. And then he remembered the honors which that

lord had bestowed on him earlier, the rich domain of the Waegmundings, every privilege over the people which his father had had. He could not hold back. His hand grasped his shield of yellow linden-wood; he took up the old sword which had been the legacy among men of Eanmund, Ohthere's son. With the edge of his sword, Weohstan had been the death of that lordless exile, and had borne off to his kinsmen his helmet of burnished plate, his ringed mail-shirt, and his old sword of giant make. Onela gave him that war-gear belonging to his kinsman, that armor ready for use; he did not say a word about the feud, although Weohstan had killed his brother's son. He kept those precious things many years, that blade and mail-shirt, until his son was able to do the heroic thing, as his father had before him. When he was taking leave of this life, old 2625 and on the way out, he gave Wiglaf an untold amount of war-gear of every kind among the Götar. This was the first time for the young champion that it fell his duty to carry out a raid with his lord. His heart did not turn soft, nor did his father's legacy grow blunt in that warfare. The serpent discovered that, once they had come together.

Wiglaf made an address; he spoke many words to his comrades about their duties. The heart in him was grieving: "I remember the time in which we were taking our mead, when in that hall of noble toasts we promised this lord of ours who gave us these golden armbands that we would repay him for these arms, these helmets and hard swords, if need like this should ever befall him. That is why of his own free will he chose us for this expedition from among the whole army, believed us worthy of honor, and gave me these treasures; that is why he held us great soldiers, his brave-helmeted men, even though as lord over us and keeper of his people, he planned to do this deed of daring on his own, since he had achieved the greatest feats among men, desperate undertakings. Now the day has come when our liege-lord stands in need of the strength of great soldiers. Let us go and help our prince of battles. As long as that heat lasts, that cruel and terrible fire, God knows that for 2650 my part I would much rather the flame embraced my flesh together with that of my treasure-giver. I do not feel it decent that we carry our shields back home, unless we first are able in some way to bring this foe to the ground and save the life of the lord of the Weders. I certainly know that his deserts over long years are not such that he alone of the veteran soldiers of the Götar should suffer agony and fall in battle. This sword and helmet, this mail-shirt and armor will be shared by us both."

Then he moved forward through the killing smoke; he wore his helmet to his prince's aid. He spoke these few words: "Dear Beowulf, make it all good, following out what you said in the time of your youth, that never as long as you lived would you let your glory drag in the dust. Now bold in your deeds, a prince with one thing in mind, you must fight with all your strength to save your life. I will stand by you to the full."

After those words, the furious serpent, a cruel demon of malice, came blazing with surges of fire to attack its foes, the men it hated, a second time. His shield was burned to the rim by the waves of fire; his shirt of mail could not possibly have helped the young warrior, but the young man managed with daring to get behind his kinsman's shield when his own had been burnt to ashes by the flames. Then once more the king of battles fixed his mind on renown. With all his might and main, he struck so hard with his war-sword that it stuck in the serpent's head, driven in by the force. Naegling fell to pieces. Beowulf's old and iron-colored sword failed him in the fight. It was not granted him that the edge of any iron might help him in battle. The hand was too strong, and, as my story has it, sought too much in its swing from every kind of blade. Even when he bore into battle a weapon tempered by blood, he was not the least better off for it.

Then the destroyer of that people, the ferocious fire-dragon, was bent on attack a third time. It rushed at the brave man, when the chance was given it; hot and vicious in battle, it took hold of his whole neck with its sharp teeth. He was soaked with his life's blood; his blood welled out of him in waves.

Then I have heard that the good soldier of that great king standing beside him made plain in his lord's time of need the daring, the skill and the courage that was his by nature. He paid no heed to the dragon's head; the hand of the great-hearted man was badly burned when he came to his kinsman's aid. Soldier-like in his armor, he struck the vicious demon a little below the head, so that the sword sank in deep, bright and plated with gold, and the fire then began to slacken. Then the king himself once more came to his senses: he drew the murderous knife, keen and sharpened for battle, which he wore on his mail-shirt. The bulwark of the Weders cut the serpent in half. They had struck down their enemy—their daring had driven the life out of it—and they both had killed it, princes bound by ties of blood. So a soldier should be, a true retainer in time of need. 2700

For that lord, that was the last moment of victory won by his own deeds, the last of his work in the world. The wound which the earth-dragon had just given him began to burn and swell. He grasped at once that the venom was working deep within his breast with deadly force. The prince then made his way to a place where deep in wise thought, he sank down on a seat beside the rampart. He looked at that work of giants, saw how that hall of earth held within it arches of stone, firm on their stanchions. It was then that with his own hands, that noble retainer, good beyond measure, washed him in the water, his famous prince, his lord and his friend, spattered with blood, sick to death of battle. And he unclasped his helmet.

Beowulf made an address. Despite the gashes on him, his sad mortal wounds, he spoke. He was well aware that he had lived through the last of moments in daylight, of delight in the earth. His whole tally of days had run out; death was near beyond measure. 2725

"I would now have given these arms to my son, if it had been granted me that any heir of my body should succeed me. I have ruled these people fifty years. There never has been a single great king among those dwelling round us who ever dared to meet me with his troops or make me terrible threats. In my own land, I have stood up to the decrees of Fate which time brought. I have kept well what was mine. I have never gone looking for contrived quarrels, and I have never sworn oath upon oath in any unjust pursuit. Sick with mortal wounds though I am, I can take comfort in all that, for the Ruler of men need never punish me for the vicious murder of kinsmen, when my life passes from my body. Now, go quickly, dear Wiglaf, to take a good look at the hoard beneath the gray stone. Now the serpent lies dead, sleeps, sorely wounded, its treasure taken from it. Hasten now that I may have some sense of those riches of old, those golden possessions, that I may have a full

2750 sight of those rare and glittering jewels, and because of the wealth of that treasure, may more easily be able to relinquish this life of mine and this princely dignity which I have held so long."

Then after those words, I have heard that the son of Weohstan quickly obeyed his wounded, battle-sick prince; and wore his coat of mail, his woven battle-shirt under the barrow's roof. When he had gone past the seat, the brave noble retainer, glorying in victory, caught sight of yellow jeweled treasures: gold glittering upon the ground, a rare tapestry upon the wall. And then he saw the den of the serpent, the old flier through the half-light, pitchers standing in it, flagons of men long gone, with no one to burnish them, their golden designs fallen off them. Many a helmet was there, old and mottled with rust, many an armband, twisted with mastery. Bury it who will, treasure, gold in the ground, can easily prove stronger than any of the race of men.

He saw, besides, a banner of pure gold swaying high above the hoard, the greatest of rarities from a man's fingers, woven with a genius for handwork: from it shot a radiance by which he could get a true sense of the floor of the cave, and look closely at the precious things. There was no sign of the serpent there; for the sword's edge had taken him. Then, I have heard, that single man rifled the hoard,

2775 the old work of giants: he loaded cups and dishes of his own choosing against his breast. He also took the banner, the brightest of standards. The sword of his old prince—its edge was iron—had earlier killed the creature which had long been the guardian of those treasures. It had waged a fiery reign of terror, blazing before the hoard, breaking into battle in the middle of the night, till the day it had died in agony. The messenger was in haste, anxious about getting back, made more so by the treasures. Worry tormented him whether, his heart rising, he would find the lord of the Weders alive in that cleared place where he had just left him desperately sick.

Then with the treasure in his arms, he found the famous lord, his prince, soaked with blood and at the end of his life. Again he splashed him with water till the beginnings of speech broke from the treasury of his heart. Then in his grief, the old soldier spoke—he had looked closely at the gold: "In these words, I will speak my thanks to the Prince of All, the King of Glory, the Lord Everlasting, for these beautiful things of great price that I here fix my eyes on, because I have been allowed to win such wealth for my people before the day of my death. Now that I have sold my old life for this hoard of treasures, keep on looking after   2800 the needs of my people. I have not the strength to stay here any longer. After my burning, have my famous soldiers build me a barrow on that spit in the sea. It is to tower as my memorial with my people high above Hronesness, so that seafarers who drive their steep ships from far off through the shadowy fogs on the flood will call it Beowulf's Barrow in after years.

With his mind composed, the lord took from his neck his ring of twisted gold; and gave the young soldier, his retainer, his gold-encrusted helmet, that neck-ring, and his shirt of mail. He bade him make good use of them: "You are the last of our family left, of the Waegmundings. Fate has lured all my kinsmen to their death, great soldiers in their daring. I must go after them."

That was the old man's last expression of the thoughts within his heart, before he took his turn upon the pyre, in the hot, battling waves. The soul went out of his breast to seek judgment among the just.

It went hard for the young soldier when he saw the man he loved most on earth pathetically bearing up at the end of his life. The killer also lay dead, the terrible earth-   2825 dragon, robbed of its life, driven to its last misery. That serpent with its wicked coils might have charge of the treas-

ure no more, for the edges of their iron swords had taken
it, the hard blades left by the hammer, notched by battle,
so that the flier-afar fell to the earth near its treasure-hall,
stilled by its wounds. No more did it move through its
courses, flying the midnight air, no more did it flare like a
vision, proud of its wealth of treasures, for it had fallen to
earth by the deed of the hand of that war-lord. Never a man
in that land, as my story has it, even among those gifted
with great strength, daring though he might be in every
kind of action, was so endowed that he would have made
that rush full into the breath of the venomous foe, or disturbed that hall of rings with his hands, if he had come
upon its guardian standing watch in the barrow. That portion of noble treasure had been paid for by Beowulf with
his death. Each of them had to come to the end of this
life which is lent us.

It was not long till the time that the men who hung back
from the battle left the woods, those spineless breakers of
faith, ten altogether, who before had not dared bring their
spears into play in their lord's great need. But here they
2850 were, feeling their shame, wearing their shields and their
war-gear to where the old man lay dead. They looked at
Wiglaf. Exhausted, the champion sat near his prince's shoulders. He was trying to rouse him with water; he did not
succeed in the least. Never on earth could he have kept life
in that leader of spearmen, no matter how deeply he wished
to, nor could he set aside one jot decreed by the Ruler. The
Judgment of God ruled every man's deeds by His will,
even as it now does.

It was easy then for the man who had lost heart before
to get a savage answer from the young retainer. Wiglaf
made an address, Weohstan's son, that broken-hearted
soldier—he looked at the men he loathed: "A man who
has a mind to tell the truth can well say that the liege-lord
who gave you those treasures, those fighting outfits you are
standing in there, when at the ale-bench, a true lord to his
retainers, he gave those dwelling in his hall one helmet
and mail-shirt after another of the stoutest make he could
find, far or near, completely threw that armor away as

protection when war came upon him. No call to boast at all
had this great king in his comrades-at-arms. Yet God, the
Lord of Victories, granted it to him that he alone should 2875
avenge himself with his knife's edge, when he was in need
of his daring. I could give him but little protection in battle; nevertheless, beyond my scope, I undertook to be of
some help to my kinsman. When I struck his mortal enemy
with my sword, it was always the worse off for it: less
fiercely the fire surged from the seat of its senses. Too few
protectors crowded around their lord when that bad time befell him. Now receiving of treasure and giving of swords
shall cease for your kin; all their joy in domain, all that they
love shall fail them. Every man on your family estates must
move on, stripped of all rights to his land, when nobles hear
from afar the news of your flight, that deed without honor.
For any true soldier, death is better than a life of reproach."

He then had the outcome of battle announced in the
compound up over the sea-cliff, where the troop of good
soldiers had sat the day through since morning, expecting
both things by turns, the last day on earth of the man they
loved, and his return to them. He who rode up to the ridge
of the headland kept little of the strange news unspoken,
but told it faithfully before them all:

"Now the giver of joy of the Weder People, the lord of 2900
the Götar, lies fast in the sleep of death. He keeps his fatal
bed through the deeds of the serpent. Beside him, fallen
sick of the knife-wounds, the foe to his life lies dead. He
could by no means with his sword make a mark on that
terrible creature. Wiglaf, Weohstan's son, sits over Beowulf,
one noble soldier above the other's corpse: he stands
guard over the head of friend and foe with the heart gone
out of him. Now what the people have to expect is a time
of war, once the fall of the king becomes plain far and wide
to the Franks and the Frisians. This serious trouble was
first brought into being when Hygelac went sailing with an
invading force into the Frisian country, at which time the
Hetware fell upon him in battle, and because of their
greater force, quickly managed it that the mailed warrior
had to fall back. He fell in the midst of his troop: no pre-

cious things did that lord give his tried and true soldiers. The favor of the Merovingian has ever since been denied us.

"Nor do I look to the Swedish People for friendship or good faith, for it has become widely known that it was Ongentheow who had the life of Haethcyn, Hrethel's son, at Ravenswood, when the Götar troops in their pride first marched on the fighting Swedes. The shrewd father of Ohthere, old and fearsome, brought the counterattack at once. He killed the invading king, and, old as he was, rescued the old woman, his wife, the mother of Onela and Ohthere, who had been robbed of her golden jewels. And then he tracked down his mortal enemies to the point where, in hard straits and leaderless, they had escaped into Ravenswood. There with a huge force, he besieged those the sword had left exhausted from wounds. All through the long night he threatened one misery after another to the sad company. He said that next day he would drain the life from them with the sword's edge, and hang certain of them on the gallows-tree as sport for the birds. Relief came to those troubled hearts at daybreak, when they heard a call, the horn and trumpets of Hygelac as the great man came marching on their trail with men from his veteran troop.

"The bloody wake left by both Swedes and Götar, that murderous onslaught of men, was plain to see far and wide, how those armies kept the feud between them alive. When, old and down-hearted, the great man went looking with his kinsmen for their place of refuge, Lord Ongentheow turned to higher ground. He had heard tell of Hygelac's strength in battle, the skill of that proud man in war. He had no faith in his staying power, no faith that he could hold out against the raiders, make a stand for his treasure, his son and his wife. The old man next drew back behind an earthen embankment. Then chase was given to the Swedish troops. The standards of Hygelac passed right over the entrenchment, once Hrethel's avengers had crowded to the compound. Then by the sword's edge, gray-haired Ongentheow was driven to such a pass that the great king had to suffer the judgment passed on him by one man, Eofor.

Wulf, Wonred's son, had cut him so furiously with his
weapon that blood from the blow kept spurting out beneath
his hair in streams. Nevertheless the old Swede was not
shaken by fear, but when he had turned around, the great
king quickly repaid the murderous blow with one even
worse in return. The bold son of Wonred could make no
counterattack, because before he could, Ogentheow had so
shattered his helmet that, soaked with blood, it was his fate
to sink to the ground. He fell to the earth, but he was not   2975
yet doomed. He recovered, although the wound had struck
deep. When his brother was lying there, Eofor, that stern
retainer of Hygelac, having got beyond the wall of shields,
split the giant helmet with his broad blade, with his old
sword of giant make. Then it was the king, the keeper of
the people, who sank to the ground. He was struck to
the brains. When the field had been so cleared that they
had won control of the battle-ground, there were many then
at hand bandaging his brother, and lifting the powerful man
up. Meanwhile, one hero was pillaging the other: he took
the mail-shirt of iron off Ongentheow, and the hard, hilted
sword and the helmet with it. He bore the old man's decora-
tions to Hygelac. Hygelac took the precious things, and
made him handsome promises of reward among the troops.
And thus he stood by those promises: when he reached
home, the lord of the Götar, Hrethel's son, paid Eofor and
Wulf for that battle-charge with treasure beyond counting.
He gave them each a hundred thousand in land and meshed
rings. No man on earth felt the need to reproach him for
that gift, since they had won those glories in the field. And
then he gave Eofor his only daughter to do honor to him
in his domain and to pledge him his favor.

"That is the state of feud and enmity, murderous hatred   3000
towards men, which, I have every expectation, the Swedish forces will seek us out with, once they learn that our
prince is dead who in the past after the fall of our heroes
protected this treasury and realm against its foes and who
protected the valiant Scyldings. Not only did he do what
was best for the people but he also did what was heroic.

"Now haste is our best course, that we may look deep at
our great king, and bring him who gave us these golden

armbands on his way to the pyre. No single man's portion will melt with that great heart, for there is a hoard of treasures there, gold beyond counting, grimly purchased. And since at the last, he bought those golden armbands with his own life, the blaze must then devour them, the flame roof them over. No good soldier shall wear that treasure in his memory, nor lovely girl have a necklace from it on her neck, for with grieving heart, stripped of her gold, she must walk foreign soil not once but over and over, now the lord of the army has laid aside laughter, delight, and the sound of men telling tales. Because of that, many a spear, cold in the morning, shall be grasped by our fists and raised in our hands. No crowding swell of the harp shall awaken warriors; but the dusky raven, speeding above the doomed,

3025 shall have much to say to the eagle of how he sped in his feeding when he rifled the slain with the wolf."

Thus the brave soldier told his hateful news. He got little wrong in his prophecies and stories. The troop all arose. Sadly they marched beneath Earnaness to look at the strange sight, the tears pouring from them. They came on him then in the sand, the soul gone from him, the man who gave them their golden armbands in days gone by, keeping his bed of rest. The last day had really befallen that great man, then; the lord of the Weders had indeed died a mysterious death. Before, they had seen the strange creature, the loathsome serpent, lying dead on the ground opposite that place. The fire-dragon, frighteningly mottled with gruesome colors, was scorched by its own embers. It was fifty feet long stretched out. Once it had taken delight in the sky at night, and sank to return to its den. Now it slept fast in death: the earth-dragon had passed through its last tour of duty. By it stood goblets and beakers; by it lay chargers, and swords of great price, rusted and eaten through

3050 as if they had lain a thousand years there in the earth's embrace. That vast heritage was also bound by a spell, gold of men long gone, which no man might touch in that hall of rings unless God Himself, the True Lord of Victories, granted it one whom He had willed to open the hoard, some man who seemed fit to Him.

By then it was evident that the course of him who had

wrongly hidden the jewels deep beneath the wall had not
prospered. First, its guardian had killed a very great man,
then that attack was savagely avenged. It is a mystery
where a great soldier, bent on daring, will come to the end
of the fortunes of life when a man can no longer dwell with
those of his blood in the mead-hall. Thus it was with Beowulf, when he sought the guard of the barrow and frays
hard to plan for. He himself did not know how his cutting
off from the world should come to pass.

Thus did the great lords who put the treasure there lay a
grave curse upon it till the Day of Doom: the man who
plundered that ground would be convicted of great crime,
imprisoned in demon haunts, bound fast in the bonds of
hell, and wickedly tormented. Not that he who was greedy
for gold would have any more readily first consulted the   3075
owner's good will.

Wiglaf made an address, Weohstan's son: "Often through
one man's will, many a good soldier must suffer such misfortune as has befallen us. We could not have brought the
keeper of this realm, this lord we loved, to any course by
which he would not have attacked the guardian of the gold,
but let it lie, as it long had, keeping its haunts till the end
of the world. He held true to his noble fate. The hoard has
been opened to our sight, cruelly won. The fate was too
hard which drove the great king there. I have been in
there; and I looked through it all, the precious goods in that
building, when the chance was given me. In no kindly way
was the right of entry deep beneath that wall of earth
granted me. I hastily took in my hands a great and mighty
load from that hoard of treasures, and carried it out here to
my king. He was then still alive, sound of mind and senses.
The old man in his grief had his full say about many things,
and ordered me to greet you, and gave the command that
you should build in the place of his burning a barrow befitting the deeds of your lord and friend, noble, great and
glorious, since he was the soldier most honored among men
far and wide throughout earth, for as long as he was given   3100
to enjoy the wealth of his stronghold. Now let us hasten,
and see and look through that mass of curious jewels a
second time, that rare sight beneath the wall. I will show

you the way, that you may get a close enough look at the armbands and heavy gold. Let the bier be ready, the fire laid, when we come out; and then let us carry our lord, this man we loved, to where he will long remain in the Master's keeping."

Then Weohstan's son, that hero brave in battle, had the order proclaimed to many men who had domains in their charge and men at their command that they should bring to the great man from far and wide wood for his pyre: "Now must the blaze devour, its smoky flame fattening, this prince of soldiers, who lived through shower on shower of iron, when the storm of arrows, shot with power, broke against the shield-wall, and the shaft, speeded by flanges of feathers, did its duty, did the arrow service."

The wise son of Weohstan did indeed choose from the troop seven men altogether, the finest of the king's retainers. He went beneath the hated roof as the eighth of those war-heroes. One man who was walking in front carried a blazing torch. It was not by lot that anyone rifled the treasure. Once the men caught sight of any portion of it lying there wasting away, none of them took much thought, but carried the treasures of great price outside. They also shoved the dragon, the serpent, over the sea-wall. They let the wave take it, the flood embrace the guardian of treasures. Then the twisted gold was loaded on a wagon, a mass beyond counting in every respect; and the prince, the gray war-hero, was borne to Hronesness.

The men of the Götar then prepared him a noble pyre, hung around, as he had asked them, with helmets, battle-shields, and gleaming coats of mail. Wailing, the heroes then laid their famous prince, the lord whom they loved, in the midst of those things. Then on the barrow the warriors began to kindle the largest of funeral fires. Black above the blaze, the wood-smoke rose. The fire roaring was threaded with the sound of tears—all stir in the wind had died—until hot to its heart it had shattered the flesh he was housed in. With hearts gone dead, they gave way to the grief in their minds, and wailed for their liege-lord. Over and over, besides, the queen of the Götar, her hair around her, broken with sorrow, sang her grieving song. She sang that she, for

her part, stood in sore dread of more days of mourning, of
many slaughters, a reign of armed terror, humiliation, and
forced enslavement. Heaven swallowed the smoke.

Then the Weder people built his shelter on the headland.
It was tall and large, and could be seen by seafarers far
out to sea. And in ten days they raised that beacon to the
man brave in battle. Around what the fire left, they built a
wall of the worthiest kind their most discerning men could
devise. Golden armbands and jewels, they put into that
barrow, all such adornments as men bent on trouble had
taken before. They let earth keep the treasure of heroes,
left the gold in the ground, where it lives on still to this day,
as useless to men as it earlier was. Then around the barrow
rode the children of princes, men bold in battle, twelve in
all. It was their desire to give vent to their grief, to cry out
for their king, to put their words into song and tell about
the man. They paid honor to his heroism and his daring
achievement. Manfully they praised him, since it is fitting
that one should put into words praise of his lord and friend,   3175
show love from the heart, when that lord's fate is to be led
forth from his body. The men of the Götar, his household
retainers, thus lamented their lord's downfall: they said that
he was, of the kings of the world, the gentlest of men and
the most obliging, the most gracious to his people and most
bent on winning praise.

THE SONG
OF ROLAND

Translated, and with an introduction by,
W. S. Merwin

For Alice Lowell and Annella Brown

Introduction

Some time near the end of July, Charles (Charles the King, Charles the Emperor, Charles the Great, Charlemagne) turned his army north toward the Pyrenees and France. The year was 778. He was thirty-six years old and he was not used to failure, but even the royal chroniclers would have difficulty in trying to describe his ambitious summer campaign in Spain as though it had been a success.

It had not been hastily conceived. Suleiman, the Moorish governor of Barcelona, had visited Charles in the spring of 777 to urge him to cross the Pyrenees, and the request, and Charles' response to it, were both influenced by dynastic and religious promptings which had histories of their own.

Suleiman was a member of the Abassid dynasty, descended from an uncle of Mohammed. Earlier in the century the Abassids had overthrown the reigning Umayyad dynasty and assassinated every member of it except one, Abdur Rahman, who had escaped to Spain and established himself there as the Emir. Suleiman's hatred of Rahman was understandable, and it had already led him to seek and to obtain the protection of his Christian neighbor, King Pepin of France, Charles' father.

There were other reasons why Charles would have been sympathetic to Suleiman. He was himself a member of a young dynasty, a matter of subtle importance in a world governed to a great degree by tradition. And then, Abdur Rahman, as the last representative of the Umayyads, stood for the family which, half a century before, had commanded the great Moorish invasion of France. At that time the apparently invincible Umayyads had forced their way as far north as Tours before Charles' grandfather, Charles Martel, turned them back. It was the Umayyads whom Charles' father, Pepin, had fought and at last driven from France.

But doubtless none of these considerations would have impelled Charles to cross the Pyrenees if it had not been for a more powerful and obvious motive: his own ambition. In the first nine years of his reign he had conquered Aquitaine, beaten the Saxons and the Lombards, and become the official guardian of Christendom, whose boundaries he had extended to the north and east. An expedition into Spain would give him a chance to unify the different parts of his realm in a common effort, and incidentally to conquer the as yet unsubjected Basque provinces. Suleiman probably stressed the apparent fact that Rahman was a menace to Charles' southern frontier, and very possibly he would have told the French king that if he were to attack Rahman now he could not help succeeding, that the Abassids themselves were raising an army of Berbers to send against the Umayyad, and that the people of Spain were on the point of rebellion. The exact details of the embassage and the terms of the agreement that was reached are not known. But by Easter 778 Charles was in Poitou with an immense army recruited from every part of his kingdom: it included Goths, contingents from Septimania and Provence, Austrasians, Neustrians, Lombards, Burgundians, and Bavarians. After Easter he crossed the western end of the Pyrenees, through the Basque country, at the head of half his army. He sent the other half around the eastern end of the mountains. They were to meet before Saragossa.

Just what happened that summer was carefully obscured in the accounts and will never be known. Certainly there were no great triumphs. The Christian natives of Spain did not hasten to overthrow the tolerant Moorish rule and welcome the Franks; on the contrary, the Christians of the kingdom of Asturias preferred their own independence to the presence of a foreign army however dear to the Pope. It is also possible that they were in league with Rahman. At any rate they resisted the Franks. The Christian city of Pampelona refused entry to Charles and had to be stormed; it was the only city in the entire campaign which was actually taken. The native rebellion against Rahman never amounted to much and Suleiman himself had a falling out with his Moorish allies on the African continent. When the Frankish army assembled before Saragossa the city defied it, despite Suleiman's diplomatic efforts; it is not known how hard Charles tried to take it, but he had no siege machinery, and he failed. By some time in July he had received the formal surrender of a few cities—a gesture which may have owed as much to his alliance with Suleiman as it did to his own army—and he had gained some hostages, and little else. There is no way of knowing just why he abandoned the campaign so early in the summer. It is possible that he saw nothing to be gained by staying, in the circumstances, and was simply cutting his losses. Supplies may have run dangerously low. It is conceivable that the campaign had turned out far worse than the accounts would lead us to suppose, and that the army was in fact retreating. Even if that were so it cannot have been a rushed or disorderly retreat: in August the army stopped at Pampelona long enough to raze the walls of the city to punish the inhabitants for their resistance, and no doubt to weaken the Spanish side of the frontier. It has been suggested (by Fawtier) that if Charles had not been in a hurry, for some reason, he would have paused long enough to celebrate the important feast of the Dormition of the Virgin on August 15th. At any event he did not do so, but pushed on into the Pyrenees.

What happened next is one of the great riddles.

In the earliest history of Charles' expedition, the one included in a chronicle known as the *Annales Royales,* there is no reference to any military action whatever in the Pyrenees. All later writers on the subject have agreed that the author had something of importance to be silent about. Of such importance, in fact, that his immediate successors evidently felt that mere silence would not serve to conceal it, and set about explaining it. The original *Annales* were rewritten and expanded roughly a quarter of a century after they were first compiled. It was long thought that the rewriting was done by Charlemagne's biographer Einhard, and though it is now certain that the changes are not his, the second edition of the chronicle is still referred to as the *Annales dites d'Einhard*. In this work there is a brief and contradictory account of something which happened on the way back from Spain. The Basques, it says here, from positions at the tops of the mountains, attacked the rear guard and put the whole army in disorder; the Franks were caught at a disadvantage and did badly; most of the commanders of the different sections of the army were killed, and the enemy, helped by the nature of the terrain, managed to carry off the baggage and escape. There is a reference, too, to the bitterness of Charles' grief.

Then there is Einhard's own account. In the first place he is more ingenious than his predecessors at making it sound as though the Spanish campaign had been a success; then, having built up the picture, he sets against it the Pyrenean ambush on the way back as a relatively minor mishap. It was the treacherous Gascons, he says; they waited until the army was spread out in a long line in the gorges, and then they rushed down and threw the baggage train and the rear guard into confusion. There was a battle in the valley and the Franks were thrown back. The Gascons killed their opponents, the rear guard, to a man, seized the baggage, and scattered under cover of night. Their flight was made easier by their light armor and the nature of the terrain. And then Einhard says, "In this battle Egginhard the royal seneschal, Anselm the Count of the Palace, and Hruodland, the Warden of the Breton Marches, were killed, with very many others." It is one of the only two glimpses in history of the knight whose name would come to evoke one of the richest bodies of legend in the Middle Ages, and one of its greatest poems. The other is a coin, worn, but still displaying on one side the name *Carlus,* and on the reverse, *Rodlan.*

One final mention of the battle, by the chroniclers, is of interest. While the army was making its way back from Spain, Charlemagne's wife, in France, gave birth to a son, Louis, who would be his heir. Sixty years after the battle Louis' own biographer, a writer known as The Astronome, in speaking of it said that the names of those who fell in that action were so well known that there was no need to repeat them.

Of all the battles of the period, this one probably has excited most curiosity, and almost nothing about it is definitely known. It is not mere historical interest in the sources of the Roland story which still draws the speculation of scholars to what scanty evidence has come down to our times. In this case the theories of how the legend developed from the event are even more than usually dependent upon a notion of what the event was: a bitter but militarily unimportant misfortune, on the one hand, or one of the critical defeats of Charlemagne's reign, on the other.

Bedier, one of the great students of medieval literature in modern times and the editor of the Oxford text of *La Chanson de Roland*, propounded the theory of the development of the legend which was generally accepted for years. The battle, he believed, was a minor event which had been remembered in the area near the battlefield and had become a local legend; from those beginnings it had been retold and developed in monasteries and pilgrim sanctuaries along the route leading to Santiago de Compostella, in Spain; the route crossed the Pyrenees at Roncevaux—the Roncesvalles associated with the Roland story. Bedier, incidentally, was convinced that a number of the French *chansons de geste* developed in more or less the same way and may have been written by monks, or at least in collaboration with monks. With reference to the *Roland,* in particular, he cites the fact that the pass at Roncevaux was commended for admiration (complete with a monumental cross said to be Carolingian and other relics claiming descent from Roland and the battle) by the monks at Roncevaux in the twelfth century; he points out that one variant of the Roland legend is contained in a twelfth-century guide written for the benefit of pilgrims to Santiago de Compostella.

Bedier's theory was published just before World War I. It was subjected to criticism in the following decades by a number of scholars; one of the most interesting countertheories was put forward by Fawtier (*La Chanson de Roland*) in 1933. Fawtier analyzes the chroniclers' references to the battle and bases his conclusions, in great part, on the weaknesses in their accounts. The chroniclers, he insists, cannot have it both ways. Was it merely a massacre of the rear guard, or did it in fact involve the whole army and "throw it into disorder"? He poses some other interesting questions. Why, for instance, should the baggage train have been at the rear of the march, when it was usual to have it in the middle, especially in mountain country? Why should so many of the leaders of the different sections of the army have been in the rear guard (of course the legend itself, with its story of the Ganelon-Roland dispute, answers this one, but the legend in its final form came much later and a great part of it is concerned with the peculiar drama of this very situation). How many of these details, and how much of the picture of the lightning raid from the mountain tops may have been attempts to minimize and explain away a terrible defeat which had happened while Charles himself was in command?

In Fawtier's view, the battle, whether it took place at Roncevaux or elsewhere, was one of the great disasters of Charlemagne's career. The army, hurrying into the Pyrenees, was caught in a classical ambush: the van was blocked, the rear was then attacked, and the Franks had to fight their way forward, section by section, suffering losses so appalling that Charles never really managed to reassemble the survivors on the other side of the mountains, and instead set about hastily reorganizing the strong points in Aquitaine as though he expected further troubles from Spain. In fact the magnitude of the defeat was one of the things about the action which caught the popular imagination and contributed to the growth of the legend around the heroic figure of the doomed commander of the rear guard, Hruodland, Rodlan, Roland.

The legend may have grown in the region around Roncevaux, but it was elaborated in other parts of the kingdom too. By the late eleventh century, when the poem was written, it was possible for the poet to display, without fear of correction, an ignorance of the geography of Spain and, for that matter, of southern France, which indicates not only that he himself came from somewhere far from that part of the world, but also that the story and its heroes had long been familiar in places remote from the original battlefield. An audience at Roncevaux might just have been able to go along with the poet's assumption that Córdoba was near the hill city of Saragossa, which in turn was on the sea; it is unlikely that, even in the Middle Ages when simple experience was so meek an authority, they would have heard without a murmur that Narbonne and Bordeaux both lay on the same road north from Roncevaux. Furthermore, this shows a total ignorance of the Santiago pilgrim route and its monasteries, an interesting fact in view of the theory that the poem was composed in one of those places, on that route.

In Fawtier's opinion the story of the defeat was carried across France by its veterans, and in various localities, as it took on the character of legend through repetition, it was cast, in whole or in part, into the form of ballads. It is true that none of these survive, but then very little of the popular literature of the time has survived. The monks had nothing to do with the composition of *La Chanson de Roland* itself (although two other, later variants of the legend were composed by clerics). On the contrary, it was the legend, and perhaps the poem itself, which prompted the ecclesiastics at Roncevaux to exploit the pass as a pilgrim attraction—an enterprise which may have contributed to the poem's preservation.

There has been considerable controversy as to just when *La Chanson de Roland* was written. It must have been some time in the latter half of the eleventh century, but it is not possible to be much more definite than that. The poem apparently was already well known in 1096 when, at the Council of Clermont, Pope Urban II made use of it in his appeal to the chivalry of France to follow in the steps of Charlemagne and send an army against Islam. Many of the crusaders who responded to Urban's summons, and many who came later, must have been following an image of themselves which derived, at least in part, from the legendary last battle of the now transfigured Hruodland.

The poem, in its original form, has not survived. Modern knowledge of it is confined to six different versions, whose separate relations to the original are not plain. There is, for instance, a twelfth-century German translation by a Bavarian priest named Konrad. There is a Norse translation of the thirteenth century. There is a version in Franco-Italian, in the library of San Marco in Venice, which ends differently from the others. And there are three versions in French. One of them, known as *Recension O,* or the Oxford version, has survived in a single copy, Digby Mss 23, at the Bodleian Library, Oxford. It is supposed that it was a *jongleur's* copy of the poem. It is the oldest of all the versions, the most beautiful, and must have been much the closest to the original. Bedier's famous edition of the poem (the one I have used in making my translation) is based on the Oxford version, which Bedier compares at all points with the others.

Two other medieval retellings of the Roland legend are extant. One of them, the so-called *Pseudo-Turpin,* comes from Book IV of the twelfth-century *Guide to the Pilgrims of Santiago de Compostella,* to which I have already referred. It is in Latin prose and purports to have been written by the Archbishop Turpin himself. This worthy, as here presented, was with Charlemagne when Roland was attacked, and he had a vision in which he saw the soul of

King Marsiliun being carried off by demons and the soul of Roland by angels. The narrative is clumsy, ill written, and encumbered with theological baggage. The other variant of the story, the *Carmen de prodicione Guenonis,* is also in Latin prose, but is shorter and more vigorous; it is possible that it is a translation of a lost French poem. A great deal of attention is paid to the character and actions of Ganelon. These two accounts, and the six surviving descendants of the *Chanson* itself were compared by Gaston Paris, who concluded that the author of the *Pseudo-Turpin* knew the *Chanson* but that the author of the *Chanson* did not know the *Pseudo-Turpin* variant; that there was no evidence of any relationship between the *Pseudo-Turpin* and the *Carmen;* that there was no way of establishing any relationship between the *Carmen* and the *Chanson.*

No decision about the spelling of characters and places could have satisfied everyone, and between the two extremes of modernizing and Anglicizing everything, on the one hand, or of keeping to the medieval versions in every case, on the other, I have not even been consistent. It would have struck me as affected and pointlessly archaic to have insisted on the original versions of names which have become familiar in modern English—Roland, Charles, Ganelon, Reims, Bordeaux. The work, after all, is a translation to begin with. But with names which, in my judgment, had not acquired such familiarity, I have either followed one of the original versions (sometimes there are several: Marsile, Marsilies, Marsilie, Marsiliun, Naimun, Naimon, Neimes, Naimes) or Bedier's standardized modern French version (Blancandrin, Balaquer, Thierry, Seurin), depending on which seemed preferable in the circumstances.

The *Chanson de Roland,* as it has survived in the Oxford version, consists of just under 4000 lines, arranged in *laisses,* or groups of lines all ending on the same assonance. The metrical pattern is based on a ten-syllable line with a clear strong beat. There are several drawbacks to trying to reproduce anything of the kind in English. For one thing, the assonance patterns: English is far more meager than are the Romance languages in the number of similar assonances which can be found for any given word ending. There have been translations of *La Chanson de Roland* which have aimed at producing assonance patterns like those in the original, but the results have been gnarled, impacted, and stunted, as the

original certainly is not. It would also have been possible—and this too has been done—to translate the poem into a ten-syllable line more or less resembling that of the original. The trouble is that the associations of the ten-syllable line in English are not at all what they are in French. It would have been very difficult not to invoke the tradition of iambic pentameter in English literature, a gallery of connotations which would not only have been irrelevant to the poem but which also could not help disguising it. This is quite apart from my own strong disposition against even reading another transposition of *La Chanson de Roland,* or most anything else, into a sort of blankish verse.

I am not questioning the splendor of the verse in the Oxford version, the magnificence of the noise it makes. It would be boorish of me to do so after the pleasure they have given me. But the qualities of the poem which finally claim me are all related to a certain limpidity not only in the language and the story but in the imagination behind them, to a clarity at once simple and formal, excited and cool, to characteristics which I find myself trying to describe in terms of light and water. These qualities obviously could not be reproduced in any translation but I wanted to suggest them, and it seemed to me that I should try to do it in prose.

W. S. MERWIN

THE
SONG OF ROLAND

I

Charles the King, our great emperor, has stayed seven whole years in Spain and has conquered the haughty country as far as the sea. Not a single castle resists him any longer; not one wall has yet to be broken nor one city taken, except Saragossa, which is on a mountain and is held by King Marsiliun, who does not love God. Marsiliun serves Mahomet and prays to Appolin. But he cannot prevent harm from overtaking him.

II

King Marsiliun, in Saragossa, has gone out into the shade of an orchard. He reclines on a bench of blue marble. There are more than twenty thousand men around him. He summons his dukes and his counts: "Lords, hear this, regarding the scourge which has come upon us. The emperor Charles has come to this country from sweet France to destroy us. I have no host with which to offer him battle, nor such an army as could crush his. Give me counsel, my men of wisdom, to save me from death and shame!"

None of the pagans says a word in reply, except Blancandrin, from the Castle of Val-Fonde.

III

Blancandrin was one of the wisest of the pagans. He was well endowed with the kind of courage which befits a knight, and he had shrewdness and judgment to bring to the aid of his lord. And he said to the King: "Do not give way to alarm! Send promises of faithful service and great friendship to Charles, the proud, the haughty. Send him bears and lions and dogs, seven hundred camels and a thousand new-molted falcons, four hundred mules weighed down with gold and silver, fifty wagons for him to range in a wagon train. He will be able to pay his mercenaries well. Tell him that he has made war long enough in this country, that he would do well to return to Aix, in France. Tell him that you will meet him there at Michaelmas and bow to the law of the Christians and become his vassal, in all honor and good faith. If he demands hostages send him ten or twenty to gain his confidence. Let us send the sons of our own wives. I will send my own son, even at the risk of his life. It is far better that our children should lose their heads than that we should forfeit our honor and possessions, or be reduced to begging."

IV

Blancandrin said: "I will swear by this right hand, by this beard which the wind flutters at my breast, that you will see the French army break camp at once. The Franks will go back into France, to their country. When each man has returned to the place which is dearest to him, at Michaelmas Charles will hold high court in his chapel at Aix. The day will arrive, the allotted time will run out, and Charles will receive no word from us, no tidings. The King is proud, and he has a hard heart. He will command them to take our hostages and strike off their heads. It is far better that they should lose their heads than that we should forfeit serene lovely Spain or endure suffering or distress!"

The pagans say: "Perhaps he is right."

V

King Marsiliun has brought his council to an end. He summons Clarin of Balaguet, Estamarin and his friend Eudropin, and Priamun and Guarlan the Bearded, and Machiner and his uncle Maheu, and Jouner, and Malbien from across the sea, and Blancandrin, to speak in his name. He calls to one side ten of the wiliest and most treacherous. "My lords, barons, you will go to Charlemagne. He is laying siege to the city of Cordres. You will approach him carrying olive branches in your hands to signify peace and humility. If you are cunning enough to arrange an agreement for me, I will give you as much gold and silver as you could wish for, and as much land, and as many possessions."

The pagans answer: "We are more than satisfied!"

VI

King Marsiliun has brought his council to an end. He says to his men: "Go, my lords. You will carry olive branches in your hands. In my name you will speak to King Charlemagne, asking him to have mercy on me in the name of his God. Tell him that he will not see the end of this first month before I have joined him with a thousand of my followers, and that I shall bow to the law of the Christians and become his vassal in all friendship and good faith. If he demands hostages he may have them."

Blancandrin says: "It will be to your advantage."

VII

Marsiliun commands his servants to lead out ten white mules which had been given to him by the King of Suatilie. The bits are made of gold, and the saddles are overlaid with silver. The messengers mount, bearing olive branches in their hands. They have come to Charles, who has France for his domain. They will deceive him to some extent; it cannot be helped.

VIII

The Emperor has become light-hearted and gay. He has taken Cordres and smashed its walls, and with his catapults he has battered down its towers. His knights have seized great quantities of plunder: gold and silver and rich garments. There is not a pagan left in the city: every one of them was either killed or became a Christian. The Emperor is in a broad orchard, and with him are Roland and Oliver, the Duke Sansun, and the proud Anseis, and Gefrey of Anjou, the King's standard-bearer. Gerin and Gerer are with them also, and many others. There are fifteen thousand from sweet France. The knights are seated on white silk carpets. The clever and the elderly are amusing themselves at backgammon and chess; the quick-blooded young men are fencing. Under a pine tree near an eglantine they have set a throne of pure gold, and there sits the King who rules sweet France. His beard is white and his hair is in full flower. His body is noble and his bearing is princely. If a man were to come looking for him, there would be no need to point him out. The messengers dismount and greet him, making protestations of friendship and good will.

IX

Blancandrin speaks before any of the others, and he says to the King: "Hail in the name of the glorious God whom we should adore! This is the message which the worthy King Marsiliun sends to you. He has inquired deeply into the law of salvation. He wishes to shower you with gifts chosen from among his own possessions: bears and lions, leashed boarhounds, seven hundred camels and a thousand falcons lately mewed, four hundred mules weighed down with gold and silver, fifty wagons to range in a wagon train, every one of them groaning with gold coin. You will be able to pay your mercenaries well. You have been in this country long enough. It would be better if you went back to Aix, in France. My lord promises that he will join you there."

The Emperor lifts up his hands to God, then he bows his head and begins to ponder.

X

The Emperor sits with head bowed. He was never hasty of speech. It is his custom to speak only in his own good time. When he raises his head his face is filled with pride. He says to the messengers: "You have spoken well. But King Marsiliun has proved that he is my enemy. What should make me put any confidence in this message which you bring?"

"Hostages," says the Saracen. "You may have ten, or fifteen, or twenty. I will send one of my own sons, even at the risk of his life, and I am certain that you will be given others who are yet better born than he. When you are in your royal palace, my lord promises that he will join you at the high feast of Saint Michael of Peril. And there, in the baths which were made for you by God himself, he will become a Christian."

Charles answers: "He may yet be saved."

XI

The evening was fair, the sun shone brightly. Charles commands his servants to stable the ten mules. He orders them to pitch a tent in the broad orchard, and he lodges the ten messengers there, sending twelve sergeants to wait upon them. There they have stayed through the night, until the coming of the bright day. The Emperor rises in the morning, hears mass and matins, and then goes under a pine and calls his barons together to council. He wants whatever he does to be in keeping with the advice of his Franks.

XII

The Emperor goes under a pine and calls his barons to council: Duke Oger and Archbishop Turpin, Richard the Elder and his nephew Henry, and Acelin the brave Count of Gascony, Tedbalt of Reims and his cousin Milun. Gerer and Gerin came too, and with them Roland, and the good, the noble Oliver. There were more than a thousand Franks, come from France. And Ganelon came—the author of the betrayal. Then the council began which led to disaster.

XIII

Charles, the Emperor, speaks: "My lords, barons, King Marsiliun has sent his messengers to me. He wishes to present me with a splendid gift out of his own possessions: bears and lions, boarhounds which can be led on the leash, seven hundred camels and a thousand falcons for the mews, four hundred mules weighed down with gold from Arabia, and more than fifty wagons besides. But he asks me to return to France. He says he will join me at Aix in my palace, and will submit to our most holy law and become a Christian, and hold his lands under me as my vassal. But I cannot tell what he has in his heart."

The French say: "We must be on our guard."

XIV

The Emperor has ended his speech. Count Roland is not in favor of the proposal. He gets to his feet at once and comes forward to argue against it. He says to the King: "If you believe Marsiliun you will live to regret it. Here we have been for seven whole years in Spain, and I have conquered Noples and Commibles for you, and Valterne and the country of Pine, and Balasgued and Tuele and Sezilie. And King Marsiliun has already betrayed us. He sent fifteen of his pagans, each carrying an olive branch, and they all said these same words to you. And you did as your Franks suggested—they must have been light-headed when they advised you. You sent two of your counts to the pagan, one of them was Basan and the other Basilie. He cut off their heads there in the mountains below Haltilie. Carry on with the war as you began it. Take the host which you have assembled and attack Saragossa and lay siege to the city. Let the struggle continue for the rest of your life, if necessary, but avenge those whom this villain murdered."

XV

The Emperor sits with his head bowed and strokes his beard and smooths his mustache. He neither agrees nor disagrees with his nephew; he does not answer him. None of the Franks says a word, except Ganelon. He gets to his feet and comes before Charles. He begins his speech in a haughty manner, saying:

"You will live to regret it if you lend your ear to some good-for-nothing, myself or another, who does not have your best interests at heart. When King Marsiliun sends to tell you that he is willing to clasp hands and become your vassal, when he offers to rule all of Spain through your gift and says that he will submit to our law, then whoever tells you that we should reject his offer, Sire, does not much care what kind of death we may die. It is not right that the promptings of arrogance should prevail. Let us ignore the fools and cleave to the wise!"

XVI

After this Naimes comes forward. There is not better vassal in the court. And he says to the King:

"You have heard Ganelon's answer. There is wisdom in what he says, if it is properly understood. King Marsiliun is beaten. You have taken all his castles, your catapults have smashed his walls, you have burned his cities and routed his followers. When he begs you to have mercy on him it would be a sin if you were to go on. Since he offers to give you hostages as security, this great war should not go any further."

The French say: "The Duke has spoken well."

XVII

"My lords, barons, who shall we send to King Marsiliun in Saragossa?"

The Duke of Naimes answers: "I will go, if you will send me. Give me the glove and the staff."

The King answers: "You are a wise man. And by this beard and by this mustache of mine you will not get so far from me so quickly. Go and sit down, since no one sent for you!"

XVIII

"My lords, barons, whom can we send to the Saracen who rules Saragossa?"

Roland answers: "Certainly I can go."

"Indeed you shall not go," Count Oliver says. "Your temper is rough and haughty. I am afraid you would start a quarrel. If the King wishes, I can certainly go."

The King replies: "Be still, both of you. Neither you nor he will move a step. By this white beard, I will curse any man who names one of the twelve peers!"

The French are silenced. They say nothing.

XIX

Turpin of Reims rises, comes from his rank, and says to the King:

"Let your Franks rest for a little while. You have been in this country for seven years and they have endured hardship and suffering. Give me the staff and glove, Sire, and I will go to the Saracen of Spain. I would be glad to see what he looks like."

The Emperor answers him in anger: "Go and sit down on that white carpet, and do not speak again unless I ask you!"

XX

"French knights," the Emperor Charles says, "Choose me a baron from my own country to carry my message to Marsiliun."

Roland says: "You could send my stepfather, Ganelon."

The French say: "Indeed, he could do it. If you do not send him you will not find anyone better."

And Count Ganelon is distraught. He throws off the great sable mantle from around his neck, and stands up in his silk shirt. His eyes are gray and his face is haughty; a noble carriage, a broad chest. He is so handsome that all the peers stare at him. He says to Roland:

"You great fool! What set you raving? I am your own stepfather, as everyone knows, and yet you single me out to be sent to Marsiliun. If God permits me to come back from there I will see to it that misfortune follows you for the rest of your life."

Roland answers: "Pride and foolishness! Everyone knows how little I care for threats. But since the messenger ought to be a man of sense, if the King will let me I will go in your place."

XXI

Ganelon answers: "You will do nothing of the kind! You are not my vassal nor am I your lord. It is Charles who commands me to perform this service, and I will go to Saragossa, to Marsiliun. But before this anger of mine is appeased I shall have played a trick of my own."

And at these words Roland laughs.

XXII

At the sight of Roland laughing, Ganelon is convulsed with rage. Beside himself with fury, he says to the Count:

"Do not think I have any love for you. You have settled this undeserved choice on me. Just Emperor, here I am before you. I wish to do your bidding."

XXIII

"I know that I am the one who must go to Saragossa, and whoever goes there will not come back. But above all remember that my wife is your sister, and that by her I have a son named Baldewin. No one is more handsome than he. He will make an excellent knight. I leave my lands and fiefs to him. Take good care of him. I shall not see him with these eyes again."

Charles answers: "You are too tender-hearted. I have given the command. You must go."

XXIV

The King says to Ganelon: "Come here before me and receive the staff and the glove. You have heard the Franks choose you."

Ganelon says: "Sire, it was Roland's doing. I will lose no love on him as long as I live, nor on Oliver either, for being his comrade. And here, Sire, before your eyes I defy the twelve peers because of the great love they bear him."

The King says: "Your anger exceeds all moderation. Now go, since I have given the command."

"I will go, and with no better prospect of safety than Basilie had, or his brother Basan."

XXV

The King holds out his right glove to Ganelon, but the Count is intent upon wishing that he were somewhere else, and when he puts out his hand to take it, it falls to the ground.

The French say: "Oh God, what can that mean? This embassage will bring disaster upon us."

"Lords," Ganelon says, "You may expect news!"

XXVI

"Sire," Ganelon says, "Give me your leave to depart. Since I must go, there is no use delaying."

"Go," the King says, "In Jesus' name and mine."

With his right hand he absolves the Count and makes the sign of the cross. Then he gives him the staff and the letter.

XXVII

Count Ganelon goes to his tent and begins his preparations, putting on his richest equipment, fastening gold spurs to his feet and girding his sword Murglies to his side. Then while his uncle Guinemer holds the stirrup, he mounts Tachebrun, his charger. There you would have seen many knights weeping, saying to him:

"We are grieved that this has befallen you! You have been in the King's court for a long time, and all have spoken of you as a noble vassal. Charlemagne himself cannot save or protect the man who chose you to go to Marsiliun. Count Roland should never have thought of suggesting you, who are descended from so exalted a lineage."

Then they say: "Sire, take us with you."

Ganelon answers: "No, in the name of God! It is better that I should die alone than that so many excellent knights should perish too. When you return to sweet France, my lords, greet my wife for me, and Pinabel my friend and comrade, and my son Baldewin, whom you know. Give him your allegiance and serve him faithfully."

He spurs into the path and sets out on his way.

XXVIII

Ganelon rides under a tall olive tree, and there he joins the Saracen messengers. Blancandrin reins in beside him, and the two converse with great cunning.

Blancandrin says: "Charles is a wonderful man. He has conquered Puille and the whole of Calabria, and crossed the salt sea into England, where he exacted tribute for Saint Peter. What does he want from us, here in our country?"

Ganelon answers: "Such is his nature. There was never a man to equal him."

XXIX

Blancandrin says: "The Franks are noble and admirable. But these dukes and counts bring great harm upon their lord, counseling him as they do. They waste his resources and they mislead him and others."

Ganelon answers: "That is true of no one, to my knowledge, except Roland, who will suffer shame for it one day. Yesterday morning when the Emperor was sitting in the shade, his nephew came up to him, wearing a mailed tunic, bringing him booty from Carcassonne. He held out a red apple in his hand.

" 'Take it, fair Sire,' Roland said to his uncle. 'I present you with the crowns of all kings.'

"His arrogance should be his undoing, for there is never a day when he does not risk death. If someone were to kill him we could live in peace."

XXX

Blancandrin says: "Roland is utterly evil. He wants to make all nations bow down to him. He wants to leave no country unchallenged. What people does he expect to help him in all this?"

Ganelon answers: "The French. They have such love for him that they would not willingly fail him in anything. He lavishes gold and silver on them, and mules, and war horses, and silks, and armor. Even the Emperor lets him have his way, for Roland will conquer countries for him from here to the Orient."

XXXI

They ride along together and in the end Ganelon and Blancandrin swear to each other that they will try to find some means of bringing about the death of Roland. They ride on down the roads and paths until they come to Saragossa and dismount under a yew tree. There, in the shadow of a pine, is a throne covered with Alexandrian silk. On it sits the King who rules over all of Spain. Around him are assembled twenty thousand Saracens, in absolute silence, waiting to hear the news.

Ganelon and Blancandrin arrive.

XXXII

Blancandrin, leading Count Ganelon by the fist, comes before Marsiliun and says to the King:

"Salutations in the name of Mahomet and in the name of Apollin, whose holy laws we keep. We have delivered your message to Charlemagne. He raised both his hands to heaven and gave praise to his God, and made us no other answer. Here he sends you one of his noble barons, a great man of France, from whom you will hear whether or not you will have peace."

Marsiliun answers: "Let him speak. We will listen."

XXXIII

Ganelon had laid his plans with care. Now he begins to speak, and he does it artfully, for he is skilled in the ways of eloquence. He says to the King:

"Salutations in the name of God, the Glorious, to whom we owe adoration. Here is the message which the worthy Charlemagne sends you. Receive the holy Christian faith and he will give you half of Spain as your fief. Refuse, and you will be taken by force and bound and transported to the city of Aix, where sentence will be pronounced upon your life and you will die a vile and shameful death."

King Marsiliun is filled with dread. He seizes a gold-fletched javelin and raises it, and nothing but the hand of one of his courtiers prevents him from hurling it.

XXXIV

King Marsiliun has turned pale. He brandishes the shaft of his javelin. At this sight Ganelon grasps his sword and draws it two finger lengths out of the sheath, and says to it:

"Oh fair bright blade which I have worn in the King's court all these years! The Emperor of France will never hear it said that I died alone in a strange country without your having made them pay some of their best blood."

The pagans say: "Let us not come to blows."

XXXV

The best of the Saracens have at last prevailed on Marsiliun to seat himself again on the throne. The Caliph says:

"You discredit us, offering to strike the Frank. You should lend him your attention, and listen."

"Sire," Ganelon says, "I have no choice but to suffer all this. But if I am allowed to speak, not all the gold that God made, nor all the riches of this country, will dissuade me from delivering the message which Charles, the mighty King, sends through me to his mortal enemy."

He is wearing a cloak of sable covered with Alexandrian silk. He flings it aside; Blancandrin catches it. But he keeps his sword, his right hand grasping the gold hilt.

The pagans say: "Here indeed is a noble baron!"

XXXVI

Ganelon approaches the King and says to him:

"You are wrong to be angry, for Charles, who rules France, sends to tell you that if you will receive the law of the Christians he will give you half of Spain in fief. The other half will go to his nephew Roland: you will certainly have an arrogant partner! If you reject this offer, Charles will advance on Saragossa and besiege you here, and you will be taken by force, bound, and without further ceremony brought to the city of Aix. You will have neither palfrey nor war horse, mule nor she-mule to ride on the way there. You will be thrown onto a wretched beast of burden, and when you arrive you will be sentenced and your head will be struck off. Our Emperor sends you this letter."

In his right hand he holds it out to the pagan.

XXXVII

Marsiliun, pale with anger, breaks the seal, flings the wax aside, looks at the letter and sees what is written there:

"Charles, who has France for his domain, bids me remember his grief and anger when I cut off the heads of Basan and his brother Basilie, in the mountains of Haltilie. Now if I wish to purchase my life I must send him my uncle the Caliph. Otherwise I need never hope for his favor."

Then Marsiliun's son speaks. He says to the King:

"Everything which Ganelon has uttered is foolishness. He has gone too far. He should not be allowed to live any longer. Give him to me. I will do justice upon him."

When Ganelon hears this he sets his back against the trunk of a pine tree and brandishes his sword.

XXXVIII

Marsiliun withdraws into the orchard, taking with him the best of his vassals. Gray-haired Blancandrin goes with him, and Jurfaret, the King's son and heir, and Marsiliun's uncle the Caliph and his followers.

Blancandrin says: "Call the Frenchman here. He swore to me that he would help us."

The King says: "Go yourself and bring him."

Blancandrin takes Ganelon by the hand and leads him from the dais into the orchard, to the King. There they plot the unpardonable betrayal.

XXXIX

"Fair sir, Ganelon," Marsiliun says to him, "in the heat of my anger I behaved somewhat rashly toward you, threatening to strike you as I did. I swear to you by these sable skins, whose gold mountings are worth more than five hundred pounds, that before tomorrow night you will have been given a handsome compensation."

Ganelon answers: "I shall not refuse it. May God be pleased to reward you for it."

XL

Marsiliun says: "Ganelon, the truth is that I should be happy to take you into my favor. Now tell me about Charlemagne. He is very old. He has outworn his time. To my certain knowledge he has been alive for over two hundred years. He has taken his body to so many countries, he has received so many blows on his shield, he has reduced so many rich kings to beggary—will he never grow tired of making war?"

Ganelon answers: "Charles is not as you suppose. Everyone who sees him and comes to know him agrees that the Emperor is a great man. It would be impossible for me to exaggerate his glory and his virtues, or to praise them too highly. His courage is beyond description. And God has kindled such nobility in him that he would rather die than fail his barons."

XLI

The pagan says, "I am filled with amazement, and I have good reason. Charlemagne is old and his beard is gray and his hair is white. To my certain knowledge he has been alive for two hundred years and more. He has dragged his body to so many lands, he has taken so many blows from lances and from spears, and he has reduced so many kings to begging—when will he be tired of making war?"

"Never," says Ganelon, "as long as his nephew is alive. There is not another vassal to compare with him under the hood of heaven. And his companion Oliver, too, is an excellent knight. And the twelve peers, whom Charles holds in such tender esteem, and twenty thousand knights with them, make up his vanguard. Charles is safe. He is not afraid of any man alive."

XLII

The Saracen says: "I am filled with astonishment at Charlemagne, with his gray and white locks. He has been alive, to my certain knowledge, for two hundred years and more. He has traveled through so many countries, conquering them, and he has taken so many blows from good sharp spears, and he has killed so many kings and overthrown them on the field—will he never grow tired of making war?"

"Never," Ganelon says, "as long as Roland is alive. There is not another vassal to compare with him from here to the Orient. And worthy Oliver, his companion, is another excellent knight. And the twelve peers, who are so precious to Charles, and twenty thousand knights with them, make up his vanguard. Charles is safe. He fears no man alive."

XLIII

"Fair sir, Ganelon," King Marsiliun says, "never will you see an army more splendid than mine. I can assemble four hundred thousand knights. Do I dare give battle to Charles and the French?"

Ganelon answers, "Do nothing of the kind, for the moment. You will lose great numbers of your pagans. Turn from folly and cleave to wisdom: out of your wealth present the Emperor with so rich a gift that all the French marvel at it. If you send him twenty hostages the King will return to sweet France. He will leave his rear guard behind. Unless I am wrong Count Roland his nephew will be there, and brave courtly Oliver, and if I can find someone who will listen to what I have to say, both of them will be killed. Charles will behold the downfall of his great pride, and he will have no heart for making war against you any more."

XLIV

"Fair sir, Ganelon, how can I kill Roland?"

Ganelon answers: "I can tell you that, without any doubt. The King will proceed to the main pass through the mountains, at Sizer, leaving his rear guard behind him, with his nephew Count Roland, and Oliver, in whom Roland places such trust. There will be twenty thousand Franks in their company. Send a hundred thousand of your pagans against them and engage them in a first battle. The French host will be battered and shaken, and I must tell you now that your own men will suffer great losses. But send the same number against them a second time and give them battle. Whether in the first onslaught or the second, Roland is sure to be killed, and you will have achieved a noble and knightly deed, and will be free of war for as long as you live."

XLV

"If anyone could bring about the death of Roland, Charles would have lost his own body's right arm. There would be no more of these awe-inspiring armies. Charles would never again assemble these great hosts, and France, the land of our sires, would be left in peace."

When Marsiliun hears this he kisses Ganelon on the neck, and then turns to where his treasures are kept.

XLVI

Marsiliun says: "Whatever we say, all our agreements are worthless unless you will swear to me to betray Roland."

Ganelon answers: "I will do as you wish." On the holy relics in his sword Murglies he swears to betray Roland, and so his treachery is sealed.

XLVII

There is an ivory throne there. Marsiliun sends for a book containing the laws of Mahomet and Termagant, and he, the Saracen of Spain, swears that if he finds Roland in the rear guard he will attack with his entire army and kill him if he can.

Ganelon answers: "May your wish be fulfilled!"

XLVIII

Then Valdabrun, a pagan, comes forward and approaches King Marsiliun. Laughing pleasantly, he says to Ganelon:

"Take this sword. No man has a better one. The hilt alone is worth more than a thousand of our gold pieces. Fair sir, I give it to you as a token of friendship, so that you will help us to deal with Roland: make sure that we are able to find this baron in the rear guard."

"It shall be done," Count Ganelon answers. Then they kiss each other's cheeks and chins.

XLIX

After that Climorin, a pagan, approaches and, laughing pleasantly, says to Ganelon:

"Take my helmet. I have never seen a better one. And lend us your help against this Roland, lord of the marches, so that we may bring him to shame."

"It shall be done," Ganelon answers. Then they kiss each other's mouths and faces.

L

Then Bramimunde, the Queen, approaches.

"Sir," she says to the Count, "my lord and all his men hold you high in their favor, and my love for you, accordingly, is great. I send your wife these two necklaces heavy with gold, amethysts and jacinths. They are worth more than all the riches of Rome. Your Emperor never owned any to compare with them."

He takes them and puts them into his pouch.

L I

The King summons Malduit, his treasurer: "Have you made ready the gifts which are to be sent to Charles?"

And he replies: "Yes, Sire, they are ready: seven hundred camels laden with gold and silver, and twenty hostages chosen from the noblest under heaven."

L I I

Marsiliun takes Ganelon by the shoulder and says to him:

"You are very brave and very wise. In the name of that law which to you is most holy, do not withdraw your heart from us. I will lavish gifts on you out of my own possessions: ten mules laden with fine gold from Arabia. And not a year will pass but I will send you the same again. Here, take the keys of this wide city. Present these treasures to King Charles. Then arrange matters so that Roland is in the rear guard. If I can find him in any pass or ravine, I will attack and fight him to the death."

Ganelon answers: "I must not delay my return any longer."

Then he mounts and sets out on his way.

L I I I

The Emperor, starting his homeward journey, comes to the city of Galne, which Count Roland had taken for him and destroyed. After the day of its overthrow the city was deserted for a hundred years. The King waits for news of Ganelon, and for tribute from the great land of Spain. As dawn breaks and the day brightens Count Ganelon rides into the encampment.

LIV

The Emperor rises in the morning. The King hears mass and matins and then stands on the green grass before his tent. Roland is there, and brave Oliver, the Duke Naimes, and many of the others. Ganelon, the villain, the traitor, comes and begins a cunning speech, saying to the King:

"Salutations in the name of God! Here I bring you the keys of Saragossa, and all this treasure, and twenty hostages—let them be well guarded. And the brave King Marsiliun begs you not to blame him for failing to send you the Caliph, for with my own eyes I have seen four hundred thousand armed men, in their hauberks, and many of them with their helmets laced, wearing swords with hilts of carved gold, go with the Caliph and embark on the sea. They fled from Marsiliun rather than become Christians. Before they were four leagues out on the water, storm and tempest swallowed them up. They were drowned. You will never see any of them again. If the Caliph had been alive I would have brought him to you.

"As for the pagan king, Sire, you may be certain that you will not see this first month pass without his following you to the Kingdom of France, where he will bow to the law which you observe, and where with clasped hands he will become your vassal, to rule the Kingdom of Spain as your tributary."

The King says: "God be thanked. You have done well. You will be well rewarded."

At his command a thousand trumpets sound through that host. The Franks break camp, load their beasts of burden, and all set out on the road for sweet France.

LV

Charles the Great has ravaged Spain, seized its castles, sacked its cities. Now the King declares that his war is over. The Emperor rides toward sweet France.

Count Roland has fixed his pennon to his lance, and on the top of a mound he lifts it toward the sky. At this signal through all the surrounding country the Franks pitch camp.

Through the broad valleys the pagans ride, hauberks on, helmets laced, swords girded, their shields at their necks and their lances adorned with pennons. They halt in a wood high in the mountains, four hundred thousand of them, and wait for the dawn to break. Oh God, how terrible that the French know nothing of their presence!

LVI

The day passes, the night grows dark, and Charles, the mighty Emperor, sleeps. He dreams he is at the great gorges of the pass at Sizer, holding his ashen lance in his fist, and that Count Ganelon comes and seizes the lance and twists and shakes it so violently that the splinters fly toward heaven.

Charles sleeps on and does not wake.

LVII

After this vision he has another dream. He is in France, at Aix, in his chapel, and a fierce wild boar is biting his right arm. He sees a leopard come from the side toward the Ardenne, and savagely attack his body. Within the hall itself a boarhound descends, bounds toward Charles at a full run, tears the right ear from the first beast, and in a great rage attacks the leopard. The French declare it a marvelous combat and wonder which of the two will win.

Charles does not wake but sleeps on.

LVIII

The night passes and when the bright dawn appears the Emperor rides proudly through that host.

"My lords, barons," the Emperor Charles says, "you see before us the passes and narrow gorges. Who shall remain here in the rear guard?"

Ganelon answers: "Roland, my stepson. You have no braver vassal."

When the King hears this he stares hard and coldly at Ganelon and says to him: "You are a devil incarnate! Some deadly passion possesses your body. And who, then, should go before me in the vanguard?"

Ganelon answers: "Oger of Denmark. No baron of yours could better perform that service."

LIX

When Count Roland hears himself named he speaks as becomes a knight:

"Stepfather, my lord, my debt of affection to you is greater than ever, now that you have named me to the rear guard. I assure you that Charles, the King who rules France, will lose neither palfrey nor war horse, nor saddle mule, male or female, nor draft horse nor pack horse that has not first been bargained for with swords."

Ganelon answers: "I know what you say is true."

LX

When Roland hears that he will be in the rear guard he turns to his stepfather in anger and says:

"Ah, slave and coward, malicious heir of dishonored ancestors, did you think I would let the glove fall to the ground as you did the staff when you stood before Charles?"

LXI

"Just Emperor," says Roland, the baron, "give me the bow which you are holding in your fist. I am sure that no man will be able to reproach me with having dropped it, as Ganelon dropped the staff when he reached out his right hand to take it."

The Emperor's head is bowed. His hands drag at his beard and twist his mustache. He cannot keep the tears from flowing down his face.

LXII

After that Naimes comes forward. There is no finer vassal in the entire court. And he says to the King:

"You have heard how matters stand. Count Roland is in a fury.

He has been named for the rear guard and no baron of yours can change that now. Give him the bow which you have bent and find him those companions who will be of most help to him."

The King holds it out and Roland takes it.

LXIII

The Emperor speaks to his nephew Roland.

"Fair sir, nephew, listen to my decision. I will make you a present of half of my army. Keep them with you and you will be safe."

To this the Count replies: "I will do no such thing. God confound me if I shame my ancestors! I will keep with me twenty thousand Franks noted for their bravery. And you may go on your way through the pass in utter confidence, and fear no man as long as I am alive."

LXIV

Count Roland has mounted his charger. His companion Oliver comes to join him. And Gerin and the brave Count Gerer also come to join him, and Otun and Berenger come to join him, and Astor and old Anseis come to join him, and the proud Gerard of Roussillon comes to join him, and the rich Duke Gaifer comes to join him.

The Archbishop says: "My head upon it, I am with you!"

"And I along with you," says Count Gualter. "I am Roland's vassal. I must not fail him."

Then among them they choose twenty thousand knights.

LXV

Count Roland summons Gualter of Hum.

"Take a thousand Francs from our land of France and hold the defiles and the heights so that the Emperor may not lose a single man."

Gualter answers: "I will do as you bid me."

Along the defiles and on the heights Gualter has ranged a thousand French from their land of France. However bad the news he will not descend from his positions before seven hundred swords have been unsheathed. Before that terrible day is over King Amaris from the kingdom of Belferne will launch a battle against him.

LXVI

The peaks are high and the valleys are dark, the gorges awesome under dun rocks. That day the French proceed sorrowfully through the pass. The sound of them can be heard fifteen leagues away. And they emerge at last in the land of their fathers and see Gascony, the domain of their lord, and then they remember their fiefs and honors, and girls and noble wives, and there is not one of them who is not so filled with pity that he weeps.

But more than any of the others Charles is racked with anguish because he has left his nephew in the gorges of Spain. Pity overcomes him. He weeps and cannot help it.

LXVII

The twelve peers have stayed behind in Spain, and twenty thousand Francs with them, fearless to a man and with no dread of death.

The Emperor returns into France, hiding his sorrowful face in his mantle. Duke Naimes rides beside him and says to the King: "What is the cause of your grief?"

Charles answers: "It is wrong of any man to ask me! My sorrow is so great that I cannot bear it in silence. Ganelon will be the destruction of France. Last night an angel sent me a vision in which I saw Ganelon shatter my lance from between my fists. And he has named my nephew for the rear guard, and I have left Roland beyond the frontier in a foreign country. Oh God, if I lose him no one will take his place for me!"

LXVIII

Charles the Great weeps and cannot help it. At the sight of him a hundred thousand Franks are filled with tenderness and with an unreasoning fear for Roland. The villain Ganelon has betrayed him, and has accepted rich gifts from the pagan king: gold and silver, mantles and silks, mules, horses, camels and lions.

From all of Spain Marsiliun has summoned his barons, his

counts, viscounts, dukes and commanders, his emirs, and the sons
of the nobility. He has assembled four hundred thousand of them
in three days. He gives orders to sound the drums in Saragossa. On
the highest of the towers they raise an image of Mahomet, and every one of the pagans prays to it and worships it. Then they file out
and ride with all possible speed through the land of Certeine, down
the valleys and across the mountains, until they can see the pennons of the French. The rear guard under the twelve companions
will not fail to offer them battle.

LXIX

Marsiliun's nephew comes forward, riding a mule which he urges
along with a staff. His manner is pleasing, and with a laugh he says
to his uncle:

"Fair Sire, King, I have served you long and have known suffering and hardship, and battles fought and won on the field. Grant
me one favor: the first blow at Roland. I will kill him with my
sharp spear. If Mahomet will protect me, I will strike off the fetters from the whole of Spain, from the Spanish passes all the way
to Durestant. Charles will lose heart. The Franks will yield. You
will have no more war as long as you live."

King Marsiliun has given him the glove.

LXX

Marsiliun's nephew holds the glove in his fist and addresses
proud words to his uncle:

"Fair Sire, King, you have accorded me a great gift. Choose
twelve of your barons to ride with me and give battle to the twelve
companions."

Before any of the others have spoken, Fulsarun, the brother of
King Marsiliun, answers:

"Fair Sire, nephew, you and I will go together against the rear
guard of Charles' great host, and indeed we will give them their
battle. It is decided: we will be the death of them."

LXXI

From another side King Corsalis comes forward. He is a native
of Barbary, an adept of the black arts. He speaks like a true vassal.

Not for all the gold of God, he says, would he be a coward . . .
. . . .

Look now: Malprimis of Brigant spurs forward, who on foot can run faster than a horse. Before Marsiliun he calls out at the top of his voice:

"I will take my body to Roncesvalles. If I come upon Roland I will know how to dispatch him."

LXXII

There is in that company an Emir from Balasquez whose body is noble and handsome, and whose face is bold and open. When he is mounted on his horse he carries his arms proudly. He is renowned for his courage. If only he were a Christian he would be an excellent knight. He comes before Marsiliun and shouts:

"I will go and risk my body at Roncesvalles. If I find Roland he will meet his death then and there, and the same is true of Oliver and the twelve peers. The French will perish in sorrow and shame. Charles the Great is an old man in his dotage, and will have no more stomach for waging war. And Spain will be free, and will be left to us."

King Marsiliun has thanked him profusely.

LXXIII

There is in that company a commander from Moriane, and there is no greater villain in the land of Spain. He has made his boast before Marsiliun:

"I will lead my company to Roncesvalles: we are twenty thousand with shields and lances. If I find Roland I swear I will kill him and never a day will pass but Charles will grieve."

LXXIV

From another direction comes Turgis of Turteluse, a count; the whole city whose name he bears belongs to him. He nurses a deep hatred of Christians, and in the presence of Marsiliun he joins the others, saying to the King:

"Have no fear. Mahomet is worth more than Saint Peter of Rome. Serve him and the field and its honors are ours. I will go to

Roncesvalles and meet Roland and no man will be able to save him from death. Look: here is my sword. It is a good sword; it is long. I will measure it against Durendal and you will hear soon enough which one overtopped the other. The French will die if they venture against us, and Charles the Old will suffer grief and shame, and never wear crown again on this earth."

LXXV

From the opposite side comes Escremiz of Valterne, a Saracen, and lord of the land whose name he bears. From among all those who are assembled before Marsiliun, he shouts:

"I will go to Roncesvalles to bring pride to destruction. If I find Roland he will not bear away his head, nor will Oliver, who commands the others. The twelve peers are doomed, all of them. The French will die, France will be ruined, Charles will lack for good vassals."

LXXVI

From another direction comes Esturgant, a pagan, and with him Estramariz, one of his companions, villains both of them, and deceitful and treacherous. Marsiliun says to them:

"Approach, my lords! You will go to the gorges of the pass at Roncesvalles and lend your help in conducting my troops."

And they answer: "We will do as you command. We will attack Oliver and Roland, and nothing will save the twelve peers from death. We have good swords, they are sharp, they will run red with warm blood, the French will die, sorrow will settle upon Charles, we will give you the land of their fathers as a present. Come with us, King. You will see. It is true. We will give you the Emperor himself as a present."

LXXVII

Margarit of Seville, who rules over lands as far as Cazmarine, comes on the run. Because of his beauty he is a favorite with the ladies: there is not one of them who does not brighten and laugh with pleasure at the sight of him. No pagan is so excellent a knight.

He enters the crowd before the throne and shouts to the King above all the others, saying:

"Have no fear! I will go to Roncesvalles to kill Roland, and Oliver will not bear away his life. The twelve peers are set aside for slaughter. Look: here is my sword. Its hilt is made of gold. It was a gift of an Emir of Primes. I promise you that it will be bathed in crimson blood. The French will die, France will be brought to shame, Charles the Old, with his beard in full flower, will know sorrow and rage every day for the rest of his life. Before a year is over we will have seized France and will be able to take our ease in the town of Saint-Denis."

The pagan king bows low to him.

LXXVIII

Chernuble of Munigre comes from the other side. His flowing hair reaches to the ground. When he is feeling playful he is able to lift and carry weights, merely in sport, that are heavier than the packloads of four sumpter mules. It is said that in the country from which he comes the sun does not shine, the wheat cannot grow, the rain does not fall, dew never forms, and all the stones are black. Some say that the land is inhabited by devils. Chernuble says:

"I have girded on my good sword, and I will dye it crimson at Roncesvalles. If I find the bold Roland in my path and do not attack him, never believe me again. I will strike down Durendal with my own blade. The French will die and France will be ruined."

When he has spoken, the twelve pagan peers assemble, and with them a hundred thousand Saracens, eager and impatient for battle. They go into a grove of pines and arm themselves.

LXXIX

The pagans arm themselves in Saracen hauberks, most of them made of three thicknesses of chain mail. They lace their fine Saragossa helmets. They gird on their swords made of steel from Viana. They carry resplendent shields and Valencian lances with white and blue and crimson pennons. They leave behind their saddle mules and palfreys and mount their war horses and ride in closed ranks.

The day was clear and the sun was fair. The light flashed from every piece of armor. A thousand trumpets are sounded, to add to the splendor. The din is tremendous, and it reaches the ears of the French. Oliver says:

"Sir, my companion, I believe the Saracens intend to do battle with us."

Roland answers: "Pray God that it may be so! For the sake of our king we are bound to remain here. For the sake of his lord a man is bound to suffer hardship, to endure the extremes of heat and of cold, and to lose, if he must, both hair and hide. Now let every man see to it that the blows he deals are heavy, lest a shameful song be sung of us. The pagans are in the wrong and the Christians in the right. No one will ever be able to say of me that I set a bad example."

LXXX

Oliver has climbed a peak, and looking to his right along a grassy valley, he sees the pagan host approaching. He calls to his companion Roland:

"From the side that is toward Spain there is a great noise coming, and I see approaching us so many bright hauberks, so many flashing helmets—they will bring bitter suffering to our Franks. Ganelon knew of this, that villain, that traitor, when he stood before the Emperor and named us for the rear guard."

"Silence, Oliver," Count Roland answers. "He is my stepfather. I will not have you say a word against him."

LXXXI

Oliver has climbed one of the heights, and from it he can see all the way into the kingdom of Spain, and he can see the enormous host of the Saracens. Their helmets are shining, studded with jewels set in gold; and their shields and their gilt-varnished hauberks are shining, and their lances and the pennons that are fastened to them. It is not possible to count even the separate companies of that host; the battalions are past numbering, there are so many. Oliver is greatly troubled at the sight. As fast as his horse will carry him he rides down from the peak and returns to the French and tells them what he has seen.

LXXXII

Oliver says: "I have seen the pagans. No man on earth ever saw more. In the vanguard are a hundred thousand with their shields ready, their helmets laced, their limbs in shining hauberks, the shafts of their lances raised and the burnished spears gleaming. You will have such a battle as was never seen before. Lords of France, God give you strength! Hold the field, let us not be beaten!"

The French say: "A curse on the man who runs away! Until death itself not one of us will fail you."

LXXXIII

Oliver says: "The pagans have a huge army, and our French appear to be very few. Therefore Roland, my companion, sound a blast on your horn. Charles will hear it, and he will return with his host."

Roland answers: "That would be the act of a fool! I would forfeit the fame I have in sweet France. Soon I will be striking great blows with my sword Durendal, and blood will cover the blade up as far as the hilt. These villainous pagans will suffer for coming to this gateway through the mountains. I promise you, they are all marked out for death."

LXXXIV

"Roland, my companion, sound your ivory horn, and Charles will hear it and command the army to return, and the King will come to our help with all his barons."

Roland answers: "God forbid that my ancestry should be shamed by an act of mine, or that I should make sweet France an object of scorn! Instead I will attack unsparingly with my good sword Durendal, which I have girded on here at my side. You will see this weapon running with blood from one end to the other. These villainous pagans will suffer for massing against us. I promise you, they are all marked out for destruction."

LXXXV

"Roland, my companion, sound a blast on your ivory horn. Charles will hear it as he marches through the pass, and I promise you the Franks will return."

Roland answers: "God forbid that any man living should be able to say that because of the pagans I blew my ivory horn! No one will ever be able to shame my family with the mention of such a thing. When I have joined in the massed battle I will strike a thousand blows and follow them with seven hundred more, and you will see the steel of Durendal running with blood. The French are brave, they will fight hard and well, and those who have come from Spain will not be saved from death."

LXXXVI

Oliver says: "I see nothing shameful in your sounding a blast now on your horn. I have seen the Saracens of Spain. The valley is covered with them, and the mountains, and the hills, and the plains. The foreigners have an enormous army, and there are few, very few, in our company."

Roland answers: "That makes me still more eager for battle. May God in heaven and his angels forbid that the fame of France should be diminished because of me! I would rather die than be brought to shame. The Emperor's love will go to those who strike hardest."

LXXXVII

Roland is bold, and Oliver is wise. Both of them are renowned for their bravery. When they are armed and mounted no fear of death ever made them shrink from a battle. They are men of worth, these counts, and they speak proud words.

The villainous pagans ride on in great fury.

Oliver says: "Roland, now you can see a few of them. And they are near us, and Charles is far away. You would not deign to sound a blast on your ivory horn. If the King were here we would come to no harm. Look up along the pass that rises out of Spain, to the rear guard. You can see the sadness in their faces. Those who fight in this battle will never fight in another."

Roland answers: "No more of that vile talk! A curse on the heart which turns coward in its breast now! We will stay where we are, in our place. We will keep the field. And we will meet them with swinging swords and with blows of weapons."

LXXXVIII

When Roland sees that there will be a battle, his pride surpasses that of any lion or leopard. He calls out to the French and to Oliver:

"Sir, my companion, my friend, do not say such things! The Emperor set aside a full twenty thousand of his Franks to leave behind with us, and he knew that not one of them was a coward. For the sake of his lord a man must be prepared to suffer great hardships and to endure extreme cold and great heat. For the sake of his lord a man must be prepared to sacrifice even his blood and his flesh. Strike with your lance! And I will attack with my good sword Durendal, which the King gave me. And if I die, whoever takes it then will be able to say, 'It belonged to a noble knight.' "

LXXXIX

From another side Archbishop Turpin spurs his horse up a little hill, and there he raises his voice to preach a sermon to the French:

"Barons, my lords, Charles has left us here and if need be we must die for our King and to uphold Christendom! None of you can doubt that there will be a battle: now you can see the Saracens before you. Confess your sins and call upon God for his mercy, and for the salvation of your souls I shall grant you absolution. If you die, you will be holy martyrs and will sit in the topmost parts of Paradise."

The French dismount and kneel on the ground and the Archbishop blesses them in the name of God, and as a penance he bids them strike hard.

XC

The French straighten and rise to their feet, absolved and freed of their sins, and the Archbishop blesses them in the name of God. Then, armed according to the prescriptions of knighthood, and armored for battle from head to foot, they mount their chargers. Count Roland calls out to Oliver:

"Sir, my companion, you were right when you said that Ganelon had betrayed us all. He has received gold and possessions and money for his treachery, and may the Emperor take vengeance upon him on our account. King Marsiliun has bargained for our lives, but he will require swords when it comes to collecting his purchase."

XCI

Where the pass leads up out of Spain Roland has mounted Veillantif, his good swift horse. He has taken up his arms; his armor becomes him. Now with a flourish Roland the bold raises the point of his lance to heaven. Laced to the shaft is a white pennon whose fringes sweep down to his hands. He bears himself nobly; his countenance is candid and smiling. Behind him comes his companion, and the French, who regard him as their salvation. He turns and looks fiercely at the Saracens, and then humbly and sweetly at the French, whom he addresses courteously:

"My lords, barons, gently, and reined in to a walk, advance. These pagans are rushing upon their own destruction. Before nightfall we shall have seized spoils so rich and magnificent as to surpass in splendor any that were ever taken by a king of France."

At these words the two armies come together.

XCII

Oliver says: "I have no heart for talk. You would not deign to sound a blast on your ivory horn, and if you do not have Charles here at your side it is no fault of his, for that brave king knows nothing of what is happening here. And these knights who have stayed with us are blameless, whatever happens. Well then, let us ride with all our might against these Saracens. My lords, barons,

keep the field! In the name of God I pray you, let every man resolve to strike hard and return blow for blow! Now let us not forget
Charles' battle cry!"

At his words the French raise the battle cry "Mountjoy," and no
man who had heard them could ever have forgotten the brave
sound. Then—and oh God how fiercely—they charge. They spur
their horses on faster and faster, and attack—what else could they
do? And the Saracens receive their charge without flinching. Now
the Franks and the pagans have come together.

XCIII

Marsiliun's nephew Aelroth is the first to ride out in front of the
Saracen host and taunt our French with vicious words:

"Villainous French, today you will have a battle with us! You
have been betrayed by him whose duty it was to protect you, and
the king who left you here in the pass is a fool. Today France will
be shorn of her fame, and Charles the Great will lose his body's
right arm."

When Roland hears this, oh God what a rage fills him! He sets
spur to his horse, lets it out to its best speed, and rides to hurl
against the Saracen count the full fury of his attack. He smashes
the shield, bursts apart the hauberk, rips up the breast, crushes the
bones, forces the whole backbone out through the back, and with
his spear drives out the soul. He spits the Saracen on his lance, and
hoisting the body into the air, flings the corpse a spear's length
from its horse, and the neck splits into two pieces. And still he does
not leave it but addresses it in these words:

"Low wretch! Charles is no fool, and no lover of treachery! It
was the act of a brave man to leave us at the pass, and France will
lose none of her glory today. Now strike, Franks; let the first blows
be ours! The right is with us, and this rabble is in the wrong."

XCIV

There is in that company a duke named Fulsarun, a brother of
King Marsiliun's, who rules over the land of Dathan and Abiron.
There is not a bloodier villain under heaven. His forehead, between his eyes, is enormous: if a man were to measure it it would
prove to be over half a foot wide. At the sight of his nephew's death

he is filled with grief and rides forward out of the ranks to offer combat to any who will fight with him; as he does so he shouts the pagan battle cry and flings a sharp taunt at the French:

"This very day sweet France will be shorn of her glory!"

Oliver hears him and is seized with anger. He claps his gilded spurs to his horse and like a true knight rides to fight with him. He breaks the shield, tears through the hauberk, drives lance, pennon, and all, into the body, and hurls the corpse a full spear's length out of the saddle. He looks down at the villain lying on the ground and makes him a proud speech:

"Low wretch, so much for your threats. Now strike, Franks, for they are surely ours!" And they shout, "Mountjoy!" which is Charles' battle cry.

XCV

There is in that company a king named Corsablis, from Barbary, that remote country. He calls out to the other Saracens:

"Surely we can win this battle, for there are so few of the French that we would be wrong not to hold them in contempt. Not one of them will Charles be able to save. The day of their death is here."

Archbishop Turpin hears every word and at once hates him worse than any man under heaven. He sets his spurs of fine gold to his horse and rides out bravely against him, breaks the shield, plows through the hauberk, drives his great lance into the body, skewers it, heaves it up, dead, and pitches the corpse onto the path a spear's length away. He turns and looks back at the villain on the ground. He will not leave him without addressing him, and he says:

"Pagan wretch, you lied! Charles, my lord, is our protector still, and our French have no wish to flee. We will leave your companions, every one of them, stalled in their places. Now learn this: death is your portion. Strike, Franks! Remember who you are! Give thanks to God: this first blow is ours!"

They raise the shout of "Mountjoy!" resolved to keep the field.

XCVI

And Gerin charges against Malprimis of Brigal, whose good shield, upon the impact, is not worth a farthing to him. Its crystal boss shatters; half of it falls to the ground. With his good lance Gerin rips through the hauberk into the flesh, spits the body; the pagan falls to the ground, a dead weight, and Satan carries off his soul.

XCVII

And his companion Gerer charges against the Emir, breaks his shield and parts the hauberk. His good lance drives on into the entrails, digs deep, passes clear through the body, and he leaves the corpse on the field a good spear's length away.

Oliver says: "We are fighting nobly!"

XCVIII

Duke Sansun rides to attack the Saracen general, breaks his shield which is gilded and painted with flowers, and his good hauberk protects him no better, but the spear splits heart, liver and lungs and leaves a corpse, whether any man mourns it or not.

The Archbishop says: "That was a stroke worthy of a knight!"

XCIX

And Anseis gives rein to his horse and rides to attack Turgis of Turteluse. He breaks his shield under the gilded boss, plows through his double hauberk, buries the head of his lance in the Saracen's body, drives it in deeper and out through the back, and tips the dead body into the field a good spear's length away.

Roland says: "That was a stroke worthy of a brave man!"

C

And Engeler, the Gascon from Bordeaux, sets spur to his horse, slackens the reins, rides out to attack Escremiz of Valterne, breaks the shield at his neck so that the pieces fly apart, smashes through the hood of his hauberk and into the throat between the collarbones. He knocks the corpse a good spear's length from the saddle, and then says to it:

"Now Hell has swallowed you up!"

C I

And Otun attacks a pagan by the name of Estorgans, strikes the leather cover of his shield and rips the crimson and white blazon into shreds, breaks through the skirt of his hauberk, runs his good sharp spear through the body and hurls the corpse from its swift horse. Then he says to it:

"Now nothing can save you!"

C I I

And Berenger attacks Estramariz, breaks his shield, plows through his hauberk, runs his strong spear through the body and flings down the corpse in the middle of a thousand Saracens. Ten of the twelve pagan champions have been killed, and only two, Chernuble and Count Margarit, are still alive.

C I I I

Margarit is a brave knight, handsome and strong, agile and nimble. He sets spur to his horse and charges against Oliver, breaks his shield under the golden boss, and drives the spear close to Oliver's side. But God preserves Oliver so that his body is not touched. The spear shaft breaks; Oliver keeps his saddle, and Margarit passes on, unchecked, and sounds his horn to rally his followers.

C I V

The battle becomes general, and magnificent. Count Roland does not spare himself; he fights with his spear as long as the shaft lasts, but after the fifteenth stroke it shatters and becomes useless. Then he draws his good sword Durendal, he bares the blade, and spurs his horse and charges against Chernuble. He cleaves the helmet glittering with carbuncles, sheers through the steel hood and leather coif, splits the skull and face between the eyes, and carving down through the polished hauberk made of fine mail, halves the whole body all the way to the groin. His sword plunges on, and passing through the saddle covered with beaten gold, sinks into the horse, severs its spine, grinding through no joint but through solid bone, and Roland hurls down horse and man, dead, on the rich grass of the meadow. Then he says to the corpse: "Wretch, you came here to your sorrow, and you will have no help now from Mahomet! It is not by such scum as you that a battle is won, and won quickly."

C V

Count Roland rides over the field, with Durendal, that good carver and cleaver, in his hand, and he wreaks carnage among the Saracens. You would have seen him fling corpse upon corpse, and the clear blood cascading into pools. His hauberk and both his arms, and the neck and shoulders of his horse, are covered with blood.

And Oliver fights on without resting. And the twelve peers deserve no reproach. And the French fight hard and furiously. There are pagans killed and others who grow faint. And the Archbishop says:

"A blessing upon our knights!"

And he cries, "Mountjoy!" which is Charles' battle cry.

C V I

And Oliver rides through the battle, with his spear shattered to a stump, charges against Malun, a pagan, breaks his gilded shield with the flowers painted on it, knocks the eyes out of his head and brings his brains tumbling down to his feet. He throws down the corpse among seven hundred other dead pagans, and turns and kills Turgis and Esturguz. But then even the stump of his spear snaps, and splits all the way down to his fist.

Roland says to him: "My companion, what are you doing? In a battle of this kind a club is not to my taste. Only iron and steel are worth anything. Where is your sword Halteclere with its guard of gold and its crystal pommel?"

"I have not had time to draw it," Oliver answers. "I have been too occupied with fighting."

CVII

Sir Oliver has drawn his sword at the urgent promptings of his companion Roland, and he displays its uses in knightly fashion. He attacks Justin of Val Ferree, a pagan, splits the whole of his head in two, cleaves the body, the gilt-varnished coat of mail, and the good saddle studded with jewels set in gold, severs the horse's spine, and hurls down onto the meadow before him the corpses of horse and rider.

Roland says: "Now I recognize you, brother! It is for blows like that one that the Emperor loves us."

And on all sides the shout of "Mountjoy!" goes up.

CVIII

Count Gerin, mounted on his horse Sorel, and his companion Gerer, on Passecerf, slacken their reins, dig in their spurs, and charge against a pagan named Timozel. One strikes his shield, the other his hauberk; both of their spears break off in his body, and they tip his corpse out of the saddle and leave it in a furrow. I have not heard it said, and I do not remember which of those two was swifter and more nimble.

And then Esprieris was killed by Engeler of Bordeaux.

And the Archbishop kills Siglorel for them, a magician who had already descended once into Hell, guided by Jupiter, whom he had compelled to the task by means of enchantments. Turpin says: "He was marked out to be our victim."

Roland answers: "The wretch is finished. Brother Oliver, such blows as that one are a delight to see!"

CIX

The battle grows still more furious, with Frank and pagan giving and receiving tremendous blows, some attacking and others defending themselves. There are so many spears shattered and bloodied, so many pennons torn, and so many battle flags, so many good French cut down in their youth, who will never see their mothers nor their wives again, nor the Franks who are waiting for them in the pass.

Charles the Great weeps, he laments, but what good will that do? There will be no help for the rear guard. Ganelon did them a bad turn, that day when he went to Saragossa and sold his own vassals. And for that he will lose his life and his limbs. In the court at Aix he will be sentenced to be hanged, and thirty of his family with him, who never expected such a death.

C X

The battle is crushing and tremendous. Oliver and Roland fight magnificently, the Archbishop strikes a thousand blows and more, the twelve peers never pause for breath, and the French fight as one man. The pagans die by hundreds and thousands and their only safety is in flight. Their days are cut off, whether it meets their pleasure or not.

The French lose the very pillars of their strength, knights who will never again see their fathers or their families, or Charlemagne, who is waiting for them in the pass.

And in France a terrible uproar breaks loose: a storm of thunder and wind, with rain and hail falling in cloudbursts. There is scarcely a pause between the strokes of lightning, and indeed the earth quakes. From Saint Michael of Peril to Sens, from Besançon to the port of Guitsand, there is not a house without a broken wall. At high noon there is a great darkness and no light at all except when the sky is split with lightning, and no man sees it without terrible dread. Some say:

"This is the last day, and the end of the world has come."

But they know nothing; there is no truth in their words. For it is the great lamentation of the elements for the death of Roland.

C X I

The French have fought courageously and with a will, and the pagans have been slaughtered by thousands and by multitudes: out of the hundred thousand there are not even two still left alive.

The Archbishop says: "Our men are brave; there are no better under heaven. Our Emperor's noble virtues are written into the Chronicle of the Franks."

They ride over the field, they look for those whom they know, they weep over their kinfolk with sorrow and pity, and with full hearts, and with love.

King Marsiliun with his great host moves out against them.

CXII

Marsiliun advances along a valley with the enormous host which he has assembled. The king has divided his army into twenty battle formations. Their helmets shine, studded with jewels set in gold, and their shields gleam, and their gilt-varnished coats of mail. Seven thousand trumpets sound the charge and the whole countryside echoes with the huge sound.

Then Roland says: "Oliver, my companion, my brother, the traitor Ganelon has sworn that we shall be killed, and his betrayal can no longer be hidden. The Emperor will take a terrible vengeance upon him. But for our part, we have before us a battle so rough and furious that no man ever faced one like it. I will attack them with my sword Durendal, and you, my companion, fall upon them with your blade Halteclere—through how many lands we have borne them, and how many battles we have won with their help! They do not deserve to have a bad song sung of them."

CXIII

Marsiliun, seeing the massacre of his knights, commands the trumpets and horns to sound, and rides forward with the great host of his vassals. In front rides a Saracen named Abisme: there is not a man in that company who is more wicked. He is distinguished for his evils and terrible crimes. He does not believe in God, the son of Saint Mary. He is as black as melted pitch. He prefers treason and murder to all the gold of Galicia. No man ever saw him play or laugh. He is brave, and bold in the extreme, which endears him to the wicked King Marsiliun. He bears a dragon as his device, and his followers rally around it. The Archbishop hates him on sight, longs to attack him, and says to himself, under his breath:

"That Saracen looks a heretic from head to foot. The best thing would be for me to kill him. I never loved cowards nor cowardice."

CXIV

Mounted on the horse which he took from King Grossaille whom he killed in Denmark, the Archbishop begins the battle. His war horse is swift and spirited, with cupped hooves and flat legs, short in the thigh, broad in the rump, deep-chested and high-backed, with a white tail, a yellow forelock, small ears, and his head fawn-colored all over; when the reins are loosened there is no horse who is his equal. The Archbishop touches him with the spurs, and oh God how bravely he rides forward! Nothing can turn him aside: he charges against Abisme and strikes him on the shield studded with amethysts, topazes, tourmalines and blazing rubies, which a devil in Val Metas had given to the Emir Galafres, who in turn had presented it to Abisme. Turpin strikes him; he does not spare him; and after one blow I do not think the shield was worth a farthing. He chops through the body from one side to the other and knocks the corpse onto the bare ground.

The French say: "That was a noble stroke! The cross will not suffer while the Archbishop is there to protect it."

CXV

Now the French can see the full size of the pagan host, spreading over the entire plain. Again and again they call upon Oliver and Roland and the twelve peers to lead them to a place of safety. And the Archbishop speaks his mind to them:

"My lords, barons, do not give way to ignoble thoughts! In the name of God I beg you, do not flee; do not prompt them to sing contemptuously of our courage. It is far better that we should die fighting, for we are told that our end will be soon in any case, and we shall not survive that day, but of one thing I can assure you: the sacred land of Paradise stands open to receive you and you will be seated beside the Holy Innocents."

At these words the French rejoice, and as one man they raise the shout of "Mountjoy!"

CXVI

There was a Saracen there who was lord of half the city of Saragossa; his name was Climborin, a vile and ignoble man. It was he who received the oath of Count Ganelon and afterwards kissed him on the mouth and gave him his helmet and his ruby. He has boasted that he will bring shame upon the "Land of the Fathers" and that he will relieve the Emperor of his crown. He is mounted on his horse Barbamusche, which is swifter than any sparrow hawk or swallow; he digs in his spurs, slackens the reins, and charges against Engeler of Gascony, whose shield and coat of mail are powerless to protect him. The pagan stabs him with his spear, runs him through so that the blade emerges through the other side of his body, and tips his corpse into the field a spear's length away. Then he shouts:

"This rabble is ours to destroy! Charge, pagans, and break their ranks!"

The French say: "Oh God, what a brave knight we have lost!"

CXVII

Count Roland calls to Oliver: "My lord, companion, now Engeler is dead, and we had no braver knight."

Oliver answers: "God grant that I may avenge him!"

He strikes his horse with his spurs of pure gold, grips Halteclere, its blade running with blood, and with immense force strikes the pagan. He wrenches the sword loose and the Saracen falls, and the Adversary carries away his soul. After that he kills Duke Alphaien, splits Escababi's head, and unhorses seven Arabs—they will never be of use again in a battle.

Roland says: "My companion is angry! He is worthy of his fame which is coupled with my own. It is for fighting like that that Charles loves us."

Then he shouts aloud: "Strike them, knights!"

CXVIII

On another side there is a pagan named Valdabrun, King Marsiliun's godfather. He is the lord, at sea, of four hundred galleys, and every sailor on those vessels is a bondsman of his. He had taken Jerusalem by treachery and violated the temple of Solomon, murdering the patriarch beside the font. He is the one who, having received Count Ganelon's promise, gave him his own sword and a thousand gold pieces. Mounted on his horse named Gramimund, which is more swift and nimble than any falcon, he digs in his sharp spurs and charges forward to attack the rich Duke Sansun, breaks his shield, rends his hauberk, drives the tails of his pennon into the Duke's body, and flings him, dead, a good spear's length away from his saddle.

"Strike them, pagans, for we are sure of victory!"

The French say: "Oh God, we have lost a brave knight!"

CXIX

You may know that when Count Roland sees that Sansun is dead he is filled with grief, and with Durendal in his hand, which is worth more than its weight in fine gold, he spurs his horse and charges furiously at the pagan. With all his might the brave Count bears down upon the other and his blow falls on the helmet studded with jewels set in gold, splits the head and the coat of mail and the body and the good saddle studded with jewels set in gold, and cleaves deep into the horse's back. He kills both horse and rider, for what blame or praise it may be worth.

The pagans say: "That stroke was a bitter one for us!"

Roland answers: "I have no fondness for you, vainglorious as you are, and in the wrong."

CXX

There is an African there, come from Africa, whose name is Malquiant, King Malcud's son. His armor is plated all over with gold and shines to heaven above all the rest. Mounted on his horse called Saut-Perdu, who has no peer for speed, he charges against Anseis and strikes him on the shield. He cuts through the crimson and azure blazon, breaks the skirts of his hauberk and jams into the body both the head and the shaft of his spear. The Count is dead. His days are ended.

The French say: "Noble knight, we grieve for you."

CXXI

Turpin the Archbishop rides over the field—no tonsured priest who ever sang mass could put his body to so brave and warlike a use.

He says to the pagan: "God load you with every misfortune! You have killed a man whom my heart mourns for."

He urges forward his good horse, strikes the pagan on his Toledo shield, and hurls the corpse onto the green grass.

CXXII

On another side there is a pagan named Grandonies, who is the son of Capuel, the King of Cappadocia. Mounted on a horse called Marmorle, which is more swift and nimble than any bird that flies, he slackens the reins, digs in his spurs, and rides out to strike Gerin with great force, breaking his vermilion shield and tearing it from his neck, shearing away his coat of chain mail, and driving his blue pennon into the body, then hurling the corpse onto a high rock. After that the pagan kills Gerin's companion Gerer, and Berenger, and Guiun of Saint Anthony, and then turns to attack a rich duke named Austorie, lord of Valence and Envers-on-Rhone, and hurls him to the ground, dead, to the great rejoicing of the pagans.

The French say: "What a loss to our company!"

CXXIII

Count Roland grips his blood-drenched sword. He has heard the dismayed exclamations of the French, and his own heart is bursting with grief.

He says to the pagan: "God visit all misfortunes upon you! You have killed a man for whose death I will make you pay dearly!"

He spurs his horse and it leaps forward. One knight or the other must triumph, for now they have come together.

CXXIV

Gradonies was bold and brave, a strong and intrepid fighter. Now he finds himself faced with Roland. And though he has never seen him before, he recognizes him by his proud face, his noble body, his regard, his bearing, and he is filled with an uncontrollable dread and tries to escape, but fails, for the Count strikes him with such force that the blow splits his helmet, nose piece and all, cleaves through his nose, and his mouth, and his teeth, and his whole body and the coat of linked chain mail encasing it, the gilded saddle, both sides of the silver saddle tree, and deep into the horse's back. He kills them both; nothing could have saved them. And the knights from Spain all cry out in their grief.

The French say: "He strikes hard, our champion!"

CXXV

The battle is awesome and furious; the French strike with zeal and rage, cutting through wrists, bodies, spines, piercing garments to carve into living flesh. And the bright blood flows onto the green grass.

" 'Land Of The Fathers,' Mahomet's curse upon you! There is no people on earth which can match yours for bravery!"

And there is not a pagan there who does not cry out: "Marsiliun! Ride forward, King! We are in need of help!"

CXXVI

The battle is awesome and vast; the French fight hard with their burnished spears. There you would have seen terrible suffering, so many men maimed and bleeding, lying piled on each other, face up, face down. The Saracens can endure it no longer, and whatever their resolutions may have been, they forsake the field. The French, with all their strength, pursue them.

CXXVII

Count Roland calls out to Oliver: "My lord, companion, surely you must admit that the Archbishop makes a magnificent knight—

there is none better on earth under heaven. He knows how to put both his spear and his lance to good use."

"And for that very reason," Count Oliver answers, "let us lend him our help!"

At his words the Franks renew their efforts, and the blows are deadly, the struggle is fierce and bloody, and the Christians suffer heavily. There you would have seen Roland and Oliver cleaving and hacking with their swords, and the Archbishop lunging with his spear. The number of those whom they killed can be determined, for it is written in the records and the accounts, and the Chronicle says that there were more than four thousand. Through the first four assaults they hold their ground and acquit themselves well, but the fifth presses them hard and taxes them severely: all of the French knights are killed except sixty, whom God still spares. Before they die the pagans will have had to pay dearly for their lives.

CXXVIII

When Count Roland sees the slaughter of his knights he calls to his companion, Oliver:

"Fair sir, dear companion, in God's name what do you think now, seeing so many good vassals lying on the ground? We may well mourn for sweet fair France, which is despoiled of such noble knights as these! Oh King, my friend, I grieve that you are not here. Oliver, my brother, what can we do? How can we send word?"

Oliver says: "I do not know. I would rather die than bring shame upon us."

CXXIX

Then Roland says: "I will sound my ivory horn and Charles will hear it as he makes his way through the pass, and the Franks, I promise you, will return."

Oliver says: "That would bring great shame and opprobrium on all your kin, which they would have to bear for the rest of their lives. When I asked you to do it you refused. If you do it now it will not be at my bidding. There would be no bravery in sounding your horn. But look: both your arms are running with blood!"

Count Roland answers: "I have dealt heavy blows."

CXXX

Then Roland says: "The battle is fierce. I will sound my horn and King Charles will hear it."

Oliver says: "That would be an ignoble action! When I asked you to sound a blast, companion, you would not deign to do it. If the King had been here no harm would have come to us. Those knights lying there on the ground cannot be blamed."

Oliver says: "I swear by my beard that if ever again I see lovely Alde, my sister, you may give up all hope of lying in her arms!"

CXXXI

Then Roland says: "Why are you angry with me?"

And he answers: "Companion, it is your own doing, for knightly courage used with prudence is one thing and folly is another, and tempered judgment is more to be valued than the rashness of arrogance. Those French are dead because of your heedlessness, and we will never act again in Charles' service. If you had listened to me my lord would have returned and we would have won this battle and King Marsiliun would have been captured or killed. Woe to us, Roland, that we ever saw your bravery! Charles the Great, a man whose like will never be seen again until God judges the world, will no longer be able to rely on our help, and you will die, and shame will come to France. Today our faithful friendship will end, and before evening we will have parted in sorrow."

CXXXII

The Archbishop has heard their argument, and he sets his spurs of fine gold to his horse and rides over to them and reproaches them:

"My lord Roland, and you, my lord Oliver, in the name of God I beg you, do not fall to quarrelling! It is too late for a blast of the horn to save us, but it would be best if you were to blow it nevertheless, for the King will then return and avenge our deaths, and those who have come from Spain must not be allowed to leave the field rejoicing. Our French will dismount, they will find us dead and our bodies mangled, and they will lift us onto biers on the backs of pack mules, and will weep for us in sorrow and pity, and bury us in the aisles of minsters, and we will not be eaten by wolves or pigs or dogs."

Roland answers: "My lord, what you say is wise."

CXXXIII

Roland has set his ivory horn to his mouth; he puts his lips hard against it and blows with all his strength. The mountains are high, and over them the voice of the horn rings long, and more than thirty leagues away its echo answers. Charles hears it, and all the knights in his company.

The King says: "Our men are fighting!"

And Ganelon, contradicting him, answers: "If anyone else had said so I would say he was lying."

CXXXIV

Count Roland, in pain and anguish, and in great sorrow, blows a blast on his ivory horn, and the bright blood flows from his mouth, and the veins burst on his forehead, but the sound of the horn swells and mounts, and Charles hears it as he makes his way through the pass, and Duke Naimes hears it, and it comes to the ears of the Franks.

Then the King says: "I hear the sound of Roland's horn, and he would not blow it unless there were a battle."

Ganelon answers: "Battle? There is no battle! You are old and your beard and hair are white and flowery, and when you speak like that you sound like a child. You are well aware of Roland's vast pride—it is a wonder that God has endured him for so long. Did he not seize Noples without waiting for your command? The Saracens rode out on that occasion and joined battle with Roland, and that good vassal flooded the meadows afterwards to wash away the gory remains . . . A single rabbit has been known to set him blowing his horn from one end of the day to the other. At the moment he is performing some kind of sport before his peers. Who under heaven would dare to take the field against him? Ride on! Why should you pause? The 'Land of the Fathers' is still a long way off."

CXXXV

Count Roland's mouth is streaming blood and the veins on his forehead have burst. In sorrow and pain he blows his ivory horn. Charles hears it, and his French hear it.

Then the King says: "That horn has a long breath!"

Duke Naimes answers: "Some knight is in anguish. There is a battle, I am sure of it, and he who has betrayed the knights in the rear guard is the same who now counsels you to fail them. Arm, sound your battle cry, and go to the help of your noble followers. You have heard enough. That horn is the sound of Roland's despair!"

CXXXVI

The Emperor has commanded them to sound their horns, and the French dismount and put on their coats of mail and their helmets, and gird on their swords chased with gold. They have resplendent shields and large strong spears with white and vermilion and blue pennons. All the knights in that host mount their war horses and spur them along the pass, saying to each other:

"If we can get to Roland before he dies, together we will deal them great blows!"

What good are their words? For they have waited too long.

CXXXVII

The evening lengthens, the day draws out, and their armor shines against the sun, their hauberks and helmets flashing fire, and their shields also, which are elaborately painted with flowers, and their spears with the pennons worked in gold. The Emperor rides on in wrath, and the French in sorrow and rage, and there is not one of them who is not weeping bitterly, in fear for Roland. The King has bidden them sieze Ganelon, and turns him over to the cooks of the royal household, whose chief, a man named Besgun, he summons to his presence:

"Guard him well for me, as a villain like that ought to be guarded. He has betrayed vassals of my own household."

They take the traitor and surround him with a hundred kitchen hands of the best and the worst, and tear out his beard and mustache, and each one of them gives him four blows of his fist; they beat him soundly with clubs and staves, and put a chain on his neck as though he were a bear, and they fling him over a pack mule to shame him. They guard him in this way until the day when they give him back to Charles.

CXXXVIII

The peaks are high and dark and huge, the valleys deep, and the torrents dash through them. They sound their trumpets at the head of the column and at the rear, and all together blare in answer to Roland's ivory horn. The Emperor rides on, wrathfully, and the French ride on in rage and sorrow, and there is not one of them who is not weeping grievously and praying to God to protect Roland until they reach the battlefield; then indeed he and they will strike together. But what good is their talk? Their words are useless. They have waited too long. They will be too late.

CXXXIX

Charles the King rides on in great wrath, with his white beard spread out over his chain mail, and all the knights of France spurring forward around him. There is not one of them who does not furiously lament that he is not with Roland the captain, who is fighting against the Saracens of Spain, and who is in such agony that his soul cannot remain much longer in his body. Oh God, what fighters they are, those sixty knights in his company! No better men ever served king or captain.

CXL

Roland gazes at the mountains and the hillsides, and there he sees so many French dead lying, and as a noble knight he weeps for them:

"My lords, barons, God have mercy upon you and admit your souls without exception into Paradise and lay you down on the holy flowers. I never saw better vassals than you were, who have served me for so long without respite and have conquered so vast a domain in the name of Charles! The Emperor brought you up to sorrow. And you, land of France who have no peer for sweetness, today you are made desolate by calamity! Barons of France, I see you dying for my sake and I cannot defend you nor protect you. May God, who never lied, be your help! Brother Oliver, I must not fail you. I will die of sorrow if nothing else kills me. My lord, companion, let us strike them again!"

CXLI

Count Roland has returned to the battle, and with Durendal in his fist he strikes blows worthy of a knight. He has hewn in half Faldrun of Pui and twenty-four others from among the pick of the Saracens. No man ever burned so to avenge himself. As stags before the dogs the pagans run before Roland. The Archbishop says:

"You have fought well! That is the kind of courage which a knight should have who bears arms and bestrides a good horse. He must be strong and overbearing in battle or he is not worth a farthing and would do better as a monk in some monastery praying daily for our sins."

Roland answers: "Strike, and do not spare them!"

At this word the Franks resume the battle. The Christians suffer terrible losses.

CXLII

In a battle such as this one where it is known that no prisoners will be taken, the knights defend themselves furiously, and for this reason the Franks are as fierce as lions. And now Marsiliun himself approaches as a knight. He is mounted on his horse named Gaignun. He digs in his spurs and rides to strike Bevun, the lord of Belne and Digun. He breaks his shield, smashes through his hauberk, and hurls him down, dead, without another stroke. Then he kills Yvoerie and Ivun, and Gerard of Roussillon with them. Count Roland is not far away, and he says to the pagan:

"May the Lord God lay his curse upon you, who have villainously slaughtered so many of my companions! Before we part you will have been dealt a blow and will have learned the name of my sword!"

Like a true knight the Count rides to strike him and slices off his right hand. Then he turns to Jurfaleu the Blond, the son of King Marsiliun, and cuts off his head. The pagans shout:

"Help us, Mahomet! And you, our gods, for our sake wreak vengeance upon Charles, who has stocked this land with evil men who would rather die than quit the field!"

One of them says to the other: "Let us flee!" And at that word a hundred thousand take to flight, and will not return, whoever calls.

CXLIII

And what difference will it make? For even if Marsiliun himself flees there is still his uncle Marganice, the lord of Carthage, Alfrere, Garmalia and Ethiopia, an accursèd country. The black races are under his command. They have large noses and broad ears. There are more than fifty thousand of them. They ride fiercely, furiously, and they shout the pagan battle cry. Then Roland says:

"Here is our death bearing down upon us, and now I know beyond any doubt that we can live no longer. But he is a traitor who does not sell his life dearly! Strike, my lords, with your polished blades, and contend for your lives and your deaths, so that sweet France may not be shamed on our account! When Charles my lord comes to this field he will see that such punishment has been wrought on the Saracens that for every one of our dead there are fifteen of theirs, and he will not fail to pronounce his blessing over us."

CXLIV

When Roland sees the accursed people who are blacker than ink, with nothing white about them except their teeth, the Count says:

"Now I know beyond any doubt that we shall die today. Now I am sure. Strike, French knights, for now I lead you once more against them!"

Oliver says: "A curse upon the slowest!"

At this word the French charge into them.

CXLV

When the pagans see how few of the French are left they feel proud; they take heart. They say to each other:

"The Emperor is in the wrong."

Marganice, mounted on a sorrel horse, digs in his golden spurs and strikes Oliver from behind, in the middle of his back. The shining hauberk parts, laying bare the body, and the spear passes through and out at the breast. Then the pagan says:

"You were hit hard that time! Charles the Great left you here in the pass to your sorrow! He has done us wrong, but he will have no reason to congratulate himself, for in your death alone I have avenged all of ours."

CXLVI

Oliver knows that he has been given a deadly wound, and he grips Halteclere and with its burnished blade strikes Marganice on the sharp-pointed golden helmet, smashes through its flowers and gems and cleaves the head from here down to the front teeth. He gives the sword a wrench and hurls down the corpse. And then he says:

"A curse on you, pagan! I cannot say that Charles has suffered no loss, but you at least will never go back to the kingdom from which you came and brag to any wife or woman that you left me the poorer by so much as a farthing, nor that you did me or any-one else any harm!"

Then he calls to Roland to come to his help.

CXLVII

Oliver knows that he has been dealt a mortal wound and his passion to avenge himself is insatiable. He charges into the thick of the pagans, striking out like a brave knight, shearing through the shafts of their spears, and their shields and their feet and their wrists and their saddles and their ribs. Any man who had seen him then dismembering Saracens, flinging corpse upon corpse, would have been able to remember a noble knight. He does not neglect to raise Charles' battle cry, but shouts, "Mountjoy!" loud and clear. He calls to his friend and his peer, Roland:

"My lord, companion, come to my side, for today in bitter grief we must separate."

CXLVIII

Roland looks at Oliver's face and sees that it has turned gray, livid, colorless, and pale, and he sees the bright blood streaking down Oliver's body and falling in streams to the ground. The Count says:

"Oh God, what can I do now! My lord, my companion, your courage has been brought to grief, and no man will ever be your equal. Ah sweet France, what a loss of noble knights you have suffered today, and how stricken and wasted you are now! What a heavy blow this will be to the Emperor!"

And with these words he faints on his horse.

CXLIX

Look now: Roland has fainted on his horse and Oliver has been dealt a mortal wound and has lost so much blood that his sight has become confused. He can no longer see anything clearly, whether it is far away or near. He can no longer recognize any living man, and finding his companion in front of him, he strikes with all his strength at the helmet with its jewels set in gold, and he splits it down to the nose piece but does not touch the head. Roland, when the blow has struck him, looks Oliver in the face and softly and gently asks him:

"My lord, companion, did you mean to strike me? It is I, Roland, who have loved you dearly for so long. You never warned me nor challenged me."

Oliver says: "Now I hear you speak, but I cannot see you. May the Lord God keep you in His sight! I have struck you and I beg you to forgive me!"

Roland answers: "I have suffered no harm. Here and before God I forgive you."

With these words they bow to each other.

And look: it is thus, tenderly, that they part.

CL

Oliver feels the pains of death encroaching upon him. His eyes reel in his head. He loses his hearing. He can no longer see anything. He dismounts and reclines on the ground, and there in a loud voice, with his hands clasped and lifted up toward heaven, he confesses his sins and prays to God to receive him into Paradise, and he blesses Charles and sweet France and above all other men his companion Roland. His heart fails, his helmet sags, his whole body slumps onto the earth. The Count is dead. He is there no longer. Roland, that brave knight, weeps for him and gives way to his grief. Never in this world will you hear a more sorrowful man.

CLI

Now Roland sees that his friend is dead and lying face down on the ground, and with great tenderness he speaks his lament and farewell:

"My lord, companion, your tempered courage has been brought to grief! We have been together for days and years and you never did me any wrong, and I never did you any, and now that you are dead it is a grief to me to be alive."

At this word Roland, the baron, faints, sitting on Veillantif his horse, and his stirrups of fine gold hold him up, so that whichever way he leans he cannot fall.

CLII

Before Roland returns to himself and recovers from his faint, terrible losses have been inflicted on his force, for the French are dead, they are all lost except the Archbishop and Gualter of Hum. Gualter has come down from the heights. He has fought hard against the Saracens of Spain; all his men are dead, overwhelmed by the pagans, and whether he wishes to or not he flees toward the valleys there and calls out to Roland to help him:

"Ah noble Count, man of courage, where are you? I was never afraid where you were. It is I, Gualter, who conquered Maelgut! It is I, the nephew of old white-haired Droun, and you used to love me for my courage. My lance is splintered, my shield is pierced, my hauberk is broken and rent, and as for my body . . . I will die in any case, but I have sold my life dearly."

Roland hears these words, and he spurs his horse and rides toward Gualter.

CLIII

Roland, in his grief and his rage, strikes into the midst of the pagans and hurls down twenty of the Saracens of Spain, dead. And Gualter kills six, and the Archbishop five. The pagans say:

"These men are monstrous! Lords, take care that they do not get away alive! Any man who does not attack them now is a traitor, and he who lets them escape is a coward!"

Then they renew the hue and cry and ride to attack from all sides.

CLIV

Count Roland is a noble warrior, Gualter of Hum is a superb knight, and the Archbishop is a brave and proven fighter. None of them would forsake the others on any account, and they charge into the midst of the pagans. A thousand Saracens dismount, and there are forty thousand on horses, and I swear it, they are afraid to approach. Instead they throw lances and spears, and bolts and javelins and arrows and sharp missiles and long darts. One of the first of these kills Gualter. Turpin of Reims has his shield pierced by another. And then another smashes his helmet and passes through to wound him in the head, and his hauberk is rent and broken, and four spears pass through his body. They kill his war horse under him. Now there is cause for grief, as the Archbishop falls.

CLV

Turpin of Reims knows that he has been mortally wounded. Four spears have passed through his body. That brave peer gets to his feet again, looks for Roland, runs to him, and says:

"I am not beaten! A good vassal never yields while there is still life in him."

He draws his sword Almace, with its burnished blade, and in

the thick of the pagans he strikes a thousand blows and more. Charles said afterwards that Turpin of Reims spared none of the pagans, for he found four hundred of them lying around the Archbishop, some wounded, some cleft in two, some headless. That is what the Chronicle says, which was written by one who had seen the field: the worthy Gilie, for whom God performed wonders. He wrote the account in the monastery of Laon, and any man who does not know that is ignorant of the whole story.

CLVI

Count Roland fights nobly, but his body is hot and running with sweat, and his head has been throbbing with fierce pains since he blew his horn and the veins burst on his temples. But he wants to know whether Charles is on his way, and he takes his ivory horn and blows it, feebly. The Emperor halts and listens.

"My lords," he says, "it is going badly for us! Today Roland, my nephew, is lost to us. From the sound of his horn I can tell that he does not have much longer to live. Any man who hopes to find him alive must ride fast. Now sound every trumpet in this host!"

Sixty thousand trumpets blare, and the sound crashes through the mountains, and the valleys echo. The pagans hear that note, and they are not moved to laughter. They say to each other:

"Charles is upon us!"

CLVII

The pagans say: "The Emperor is returning! Listen: you can hear the trumpets of the French! If Charles comes our losses will be heavy, and Roland, if he survives, will renew the war, and our land of Spain will be lost to us."

Four hundred of them who pride themselves on being the best fighters in the field, mass together, helmet by helmet, to launch a single fierce, crushing attack on Roland.

This time the Count will have no leisure.

CLVIII

Count Roland sees them coming and his strength and pride and courage mount. He will never yield to them as long as there is life in him. Astride his horse whom men call Veillantif, he digs in his spurs of fine gold and charges into the thick of them, and Turpin, the Archbishop, with him.

The pagans say to each other: "Now let us go, friend! We have heard the horns of the knights of France, and Charles, the mighty King, is returning."

CLIX

Count Roland never loved a coward, nor a proud man, nor a man of ill will, nor any knight who was not a brave fighter. He calls to Archbishop Turpin:

"My lord, you are on foot and I am mounted, and out of love for you I will stay beside you and together we will take what comes, good or evil, and no man made of flesh will force me from you. Let us go together to attack the pagans. Durendal still strikes hardest!"

The Archbishop says: "He who holds back now is a traitor! Charles is returning. He will avenge us."

CLX

The pagans say: "Woe to us that we were ever born! What an evil day has now risen above us! We have lost our lords and our peers. Charles the brave is returning with his great host and we can hear the clear trumpets of the knights of France, and the shout of 'Mountjoy' rings loud in our ears. Such is the fierce bravery of Count Roland that no man made of flesh will overcome him. Let us hurl our weapons at him and then leave him where he is."

And they throw javelins at him in great numbers, and spears and lances and feathered darts, and they have pierced Roland's shield and smashed it, and broken and rent his hauberk, but their weapons have not touched his body. But Veillantif is wounded in thirty places: they have killed the Count's horse under him. The pagans flee, leaving him on the field. Count Roland is left there, on foot.

CLXI

Smarting with anger and rage, the pagans flee headlong toward Spain, and Count Roland, having lost Veillantif and been forced to dismount whether he likes it or not, cannot give chase. He goes to Archbishop Turpin to help him, unlaces the gold helmet from his head, draws the light, shining hauberk from his body, and cuts his tunic to pieces, which he stuffs into the gaping wounds. Then he draws the Archbishop to his breast and gently lays him down on the green grass. Then tenderly Roland begs a favor of him:

"Ah noble lord, give me leave to go from you! Our companions who were so dear to us are dead now, and we should not leave them where they are. Let me go and look for them and identify them, and bring them here before you and arrange them in a row."

The Archbishop says: "Go and return! The field is yours—I thank God—yours and mine."

CLXII

Roland leaves him and goes off over the field alone, through the valleys, along the mountains, looking . . . There he finds Yvoerie and Ivun, and after him Engeler of Gascony. There he finds Gerin, and Gerer his companion, and Berenger and Otun. There he finds Anseis and Sansun, and after them Gerard the Old, from Roussillon. One by one he takes them up, that brave knight, and brings them all to the Archbishop, and sets them in a row before his knees, and the Archbishop cannot hold back the tears. He lifts up his hand and offers a benediction, and then he says:

"My lords, you were brought to grief, and now may God the Glorious receive your souls every one and lay them on the holy flowers in Paradise! Now the pains of my own death are upon me and I will never again see the Emperor in his might."

CLXIII

Roland leaves him and goes off over the field, looking. And he has found his companion, Oliver. He draws him to his breast, in his arms, and makes his way to the Archbishop as best he can, and lays Oliver on a shield beside the others, and the Archbishop absolves him and blesses him. Then sorrow and pity well up, and then Roland says:

"Fair companion, Oliver, you were the son of Duke Reiner who ruled the marches of the Valley of Runers. To shatter a lance and pierce a shield, to strike down the proud and fill them with terror, and to sustain the brave and give them counsel, and to strike down base and vile men and fill them with terror, there is no better knight in any country."

CLXIV

When Count Roland sees all the peers dead, and Oliver whom he had loved so dearly, tenderness wells up in him and he begins to weep. His face has grown pale, and his sorrow is so great that he cannot keep to his feet any longer, but his will forsakes him and he falls to the ground in a faint. The Archbishop says:

"Brave knight, I grieve for you!"

CLXV

When the Archbishop sees Roland fall down in a faint his sorrow becomes even greater than it had been at any time before. He stretches out his hand and takes the ivory horn.

There is a stream at Roncesvalles, and the Archbishop wants to fetch some water to Roland. He walks away with little steps, swaying on his feet, so weak that he cannot go forward, having lost so much blood that all the strength has gone out of him, and after less time than it takes a man to cross an acre of ground his heart fails him, he falls forward, and the terrible agony of his death seizes him.

CLXVI

Count Roland recovers from his faint and gets to his feet, though in great pain, and looks around him, down along the valleys, up to the mountains, over the green grass, beyond his companions. And he sees on the ground that noble knight, the Archbishop, who had been ordained in the name of God. Gazing upwards, with his clasped hands lifted toward heaven, the Archbishop makes his confession and prays to God to receive him into Paradise. Now Turpin, Charles' warrior, is dead. In great battles and in beautiful sermons, all his life he was a champion of Christendom against the pagans. May God grant him His holy blessing!

CLXVII

Count Roland sees the Archbishop on the ground and the bowels sagging out of his body and the brain oozing over his forehead. On the breast, between the two collarbones, he crosses the white and shapely hands. Then, following the custom of his country, Roland speaks a lament over him:

"Ah noble sir, knight born of honored ancestors, today I commend you to the Glorious King of Heaven. No man ever served him with a better will. Never since the days of the saints was there such a man of God for maintaining the laws and drawing men to the faith. May your soul not suffer, and may the door of Paradise be open to you!"

CLXVIII

Now Roland feels death near him. His brains have begun to seep out through his ears. He prays for the peers, asking God to summon them to His presence, and then for himself he calls upon the angel Gabriel. He takes his ivory horn, so that no one may be able to bring shame on him by showing it, and in the other hand he takes his sword Durendal. A little farther away than a man might shoot with a crossbow, on the side toward Spain, there is a grassy place. Roland goes to it and climbs a little mound. There is a beautiful tree there and there are four great stones of marble under it. On the green grass he has fallen backward, and he has fainted there, for death is near him.

CLXIX

The mountains are high, and the trees are tall, and there are four great stones of marble there, shining. Count Roland faints on the green grass.

A Saracen has been watching him closely from among the

corpses, where he has been lying with his body and face smeared with blood, pretending to be dead. He gets to his feet and begins to run. He is a man of handsome appearance and great courage. It is pride which spurs him on to this fatal folly. He seizes Roland by his arms and body and he says:

"Charles' nephew is beaten! I will take this sword to Arabia."

As he draws it the Count returns somewhat to his senses.

CLXX

Roland feels the sword being taken away from him and he opens his eyes and says to the other:

"You do not look like one of ours."

He grips his ivory horn, which he had not wanted to leave behind, and with it he strikes the pagan on the helmet, which is covered with jewels set in gold, and smashes the steel and the head and the bone so that both the eyes burst from the face and the body falls dead at his feet. Then he says:

"Base pagan, what made you so rash as to seize me, whether by fair means or foul? Whoever hears the story will take you for a fool. But the mouth of my ivory horn is shattered, and the crystal has fallen from it, and the gold."

CLXXI

Now Roland feels the sight of his eyes forsaking him, and with a great effort he gets to his feet. All the color has left his face. He sees before him a gray stone. In sorrow and bitterness he strikes it ten blows with his sword, and the steel grates but will not break nor be blunted.

"Ah," says the Count, "Saint Mary help me! Ah Durendal, my good sword, you have fallen on sad days, for I am dying and you will no longer be in my keeping. With you I have won so many battles in the field and conquered so many broad lands which white-bearded Charles rules over! May you never fall into the hands of any man who will flee before another, for you have been owned by a brave knight for a long time, and holy France will never see another like you."

CLXXII

Next Roland strikes the great blood-red stone, and the steel grates but will not break nor be blunted. When he sees that he cannot break the sword, Roland begins to grieve over it:

"Ah Durendal, how beautiful you are, and how bright, and how dazzling, glittering and flashing in the sunlight! Charles was in the Valley of Moriane when God in heaven sent an angel to tell him to give you to a count, one of his captains, and it was then that you were girded upon me by that noble king, that great king.

"With this I conquered Anjou and Brittany for him, and for him I conquered Poitou and Maine. With this I conquered proud Normandy for him, and for him conquered Provence and Aquitaine and Lombardy and the whole of Romagna. With this I conquered Bavaria and all of Flanders for him, and Burgundy, and Poland from one end to the other, and Constantinople, from which he received homage, and in Saxony his command is obeyed. With this I conquered Scotland for him, and . . . and England, which he held as his own place. With this I have conquered so many lands for him, so many countries, and white-bearded Charles rules over them. And now I am full of grief and sorrow because of this sword, for I would rather die than let it fall into the hands of the pagans. God, Father, do not allow France to be thus dishonored!"

CLXXIII

Roland, striking harder than I can say, brings the sword down on a gray stone, and it grates, but is neither chipped nor shattered. It rebounds toward heaven. When the Count sees that it will not be broken, very softly he grieves over it:

"Ah Durendal, how beautiful you are, and how blessed, with the holy relics in your golden hilt—there is a tooth of Saint Peter's there, and some of Saint Basil's blood, and several hairs of my lord Saint Denis, and a bit of a garment of Saint Mary's. It would not be right if you were to fall into the hands of pagans; you should be in the keeping of Christians. May no coward ever possess you! With you I have conquered many broad lands which Charles rules over. His beard is in flower. Because of you the emperor is venerable and mighty."

CLXXIV

Now Roland feels death taking everything from him, descending from his head into his heart, and he runs under a pine tree and lies down with his face to the green grass. Underneath him he places his sword and ivory horn. He turns his head toward the pagans, so that Charles and all his knights may say:
"The noble knight died a conqueror."
He makes his confession, carefully, over and over, and he offers his glove, as a token of his sins, to God.

CLXXV

Now Roland feels that the end of his life has come. He has lain down on a steep hill with his face toward Spain and with one hand he beats his breast:
"God, I acknowledge my guilt and I beg for Thy mercy for all the sins, greater and lesser, which I have committed from the hour of my birth until this day when I lie here overcome by death!"
He has held out his right glove to God.
Angels descend out of heaven and come to him.

CLXXVI

Count Roland has lain down under a pine tree, turning his face toward Spain. Many things come to his memory—so many countries which he had conquered as a brave knight, and sweet France, the land of his ancestors and of Charlemagne, his lord, who had reared him. He cannot hold back the tears and the sighs.
But he does not wish to forget himself. He confesses his sins and prays to God for mercy:
"True Father, who never lied, who raised Saint Lazarus from the dead, and saved Daniel from the lions, save my soul in spite of all the perils which I have incurred with the sins of my life!"
He offers his right glove to God, and Saint Gabriel takes it from his hand. His head sinks onto his arm. With clasped hands he comes to the end of his life. God has sent His angels, Cherubim

and Saint Michael of Peril, and Saint Gabriel with them, and they bear the soul of the Count to Paradise.

CLXXVII

Roland is dead and God has taken his soul into heaven.

The Emperor reaches Roncesvalles. There is not a track nor a path, nor a yard nor even a foot of empty ground without a Frank or a pagan lying on it.

Charles calls out: "Where are you, fair nephew? Where is the Archbishop? And Count Oliver? Where is Gerin? And his companion Gerer? Where is Otun? And Count Berenger? Ivun and Yvoerie, who were so dear to me? What has become of Engeler of Gascony? And Duke Sansun? And the brave Anseis? Where is Gerard the Old, from Roussillon? Where are the twelve peers whom I left here?"

What good is it to call? Not one of them answers.

"Oh God!" the King says, "what reason I have now to lament that I was not here when the battle began!"

In his passion he tears at his beard. His brave knights weep. Twenty thousand of them faint to the ground. Duke Neimun is overcome with grief.

CLXXVIII

There is no knight or baron there who is not shaken with grief and bitter weeping. They are weeping for their sons, for their brothers, for their nephews and their friends and for their lords, and many of them faint to the ground out of sorrow. Now Duke Naimes conducts himself worthily, for he is the first to say to the Emperor:

"Look before you. You can see the dust rising over the main roads two leagues away, there are so many of the pagans. Now ride! Avenge this sorrow of ours!"

"Oh God," Charles says, "they are so far already! Now render me the obedience and honor which you owe me, for they have stolen from me the flower of sweet France."

The King summons Gebuin and Otun, Tedbalt of Reims and Count Milun:

"Guard the field, and the valleys, and the mountains. Leave the dead where they are lying and let no beast nor lion touch them. Let no squire nor foot soldier be touched, nor any man be touched until God permits us to return to this field."

And they answer with sweet and loving reverence:

"Just Emperor, dear lord, we shall do it!"

They keep a thousand of their knights with them.

CLXXIX

The Emperor commands the trumpets to sound, and then that brave king rides forward with his enormous host. The Saracens of Spain have turned their backs; the Franks set out in pursuit, all riding together. When the King sees the dusk descending he dismounts on the green grass of a meadow and lies down on the ground and prays to the Lord God to make the sun stand still and the night wait and the day go on. Then an angel who had spoken to him many times before comes and says to him:

"Ride on, Charles, for the light will not fail you. God knows that you have lost the flower of France. You can wreak vengeance upon the evildoers."

When he hears these words the Emperor mounts.

CLXXX

For Charlemagne's sake God has performed a great miracle, for the sun is standing still where it was. The pagans flee and the French give chase furiously and catch them in Val Tenebrus and drive them on toward Saragossa, having cut off the main roads and lanes by which they might have escaped. All along the way the Franks harry them with fierce blows, and slaughter them. Now the pagans are confronted by the deep, awesome and swiftly flowing waters of the Ebro, and there is neither barge there, nor boat, nor galley. The pagans call upon their god Termagant, and then they leap in, but no divinity protects them. Those who are in full armor are the heaviest, and great numbers of them sink to the bottom, and others are swept off by the current, and they are the lucky ones who drink their fill at once, for in fact all of them drown, and in fearful anguish. The French shout:

"Roland, we grieve for you!"

CLXXXI

When Charles sees that all the pagans are dead, many of them killed, and the greater part of them drowned, and when he sees the vast spoils which his knights have taken, the noble King dismounts and lies down on the ground and gives thanks to God. When he stands up again the sun has set. The Emperor says:

"It is time to make camp. It is too late to return to Roncesvalles. Our horses are tired and listless. Take off their saddles. Take the bits from their mouths. Let them refresh themselves in the meadows here."

The Franks say: "Sire, you have spoken wisely."

CLXXXII

The Emperor has pitched his camp. The French dismount in the empty country and take the saddles from their horses and the golden bits out of their mouths and turn them loose in the meadows where there is cool grass in plenty. There is nothing more that they can do for them. Then whoever is tired goes to sleep on the ground. That night no one mounts guard.

CLXXXIII

The Emperor has made his bed in a meadow. The brave King sets his massive spear at his head, not wishing to lay aside his arms that night. He does not remove his shining gilt-varnished hauberk; his helmet, studded with jewels set in gold, is laced to his head, and his sword Joyeuse is girded to his side. There was never another like it. Its brilliance changes color thirty times a day. We have heard of the lance which wounded Our Lord, on the cross: by the goodness of God the point of it has come into Charles' keeping, and he has caused the point of it to be mounted in the golden pommel of his sword. And it is because of this honor and this grace in it that the sword was given the name Joyeuse. The knights of France are not likely to forget it, for from it came their battle cry of "Mountjoy!" and therefore no people can stand against them.

CLXXXIV

The night is clear and the moon is shining. Charles has lain down, but his sorrow for Roland comes over him, and he grieves bitterly for Oliver and the twelve peers, and for the French knights whom he had left in their blood at Roncesvalles. He weeps, he laments, he cannot help it, and he prays to God to save their souls. The King is tired, he is weighed down with heavy grief, and he sleeps because he can no longer stay awake. And over all those meadows the Franks lie sleeping. Not one horse is able to keep to its feet. Those that want grass crop it lying down.

He who has endured great suffering has learned much.

CLXXXV

Charles sleeps the sleep of the weary. God sends Saint Gabriel to keep watch over the Emperor, and all night the angel stands at his head, and by means of a vision, whose significance is made plain in terrible omens, foretells a battle which will be fought against him.

Charles looks up toward heaven and sees thunderbolts, hail, rushing winds, storms and awesome tempests, and fires and flames appear to him, falling suddenly upon his whole army. The lances of ash wood and of apple wood catch fire and burn, and the shields, even to the gold bosses on them. And the shafts of their sharp spears are splintered, and their hauberks and their steel helmets are broken; and he sees his knights in great distress. Then bears and leopards come to devour them, serpents and vipers, dragons and devils, and more than thirty thousand griffons, and all of them fling themselves on the French. And the French cry out:

"Charlemagne, help us!"

The King is filled with sorrow and pity. He longs to go to their help, but he cannot, for his way is blocked by a huge lion which comes out of a wood toward him, raging and proud and fierce, and springs at his body and seizes him, and they fall to grips and struggle and he cannot say which of them is on top and which of them is underneath. And the Emperor does not wake.

CLXXXVI

After that, another vision comes to him: he is in France, at Aix, on a dais, and is holding a bear by two chains. He sees thirty other bears emerge from the Ardenne and come toward him, each one talking like a man. They say to him:

"Sire, give him back to us! It is not right that you should keep him for so long. He is our own kin, and we are bound to come to his help."

Out of his palace a greyhound dashes, and choosing the largest of the bears, on the green grass, beyond its companions, attacks it. Then the King sees a fearful combat, but he cannot tell which of them wins and which is beaten.

This is what the angel shows to the noble lord. Charles sleeps on until the morning, and the bright day.

CLXXXVII

King Marsiliun flees to Saragossa, and there he dismounts in the shade of an olive tree. His sword is broken, and his helmet, and his coat of mail, and he lies down in wretchedness on the green grass. He has lost the whole of his right hand, and he faints from pain and loss of blood. Bramimunde, his wife, comes before him, weeping and crying out, and uttering loud laments, and there are more than twenty thousand men with her, all of them cursing Charles and sweet France. And they run to the image of Apollin which is in the crypt there, and fall to berating it and horribly abusing it:

"Oh wicked god, why have you visited such shame upon us? Why have you allowed our King to be overthrown? Let a man give you long and faithful service and you will give him an ill reward!"

Then they strip from it its scepter and its crown, and hang it by the hands on a column, and topple it into the dirt among their feet, and beat it and smash it with clubs. And they tear out Termagant's carbuncle and hurl the image of Mahomet into a ditch for pigs and dogs to devour and befoul.

CLXXXVIII

Marsiliun recovers from his faint and has himself carried into his vaulted bedroom, painted and inscribed in many colors. And Bramimunde, the Queen, weeps because of him, and tears her hair, and calls herself a wretch, and cries out, shrieking every word:

"Oh Saragossa, now you are bereft of that noble king who had you in his keeping! Our gods have betrayed us, for this morning they failed him in battle. And the Emir is a coward if he does not come now and fight with these bold people who are so proud that they are careless of their lives. The Emperor with the flowering beard is brave; he is foolhardy. He will never flee from a battle. Oh what a pity that someone does not kill him!"

CLXXXIX

The Emperor, by the exercise of his great power, has stayed seven whole years in Spain and taken castles and many cities, though Marsiliun has made every effort to resist. Ever since the first year the Saracen King has been sending sealed messages to Babylon, to the ancient Emir Baligant, who has survived both Virgil and Homer, urging him to come to the relief of Saragossa. Otherwise, the messages continue, Baligant's gods and all the idols which he adores will be abandoned, and Marsiliun will accept Christianity and come to terms with Charlemagne. But Baligant is far away, and he has taken a long time. He has gathered together his people from out of forty kingdoms, and he has had his great transport vessels made ready, and has equipped barges and galleys and ships. Below Alexandria there is a port giving onto the sea, and there he has assembled his entire fleet. It is in May, on the first day of summer, that he embarks with his whole army.

CXC

That race of the devil is sending an enormous host.

They scud along with sails and oars, maintaining their course, and their mastheads and their tall prows gleam with carbuncles and lanterns which flash so brightly into the sky that at night they adorn the sea. And as the vessels approach the land of Spain, this brilliance floods the whole coast, so that it shines.

The news of their arrival reaches Marsiliun.

CXCI

Rather than anchor, the pagans sail on and, leaving the sea, enter fresh water, sail past Marbrise and Marbrose, and ascend the Ebro with their entire fleet, which is spangled with lanterns and carbuncles so that it gleams brightly all night. With daylight they sail on to Saragossa.

CXCII

The day is clear, with brilliant sunlight. The Emir has disembarked from his vessel. On his right he is escorted by Espaneliz, and seventeen kings follow behind him, and more counts and dukes than I can say. Under a laurel tree which is growing in the middle of the camp they toss a white silk robe onto the green grass, and on it they place an ivory throne, and on that Baligant the pagan is seated. All the others remain standing. Their lord speaks first:

"Brave and open-hearted knights, listen now to what I have to say! Charles the King, the Emperor of the Franks, has no right even to eat except at my command, and he has waged a great war against me throughout all of Spain. I will march into sweet France and seek him out, and the war will not end in my lifetime except with his death or his admission of defeat."

He strikes his knee with his right glove.

CXCIII

And having said it, he is as good as his word, and all the gold under heaven would not dissuade him from going to Aix, where Charles is holding court. And his men applaud his decision and advise the same thing. Then he summons two of his knights, one named Clarifan and the other Clarien.

"I command you, the sons of King Maltraien who in the old days was happy to be my ambassador, to go to Saragossa and inform King Marsiliun, in my name, that I have come to help him against the French. If I can come face to face with them there will be a great battle. Give him this folded glove threaded with gold, and tell him to wear it on his right fist. Take him this staff of pure gold and tell him to come and acknowledge his fealty to me. I will go to France and carry the war to Charles, who will either kneel at my feet and beg for mercy, and renounce the Christian faith, or else I will take the crown from his head."

"Sire," the pagans answer, "you have spoken well."

CXCIV

Baligant says: "My lords, to your horses! Let one take the glove and the other the staff."

And they answer: "Beloved lord, we shall do it."

They ride until they come to Saragossa. They go through ten gates and over four bridges and along all the streets where the townspeople live, and as they approach, at the top of the city, they hear a loud voice coming from the palace. There the pagans have assembled in great numbers, and they are weeping and moaning and showing all the signs of deep mourning. They lament the loss of Termagant and Mahomet and Apollin, their gods, which they no longer possess. And they say to each other:

"What will become of us, wretches that we are? Calamity has come upon us! We have lost King Marsiliun. Yesterday Count Roland cut off his right hand. And Jurfaret the Blond is lost to us as well. After today all of Spain will be at their mercy!"

The two messengers dismount before the steps of the palace.

CXCV

They leave their horses under an olive tree, and two Saracens take the reins. They lay hands on each other's cloaks and then go up into the lofty palace. As they enter the vaulted bedroom their fair good will leads them to utter an unfortunate greeting:

"May that Mahomet who reigns over us, and Termagant, and Apollin, our sire, protect the King and watch over the Queen!"

Bramimunde says: "What folly is this that I hear? Those gods of ours betrayed us. The miracles which they worked at Roncesvalles were disastrous! They allowed our knights to be slaughtered, and look at my lord here whom they failed in battle. He has lost his right hand. It is gone. It was cut off by that great peer Count Roland. Now Charles will rule over all of Spain and what will become of me, miserable wretch that I am? Oh alas, if only someone would kill me!"

CXCVI

Clarien says: "Lady do not talk so much! We are messengers from the pagan Baligant, who announces that he has come to protect Marsiliun, and has sent his staff and his glove as tokens. We have four thousand vessels anchored in the Ebro, and boats and barges and galleys, and there are more transports than I can say. The Emir is rich and mighty, and is going into France to seek out Charlemagne, determined either to kill him or force him to surrender."

Bramimunde says: "It would be wrong to go so far! You will be able to find the Franks much closer to here. They have been in this country for seven years now. Their Emperor is brave and a fighter and would rather die than flee from the field. There is not a king under heaven whose strength Charles considers any more highly than that of a child, and he is not afraid of any man alive."

CXCVII

"Enough!" says King Marsiliun. To the messengers he says:

"My lords, address your words to me. As you see, the grip of death is upon me and I have neither son, nor daughter, nor heir, and the one whom I had was killed yesterday evening. Tell my lord the Emir to come and see me. He has a right to the land of Spain, and I will freely give up the kingdom in his favor, if he will have it, since he means to defend it against the French. As concerns Charlemagne, I will give him such good counsel that the Emperor will be his prisoner within the month. Take him the keys of Saragossa and tell him not to go away, if he puts any faith in my words."

They answer: "Sire, you have spoken wisely."

CXCVIII

Then Marsiliun says: "Charles the Emperor has killed my men, laid waste my kingdom, and razed and plundered my cities. Last night he camped on the banks of the Ebro, not more than seven leagues away from here, by my own count. Tell the Emir to come with his army, and in my name urge him to join battle with the Franks."

He has given them the keys of Saragossa. When he has finished speaking both of the messengers bow and take their leave.

CXCIX

Both messengers mount their horses and quickly ride out of the city, and in great agitation they come to the Emir and present him with the keys of Saragossa.

Baligant says: "What have you found out? Where is Marsiliun, whom I sent for?"

Clarien says: "He is wounded and on the point of death. Yesterday the Emperor rode into the pass intending to return to sweet France, and he left behind him a rear guard which would do him great honor. Count Roland, his nephew, remained behind there, and Oliver and all of the twelve peers, and twenty thousand armed Franks. The brave King Marsiliun attacked them; he and Roland met on the battlefield, and Roland gave him a blow with Durendal which severed his right hand. And the Count killed the King's son who was so dear to him, and the knights whom he had taken with him, and Marsiliun was unable to keep the field, and returned in full flight with the Emperor in close pursuit. The King requests your help, and in return he will freely give up the kingdom of Spain in your favor."

And Baligant falls to pondering what he has heard, and his sorrow almost deprives him of his senses.

CC

"My lord Emir," says Clarien, "there was a battle at Roncesvalles yesterday. Roland is dead, and Count Oliver, and the twelve peers who were so dear to Charles, and twenty thousand of their

Franks. King Marsiliun lost his right hand, and the Emperor pursued him closely. There was not a single knight from this country who was not either killed or drowned in the Ebro. The Franks are encamped on the far shore. They have come so close to us in this country that if you chose to attack they could not get away without difficulty."

And Baligant's countenance grows proud, and his heart fills with joy and delight. From his throne he rises to his feet and calls out:

"Barons, lose no time! Descend from the ships, mount, and ride! If old Charlemagne does not flee, King Marsiliun will soon be avenged. For the loss of his right hand I will give him the Emperor's head."

CCI

The pagans from Arabia have disembarked and have mounted their horses and mules, and they ride—what more could they do? The Emir, who has wrought them up to a high pitch of excitement, summons Gemalfin, one of his favorites:

"I put all my hosts under your command."

Then he mounts his sorrel charger and with four dukes in his escort he rides to Saragossa and dismounts on a marble step with four counts holding his stirrup, and goes up the stairs into the palace. Bramimunde comes running to meet him and says to him:

"Oh miserable wretch that I am! I have lost my lord, Sire, and in a shameful manner!"

She falls at his feet and the Emir lifts her up; together, grieving, they come to the bedchamber.

CCII

When he sees Baligant, King Marsiliun calls to two Saracens of Spain:

"Take me in your arms and lift me up until I am sitting."

He has taken one of his gloves in his left hand. Then Marsiliun says:

"King, Emir, my lord, receive with this glove all my domains and Saragossa, and all the lands and titles pertaining to it. I am lost to myself and I have lost all my people."

And the other answers: "The greater is my sorrow. But I cannot stay long to talk with you, for I am sure that Charles will not wait for me. I will take your glove, though, in any case."

He turns away, weeping with grief, and descends the palace steps, mounts his horse and, digging in his spurs, rides off to rejoin his army, and at such a speed that he arrives before any of the others, and as he does so he calls out over and over:

"Come, pagans, for they are fleeing from us already!"

CCIII

In the morning, at the first light of dawn, Charles wakes, and Saint Gabriel, whom God had sent to guard him, raises one hand and blesses him with a sign. The King rises and lays aside his arms, and on all sides throughout his host his knights follow his example and disarm. Then they mount and ride at a good pace over the long highways and the broad roads until they come within sight of the terrible carnage at Roncesvalles, where the battle was.

CCIV

Charles has come to Roncesvalles, and at the sight of the dead he begins to weep. He says to the French:

"My lords, rein in your horses and ride slowly, for I must go in front and look for my nephew. It was at Aix, on a holiday, when my brave knights were boasting in my presence about great battles and furious combats, that I heard Roland describe how, if he were to die in a foreign kingdom, he would be found lying beyond his knights and his peers, on the side toward the enemy and with his head turned toward their country, and that thus the brave warrior would meet his end as a conqueror."

About as far beyond the others as one might throw a staff, the Emperor climbs a little hill.

CCV

As the Emperor goes looking for his nephew, all over the meadow he finds wild flowers which are crimson with the blood of our knights. He is overcome with pity. He weeps and cannot help it. He reaches the shade of two trees. On three stones he recognizes the strokes of Roland's sword, and then he sees his nephew lying on the grass. What wonder if Charles is torn with grief? He dismounts and runs to him, and between his two hands . . . and in his anguish he faints across the body.

CCVI

The Emperor revives, and Duke Neimun, Count Acelin, Gefrey of Anjou and his brother Henry take him up, and under a pine tree they raise him to his feet. He looks down onto the ground and sees his nephew lying there, and very tenderly he speaks his lament and farewell:

"Friend Roland, may God be merciful to you. No man ever saw such a knight as you were for forcing great battles and winning them. Now my honor has begun its decline."

Charles faints; he cannot help it.

CCVII

Charles the King recovers from his faint and four barons hold him up with their hands. He looks at the ground where his nephew is lying. The body is beautiful but it has lost all its color, and the eyes are turned upward and filled with darkness. In faith and in love Charles mourns him, saying:

"Friend Roland, may God set your soul among the flowers in Paradise, with the glorious! What an unworthy lord you followed into Spain! Not a day will pass without my grieving for you. What a falling-off there will be now in my strength and my spirit! There will be no one to maintain my honor, indeed it seems as though I had not a single friend now under heaven, and though I have kin, none of them is your equal for bravery."

With both hands he tears out his hair. A hundred thousand Franks are filled with such sorrow that there is not one of them who is not weeping.

CCVIII

"Friend Roland, I will return to France, and when I have come to Laon, to my own domain, foreign vassals will come from many kingdoms, asking:

" 'Where is your captain, the Count?'

"And I will tell them that he lies dead in Spain. And after today I will rule in great sadness, and not a day will pass but I will weep and mourn."

CCIX

"Friend Roland, brave knight, fair youth, when I have come to Aix and have entered my chapel my vassals will arrive and ask for news, and I will tell them dreadful and awesome tidings:

" 'My nephew is dead, who conquered so many countries in my name.'

"The Saxons will rebel against me, and the Hungarians, and the Bulgarians, and many other devilish races, and the Romans, and the Poles, and all those who live around Palermo, and those of Africa and those of Californe, and my troubles and my sufferings will never leave me. Who will lead my armies with such force now that he who always rode before us is dead? Ah France, how utterly you are despoiled of men, and my own grief is such that I would rather be dead!"

He falls to tearing his beard and the hair of his head with both hands. A hundred thousand Franks faint on the ground.

CCX

"Friend Roland, may God be merciful to you and set your soul in Paradise! Whoever killed you made desolate the whole of France. And my grief for the knights of my household who have died for my sake is such that I would rather not be alive. Now, today, before I reach the great pass at Sizer, may God the son of Saint Mary be so gracious to me as to part my soul from my body and set it among their souls and give it a place there, and may my flesh be buried beside theirs."

He weeps from his eyes, he tears his white beard, and Duke Naimes says:

"Charles is in torment!"

CCXI

Then Gefrey of Anjou says: "My lord, Emperor, do not allow yourself to be so carried away with grief! Send to every part of the field and let a search be made for our men whom the Saracens of Spain killed in the battle, and have them carried to a single grave."

Then the King says: "Sound a blast on your horn."

CCXII

Gefrey of Anjou has sounded his trumpet, Charles has given the command, and the French dismount. All of their friends whom they find dead they carry to a single grave. There are many bishops and abbots present, and monks, canons, and tonsured priests, who absolve the dead and bless them in the name of God, and cause myrrh and incense to be kindled, and rich clouds of scented smoke to envelop the bodies, which are then buried with great honors and so left. What more could have been done?

CCXIII

The Emperor has Roland made ready for burial, and also Oliver and Archbishop Turpin. He orders all three of them to be opened in his presence, and he has their hearts brought to him, and he wraps them in silk and places them in a casket of white marble. Then the bodies of the three barons are taken and washed in wine and spices, and the lords are laid in stag skins. The King commands Tedbalt and Geboin, Count Milun and Marquis Otun:

"Let them be placed on three wagons, and you lead them."

The bodies are covered with silken palls from Galaza.

CCXIV

The Emperor is about to depart when suddenly he is confronted with the pagan vanguard. Out of their front rank ride two messengers, and in the name of their lord the Emir they announce battle:

"Haughty King, do not imagine that you will be allowed to depart. Look, here is Baligant riding behind you with the great hosts which he has brought from Arabia. Today we shall see what your courage amounts to."

Charles the King lays his hand on his beard. He calls to mind all his grief and all that he has lost. Proudly he surveys his whole army, and then in a loud ringing voice he shouts:

"Barons of France, to arms and mount!"

CCXV

The Emperor is the first to arm. Quickly he dons his coat of mail, laces on his helmet, girds on his sword Joyeuse, whose brightness even the sun does not eclipse, and around his neck he hangs a shield from Biterne. He grips his lance and brandishes it. Then he mounts his good horse Tencendur, which he had won at the ford below Marsune, hurling Malpalin of Narbonne out of the saddle, dead. He slackens the reins and spurs forward eagerly, and brings his horse to a full gallop with a hundred thousand men looking on. He calls upon God and the Apostle of Rome.

CCXVI

All over the field the French dismount, and together they arm. There are more than a hundred thousand of them, and their arms leave nothing to be desired. They have swift horses and superb weapons. They mount and go through their paces, showing their skill with their weapons, and their horsemanship. If the occasion offers they will do their part in a battle. The hanging pennons reach to their helmets.

When Charles sees the splendor of their appearance he calls to Jozeran of Provence, Duke Naimes and Antelme of Maience:

"A man can put his trust in vassals such as these, and with such knights around him only a fool could be faint-hearted. If the Arabians do not go back on their decision we will make them pay dearly for Roland's death!"

Duke Naimes answers: "God grant that we may!"

CCXVII

Charles calls to Rabel and Guinemans. Then the King says to them:

"My lords, I command you to take up Roland's position, and Oliver's. One of you carry the sword and the other the ivory horn. Ride in front, ahead of the others, and take fifteen thousand Franks with you, and let them be young, and chosen from among the bravest of your knights. And behind you will come as many more, with Geboin and Lorant leading them."

Duke Naimes and Count Jozeran form up the two battalions. If the occasion offers, the battle will be tremendous.

CCXVIII

The first two battalions of the French have been formed. They are made up of Franks from France. And after them comes the third, which is composed of some twenty thousand knights: vassals from Bavaria. The battle will not languish on their account. Except for the French themselves, who have conquered kingdoms for him, none of his followers are dearer to Charles. At their head is Count Oger the Dane, a superb fighter, for they are a proud company.

CCXIX

Charles, the Emperor, has formed three battalions. Now Duke Naimes organizes the fourth. It is made up of German barons, from Germany, men of great courage, and their number, by common consent, is put at twenty thousand. They are well armed and well mounted, and in the face of death itself they would not give ground in a battle. Herman, the Duke of Trace, will lead them: a man who would rather die than play the coward.

CCXX

In the fifth battalion Duke Naimes and Count Jozeran have placed the Normans; according to the Frankish estimate there are twenty thousand of them, magnificently armed and mounted on fast horses. The threat of death will not make them retreat. No people under heaven can give a better account of themselves on a battlefield. Richard the Old will lead them out to the fight and will strike hard blows himself with his sharp lance.

CCXXI

The sixth battalion is made up of Bretons: a force of thirty thousand knights. There is no doubt that these are barons: you can see it as they ride out. The shafts of their lances are painted, the

pennons are fixed to them. Their lord is named Oedun. He calls out
to Count Nevelun, Tedbalt of Reims and Marquis Otun:
"Lead my vassals. I accord you this honor."

CCXXII

The Emperor now has six battalions ready. Duke Naimes prepares a seventh, which is made up of some forty thousand knights
from Poitou and barons from the Auvergne, mounted on good
horses and superbly armed. They form up in a little valley behind a
hill and Charles blesses them with his right hand. Jozeran and
Godselme will lead them.

CCXXIII

Duke Naimes has put the eighth battalion in order, composing
it of Flemings and of Freisian barons. They number more than
forty thousand knights, and the line will not falter where they
hold the field. Then the King says:
"There is a company which will serve me well."
Rembalt and Hamon of Galicia will lead these fighters, and they
will do it in a manner worthy of knighthood.

CCXXIV

Naimes and Count Jozeran have formed the ninth battalion,
which is made up of brave vassals from Lorraine and Burgundy.
They muster fifty thousand knights, with helmets laced, wearing
their coats of mail, carrying stout spears with short shafts. If the
Arabians do not repent their decision, these will hit them hard
when they have hurled themselves into the charge. Thierry, Duke of
Argonne, will lead them.

CCXXV

The tenth battalion is composed of the barons of France: one
hundred thousand of our best captains, with handsome bodies and
proud faces, flowing hair and white beards, wearing hauberks and
double tunics of chain mail, and at their waists swords forged in

France or Spain. They carry magnificent shields painted with heraldic devices. They mount. They are impatient for battle, and they raise the cry of "Mountjoy!" It is in their company that Charlemagne will ride. Gefrey of Anjou will carry the red silk banner of Saint Denis, which is the Emperor's battle flag. At one time it was Saint Peter's and was called "Rommaine," but later it too answered to the name of "Mountjoy."

CCXXVI

The Emperor dismounts and lies down on the green grass with his face turned toward the rising sun, and with all his heart he calls upon God:

"True Father, protect me today, you who delivered Jonah from the whale which had him in its body, who spared the king of Nineveh, and saved Daniel from terrible suffering when he was in the pit among the lions, and the three children in the burning oven! Keep your love close to me today, and by your grace, if it is your pleasure, grant that I may avenge my nephew Roland."

When he has made his prayer he gets to his feet and makes the sign of the cross on his brow—that sign whose powers exceed all others. Then, while Naimes and Jozeran hold the stirrup, the King mounts his swift horse and grasps his shield and his sharp lance. His body is noble and handsome, and he bears himself well. His countenance is forthright and determined. When he rides he sits his horse with assurance. The trumpets sound through the host, in the rear, in the van, and above all the others Roland's ivory horn rings out, and the Franks weep out of pity for Roland.

CCXXVII

The Emperor rides with a noble air. He has spread his beard outside his chain-mail tunic, and in their love for him all his knights do the same. Thus the hundred thousand Franks may be told apart from the others. They ride past the peaks and the rocky heights, the deep valleys, the tortuous defiles. They ride forth from the pass and the wild country and their battalions move out into Spain, where they take up positions on a stretch of open, level ground.

Baligant's scouts return to him and a Syrian delivers the message:

"We have seen Charles, the arrogant King. His men are proud; they are not of a mind to fail him. Arm, for there will be a battle, and soon."

Baligant says: "That is bravely spoken. Sound your trumpets. Let my pagans hear the news."

CCXXVIII

All through that host the drums sound, and their horns and their clear trumpets, and the pagans dismount to put on their armor. The Emir bestirs himself, not to be the last. He puts on his coat of mail with its gilt-varnished skirts, laces his helmet which is studded with jewels set in gold, and then girds his sword onto his left side. He has heard of Charles' sword, and his pride has found a name for his own: "Precieuse." The word has become his battle cry; he has commanded his knights to shout "Precieuse." He hangs from his neck his great broad shield with its golden boss and crystal border; it is swung on a thick strap of silk embroidered with circles. He grasps his spear named Maltet, with its shaft as thick as a club. Its iron head alone would make a full load for a pack mule. Then, while Marcules, from across the sea, holds his stirrup, Baligant mounts his war horse. He has a good broad stride in the saddle, this brave knight. He is narrow in the hips, but big-ribbed, and his chest is deep and beautifully molded, his shoulders are massive, his color is fair and his face proud. His curling hair is as white as a summer flower. His courage has been proved many times. God, what a baron, if only he were a Christian! He digs his spurs into his horse until the clear blood runs. He brings it to the gallop and jumps a ditch measuring fifty feet across. The pagans cry:

"There is the man to defend the marches! Any Frenchman who dares to cross arms with him will die for it, like it or not. Charles is a fool not to have fled."

CCXXIX

You can see at a glance that the Emir is a noble baron. His beard is white as a flower. He rules with learning and wisdom, and in battle he is proud and overbearing. His son Malprimis is an ardent and accomplished knight. He is big and strong, and resembles his ancestors. He says to his father:

"Sire, now let us ride! I will be very much surprised if we see Charles at all."

Baligant says: "We will see him, for he is a very brave man. There are many stories about him which redound to his great honor. But his nephew Roland is no longer with him, and he will not be able to hold the field against us."

CCXXX

Then Baligant says: "Fair son Malprimis, yesterday Roland, that good vassal, was killed, and so was brave noble Oliver, and so were the twelve peers who were so dear to Charles, and so were twenty thousand warriors of France. As for all the others, I would not give a glove for them. It is true, the Emperor has returned: my messenger, the Syrian, has brought me word. Charles has ten huge battalions. Someone is sounding Roland's ivory horn. He is a brave man. And his companions give answer with the clear note of a trumpet, and those two ride out ahead of the others, and fifteen thousand Franks with them, knights in the first strength of their youth, whom Charles calls his sons. Behind them come the same number again. They will attack with pride."

Malprimis says: "Grant me the first blow."

CCXXXI

Baligant says to him: "My son, Malprimis, I grant what you ask. Ride to attack the French, and take with you Torleu, the Persian King, and Dapamort, the King of Lycia. If you can smash the towering pride of the first battalions, I will give you a piece of my own domain, from Cheriant to Val Marchis."

The other answers: "Sire, receive my thanks!"

He advances and accepts the gift: a piece of land which had once belonged to King Flurit. As for Malprimis, it did not bring him luck, for he never set eyes on it. It never became his, and he was never its lord.

CCXXXII

The Emir rides through that host, with his tall son behind him. King Torleu and King Dapamort form up thirty battalions at once, filling them with vast numbers of men: in the smallest of those companies there are fifty thousand knights. The first is made up of warriors from Butentrot; the one which follows it is composed of vassals from Micenes, with big heads. Like hogs, they have bristles all along their spines. And the third battalion contains the vassals from Nubles and Blos, and the fourth those from Bruns and Esclavons, and the fifth those from Sobres and Sores, and the sixth the Armenians and the Moors, the seventh the knights from Jericho, the eighth those from Nigres, the ninth those from Gros, and the tenth is made up of vassals from the stronghold of Balide, whose people have always been a race of malefactors. The Emir swears by all that he holds sacred, by the miracles and body of Mahomet:

"Charles is a fool to ride against us! Unless he breaks and runs now, there will be a battle and he will never again wear a golden crown."

CCXXXIII

Then they assembled another ten battalions. The first musters the ugly men of Canaan, who have come by way of Val Fuit, crossing it from one side to the other. Next comes the battalion of Turks. And third, the Persians. And the fourth is composed of Pincenians and . . . and the fifth of Solterans and Avars, and the sixth of Ormalians and Eugles, and the seventh of the people of Samuel, and the eighth of the vassals from Brusse, and the ninth of the vassals from Clavers, and the tenth is made up of those who come from the desert of Occian, a people who do not serve the Lord God, and as villainous a race as you will ever hear mentioned. Their skins are as hard as iron, so that they do not need either helmet or hauberk, and they are brutal and headstrong in battle.

CCXXXIV

The Emir has drawn up another ten battalions. In the first of them are the giants from Malprose, in the second the Huns, in the third the Hungarians, and in the fourth are the vassals from Long Baldisa, and in the fifth those from Val Penuse, and in the sixth those from . . . Maruse, and in the seventh those from Leus and Astrimonia. The eighth is made up of warriors from Argoilles, and the ninth of those from Clarbone, and in the tenth are assembled the long-bearded knights from Fronde, a race which never loved God. And thus, according to the Chronicle of the Franks, they mustered thirty battalions. From one end of that enormous host to the other the trumpets sound, and the pagans ride out bravely.

CCXXXV

The Emir has vast powers at his command. He sends his standard bearers before him with his dragon and the banner of Termagant and Mahomet, and an image of the villain Apollin. Ten Canaanites ride with the banners, chanting in loud voices:

"Let every one who hopes for the protection of our gods pray to them now and cast himself down in their worship!"

The pagans bow their heads and their chins to them, and incline their shining helmets.

The French say: "Base wretches, you are close to death! May utter destruction overwhelm you today! Oh Lord Our God, defend Charles, and in his name may this battle be . . .

CCXXXVI

The Emir is a man of great wisdom. He calls to his son and the two kings:

"Barons, my lords, ride before us and lead all my battalions except three of the best which I shall keep with me: the first of them made up of Turks, the next of Ormalians, and the third of the Malprosian giants. And the knights from Occian will go with me and fight against Charles and the French. If the Emperor contests the field with me he will lose the head from his shoulders. It will be done, and that will be all, and that will end his claims."

CCXXXVII

Huge are the hosts and beautiful their battalions, and between the two armies there is neither mountain nor valley nor hill nor forest nor wood. Nothing and no one can be hidden; they are all in plain sight, with open country around them.

Baligant says: "Pagans, my vassals, ride forward now and join battle."

Amborres of Oluferne carries his standard, and the pagans raise the battle cry of "Precieuse!"

The French say: "May your losses be heavy today!" and with loud voices they renew the shout of "Mountjoy!" The Emperor gives the command for his trumpets to sound, and with them Roland's ivory horn, which rings out above all the others.

The pagans say: "Charles has a magnificent army. Our battle will be fierce and bitter."

CCXXXVIII

They are on a broad plain, in open country, and their helmets studded with jewels set in gold, and their shields and their gilt-varnished tunics of chain mail and their spears and the banners fixed to them are all shining. The trumpets sound, raising their clear voices. The high note of Roland's ivory horn sounds the charge. The Emir calls to his brother, Canabeus, the King of Floredee, whose domain extends as far as Val Sevree, and shows him Charles' battalions.

"Look! There is the pride of famous France, and there is the Emperor riding boldly. He is toward the rear, among those knights who have let their long snow-white beards flow loose over their tunics of chain mail. They will strike with lances and with swords, and the battle between us will be so fierce and furious that no man will ever have seen the like."

Baligant rides on ahead of his knights until he is a little farther in front of them than a man might throw a peeled wand, and then he calls out:

"Come, pagans, for I am on my way!"

He brandishes the shaft of his spear, and then he turns the point toward Charles.

CCXXXIX

When Charles the Great sees the Emir and the dragon and the banner and the standard, and when he sees the host of the Arabians and how vast it is, spreading over the countryside everywhere except where the Emperor's own army is waiting, the King of France calls in a loud voice:

"Barons of France, you are good vassals and you have fought

many battles in the field. You can see the pagans: they are evil and cowardly and their whole credo will not do them a farthing's worth of good. What difference does it make, my lords, if they come in great numbers? If any man does not wish to come with me let him go now!"

Then he spurs his horse, Tencendur, which bounds forward in four great leaps.

The French say: "Here is a noble king! Ride, brave knights! Not one of us will fail you!"

CCXL

The day was clear and the sun was bright. Beautiful are the hosts and huge their battalions, and the first ranks of the two armies are face to face. Count Rabel and Count Guinemans give rein to their fast horses and spur forward, and with that the French charge, hurling themselves forward to strike with their sharp spears.

CCXLI

Count Rabel, that bold knight, digs in his spurs of pure gold and rides to attack Torleu, the Persian king. Neither shield nor chain mail withstand the blow, but the gilded spearshaft drives through the pagan's body and the corpse is flung down onto a little bush.

The French say: "May the Lord God be our help! Charles is in the right. We must not fail him."

CCXLII

And Guinemans charges at the King of Lycia and smashes his shield painted with flowers, and he bursts the pagan's chain-mail tunic and buries the whole of his pennon in the other's body, killing him, let men mourn or laugh as they will. At the sight of that blow the French shout:

"Strike, baron, and do not spare! Charles is in the right, fighting against these . . . God has chosen us to be instruments of His true justice."

CCXLIII

Malprimis, mounted on a pure white horse, hurls himself into the thick of the Frankish host, dealing hard blows first on one side, then on another, and flinging corpse upon corpse without pausing. Before any of the others raises his voice, Baligant shouts:

"My barons, for a long time I have fed you at my table. Look: my son is making his way toward Charles, wielding his arms in defiance of so many knights. I could not ask for a better vassal. To his help now with your sharp spears!"

At this word the pagans advance. They strike hard blows. There is vast slaughter. The battle is crushing and awesome, and such a struggle has never been seen before or since.

CCXLIV

Huge are the hosts and fierce are their companies, and by now all of the battalions on both sides have met, and the pagans strike hard. Oh God, there are so many spear shafts splintered, shields smashed and mailed tunics burst apart! The ground is littered with them, and the green tender grass of the field. The Emir calls out to his vassals:

"Strike, barons, against the Christian host!"

The battle is furious, with neither side giving ground. Never before nor since has there been a struggle like this one. It will go on without a pause until nightfall.

CCXLV

The Emir calls to his knights:

"Strike, pagans! That is what you came for! I will give you noble and lovely wives, and I will give you domains and honors and lands!"

The pagans answer: "It is our duty to obey."

With the shock of heavy blows, spear after spear has splintered, and then over a hundred thousand swords are drawn. Now the slaughter becomes grim and terrible, and any man who is in the midst of that fighting learns what a battle is.

CCXLVI

The Emperor calls out to the French:

"Barons, my lords, my love for you is great, and I have faith in you. You have fought so many battles for me, you have conquered so many kingdoms and dethroned so many kings. I have not forgotten that the reward I owe you is nothing less than myself: body, lands, and possessions. Avenge your sons, your brothers, your heirs who were killed the other evening at Roncesvalles! You know that I am in the right, fighting against the pagans."

The Franks answer: "Sire, what you say is true."

And twenty thousand of those who are closest to him pronounce a solemn oath together, swearing that they will not fail him though they are faced with death or pain. Every one of them puts his spear to good use, and then they strike with their swords, and the battle grows bloody and awesome.

CCXLVII

And Malprimis rides over the field inflicting terrible slaughter on the Franks, until Duke Naimes turns a proud glance upon him and rides bravely to attack him. The Duke smashes through the top part of the pagan's shield and cleaves through both thicknesses of his double hauberk, burying the whole of his spear to the end of its yellow pennon in the other's body and hurling down his corpse among seven hundred others.

CCXLVIII

King Canabeus, the Emir's brother, digs his spurs into his horse. He has drawn his crystal-pointed sword, and with it he strikes Naimes on the top of the helmet, which splits apart into two pieces. His steel blade cuts through five of the helmet laces and, slicing through the hood of chain mail as though it were nothing, parts the cap, comes to the flesh and hacks off a piece, which is hurled to the ground. The Duke is stunned by the heavy blow, and is about to fall, when God helps him, and he grips the neck of his horse with both arms. If the pagan can rein up and return once more the noble vassal will be killed. But Charles of France comes to his aid.

CCXLIX

Duke Naimes is in great distress, and the pagan rushes to strike him again. Charles says:

"Base wretch, that blow will call down sorrow upon you!"

And the Emperor rides bravely to strike him, and breaks his shield, crushing it against his heart, and smashes the lower part of his helmet, and hurls his corpse to the ground, leaving the saddle empty.

CCL

Charlemagne the King, when he sees Duke Naimes wounded before his eyes and the bright blood falling onto the green grass, is filled with bitter grief. The Emperor says to him:

"Naimes, fair sir, ride along beside me. That base creature who was about to attack you in your distress is dead now. This time I ran my spear through his body."

The Duke answers: "Sire, I put my trust in you. If I survive this, your help to me will be rewarded."

Then in love and in faith they ride along together, and with them twenty thousand of the French, every one of them cleaving and hacking as he goes.

CCLI

The Emir rides over the field and charges to attack Count Guinemans, smashing his white shield against his breast, bursting the folds of his hauberk, splitting his chest in two and hurling him, dead, from his running horse. After that he kills Geboin and Lorant, and Richard the Old, the lord of the Normans.

The pagans shout: "Brave Precieuse! Strike, barons, for our defense is with us!"

CCLII

Then what a sight to see the warriors of Arabia and the ones from Occiant and from Argoille and Bascle, striking and thrusting

with their spears! The French are not tempted to flee; many die
on the one side and on the other, and the battle rages in full fury
into the evening. Great numbers of the Frankish barons are killed.
The grief will be worse before it is over.

CCLIII

Both the French and the Arabians fight hard, and their shafts
and polished lances are snapped. And if you had been there what
a sight you would have seen of smashed shields, and what a din
you would have heard of hauberks hacked apart and of shields
grating against helmets. You would have seen knights falling, and
men howling and dying on the ground, and you would have
brought away a memory of great suffering! It is a harsh and terrible
battle to live through. The Emir calls upon Apollin and upon
Termagant and Mahomet as well:

"My lord, my god, I have served you for many years. Now I
will have your images made of pure gold . . ."

Gemalfin, one of his favorites, appears before him bearing bad
news, and says:

"Baligant, sire, sorrow has come to you. You have lost Malprimis, your son, and Canabeus, your brother, has been killed.
Two of the French have been lucky and have struck them down,
and one of the two, I believe, was the Emperor. He was large of
stature, and his bearing was that of a ruler, and his beard was as
white as a flower in April."

The Emir bows his helmet, and after that his face darkens. His
grief is so terrible that it seems as though he were dying. Then he
calls to Jangleu from Outremer.

CCLIV

The Emir says: "Jangleu, come before me. You are a brave
knight, and very wise, and I have always . . . heeded your counsel. What do you think of the Arabians and the Franks: will victory be ours on this field?"

And the other answers: "Baligant, you are a dead man! Your
gods will not protect you. Charles is proud, and his men are brave,
and never have I seen an army fight as this one is fighting. But
call up the barons from Occian, and the Turks and Enfruns, the

Arabs and the Giants. What is fated will happen, but do not waste time in waiting."

CCLV

The Emir has spread his beard out over his chest, and it is as white as any thorn flower: whatever happens he does not want to be hidden. He sets his clear-voiced trumpet to his mouth and blows a ringing blast so that all his pagans may hear it, and from all over the field his vassals rally to him. Those who have come from Occian bray and whinny, and those from Argoille yelp like dogs, and they hurl themselves recklessly into the thick of the Franks and break and scatter them, in this one charge flinging down seven thousand dead.

CCLVI

Count Oger was never a coward, and no better knight ever wore a coat of mail. When he sees the French battalions scattered he calls to Thierry, the Duke of Argonne, and to Gefrey of Anjou and Count Jozeran, and with great pride he addresses Charles:

"See how the pagans are slaughtering your men! May it grieve God to see the crown on your head if you do not strike now to avenge your shame!"

No one says a word in reply to this, but they all dig in their spurs and give rein to their horses and ride to attack the pagans wherever they may find them.

CCLVII

Charlemagne the King strikes hard and well, and so does Duke Naimes, and so do Oger the Dane and Gefrey of Anjou, who carries the standard. And the bravery of Oger the Dane is without peer. He spurs his horse, gives it full rein, and strikes Amborres, the pagan standard-bearer, with such force that the other is hurled to the ground head first, and with him the dragon and the pagan King's ensign. Baligant sees his pennon fall and the standard of Mahomet struck down, and at that moment the Emir perceives that he is in the wrong, and that Charlemagne is in the right. The pagans from Arabia give ground . . .

The Emperor calls out to the French: "Tell me, my barons, in the name of God will you lend me your help now?"

The French answer: "What is the good of asking? A curse on any man who does not strike with all his heart!"

CCLVIII

The day passes, the evening comes, and Franks and pagans fight on with their swords. Those who have led these two hosts into battle are brave men. They have not forgotten their war-cries: the Emir shouts, "Precieuse!" and Charles raises his famous battle cry of "Mountjoy!" And by their clear ringing voices the two men recognize each other, and they meet in the middle of the field and ride to attack each other, and exchange heavy blows, each one's spear smashing into the other's ringed shield. And each shield is pierced above the broad boss, and the folds of both of their hauberks are rent, but on neither side do the spears enter the flesh. Their cinches break and their saddles tip over and both kings fall to the ground, but they leap to their feet at once and bravely draw their swords. Now nothing can separate them, and the fight cannot end except with the death of one or the other.

CCLIX

Charles of sweet France is gifted with great courage, and the Emir shows neither dread nor hesitation. They draw their swords, showing the naked blades, and they deal each other heavy blows on their shields, cutting through the leather coverings and the two outer layers of wood, so that the nails fall and the buckles are broken in pieces. Then, bare of shields, they hack at each other's coats of mail, and the sparks leap from their bright helmets. This combat cannot be brought to an end without one or the other confessing that he is in the wrong.

CCLX

The Emir says: "Charles, consider the matter carefully and make up your mind to repent for what you have done to me. You have killed my son, if I am not mistaken, and you are wrongfully disputing with me the possession of my own country. If you will become my vassal [and swear fealty to me] you may come with me and serve me from here to the East."

Charles answers: "To my way of thinking that would be vile and base. It is not for me to render either peace or love to a pagan. Submit to the creed which God has revealed to us, become a Christian, and my love for you will never end as long as you put your faith in the omnipotent King and serve Him."

Baligant says: "You have begun a bad sermon!" Then they raise their swords and resume the fight.

CCLXI

The Emir is a strong and skillful fighter. He strikes Charlemagne upon his helmet of burnished steel and splits and smashes it above his head, bringing the sword down into the fine hair, sheering off a palm's breadth and more of flesh, and laying bare the bone. Charles staggers and almost falls, but it is not God's will that he should be killed or beaten. Saint Gabriel comes to his side, asking:

"Great King, what are you doing?"

CCLXII

When he hears the holy voice of the angel, Charles loses all fear of death, and his vigor and clearness of mind return. He strikes the Emir a blow with the sword of France, cleaves the helmet flashing with jewels, cuts open the head and spills the brains, and splits the whole face down through the white beard. It is a corpse, past all hope of recovery, which that stroke hurls to the ground. Charles calls "Mountjoy!" to rally his vassals, and at his shout Duke Naimes comes to him bringing with him the Emperor's horse Tencendur, and the King mounts.

The pagans flee. It is not the will of God that they should remain. Now the French have achieved the triumph which they had hoped for.

CCLXIII

The pagans flee, for such is the will of the Lord God, and the Franks, and the Emperor with them, give chase. Then the King says:

"Now, my lords, avenge your griefs. Show your wills now and the passions of your hearts, for this morning I saw the tears running from your eyes."

The Franks answer: "Sire, we must do so."

And each of them strikes blow after heavy blow, with all his heart, and of the pagans who are there, few escape.

CCLXIV

In the fierce heat the dust rises. The pagans flee; the French harry them, and the pursuit continues as far as Saragossa.

Bramimunde has climbed to the top of her tower. She has with her there her clerics and canons of the false religion which God never loved. They have not been ordained and their heads are not tonsured. When she sees the rout of the Arabians she calls out in a loud voice:

"Help us, Mahomet! Ah noble King, our men have been beaten, and the Emir has been killed, to add to the shame of it!"

When Marsiliun hears her he turns to the wall with the tears running from his eyes, his head sinks, and he dies of sorrow with the weight of his sin upon him. His soul is given to the quick demons.

CCLXV

The pagans are dead. Many of them . . . And Charles has won his battle. He has beaten down the gate of Saragossa and he knows beyond any doubt that it will not be defended. He occupies the city. His army enters its walls. His men lodge there that night by right of conquest. The white-bearded King is filled with pride, for Bramimunde has surrendered her towers to him—the ten enormous ones and the fifty smaller ones.

He whom the Lord God helps will triumph.

CCLXVI

The day passes. The night has grown dark. The moon is bright and the stars shine. The Emperor has taken Saragossa.

He sends a thousand French, bearing hammers and iron mallets, to search through the city's mosques and synagogues and to smash the images and all the idols, sparing nothing which pertains to the black arts and false creeds of the heathen. Because the King believes in God, he is eager to serve Him, and his bishops bless water, and the pagans are led into the baptistry. If anyone resists Charles, he is hanged or burned or put to the sword, and more than a hundred thousand of them are baptized and become true Christians. But not the Queen. She is to be led captive into sweet France, where the King hopes that she will be converted by love.

CCLXVII

The night passes and the bright day appears. Charles garrisons the towers of Saragossa, leaving a thousand intrepid knights to guard the city in the Emperor's name. The King and all his men mount their horses, and Bramimunde with them, whom he is taking in his company, a prisoner, though it is not his will that anything except good should befall her. Rejoicing and triumphant, they return toward France. In their strength and vigor they seize Narbonne and pass on, and reach Bordeaux, the city . . . On noble Saint Seurin's altar he lays Roland's ivory horn filled with gold and with gold pieces; the pilgrims who go there can see it still. He and his army enter into the great ships which are there and cross the Gironde. As far as Blaye he carries his nephew's body, and the body of his noble companion Oliver, and the body of the wise and brave Archbishop. There he commands them to enclose the three lords in white sarcophagi, and they are lying there still at Saint-Romain, those noble knights. The French commend them to God and to His holy name.

After that, Charles rides through the valleys and over the mountains, refusing to break his journey until he has come to Aix, and at last he dismounts on his own threshold. And when he has entered the royal palace he sends messengers to summon his judges, Bavarians and Saxons, and those from Lorraine and Freisia. He sends to the Germans, he sends to the Burgundians, and to the Poitevins and the Normans and the Bretons, and to the judges of France, whose wisdom is unsurpassed. Then the trial of Ganelon begins.

CCLXVIII

The Emperor has returned from Spain and has come to Aix, which is without peer among the seats of France. He climbs the steps and goes into his palace and enters the hall. Now Alde, a beautiful girl, approaches him, and she says to the King:

"Where is Roland, the captain, who swore that he would take me to be his wife?"

Charles is filled with sorrow and grief. The tears run from his eyes and he rends his white beard.

"Sister, beloved friend, you are asking for a dead man. In his place I will give you a vassal who is even more nobly born than Roland was, and that is Louis, and better than that I cannot say. He is my son, and it is he who will rule my marches."

Alde answers: "Your words are strange to me. May it not please God nor His saints nor His angels that I should continue to live when Roland is dead!"

The color drains from her face, and she falls at Charlemagne's feet and dies. May God have mercy on her soul! The French barons weep and mourn for her.

CCLXIX

Alde the Lovely is no longer alive. And the King pities her, thinking that she has fainted; the Emperor weeps for her and takes her by the hand and draws her up. Her head falls onto her shoulders. When Charles sees that she is dead he sends at once and summons four countesses, and they bear Alde's body to a nuns' convent. There a watch is kept over her all night and into the dawn. Then, beside an altar, she is buried with great ceremony, and the King accords her many honors.

CCLXX

The Emperor has returned to Aix. Ganelon, the villain, is brought in iron chains into the city, and taken before the palace, where the serfs bind him to a stake, tying his hands with deer-hide thongs. Then they beat him soundly with wooden clubs and cudgels. Certainly he has earned no better reward. And there in great pain he awaits his trial.

CCLXXI

It is written in the old story that Charles sent into many lands to summon his vassals. They have assembled at Aix, in his chapel. It is a holiday, an occasion of high solemnity—many say that it is noble Saint Sylvester's day. Then the trial and the giving of evidence concerning Ganelon, the traitor, begin. The Emperor has the man dragged before him.

CCLXXII

"Barons, my lords," says King Charlemagne, "consider the rights of the case and judge Ganelon for me. He came with me into Spain in the army, and his presence cost me twenty thousand of my French knights, and my nephew, whom you will never see again, and brave, courteous Oliver, and he betrayed the twelve peers for gain."

Ganelon says: "I would be ashamed to deny what I have done! Because of Roland I had lost gold and possessions, and it was for that reason that I set about to cause his death and his ruin. But as for treachery, I will not admit to anything of the kind."

The French answer: "We will deliberate upon the matter."

CCLXXIII

There stands Ganelon, before the King. His body is handsome, his color is fresh and fair, and if only he had been loyal his appearance would be in every respect that of a noble knight. He looks at the French vassals and at all his judges, and at the thirty members of his own family who are there on his account, and then he calls out in a loud voice:

"Barons, for the love of God listen to me! My lords, I was in the host with the Emperor and I served him in faith and in love. His nephew Roland conceived a hatred for me and contrived my death and sorrow. I was sent as an envoy to King Marsiliun, and nothing but my own wit saved me. I challenged Roland, that fearless and skillful fighter, and I challenged Oliver and all their companions. Charles and his noble barons heard me. And I have avenged myself, but there has been no treachery."

The French answer: "We must put it to debate."

CCLXXIV

When Ganelon sees that the great trial is about to begin there are thirty of his relatives there with him. Pinabel, from the castle of Sorence, is the spokesman for the rest, for he is an eloquent and persuasive speaker, and a brave knight when it comes to trials of arms. Then Ganelon says to him:

"In you . . . friend . . . Now save me from death and calumny!"

Pinabel says: "You will be saved, and it will not take long. No Frank will condemn you to be hanged, or if he does the Emperor will set our two bodies in the lists together and I will give him the lie with my steel blade."

Count Ganelon bows down at his feet.

CCLXXV

The Bavarians and the Saxons have entered into council, and the Poitevins and the Normans and the French. There are many Germans and Teutons there, and the vassals from the Auvergne are the most courteous of all. They all speak more softly, because of Pinabel. One says to another:

"It would be best to leave things as they are. Let us abandon the trial and ask the King to allow Ganelon to go free this time. Then let him serve the Emperor with love and faith in the future. Roland is dead; you will never see him again, and no gold and no riches will bring him back. Any man who . . . would put it to the combat is a fool many times over."

And everyone agrees except Thierry, Gefrey's brother.

CCLXXVI

The barons return to Charlemagne and say to the King:

"Sire, we beg you to acquit Count Ganelon of this charge. Let him serve you with love and faith in the future. Grant him his life, for he comes of a noble line. Besides, his death will not bring Roland back to you, nor will any riches restore your nephew."

Then the King says: "You are despicable villains."

CCLXXVII

When Charles sees that they have all failed him, he bows his head and his face in grief, and in his sorrow he cries out:

"Alas, what a wretch I am!"

It is then that a knight named Thierry, the brother of the Angevin Duke Gefrey, stands up before the King. He is gaunt of limb, and wiry, and quick, with black hair, and his face is swarthy. He is neither very tall nor very short. In a courteous manner he says to the Emperor:

"Fair sire, King, do not thus abandon yourself to despair! You know that I have served you long and well, and I owe it to the honor of my ancestors to uphold your accusation. However Ganelon may have had cause to complain of Roland, Roland was your officer, which in itself should have rendered him inviolable. And Ganelon is a villain for having betrayed him and for having lied to you and for having broken his oath to you. Therefore I condemn him to be hanged until he is dead, and his body put . . . like any common criminal. If any of his kin wish to contest what I say I will defend my judgment at once with this sword which I have girded to my side."

The Franks answer: "Now you have spoken well."

CCLXXVIII

Pinabel has come to stand before the King. He is tall and strong and brave and quick, and if he strikes a man a blow, the other has come to the end of his days. He says to the King:

"Sire, this is your trial. Command them to make less noise! With regard to Thierry, here, who has pronounced judgment, I declare his sentence to be false, and I will fight him."

He hands the King the deer-skin glove from his right hand. The Emperor says:

"I must have sufficient pledges."

Thirty of Ganelon's relatives offer themselves as loyal hostages. Then the King says:

"You may go free while these stand surety for you."

And he has the hostages put under guard until justice is done.

CCLXXIX

When Thierry sees that there will be a trial by arms, he gives Charles his right glove, and the Emperor himself stands surety for him and allows him his freedom. Then the King has four benches brought into the place and those who are to fight go and sit there. All who are present agree that the challenge has been given and accepted according to the rules. Oger of Denmark repeats the words of defiance in the names of both parties. Then the combatants send for their horses and their arms.

CCLXXX

When they have got ready for the combat they make confession and receive absolution and a benediction, and hear mass and take communion. Each of them makes a large offering to his church. Then both of them come before Charles.

They have put their spurs on their feet and donned their strong, light, shining hauberks, and laced their helmets onto their heads. They have girded on their gold-hilted swords and hung their shields, with the quarterings painted on them, around their necks. They take their sharp spears in their right hands. Then they mount their swift horses.

As they do, a hundred thousand knights fall to weeping, in pity for Roland and Thierry.

God knows how the fight will end.

CCLXXXI

Below the city of Aix there is a broad meadow, and there the two barons come together to fight. Both of them are noble and courageous, and their horses are swift and high-spirited. They dig in their spurs and loosen the reins all the way, and with all their might they charge at each other. Their shields are shattered and smashed, their hauberks are rent. And the cinches are burst so that the saddlebows are overturned and the saddles fall to the ground. A hundred thousand men weep as they watch them.

CCLXXXII

Both knights have fallen to the ground, but they leap to their feet at once. Pinabel is strong and light and quick. They rush at each other on foot, and with their gold-hilted swords they hew and hack at each other's steel helmets. The blows are heavy, and the helmets are gashed and rent. And the French knights raise loud laments.

"Oh God," says Charles, "reveal the right!"

CCLXXXIII

Pinabel says: "Thierry, admit yourself beaten! I will become your vassal in all love and faith, and will give you as much of my wealth as you please, but make peace between Ganelon and the King!"

Thierry answers: "I will not long debate the matter. May the name of a villain belong to me many times over if I agree to the smallest detail of what you ask. And may God this day show which of us is in the right!"

CCLXXXIV

Then Thierry says: "Pinabel, you are noble and knightly, you are tall and strong, your body is well molded, and your peers are in no doubt as to your courage. Abandon this fight now. I will make peace between you and Charlemagne. But Ganelon will have justice meted out to him, and in such a manner that a day will never pass without its being retold."

Pinabel says: "The Lord God forbid! I will uphold the honor of my family, and I will not yield for any mortal man. I would rather die than suffer disgrace."

They raise their swords again and strike each other on the helmets which are studded with jewels set in gold, and the bright sparks fly up toward heaven. Now there is nothing that can separate them, and the fight cannot end without the death of one or the other.

CCLXXXV

Pinabel of Sorence is strong and fearless. He strikes Thierry on the helmet, which comes from Provence, and the sparks leap and set fire to the grass. Then he lunges with the point of his sword and strikes Thierry a blow on the forehead [and cuts off] a piece of his face, leaving the right cheek streaming blood, and covering Henry's hauberk with blood as far down as the waist. God alone saves him from being killed on the spot.

CCLXXXVI

Thierry sees that he has been wounded in the face, and that his bright blood is falling onto the grass of the meadow. He strikes Pinabel on the burnished steel helmet and splits it down as far as the nose piece, spilling the brains out of the head. Then he wrenches the blade in the wound and hurls down his opponent, dead. With that blow he has won the fight.

The French shout: "God has wrought a miracle! Justice demands that Ganelon should be hanged, and with him his kinfolk, who took his part."

CCLXXXVII

When Thierry has won his battle the Emperor Charles comes to his side, and four of his barons come with him: Duke Naimes, Oger of Denmark, Gefrey of Anjou, and William of Blaye. The King embraces Henry, and wipes Henry's face with his great sable mantle. Then he lays that mantle aside and puts on another. Very gently the knight is disarmed, and they mount him on a mule from Arabia. And they return, celebrating and rejoicing, and come to Aix, and dismount in the square.

Then the execution of the others begins.

CCLXXXVIII

Charles summons his counts and his dukes.

"What do you suggest that I should do with those whom I have under guard? They came here to maintain Ganelon's case, and they gave themselves up to me as hostages for Pinabel."

The Franks answer: "It would be wrong to spare the life of a single one of them."

The King sends for one of his officers, named Basbrun:

"Go and hang all of them on the malefactors' tree, and by this white beard I will see you dead and cursed to damnation if any one of them is allowed to escape."

The other answers: "I have no choice but to obey." He takes a hundred sergeants and drags the condemned men by main force to the place of execution. There are thirty of them who are hanged. The traitor brings death upon himself and upon others.

CCLXXXIX

And after this the Bavarians and the Germans and the Poitevins and the Bretons and the Normans, but first and most particularly the Franks, agree that Ganelon should be executed in some terrible and painful manner. They bring four war horses, and to them they tie Ganelon's feet and hands. They are proud, swift horses. Four sergeants urge them on toward a stream in the middle of a field. Ganelon comes to a terrible end. All his nerves are distended and every limb of his body is broken. His bright blood streams out over the green grass. Ganelon dies like a wretched felon. If a man is a traitor, it is not right that he should live to boast of it.

CCXC

When the Emperor has taken his vengeance he summons to him the bishops of France, Bavaria and Germany:

"There is a noble prisoner in my house who has heard so many sermons and parables that she has come to believe in God and has asked to be made a Christian. Baptize her, so that God may receive her soul."

They answer him: "Let her be provided with godmothers."

. . . .

In the baths at Aix there are great . . . There they baptize the Queen of Spain, giving her the name of Julienne, which they have chosen for her, and by virtue of her true knowledge of the faith she is made a Christian.

CCXCI

When the Emperor has meted out his justice and satisfied his great wrath and has had Bramimunde baptized a Christian, the day is over and the night has darkened.

The King has gone to bed in his vaulted bedroom. God sends Saint Gabriel to him, to say to him:

"Charles, summon all the hosts of your Empire and enter the land of Bire by force of arms, and rescue King Vivien, for the pagans have laid siege to him in the city of Imphe, and the Christians there are pleading and crying out for you."

The Emperor does not wish to go.

"Oh God," says the King, "my life is a burden!" And the tears run from his eyes and he rends his white beard.

The story which Toruldus set down ends here.

THE
NIBELUNGENLIED

Translated, and with an introduction by,
Helen M. Mustard

Introduction

Who wrote the *Nibelungenlied* we do not know, and in all probability never shall, despite numerous and diligent efforts to discover the poet's identity. The work itself is Austrian, and the author may have lived in Passau, or possibly in Vienna. In either city he would have had a distinguished audience. At any rate, he knew the region along the Danube in Austria very well, for he described it in the poem in such detail that one can easily trace the journey of the Burgundians on a map. This is in sharp contrast to the less definite, sometimes even inaccurate geography of territory west of Passau. From the work itself one can see that he was a cultivated man, acquainted with courtly society and with the popular literature of the day, French as well as German. It is even possible that he could read Latin, as some critics assume from his frequent references to Walther of Spain, hero of the Latin epic *Waltharius*. On the other hand, he alludes to the story so casually that it, like the stories of Dietrich of Bern, must have been very familiar to his audience, and this points to other sources than Latin.

His attempt to create a courtly epic out of German sources, remote in time and atmosphere from the world of chivalry, though not completely successful, nevertheless produced the only heroic epic in German which even remotely approaches the stature of the two contemporary Arthurian epics, the finest in medieval German literature, *Parzival* by Wolfram von Eschenbach and *Tristan* by Gottfried von Strassburg.[1] All three works probably date from the first decade of the thirteenth century. The *Nibelungenlied* was the first to be completed, approximately 1203; *Parzival* and *Tristan*, the latter left incomplete presumably because of Gottfried's death, were finished by about 1210.

The last third of the twelfth century and the first half of the thirteenth were important years for German literature. For the first time German authors are truly poets, and for the first time German literature is art. It is not an accident that this first flowering coincides with the advance of the knightly class under the Hohenstaufen emperors, whose rule had begun in 1138. Courts in Germany and Austria were centers of culture, providing encouragement, patronage, and an audience for the new class of writers, themselves knights, composing for an aristocratic society receptive to works which entertained, while at the same time reflecting the brilliance and the ideals and interests of courtly life. To be sure, knighthood did not begin with the reign of the Hohenstaufens, nor had there been a lack of secular literature addressed to a courtly audience. As early as the middle of the eleventh century a Latin narrative poem, *Ruodlieb,* presents a picture of an idealized knightly type, and German epic poems before 1170, such as the *Alexanderlied* or the *Rolandslied,* also portray knights living according to knightly ideals. But the authors of these tales were clerics who wrote, it is true, for a courtly society, but were not primarily artists. Only commencing with Heinrich von Veldeke, the father of courtly German literature, who began his *Eneit* about 1170, was German literature produced by actual members of the knightly class,[2] among them some of the greatest medieval poets, and only after that was it possible for German literature to attain

---

[1] Both are available in recent English translations, *Parzival,* translated by Helen M. Mustard and Charles E. Passage, New York, 1961, and *Tristan,* translated by A. T. Hatto, Penguin, 1960.

[2] To be sure, Gottfried of Strassburg was not a knight. He was either a bourgeois or a cleric, but he was a very cultivated man and a consummate artist.

the mastery of form and style, the subtlety and profundity of thought, apparent in *Parzival* and *Tristan* and in the best lyrics of the period.

These were the two most popular forms, the epic and the lyric. Both undoubtedly owe a great deal to the French, who developed the courtly epic and lyric earlier than the Germans and Austrians. Even the poet of the *Nibelungenlied,* though drawing from German sources, was apparently familiar with French literature and seems to have made occasional use of French sources in certain episodes. The astonishing thing, however, is that, while following the common medieval practice of using sources, the German and Austrian poets within a comparatively brief span of years achieved in their best works an originality and distinction of the highest order.

This flowering period was all too short. By 1250 it had already begun to decline. Social and religious unrest and conflict, changes within the Catholic church such as the founding of the Franciscan and Dominican orders and the development of scholasticism and mysticism, later the spirit of the Renaissance, the increasing power and importance of a prosperous middle class, and the ever lessening role of the knightly class, completely altered the intellectual and artistic climate and made courtly literature obsolete. Indeed, it was not until the latter half of the eighteenth century, with Goethe and Schiller, that German literature could again be called a great literature.

The *Nibelungenlied* must have been very widely read, for thirty-four manuscripts or fragments of manuscripts have been preserved, dating from the thirteenth to the early sixteenth century. This popularity is not difficult to understand. The poem contains some of the most unforgettable characters in medieval literature and some very dramatic and impressive scenes. It ranges in appeal from charming love scenes of a decorousness and restraint not surpassed in courtly romance, to Brunhild's earthy, yes, even vulgar display of muscularity and contempt for men, to the blind and ruthless passion for revenge which is responsible for Siegfried's death and the final catastrophe. The numerous and lengthy descriptions of clothing, weapons, courtly customs and etiquette, though boring to the modern reader, may have been very pleasing to a medieval audience, and the exploits in combat, recounted with such relish and to the last brutal detail, could only have added to its attractiveness. The *Nibelungenlied* is not a profound work; it has no "meaning" beyond the power of the story itself. The subtlety and depth which both Wolfram and Gottfried show, Wolfram's keen sense of humor and sensitive understanding of human beings, Gottfried's sophisticated irony and complexity of thought —all these the poet of the *Nibelungenlied* lacks. In fact, one is even tempted to question whether the author was a real poet, so clumsy is he at times, so repetitious and tedious at others, so apparently unaware of inconsistencies which should have disturbed a more skillful artist. Nevertheless, this unknown author gave us a story that might otherwise never have been told and that does not lose its force despite some faults in the telling.

Like all heroic epics, the *Nibelungenlied* owes its origin in part to actual events and persons, but it shows a characteristic unconcern for the facts of history. History has become legend, and historical personages are transformed into representative or exemplary types. The Burgundians were, in fact, almost completely destroyed by the Huns in 437, though not under Attila's leadership, but in the poem the Huns are not the enemies of the Burgundians. It is Kriemhild, sister of the Burgundian kings, who is responsible for their ruin. Etzel (Attila) is drawn into the conflict against his own will, and in German legends is nowhere described except as a good and kindly king, known for his hospitality to exiles from other lands. Dietrich of Bern (Verona) was in real life Theoderic the Great, King of the Ostrogoths. Commissioned by the Emperor, he led a successful campaign against Odoacer in Italy, murdered him, and added King of the Romans to his title. In the legends about him his fortunes are reversed and his character altered. Exiled from his kingdom in northern Italy, he lives at Etzel's court, and in the *Nibelungenlied* is a notable example of an honorable knight and a man of peace as well. Nor does it disturb the makers and tellers of legend that Attila and Theoderic were not even contemporaries. In like manner the *Nibelungenlied,* as is the way of legend, treats other historical events and people. The Burgundian kings have counterparts in history, as do the Margraves Gere and Eckewart, Bishop Pilgrim, possibly Volker, Rudeger, and others, but their derivation from actual persons sheds no light on their roles in the poem.

The *Nibelungenlied* is a national epic only in that its sources are Germanic. It does not celebrate a national hero, like the *Cid,* or transform a minor historical figure like Roland into a national hero. No figure in the German epic owes his significance to being a representative of a particular people. There is no national awareness in the poem except perhaps for the implication that the Hunnish warriors are not the equal of the Burgundians or the occasional slurs cast at the Bavarians for their reputation as highway robbers. The war with the Saxons and the Danes, conducted in a very gentlemanly fashion, simply provides Siegfried an opportunity to demonstrate his knightly prowess. Even the fall of the Burgundians is not the fall of one nation at war with another; it is the destruction of brave heroes, victims of a woman's vengeance.

The individual personality is always in the foreground. Conflict and catastrophe develop out of personal motivations: jealousy and suspicion on Brunhild's part because her sister-in-law Kriemhild is allowed to become the wife of a man she believes to be her husband's vassal, the quarrel of the two queens over this question of precedence, Hagen's ruthless loyalty to his lady, which leads to the betrayal and murder of Siegfried, this in turn causing Kriemhild's desire for revenge and thus motivating the entire action of the second part of the work. The chief concerns are personal and social, not national or political.

One of the poem's curious charms is the contrast, even clash, between the courtly tradition and elements of the story stubbornly incompatible with that tradition. By this I do not mean the brutality of the blood-bath at the close, ancient as its origins are. The descriptions of combat in the *Song of Roland,* though not so lengthy, are fully as cruel, and such scenes belong to the heroic epic. It is in figures like Hagen or the Kriemhild of the second half of the poem that one finds primitive urges and deeds very remote from the ideals of chivalry. Yet for all their vindictiveness, the two chief protagonists are not villains, and it is to the author's credit that he does not portray them as such. An occasional reproach, which he cannot restrain, does not diminish their stature. They dominate the poem from beginning to end and are permitted to play out their great scenes as antagonists worthy of each other. They stand as peers beside the representatives of the highest ideals of the poet's world, Dietrich and Rudeger, knightly heroes at their best. Dietrich can shame Kriemhild into silence, and his sympathies are clearly with the Burgundians, but he saves Kriemhild's life at the outbreak of hostilities in the hall, refrains from taking sides in the struggle, and delivers Gunther and Hagen as hostages into her hands. Neither he nor Rudeger, by remaining true to their knightly principles, function in any sense as a standard by which to judge, much less condemn, Hagen or Kriemhild, governed by laws so different. Two worlds exist here side by side, and if not always in harmony, at least in interesting conflict.

The poet did his best to mold his materials to fit the courtly fashion, and in all externals and in characters like Dietrich, Rudeger, Siegfried, and others, he succeeded admirably. The finest court etiquette is meticulously observed, more than ample attention is paid to fashionable and costly clothing, rulers and lords treat their vassals with the greatest generosity and receive in turn devoted service. The young Kriemhild and Rudeger's daughter behave with proper maidenly modesty and good breeding, and the love scenes would fit as well into any Arthurian romance. Moreover, Christian rites and customs are faithfully followed and emphasized, though it is questionable whether Christianity actually goes more than skin deep in the poem. Goethe once remarked that the Nibelung heroes and heroines went to church only to start a fight, and even a casual reader will sense the incongruity when Hagen is the one to admonish his fellow Burgundians to go to church at Etzel's court and confess their sins, since this will be the last time they will ever hear mass. Rudeger is usually cited as the one genuinely Christian figure in the poem; he does speak movingly of the risk of losing his soul if he fights against his friends, and he utters the only prayer in the poem, that God may instruct him what to do. Yet his choice lies ultimately between two loyalties, to his friends or to his lords, and his final decision to abide by his primary loyalty, that to his king and queen, is in the best feudal and also heroic tradition. Whether it has anything to do with Christianity is another question.

The main action is motivated by a morality clearly remote from either Christianity or chivalry, and the sense of impending doom, particularly in the second part, the fearless, even defiant, acceptance of the workings of a relentless fate from which there is no escape and which offers no hope of a hereafter, clearly belong to a pre-Christian world. Even the more civilized ideals present in the poem, the mutual loyalty of lord and vassal, the unwavering friendship between the two comrades Hagen and Volker, the respect for an esteemed opponent which leads Hagen to refrain from combat with Rudeger, are not only ideals of European chivalry, but are to be found everywhere in the heroic tradition.

Only in the young Kriemhild and her love for Siegfried do the courtly ideals go deeper than the surface. She is a sister of many women of courtly romance and lyric, noble and beautiful, the pride of the Burgundian court, surrounded by admiring knights, worshiped by Siegfried from afar. The description of the courtship and of her devoted love for her husband is a genuine and sensitive reflection of the important and idealized role of women in the world of chivalry.

A much disputed matter has been and still is how to reconcile the gentle Kriemhild of the first part of the poem with the vengeful and unscrupulous Kriemhild of the second part. Some critics point to the fact that the two parts derive from separate sources which remained separate for a long time and look on the two Kriemhilds as two different characters, so to speak. Others maintain that the poet has carefully prepared for the transition by emphasizing the intensity of her love for Siegfried and the long years of grief after his death. It does seem evident from the work itself that the poet tried his best to explain and motivate the discrepancy, but given the legend of the second part as he must have known it, he could not have succeeded without ruining the story. It is certainly a mistake to look in a work like this for anything like a psychological development, as we now understand the term.

After a popularity which lasted into the sixteenth century, a period of over three hundred years, the *Nibelungenlied* was completely forgotten until a Swiss scholar, Johann Jacob Bodmer, rescued it from oblivion by publishing a portion of it in 1757. It met with no interest in Germany, and even the publication of the complete epic in 1782, in a volume also containing Veldeke's *Eneit,* Wolfram's *Parzival,* and Hartman's *Der arme Heinrich,* aroused no real enthusiasm. This publication had been dedicated by its editor, a young friend of Bodmer's, to Frederick the Great and a copy sent to him. The king acknowledged it with his characteristic disdain for things German, saying the poems were not worth a shot of powder and that he would not have such worthless trash in his personal library. Not until the early 1800's, with the increased interest in the German past, its history and its culture, did the epic gradually begin to find in its own country the recognition it deserved.

German scholars have not spared effort or imagination in pursuit of the sources and genesis of the *Nibelungenlied,* yet the fact remains that the most widely accepted theory, Andreas Heusler's,[3] is based on the assumption of earlier German versions which do not actually exist. The beginnings of the Nibelung story were very likely short songs, preserved and no doubt varied by oral tradition, but exactly what these songs were like and what the intervening stages were between them and the epic of the thirteenth century is not known, for there is no written version in German of any part of the story earlier than the *Nibelungenlied.* And no two scholars in this area agree completely in their opinions on probable earlier versions or the relation between these and Scandinavian versions which have been preserved. By the very nature of the case, the problem is insoluble.

The Nibelung story, or stories, undoubtedly originated in western Germany. The destruction of the Burgundians by the Huns in the fifth century is a historical fact, and in Scandinavian versions the court of the Burgundian kings is the locale for the wooing of Kriemhild. From Germany the tales, or songs (for the story of Brunhild and the story of the destruction of the Burgundians were at first not connected with each other), went by way of the Vikings to Norway and spread widely through the Scandinavian countries. The tales must have been extremely popular in German-speaking lands and in Scandinavia. German versions, oral or written or both, must have existed and retained their popularity; otherwise the Austrian poet would not have been drawn to this material. And the number of songs and tales relating to the Nibelung story which have been preserved in Iceland and Norway, dating from the tenth to the thirteenth century, bespeak its popularity there.

Interesting as the comparison between the various Scandinavian versions and the *Nibelungenlied* is, it adds little to an understanding of the German poem. In Scandinavia the story was not developed into an epic until some time after the completion of the *Nibelungenlied.* The three works which do contain a complete saga of the Nibelungs, in prose, not in verse, are the so-called *Younger Edda,* a textbook for young skalds composed by an Icelander about 1230-1240, the *Thidrekssaga,* written by a Norwegian about the middle of the thirteenth century, and the *Volsungasaga,* written by

[3] *Nibelungensage und Nibelungenlied,* first published 1921, revised edition 1923, reprinted 1929 and later.

an Icelander in Norway about 1260. Of these none can compare in artistic merit with the *Nibelungenlied.* The older Scandinavian sources are songs about incidents or characters from the Nibelung story to be found in the *Older Edda,* in an Icelandic manuscript dating from 1270. Some of these songs are very old, possibly going back as far as the eighth or ninth centuries. There is, however, no evidence that Norse materials had any influence on the German poem. The author of the *Thidrekssaga* refers to German sources, and some scholars believe that he and the writer of the *Nibelungen-lied* may have had access to similar sources and that some idea of their content may be deduced from the Norwegian saga. Other scholars dispute this, and Friedrich Panzer believes that the author of the *Thidrekssaga* drew on the *Nibelungenlied* as a source.[4]

The problem of sources, German or others, and the question as to how much help Scandinavian versions can be in deducing the nature of German sources are matters far too complicated to be dealt with here, but it is perhaps worth while to mention the main differences to be found in Norse versions of the story. Since these versions differ among themselves, I must, for brevity's sake, simplify as much as possible. In some accounts young Siegfried is not brought up at a court, but lives in a forest, where he is reared by a dwarf, a smith, and there acquires his famous sword, kills a dragon, possessor of the treasure, and takes it from him. The motif of invulnerability is not found in the Northern tradition. Siegfried becomes, in the North as in Germany, the proxy in wooing Brunhild for Gunther. Assuming Gunther's form, he rides through a wall of flames to reach her, remains with her three nights, but with his sword separating them, then takes her to Gunther, but not without first removing her ring, which he later gives to Kriemhild. The version which relates that Siegfried first won Brunhild for himself and was afterward given a magic potion by Kriemhild's mother which caused him to forget his betrothal, that Brunhild's unhappiness at the Burgundian court is due to Siegfried's betrayal of her love, and that she commits suicide herself after the murder of Siegfried, is a later addition to the original story. The mythological elements in some of the Norse tales, the appearance of the gods as characters in the Siegfried story, Brunhild as the Valkyrie, daughter of Odin, have also been shown to be later additions. Incidentally, Wagner

[4] *Das Nibelungenlied. Enstehung und Gestalt,* Stuttgart, 1955.

drew chiefly on Scandinavian sources for *Der Ring des Nibelungen,* hence his tetralogy bears no resemblance to the German epic.

The Icelandic accounts of the second part of the Nibelung story differ radically from the *Nibelungenlied.* Etzel is portrayed as a cruel and treacherous man, and it is he who, after marrying Kriemhild, invites her brothers to his court in order to get possession of the Nibelung treasure. He is then the instigator of the battle with the Burgundians, and when only Gunther and Hagen (here brothers, not lord and vassal) are left alive, he kills both when they refuse to reveal the whereabouts of the treasure. This scene is similar to that in the *Nibelungenlied* except that the roles of Gunther and Hagen are reversed. Hagen is the first to die, and Gunther makes the final defiant speech which is given to Hagen in the German version. Kriemhild takes revenge on Etzel by serving him a meal of the flesh of their two sons, stabs him to death in the night while he lies in a drunken sleep, then sets fire to the hall and dies herself in the flames.

To return to the German poem—it divides naturally into two parts, the second part beginning at chapter XX with Etzel's decision to court Kriemhild. There are some signs that the poet gave deliberate attention to structural elements,[5] though he fell far short of the artistry of composition in a work like *Parzival.* The two parts are of approximately equal length, the first containing 4568 lines, the second 4748. Certain scenes and actions in the two parts are obvious parallels to each other and thus add to the symmetry of structure. There are two courtships, Siegfried's and Etzel's; two invitations to a festival, Gunther's to Siegfried and Kriemhild, Etzel's to the Burgundians; two betrothal scenes; two premonitions of disaster in dreams, Kriemhild's warning to Siegfried before the hunt, Ute's warning to the Burgundians before they leave for Etzel's court. Yet there is other evidence of a lack of feeling for what detracts from the effectiveness of the story, for instance, the very long and in part tedious chapter on the war with the Saxons and Danes and the section describing Siegfried's trip from Isenland to fetch his Nibelung men.

[5] I pass over here the unanswerable question as to whether the last poet or one of his predecessors is responsible for changes and additions, and speak of "the poet" in the anonymous and indefinite sense this word must necessarily have in connection with the *Nibelungenlied.*

The verse form is not the rhymed couplets used in the Arthurian epics, but a four-line stanza otherwise found only in the lyrics of Austrian poets and, somewhat varied, in other epics. Each line is divided by a caesura into two parts, and each half-line contains in principle four accents, though only in the last half-line of the stanza are the four accents fully stressed. In the first half-lines the fourth accent frequently falls on a syllable which would not usually be stressed. In the second half-lines of the first three lines the final, fourth, accent is usually replaced by a pause. The number of unaccented syllables is irregular, and not infrequently one stressed syllable follows directly on another. The rhymes are masculine, aabb, and some lines contain internal rhymes.

Owing to the choice of this stanza form, and possibly also to the natural inclination of the poet, there is a great amount of padding. Since the stanza is usually a unit, the poet, having arrived at the fourth line of a stanza with nothing new to say about the topic at hand, all too frequently uses the line to repeat, with variations, something which has already been said, before going on to a new topic in the next stana. Very often half lines are also used simply as fillers. Repetition and the use of stereotyped phrases are to some extent characteristic of all medieval epics and were no doubt an aid for the listener, but in no other epic that I know is there such an amount as here.

Dialogue occupies a great part of the poem, though never do the characters deliver such long speeches as they do in the German Arthurian romances, and much of the action is conveyed through the dialogue, often very effectively and dramatically. Straight narrative passages are comparatively brief, except for the descriptions of battles. The reader may be surprised occasionally by the lack of motivation, but this is characteristic of the style of the poem. Gernot's proposal in chapter XIX, for instance, to sink the treasure in the Rhine, is completely unprepared for, and only the demands of the legend can explain it. Giselher's behavior in this same passage is not consistent with what we have heard of him before. Hitherto he has always been on Kriemhild's side, yet here he evades her appeal for help and with his brothers absents himself from the scene while Hagen disposes of the treasure.

Unlike the geography of the Arthurian romances, which tends to be exotic, fanciful, or vague, the location of events in the

Nibelungenlied, as in epics like *Roland* and the *Cid,* is definite and fairly accurate.[6] Only the fictitious Azagouc and Zazamanc[7] are clearly fanciful. As has been mentioned before, the author knew the region between Passau and Hungary extremely well. He was less certain of his facts about places west of Passau, making some curious mistakes, such as locating the Wasken woods (Vosges mountains) on the eastern side of the Rhine. The location of Isenland, Brunhild's country, is very vague, and the mention in chapter XII of Siegfried's castle in the march of Norway is puzzling, since otherwise his kingdom is located on the lower Rhine. But for the most part the geography is realistic and must have strengthened for the contemporary audience the realism also evident in descriptions of battles, weapons, clothing, court etiquette, etc.

The language is far less difficult than that of some other medieval German epics, notably *Parzival* and *Tristan.* The style is simpler, the syntax not so intricate, though there are, of course, ambiguous and confusing passages. The main problem of translation is, however, not comprehension, but the difficulty of transforming an extremely repetitive style and an often monotonous syntax into a readable English. I found myself forced to abandon to some degree a principle of translation I firmly believe in, fidelity to the original, realizing that if I adhered to it strictly, the translation would be unbearably verbose and dull. I have taken the liberty of omitting a considerable number of the most frequently repeated clichés, epithets like "the good warrior," "the mighty Siegfried," which add nothing to the meaning, even in the German, but I have tried to keep enough such expressions to maintain the flavor of the original without, I hope, tiring the reader. I have also occasionally omitted lines, once an entire stanza, which merely repeated what had just been said before. It was no small comfort to me to discover later that Goethe had more than once urged a prose translation of the *Nibelungenlied* which would omit all padding and thus enable the story to appeal more immediately and forcefully to the modern reader.

I have also taken a second liberty which I felt necessary. The

[6] For further detail concerning geography consult Index of Names, below.

[7] Scholars are not agreed as to whether Wolfram von Eschenbach took these from the *Nibelungenlied* or whether the author of the latter was the borrower, but since Wolfram is noted for his love of fantastic names and coined more than one himself, it seems more likely that he is also responsible for these.

vocabulary is extremely small, particularly in view of the length of the poem, and many words or expressions are repeated so often that even in the German text they become monotonous. A greater contrast to Gottfried von Strassburg, who had a seemingly inexhaustible repertoire of synonyms, can scarcely be imagined. It is only a slight exaggeration to say that the *Nibelungenlied* is written in a kind of Basic Middle High German. To have used the same English word for every repetition of a German word would actually have produced a distortion of the original by turning it into an absurdity, for however simple and unsophisticated the style, it is not absurd. The contemporary audience may well have perceived in the repetition of a word or phrase, but in a different context, a fresh nuance of meaning, but to convey such shifts of meaning, mere repetition of the English word would not suffice. I have therefore frequently varied the translation of identical words or phrases, but have used the same word in English whenever I felt that the repetition in the original was significant or when it seemed unavoidable, as in the frequent mention of maidens, ladies, warriors, and the like.

The vocabulary is interesting for its use of archaic words, rarely or never found in the Arthurian epics, side by side with modern, courtly vocabulary of the poet's own time. Unfortunately, I saw no way, short of a stilted artificiality I wished to avoid, of conveying this meeting of two worlds on a linguistic level, parallel to their meeting on other levels.

Of the existing manuscripts three have been published, A, B, and C. One of the rare points of agreement among scholars of the *Nibelungenlied* is that manuscript B, though certainly not the original, is closest to it. Two editions are available, and I have made use of both, the original edition edited by Karl Bartsch (3 vols., Leipzig, 1870-1880) and a recent revision of this edition by Helmut de Boor (Wiesbaden, 1956, and reprinted often since then).

Since the title *Nibelungenlied* (Song of the Nibelungs) is the one most commonly used, I have retained it to avoid confusion, even though it is not accurate. The various manuscripts have been divided into two groups, one called the *liet*-group because the final half line reads *daz ist der Nibelunge liet* (this is the song of the Nibelungs), the other called the *nôt*-group because the close is *daz ist der Nibelunge nôt* (this is the fall of the Nibelungs). The traditional title was derived from a manuscript belonging to the first group, but the standard text, based on manuscript B, belongs in the second group. The poem should therefore more properly be called *The Fall of the Nibelungs*. In the title the word "Nibelungs" refers of course to the Burgundians, a use the word takes on only in the second half of the work. In the first half it generally means Siegfried's vassals from the Nibelung land.[8]

In the German editions of the original each section or chapter is called an *âventiure*. I omit the word, or even the word "chapter" in the text, for two reasons. This Middle High German word is not found in manuscript B and, what is more important, the word never once occurs in the whole manuscript. It is a term from courtly vocabulary, meaning a special or extraordinary incident, such as a knightly adventure, and is not an appropriate heading for most sections of this poem, which is organized quite differently from some of the medieval romances, in which there are sequences of "adventures" in the courtly sense of the word. I have, however— and I admit the inconsistency—retained the chapter titles, another convention in most editions of the poem, though they are also not to be found in manuscript B, where the divisions are indicated only by a large initial letter. The titles seem to me helpful for practical purposes, as a brief indication of the content of a section, and do not seem, to me at least, as out of place as a word this poet so studiously avoids, in spite of his obvious familiarity with the courtly vocabulary. I have used the chapter headings as given in de Boor's edition, except that I have supplied a title for the first section, which for some reason bears no title in any manuscript.

A number of English translations of the poem have been made, both prose and verse, but none of recent date. The most readable, though not the most accurate, is probably the prose translation by Margaret Armour, first published in London, 1908, no longer in print. There is, oddly enough, no good translation into modern German.

Readers interested in pursuing the subject of the *Nibelungenlied* and related questions will find a selceted bibliography in W. T. H. Jackson's *The Literature of the Middle Ages* (New York, 1960). Unfortunately, the basic works are accessible only to those who can read German.

HELEN M. MUSTARD

---

[8] For further details consult the Index of Names, below.

I

Concerning Kriemhild

In ancient tales many marvels are told us of glorious heroes, of arduous trials, of joys and festivals, of weeping and lamenting, of combats between brave warriors. Listen now to the telling of these marvels.

There grew up in Burgundy a noble maiden. In no land was there a fairer. Kriemhild was her name. She became a beautiful woman, for whose sake many heroes were to lose their lives. The charming maid well deserved to be loved. Bold warriors desired her, and no one disliked her. She was lovely beyond measure, and her maidenly virtues[1] would have been a credit to any woman.

Three noble and powerful kings had her in their keeping, Gun-

---

[1] The word *tugende* includes both character and good breeding.

ther and Gernot, valiant warriors, and young Giselher, a peerless hero. The lady was their sister, and the princes watched over her. They were generous,[2] of lofty lineage, and possessed of extraordinary strength and courage. Their kingdom was called Burgundy. Later, in Etzel's[3] land, they performed marvelous deeds.

They lived in fullness of power at Worms[4] on the Rhine, and many proud knights from their lands served them with laudable honor until their end had come. Through the hate of two noble ladies they were to die a wretched death.

Their mother, Lady Ute, was a mighty queen. Their father's name was Dankrat, a very valorous man, who in his youth had also won great renown and who after his death left them lands and wealth.

The three kings, as I have said, were of very high courage. Subject to them were the best warriors of whom poets have ever sung, strong and brave, and undaunted in sharp combat. There was Hagen of Troneg, and his brother, the powerful Dankwart, Ortwin of Metz, the two margraves Gere and Eckewart, and Volker of Alzei, endowed with faultless strength. Rumolt, the master cook, a splendid warrior, and the lords Sindolt and Hunolt, vassals of the three kings, had to tend to the court and its dignity. They had many other warriors too, whom I cannot name. Dankwart was marshal, and his nephew, Ortwin of Metz, was the king's steward. Sindolt was cup-bearer, an excellent fighter, and Hunolt served as chamberlain. These knew how to uphold the court's high dignity. Of the glory of the court and its far-reaching power, of the great honor and of the chivalry the lords cultivated joyously[5] all their life long—on my word, of these things no one could give you a full description.

In the midst of these splendid surroundings Kriemhild had a dream, of how she reared a falcon,[6] strong, handsome, and wild, which two eagles tore to pieces before her very eyes. No greater sorrow could befall her in all this world. She told the dream to her

[2] A most important virtue in a medieval ruler.

[3] Etzel is the German form of the name of the historical Attila, king of the Huns.

[4] In the fifth century Worms was the capital of the Burgundian kingdom, but was destroyed by the Huns in 437.

[5] Joy (*vröude*) is a very important concept in knightly life. It means a rich and full enjoyment in participating in knightly society.

[6] In the early *Minnesang* the falcon was a symbol of the lover.

mother Ute, who could give the good maiden no better interpretation than this: "The falcon which you rear is a noble man. If God does not protect him, you will soon have lost him."

"Why do you speak to me of a man, my dear mother? I wish always to be without a man's love. Until my death I wish to remain as beautiful as I am now, and I never want to suffer grief from the love of a man."

"Now don't renounce this too firmly," said her mother. "If ever in this world you are to be happy with all your heart, that will come about through a man's love. You will become a beautiful woman if God grants you a truly worthy knight."

"Do not speak so, my Lady," [7] she said. "We have often seen with many women how in the end joy can reward one with sorrow. I shall shun them both, then no misfortune can befall me."

So in her heart Kriemhild renounced all love, and the maid now lived many a happy day without knowing any man whom she cared to love. In later times she became in all honor a valiant warrior's wife. He was that same falcon she had seen in the dream which her mother interpreted for her. How violently she took revenge on her nearest kin, who slew him! For the death of this one man many a mother's son died.

II

Concerning Siegfried

There grew up in Netherland the son of a noble king. His father's name was Siegmund, his mother's Siegelind. They lived in a mighty castle called Xanten, on the lowlands of the Rhine, which was known far and wide. Siegfried was the name of this brave and excellent warrior. Being strong of body, he rode into many lands and with valiant spirit tried his fortune in many a realm. Oh, what bold fighters he later found among the Burgundians!

[7] The daughter addresses the mother very politely and formally.

Great marvels could be told of Siegfried at his prime, in the days of his youth, how his reputation grew, and how handsome he was. Many a lovely woman lost her heart to him.

He was reared with the care which befitted him, but by his own nature what virtues he attained! For proving to be so distinguished in every respect, he was an honor to his father's land. He had now grown old enough to appear at court. The people were glad to see him, and many a lady and many a maid wished that his desire would always bring him there. Plenty of them were partial to him. Of this the young nobleman was well aware.

Never was the youth permitted to ride alone without escort. By order of Siegmund and Siegelind he was always richly dressed, and experienced men who knew the meaning of honor had him in their charge. Thus he deserved to inherit people and kingdom.

He was now strong enough to bear weapons. The qualities needed for this he possessed in abundance. And he very sensibly began to pay court to beautiful women. To love the bold Siegfried would have done them honor.

Then his father, Siegmund, sent the announcement to his vassals that he intended to hold a festival with dear friends present. This news was carried to the lands of other kings, and to the foreigners and to his own people as well he gave horses and fine apparel. Wherever any youth was found of a rank equal to Siegfried's family and ready to become a knight, these young noblemen were invited to the kingdom for the festival, and with the young king they received their swords.[1]

Wondrous tales could be told of the festival. Siegmund and Siegelind won great honor with the lavish gifts they dispensed. On this account many strangers rode into their land. Four hundred squires, ready to bear swords, were to wear knightly garb with Siegfried. Lovely maidens were busily at work, for they were fond of him, and the ladies set quantities of precious stones into the gold of the edgings to be embroidered on the garments of the proud young warriors. The host bade seats be set up for the valiant men. It was the time of the summer solstice when his son won the title of knight.

Now many a high-born squire and many a noble knight pro-

---

[1] This is of course the ceremony of knighting.

ceeded to the minster. The experienced warriors quite properly served the inexperienced as they had been served in their time. They were looking forward to knightly sports and other pleasures, too. First, to do honor to God, a mass was sung. After this there began a mighty thronging among the people when the squires became knights according to knightly usage and with splendor so great as would scarcely be seen again.

Then they hastened to where they found horses saddled, and the bohourt[2] at Siegmund's court became so violent that palace[3] and hall resounded. The high-spirited warriors created a prodigious tumult. From old and young many a clash was heard, and the cracking of spearshafts filled the air. Splinters were seen flying far, right up to the palace, from the fighters' hands. These games were played with zest. At last the host ordered them stopped, and the horses were led away. Many a sturdy shield's boss could be seen there, shattered, and precious stones from the gleaming shield plates, hurled onto the grass from the impact of the onslaught.

The guests now went to the seats assigned them. A variety of excellent foods and the very best of wine, which was served them generously, freed them from their fatigue. Both strangers and the host's own people were treated with great honor. Though they had had much entertainment throughout the day, many traveling minstrels now gave themselves no rest. They were doing service for the magnificent presents they received there, and Siegmund's whole land was honored by their praise.[4]

The king bade the young Siegfried confer as fiefs land and castles, as he himself had done formerly. On his comrades of the sword[5] his hand bestowed much, and they were glad of the journey they had taken to this land. The celebration lasted until the seventh day. In honor of her son the rich Siegelind, following the old custom, distributed red gold; she knew how to earn for him the devo-

2 The *bûhurt* was jousting in groups.

3 The *palas* was a large building containing the great hall, *sal,* the large reception room where court was held, meals were served for the whole court, and indoor entertainments took place. Often, however, in this poem and in others, *palas* is also used to refer to the hall itself.

4 A good ruler was always known for his generosity to such people as the traveling minstrels, who were dependent on their patrons for a living.

5 I.e., the young men who became knights at the same time as he did.

tion of the people. Not a single poor man was now to be found among the wandering folk.[6] Horses and clothing flew out of the hands of the hosts, as if they were not to live one day longer. Never, I think, did a household practice such generosity.

The festival came to a glorious close. The powerful noblemen were afterward heard to say that they would like the youth as their master, but Lord Siegfried had no desire for this. As long as both Siegmund and Siegelind were alive, their beloved child did not wish to wear the crown; yet he did want to be the leader in resisting all violence, which he feared might break out in his lands.

III

How Siegfried Came to Worms

No heart's grief had ever troubled the young hero. Then he heard reports that there was in Burgundy a lovely maiden of incomparable beauty. From her he afterward reaped much joy, and distress as well. Her extraordinary beauty was known far and wide. Many a man also felt her nobility of spirit, and this alone attracted many guests to Gunther's land. Despite all the knights who wooed her love, Kriemhild never owned in her heart that she wished to have any one of them as her beloved. He to whom she was later to belong was as yet unknown to her.

Now Siegelind's son aspired after noble love,[1] and the wooing of all the others was as a breath of wind to his. He was indeed worthy of a beautiful woman. Before long Kriemhild became Siegfried's

[6] This general term, *die varnden*, can include wandering minstrels and players and any of the poor people, not belonging to the knightly class, who accompany the retinue of a rich nobleman.

[1] The poet uses here a phrase from the vocabulary of chivalry, *hôhe minne*. In its conventional use it means courtly love, an idealized, platonic relationship, in which a knight serves a lady as her admirer, but not necessarily with a view to marriage. In this passage, however, *hôhe minne* is associated with marriage.

wife. His kinsmen and many of his vassals counseled him, since he was desirous of steadfast love, to court a lady of equal rank.

To this Siegfried responded, "Then I will take Kriemhild, the fair maid of Burgundy, for her beauty beyond measure. I know very well there was never an emperor so powerful that it would not be fitting for him, if he wanted a wife, to love this noble queen."

From the talk among his followers Siegmund heard of the matter and thus discovered his son's intention to woo the maid. It was a bitter grief to him. Siegelind heard of it too, and feared greatly for her child, since she knew Gunther and his men well. So they tried to turn him from his venture.

Then the bold Siegfried said, "My dear father, I would rather be without the affection of noble ladies forever if I cannot woo her for whom my heart feels ardent love. You may say what you like—this has to be."

"If you will not desist," said the king, "then I will be truly glad at your intent and will help you as best I can to carry it through, but King Gunther has many a haughty vassal. Even if there were no one else but the warrior Hagen, he can be so arrogant in his pride that I very much fear we shall suffer if we try to woo the high-born maid."

"Why should that hinder us?" said Siegfried. "What I can't get from them in friendship, I can win with my strength. I'm sure I can take from them by force both their people and their land."

"Your words do not please me," said King Siegmund. "If these things were reported on the Rhine,[2] you would never dare to ride into that land. I have known Gunther and Gernot for a long time. No one can win the maid with force. This I have been told. But if you wish to ride to the land with warriors, all the friends we possess shall be summoned immediately."

"I have no thought," said Siegfried, "of having warriors accompany me to the Rhine in any military expedition with which to take the maid by force. That would not suit me at all. My hand alone can win her. I will go to Gunther's land with twelve companions. In this you shall help me, father Siegmund."

Then his warriors were given garments of fur, both gray and variegated. Now his mother Siegelind also heard this news. She

[2] I.e., in Worms.

began to mourn for her dear child, whom she feared to lose at the hands of Gunther's men, and the queen wept bitterly.

Lord Siegfried went to where she was and said to his mother gently, "Lady, you mustn't weep for me. Believe me, I shall have nothing to fear from those warriors. Help me with the journey to the Burgundian land, so that my men and I may have such clothing as proud heroes can wear with honor. For this I shall be truly grateful to you."

"Since you will not turn back," said Lady Siegelind, "I'll help you to the journey, my only child, with the best garments a knight ever wore, for you and your companions. You shall have enough."

Young Siegfried bowed his thanks to the queen and said, "I shall take no more than twelve warriors for the trip. Have clothing prepared for them. I want very much to find out everything pertaining to Kriemhild."

Then night and day beautiful ladies sat, and none of them had any rest until Siegfried's garments had been made. He had no intention of giving up his journey. His father bade that the knightly garb in which he would leave the land be splendidly adorned. The gleaming breastplates, too, were put in order, and their sturdy helmets and beautiful broad shields.

The time for their journey to Burgundy was now approaching. Men and women alike were anxious lest they should never return to their homeland again. The warriors ordered their pack horses to be loaded with weapons and clothing. Their riding horses were handsome, bridles and saddles red with gold. No one had more right to live proudly than Siegfried and his men. Then he asked leave to depart for Burgundy, and the king and his wife sadly granted his request.

Lovingly he consoled them both, saying, "Don't weep for my sake. You must never fear for my life."

The warriors, too, were downcast, and many a maiden wept. I think their hearts told them rightly that many of their friends would perish from this journey. Quite justly they lamented; they had good reason to.

On the seventh morning the brave men rode onto the sandy shore at Worms. All their apparel was red with gold, and their riding gear magnificent. Smoothly their horses trotted along. Their shields were new, shiny, and broad, and their helmets exceedingly fine.

Thus the bold Siegfried rode to Gunther's court. Never had heroes been seen wearing such splendid clothing. The tips of their swords hung down to the spurs, and they carried sharp javelins. Siegfried bore one fully two spans wide with edges that cut fearfully. In their hands they held gold-colored reins, and the horses' breast straps were of silk.

On all sides the people stared at them, and many of Gunther's men ran to meet them. Spirited warriors, both knights and squires, went toward the guests, as was proper, welcoming them to the land of their lords and taking their horses and shields.

They meant to lead the horses away to rest, but Siegfried quickly spoke up, "Let our horses remain here. We want to leave very soon. That is my firm intention. Whoever knows, let him not conceal it from me, but tell me where I can find the king, the mighty Gunther of Burgundy."

Then one who knew informed him, "If you want to find the king, that can easily be done. I saw him there in the great hall with his warriors. Go there, and you will find with him many an excellent man."

Now word had been brought to the king that very distinguished knights had arrived wearing sparkling coats of mail and magnificent attire. No one in Burgundy knew them. Gunther was surprised and asked where these warriors had come from with their brightly colored garments and such fine shields, new and broad. He was displeased that no one could tell him.

Ortwin of Metz answered the king, "Since we don't know them, send for Hagen, my uncle, and let him see them. He is acquainted with all kingdoms, and foreign countries too. If he recognizes these noblemen, he will tell us who they are."

The king commanded that he and his vassals be summoned, and Hagen appeared, coming to court in stately fashion with his warriors. He asked what the king wished of him.

"There are strange warriors in my castle yard whom no one here knows. If you have ever seen them, Hagen, tell me the true facts about them."

"That I will do," said Hagen. He went to a window and let his gaze rest on the strangers. Their dress and their whole appearance pleased him, but they were strangers to him too. He said wherever the warriors had come from in their journey to the Rhine, they were probably princes or envoys of princes, for their horses were handsome and their garments very fine, and whatever their origin, they were high-spirited men.

Having said this, Hagen continued, "I am inclined to say, although I have never seen Siegfried, yet I do believe nevertheless, that he is the warrior walking there with such a noble bearing. He will bring rare tales to our land. This hero's hand slew the valiant Nibelungs, Schilbung and Nibelung, mighty sons of a king. Since then he has performed great exploits with his enormous strength. Once, as he rode alone, without any assistance, he found at the foot of a mountain, so I was told, Nibelung's treasure and many a venturesome man. They were strangers to him until he came to know them there.

"The whole of Nibelung's treasure had been carried out of a hollow mountain. Now listen to the marvelous tale of how the Nibelungs wanted to divide the treasure. Siegfried saw them and became curious. He came so close to them that he could see the warriors, and they could see him too. 'Here comes the mighty Siegfried,' said one of them, 'the hero of Netherland.' He had strange adventures with the Nibelungs. Schilbung and Nibelung welcomed him warmly, and in mutual agreement the young princes requested him to divide the treasure. They urged him eagerly, and he gave them his promise.

"He saw so many precious stones, as we heard the tale, that a hundred wagons could not have carried them, and there was even more red gold from the Nibelung land. All of this Siegfried was to divide between them. As a reward they gave him Nibelung's sword, but they were paid very poorly by the service which Siegfried was supposed to render them. He could not perform it, for they became angry.[3] Among their friends they had twelve bold men who were powerful giants, but what good could that do them? In wrath Siegfried slew them, and with his good sword Balmung he vanquished seven hundred warriors from the Nibelung land.

---

[3] The reason for their anger, though not clear here, becomes apparent in another version of the story given in *Biterolf*. A quarrel arose between Siegfried and the Nibelung brothers because, according to ancient law, Siegfried acquired with the sword the rights of the first born, which the brothers, however, refused to grant him. The author of the *Nibelungenlied* obviously assumes that his audience is already familiar with some similar version of the story.

Moreover, he killed the two mighty kings. Alberich then drove him to sore straits, hoping to avenge his lords immediately, but he soon discovered how strong Siegfried was. The sturdy dwarf was no match for him. Like two wild lions they raced toward the mountain, where Siegfried robbed Alberich of the cloak of invisibility.[4] Then because of the great fear which many young warriors had of the sword and the valiant man, they made the land and its castles subject to him.

"Thus Siegfried, the dreadly man, became master of the treasure. All those who had ventured to fight were dead. He ordered Nibelung's men to return the treasure to the place where they had gotten it, and the mighty Alberich became its guard. He had to swear Siegfried an oath that he would serve him like a servant. Any kind of task he stood ready to perform."

And Hagen continued, "All these things Siegfried did. Never has any warrior possessed greater vigor. And I know still more about him. He slew a dragon and bathed himself in the blood, whereupon his skin became hard as horn. For this reason no weapon can cut him; that has been proved. We should welcome him all the more warmly so that we may not reap the young warrior's wrath. He is so courageous that we should try to gain his good will. By his strength he has performed many a marvelous deed."

"You may be right," said Gunther. "Just look how warrior-like he stands there, eager for battle, this bold man, and his companions too. Let us go down to meet him."

"That you can do in all honor," said Hagen. "He is of noble lineage, son of a powerful king. His bearing is such that in my opinion he has not ridden here for any trivial matter."

"May he be welcome here," said the king. "He is noble and brave, so I have just been told. This shall be to his advantage in the Burgundian land."

Then King Gunther went to where Siegfried stood. The host and his warriors welcomed the guest in such fashion that nothing was lacking in their courtesy, and the excellent man bowed in thanks to them for greeting him so cordially.

"I am curious to hear," said the king at once, "where you came

---

[4] There is no English equivalent, so far as I know, for the *tarnkappe*, a magic cloak which covers the whole body, makes the wearer invisible, and gives him the strength of twelve men.

from into this land, noble Siegfried, and what purpose brought you to Worms on the Rhine."

"I shall not conceal it from you," replied the guest. "I was told in my father's land that here with you were the boldest warriors a king had ever acquired. This I have often heard, and wanting to see for myself, I came here. I have also heard great bravery attributed to you, that a more courageous king has never been seen. Throughout all these lands the people talk about it. So now I will not rest until I have found out for myself. I am a warrior too and could wear a crown, but I want it to be said of me: He has earned the right to rule a people and a land. For this my honor and my head shall be security. Now since you are so courageous, as I have been told, I don't care whether anyone likes it or not—I intend to' take by force everything you possess; land and castles shall be subject to me."

The king was astonished, and his men as well, when they heard that Siegfried was determined to take their land from them. His warriors grew angry as they listened.

"How do I deserve this," said Gunther, "that we should lose, through the strength of one man, what my father long ruled in honor? Then we would prove very poorly that we too pursue the art of knighthood."

"I will not desist," answered the bold man. "Unless your valor can secure peace for the land, I intend to rule it all. On the other hand, if you can win my inheritance with your power, it shall be subject to you. Your heritage and mine shall lie at balance on the scales. Whichever one of us can gain the victory over the other, the two lands and peoples shall serve."

Hagen and Gernot immediately spoke in opposition. "We have no desire," said Gernot, "to conquer any lands by letting one warrior fall at the hand of another. We have rich territories which give us our due service, and to no one else do they more rightfully belong."

With anger in their hearts his friends stood there, among them Ortwin of Metz, who said, "I don't like this attempt at settlement. The mighty Siegfried has challenged you without cause. Even if you and your brothers did not have enough men to defend you, and even if he brought along a whole king's army, you may be sure I would force him in battle to abandon this arrogant behavior."

The hero of Netherland was enraged at this and said, "Don't

you dare raise your hand against me. I am a powerful king, and you but a king's vassal. Twelve of your sort could not withstand me in battle."

Ortwin called loudly for swords, thus showing he was indeed the son of Hagen's sister. The king was disappointed that Hagen had remained silent so long.

Then Gernot interrupted and said to Ortwin, "Let your anger be. Lord Siegfried has not done anything to us but what we can settle in all propriety and still keep him as a friend. This is my counsel and would be far more to our credit."

Then Hagen said, "We and all your warriors have good reason to be offended that Siegfried rode here to the Rhine to pick a quarrel. He shouldn't have done it. My masters would not have done *him* such wrong."

Siegfried answered, "If you are displeased at what I have said, Lord Hagen, then I'll show you that I will rule supreme here in Burgundy."

But Gernot intervened again and said, "I will prevent this, unassisted," and he forbade all his warriors to speak any arrogant words that might irritate Siegfried.

Siegfried, too, then bethought himself of the noble maid.

"How could we, in all decency, fight against you?" Gernot continued. "No matter how many heroes should fall in the battle, we would gain little honor and you very small profit."

Siegfried, son of Siegmund, answered, "Why are Hagen and Ortwin waiting? Why don't they make haste to fight, they and their friends, of whom they have so many here in Burgundy?"

These knights had to hold their tongues, for that was Gernot's advice.

"You are welcome among us," said Ute's son,[5] "and your fellow warriors who have come with you. My kinsmen and I will gladly be of service to you."

Then the command was given to pour Gunther's wine for the guests, and the lord of the land said, "Everything we have, if you desire it in an honorable fashion, shall be at your disposal, and we will share with you our life and our possessions."

At this Lord Siegfried's temper became a little milder. All their equipment was now ordered into safe-keeping, and lodging was

---

[5] I.e., Gernot.

provided for Siegfried's squires, the best to be found, where they could rest in comfort.

Thereafter this guest was heartily welcome in the Burgundian land. He was shown great honor for many and many a day, a thousand times more than I can tell you. Believe me, his valor deserved this. No one who ever saw him could feel unfriendly toward him.

The kings and their vassals occupied themselves with knightly sports, and whatever they did, Siegfried was always the best. No one could rival him, so great was his strength, whether in hurling the stone or in casting the spear.[6] When, to show their knightly breeding, the accomplished knights engaged in sports in the presence of the ladies, the hero of Netherland was always seen with pleasure. His whole striving was bent on noble love. He was ready for every game that was played, but he bore in his thoughts a lovely maid, whom he had never seen. And she, too, thought of him and in private often spoke kindly of him. When the youths, both knights and squires, played their knightly games in the courtyard, Kriemhild, the noble queen, often watched from the windows. During these times she needed no other entertainment. Had he known that she whom he bore in his heart was watching him, that would have been enjoyment enough for him. And if his eyes had seen her, I am sure nothing sweeter could have happened to him in this world.

Whenever he stood in the court among the warriors, as people still do today to pass the time, Siegelind's son bore himself so charmingly that many a maiden's heart was filled with yearning for him.

Often he thought, "How shall it come to pass that I can see the noble maid with my own eyes? She whom I love with all my heart and have loved for a long time is still a stranger to me, and so I remain sad."

Whenever the kings rode out into their land, all the warriors had to accompany them, and Siegfried likewise. This grieved Lady Kriemhild, and he also, for love of her, often suffered distress. Thus he lived with the lords in Gunther's land—this, I assure you, is true—for an entire year without once seeing, in all this time,

---

[6] These were popular sports of the age of chivalry. They are also significant here as an anticipation of Siegfried's later role in the wooing of Brunhild.

the lovely maid from whom much joy was to come to him, and much sorrow too.

IV

How He Fought with the Saxons

Strange news now approached Gunther's land, brought by envoys who had been sent to the Burgundians from far away by warriors they did not know but who bore them hate. When they heard the message, they were greatly dismayed.

I will tell you their names. They were Liudeger, a mighty prince from the land of the Saxons, and King Liudegast of Denmark. They took with them on their campaign many an excellent fighter.

The envoys had arrived in Gunther's land, sent there by his enemies, and people asked the strangers what message they brought and bade them to go quickly to court to see the king.

He greeted them kindly and said, "You are welcome. Tell me who sent you here. I have not been informed of this."

Thus the king spoke, but they were much afraid of his anger. "If you will permit us, O King, to give you the message we bring, we will not be silent but will name you the lords who sent us here —Liudegast and Liudeger. They intend to invade your land. You have earned their wrath. In fact, we have been told that both rulers bear you great hate. They plan to march against Worms on the Rhine, and many warriors will aid them—of this we assure you. Within twelve weeks the campaign will take place. If you have good friends who will help you protect your castles and your lands, you had better show this speedily, for many a helmet and shield will be slashed here by our lords. Or if you wish to negotiate with them, send them word, and the vast hosts of your powerful enemies will not ride so near to you to do you grievous injury from which many a good knight must lose his life."

"Wait for a while," said the king, "until I consider the matter further. Then I will announce my intention to you. If I have loyal friends, I shall not conceal this important news from them but shall make lament of it."

Deeply troubled, Gunther kept the message a secret in his heart. He summoned Hagen and others of his men and also sent for Gernot to come to court at once. Then came the most distinguished men, as many as could be found there.

"Our land is to be attacked by powerful armies," said Gunther. "Take this to heart."

Gernot made answer, "We'll prevent that with our swords. Only those destined for death will fall. Let them die—I can't forget my honor for their sake. Our enemies shall be welcome."

"I don't agree," said Hagen. "Liudegast and Liudeger are very arrogant. And we cannot summon all our men in such a short time. Why don't you tell Siegfried about it?"

Orders were given to quarter the messengers in the town. Gunther bade that they be well cared for, no matter how hostile one felt toward them—and this was well done—until he learned from his friends who among them would assist him. Yet with his fears the king was very troubled. Then a good knight,[1] who could not know what had happened, saw him grieving and asked the king to tell him about the matter.

"I am greatly surprised," said Siegfried, "at how you have changed the joyful manner that has long been your custom with us until now."

Gunther answered, "I cannot confide to everyone the sorrow I must bear secretly in my heart. Only to steadfast friends should one lament his heart's distress."

At this Siegfried's color turned first pale, then red, and he said to the king, "I have never refused you anything. I will help you ward off all your sorrows. If you are seeking friends, I shall be one of them and am certain of fulfilling this pledge with honor as long as I live."

"May God reward you, Lord Siegfried. Your words please me. And even if your prowess should never aid me, I am happy to hear that you are so friendly toward me. If I live a while longer, you will be rewarded for this. I will tell you why I am sad. I have heard from messengers of my enemies that they intend to make war on me. Never before did warriors do that to us in this land."

[1] Siegfried.

"Don't be concerned about it," said Siegfried. "Put your mind at ease and do as I request—let me win for you honor and profit, and command your men to come to your aid. Even if your mighty enemies had thirty thousand warriors to help them, I would withstand them if I had only a thousand. Rely on me for that."

"I shall always repay you with my service," said King Gunther.

"Then summon a thousand of your men, since I have only twelve of my own with me, and I will protect your land. Siegfried's[2] hand shall always serve you loyally. Hagen shall help us, and also your good warriors Ortwin, Dankwart, and Sindolt. And brave Volker shall ride along. He shall carry the banner. There's no one I'd rather entrust it to. Let the messengers ride home to their master's lands, and send word that they will see us soon so that our castles may be left in peace."

The king gave orders to summon both kinsmen and vassals. Liudeger's envoys now came to court. They were overjoyed that they were to return home. King Gunther offered them rich gifts and provided them with safe conduct. At this their spirits rose.

"Tell my enemies," said Gunther, "to give up their journey and remain at home. But if they insist on invading my lands, they will come to grief unless my friends desert me."

Costly gifts were brought out for the messengers. Of these Gunther had an abundance to give, and Liudeger's men dared not refuse them. When they had been dismissed, they went away happy.

Now when the envoys had arrived in Denmark and King Liudegast was told with what message they had come from the Rhine, he was extremely annoyed at the great arrogance of the Burgundians. The envoys reported that they had many valiant men and that among them they had seen a warrior called Siegfried, a hero from Netherland. Liudegast was not pleased to hear this news.

When the men of Denmark learned of it, they hastened to fetch even more of their friends, until at last Lord Liudegast had gathered twenty thousand of his brave warriors for his journey. King Liudeger of Saxony also summoned his men till they had forty thousand or more with whom they meant to ride to Burgundy.

Here at home likewise King Gunther had assembled his kinsmen and his brother's vassals, whom they intended to lead to battle, and also Hagen's men. Because of this, warriors were soon to

[2] This curious expression, a reference to oneself in the third person, occurs quite often in the *Nibelungenlied*.

meet their death. They prepared for the journey, and when they were ready to ride from Worms across the Rhine, bold Volker bore the banner, and Hagen of Troneg was marshal of the troop.[3] With them rode Sindolt and Hunolt, who knew well how to earn Gunther's gold, and Hagen's brother Dankwart and Ortwin, too, served with honor in the campaign.

"Sir King, remain here at home," said Siegfried, "since your warriors are willing to follow me. Stay with the ladies and have full confidence. I assure you, I will protect both your honor and possessions. I'll see to it that those who planned to attack you at Worms on the Rhine will have reason to stay at home. We'll ride into their land so close to them that their overbearing pride will turn to fear."

From the Rhine they rode with their warriors through Hesse toward Saxony, where battle later took place. With fire and pillage they so ravaged the land that both princes were deeply distressed when they were told of it.

They had now reached the border. The squires came marching along.

"Who shall take command of this following?" asked Siegfried.

"Have Dankwart protect the lads on the way," they said. "He is a valiant fighter. We'll lose all the less through Liudeger's men. Have him and Ortwin guard the rear." [4]

"Then I will ride myself," said Siegfried, "and reconnoiter until I discover where our enemies are."

He was soon armed, and when he was ready to leave, he placed the troops[5] in Hagen's and Gernot's charge. Then he rode alone into the Saxon land, and many a helmet strap did he sever that day. Soon he saw the mighty host that was encamped upon the plain and far outnumbered his own forces. There were forty thousand or even more. Siegfried, in high spirits, rejoiced at the sight.

There also a warrior, fully armed, had set out toward the enemy to reconnoiter. Lord Siegfried caught sight of him, and he saw Siegfried too. Each began to eye the other hostily. I will tell you who it was who was scouting there. He bore a bright shield of gold in his hand. It was King Liudegast, guarding his troops. The noble

---

[3] Siegfried is of course the commander in the campaign.

[4] When a battle was imminent, the squires remained behind, not taking part in the battle.

[5] The warriors, in contrast to the squires mentioned just before.

stranger[6] urged his horse toward him. Lord Liudegast had also watched him with enmity. Both now dug the spurs into their horses' flanks and couched their spears against the shields. At this the mighty king was seized with great fear. After the thrust the horses carried the princes past each other as if blown by the wind. Then in true knightly fashion, using the bridles, the two fierce men wheeled about and took a try with their swords. Lord Siegfried struck so hard that the whole plain resounded, and from the helmet flew flame-red sparks as if from mighty fires. Each had met his match in the other. Lord Liudegast, too, dealt Siegfried many a furious blow. The strength of both fell heavy on the shields.

Meanwhile thirty of Liudegast's men had ridden out on patrol, but before they could come to his aid, Siegfried gained the victory with three severe wounds which he dealt the king through his splendid, gleaming breastplate. Along both edges the sword drew blood from the wounds, and King Liudegast was sad at heart. He begged Siegfried to let him live and offered him his lands and told him his name was Liudegast.[7] His warriors now came up, having seen clearly what happened between the two on their scouting trip. As Siegfried was about to take Liudegast away, he was set upon by the thirty men, but he guarded his royal hostage with mighty blows. Then he did them even worse harm. In self-defense he killed the thirty warriors. He left only one alive, who speedily rode away and brought the news of what had happened there. The truth of his story could be seen by his reddened helmet. The men of Denmark were deeply grieved when they heard that their lord had been taken prisoner. His brother was told of it too, and he began to rage with a boundless wrath at the injury that had been done him.

Siegfried took Liudegast by force to Gunther's men and delivered him into Hagen's charge. When they were told it was the king, they were but moderately grieved. The Burgundians were ordered to tie on their pennants.[8]

"Up now," called Siegfried. "More shall be done here before the day ends, if I am still alive, and it will sadden many a woman in the Saxon land. Listen to me, warriors from the Rhine. I can guide you well to Liudeger's host, and you will see helmets slashed

---

[6] I.e., Siegfried.
[7] The loser in a combat gives his name as token of his surrender.
[8] This is the signal for the attack.

by the hands of good fighters. They'll learn what fear is before we return home."

Gernot and his men hastened to their horses. At once Lord Volker, the stalwart minstrel, seized the banner and rode at the head of the troops. The whole army was splendidly equipped for battle. Yet they had no more than a thousand men, and Siegfried's twelve warriors besides. Clouds of dust rose up from the roads as they galloped across the land. Many a fine shield could be seen glittering from their ranks.

The Saxon troops had also come up, with well-sharpened swords, as I have since been told, that cut fearfully in the warriors' hands. They meant to defend castles and land against the strangers. Marshals of the two rulers led the troops forward.

Now Siegfried came up with his men whom he had brought from Netherland. Many hands were bloodied that day in battle. Sindolt and Hunolt, and Gernot as well, struck many a warrior dead in combat before he actually realized how courageous they were. Noble ladies later wept over this. Volker and Hagen, and Ortwin too, these battle-bold men, dulled with streaming blood the gleam of many a helmet. And Dankwart performed marvelous deeds.

The men of Denmark put their hands to the test, and shields were heard resounding from the hurtling clash and from the sharp swords wielded there. The daring Saxons did damage enough in the fray. As the Burgundians pressed forward to the fight, they hewed many a gaping wound, and blood flowed across the saddles. Thus the brave knights strove for honor. Their keen-edged weapons ringing loudly in their hands, the men of Netherland pushed through the mighty host to follow their lord. Valiantly they made their way with Siegfried, but not one of the men from the Rhine was able to keep up with him. Bloody streams were seen pouring through the bright helmets from the strength of Siegfried's hand before he came upon Liudeger at the head of his battle comrades. Three times he had fought his way through the host from end to end. Now Hagen appeared and helped him to satisfy his thirst for strife. Many excellent knights were to die at their hands that day.

When the mighty Liudeger caught sight of Siegfried and saw that he held the good sword Balmung high in his hand and was killing so many of the Saxons, he became fiercely angry. There was a great press and loud clang of swords as their followers thrust against each other. The two warriors now tried their mettle on one another. The troops gave way for them, and a savage combat began. The ruler of the Saxons had been told that his brother was a prisoner, and he was deeply grieved. He did not know[9] that Siegelind's son had done it. People had blamed Gernot, but he later learned the truth. Liudeger's blows were so powerful that Siegfried's war horse staggered beneath the saddle. When the horse had recovered, Siegfried turned furiously to the attack. Hagen and Gernot helped him well, and Dankwart and Volker too. Many a man fell at their hands. And Sindolt, Hunolt, and Ortwin struck down many in the struggle. The princes remained unseparated in the battle. Hurled by warriors' hands, spears flew above helmets right through the bright shields, many of which were stained with blood. Many men dismounted from their horses during the violent battle,[10] and Siegfried and Liudeger also rushed at one another. Then off flew the shield plates from the force of Siegfried's blow. He thought to win the victory over the valiant Saxons, many of whom were wounded. Oh, how many shining armor rings the bold Dankwart broke! Now Lord Liudeger recognized a crown painted on the shield in Siegfried's hand and knew who this mighty warrior was.

He began to call out loudly to his friends, "Cease your fighting, all my vassals. I have seen Siegmund's son here. I have recognized the powerful Siegfried. The wicked devil sent him here to Saxony."

He bade the banners be lowered and asked for peace. It was then granted him, but he had to become a hostage to Gunther's land. To this Siegfried had compelled him. By mutual agreement they put an end to the battle and laid aside their riddled helmets and their broad, battered shields, all of them red with blood. The Burgundians took prisoner whomever they wished, for they had the power. Gernot and Hagen gave orders for the wounded to be placed on stretchers. Five hundred knights they took with them as prisoners to the Rhine. The defeated warriors now rode back to Denmark.[11] Nor had the Saxons fought so well that one could give

[9] All the manuscripts have *wol wesser,* "he knew well," but the *wol* is undoubtedly wrong. Liudeger does not know at this point that Siegfried had captured his brother, nor does he even recognize Siegfried until later.

[10] In order to continue fighting on foot.

[11] Except for the prisoners and the wounded, the opposing armies are allowed to return home.

them any praise, and they were downcast. The dead were greatly mourned by their friends.

The Burgundians had their arms loaded on pack horses for the journey to the Rhine. Siegfried and his men had acquitted themselves well, and *he* had distinguished himself. This all Gunther's warriors admitted. Lord Gernot sent messengers to Worms to tell his friends how successful he and his men had been and how the brave knights had fought as honor demanded.

The squires made haste and told the news. Those who had earlier been troubled, now exulted for joy at the welcome tidings that had reached them. Many questions were heard from noble ladies as to how the king's vassals had fared.

One of the messengers was now sent to Kriemhild. This was done in great secrecy; she did not dare do it openly, for she had among the warriors her own heart's beloved.

As she saw the envoy come into her chamber, she said graciously, "Now tell me good news, and I will give you my gold. If you do this without deceit, I will always be friendly to you. How did my brother Gernot and my other kinsmen come out of the battle? Are many of our men dead? Who performed best? Tell me."

Quickly the messenger answered, "We did not have a single coward, but no one rode so well in the battle, noble Queen, since you wish me to tell you, as the distinguished stranger from Netherland. Siegfried did great marvels. Whatever all the warriors achieved in the battle, Dankwart and Hagen and others of the king's vassals, however gloriously they fought—this is as nothing compared with Siegfried alone, King Siegmund's son. They killed many warriors, but no one could tell you the marvelous deeds that Siegfried performed whenever he rode into the fight. He brought ladies grievous sorrow through their kin, and many a lady's lover fell there. You could hear his blows ringing so loudly on the helmets that they drew blood streaming from the wounds. He is a brave and worthy knight, possessed of every noble quality. Whatever deeds Ortwin of Metz did there—and everyone he could reach with his sword fell sorely wounded, most of them dead—it was your brother who wrought the greatest injury that could ever be done in battle. In all truth one must say of these excellent warriors—the proud Burgundians acquitted themselves so as to preserve their honor from any disgrace. You could see many a saddle empty before their hands, while the plain resounded loudly with the flashing swords.

The warriors from the Rhine rode so well that their enemies would have done better to avoid the conflict. The brave men of Troneg inflicted tremendous damage when the massed forces of the two armies met. Bold Hagen killed many a warrior. Much could be told of this here in Burgundy. Sindolt and Hunolt and the daring Rumolt did such deeds that Liudeger will always have reason to regret that he declared war on your kinsmen on the Rhine. But the very best fighting that was done there anywhere, from beginning to end, the best you ever saw, was done most willingly by Siegfried's hand. He is bringing mighty hostages to Gunther's realm. With his own strength he vanquished them, and because of this King Liudegast must suffer, and his brother Liudeger from Saxony as well. Now listen to my story, noble Queen. Siegfried captured both of them. Never were so many hostages brought to this land as are now coming to the Rhine through his doing."

This news could not have pleased her more.

"They are bringing to our land five hundred prisoners or more, uninjured, and not less than eighty blood-red stretchers with the severely wounded. Most of these Siegfried's hand struck down. Those who out of arrogance sent a declaration of war to the Rhine must now be Gunther's captives. They are being brought here in triumph to this land."

Kriemhild's radiant coloring blossomed. Her lovely face turned rose-red as she heard how Siegfried had so luckily escaped from the grave peril. She rejoiced too for her kinsmen, as was fitting.

Then the fair maiden said, "You have given me good news, and you shall have as reward rich attire and ten marks[12] of gold. I'll order them brought for you."

For such compensation a messenger is glad to bring noble ladies good news. He was given his reward, the garments and the gold. Then many a maid went to the windows to look out upon the road, where a host of high-spirited knights could be seen riding into the Burgundian land. There came the warriors, the wounded as well as the sound. They had no need to be ashamed on hearing greetings from their friends.

The host rode out jubilantly to meet his guests. His great fears had ended in joy. Cordially he greeted his vassals and the strangers, too, for no other behavior befitted the mighty king than to

[12] A mark was half a pound of gold or silver.

give warm thanks to those who had come to his aid and had won with honor the victory in the battle. Gunther asked his kinsmen which of his men had been killed in the campaign. He had lost only sixty, and to this they had to be reconciled, just as one must today when warriors die. Even those who were uninjured brought back to Gunther's land many a battered shield and riven helmet. They dismounted before the king's hall, and the happy tumult of a joyous welcome could be heard.

The command was given to lodge the warriors in the town. The king bade that his guests be well tended, the wounded cared for and provided with comfortable quarters. His knightly courtesy was clearly to be seen in the treatment of his foes.

"Welcome," he said to Liudegast. "Because of you I have suffered severe loss. For this I shall now be compensated, if fortune continues to favor me. May God reward my friends, for they have done me good service."

"You have every reason to thank them," said Liudeger, "for never did a king win such noble hostages. We will give you great wealth in return for good treatment and we ask you to act graciously toward your enemies."

"I will allow you both to go about freely," said Gunther, "but I must have surety that my enemies will remain here with me and not leave my land without permission."

To this Liudeger gave his hand as pledge. They were now taken to their lodgings and provided with every comfort. Good beds were prepared for the wounded, and mead and fine wine were served to those who were unharmed. The warriors could not have been in better spirits. Their battered shields were carried away for safekeeping, and the bloody saddles were hidden so that the ladies might not weep. Many a good knight had returned weary from the march. The king tended his guests most assiduously. The land was full of strangers and his own vassals. He ordered that the seriously wounded be nursed very carefully. Their overweening pride was now laid low. Rich reward was offered to those who practiced medicine, unweighed silver[13] and shiny gold, if they would heal the warriors after the stress of battle. Moreover, the king gave the strangers generous gifts. Those who wished to return home were urged to stay, as one does with friends. The king now took counsel

[13] The giving of unweighed silver or gold was an indication of extreme generosity.

as to how he should reward his men, for they had fulfilled his desire
with all honor.

"Let them ride away," said Lord Gernot. "Announce to them
that in six weeks they are to return for a festival. Then many who
are now in bed, badly wounded, will be healed."

Siegfried also asked permission to leave, but when King Gun-
t'er learned his wish, he urged him warmly to stay. Had it not
been for the king's sister, Siegfried would not have done it. He was
too rich to accept any reward, yet he had well deserved the king's
friendship. Gunther's kinsmen liked him too, for they had seen
what had been accomplished in the battle by his strength. For the
fair maiden's sake Siegfried decided to remain, in the hope of seeing her. This soon came about, and according to his desire, he
learned to know the maid. Later he rode back joyfully to Siegmund's land.

The host ordered knightly sports to be practiced every day, and
many a young warrior complied willingly. And he bade seats be
set up on the sandy shore before Worms for the guests who were
to visit him in Burgundy. At the time when they were to come,
Kriemhild heard that the king intended to hold a festival for his
dear friends. Then lovely ladies busily prepared garments and
headdresses that they were to wear. The noble Ute was also told
of the proud warriors who were expected, and many splendid
gowns were taken from their wrappings. For the sake of her sons
she bade garments made ready with which to adorn many a lady
and maid and many a young knight of the Burgundian land. And
for many of the strangers also she had rich attire prepared.

V

How Siegfried First Saw Kriemhild

Now every day knights were seen riding to the Rhine who wanted
to be present at the celebration. To many of those who came to the
land for the sake of the king, horses were given and sumptuous

apparel. Seats were prepared for them all, and for the noblest and most distinguished guests, so we have been told, the two and thirty princes there for the festival. The beautiful ladies bedecked themselves in anticipation, vying with each other.

The youth Giselher was anything but idle. He and Gernot and their vassals welcomed warmly strangers and friends, greeting them with due ceremony. These warriors brought with them many saddles adorned with red gold, magnificent shields, and splendid attire to the festival on the Rhine. Many a wounded man now appeared there, joyful once more. Even those who lay in their beds suffering the torture of wounds came to forget how bitter death is. People ceased to mourn for the sick and rejoiced at the prospect of festive days and how well they would fare at the feasting. Delight without limit and overabundance of joy would be the lot of everyone. Thus great jubilation arose throughout all of Gunther's land.

On a Whitsuntide morning[1] many men were seen going forth to the festival, five thousand or more, splendidly arrayed, and everywhere knightly games of rivalry commenced.

The host was discerning enough to know how fondly, though he had never seen her, the hero of Netherland loved his sister, whose great beauty, everyone said, surpassed that of all other maidens.

Ortwin now said to the king, "If the honor you gain by this festival is to be complete, you must allow the charming maids to appear, who are the great glory of Burgundy. What would be man's delight, what could give him pleasure, if not lovely maidens and noble ladies? Let your sister appear before your guests." This counsel met the approval of many a warrior.

"I will gladly follow your advice," said the king, and all who heard this rejoiced.

He sent a message to Lady Ute and her daughter that they should come with their maidens to court. Then fine garments were fetched from the coffers, all the choice apparel that had been stored away. Bracelets and galloons in abundance lay ready, and the maidens adorned themselves eagerly.

Many a novice knight had such hopes on that day of appearing to advantage before the ladies that he would not have exchanged this chance for a rich king's land. And the young knights took

---

[1] This is also the favorite time for festivals in the Arthurian romances.

great pleasure in gazing on these ladies whom they had not known till now.

Then the king bade a hundred of his men, his and his sister's kinsmen, to escort Kriemhild, sword in hand, and put themselves at her service. These were the courtiers of the Burgundian land. Lady Ute was seen coming with her; she had as companions beautiful ladies, fully a hundred or more, wearing rich robes. And many fair maidens also followed in her daughter's train. As they left the ladies' apartments, the knights surged forward, hoping, for their own delight, to catch sight of the noble princess if that were possible.

Now came the lovely maiden, like the red of dawn appearing from out of murky clouds, and he who bore her in his heart, as he had done for so long, was delivered from great torment when he saw her standing there in all her splendor. From her gown flashed many a precious stone, and her rose-red coloring glowed with a charming radiance. Even had anyone wished to, he could not have said he had ever in this world seen anything more beautiful. As the bright moon outshines the stars, when its brilliant gleam pierces through the clouds, so she now outshone many a fine lady. This enchanting sight rejoiced the heroes' hearts. Stately chamberlains preceded her, but the warriors in high spirits never ceased pressing forward to catch a glimpse of her.

Lord Siegfried felt both joy and sadness, and to himself he thought, "How would it ever be possible for me to win your love? That is an idle hope. Yet if I must remain a stranger to you, I would rather be dead."

At these thoughts he paled and blushed by turns. Siegmund's son stood there as winsomely as if he were painted on parchment with the skill of a great master; and indeed everybody declared that no one had ever seen such a handsome man.

Those escorting the ladies ordered the way to be cleared on all sides, and the warriors obeyed. Many a man's heart thrilled for joy, as with perfect decorum the ladies passed by.

Then Lord Gernot said, "Gunther, dear brother, you should make recompense before all these warriors to him who so kindly offered you his service. Of this counsel I shall never be ashamed. Bid Siegfried approach my sister so that the maid may greet him. This will profit us. She who has never greeted a warrior shall now greet him, and by this means we'll secure the good knight for us."

The host's kinsmen now went to find Siegfried and said, "The king has given you permission to come to court. His sister shall give you greeting. This is done as an honor to you."

The young nobleman was pleased, and in his heart he bore joy without sorrow that he was to see fair Ute's child. With charming propriety she greeted the proud warrior, but when she looked full at him as he stood there before her, his color flamed.

"Welcome, Lord Siegfried, good and noble knight," said the maid.

At this greeting his spirits rose, and he fervently bowed his thanks. She took him by the hand, and how gallantly he walked by the lady's side! With fond glances they looked at each other, the lord and the lady, though very covertly. Was a white hand pressed ardently out of heartfelt love? I do not know. Yet I cannot believe it was not, for she had very quickly revealed her liking for him. Never again in the summertime, around the days of May, was he to hold such high rapture in his heart as he felt now when she whom he wished to call his love walked with him hand in hand.

Many a warrior thought, "Oh, if only the same thing had happened to me, to walk beside her, as I have seen him do, or perhaps to lie with her! To that I would not be averse."

Never did a warrior serve better to win a queen. From whatever kingdom the guests had come, they had eyes only for these two. She was now permitted to kiss the excellent knight, who had never in all the world met with anything so sweet.

Then the king of Denmark said, "Because of this solemn greeting many men lie wounded by Siegfried's hand—this I have experienced myself. May God grant that he never come to my lands again!"

The order was given to yield the way for Kriemhild, and many warriors were seen escorting her decorously to church. Soon Siegfried was parted from her,[2] and she entered the minster, followed by her ladies. So beautifully was she attired that many an aspiring wish was nursed in vain. She was born to delight warriors' eyes. Siegfried could scarcely wait for the mass to be sung. He might indeed thank his good fortune that she whom he cherished in his heart had such regard for him, and he, too, held her dear, as she well deserved. When she left the minster, he was already outside

---

[2] Knights and ladies sat separately in church.

and was invited to join her again. Now the maid thanked him with all her heart for fighting so splendidly at the vanguard of her kinsmen.

"May God reward you, Lord Siegfried," she said, "for having earned the loyalty and true devotion of the warriors, as I hear them say."

He glanced tenderly at Kriemhild and answered, "I shall always serve them and will never lay my head to rest, so long as I live, till I have done their will. This I do, my Lady Kriemhild, to win your favor."

For twelve days, on each and every day, one saw the girl and the warrior together whenever she went to court to meet her kinsmen. Because of their great affection for him this distinction was granted.

Day after day nothing but joy and delight were seen before Gunther's hall, and outside and in could be heard the festive tumult of many valiant men. Ortwin and Hagen performed marvelous deeds, and whatever sport was chosen, they were always ready to join in with abandon. Thus they became well known among the guests, and Gunther's whole land gained honor thereby. Those who had lain wounded were now seen coming forth. They wanted to join the company in the knightly games, hold their shields before them, and shoot their shafts. They had plenty to help them, for knights were there in great numbers.

During the festival time the host bade the best of food be served and kept himself free of any reproach that a king might meet. One could see him moving about graciously among his guests.

And he said to them, "Good warriors, before you depart, accept my gifts. I wish always to be of service to you. Do not disdain my possessions. I am most willing to share them with you."

The men of Denmark spoke up immediately, "Before we ride home again to our land, we would like a lasting peace. This we need, for we have lost many dear kinsmen at the hands of your warriors."

Liudegast was healed of his wounds, and the lord of the Saxons had recovered from the battle, but they left many dead behind them in this land.

King Gunther now went to Siegfried and said, "Advise me what to do. Our enemies wish to leave early tomorrow, and they desire lasting peace with me and my vassals. Now counsel me, warrior

Siegfried, what you think wise in this matter. I will tell you what the lords offer. If I set them free, they would be ready to give me as much gold as five hundred pack horses can carry."

"That would be ill done," said Siegfried. "Let them go without ransom, but have the two lords give you their word and their hand-clasp as pledge that henceforth they will refrain from any invasion of your land."

"I will follow your counsel."

With this they walked away, and Gunther's foes were informed that no one wished the gold they had offered. At home their dear friends were longing for the battle-weary men.

Many shields full of treasure were brought, and Gunther portioned it out in abundance, unweighed, to his friends, about five hundred marks, and to many he gave even more. This was what Gernot had advised him to do. Now wishing to depart, the guests all took their leave and were seen going to Kriemhild and to where Lady Ute, the queen, was seated. No warriors were ever given a finer farewell. The lodgings were emptied as they rode away, yet in royal splendor the king remained there at home with his kinsmen. And every day they went to Lady Kriemhild.

Siegfried now also wanted to depart, for he despaired of winning what his mind was set upon. The king heard of his intention, but then young Giselher dissuaded him from the journey.

"Where are you going, noble Siegfried? Do as I ask and remain with the warriors, with Gunther, the king, and his vassals. There are many beautiful ladies here whom we'll gladly let you see."

Then Siegfried said, "Let the horses stay where they are. I meant to leave, but I'll give it up. And take the shields away. I intended to go to my land, but Lord Giselher with his great friendship has turned me from this purpose."

So Siegfried remained there to please his friends. In no other land would he have been so contented, the reason being that he now saw the lovely Kriemhild every day. He stayed for the sake of her surpassing beauty. With many a pastime they whiled away the hours; yet love of her oppressed him and often caused him grief. For this same love the brave man was to die a wretched death.

VI

How Gunther Went to Isenland to Woo Brunhild

Fresh tidings came over the Rhine. Tales were told of the many fair maidens yonder, and King Gunther was of a mind to win one for himself. This thought filled his heart with joy.

A queen lived across the sea whose like was not known anywhere. She was beautiful beyond measure, and her strength was exceedingly great. With sturdy warriors she shot the shaft; her love was the prize. She hurled the stone afar and leaped a great distance after it. Whoever desired her love had to win three games from her without fail. If he lost in one, he forfeited his head. This had happened many a time, when one day it reached the ears of a handsome knight [1] on the Rhine, who fixed his desire on the lovely lady. For this heroes later lost their lives.

The lord of the Rhine said, "I want to go down to the sea to Brunhild, however I may fare. I'll risk my life for the sake of her love, and lose it if she does not become my wife."

"I would advise against it," said Siegfried. "The queen is so cruel that whoever courts her love pays for it dearly. For this reason you should forgo the journey."

"*I* would advise you," spoke up Hagen, "to ask Siegfried to share the heavy burden with you. This is *my* counsel, since he knows so much about Brunhild."

"Will you help me, noble Siegfried," said Gunther, "to woo the fair maid? If you do what I ask of you and if she becomes my beloved, I will hazard for your sake my honor and my life."

Siegfried answered, "If you give me your sister, the lovely Kriemhild, I will do it and ask no other reward for my labors."

"That I promise, Siegfried," said Gunther, "with my handclasp

---

[1] Gunther, of course.

as pledge. If Brunhild comes here to this land, I will give you my sister as wife, and you can live happily with her ever after."

To this the warriors swore an oath. And now their troubles were greatly increased till at last they brought the lady to the Rhine. And because of this undertaking the valiant men were later in grave peril.

They made ready for the trip. Siegfried took with him the magic cloak which he had acquired at great risk from the dwarf called Alberich. When he wore it he had strength enough, the might of twelve men besides his own. With great cunning he won the proud maid. This cloak was of such a nature that any person wearing it could do what he liked without being seen by anyone. Thus he won Brunhild, which was to cause him great suffering.

"Now tell me, Siegfried, before my journey begins, shall we take warriors with us into Brunhild's land so that we may go to the sea in full honor? Thirty thousand men can be summoned immediately."

"However large a host we might take," answered Siegfried, "the queen is so fierce that they would die in any case through her arrogance. I'll give you better counsel. Let us go down the Rhine valley as wandering fighters. Four warriors in all, we'll go to the sea, and I will tell you who they shall be. Thus we will win the lady, whatever may happen to us afterward. I shall be one of the comrades, and you the second. The third shall be Hagen—then we can hope to come out alive—and the fourth shall be the valiant Dankwart. A thousand others would never dare to withstand us in combat."

"I would like to know before we leave," said the king, "what kind of clothing would be proper for us in Brunhild's presence. Inform Gunther about this."

"The very best apparel that was ever seen is worn at all times in Brunhild's land. We must wear rich garments in the lady's presence so that we shall not be disgraced when people tell about us."

"Then I will go myself to my dear mother," said Gunther, "to see if I can prevail upon her to have her maidens help prepare clothing for us which we may wear with honor before the proud Brunhild."

Hagen of Troneg spoke up imperiously, "Why do you want to ask your mother for such services? Let your sister know of your intention, and she will serve you well for this journey to court."

Gunther sent word to his sister that he and Siegfried wished to visit her. Before receiving them, the maid arrayed herself to perfection. The coming of the valiant men was not displeasing to her. And her attendants too were adorned as befit them. When she was told the two princes had arrived, she rose from her seat and went courteously to greet her brother and the guest.

"Welcome, my brother, and your companion as well," said the maiden. "I would like to know what you desire, that you now come to my court. Tell me how I may be of service to you noble warriors."

Then King Gunther said, "Lady, I will tell you. We are very much concerned, in spite of our happiness. We want to go courting afar to foreign lands and would like to have fine garments for the journey."

"Sit down, dear brother," she said, "and tell me exactly who these ladies are whom you desire to court in the lands of other kings."

She took them by the hand and went with them to where she had sat before. They seated themselves on sumptuous couches, wrought, I assure you, with fine designs embossed in gold. Here they could nicely while away the time with the ladies. Many a fond glance and kind look passed between the two.[2] He bore her in his heart, and she was as dear to him as his own life. Later the lovely Kriemhild became mighty Siegfried's wife.

Then the king said, "My dear sister, without your help we cannot carry out our plan. We want to seek knightly adventure in Brunhild's land, and we need rich attire to wear in the presence of ladies."

"My dear brother," answered the maiden, "I shall convince you that I am ready to give you whatever help I can. It would grieve Kriemhild if anyone refused you. Noble Knight, you need not ask me timidly. Command me as my lord. I am ready and willing to do anything that would please you."

"Dear sister, we wish to wear fine garments, and these you shall help to prepare. Have your maidens make them to fit us properly, for we cannot give up this journey."

---

[2] I.e., Siegfried and Kriemhild.

"Now pay attention to what I say," she replied. "Silks I have myself. See to it that precious stones are brought to us on shields, and we will make the garments."

Gunther and Siegfried agreed to this.

"Who are the comrades," she asked, "who will appear with you in courtly dress?"

"I shall be one of four," answered Gunther. "My two vassals Dankwart and Hagen will go with me to court. Mark well what I say to you, Lady. We four need for each of four whole days three changes of apparel, clothing so splendid that we may quit Brunhild's land without disgrace."

She bade the knights a gracious farewell, and they took their leave. Then she summoned from their chamber thirty of her maidens who had a great gift for such work. Into Arabian silks, white as snow, and fine silks from Zazamanc,[3] green as clover, they set precious stones, and from these fabrics fashioned sumptuous robes. Kriemhild herself cut them out. As many handsome linings as they could get, from the skins of foreign fish,[4] rarely seen there, they covered with silks, for thus they were meant to be worn. Now hear great wonders concerning this lustrous attire. From the land of Morocco and from Libya too, they had an abundance of the very best silks any king's kinsman had ever acquired. Kriemhild did indeed show plainly that she was well disposed toward the knights. Since the proud journey was now their desire, she thought ermine furs not fine enough and covered them with pfellel silk, black as coal, which would still today be fitting for valiant heroes at festival times. Many precious stones sparkled from their settings of Arabian gold. The ladies' labor was not slight; within seven weeks they finished the garments. And at the same time the warriors' weapons were in order.

When they were equipped, there was built for them on the Rhine with unsparing toil a sturdy little ship which was to carry them right down to the sea. The maidens were exhausted from their exertions. Then the warriors were told that the garments they were to wear

---

[3] A fictitious land, mentioned only here and a few times in Wolfram's *Parzival*.

[4] In the Middle Ages the word "fish" was a much broader term than it is today; it included, for example, the otter and the beaver. Furs and fish skins were often used as linings and covered, as described here, with silk or other cloth.

were ready for them, just as they had wished. Now that everything was completed, they did not want to linger longer by the Rhine. A messenger came to the comrades to ask if they wished to look at their new clothing to see if it were too short or too long. It fitted precisely, and for this they thanked the ladies. All who saw them had to admit they had never seen better garments anywhere. They could rightly take pleasure in wearing them at court and did not fail to give generous thanks. Then with knightly courtesy they begged leave to go. Bright eyes now grew dim and moist from weeping.

"Dear brother," said Kriemhild, "you had better remain here and pay court to other ladies, where your life would not hang in the balance—that I would call well done. You could find nearer home a wife just as highly born."

I think their hearts told them what would come of this. All wept alike, no matter what anyone said, and the gold upon their breasts was tarnished from the tears that poured down in streams from their eyes.

"Lord Siegfried," she said, "I commend my dear brother to you, to your loyalty and good will, that nothing may harm him in Brunhild's land."

This the brave hero pledged in Lady Kriemhild's hand and said, "If I remain alive, Lady, you shall be free of all care. I'll bring him back to the Rhine unharmed, be assured of that."

She bowed to him in gratitude.

Their gold-colored shields were carried out to the sandy shore, and all their armor was brought them. Orders were given to lead up their horses, for they were ready to ride away. Beautiful ladies now wept profusely, and at the windows stood the charming maids. A high wind stirred their ship with its sail, and the warrior comrades embarked upon the Rhine.

Then King Gunther said, "Who shall be the ship's captain?"

"I will," said Siegfried. "I can steer you well on the flood, you may be sure. The right waterways are very familiar to me."

So with light hearts they left the Burgundian land. Siegfried quickly seized a pole and began to push away from the shore, and Gunther himself took an oar. Thus the brave knights set forth from land. They took with them choice food and excellent wine, the best to be found along the Rhine. Their horses stood in comfort and could rest well. Their ship moved very smoothly, so that they had no discomfort. They stretched the stout sheet-ropes taut and sailed twenty miles with a good wind down toward the sea before it became night. This arduous enterprise later brought them grief.

On the twelfth morning, so we are told, the winds had borne them far away to Isenstein in Brunhild's land, which was known to none of them except Siegfried.

When King Gunther saw so many castles and the broad domains as well, he quickly asked, "Tell me, friend Siegfried, do you know to whom these castles and this splendid land belong?"

"I know very well," answered Siegfried. "People and land are Brunhild's, and the fortress is Isenstein, of which you have heard me speak. There you can see today many beautiful ladies. And I want to give you warriors some advice—come to an agreement on what you intend to say. This would be to the good, I'm sure. For if we appear today before Brunhild, the queen, we shall have reason to be apprehensive in her presence. When we see her with her retinue, you must all say this one thing: that Gunther is my liege lord and I am his man. Then what he hopes will all come true."

They were ready for whatever he bade them vow, and no one of them failed, through arrogance, to speak as Siegfried had asked. Hence they fared well when King Gunther met Brunhild.

"I pledge this[5] not so much to oblige you as for the sake of your sister, the lovely maid. She is to me as my soul and as my own body, and I will do anything to deserve that she become my wife."

[5] Siegfried is speaking, and the pledge refers to the assurance he has just given that Gunther's desires will be fulfilled.

VII

How Gunther Won Brunhild

Meanwhile their ship had come so close to the castle that the king saw many beautiful maidens standing above at the windows and was vexed that he did not know any of them.

He asked his comrade Siegfried, "Do you know anything about the maidens there, looking down at us on the water? Whoever their lord may be, they have a noble air."

"Observe the maidens secretly," said Lord Siegfried, "and tell me then which you would like to have if it were in your power."

"I will," said Gunther. "In that window there I see one of them, dressed in snowy white. She is so fair that my eyes choose her for her beauty. If I had the power, she would become my wife."

"The light of your eyes has chosen quite rightly for you. That is the noble Brunhild, for whom your heart strives, your mind, and your desire."

All her bearing seemed to Gunther good. Then the queen bade her maidens step away from the windows and not stand there for the strangers to stare at. They obeyed her, and we have since been told what they did next. As has always been the way of fair maidens, they adorned themselves for the meeting with the strangers. Then they went to the narrow embrasures, where they gazed curiously at the heroes.

There were only four who entered the land. Through the window slits the ladies saw how Siegfried led a horse onto the shore,[1] and at this King Gunther felt his honor enhanced.[2] Siegfried held it by the bridle, the magnificent battle horse, excellent and handsome, and very large and strong, until Gunther had seated himself in the sad-

---

[1] Siegfried leads Gunther's horse off the ship in order to make it appear obvious that he is Gunther's vassal.

[2] So important was it to Gunther that the ladies were observing this service of Siegfried's, a symbol of Gunther's importance.

dle. Thus Siegfried served him, which the king later quite forgot. Then he led his own horse from the ship. Never had he done such service before, standing at any man's stirrup. The ladies watched this through the windows.

Well matched and just alike, of snow-white hue, were the horses and garments of these valiant heroes,[3] and their handsome shields gleamed in their hands. Proudly they rode up before Brunhild's hall, their saddles set with precious stones, the horses' breast straps narrow, with bells dangling from them of bright and ruddy gold. They arrived in this land as their valor bade them, with spears freshly sharpened and well-fashioned swords, keen-edged and also broad, which hung down to their spurs. All this Brunhild saw.

Dankwart and Hagen came with them. These warriors—so we heard the tale—had rich clothing of raven-black hue, and their shields were large and shiny, solid and broad. They wore precious stones from the land of India which blazed brilliantly as they moved. They had left their little ship unguarded by the water.

Thus they rode to the castle. Six and eighty towers they saw within, three vast palaces, and a stately hall of costly marble green as grass, in which Brunhild herself sat with her retinue. The castle was open and the gates flung wide. Brunhild's men ran to meet them and welcomed the strangers into their lady's land. Orders were given to put up their horses and take the shields from their hands.

A chamberlain said, "Give us your swords and your shining breastplates, too."

"This we refuse to do," said Hagen of Troneg. "We intend to keep them on."

Then Siegfried explained to him what was here considered proper. "It is the custom in this castle that no guests are allowed to bear arms. It would be best to let them be taken away."

Reluctantly Hagen obeyed. Now wine was poured for the guests and lodging prepared for them. From all sides warriors[4] were seen coming to court in princely attire, and many an eye was turned toward the strangers.

Then Lady Brunhild was told that unknown warriors in sumptuous attire had come sailing on the waters, and she began to ask about this.

[3] I.e., Gunther and Siegfried.
[4] I.e., Brunhild's men.

"Tell me," said the queen, "who these unknown warriors are that stand so proudly in my castle. And why have they come here?"

"Lady," said one of her vassals, "I can say with certainty that I have never seen any of them before, but one resembling Siegfried is among them. Receive him well. This is my loyal counsel. The second of the comrades is so distinguished that if he had the power and could possess them, he might well be a mighty ruler over broad and princely lands. You can see him standing there near the others with a lordly air. The third of the comrades is terrifying—yet handsome of person, noble Queen—because of the fierce glances he so often casts. I would imagine he is savage in spirit and temper. The youngest among them merits praise. He stands there so charmingly, with a maidenly courtesy and excellent bearing. Yet we might all have cause for fear, had anyone here done him harm, for however courteously he may practice chivalry and however pleasing he may be of person, he could bring many a woman to tears if he should grow angry. To judge from his appearance, with all his gentle breeding he is a warrior both bold and brave."

Then the queen said, "Bring me my ceremonial robes. If the mighty Siegfried has come into this land to win my love, he risks his life. I am not so afraid of him as to become his wife." [5]

Brunhild was soon richly dressed, and with her came many maidens, beautifully adorned, a hundred at least, eager to see the strangers. Warriors from Isenland escorted them, Brunhild's men-at-arms, five hundred or more. They carried swords in their hands, which disturbed the strangers. Now the valiant heroes rose from their seats.

When the queen caught sight of Siegfried—listen to what she said, "Welcome, Siegfried, to this land. What is the meaning of your journey? That I would like to know."

"You do me too great honor, my Lady Brunhild, gracious Queen, that you deign to greet me first before this noble warrior who stands here in front of me,[6] for he is my liege lord. This honor I gladly forswear. By birth he is from the Rhine; what more need I say? For the sake of your love we have come here. He intends to woo you, whatever may befall him. Now weigh this well, while there is still time, for my lord will not renounce you. Gunther is his name, and he is an illustrious king. If he won your love, he would

---

[5] I.e., willingly, without combat.
[6] Siegfried, posing as Gunther's vassal, quite properly stands behind him.

desire nothing more. It was at his bidding that I made this journey. I would gladly have forgone it if I could have refused."

"If he is your lord," she said, "and you are his man, and if he ventures to undertake the contests I propose to him and gains the mastery, then I will become his wife. But if I win, you shall all lose your lives."

Then Hagen of Troneg said, "Lady, let us see your hazardous games. Things would have to be very bad before Gunther, my lord, would concede you the victory. He is confident of winning so fair a maid as you."

"He must throw the stone and leap after it and compete with me in hurling the spear. Do not be too hasty. You could easily lose your honor as well as your lives. Consider this well," she said.

Siegfried stepped up to the king and bade him declare to the queen his firm intention and told him to have no fear. "I'll guard you well against her with my arts."

Then King Gunther said, "Noble Queen, impose your conditions. And even if there were more, I would undertake all for the sake of your beauty. I'll gladly lose my head if you do not become my wife."

When the queen heard his words, she bade them make haste with the games, as was proper, and ordered good armor to be brought her, a breastplate of red gold and a sturdy shield. She then put on a gambeson of pfellel silk from Libya, which no weapon had ever cut in any combat, beautifully fashioned. On it glittered bright embroidered edgings.

Meanwhile arrogant threats were flung at the strangers, and Dankwart and Hagen stood there downcast. Their hearts were troubled as to how the king would fare, and they thought, "This journey bodes no good for us."

During this time, without anyone's noticing it, Siegfried had gone to the ship, where his magic cloak was concealed. Quickly he slipped into it, and so was known to none. He hastened back again and found a crowd of warriors at the place the queen had set for her dangerous games. With his magic arts he stole in secretly among them, so that no one there saw him.

The ring had been measured out where the games were to be held in the presence of many warriors, more than seven hundred, all bearing weapons. They were to judge who won in the contest.

Brunhild had now appeared, armed as if she meant to battle for all royal realms. On her silken coat she wore many a clasp of gold, and her lovely coloring shone radiantly beneath her armor. Then came her attendants bringing her a shield, all red with gold, with steel-hard ribs, large and broad, beneath which she would play at the games. Her shield thong was a costly band, on which were precious stones, green as grass, that sparkled brightly, rivaling the gold. He had to be bold indeed to whom this lady gave her love. Beneath the boss, as we are told, the shield she was to bear was three spans thick, so rich in steel and gold that her chamberlain with three helpers could scarcely carry it.

When Hagen saw the shield brought up, he said grimly, "How now, King Gunther? We are as good as dead! She you wish to love is the devil's bride."

Let me tell you more about her garments, of which she had an abundance. She wore a surcoat of silk from Azagouc,[7] sumptuous and costly, and from its gleaming surface there shone on the person of the queen many a splendid stone.

A sharp spear was brought for the lady, heavy and large, which she was used to hurl. It was sturdy and unwieldy, huge and broad, and its edges cut most fearfully. Now hear marvels of its heaviness. Three and a half weights of iron[8] were consumed in the making, and three of Brunhild's men could hardly carry it.

Gunther began to be very afraid and thought to himself, "What will come of this? Not even the devil from hell could escape from this fix with his life! If only I were safe and sound in Burgundy, she would be free of my love for a very long time."

Then Dankwart said, "I deeply regret the journey to this court. Until now we have always been called warriors! What a shameful death for us if we die here at the hands of women! I am very angry that I came to this land. If only my brother Hagen had his sword in hand and I had mine, Brunhild's men would walk softly in their arrogance. They would restrain themselves—of this you may be sure. And even if I had sworn peace with a thousand oaths, before I would see my dear lord die, that maiden would lose her life."

"We might well escape from this land uncaptured," said Hagen, "if we had the armor we need for battle and also our good swords.

[7] Like Zazamanc, a fictitious land. This name is also found in Wolfram's *Parzival*.

[8] The Middle High German *messe*, from the Latin *massa*, refers to a certain amount of metal.

Then the powerful lady's pride would certainly be chastened."

The maid heard clearly what the warrior said, and with smiling mouth she glanced over her shoulder. "Since he thinks himself so bold, bring the warriors their armor and give them their sharp swords."

When they received their swords, as the maiden bade, Dankwart grew red with joy. "Now let them play as they like," he said. "Gunther is unvanquished since we have our arms."

Brunhild's strength was now strikingly revealed. They brought to the ring a heavy stone, large and cumbersome, huge and round, which she always threw after casting the spear. Twelve men could scarcely carry it. The Burgundians' fears were greatly increased.

"Curses!" said Hagen. "What a lady-love the king has chosen! She deserves to be in hell as the evil devil's bride."

She turned up the sleeves on her very white arms and took the shield in her hand. The spear she swung up high, and then the combat began. Gunther and Siegfried feared Brunhild's fury, and if Siegfried had not come to his aid, she would have taken the king's life. He went to him secretly and touched his hand.

This trick frightened Gunther. "What touched me?" he thought and looked all about, but saw no one standing there.

"It is your friend Siegfried. You have nothing to fear from the queen. Give me your shield and let me carry it, and pay close attention to what you hear me say. Now you make the motions, and I'll do the deeds."

When Gunther knew who it was, he was overjoyed.

"Keep my arts secret, and tell them to no one. Then the queen can win little fame from you, though that is her intention. See how the lady stands before you unconcerned."

Then with might and main the proud maiden thrust at the new shield, large and broad, which Siegelind's son bore in his hand. The sparks sprang from the steel as if blown by the wind. The edge of the sturdy spear broke right through the shield, setting fire flaming from the armor rings. Both stalwart men staggered at the blow. Save for the magic cloak they would have been dead. Blood gushed from Siegfried's mouth, yet swiftly he sprang back again, and taking the spear she had driven through the shield, he returned it to her. "I don't want to kill her," he thought, and reversing the point, he hurled the spearshaft at her armor so that it rang out loudly from the force of his hand. Sparks flew from the mail as if driven by the wind. Siegmund's son had shot a vigorous thrust, and despite all her strength she could not withstand the shock. Believe me, King Gunther could never have done it.

Brunhild sprang up quickly. "Gunther, noble Knight, I congratulate you on that blow." She thought he had done it of his own strength. But a far more powerful man had secretly pursued her. Quickly she stepped forward, full of anger, and raising the stone up high, she flung it as hard as she could a long distance from her. Then, with all her armor ringing, she sprang after the throw. The stone had fallen twelve fathoms away, but with her leap she outdid the throw.

Lord Siegfried went to where the stone lay. Gunther lifted it, but Siegfried did the throw. He was courageous, of great strength and stature. He threw the stone still farther and made a broader jump. Thanks to his remarkable arts, he had strength enough to carry King Gunther with him as he sprang. The leap was done; the stone lay there. And there was no one to be seen but Gunther.

Brunhild turned red from anger. Siegfried had prevented King Gunther's death.

Seeing him safe and sound at the edge of the ring, she called out to her retinue in an uncommonly loud voice, "Come closer at once, kinsmen and liegemen of mine. You shall all now be subject to King Gunther."

The valiant men laid aside their arms and knelt at the feet of the mighty Gunther from Burgundy. They thought he had done the games with his own strength. He greeted them graciously, for he was a man of great courtesy.

Then the maiden took him by the hand and bestowed on him full power over the land. At this bold Hagen rejoiced. She now asked the knight to accompany her to the spacious palace, and there the warriors were offered better hospitality.[9] Dankwart and Hagen submitted to this with good grace.

Siegfried was wise enough to put away his magic cloak. When he returned to where the ladies sat, he said to the king—and this was shrewdly done, "Why are you waiting, my Lord? Why don't you begin the many games the queen imposes on you? Show us at once what they are like." The cunning man behaved as if he knew nothing of them.

---

[9] I.e., in contrast to the reception earlier.

The queen said, "How did it happen, Lord Siegfried, that you didn't see the games Gunther won here?"

Hagan gave answer and said, "You had made us sad in spirit, Lady, and so Siegfried was at our ship when the lord of the Rhine gained the victory over you in the games. This is why he knows nothing about them."

"What welcome news," said Siegfried, "that your pride has thus been humbled and that there lives a man who can be your master. Now, noble maid, you must follow us to the Rhine."

"This cannot be," she answered, "until my kinsmen and vassals learn of it. I can't so easily quit my kingdom. My best friends must first be sent for."

Then she dispatched messengers all about. She summoned her friends, kinsmen and vassals, asking them to come to Isenstein without delay and bidding them all be given fine and costly apparel. Every day, late and early, they rode in troops to Brunhild's castle.

"By God!" said Hagen. "What have we done? We'll be in sore straits if we wait for Brunhild's men. If they now come into the land in force, then this maiden was born to our great peril. The queen's intent is not known to us—what if she is so angry that we shall be lost?"

"That I shall prevent," said Siegfried. "What you are fearful of, I shall not allow to happen. I'll bring help for you here to this land, from excellent warriors as yet unknown to you. Do not make any inquiries about me. I shall leave, and meanwhile may God preserve your honor. I'll return very soon and bring you a thousand of the very best warriors I have ever known."

"Just don't be too long," said the king. "We are glad for your help, and with reason."

"I shall come again in a few short days," he answered. "Tell Brunhild you have sent me away."

VIII

How Siegfried Went to Get His Vassals

Siegfried then went in his magic cloak through the gate leading to the shore, where he found a small ship. He embarked unseen and rowed it away as vigorously as if the wind were blowing it. No one saw the helmsman. The ship sped along, impelled by Siegfried's mighty strength. Everyone thought an uncommonly powerful wind was driving it, but no, it was Siegfried who did it, Siegelind's handsome son.

Rowing with might and main during that day and the one night, he reached a land a hundred long miles[1] away or even more, the land of the Nibelungs, where he owned the great treasure. He rowed alone to a broad island and quickly tieing his ship fast, he went to a hill, on which stood a castle, to seek lodging, as wayweary travelers do. He came to the gate, but it was closed. They protected their honor well, as people still do today. The stranger now began to knock on the gate. It was well guarded, for he saw within a giant who watched over the castle and who always had his arms close at hand.

"Who is knocking so violently at the gate?" asked the giant.

Lord Siegfried disguised his voice and answered, "I am a warrior. Now open up the gate, or I'll enfuriate many a man here today who would rather lie comfortably and take his rest."

The gate-keeper was irritated at Lord Siegfried's words. He had now donned his armor and put his helmet on his head. Then quickly the mighty giant seized his shield and swung wide the gate. Fiercely he rushed at Siegfried, asking how he dared to wake so many valiant men. His hand dealt out powerful blows, and the stranger took cover behind his shield. Then the gate-keeper shattered his shield plates with an iron bar, and Siegfried found himself

---

[1] The word *raste*, with the primary meaning of "rest" or "repose," is used as a measure of distance, but represents no uniform length.

in danger. He began to be very afraid of death as the gate-keeper struck so vigorously, but for this very reason Siegfried, his master, was kindly disposed toward him.[2] They fought so hard that the whole castle rang, and the noise could be heard in Nibelung's hall. At last Siegfried overcame the gate-keeper and bound him fast. This news spread through all the Nibelung land.

The brave Alberich, a wild dwarf, heard the fierce struggle from far away through the mountain. Arming himself speedily, he ran to where he found the noble stranger as he was tying up the giant. Alberich was furious and extremely powerful. He wore a helmet and coat of mail, and carried a heavy whip of gold in his hand. In all haste he raced at Siegfried. Seven heavy balls hung at the end of the whip, and with these he struck the shield in front of the brave man so fiercely that much of it broke off. The stranger feared for his life. He flung the broken shield from his hand and thrust his long sword into its sheath. Not wishing to kill his chamberlain, he was guided by his courtly breeding, as knightly virtue dictated. He rushed at Alberich and with his strong hands he seized the gray old man by the beard, jerking him so roughly that he screamed loudly. The young warrior's good breeding[3] was painful to Alberich.

"Let me live," shouted the dwarf, and added cunningly, "If I could be the bondsman of anyone else besides one warrior, to whom I swore an oath that I would be subject to him, I would serve you rather than die."

Siegfried then bound Alberich as he had the giant before. His strength hurt the dwarf grievously.

"What is your name?" asked the dwarf.

"My name is Siegfried. I thought I was well known to you."

"What good news!" said Alberich. "Now I have seen by your warrior-like deeds that you are by due right ruler of this land. If you spare my life, I will do whatever you command."

Then Lord Siegfried said, "Go quickly and bring here to me a thousand Nibelungs from among the best warriors we have."

Why he wanted this no one heard him say. He untied Alberich

---

[2] Siegfried was pleased that the gate-keeper was so reliable.

[3] This is a pun which cannot be reproduced in English. The word in the original is *zuht,* and the poet seems to have achieved a triple pun, since three meanings of the word would be equally appropriate here, "pulling," "punishment," and "good breeding."

and the giant, and Alberich ran quickly to where the warriors were.

Filled with fear, he wakened the Nibelungs, calling, "Up now, you warriors! You must go to Siegfried."

They sprang from their beds and were ready at once. A thousand valiant knights in fine attire went to where they saw Siegfried standing, and with words and acts[4] gave him cordial greeting. Many candles were lighted, and mulled wine was poured for him.

He thanked them all for coming immediately and added, "You must come with me across the sea."

He found the men quite willing. Fully thirty hundred warriors had now appeared, and from them a thousand of the best were chosen. Their helmets and the rest of their armor were brought, for Siegfried intended to take them to Brunhild's land.

"Good knights," he said, "I want to tell you something. You must wear costly garments at court, since many lovely ladies will see us there. So adorn yourselves with fine clothing."

Early on a morning they set out. What brave companions Siegfried had acquired! They took with them good horses and rich apparel and thus went proudly to Brunhild's land. On the ramparts stood lovely maidens.

Then the queen said, "Does anyone know who it is I see sailing far away there on the sea? They have splendid sails even whiter than snow."

"They are vassals of mine," said the king from the Rhine, "whom I left close by here on the way. I sent for them, Lady, and now they have come."

All eyes were turned on the proud strangers. Siegfried could be seen standing at the prow of the ship, in magnificent attire, and many other warriors besides.

"Sir King," said the queen, "tell me, shall I greet the strangers, or shall I refuse them my greeting?"

"Go to meet them before the palace," he said, "so that they will realize clearly that we are glad to see them."

The queen did as the king advised her, but she greeted Siegfried differently from the rest.[5] Lodgings were prepared for them and their armor put away. So many guests had come to the land that

---

[4] I.e., the warriors knelt before Siegfried or shook his hand.

[5] Brunhild, believing that Siegfried is only a bondsman of Gunther's, greets him less graciously than the rest.

everywhere there was a jostling throng of troops. The Burgundians now wished to set out for home.

Then the queen said, "I would be grateful if someone could distribute my silver and my gold, of which I have so much, to our guests, mine and the king's."

"Noble Queen," replied Dankwart, the brave Giselher's vassal, "let me take charge of the keys. I am so sure of knowing how to distribute it that any disgrace I may incur I shall take upon myself."

He then gave abundant proof that he was generous. Taking over the keys, Hagen's brother offered so many rich gifts that anyone who asked for one mark was given so much that all the poor could live happily on it. Amounts of fully a hundred pounds he gave away time and time again. Many walked about there in front of the hall who had never before worn such fine garments. The queen heard of this and was extremely vexed.

"Sir King," she said, "I could dispense with this—your chamberlain won't leave me any of my garments, and he is squandering all my gold. I would be grateful if someone would put a stop to it. He is giving such costly gifts he must think I have sent for death to come. But I intend to keep the treasure my father left me for a long time yet, and I can spend it quite well myself."

Never did any queen get such a generous chamberlain.

Then Hagen said, "Lady, let me tell you this. The king from the Rhine has so much gold and clothing to give that we have no need to take your garments with us."

"No," said the queen, "for my sake let me fill twenty traveling chests with gold and silks to distribute when we go across the sea to Gunther's land."

Her chests were then filled with precious stones. Her own chamberlain had to be present, for she did not want to entrust the task to Giselher's vassal. At this both Gunther and Hagen began to laugh.

Then the queen said, "To whom shall I give my kingdom in charge? You and I must provide for this before we leave."

The king answered, "Bid him who suits you best to come here, and we will make him vice-regent."

The lady saw one of her most distinguished kinsmen standing near her—it was her mother's brother—and said to him, "I put my castles and my land in your charge until the time when King Gunther shall administer justice here."

Then she chose from among her following twenty hundred men who were to go with her to Burgundy in addition to the thousand warriors from the Nibelung land. They made ready for the journey and rode out to the shore. She took with her six and eighty matrons and at least a hundred maidens. Without further delay they now made haste to depart, and many of those they left at home began to weep. With fine courtesy Brunhild quitted her land. She kissed the close friends who were with her, and after the gracious farewell they set out to sea. The lady never again returned to her fatherland.

During the trip they had all kinds of festivities and entertainment, and a fair wind helped them on their way. Brunhild did not wish to lie with her lord on the journey. Nuptial pleasures were reserved for a festival in his home in the castle at Worms, where they soon arrived happily with their warriors.

IX

How Siegfried Was Sent to Worms

When they had traveled for full nine days, Hagen of Troneg said, "Now listen to what I say to you. We are tardy in sending a message to Worms. Your messengers ought to be in Burgundy now."

"What you say is true," said King Gunther. "No one would be as suitable for this journey as you, friend Hagen. Ride to my land. No one can bring the news of our journey to the court better than you."

"I am not a good messenger," answered Hagen. "Let me be chamberlain. I'll remain on the sea with the ladies and take charge of their garments until we bring them to Burgundy. Ask Siegfried to bear the message. If he refuses to make the journey, then ask him courteously as a friend to grant the request for the sake of your sister."

Gunther sent for the warrior, who came as soon as they sought him out, and said, "Since we are getting close to my homeland, I ought to send messengers to my dear sister and to my mother to say that we are approaching the Rhine. This I ask of you, Siegfried.

Carry out my wish, and I shall always recompense you for it."

Siegfried protested until Gunther pled with him urgently and said, "Ride for my sake and for the sake of Kriemhild, the lovely maid, and she, as well as I, will compensate you for it."

When Siegfried heard this, he was entirely willing. "Send whatever message you will. Not a word of it will be withheld. I will gladly undertake this mission for the fair maiden's sake. Why should I refuse anything to her whom I hold in my heart? Whatever you command in her name is as good as done."

"Then tell my mother, Queen Ute, that we are in high spirits on this journey, let my brothers know how we have fared, and let our friends hear the news too. Do not withhold from my fair sister my greetings and Brunhild's, and also deliver them to my household and to all my vassals. How well I have accomplished what my heart always longed for! And tell Ortwin, my dear kinsman, to order seats set up at Worms on the Rhine, and inform all my other kinsmen that I intend to celebrate a great festival with Brunhild. And tell my sister as soon as she has heard that my guests and I have arrived in the land to prepare a fine reception for my bride. For this I will always be at her service."

Lord Siegfried quickly took leave of Lady Brunhild, as was fitting, and of all her following, and rode away to the Rhine. There could be no better messenger anywhere in the world. With four and twenty warriors he rode into Worms. When the word spread that he had come without the king, the whole household was oppressed with pangs of grief, for they feared their lord had died there. In high spirits the warriors sprang from their horses. The young king Giselher hastened toward them with his brother Gernot.

When he did not see King Gunther with Siegfried, he said at once, "Welcome, Siegfried. Tell me where you have left my brother, the king. I fear Brunhild's strength has robbed us of him. If so, her love, courted at such great risk, would have wrought us great harm."

"Have no fear. My comrade sends his greetings to you and all his kinsmen. I left him safe and sound. He sent me to you as his messenger bearing news to your land. Consider at once how I may in some way see the queen and your sister. I am to inform them of the message Gunther and Brunhild have sent them. Both are faring excellently."

"Just go to her," said young Giselher. "With this you will bring my sister great joy, for she is much concerned about my brother. The maid will be glad to see you—I'll warrant you that."

Lord Siegfried answered, "Anything I can do to serve her shall be done willingly and faithfully. Who will announce to the ladies that I wish to go to them?"

Giselher undertook the message and said to his mother and his sister, "Siegfried has come to us. My brother Gunther sent him here to the Rhine. He brings us tidings about how things go with the king. Permit him now to come to your court, and he will tell you the true news from Isenland."

The ladies still felt great concern.[1] They hastily sought out their garments[2] and invited Siegfried to court. He went willingly, for he was eager to see them.

Kriemhild said to him graciously, "Welcome, Lord Siegfried, excellent Knight. Where is my brother Gunther, the noble king? I fear we have lost him because of Brunhild's strength. Alas for me, wretched maiden, that I was ever born into the world."

Then the brave knight said, "Give me a messenger's reward.[3] Fair ladies, you weep without cause. I can report to you that I left him in good health. He and Brunhild sent me here to you both with messages. Noble Queen, he and his bride send you fond greetings with the affection of kin. Now cease your weeping. They will come very soon."

She had not heard such welcome news in many a day. With the snow-white hem of her gown she wiped the tears from her lovely eyes and thanked the envoy for this news that had reached her. Her great grieving and her weeping were now taken away. She bade the messenger be seated, and he willingly complied.

Then the charming maiden said, "It would please me very much if I might give you my gold as messenger's reward. You are too rich for that, but I will always be grateful to you."

"Even if I were the sole ruler over thirty lands," he answered, "I would still be glad to accept a gift from your hand."

"Then it shall be done," said the maid and bade her chamberlain fetch the messenger's recompense.

---

[1] Because they had heard no details as yet.

[2] I.e., dresses suitable for receiving Siegfried.

[3] With these words Siegfried indicates that his news is good, since his message deserves a reward.

Four and twenty arm rings with fine stones she gave him as reward. It was not his intention to keep them; he at once gave them to the members of her household whom he saw standing nearest to her in the chamber.[4]

Her mother now graciously tendered her thanks to him.

"I am to tell you," he continued, "what Gunther requests of you when he comes to the Rhine. If you will fulfill this, Lady, he will always be devoted to you. I heard him ask that you welcome his distinguished guests warmly and do him the favor of riding to meet him on the shore before Worms. By your true loyalty the king begs this of you."

"I am quite willing," said the maid. "I will not deny him any service I can do him. It shall be done with sisterly devotion." And her color flamed for joy. Never was any prince's messenger better received. She would have kissed him if she had dared. How very courteously he now took leave of the ladies!

The Burgundians did as Siegfried ordered. Sindolt and Hunolt, and the warrior Rumolt too, were busily occupied with setting up seats on the shore before Worms. Ortwin and Gere did not fail to send messengers far and wide, informing Gunther's friends of the festival that was to take place. The lovely maidens bedecked themselves in expectation. The palace and all its walls were decorated, and Gunther's hall was lavishly furnished with tables and benches for the many guests. This magnificent festival commenced most joyfully.

Now from all sides there came riding on the highways through the land the three kings' kinsmen, who had been summoned to await the approaching guests. Many rich garments were taken from their wrappings. Then the news was brought that Brunhild's friends had been seen on horseback,[5] and a great bustle arose among all the people of Burgundy. Oh, how many brave warriors were to be seen in both retinues!

Then Kriemhild said, "You maidens of mine who wish to accompany me to the reception, fetch from the chests your very best gowns so that the guests may grant us praise and honor."

The warriors now arrived and ordered splendid saddles of red

---

[4] By giving away Kriemhild's present, Siegfried shows that only the token of her gratitude is important to him, not the material reward.

[5] According to this passage, Gunther and Brunhild leave the ship to make the last stage of the journey on horseback.

gold to be brought for the ladies to ride on to the Rhine. Nowhere was there ever finer horses' gear. The bright gold gleamed on the palfreys, and from their bridles glittered many precious stones. Golden footstools, placed on fine, lustrous pfellel silk, were brought for the ladies, who were in gay spirits. Their riding horses stood ready for them in the courtyard, as I have told you, wearing narrow breast straps of the best silk anyone could tell you of. Six and eighty ladies were seen coming out, wearing headdresses and clothed in shimmering gowns. They joined Kriemhild and were followed by many a fair maid of the highest rank, fifty and four from the Burgundian land, beautifully attired and with bright ribbon bands on their flaxen hair. What the king had previously requested was diligently done. They wore before the stranger knights rich pfellel silks, the best to be found, such fine garments as well became their ample beauty. A man who could be irritated at any one of them, would be a simpleton indeed. There were many robes of sable and of ermine, and many an arm and hand was richly adorned with bracelets over the silken sleeves. No one could tell you the whole of their zeal in prinking. Many a hand wound finely wrought girdles of silk from Araby, costly and long, around lustrous gowns over sumptuous ferran[6] skirts. Through clasps their dresses were charmingly laced across the breast. Any one of them would have been pained if her own radiant color had not outshone the brilliance of her garments. No queen nowadays has such beautiful ladies-in-waiting. When the fair maids had finished dressing, those who were to accompany them promptly appeared, a great troop of light-hearted warriors, carrying with their shields many a spear of ash.

X

How Brunhild Was Received at Worms

From the other side of the Rhine the people could see the king and his guests, with their host of companions, nearing the shore and

6 A fabric of wool and silk.

many a maiden's horse being led along by the bridle. All who were there to welcome them stood ready. Those from Isenland and Siegfried's Nibelung men went across in boats and without wasting a moment hastened to the land, where, on this side of the river, they found the king's friends waiting.

Now listen to how Ute, the queen, led her ladies-in-waiting from the castle and rode with them to the shore. Many a knight and maid thus came to know each other. Duke Gere led Kriemhild's horse by the bridle till just outside the castle gate, and Siegfried attended her further. He was soon well rewarded for his service. Ortwin rode at Lady Ute's side, and many knights and maidens rode in pairs. Never were so many ladies seen together, we assure you, at such a magnificent reception. Good knights performed fine bohourts in Kriemhild's presence as they rode along, all the way to the ships—this could not well have been omitted. The ladies were now lifted from their palfreys. The king had come across, and many distinguished guests. Oh, what stout lances splintered before the ladies' eyes! And many a clash of hurtling shields was heard. Oh, what costly bosses clanged loudly in the crush!

The ladies stood by the harbor as Gunther and his guests came off the ships. He himself led Brunhild by the hand. Bright gems and gowns shone in rivalry with each other. Lady Kriemhild went most courteously to welcome Lady Brunhild and her retinue. White hands pushed back the chaplets[1] as the two kissed each other; this was done for courtesy's sake.

Then politely Kriemhild said, "You are welcome in these lands, to me and my mother, and to all our loyal friends."

Brunhild thanked her with a bow, and the ladies embraced each other again and again. No one has ever heard of such fond greetings as the two, Lady Ute and her daughter, gave the bride; they kissed her sweet mouth many times.

When Brunhild's ladies had all come to shore, stately warriors took them gallantly by the hand, and the fair maidens stood there before Lady Brunhild. It was a long time before the greetings came

---

[1] Originally garlands or wreaths of flowers, then bands or circlets, often set with precious stones, or, as here, a much larger and more elaborate headdress, such as is still a part of the costume worn by young peasant girls on Sundays or festive occasions. The *schapel* was worn only by unmarried women.

to an end, and many a rose-colored mouth was kissed. The princesses still stood side by side, and the warriors rejoiced to see this. Those who had heard people say they had never seen anything so beautiful as these two women now gazed with all their eyes and confessed it was no lie. Nor was there seen on their persons any art of deception. Those who knew how to judge feminine charms praised Gunther's bride for her beauty, but the more experienced, who had observed more carefully, maintained that Kriemhild surpassed Brunhild.

Maids and matrons joined each other, and many a lovely figure could be seen, richly adorned. The whole plain before Worms was covered with silken tents and costly pavilions. The king's kinsmen came thronging around as Brunhild and Kriemhild and all the ladies with them were bidden to go to where there was shade,[2] and the warriors from Burgundy escorted them.

Now all the guests were also mounted, and shields were pierced in splendid jousts. Dust swirled up from the plain as though the whole land had burst into flame. Many a man proved himself a hero, and the maidens looked on at what the warriors did. I imagine Lord Siegfried rode many a turn before the tents,[3] at the head of his thousand Nibelung men.

Then came Hagen of Troneg, as the host had bidden him, and courteously put an end to the jousting, so that the maidens should not be covered with dust. Willingly the guests obeyed.

Lord Gernot said, "Let the horses stand until it gets cool. Then we'll do service to the ladies and escort them to the great hall. But see to it that you are ready when the king wishes to leave."

When the jousting had ceased over all the plain, the knights went to the ladies under the high tents to pass the time in pleasant entertainment. There they whiled away the hours until it was time to go.

Before the approach of evening, when the sun was setting and it began to grow cool, they lingered no longer but set out for the castle. Many a lady was caressed by affectionate glances. And now great numbers of garments were torn by the lusty knights, jousting

---

[2] Probably to the tents.

[3] I.e., he rode through the troops of his opponents, looking for jousts, then turned back to his own forces, and repeated this procedure again. In doing so, he stayed close to the tents so that Kriemhild could see him.

as they rode, according to the custom of the land, until the king dismounted before the palace. There ladies received the service spirited heroes always give them.

The queens now separated. Lady Ute and her daughter went with their train to a spacious chamber. Everywhere loud noise of gaiety was heard.

Seats were prepared, for the king wished to go to table with his guests. At his side stood the lovely Brunhild, wearing the crown in the king's realm. For this her lineage was royal enough. Benches were set up for the warriors, so we are told, and good, broad tables laden with food. Nothing they needed was lacking. With the king were seen many distinguished guests. The host's chamberlains brought out water in basins of red gold.[4] It would be quite pointless for anyone to tell you that there was ever better service at a prince's festival—I myself would not believe it.

Before the ruler of the Rhine took the water, Lord Siegfried, as was but proper, reminded him of the promise he had given before having seen Brunhild at her home in Isenland.

"Remember what your hand swore to me," he said, "that if Lady Brunhild came to this land, you would give me your sister to wife. What has become of these oaths? I suffered great hardship on your journey."

Then the king said to the guest, "It is right that you have reminded me. My hand shall certainly not be perjured. I shall help you as best I can to bring this about."

Kriemhild was summoned to court before the king. She came with her maidens to the entrance of the hall, and Giselher sprang down the steps to meet her.

"Bid these maidens turn back," he said. "No one but my sister alone is to be here with the king."

Then Kriemhild was led to where the king was seated. Knights from the lands of many princes were present in the vast hall, and they were asked to remain. Meanwhile Lady Brunhild had stepped up to the table.

King Gunther said, "Dear sister, I appeal to your noble spirit. Help me to redeem my oath. I swore to give you to a warrior, and if he becomes your husband, then you will have done my will most loyally."

---

[4] This is water for washing the hands.

"Dear brother," answered the maiden, "you do not need to entreat me. I will always be as you command, and whatever you bid me shall be done. I will gladly pledge my troth to him whom you give me, my Lord, as husband."

Siegfried turned red at the glance of fond eyes and offered his service to Lady Kriemhild. Then they bade them stand side by side within the circle[5] and asked if she would have the knight. In her maidenly modesty she was half ashamed, yet such was Siegfried's luck and fortune that she had no wish to refuse him. And he too vowed to take her as his wife. When they had pledged their vows, the charming maid was soon lovingly clasped in Siegfried's arms, and he kissed her in the presence of the warriors.

The circle broke up, and with the Nibelungs escorting him, Siegfried took the seat opposite the king, Kriemhild at his side.[6] Many a man stepped up to do him reverence.

The king and Brunhild had now taken their seats. Then she noticed Kriemhild sitting beside Siegfried. Never had she been so sad, and she began to weep. Hot tears rolled down her bright cheeks.

"What is the matter, my Lady," said Gunther, "that the glow of your bright eyes is dimmed? You have cause to rejoice, for my land and castles and many excellent vassals are now subject to you."

"I have cause to weep," answered Brunhild. "I am grieved to the heart for your sister. I see her sitting there close beside your bondsman. I can never stop weeping if she is humiliated so."

"Say no more," said King Gunther. "Some other time I'll tell you why I have given Siegfried my sister as his wife. I know she will always be happy with him."

"I mourn for her beauty and her gentle breeding," she said. "If I knew where to go, I would like to flee, so that I would never lie with you unless you tell me why Kriemhild is Siegfried's beloved."

"I will tell you," said the king. "He has castles and vast lands, as well as I—of that you may be assured. He is a mighty king. For this reason I am glad to give him the maid as his wife."

But no matter what the king said to her, she remained unconsolable.

Many a good knight rushed away from the tables, and their

[5] This is the circle formed by the warriors mentioned above, who are now to serve as witnesses.

[6] Gunther, as king, sits at one end of the table; Siegfried has the seat of honor at the opposite end.

bohourt now grew so vigorous that the whole castle resounded. But the host was very bored with his guests. He thought it would be more pleasant to lie with his beautiful lady. He was then not without hope in his heart that through her he would know great bliss, and he began to gaze at her tenderly. The guests were requested to cease their knightly sports, for the king and his wife wished to go to bed. At the top of the stairs leading up to the hall Kriemhild and Brunhild met, as yet without hatred on either side. Their attendants followed, and without delay their chamberlains brought them lights. The vassals of the two kings now separated, and many warriors went with Siegfried as escort.

The lords both went to where they were to lie. Each thought to conquer his lady with love, and their hearts were glad. Siegfried's pleasure was very great. As he lay at Kriemhild's side and with true love caressed the maid so tenderly, she grew as dear to him as his own life, and he would not have exchanged her for a thousand other women.

I shall tell you no more of how he fondled her, but listen to how the warrior Gunther fared as he lay with Lady Brunhild. With other women he had often lain more comfortably. Their following had departed, both knights and ladies, and the chamber door was quickly locked. Gunther fancied he would now embrace Brunhild's lovely body, but it was a long time yet before she became his wife. She went to bed in a white linen gown, and he thought to himself, "Now I have everything here that I ever desired in all my days." She pleased him well in her beauty—and with reason. He veiled the lights and then joined the lady. He laid himself beside her, and great was his joy when he clasped the charming maid in his arms. He would have fondled her ardently if she had permitted it, but she became so angry that he was deeply hurt. He thought to find love; what he found was hostile hate.

"Noble Knight," she said, "give up all thought of what you have been hoping for. You won't get it. I intend to remain a virgin, remember that, until you tell me the whole story."

Then Gunther became angry. He struggled for her love and rumpled her gown. The maid now seized her girdle, a stout band that she wore about her waist, and with it inflicted great suffering on the king. Since he was disturbing her sleep, she bound his feet and hands, carried him to a nail, and hung him up on the wall.

And she refused him love. In fact, he almost perished from her strength.

Then he who had fancied himself the master began to plead, "Loosen my fetters, noble Queen. I no longer think I can gain the victory over you, fair Lady, and I will never lie so close to you again."

She did not care how he felt, for she lay very comfortably, so there he was forced to hang all through the night until the day, when the bright dawn shone through the windows. If he had ever had great strength, he had little of it now.

"Tell me, Lord Gunther," said the maid, "won't you be upset if your chamberlains find you tied fast by a woman's hand?"

"You would only get reproach," he answered, "and I would have little honor from it. For the sake of your own reputation let me come to you now. Since my caresses are so displeasing to you, I will not so much as touch your gown."

Then she quickly loosened his bonds and let him set foot on the ground. Once more he went to the bed and lay down beside the lady, but so far away that he never once touched her lovely gown. Nor would she have permitted it.

Now their attendants appeared, bringing them fresh clothing, of which a great abundance had been laid out for the morning. However happy the people were, the lord of the land was sad indeed, though he wore his crown[7] that day. According to the custom, which they quite properly observed, Gunther and Brunhild delayed no longer, but went to the minster, where mass was sung. Lord Siegfried also went, and great crowds thronged around. Everything they needed was ready for them, their crowns and robes, in keeping with their royal rank. They were then solemnly blessed,[8] after which all four could be seen standing joyful beneath their crowns. Many youths, six hundred or more, now received their swords in honor of the kings, and there was great rejoicing in the Burgundian land. Spearshafts were heard clashing in the hands of the newly sworded knights. At the windows the maidens sat and watched the gleam of many a shield flashing before their eyes.

The king had parted from his men, and no matter what the oth-

[7] The crown was worn on special occasions such as this.
[8] The marriage ceremony in church regularly took place after the actual consummation of the marriage.

ers did, he walked about in sadness. His mood and Siegfried's were very unlike. Siegfried knew well what ailed the king. He went to him and asked, "Tell me, how did you fare last night?"

"I got only shame and disgrace," said the king, "for I have brought the wicked devil home to my house. When I wanted to make love to her, she tied me up tightly, carried me to a nail, and hung me up high on the wall. There I hung in terror all night until the day, before she untied me. How comfortably she lay there! I make this complaint to you in confidence, as my friend."

"I am truly grieved," said Siegfried, "and if you allow me, I will prove it to you. I'll see to it that tonight she shall lie so close beside you that she will withhold her love from you no longer."

After all his troubles Gunther was joyful at these words.

"Everything will be all right," said Lord Siegfried. "Last night must have been quite different for the two of us. Your sister Kriemhild is dearer to me than life. Lady Brunhild must become your wife tonight. I'll come to your chamber this evening, so concealed in my magic cloak that no one will notice my arts. Send the chamberlains to their quarters. I'll put out the lights in the pages' hands, and by this you will know that I am there and ready to serve you. Then I'll tame your wife for you so that you can possess her tonight, or I'll give my life as forfeit."

"Provided you are not too free with my wife," said the king, "I agree. Do to her whatever you please. Even if you took her life, I would overlook it, for she is a terrible woman."

"I pledge on my honor," said Siegfried, "that I will not make love to her. Your sister is more to me than all other women I have ever seen."

Gunther believed completely what Siegfried said.

The knightly games brought both pleasure and strain. But now bohourt and din were halted, since it was time for the ladies to go to the hall. Chamberlains bade the crowd make way, and the court was cleared of people and horses. A bishop led each of the ladies when they went to table in the presence of the kings, and many stately warriors followed them to the seats.

The king sat there in joyful expectation, thinking of what Siegfried had promised him. This one day seemed to him fully thirty days long. He had but a single thought: enjoying his lady's love. He could scarcely wait until they left the table. At last fair Brunhild, and Lady Kriemhild too, were bidden to go to their rest. Oh, how many valiant warriors were seen walking before the queens!

Lord Siegfried sat affectionately beside his wife, in bliss without a flaw. With her white hands she caressed his, until before her eyes he vanished, she knew not when. After thus fondling him and then seeing him no longer, the queen said in astonishment to his attendants, "I wonder where the king has gone. Who took his hands out of mine?" She spoke no other word.

Meanwhile he had gone to where he found many pages standing with candles. These he began to extinguish. Then Gunther knew it was Siegfried and knew well why he was there. He bade maids and ladies depart, and that done, the king himself made fast the door and speedily shoved two strong bolts in place. Quickly he hid the lights behind the curtains of the bed. Then the sturdy Siegfried and the lovely girl began a game which there was no avoiding and which brought the king both joy and sorrow. Siegfried lay down close beside the maid.

"Now stop this, Gunther," she said, "however much you may like it, or you'll suffer the same misery as before."

The lady was soon to cause bold Siegfried great distress. He concealed his voice and did not speak a word. Gunther heard very plainly, though he could not see him, that no intimacies passed between the two. They found little rest in the bed. Siegfried behaved as if he were Gunther and clasped her in his arms. She threw him out of the bed upon a bench nearby so that his head thudded loudly against a stool. With all his might he sprang up again; he wanted to have another try. But when he now thought to subdue her, he suffered sorely for his efforts. Such resistance from a woman, I fancy, will never be seen again.

When he would not desist, she jumped up and said, "Don't rumple my white gown. You are a clumsy boor, and you will regret it—you'll see."

She seized him in her arms, intending to tie him up as she had the king, that she might have peace in the bed. The lady took thorough revenge for his having rumpled her clothes. Of what avail was his mighty brawn? She showed the warrior her overpowering strength. She carried him by force, since there was no other way, and pressed him roughly between a chest and the wall.

"Alas," he thought to himself, "if I now lose my life at a maiden's hands, then after this many a woman may be insolent to her husband, who would otherwise never do such a thing."

The king heard all this distinctly and feared for the man. Siegfried was very ashamed and flew into a rage. With tremendous force he grappled with Lady Brunhild and desperately attempted once more to subdue her. To the king the time seemed long until he conquered her. She squeezed his hands so hard that the blood spurted out from under the nails. This provoked the hero, and he soon compelled the maid to abandon the unseemly intent which she had announced before. The king heard all this, but said nothing. Siegfried crushed her against the bed so that she cried out loudly, for his strength caused her immense pain. Then she clutched at her waist where her girdle was, meaning to tie him fast, but his hand interfered in such a way that her limbs and her whole body cracked. Thus the struggle was ended, and she became Gunther's wife.

"Noble King," she said, "let me live. I will atone fully for what I have done to you. I shall no longer resist your noble love. I have discovered that you know how to master women."

Siegfried left the maid lying there and stepped away, as though he wished to remove his clothes. Without her perceiving it, he drew from her hand a golden ring. And he took her girdle too, a fine embroidered band. I don't know whether he did this out of arrogance. He gave them to his wife, and later suffered for it.

Now Gunther and the maid lay side by side. He fondled her lovingly, as was fitting, and she was forced to renounce her anger, and her maidenly shyness as well. The liberties he took with her left her a trifle pale. Oh, how through love her great strength drained away! Now she was no stronger than any other woman. Amorously he caressed her beautiful body. Even if she had tried again to resist, how could that have helped her? All this Gunther had done to her with his love. How sweetly she lay there beside him in loving embrace until the bright day!

Lord Siegfried had gone again to where he was warmly welcomed by a lovely lady. He evaded the questions she had meant to ask and for a long time withheld the things he had brought for her. But when she was crowned and ruled as queen in his land, he no longer kept to himself what destiny had ordained he should give her.

The next morning the host was in a far better mood than he had been before. At this, there was rejoicing without limit throughout his whole land among the many nobles he had invited to his court, for they were served lavishly. The festival lasted until the four-teenth day, and all the while the sound never ceased of all sorts of pleasures, whatever they wished to indulge in. The cost to the king was judged very high. At his command, his kinsmen gave presents in his honor to the wandering minstrels, clothing and red gold, horses and silver. All those who desired gifts departed well satis-fied. Lord Siegfried and his thousand men gave away all the gar-ments they had brought to the Rhine, as well as their horses and saddles; they knew how to live as lords. To those who wanted to return home the time seemed too long before all the costly gifts were bestowed. Never were more guests better entertained. Thus the festival ended, as was Gunther's wish.

XI

How Siegfried Returned Home with His Wife

When the guests had all left, Siegmund's son said to his followers, "Let us also make ready to go home to my lands."

His wife was pleased when she heard the news and said to her husband, "When are we to leave? I don't want to be in too much of a hurry. My brothers must first share their lands with me."

Siegfried was annoyed when he heard Kriemhild's demand.

The princes came to him and said, all three, "Now know this, Lord Siegfried, our loyal service will always be yours till death."

He bowed his gratitude to the warriors for treating him so gra-ciously.

"And we will share with you," said the youth Giselher, "the land and castles we own ourselves and all the broad domains under our rule. You shall have a suitable share of them together with Kriem-hild."

When Siegfried heard and saw their good intentions, he said, "God grant that your heritage will always be a source of happiness to you and to the people in these lands. My dear wife can well forgo the share you wish to give her. Where she is to wear the crown, if I live long enough, she will be richer than anyone alive. For whatever else you command, I am at your service."

Then Lady Kriemhild said, "Though you renounce my inheritance, concerning the Burgundian warriors the matter is not so simple. These a king might be proud to take to his land. My dear brothers must certainly share *them* with me."

"Take anyone you like," said Lord Gernot. "You will find here many who will gladly ride with you. Of thirty hundred warriors we will give you a thousand men to be your own retinue."

Kriemhild sent for Hagen and Ortwin to ask if they and their kinsmen were willing to be her vassals.

At this Hagen became very angry and said, "Gunther cannot give us to anyone in the world. Ask others to go with you. You know very well the custom of the men of Troneg. We are duty bound to stay here at court with the kings. We have followed them till now and we shall keep on serving them."

So they let the matter rest and prepared to leave. Lady Kriemhild took with her her royal train of two and thirty maidens and five hundred men. Count Eckewart joined Siegfried's following. They all took their leave, knights and squires, maids and ladies. With kisses they parted and in good spirits quitted King Gunther's land. Their friends and kinsmen bore them company far upon the way and ordered night quarters to be set up for them wherever they pleased throughout the whole kingdom.

Then messengers were quickly dispatched to Siegmund so that he and Siegelind might know that their son was coming with Lady Ute's daughter, the fair Kriemhild, from Worms beyond the Rhine. This news could not have been more welcome.

"How happy I am," said Siegmund, "that I have lived to see Kriemhild crowned here as queen. My heritage will be greatly enhanced by this. My son Siegfried shall himself be king."

Lady Siegelind then gave the messengers as reward a great quantity of red samite, silver, and heavy gold. She rejoiced at the news she had heard, and her ladies-in-waiting dressed themselves with care.

They were told who was coming with Siegfried to the land, whereupon they bade that seats be set up immediately, toward which he would take his course, wearing the crown in the presence of his friends. Then King Siegmund's men rode to meet him. If anyone has ever been better welcomed than were these famous heroes in Siegmund's land, I know nothing of it. With many ladies and an escort of knights, Siegelind rode to meet Kriemhild. It was a whole day's journey before the guests were sighted. Both the strangers and those at home in the land suffered some discomforts till they came to the spacious castle called Xanten, where Siegfried and Kriemhild were to wear the crown.

With smiling mouth Siegelind and Siegmund kissed Kriemhild and Siegfried time and time again for joy. Their sorrow had been taken from them. And the entire retinue received a hearty welcome. They bade the guests be brought before Siegmund's hall. The maidens were lifted down from their palfreys, for there was many a man eager to serve the ladies. However famed the splendid festival on the Rhine, the knights were given much better apparel here than they had ever yet worn in all their days. Great wonders could be told of their pomp as they sat there in all their glory with abundance of everything. What a quantity of gold-covered borders the courtiers wore on their robes, beset with pearls and precious stones! Thus did Queen Siegelind tend them zealously.

Then Lord Siegmund spoke in the presence of his friends, "To Siegfried's kin I do proclaim that he shall wear my crown before these warriors."

The men of Netherland rejoiced to hear this news. Siegmund gave his son the crown, the power of jurisdiction, and his kingdom, and Siegfried became ruler of them all. When there was a suit at law, and it was his duty to pronounce judgment, this was done in such a way that Kriemhild's husband was much feared.

In this great esteem he lived, and administered justice as king, until the tenth year, when his fair lady bore a son. Thus the desire of the king's kinsmen was fulfilled. They hastened to baptize him, and named him Gunther after his uncle. Of this name he had no need to be ashamed. Should he take after his kinsmen, that would be well for him. He was reared with care, as was but right. In these same times Lady Siegelind died, and many were grieved that death had taken her from them. Kriemhild now had all the power that is the due of such well-born ladies[1] who rule over a kingdom.

There by the Rhine also, we are told, in the Burgundian land, Brunhild had borne a son by Gunther. He was named Siegfried in honor of that hero. How carefully they watched over him! Gunther

---

[1] I.e., Siegelind and Kriemhild.

gave him masters who knew well how to bring him up to be a valiant man. Alas, of how many friends misfortune later robbed him!

Constantly tales were told of how splendidly the warriors always lived in Siegmund's land, and Gunther lived in like manner with his kin.

The Nibelung land and Schilbung's warriors, and both kings' possessions, were at Siegfried's service. None of his kinsmen was ever more powerful than he. On this account he was in all the better spirits. He now had the very largest treasure any man had ever acquired, save for those who owned it before. He had won it with his own hands in battle at the foot of a mountain, killing many a knight to get it. He enjoyed honors in abundance. Yet even had this not been so, one would have to admit in all justice that the noble warrior was one of the best that ever mounted a horse. His might was feared, and rightly.

XII

How Gunther Invited Siegfried to the Festival

And all the while Gunther's wife thought, "How can Lady Kriemhild carry her head so high? Isn't her husband Siegfried our vassal? For a long time now he has rendered us no service." [1]

These thoughts she bore in her heart but held her peace. She was very vexed that they were so far from her and that Siegfried's land sent her no tribute. She would have liked to know how that came about. Once she asked the king if it might be possible for her to see Kriemhild again. It was in private that she told him what she had in mind. Her words pleased him only moderately.

"How could we bring them here to this land?" he said. "That would be impossible. They live too far from us. I can't ask it of them."

---

[1] I.e., feudal service.

Brunhild answered shrewdly, "No matter how all-powerful a king's vassal may be, he should not refuse what his lord commands."

Gunther smiled when she said this. Siegfried's visits, however frequent, he never considered as service to him.

"My dear Lord," she said, "for my sake help me to bring Siegfried and your sister to this land so that we may see them. Truly nothing more pleasant could happen to me. How happy I am when I think of your sister's courtesy and gentle breeding and of how we sat together when I first became your wife! She does honor to herself by loving the brave Siegfried."

She pleaded long until the king said, "You may be sure that no guests were ever more welcome. You needn't beg me so urgently. I'll send my messengers to them both and ask them to come to the Rhine to us."

"Then tell me when you intend to send for them," said the queen, "and at what time our dear friends will arrive in the land. And let me know whom you plan to send there."

"I will," he said. "I shall send thirty of my men there on horseback."

He bade them appear before him and gave them a message to Siegfried's land. To their delight Brunhild presented them with rich apparel.

King Gunther said, "You warriors are to say everything with which I charge you, withholding nothing. Tell Siegfried and my sister that no one in the world can be more fond of them. And ask them both to come to the Rhine to us. For this I and my wife will always be beholden to them. Before Midsummer's Day[2] he and his men shall see many here who will do him great honor. Give my greetings to King Siegmund, and tell him that my friends and I will always be kindly disposed toward him. Also tell my sister not to fail to ride to her kin. There was never a better reason for her to come to a festival."

Brunhild and Ute and all the ladies present sent their greetings to the ladies and knights in Siegfried's land. With the consent of the king's kinsmen the messengers set out. Their horses and clothing were ready and, well equipped, they left the land. The king had given orders for them to be carefully protected by escorts, and they

---

2 The summer solstice, June 22nd.

speeded on the journey to their destination. In three weeks they came riding into the land to Nibelung's castle, to which they had been sent. There, in the march of Norway,[3] they found the warrior. The horses were very weary from the long way.

Siegfried and Kriemhild were both informed that knights had arrived, wearing clothes like those the fashion in Burgundy. She sprang up from a couch where she lay resting and bade a maid go to the window. In the court the maiden saw Gere standing with his companions. What joyful news this was for her homesick heart!

"Look at them walking in the court with Gere," she said to the king. "My brother Gunther sent them down the Rhine to us."

"They are welcome here," said Siegfried.

The whole household ran to see them, and each one greeted the messengers warmly, as best he could. Lord Siegmund rejoiced at their coming. Then Gere and his men were given lodgings, and servants were bidden to see to the horses. Having received permission to appear at court, the envoys now went to where Lord Siegfried sat with Kriemhild. The host and his wife rose at once from their seats, and Gere of Burgundy and his companions, Gunther's vassals, were cordially welcomed. They bade Gere to be seated.

"Permit us to deliver our message before we take our seats, and meanwhile let us way-worn guests remain standing. We bring you tidings which Gunther and Brunhild have sent you. All is well with them. And we also bring you word from Lady Ute. Young Giselher and Lord Gernot and your nearest kin send greetings to you from Gunther's land."

"May God reward them!" said Siegfried. "I have great trust in their loyalty and love, as one should with friends, and so does their sister too. Now tell us, are our dear friends at home in good spirits? Has anyone done my wife's kinsmen harm since we parted from them? That you must let me know. I will always help them faithfully till their foes regret my assistance."

Margrave Gere said, "They live in great honor and are so glad at heart that they invite you to the Rhine to a festival. They are

[3] Up to this point Siegfried's court has been at *Santen*, which is Xanten on the lower Rhine, and Siegfried's land has always been called Netherland. Now the poet suddenly places the court in Norway, and in this and the following chapters calls Siegfried's land sometimes Netherland, sometimes the Nibelung land. Various explanations have been offered for this confusion, but the confusion in geography is not important for the story itself. It is quite obvious that, apart from the names, the scene has not actually shifted.

longing to see you; of that you need have no doubts. And they ask my Lady Kriemhild to come with you. When the winter has come to an end, before the next Midsummer's Day, they would like to see you."

"That is hardly possible," said Siegfried.

Then Gere replied, "Your mother Ute, and Gernot and Giselher too, urge you not to refuse them. Every day I hear the lament that you live so far away. My Lady Brunhild and all her maidens will rejoice at the news that it might be possible for them to see you again. This would make them very happy."

Kriemhild was pleased with the message. Gere being her kinsman, the host bade him be seated and ordered that wine be poured for the guests. This was done at once.

Now Siegmund had also come to see the messengers and said to them graciously, "Welcome, you warriors, Gunther's men. Since my son Siegfried has won Kriemhild as his wife, we should see you more often here in this land, if you would claim friendship with us."

They said they would gladly come whenever he wished. Their immense weariness was now eased with joyous hospitality. The envoys were assigned seats, and a great plenty of food was brought them, as Siegfried had commanded. Full nine days the knights were kept there till at last they complained at not being permitted to ride back to their land.

Meanwhile King Siegfried had sent for his friends. He asked them for their advice as to whether they should go to the Rhine.

"My brother-in-law Gunther and his kinsmen have summoned me to a festival. I would like to visit him, except that his land is so far from here. They also ask Kriemhild to come with me. Now counsel me, dear friends. How is she to get there? As for me, I would put myself at their service even if I had to do battle for them in thirty lands."

"If you are inclined to take the trip to the festival," said his warriors, "we will advise you what to do. Ride to the Rhine with a thousand men. In this way you can appear with honor among the Burgundians."

Then Lord Siegmund said, "If you want to go to the festival, why don't you tell me so? Unless you are against it, I will ride there with you. I'll take a hundred warriors and so strengthen your company."

"If you wish to ride with us, my dear father," said Siegfried, "I shall be very happy. Within twelve days I will leave my lands."

Then to all who desired them, horses and apparel were given. The king having decided to take the journey, the good envoys were now bidden to ride home, and he sent word by them to his wife's kinsmen that he would gladly attend their festival. Siegfried and Kriemhild, so we are told, gave them so many presents that their horses could not carry them home to their land. He was a wealthy man. With light hearts the messengers urged the sturdy pack horses on their way.

Siegfried and Siegmund equipped their men with clothing, and Margrave Eckewart at once gave orders to seek out ladies' garments, the best that were at hand or could be obtained in all of Siegfried's land. Saddles and shields were made ready, and the knights and ladies who were to go with them were given whatever they wished, so that they lacked for nothing. Thus Siegfried brought his friends many a splendid guest.

The messengers made great haste upon their homeward journey, and Gere received a hearty welcome when he arrived in Burgundy. They dismounted from their horses before Gunther's hall. And, as people always do, young and old gathered round to ask the news.

"You will hear it when I tell the king," said the good knight and went with his companions to find Gunther.

For very joy the king sprang from his seat. Brunhild thanked them for returning so soon, and Gunther asked, "How is Siegfried, who has done so much for me?"

"He turned red for joy," said Gere, "and your sister too. No man ever sent friends a message so sincere as the one Lord Siegfried and his father have sent to you."

The queen said to the margrave, "Now tell me, is Kriemhild coming to see us? Has the fair lady still retained the gracious courtesy she knew so well how to practice?"

"Yes, she will certainly come," answered Gere.

Ute then asked the messengers to come to her at once. By the way she questioned them one could tell that she was eager to hear whether Kriemhild was still in good health. Gere told how he had found her and said she would come very soon. Nor did they keep silent at court about the presents Lord Siegfried had given them. They brought out the gold and the garments for the three kings' men to see, and Siegfried and Kriemhild were praised for their great generosity.

"It's easy enough for him to be generous," said Hagen. "He couldn't use up all his wealth even if he lived forever. He has in his possession the treasure of the Nibelungs. Oh, if that could only get to Burgundy some day!"

The whole court rejoiced that they were coming. Late and early the three kings' vassals were anything but idle, and many seats were made ready for the crowd. Hunolt and Sindolt had little rest, for during this time they had to oversee the stewards and cup-bearers in the arranging of the benches. Ortwin helped at this, and Gunther expressed his thanks. How well Rumolt, the master cook, ruled his underlings, the many huge kettles, pots, and pans! And oh, what a tremendous number there were! Thus the foods were prepared for those who were coming to the land.

XIII

How Siegfried Went to the Festival with His Wife

Let us say no more about their labors but tell how Lady Kriemhild and her maidens journeyed from the Nibelung land to the Rhine. Never did pack horses carry so many rich garments. They made ready for the way numerous travel chests, and Siegfried, accompanied by his friends and by the queen, set out for the place where they hoped to find joy. But for all of them this joy soon turned to bitter sorrow. They left their little son at home; they could not do otherwise. Their journey to the court brought him great grief. The child never saw father nor mother again. Lord Siegmund also rode with them. Had he known what was to happen at the festival, he would not have gone. No greater misfortune could ever befall dear kinsmen of his.

Messengers were sent ahead to bring the news of their coming, and many of Ute's kin and Gunther's men, a splendid host, rode out to meet them. Gunther went to great pains in preparing for his guests.

He went to where Brunhild was sitting and said, "How did my sister receive you when you came into my land? You must welcome Siegfried's wife in the same way."

"I will," she said, "for I have every reason to be fond of her."

"They will arrive early tomorrow," said the king. "If you want to greet them, there is no time to be lost if they are not to find us still here in the castle. Never have I had such welcome guests."

She bade her maidens and ladies get out fine clothing, the best they could find, to wear before the guests. I can assure you they complied willingly. Gunther gathered his warriors about him, and they all hastened away to pay their respects. The queen rode out in great splendor, and how joyfully the visitors were received! It seemed to everyone there that not even Lady Kriemhild had welcomed Lady Brunhild so graciously to the Burgundian land. Those who had never seen Kriemhild before now realized what true nobility is.

Siegfried had also arrived with his men, and over all the plain the knights could be seen coursing back and forth in innumerable bands. No one could escape the jostling and the dust.

When the host of the land saw Siegfried and Siegmund, he said with great cordiality, "You are most welcome to me and all my friends. We are very happy at your journey to our court."

"May God reward you," said Siegmund, a man who strove for honor. "Ever since my son Siegfried won you as a kinsman, my heart has urged me to visit you."

King Gunther responded, "It is my pleasure to see this now accomplished."

Siegfried was received with the high esteem that was his due, for no one there was hostile to him, and Giselher and Gernot assisted with the greatest of courtesy. No guests, I am sure, have ever been shown such friendliness.

Now the wives of the two kings approached each other, and many a saddle was emptied as knightly hands lifted the ladies down upon the grass. Any man who enjoyed serving ladies was busily occupied! The two charming women[1] now met, and many knights rejoiced that their greeting was so graceful. The royal com-

---

[1] I.e., Brunhild and Kriemhild.

pany was assembled, and each knight took his lady by the hand. Fair ladies bowed courteously to each other and exchanged fond kisses, a pleasing sight to Gunther's and Siegfried's men.

Without further delay they rode to the town. The host bade his guests be shown that they were welcome in Burgundy, and much fine tilting was performed in the presence of the maidens. Hagen and Ortwin took charge, and whatever they commanded was done. Many a service they rendered the honored guests. Shields clanged loudly from thrusts and blows before the castle gate. The host and his visitors lingered long before going inside, for the time passed rapidly with their knightly games.

Then in good spirits they rode to the magnificent palace. Coverings of fine pfellel silk, elegant and skillfully cut, hung down on either side from the ladies' saddles. Gunther's vassals now appeared, and orders were given to lead the guests at once to their chambers. Now and then Brunhild was seen to glance at Lady Kriemhild, who was indeed very lovely. Her fair coloring shone out radiantly against the gold of her gown.

Everywhere in the town of Worms could be heard the festive tumult of the court followers. Gunther bade his marshal to attend to them, and Dankwart assigned the company very comfortable quarters. Food was served both outside and inside the castle.[2] Never did guests from foreign lands receive better care; everything they desired was willingly provided. The king was so wealthy that no one was denied anything. They were served courteously, without any hostility.

The host now sat at table with his guests. Siegfried was asked to sit where he had sat before,[3] and many knights escorted him to his place. Twelve hundred warriors sat at his round table, whereat Queen Brunhild thought to herself that no liegeman could be more powerful. Yet she was still so kindly disposed toward him that she did not wish him dead.

That evening as the king sat there and the cup-bearers went from table to table, many rich robes were wet with wine. Zealously every service was given, as has long been the custom at festivals. No matter from where the guests came, the host was ready to serve them, and with friendly hospitality they were all given

[2] The knights and ladies had their meals inside the castle, the followers outside.

[3] I.e., in the seat of honor opposite the host.

aplenty. And now fine lodgings were ordered for the ladies and maidens.

When the night was ended and the day appeared, from the travel chests many a precious stone glittered on fine garments as the ladies touched them and unpacked the many sumptuous gowns. The day had not yet fully dawned when a host of knights and squires came out in front of the hall, and again there arose a joyous tumult, before the early mass that was sung for the king. So well did young heroes journey there that the king commended them. Trumpets blared shrilly, and the noise of drums and flutes swelled so mightily that the wide city of Worms re-echoed from the sound. The lusty warriors all sprang to horse, and noble games of chivalry commenced. Many were seen there whose young hearts beat high, splendid knights beneath their shields. The ladies and maidens, richly adorned, took seats at the windows and watched the men at their knightly sports. Then the host himself and his friends began to tilt. Thus they passed the time and did not think it long.

Now from the cathedral was heard the ringing of many bells. The palfreys came, and the ladies rode forth, with many men escorting the two queens. Before the minster they dismounted to the grass. Brunhild was still friendly toward her guests. Wearing their crowns, the queens entered the spacious church. Soon this affection was sundered; great hatred was the cause. After they had heard mass, they rode away again in state and were seen going happily to table. Their joy at the festival did not cease until the eleventh day.

XIV

How the Queens Quarreled

One day, before vespers, a great turmoil arose from many knights in the courtyard, where for pastime they practiced knightly sports, and a throng of men and women came running to look on. The queens had sat down together, their thoughts occupied with two splendid warriors.

Then Kriemhild said, "I have a husband who should by right have all this realm in his power."

"How could that be?" said Lady Brunhild. "If no one else were alive except for him and you, these lands might well be subject to him, but as long as Gunther lives, that could never happen."

Then Kriemhild spoke again. "Just look at how he stands and with what true majesty he surpasses the warriors as the bright moon outshines the stars. I have good reason to be happy."

"No matter how stately your husband may be, and excellent and handsome," said Lady Brunhild, "you must admit that your brother Gunther has the advantage over him. I assure you, he is the best of all kings."

Lady Kriemhild answered, "So worthy is my husband that I have not praised him without due cause. His renown is great in many respects. Believe me, Brunhild, he is easily Gunther's peer."

"Don't take offense, Kriemhild, for I did not speak thus without reason. I heard them both declare, at my first meeting with them, when the king gained the victory over me and won my love in such knightly fashion, that Siegfried was the king's vassal. He admitted it himself. So I consider him a liegeman, for I heard him say it."

"If that were so," said Kriemhild, "it would be disgraceful treatment of me. Why should my brothers have tried to make me wife to a vassal? So I ask you kindly, Brunhild, out of friendship for me, to stop talking about such things."

"I can't stop," said Brunhild. "Why should I renounce so many knights who, together with Siegfried, owe us fealty?"

Kriemhild flew into a rage. "You will have to renounce him, for he will never do you any feudal service. He is more distinguished than my brother Gunther. You ought to spare me what I have heard from you. And I am really surprised, since he is your vassal and you have such power over both of us, that he has failed to pay you tribute for so long. I have had quite enough of your arrogance."

"You are getting too high and mighty," said Brunhild. "I'll be curious to see whether people will treat you with as much respect as they do me."

Both ladies became furious, and Lady Kriemhild said, "We'll take care of that right now. Since you have declared my husband to be your vassal, both kings' men shall see today whether I dare enter the church before the queen, and you will have the proof of your own eyes that I am noble and free and that my husband is superior to yours. As for me, I don't care to be abused for what I have said. You shall see yet today how your liegewoman goes to court in Burgundy at the head of her warriors. I'll show that I am higher in rank than any queen who ever wore a crown."

Fierce hatred now flared up between the two women.

Then Brunhild spoke again. "If you insist you are not my liege-woman, then you and your ladies must separate yourselves from my retinue when we go to the church."

"We shall do that, you may be sure," replied Kriemhild. Then to her ladies-in-waiting she said, "Now attire yourselves. I must remain without reproach. Let everyone see that you have costly garments. Brunhild shall have good cause to take back the statements she has made."

They did not need urging, but sought out sumptuous gowns, and many a lady and maiden dressed herself splendidly. Then Kriemhild, also finely arrayed, set out with her train of three and forty maidens whom she had brought to the Rhine. Wearing bright pfellel silk made in Araby, the lovely maidens proceeded to the minster. Siegfried's men all waited for them in front of the castle.

The people were surprised to see the queens separated, not walking together as before, and wondered why it was. Many a warrior, because of this, later suffered dire distress. Here before the minster stood Gunther's wife, while a host of knights passed the time in dalliance with the ladies. Now came Lady Kriemhild with her proud company. Any garments the daughters of noble knights had ever worn were as nothing compared to those of her retinue. Kriemhild was so rich in possessions that the wives of thirty kings could not have displayed a splendor equal to hers. And even had anyone wished, he could not have said he had ever seen such costly gowns as her maidens were wearing at this moment. She would not have done it except to annoy Brunhild.

They met before the vast minster. With a hatred intense the mistress of the castle sharply ordered Kriemhild to halt. "No bond-woman may precede the wife of the king."

Her temper aroused, Kriemhild replied, "It would have been better for you if you could have held your peace. You have brought disgrace upon yourself. How could a vassal's mistress ever become the wife of a king?"

"Whom are you calling a mistress?" asked the queen.

"You," said Kriemhild. "Your body was first caressed by Siegfried, my husband. It was not my brother who took your virginity. What were you thinking of? It was a vile trick. Why did you let him love you if he is your liegeman? You have no right to complain."

"Gunther shall hear of this, you may be sure," said Brunhild.

"What is that to me? Your arrogance has betrayed you. With your words you have claimed me as your servant. And I tell you frankly, this will always grieve me. I refuse to keep your secret any longer out of friendship."

Then Brunhild wept. Kriemhild delayed no more, but with her retinue preceded the queen into the minster. Thus there arose great hatred, and bright eyes grew dim and moist. Whatever was done or sung there in God's service, the time seemed to Brunhild far too long, for she was greatly troubled in spirit. Many a brave hero was later to pay for this.

Brunhild went out with her ladies and stopped before the minster. "Kriemhild must tell me more," she thought, "about what she has accused me of, that sharp-tongued woman. If Siegfried has boasted about this, it will cost him his life."

Now Kriemhild came out, accompanied by many knights.

"Stop a minute," said Lady Brunhild. "You called me Siegfried's mistress. Prove it. I want you to know, your assertions have wounded me deeply."

"You would do better to let me go," said Lady Kriemhild. "I can prove it with the golden ring I have on my hand. My husband brought it to me when he first lay with you."

Brunhild had never had a more distressing day.

"This precious gold," she said, "was stolen and hidden from me out of spite for a very long time. I know now who took it."

By this time both women were in a passion.

Then Kriemhild answered, "I'll not be called a thief. You would have done better to be silent if your honor were dear to you. I'll prove that I am not lying by the girdle I wear about my waist. My Siegfried became your lover."

She was wearing the band of silk from Nineveh, set with precious stones; it was indeed magnificent. When Lady Brunhild saw it, she began to weep. Gunther now had to hear of this and all the Burgundian men.

"Ask the Prince of the Rhine to come," said the queen. "I want him to hear how his sister has mocked me. She is saying openly that I am Siegfried's mistress."

The king came with his warriors. When he saw his beloved weeping, he said gently, "Tell me, dear Lady, who has hurt you?"

"I have every reason to be unhappy," she said. "Your sister would like to deprive me of all my honor. Listen to my complaint. She claims that Siegfried, her husband, has had me as his mistress."

"Then she has done a wicked thing," said King Gunther.

"She is wearing the girdle I lost, and my ring of red gold. My Lord, I shall regret that I was ever born unless you clear me of this great disgrace. If you do, I will always be grateful to you."

Then King Gunther said, "Bid the hero of Netherland to appear here. He must admit it if he has boasted of this, or he must deny it."

Orders were given to fetch Kriemhild's husband at once. When Lord Siegfried saw the angry women, he said quickly, for he did not know the circumstances, "Why are these women weeping? That I would like to know, or for what reason the king sent for me."

"I am deeply grieved," said King Gunther. "My Lady Brunhild has told me you have boasted that you were the first to caress her body. Lady Kriemhild, your wife, says so."

"If she said this," replied Siegfried, "she shall suffer for it before I am through. And on my solemn oath I am willing to testify before all your men that I did not tell her this."

"You shall be put to the test," said the king. "If you swear here to the oath which you offer, I will acquit you of all false charges."

The Burgundians were bidden to form a circle, and Siegfried stretched out his hand for the oath.

Then the king said, "Your perfect innocence is so well known to me that I acquit you of having done what my sister accuses you of."

Siegfried replied, "If my wife does not pay for having grieved Brunhild, I shall be greatly distressed, I assure you."

The good knights of Burgundy looked at one another.[1]

"One should train women so," said Siegfried, "that they refrain from insolent words. Forbid this to your wife, and I'll do the same to mine. I am truly ashamed of her great discourtesy."

Many fair ladies were now estranged, no longer speaking to each

[1] The knights serving as witnesses are surprised that Gunther acquits Siegfried without the oath.

other. Brunhild grieved so deeply that Gunther's men were moved to pity. Hagen of Troneg sought out his lady. He found her weeping and asked what was the matter. She told him the story, and he vowed to her then and there that Kriemhild's husband should atone for this or he himself would never know happiness again. Ortwin and Gernot now joined in the talk, and all counseled Siegfried's death.

Giselher also came up, but when he heard their words, he spoke out loyally, "Good warriors, why do you do this? Siegfried has not deserved such hatred that he should therefore lose his life. Women always quarrel about trifles."

"Are we going to shelter adulterers?" [2] said Hagen. "Such good warriors as you will gain little honor from that. He has boasted of possessing my dear lady. This shall cost him his life, or I will die myself."

Then Gunther said, "He has brought us nothing but good and honor. Let him live. What purpose would it serve if I should hate him now? He has always been faithful to us, and that very willingly."

But Ortwin of Metz spoke up, "His great strength cannot help him now. If my lord will permit, I'll do him some damage."

So without cause they had declared a feud against him. Yet no one pursued the matter, except that Hagen constantly pointed out to Gunther that if Siegfried were no longer alive, many kings' lands would fall under his rule. At this the king grew sad, and so they let it be.

Knightly sports were now seen there again. Oh, how many sturdy spearshafts were shattered in the presence of Siegfried's wife, before the minster and all the way to the hall! Gunther's men were furious.[3]

"Give up this murderous rage," said the king. "Siegfried was born to our good fortune and our honor. And besides, the man is completely fearless and so frightfully strong that if he noticed anything, no one would dare withstand him."

---

[2] The original meaning of the word *gouch* is "cuckoo." Since the cuckoo is known for laying its eggs in other birds' nests, the word later took on the connotation of adulterer.

[3] Siegfried's men intentionally devote themselves to Kriemhild and maintain the festival mood. Gunther's men see in this an insult to Brunhild and become angry.

"*He* won't," said Hagen. "You need not worry. I'll undertake to arrange things in secret, so that he shall suffer for Brunhild's tears. Hagen will always be his enemy."

"How could that be done?" asked King Gunther.

"I will tell you," answered Hagen. "We'll order messengers not known to anyone here to ride into our land and declare war on us openly. Then you will say in the presence of the guests that you and your men intend to go to battle. Once that is done, Siegfried will promise to come to your aid. And for this he shall lose his life, that is, if I can get certain information from the warrior's wife."

To his misfortune, the king followed Hagen's counsel, and the knights began to plan great disloyalty before anyone was aware of it. From the quarreling of two women many a hero lost his life.

X V

How Siegfried Was Betrayed

On the fourth morning two and thirty men came riding to the court, and word was brought to Gunther that war had been declared against him. A lie caused women direst grief. Having received permission to appear before the king, the riders claimed they were Liudeger's men, whom Siegfried had once vanquished and brought as hostages to Gunther's land. Gunther greeted the messengers and bade them be seated.

"My Lord," said one of them, "permit us to stand until we have given the message we have been charged with for you. You must know that you have many a mother's son as your enemy. Liudegast and Liudeger, whom you once did such terrible injury, declare war upon you. They intend to ride with their army into your land."

The king grew angry when he heard this communication, and orders were given to lead the traitor envoys to their lodgings. How could Lord Siegfried, or anyone else, protect himself against what they were plotting? They themselves suffered greatly for this afterward. The king walked with his friends, consulting in whispers. Hagen gave him not a moment's peace. Plenty of the king's men would have liked to settle the matter amicably, but Hagen refused to give up his scheme.

One day Siegfried found them whispering and asked, "Why are the king and his men so sad? If anyone has done him harm, I'll gladly help to avenge it."

"I have reason to be sad," said Gunther. "Liudegast and Liudeger have declared war on me. They plan to ride to my land in open arms."

At this the valiant warrior said, "Siegfried's hand shall vigorously prevent this, and your honor be preserved. I'll give these warriors the same treatment as I did previously. I'll lay waste their lands and castles before I turn back. For this my head shall be your security. You and your warriors stay here at home, and let me ride against them with my own men. I'll show you that I serve you willingly. Be assured, your enemies shall suffer at my hands."

"How happy I am at what you have said!" said the king, as if he were truly glad for the aid, and the faithless man bowed his thanks deceitfully.

"You need have no worries," said Siegfried.

They now made preparations for the journey with the foot soldiers,[1] though merely for the sake of appearance, to deceive Siegfried and his men. Siegfried then bade his warriors to equip themselves, and they got out their battle attire.

"Siegmund, my father," said Siegfried, "you must stay here. If God grants us good fortune, we shall return to the Rhine soon. Remain here with the king and enjoy yourself."

They tied fast the banners as if they intended to depart. Many of Gunther's men knew nothing of why this was done. A great host could be seen assembled around Siegfried. Fastening their helmets and their breastplates to the horses,[2] many knights prepared to leave the land. Then Hagen sought out Kriemhild to bid her good-by, adding that they were about to leave.

"How glad I am," said Kriemhild, "that I won a husband who has the courage to protect my dear kinsmen as well as Lord Siegfried does. I am proud and happy at this. Don't forget, dear friend

---

[1] Since Siegfried is taking his own knights, the Burgundians provide only the rank and file.

[2] These parts of the armor are not put on until the battle begins.

Hagen, that I am wholly at your service and have never wished you ill. Let my beloved husband benefit from this. Don't make him pay for anything I have done to Brunhild. I have come to regret it since. Besides, he beat me black and blue. He has taken ample revenge that I ever said anything to offend her."

"You will be friends again after a while," he said. "Kriemhild, dear Lady, do tell me how I can serve you in regard to Siegfried, your husband. I shall be glad to do it, Lady. There is no one I would rather serve."

"I would not have any fear," she said, "that someone might take his life in battle if he weren't so inclined to be foolhardy. But for that, the brave warrior would be quite safe."

"Lady," said Hagen, "if you fear that he may be wounded, tell me by what means I can prevent this. Whether on horse or afoot, I will always watch over him."

"You are my kinsman," she said, "and I am yours. I commend to you in trust my sweet love, my dear husband, that you may guard him well."

Then she told him things which would better have been left unsaid. "My husband is courageous and very strong. When he killed the dragon on the mountain, he bathed himself in its blood, and since then no weapon has ever cut him in battle. And yet I am afraid, whenever he is in combat and spear thrusts fly from warriors' hands, that I may lose my dear husband. Alas, what great anguish I often endure for Siegfried's sake! I will reveal to you, dear kinsman, confident that you will keep faith with me, where he can be wounded. I tell you this, trusting in your loyalty. When the hot blood gushed from the dragon's wounds and Siegfried bathed in it, a broad linden leaf fell between his shoulder blades. There he can be cut, and of this I am afraid."

Then Hagen said, "Sew a small sign on his clothing. By this I will know where I must guard him when we are in battle."

She thought to save the hero. Instead, she caused his death.

"With fine silk," she said, "I'll sew a cross on his clothing, almost invisible. It is there that your hand must guard my husband when he stands among his enemies in the thick of battle."

"That I shall do, my dear Lady," Hagen replied.

And again Kriemhild thought this would help him. Instead, her husband was thus betrayed. Hagen then took his leave and went away in high spirits. And all the king's followers were well content.

No warrior, I think, will ever again plot such a treacherous scheme as Hagen did then, while Kriemhild, the queen, trusted in his loyalty.

The next morning Lord Siegfried rode forth gaily with his thousand men, thinking he was to avenge the grievance of his kinsmen. Hagen rode so close to him that he could see his clothing. As soon as he spied the sign, he sent two of his men away secretly to deliver a different message and say that Liudeger had sent them and that Gunther's land would remain at peace. How unwillingly Siegfried now rode back again without having avenged any injury to his kin! Gunther's men could scarcely persuade him to turn round.

He rode to the king, who said gratefully, "May God reward you for your intent, friend Siegfried. I shall always be thankful to you, as I rightly should, for being so ready to do what I ask of you. I trust you above all my friends. Now that we are freed from this campaign, I want to ride to the Wasken woods, as I've done very often, to hunt bear and boar."

This Hagen had counseled, the faithless man.

"Have all my guests told that we shall ride out early. Let those who wish to hunt with me get ready. But if any wish to stay here and amuse themselves with the ladies, that is quite agreeable to me."

"If you ride out hunting," said Siegfried, "I would like to go with you. Lend me a huntsman and a hunting dog, and I'll ride to the pine woods."

"Do you want only one huntsman?" asked the king. "I'll lend you four, if you like, who know the woods well and the paths where the game goes and won't let you miss the camp."

Siegfried now rode to his wife, while Hagen quickly told the king how he planned to overpower the warrior. No man should ever practice such disloyalty.

XVI

How Siegfried Was Killed

Gunther and Hagen treacherously proclaimed a hunt in the forest to go for boar, bear, and bison with their sharp spears. What could be braver sport? They took along many kinds of food. And Siegfried rode with them in splendid array. At a cool spring he was soon to lose his life, as Brunhild had urged.[1]

The brave warrior now went to where he found Kriemhild. His fine hunting gear and that of his companions were already loaded on pack horses, for they meant to cross the Rhine. Never did Kriemhild have reason to be more sorrowful.

He kissed his love on the mouth. "Lady, God grant that I see you again in good health, and that your eyes may see me too. Pass the time pleasantly with your loving kinsmen. I cannot remain here at home."

Then she thought of what she had told Hagen, though not daring to confess it, and she began to lament that she had ever been born and wept uncontrollably.

"Let your hunting be," she said. "I dreamt last night of misfortune, how two wild boars chased you over the heath, and then the flowers grew red. Truly, I cannot help weeping so. I very much fear some sort of plot. Perhaps we have offended persons here who hate us and can do us harm. Stay with me, my dear Lord. In good faith I counsel you so."

"My love," he said, "I'll return in a few short days. I know no one here who bears me hate. All your kinsmen are friendly toward me, nor have I deserved otherwise of them."

"No, no, Lord Siegfried! Truly I fear your ruin. I dreamt last

[1] Here is one of the traces of the clash between earlier and later versions of the tale of Siegfried. This passage does not seem compatible with the poet's earlier description of Hagen as the instigator of the revenge.

night of misfortune, how two mountains fell down upon you, and I never saw you again. If you leave me, it will break my heart."

He clasped the gentle lady in his arms, and kissing her tenderly, he fondled her lovely body. Very soon after, he took his leave. Alas, she never saw him alive again.

Then they rode away into a deep forest in search of manly sport. Many knights followed Gunther and his men, but Gernot and Giselher remained at home. Heavily laden horses had crossed the Rhine before them, bearing bread and wine for the company of hunters, and meats and fish and numerous other provisions, such as a king so rich naturally possesses. The hunters were instructed to make camp on a broad island [2] at the edge of the green forest, near the place where game could be started and where they were to hunt. They informed the king that Siegfried, too, had arrived. Now the hunting companions occupied their stations on all sides.

"Who is going to lead us to the game in the forest?" asked Siegfried.

"Let us separate," replied Hagen, "before we begin the hunt. Then we will know, my lords and I, who are the best hunters on this trip to the woods. Let's divide men and hounds and let everyone go where he pleases. Whoever gets the best catch shall receive our praise."

After these words the hunters did not remain together much longer.

"I need no hounds," said Lord Siegfried, "except one hunting dog that has been trained [3] to find the track of the animals through the woods. We'll get the game all right."

An experienced huntsman took a good hunting dog and in a short time led Siegfried to where there was plenty of game. All the animals that rose from their lairs the comrades caught, as good hunters do. Whatever the hound started, bold Siegfried struck down with his hand. His horse ran so hard that not a one escaped him. In the chase he won praise beyond all the rest. He excelled in everything. He killed the first animal of the hunt with his own

[2] A *wert* is a river island. This scarcely fits with the general description of the region of the hunt, but is no more puzzling than some other geographical references. See Introduction, and Index of Names below.

[3] The word *genozzen* is a hunting term meaning that the dog has been trained by feeding him the flesh of wild game so that he can find the track.

hands, a powerful half-grown boar. Shortly afterward he came upon an enormous lion.[4] When the hound started it, he shot it with his bow, in which he had strung a sharp arrow. After the shot the lion took only three more leaps, and Siegfried's hunting comrades applauded him. Then in quick succession he killed a bison and an elk, four strong auerochs,[5] and a fierce shelk.[6] His horse bore him so swiftly that nothing escaped him. Neither hart nor hind could elude him. Then the dog started a mighty boar. When it began to flee, the champion of the hunt immediately barred its path. Furiously the boar ran at him, but Kriemhild's husband slew it with his sword. For any other hunter this would not have been so easy. After he had felled it, they put the hound on its leash. And now word soon spread among the Burgundians about Siegfried's rich booty.

Then his huntsmen[7] said, "If it is possible, Lord Siegfried, leave some of the game alive for us. You'll empty our mountain today and our forest as well."

The warrior smiled at this. Now all around they heard the calls of men and the baying of hounds, and so great was the noise that mountain and wood echoed with the sound. Four and twenty packs the hunters had let loose. Many a beast lost its life that day, for each man hoped to win the prize at the hunt. But their efforts proved to be in vain as soon as the mighty Siegfried was seen standing by the fire. The hunt was over, and yet not quite. Those who went to the campfire took with them the hides of many animals, and game aplenty. Oh, what a load was carried to the kitchen for the king's retinue!

The king bade a signal be given the hunters that he wished to dine. One loud blast of a horn was blown, and with that they knew that the prince was there in camp.

"My Lord," said one of Siegfried's huntsmen, "I heard the blast of a horn summoning us to the camp. I'll give answer to it."

Again and again the horn was blown to call the company back.

---

[4] Needless to say, there were no lions in the forests of Germany. The lion is, however, a favorite beast in medieval German literature, and an encounter with a lion always helps to enhance the fame of a hero.

[5] The European bison, once widely distributed, but now nearly extinct.

[6] An extinct species of giant deer. For lack of an English word, I use an Anglicized spelling of the original.

[7] The plural here seems to be inconsistent with Siegfried's demand for only one huntsman, but the slip, if it is one, is of no great moment.

Then Lord Siegfried said, "We'll leave the woods now too."

His horse bore him smoothly as they all dashed away together. Their uproar started a savage beast. It was a wild bear.

Siegfried called back to the men behind, "I'll provide us hunters with some good sport. Let the hound loose. I see a bear that shall go to camp with us. Unless it runs like mad, it can't possibly escape."

The hound was unleashed; the bear rushed off. Kriemhild's husband tried to ride it down, but he came upon a wild ravine where he could not get at it. The powerful beast now thought itself safe from the hunter, but the knight sprang from his horse and raced after it on foot. The animal was caught off guard and could not escape him. Promptly Siegfried seized it and without getting a single wound, he bound it tight so that it could neither scratch nor bite him. Tying it to his saddle, he mounted his horse, and out of sheer high spirits he took it for sport to the campfire.

How splendidly he rode to camp! His spear was large, sturdy, and broad. A fine sword hung down to his spurs, and he carried a handsome horn of red gold. I never heard tell of better hunting gear. He wore a cloak of black pfellel silk and a hat of rich sable. Oh, what costly borders he had upon his quiver! A panther's skin formed its covering for the sake of the sweet fragrance.[8] And he carried a bow which no one could bend but himself except with a windlass. His hunting garb was all of otter[9] skin, with inserts of other-colored furs from head to toe, and from the shining fur there gleamed on either side many a golden clasp. He carried Balmung, a broad and handsome sword. So sharp were its cutting edges that it never failed when wielded against a helmet. The splendid hunter was proud and gay. Since I must tell you everything, to the smallest detail—his precious quiver was full of good arrows, the heads mounted in gold and at least a hand's breadth wide. Whatever he pierced with them was soon doomed to die.

So the knight rode along in hunter's fashion. When Gunther's men saw him coming toward them, they ran to meet him and took charge of his horse. Hanging from his saddle was the big strong bear. Dismounting, he loosened the bands from its feet and snout.

---

[8] In the Middle Ages the panther was commonly believed to give off a sweet fragrance which attracted wild game.

[9] The meaning of the word *ludem* is not known. Some scholars believe it is the fish otter.

At once all the dogs that spied it barked noisily. The beast tried to head for the woods; the people were uneasy. Frightened by the din, the bear got into the kitchen. Oh, how it drove the kitchen boys from the fire! Many a kettle was upset and many a flaming log scattered. Alas, how much good food lay there in the ashes! Then the lords and their vassals sprang up from their seats. The bear began to get angry, and the king gave orders for all the hounds to be unleashed. This would have been a happy day if only things had ended well! Delaying no longer, the men ran for the bear with bows and spears, but there were so many dogs that nobody dared to shoot. The whole mountain rang with the people's shouting. The bear began to flee before the hounds, and no one but Kriemhild's husband could keep up with it. He ran it down and killed it with his sword. Then back to the fire they carried the bear, and all who saw it declared that he was a mighty man.

The hunting companions were bidden to go to the tables. A goodly company sat there on a pretty meadow. Oh, what choice foods were carried out to the hunters! Except that the cup-bearers were tardy in bringing wine, warriors could never be better served. Had there not been false hearts among them, they would have been free of all reproach.

Now Lord Siegfried said, "I wonder, since they provide us with such abundance from the kitchen, why the cup-bearers don't bring us the wine. Unless hunters are better treated, I'll not be your hunting-partner again. I certainly deserve to have more attentive service."

From his table the king answered deceitfully, "We will gladly recompense you for what we now lack. It is Hagen's fault. He wants us to die of thirst."

"My dear Lord," said Hagen, "I thought today's hunt was to be in the Spessart. I sent the wine there. We may go thirsty today, but another time I'll be more careful."

"Little thanks you will get for that!" said Lord Siegfried. "Seven pack horse loads of mead and spiced wine were to have been brought to me here. If that was not possible, our camp should have been placed closer to the Rhine."

Then Hagen said, "Noble Knights, I know a cool spring nearby. Let's go there. And don't be angry with me."

This counsel was to bring great sorrow to many a warrior. The pangs of thirst forced Siegfried to order the table removed all the sooner so that he could go to the spring at the foot of the mountain. Treacherously the warriors had contrived this plot. They sent the game Siegfried's hand had struck down on wagons to Gunther's land, and all who saw it admitted his great prowess.

Hagen basely broke faith with Siegfried. When they were about to start for the broad linden tree, he said, "I have often been told that no one could keep up with Kriemhild's husband if he felt like racing. Give us a demonstration now."

Then Siegfried said, "You can easily test that if you run a race with me to the spring. When it is finished, he who is seen there first, shall be declared the winner."

"Let's try it," said Hagen.

And Siegfried said, "I'll lie down on the grass at your feet." [10]

How pleased Gunther was when he heard this!

"I'll go even further," said Siegfried. "I'll carry all my equipment with me, my spear and shield and all my hunting garb."

Hastily he girded on quiver and sword. The other two[11] took off their clothes and stood there in their white shirts. Like two wild panthers they ran through the clover, but Siegfried was seen to be first at the spring. In all things he outshone many a man. Quickly he laid off his sword, set down his quiver, and leaned his sturdy spear against a branch of the linden. He now remained standing by the flowing spring, for his courtesy was great. Where the spring gushed forth, he laid down his shield, but would not drink, no matter how great his thirst, until the king had drunk. *He* gave him evil thanks for that.

The spring was cool, clear, and good. Gunther bent down to the water, and having drunk, he stood up and stepped aside. Siegfried would have liked to do the same, but now he paid for his courtesy. Hagen took away both bow and sword, then dashed back to where he found the spear. Now he looked for the sign on the brave man's clothing, and as Siegfried bent over the spring and drank, he pierced him through the cross so that his heart's blood spurted out of the wound and onto Hagen's shirt. Never again will a hero

---

[10] This passage seems to mean that Siegfried is giving Hagen another advantage in the race in addition to the one mentioned just afterward, for Siegfried will now have to jump up before he can begin to run.

[11] Both Gunther and Hagen run the race with Siegfried.

commit so vile a deed. He left the spear sticking in Siegfried's heart and fled more desperately than he had ever run before from any man.

When Siegfried felt the deep wound, he sprung up raging from the spring. The long spearshaft towered from his heart.[12] He thought to find bow or sword, and then Hagen would have been repaid as he deserved. But the sorely wounded hero could not find the sword and had nothing left but his shield. This he snatched from the spring and rushed at Hagen. King Gunther's man could not escape him. Though Siegfried was wounded to death, he struck so powerfully that many a precious stone flew off the shield, and the shield itself splintered to bits.

Hagen fell to the ground, and the island echoed loudly from the force of the blow. So angry was the wounded man, as he had reason to be, that if he had had his sword at hand, it would have been Hagen's death. He had grown pale and could not stand upright. His strength had gone completely, and on his fair complexion he bore the mark of death. Many a lovely lady later wept for him.

Kriemhild's husband fell among the flowers, the blood streaming from his wound. Then he began to upbraid those who had plotted this faithless death.

"You wicked cowards," he said, "of what avail are my services now that you have slain me? I have always been true to you, and this is my reward. Alas, you have brought shame upon all your kinsmen. All who are born in later times will bear this stain. You have avenged your wrath all too bitterly upon me. In disgrace you shall be outlawed from the fellowship of noble warriors."

The knights all ran to where he lay prostrate. For plenty of them this was a joyless day. Those who knew any loyalty mourned him, as he had well deserved. Gunther also lamented his death.

Then the dying man said, "There is no need for him who did the wrong to weep about it himself. He deserves severe censure, for it would better have been left undone."

"I don't know what you are all mourning about," said Hagen. "Our fear and our suffering are now over forever. We shall find

---

[12] Despite the poet's description, one must not forget that Hagen struck Siegfried in the back. The spear is therefore projecting backward, not forward.

few who will dare oppose us now. I am glad I have put an end to his power."

"It is easy enough for you to boast," said Siegfried. "If I had perceived your murderous intent, I would certainly have protected myself against you. Nothing grieves me so much as Lady Kriemhild, my wife. Now may God have pity that I ever had a son who for all time will bear the reproach that his kinsmen treacherously killed a man. If I could, I would make complaint of this—and rightly so." And piteously the dying man continued, "Noble King, if you will show any loyalty to anyone in the world, then let my dear love be commended to your favor, and let her benefit from being your sister. For the sake of all princely honor, stand by her faithfully. My father and my men will have to wait long for me. No woman has ever suffered so because of her dear love."

The flowers all around grew wet with blood. He wrestled with death, but not for long. Death's sword had cut all too deep, and the brave warrior could speak no more.

When the lords saw that he was dead, they laid him on a shield of red gold and took counsel how they could conceal that Hagen had done the deed.

Many of them said, "Things have gone badly for us. You must all hide it and say the same thing—that robbers killed Kriemhild's husband as he rode hunting alone through the woods."

Then Hagen of Troneg said, "I'll take him back home. I don't care if she does find out. She made Brunhild sad at heart, and it matters very little to me how much she may weep."

XVII

How Siegfried Was Mourned and Buried

They waited for the night and then crossed the Rhine. Never had heroes hunted worse. Noble maidens wept over *one* beast they slew, and many good warriors were later to suffer for its sake. Now listen to a tale of overbearing arrogance and terrible revenge.

Hagen ordered that the dead Siegfried be carried to the chamber where Kriemhild was. He bade the men lay him secretly outside the door, so that she should find him there when she went before dawn to early mass, which she never missed by lying abed.

The minster bells were rung as usual. Kriemhild wakened her maidens and bade that a light be brought and also her apparel. A chamberlain now came and found Siegfried there. He saw him red with blood, his clothing all wet, but he did not know that it was his lord. Carrying the light in his hand, he entered the chamber, and from him Lady Kriemhild heard grievous tidings.

She was about to set out with her ladies for the minster when the chamberlain said, "Stop. In front of this chamber lies the body of a knight."

Kriemhild began to lament uncontrollably. Before she had even made sure that it was her husband, she thought of Hagen's question as to how he might protect him. At that moment her real suffering began. With his death she renounced all happiness. She sank to the floor without a word and lay there, bereft of joy. Her grief was beyond measure. When at last she came out of her faint, she cried out so that the whole chamber rang.

Then her attendants said, "Perhaps it is a stranger."

The blood gushed out of her mouth, from her agony of heart. "It is Siegfried," she said, "my own dear husband. Brunhild planned this, and Hagen did the deed."

The lady bade them lead her to where the warrior lay, and with her white hand she raised his handsome head. Red though it was with blood, she knew him at once. It was the hero of the Nibelung land who lay there so pitifully.

Then sadly the gentle queen cried, "Oh, alas, what grief is mine! Your shield is not slashed with swords. You lie here murdered. If I knew who had done this, I would never stop plotting his death." [1]

The whole household lamented and mourned with their dear lady, for the loss of their noble lord distressed them deeply. Hagen had cruelly avenged Brunhild's wrath.

Then the sorrowful lady said, "You chamberlains go now and speedily waken Siegfried's men. And tell Siegmund of my grief and ask if he will help me mourn the brave Siegfried."

In great haste a messenger ran to where Siegfried's warriors

[1] This does not contradict her previous statement that Hagen was the murderer. She suspects him, but has as yet no proof.

were lying, and with his painful tidings robbed them of their joy. They refused to believe him until they heard the weeping. Then the messenger went quickly to the king. Lord Siegmund was not asleep. I think his heart told him what had befallen him, that he would never again see his dear son alive.

"Wake up, Lord Siegmund. Kriemhild, my Lady, bade me go to fetch you. She has been done a wrong that cuts her to the heart, beyond any other grief. You must help her mourn, for it concerns you too."

Siegmund sat up and said, "What is this sorrow of Kriemhild's of which you speak?"

Weeping, the messenger replied, "I cannot conceal it from you. The brave Siegfried has been killed."

Then Lord Siegmund said, "For my sake stop your jesting and the spreading of such bad news. Tell no one that he was killed, for I would never be able to mourn him enough before the day of my death."

"If you do not wish to believe what you hear me say, then you can hear for yourself Kriemhild and all her household bewailing Siegfried's death."

Siegmund was deeply shocked. He and his hundred men sprang from their beds and snatched up their long, sharp swords. Then, stricken with sorrow, they ran toward the wailing. Siegfried's men came also, a thousand warriors, and only when they heard the ladies mourning so piteously did some of them become aware that they ought to be properly dressed. For very grief they had lost their wits. Great sadness lay buried in their hearts.

King Siegmund went to Kriemhild and said, "Alas for the journey here to this land! Who, at the home of such good friends, has robbed us so treacherously, me of my son and you of your husband?"

"Oh, if I knew who it was," she said, "my heart would never show him mercy. I would plot such harm to him that his friends would be forced to tears because of me."

Lord Siegmund clasped the prince in his arms, and his friends' distress grew so great that palace and hall and the city of Worms echoed with the mighty sound of their mourning and weeping. No one could console Siegfried's wife. They drew off the clothes from his fair body and washed his wounds and laid him on the bier. His people were heartsick in their great despair.

Then his warriors said, "Our hands will always be ready to avenge him. He who did it is in this castle."

The men hastened to their arms and returned with their shields, eleven hundred excellent warriors. These Lord Siegmund now had in his troop.[2] He was eager to avenge the death of his son, though they did not know whom to oppose in battle unless it were Gunther and his men, with whom Siegfried had ridden to the hunt.

When Kriemhild saw them armed, she was greatly dismayed. However deep her sorrow and however intense her distress, she feared so very much the death of the Nibelungs at the hands of her brothers' men that she intervened. She warned them kindly as one dear friend to another.

"My Lord Siegmund," said the grief-stricken woman, "what do you plan to do? Surely you do not know how many bold men King Gunther has. You will all be lost if you attack them."

With helmets bound fast they stood there, impatient for the fight. The queen begged and even commanded them to forbear, and when they refused, she was greatly distressed.

"Lord Siegmund," she said, "let this be until a better time. Then with your help I will avenge my husband. If I get proof of who robbed me of him, I shall be his ruin. There are so many arrogant warriors here on the Rhine that I advise you not to fight. They have thirty men for every one of yours. May God give them such fortune as they have deserved of us! Remain here and bear this sorrow with me. When day begins to dawn, valiant heroes, help me lay my dear husband in his coffin."

The warriors answered, "That shall be done."

No one could possibly describe to you how great beyond belief were the laments of knights and ladies, so that even in the city the sound of mourning was heard. The good townsmen hurried to the castle and mourned with the guests, for they were sorely grieved. And their wives wept there with the ladies. No one had told them of any crime of Siegfried's, for which the warrior had lost his life.

Smiths were bidden to make haste and fashion a coffin of silver and gold, very large and strong, and brace it firmly with bars of good steel. Then all the people were sad at heart.

The night had come to an end, and the dawn was about to break.

---

[2] A thousand are Siegfried's men from the Nibelung land. The remaining hundred are Siegmund's. Upon Siegfried's death, his men look to Siegmund for leadership.

Kriemhild now bade them bear Siegfried, her beloved husband, to the minster. All the friends he had there were seen weeping as they went. Many a bell rang as they took him to the church, and on all sides[3] could be heard the chanting of many priests. Then toward the sound of mourning came King Gunther with his men, and the fierce Hagen too.

"Dear sister," said Gunther, "alas for your suffering! And alas that we could not be spared this great misfortune! We shall mourn Siegfried's death forever."

"You have no reason to," said Kriemhild. "If you were grieved at this, it would never have happened. You did not think of me—this I can say for sure—when I and my dear husband were thus parted. Would to God it had happened to me instead!"

They persisted in their denial, and Kriemhild continued, "Let him who is innocent prove it. Let him go to the bier in the presence of the people. By this the truth will be known at once."

This is a great marvel, yet it happens very often. When the murder-stained man stands beside the dead, the wounds bleed again. And so it happened there, and Hagen's guilt was plain to all. The wounds bled profusely, as they had done at first, and those who had mourned before, now mourned even more.

Then King Gunther said, "I shall tell you how it was. Robbers killed him. Hagen did not do it."

"I know these robbers well," she said. "God grant that his friends may yet avenge him. Gunther and Hagen, you did the deed."

At this Siegfried's warriors wanted to attack, but Kriemhild said to them, "Bear this grief with me."

Gernot and Giselher, these two, now went to where he lay dead. They mourned him sincerely, with the others, and wept with all their hearts. It was time to sing the mass, and from all around women, men, and children were coming to the minster. Even those who did not feel his loss wept for Siegfried now.

Gernot and Giselher said, "My sister, console yourself after this death, for it cannot be changed. We will try to make up to you for it as long as we live."

But no one in the world could give her any comfort. At midday his coffin was ready, and they lifted him from the bier on

[3] Perhaps the chanting of the mass for the dead in all the churches of the city.

which he lay. The queen would not allow him to be buried yet; there were still fatiguing labors which all had to share. They wound the dead man in a rich pfellel silk. There was no one, I think, who did not weep. Ute and her entire household made heartfelt lament for him. When word spread that Siegfried had been placed in his coffin, and that mass was being chanted in the minster, a great thronging began. How many offerings were made for the sake of his soul! Even in the land of his enemies he had good friends enough.

The sorrowful Kriemhild said to her chamberlains, "Let those who wish him well and are true to me endure stress[4] for my sake. For Siegfried's soul divide his gold among them."

There was no child so small—if it was old enough to understand—that did not bring its offering before he was buried. More than a hundred masses were sung there that day. And great was the press of Siegfried's friends. When the mass was sung, the people departed.

Then Lady Kriemhild said, "Do not let me hold vigil alone tonight over this peerless warrior. With him all my joy has vanished. I wish him to remain here for three days and three nights, that I may look my fill on my beloved husband. Perhaps God will command death to take me too. Then I, wretched Kriemhild, would find an end to my grief."

The people of the town now returned to their lodgings. Priests and monks she asked to remain, and Siegfried's men as well, to keep watch over the hero. Their nights were arduous, and their days exhausting. Many a man abstained from food and drink, but those who desired it were informed that they would be served abundantly. Lord Siegmund saw to this. During the three days, so we are told, those who knew how to sing had to endure much strain. But what offerings were brought them! The very poor among them now became wealthy enough.[5] Any paupers, possessing nothing, were bidden to take gold for offerings from Siegfried's own treasure chamber. Since he was not destined to live, many thousand marks were given for his soul. Kriemhild distributed lands and revenues throughout the realm, wherever there were cloisters or the sick and the needy. The poor were given abundance

---

[4] I.e., the stress of the mourning, fasting, etc.
[5] The preceding probably refers to the priests who sang the masses.

of silver and clothing. By her deeds she showed how dearly she loved Siegfried.

On the third morning, at the hour of mass, the spacious church-yard by the minister was full of people, citizens of the land, all weeping. They served him after death as one serves dear kinsmen. In those four days, it has been said, thirty thousand marks, or even more, were given to the poor for his soul's sake. His great beauty and his life were as nothing now.

When God had been served and the mass was ended, many wrestled with violent grief. They bore him from the minster to the grave, and those who missed him most were seen to weep and mourn. Crying out loudly, the people followed him. No one there was joyful, neither man nor woman. A ritual was sung and read before they buried him. Oh, what good priests were at his burial! Before Siegfried's wife went to the grave, her faithful heart was wrung with such agony that time and again they had to sprinkle her with water from the spring. Her sorrow was immeasurably great, and it was a wonder that she ever lived. Many a lady joined in her lament.

Then the queen said, "Men of Siegfried, by your loyalty show your love for me. Allow me, after all my suffering, this small joy, to see his fair head once more."

She pleaded so long, and with an anguish so intense, that they had to break open the sumptuous casket. Then they led the lady to where he lay. With her white hand she raised his fair head, and dead though he was, she kissed the noble knight. Her bright eyes wept blood for very sorrow. It was a piteous farewell. They carried her away; she could not walk, but lay there in a faint. She could have died for grief.

Having now buried their lord, all who had come with him from the Nibelung land suffered sadness beyond compare. And never did one find Siegmund joyful. Some among them, in their great grief, neither ate nor drank for three whole days. Yet they could not neglect their bodies so completely; they recovered from their sorrow, as many still do today.

XVIII

How Siegmund Returned Home

Kriemhild's father-in-law went to where he found her and said to the queen, "We want to return to our country. We are unwelcome guests, I fear, on the Rhine. Kriemhild, dear Lady, come with me now to my lands. Though treachery robbed us of your noble husband here in this land, you shall not suffer for this. I will be kindly disposed toward you for my son's sake—have no doubt of that. Moreover, you shall have all the power, Lady, which Siegfried gave you before. The land and the crown shall be subject to you, and all of Siegfried's men will gladly serve you."

Then the squires were told that they intended to ride away, and there was a great hurrying after the horses, for they did not care to remain with their deadly foes. Ladies and maidens were bidden to pack their clothing. When King Siegmund wished to depart, Kriemhild's kinsmen began to beg her to remain there with her mother.

"That could never be," she said. "How could I bear the sight of him through whom such grief befell me, wretched woman?"

Young Giselher answered, "My dear sister, you ought to stay here with your mother out of love for her. You need no service from those who have grieved and saddened your heart. Just live from my wealth alone."

"That cannot be," she said. "I would die of grief if I had to see Hagen."

"I will protect you from that, my dear sister. You shall be with your brother Giselher, and I will comfort you for your husband's death."

"This is indeed what Kriemhild needs," answered the forlorn woman.

When young Giselher had made her such kindly proposals, Ute and Gernot and all her loyal kinsmen began to entreat her. They begged her to remain there, for she had no kin among Siegfried's men.

"They are all strangers[1] to you," said Gernot. "No one who lives is so strong but that he must die sometime. Remember this, dear sister, and console your spirit. Stay with your kin. This will be the very best for you."

She promised Giselher that she would stay. The horses had been led out for Siegmund's men since they wished to ride to the Nibelung land, and all their armor was already loaded on the pack horses.

Then Lord Siegmund went to Kriemhild and said, "Siegfried's men are waiting for you by the horses. We want to ride away now. I don't like to be here in Burgundy."

Lady Kriemhild answered, "All the loyal kinsmen I have advise me to stay here with them since I have no kin in the Nibelung land."

King Siegmund was very sad when he heard this from Kriemhild, and he said, "Don't let anyone persuade you to this. You shall wear the crown before all my kinsmen with as much sovereign power as you had before. You shall not suffer because we have lost Siegfried. And for your child's sake too, journey back with us. Lady, do not leave him orphaned. When your son is grown, he will be a comfort to your heart, and meanwhile many brave and good heroes shall serve you."

"Lord Siegmund," she said, "I cannot ride with you. Whatever may befall me, I must stay here with my kinsmen, who will help me in my grief."

These words displeased the warriors, and they said of one accord, "We would have good reason to say that only now has the sorest grief befallen us. If you were to stay here with our enemies, then never have heroes ridden to court in greater misery."

"You may go in God's care without any fear. You will be given safe conduct to Siegmund's land, and I will order that you be well protected. My dear child I commend to you warriors, trusting in your good will."

When they realized fully that she would not leave, Siegmund's men all wept, and very sorrowfully Siegmund parted from Lady Kriemhild. Grief was now his lot.

"Alas for this festival," he said. "Never again will there befall a

[1] The word *vremde*, "strangers," is here used as the opposite of *künne*, "kin." The family tie is so strong that by contrast all persons not related are strangers.

king or his kin, because of merry-making, what has befallen us. We shall never be seen again here in Burgundy."

Then Siegfried's men spoke out openly. "A journey to this land might still take place if we found out for certain who killed our lord. They have bitter enemies aplenty among his kinsmen."

Siegmund kissed Kriemhild, and when he saw that she meant to remain, he said sadly, "Now let us ride home joyless to our land. Only now do I feel the whole weight of my grief."

They rode without escort from Worms to the Rhine. The brave Nibelungs were firmly resolved to defend themselves if they were attacked by enemies. They took leave of no one, but Gernot and Giselher went cordially to Siegmund and assured him that they were grieved at his loss.

Courteously Prince Gernot said, "God in heaven knows that I was not to blame for Siegfried's death. And I never heard who was his enemy here.[2] I shall always mourn for him."

Then the youth Giselher gave them good escort and took the king and his warriors safely out of the land home to Netherland, where they found none of their kinsmen joyful.

How they fared thereafter, I cannot say, but here in Worms Kriemhild mourned without ceasing, and no one could comfort her mind and heart except Giselher, who was faithful and good. The fair Brunhild sat haughtily on her throne. She did not care how Kriemhild wept, and she never again showed her kindness or affection. But later Lady Kriemhild caused *her* the bitterest grief of heart.

XIX

How the Nibelung Treasure Was Brought to Worms

After Kriemhild was thus widowed, Count Eckewart and his men remained with her in the land and served her at all times. He also

---

[2] This statement of Gernot's is not consistent with the scene in chapter XIV where both Gernot and Giselher are aware of Hagen's plan.

often helped his lady mourn his lord. In Worms, near the minster, they built a house for her, wide and tall, costly and spacious, where from then on she dwelt joyless with her household. Of her own accord and with great devotion she spent much time in church. Every day she went with sorrowing heart—how rarely did she omit this! —to where her love lay buried, and prayed the good Lord to have mercy on his soul. In true loyalty she wept for him often and often.

Ute and her following tried always to console her, but her heart was so sorely wounded that the comfort they offered her was of no avail. She had the greatest longing any wife ever had for her beloved husband. In this her noble excellence was plain to see. Until her end she mourned, as long as she lived. Later the brave Siegfried's wife avenged herself mightily. Thus she lived in grief—and this is true—full three and a half years after her husband's death, and she spoke no word to Gunther, nor, in all this time, did she see her enemy Hagen.

Then Hagen said, "If you could win your sister's friendship, the Nibelung gold would come to these lands. You could get much of it for yourself if the queen were kindly disposed toward us."

"We'll try," answered Gunther. "My brothers often see her. We'll ask them to bring about a reconciliation, and perhaps we can prevail upon her to consent to be our friend."

"I doubt," said Hagen, "that that will ever happen."

Gunther bade Ortwin and Margrave Gere go to her court. Gernot and the youth Giselher were also sent, and as friends they made an attempt with Lady Kriemhild.

"Lady," said Gernot, "you mourn Siegfried's death too long. The king will prove to you that he did not kill him. You are constantly heard mourning so grievously."

"No one accuses him of this," she answered. "Hagen's hand slew him. When he learned from me where Siegfried could be wounded, how could I suspect that he bore him hate? Had I known, I would have taken good care not to betray his life and could cease my weeping now, wretched woman that I am. I'll never be the friend of those who did it."

Then the winsome Giselher pleaded with her.

"I will receive the king," she said.

When she had given this promise, Gunther appeared before her with his nearest kin, but Hagen did not dare come into her presence. Well he knew his guilt; it was he who had done her harm.

Since she was ready to renounce her hatred of Gunther, it would now have been only proper for him to kiss her,[1] and he could have gone up to her boldly if she had not suffered injury from his breach of faith. Never was peace between kindred made with so many tears, for her loss still grieved her. She forgave them all except one man. No one would have killed Siegfried if Hagen had not done it.

Not long afterward they contrived to have Lady Kriemhild fetch the great treasure from the Nibelung land and bring it to the Rhine. It was her marriage gift[2] and rightly belonged to her. Giselher and Gernot went to get it. Kriemhild ordered eighty hundred men to take it from where it lay hidden, guarded by the warrior Alberich and his closest kin.

When they saw the men from the Rhine coming for the treasure, Alberich said to his friends, "We dare not withhold any part of the treasure from her, for the queen has claim to it as her marriage gift. Yet this would never happen but that unfortunately we have lost with Siegfried the magic cloak he always wore. Now, alas, things have turned out badly for Siegfried because he took the cloak from us and forced all this land to serve him."

The custodian went to fetch the keys. At the foot of the mountain stood Kriemhild's men and some of her kin. They had the treasure brought to the sea, onto the ships, and bore it across the waves and up the Rhine.

Now listen to marvels about the treasure. Twelve wagons could scarcely carry it from the mountain in four days and nights, and each of them had to make the trip three times a day. It consisted entirely of precious stones and gold, and even if one had paid out of it the wages of all the world, it would still not have been reduced in worth by so much as one mark. Not without good reason had Hagen desired it. The supremely perfect piece was a wishing rod of gold. He who knew its nature could be master over every man in the whole world.

Many of Alberich's kinsmen departed with Gernot. When they stored the treasure in Gunther's land and the queen took everything in charge, chambers and towers were heaped full with it.

[1] The kiss was a sign of reconciliation.
[2] The word *morgengâbe,* which still exists in modern German, means literally "morning gift," that is, the gift the bridegroom gives the bride on the morning after the bridal night.

Never again did one hear such marvels told about any treasure. Yet even had it been a thousand times larger, if Siegfried could have been alive again, Kriemhild would gladly have remained with him empty-handed. No hero ever won a more faithful woman. Now that she had the treasure, she brought into the land many foreign warriors. Indeed, she gave so freely that such generosity was never seen again. The queen possessed noble qualities; this everyone admitted. On the poor and on the rich she now bestowed so much that Hagen remarked if she should live a while longer she would win so many men to her service that things would go hard with them.

Then King Gunther said, "Her life and property are hers. How can I prevent what she does with them? I could scarcely persuade her to become this much my friend. Why should we care to whom she gives her silver and gold?"

"A clever man would not leave the treasure to any woman," replied Hagen. "She will carry things so far with her gifts that the Burgundians may well regret it."

King Gunther said, "I swore her an oath that I would never again do her harm, and I intend to keep it, for she is my sister."

"Let me be the guilty one," said Hagen.

Some among them kept their oaths very poorly. They took from the widow her mighty fortune, and Hagen took charge of all the keys. Her brother Gernot was angry when he discovered it.

Then Giselher said, "Hagen has caused my sister much suffering. I ought to prevent it, and if he weren't my kinsman, it would cost him his life."

Siegfried's wife began to weep again.

Then Gernot said, "Rather than always be burdened with this gold, let us have it all sunk in the Rhine so that it will never belong to anyone."

Lamenting, Kriemhild stepped up to Giselher and said, "Dear brother, do not forsake me, but be the protector of both my person and my possessions."

"This I will do when we return," he answered. "Now we intend to ride out."

The king and his kinsmen quitted the land, and with them the very best men to be found there. Only Hagen alone remained, and most willingly, for the hatred he bore Kriemhild. Meanwhile, before the king returned, Hagen seized all the treasure and sunk it in the Rhine at Loche. He thought he could one day make use of it, but that was not to be.

The princes and their men returned. With her maidens and her ladies Kriemhild now began to lament her great loss, for they were solely grieved.

Giselher would have liked to keep faith with her, and they all said with one voice, "He has done a wicked thing."

Hagen avoided the princes' wrath until he regained their favor.[3] They left him unharmed, but Kriemhild hated him more than ever. Before Hagen hid the treasure, they had sworn with the strongest oaths that it should be concealed as long as one of them was still alive. Thus they could not give it to themselves later on nor to anyone else.

Kriemhild's heart was heavy with fresh grief, both for her husband's death and because they had taken the entire treasure from her. Her lamenting never ceased her whole life long down to her last day. After Siegfried died—and this is true—she lived in great sorrow for thirteen years, for she could not forget that warrior's death. She was true to him; this everyone admits.

XX

How King Etzel Sent to Burgundy for Kriemhild

It was in the days when Lady Helca died and King Etzel sought another wife that his friends counseled him to take a proud widow in the Burgundian land. Her name was Lady Kriemhild.

"Now that the lovely Helca is dead," they said, "if you wish to win a noble wife, the finest and best a king ever won, then take this very lady. The powerful Siegfried was her husband."

"How could that come about," said the king, "since I am a

---

[3] This is of course not to be taken seriously, since at least Gunther was an active partner of Hagen's, Gernot had himself suggested disposing of the treasure, and Giselher had offered no real resistance to the plan.

heathen and have not been baptized? The lady is a Christian, so she will not consent. It would be a miracle if it ever happens."

But the warriors said, "Perhaps she will do it for the sake of your exalted name and your great wealth. We should at least make the attempt, for you would do well to marry this noble and beautiful lady."

"Who among you knows the people and the land by the Rhine?" asked the king.

Rudeger of Bechelaren answered, "I have known the queen from childhood, and the good knights Gunther and Gernot. The third is called Giselher. Each of them does the best he can to uphold honor and manly virtue, as their forefathers too have always done."

Then Etzel spoke again. "Friend, tell me whether she is fit to wear the crown in my land. If she is as beautiful as they say, my best friends will never regret this."

"She compares well in beauty with my dear Lady Helca. No king's wife in all this world could be more beautiful. The man she promises to marry may well be satisfied."

"Take this upon you, Rudeger," said the king, "as I am dear to you. And if ever I lie with Kriemhild, I'll reward you as best I can. If you do this, you will have fully accomplished my desire. I'll bid you be given from my treasure chamber horses and clothing and anything you wish, so that you and your comrades may live in contentment. I'll have plenty of such things made ready for your mission."

"It would not be right for me to take from your possessions," replied Margrave Rudeger. "I will gladly be your messenger to the Rhine, but with my own possessions, which I have received from your hand."

Then the king said, "When will you set out to woo the fair lady? God keep you in all honor on the journey, and also my lady! And may Fortune help me to win her favor!"

"Before we leave this land," said Rudeger, "we must prepare such arms and apparel that we may appear with honor before princes. I will take to the Rhine five hundred men. Wherever my men and I are seen among the Burgundians, every one of them shall say, when speaking of you, that no king ever sent so many men so far, nor better equipped, than you have sent to the Rhine. And if you, mighty King, will not withdraw on this account, I will tell you that she yielded her noble love to Siegfried, son of Siegmund. You have seen him here. One must in all truth concede his superb prowess."

Then King Etzel said, "Though she was this warrior's wife, the noble prince was so excellent a man that I shall not disdain the queen. And she pleases me well for her great beauty."

"Very well," said the margrave, "then we shall set out in four and twenty days. I shall send word to Gotelind, my dear wife, that I myself will be the messenger to Kriemhild."

Rudeger dispatched the news to Bechelaren that he was to woo a wife for the king. At this the margravine was at once both sorrowful and glad. Tenderly she thought of the lovely Helca. In part, the message distressed her, and she could not restrain her tears as she wondered if she would get such a lady as before. The thought of Helca grieved her to the heart.

In seven days Rudeger left Hungary, and at this King Etzel rejoiced. Clothing was prepared for them in the city of Vienna, and that done, he delayed his journey no longer. In Bechelaren Gotelind awaited him. The young margravine too, Rudeger's daughter, wished very much to see her father and his men, and many maidens looked forward to them with joy.

On arriving in Bechelaren, the host graciously bade his traveling companions be provided with comfortable quarters. Gotelind was happy to see him come, as was his dear daughter also. She could not have been more pleased. How glad she was to see the heroes from the land of the Huns! [1]

Smiling, the maiden said, "You are most welcome to us, my father and his men." And many a knight was quick with courteous thanks for the young margravine.

Gotelind understood Rudeger well. As she lay close beside him that night, she asked sweetly where the king of the Huns had sent him.

"My Lady Gotelind," he said, "I will gladly tell you. I must woo another wife for my lord, now that Helca is dead. I am to ride to

---

[1] The word "Huns" does not, of course, have the derogatory implications it bears in English. To be sure, there are passages where one senses that the poet does not view the characteristics and abilities of the Hunnish warriors with quite the respect that he has for the Burgundians or for Rudeger's and Dietrich's men, but Etzel, though he plays a rather minor and passive role, is described as a good king and a brave hero, and is obviously esteemed by distinguished men at his court, such as Rudeger and Dietrich.

the Rhine for Kriemhild. She shall be queen here among the Huns."

"God grant that this may happen!" said Gotelind. "Since we have heard so much praise of her, she may perhaps take our lady's place in our old age. We could be happy to have her wear the crown in the Hunnish land."

"My love," said the margrave, "you must graciously offer your wealth to those who ride with me to the Rhine. When warriors travel richly equipped, they are in good spirits."

"There is no one," she said, "if he wishes it, to whom I will not give whatever he likes before you and your men leave here."

"That makes me happy," said the margrave.

Oh, what rich pfellel silks were brought out of her treasure chamber! From these the warriors were given abundance of garments, carefully lined from the neck down to the spurs.

Rudeger had chosen for the journey the men who suited him best, and on the seventh morning they left Bechelaren. Weapons and clothes aplenty they transported through the Bavarian land. Not once were they attacked on the roads by robbers, and within twelve days they reached the Rhine. This news could not be concealed. The king was informed, and also his men, that foreign guests had arrived. The host then said that if anyone knew them, he should tell him so. Their pack horses could be seen, bearing heavy loads. It was clear that they were very rich.

Quarters were immediately provided for them in the large city. When the host of strangers had been lodged, the people stared at them curiously and wondered where they had come from. The host sent for Hagen to see if he might know them.

"I haven't seen them yet," said Hagen. "As soon as we see them, I can probably tell you from where they have ridden into this land. They would have to be strangers indeed, if I did not recognize them at once."

The guests had now received their lodgings, and in sumptuous garments, most skillfully cut, the messenger and his companions now came riding to court.

Then Hagen said, "As far as I can tell, for I have not seen the lord in a long time, they ride as if it were Rudeger, the brave warrior from the land of the Huns." [2]

[2] There are several such allusions in the poem, which show that the poet was familiar with the story of the legendary Walther of Aquitania. His adventures have been preserved in the Old English *Waldere*, the Latin epic of

"How can I believe," said the king, "that the lord of Bechelaren has come to this land?"

Scarcely had King Gunther finished speaking when Hagen spied Rudeger. He and his friends all ran out to meet them. Five hundred knights dismounted from their horses and were warmly welcomed.

Hagen of Troneg called out loudly, "A most cordial welcome to all you warriors, Lord of Bechelaren and your men!"

The brave Huns were received with all honors. The nearest of kin to the king went to where Ortwin was saying to Rudeger, "Never at any time have we been so glad to see guests here, I assure you."

The strangers thanked all the warriors for their greeting and went with their following into the hall, where they found the king and many valiant men. With great courtesy the king rose from his seat and went graciously toward the messengers. Gunther and Gernot welcomed the guest and his vassals cordially, as was his due. Then Gunther took Rudeger by the hand, led him to the seat where he himself sat, and commanded that good mead be poured for the guests and the best wine to be found in the land round about the Rhine. Giselher and Gere had both come in, and Dankwart and Volker too, having heard of the arrival of the guests. They were glad at heart, and in the presence of the king they welcomed the noble knights.

Then Hagen said to his lord, "These warriors of yours should repay the service that the margrave has done us. The fair Gotelind's husband should be rewarded for it."

King Gunther said, "I cannot keep from asking—how does it fare with Etzel and Helca from the Hunnish land?"

"I will be glad to tell you," said the margrave. He rose from his seat with all his men and said to the king, "If you permit me, Prince, I will not conceal the message I bring, but deliver it willingly."

"Any message that has been sent us through you," said the king, "I permit you to give without counsel from my friends. Let me

---

Waltharius, fragments of a Middle High German epic, and the *Thidrekssaga,* and the author of the *Nibelungenlied* must have known this obviously popular tale, though almost certainly not from any version we possess today. Walther and Hagen both spend part of their youth as hostages at Etzel's court, hence Hagen's extensive acquaintance with Etzel and his court.

and my men hear it. With all honor you may fulfill your mission."
Then the good envoy said, "My lord sends to you and all your
friends on the Rhine his devoted service. This message is sent in
true fidelity. The king bade me tell you of his distress. His people
are without joy; my lady is dead, the excellent Helca, my lord's
wife. By her death many maidens have been orphaned, daughters
of noble princes, whom she had reared. On this account the land
is full of sorrow, for alas, they now have no one who will care for
them faithfully. The king's grief, I think, will not quickly subside."

"May God reward him," said Gunther, "that he so willingly
offers his service to me and my friends. I am happy to hear his
greeting, and both my kinsmen and my vassals will be glad to
reciprocate with their service."

Then Gernot said, "The world may well mourn Helca's death
because of the many virtues she possessed."

Hagen agreed with these words, and many another knight.

Rudeger now continued, "If you permit me, O King, I will tell
you more of the message my dear lord has sent you, for he has
fared so wretchedly since Helca's death. My master was told that
Lord Siegfried is dead and Kriemhild without a husband. If this is
so and if you allow it, she shall wear the crown before Etzel's warriors. This my lord bade me say to her."

The king answered courteously, "She shall hear my wish in this
matter if she is willing. I will let you know within three days. Why
should I refuse Etzel before I have learned what she desires?"

Meanwhile orders were given to provide good rest for the guests,
and they were served so well that Rudeger had to admit he had
friends there among Gunther's men. Hagen served him gladly;
Rudeger had done the same for him in the past.[3] So Rudeger remained there until the third day. The king acted wisely and called
his council to ask his kinsmen whether they thought it a good thing
for Kriemhild to take King Etzel as her husband.

All approved of it except Hagen, who said, "If you are sensible,
you will take care never to do this even if she should consent."

"Why shouldn't I consent?" asked Gunther. "I have no reason
to begrudge the queen any good fortune that may befall her. She is
my sister. We ourselves ought to bring it about if it is to her honor."

"Stop talking this way," said Hagen. "If you only knew Etzel as

---

[3] This is another reference to Hagen's earlier stay at Etzel's court.

I do! If she marries him, as I hear you say, then you will really have reason for fear."

"Why?" said Gunther. "I'll see to it that I don't get close enough to him to be forced to endure any hatred on his part even if she became his wife."

"*I'll* never counsel *this*," said Hagen.

Gernot and Giselher were now summoned to see if they were in favor of Kriemhild's marriage to the king. Hagen still advised against it, but no one else besides.

Then Giselher said, "Now show her loyalty for once, friend Hagen. Make good to her the wrong you did her. Any good fortune she may have you should not oppose. You have caused my sister so much sorrow that she would have every reason to be angry with you. Never did a man rob any woman of greater happiness."

"I will tell you one thing I know for certain. If she takes Etzel and lives long enough, she'll do us great injury in one way or another, for a host of valiant men will be in her service."

Gernot answered Hagen, "They may both be dead before we ever ride to Etzel's land. Let us be loyal to her, for that does us honor."

Again Hagen spoke. "No one can convince me otherwise. If Kriemhild wears Helca's crown, she will do us harm in any way she can. Let this thing alone; it will be far better for you warriors."

Angrily Giselher replied, "Let's not all act treacherously. We ought to be glad of whatever honors befall her. No matter what you say, Hagen, I will serve her faithfully."

Hagen was annoyed at these words. The good knights Gernot and Giselher, and the mighty Gunther, finally declared that if Kriemhild agreed to the marriage, they would not oppose it.

Then Gere said, "I will tell the lady to look with favor on King Etzel. Many a warrior serves him in fear as vassal. He may well compensate her for all the suffering she has had."

He went to Kriemhild, who received him kindly. "You have good cause to greet me cordially and give me a messenger's reward," said Gere. "Fortune will soon part you from all your grief. Lady, one of the best men who ever won a kingdom in great honor or ever wore a crown has sent here to sue for your love. Noble knights have come wooing you. This your brother bade me tell you."

The sorrowful lady replied, "God forbid you and all my friends to make sport of me, wretched woman. What could I be to a man who had once known happiness of heart through the love of a good woman?"

She opposed it firmly. Then Gernot and Giselher came and lovingly begged her to take comfort, for it would truly be to her good if she should take the king. But no one could persuade her to marry any man.

"If you do nothing more," pleaded the warriors, "consent to see the messenger."

"I'll not deny," she said, "that I will be happy to see Rudeger because of his great courtesy. If any other messenger had been sent here in his place, I would remain a stranger to him. Ask him to come to my chamber tomorrow. I will inform him frankly of my decision and tell it to him myself." Then her bitter grieving began afresh.

For his part, Rudeger desired nothing else but to see the queen. If this could only come about, he knew he was clever enough to succeed in persuading her. Early the next morning, after mass had been sung, a great crowd pressed round as the envoys appeared, bound for the court with Rudeger. He found her in the clothes she wore every day,[4] though her retinue was richly dressed. She stepped to the door to meet him and welcomed him graciously. With only eleven companions he went in to her. He was shown great honor, for they had never received more distinguished envoys. They bade the lord and his men be seated. In front of the queen stood the two margraves Eckewart and Gere. Because of the lady of the house no one was gay of spirits. Many ladies were seated around Kriemhild, but she only clung to her grief. Rudeger saw that her dress, where it covered her breasts, was wet with hot tears.

"Most noble Queen," he said, "permit me and my companions who have come with me to stand before you and tell you the reason for our coming here."

"You shall be allowed to say what you like," said the queen. "I am of a mind to hear it, for you are a good messenger."

But as she spoke, all the others noticed her reluctance.

"Lady, the great king Etzel assures you of his faithful and pro-

---

[4] I.e., she was in mourning.

found devotion. He has sent many good warriors to this land to sue for your love. With all his heart he offers you love without sorrow and is ready to give you steadfast affection as he did to Lady Helca, who was very dear to him. In longing for her virtues he has many a sorrowful day."

"Margrave Rudeger," said the queen, "anyone who had known the piercing anguish that I feel would not ask me to love another man. I lost one of the best a woman ever had."

"What can comfort sorrow," answered the bold knight, "but affectionate love if one can find it and chooses a person who is right for him? Nothing is so healing for a grieving heart. And if you consent to love my noble lord, you will have the power over twelve mighty crowns. In addition, my lord will give you the lands of thirty princes, all of them conquered by his brave hand. You shall become mistress over many worthy vassals who were subject to my lady Helca and over many ladies who were under her rule, the kin of high princes. Besides, my lord will give you—this he bids me say—if you consent to wear the crown with him, the supreme power that Helca possessed. You shall wield it with all authority over Etzel's men."

"How could I ever desire to become a hero's wife?" said the queen. "Death brought me through the one such sorrow that I must live without joy until my very end."

The Huns answered, "Noble Queen, if you marry Etzel, your life with him will be so glorious that you will know nothing but bliss. The mighty king has a host of valiant men. If Helca's maidens and yours should form one retinue, the warriors would have good reason to rejoice. Follow our counsel, Lady; it will be to your advantage."

Courteously she said, "Let the matter rest until tomorrow morning. Come to me then, and I will answer you concerning your purpose."

To this the warriors had to consent. As soon as they had all gone to their lodgings, Kriemhild sent for Giselher and her mother and told them both that her only desire was to weep and nothing else besides.

"Sister," said Giselher, "I have been told, and I am ready to believe it, that King Etzel will drive away all your sorrows if you take him as your husband. I think this is what you should do, whatever others may advise. He will be able to make you forget your grief. There is no king so powerful as he, from the Rhone to the Rhine, from the Elbe to the sea. You can be very glad if he makes you his wife."

"Dear brother," she said, "why do you counsel me thus? Mourning and weeping are far more fitting for me. How could I appear at court there before the warriors? If I was ever beautiful, I have lost my beauty now."

Then Lady Ute said to her daughter, "Do as your brothers counsel, dear child. Follow the advice of your kinsmen, and all will go well with you. I have seen you too long in your great sorrow."

Then over and over Kriemhild prayed God to grant her the means for distributing gold and silver and apparel as she had before when her husband was still alive, though never again would she know such happy hours.[5] Yet she thought to herself, "Shall I, a Christian woman, give myself to a heathen? Then I would be disgraced before everyone. Even if he gave me all the kingdoms on earth, I will never do it."

She kept to this decision. All night long until the day she lay brooding on her bed. Her bright eyes were never dry till morning when she went to early mass. At this time the kings had come and taken their sister in hand again. They urged her to wed the king of the Hunnish land, but none of them saw in the lady the slightest sign of joy.

Then they summoned Etzel's men, who were now eager for permission to leave, with their mission accomplished or thwarted, as the case might be. Rudeger set out for the court. His companions advised him to learn Gunther's will, and to do this promptly, for it was a far way back to their land. All agreed that this counsel was good. Rudeger was escorted to Kriemhild, and he begged her most courteously to tell him what message she wished to send Etzel. I think he got nothing from her but No, she would never marry any man.

---

[5] The emphasis here on Kriemhild's desire for wealth seems, at first glance, to be inconsistent with the poet's picture of her as a grief-stricken woman, but, as her second conversation with Rudeger shows, the thought of revenge now begins to motivate her actions. Only by acquiring wealth and power can she hope to avenge Siegfried's death.

"That would be a mistake," said the margrave. "Why let such beauty go to waste? You can again become with honor the wife of a valiant man."

Their pleading was of no avail until Rudeger told her in private that he would make amends for any wrongs that had been done her. At this her great distress subsided a little.

"Cease your weeping," he said to the queen. "Even if you had no one among the Huns but me and my loyal kinsmen and vassals, anyone who had ever done you harm would have to pay dearly for it."

Kriemhild's heart grew lighter, and she said, "Then swear on your oath that if anyone does me any harm, you will be the first to avenge my wrongs."

"Lady, I am ready to do so," replied the margrave.

Then Rudeger and all his men swore to serve her loyally always, and with his hand he pledged her that the warriors from Etzel's land would never deny her anything that would be to her honor.

The faithful Kriemhild thought, "Since I, wretched woman, have won so many friends, I'll let the people say what they like. Perhaps my dear husband will still be avenged. Etzel has so many warriors that if I rule over them, I can do as I please. And he is so rich that I shall have gifts to bestow. That detestable Hagen has robbed me of my wealth."

To Rudeger she said, "If I had not heard he was a heathen, I would gladly go wherever he liked and take him as my husband."

"Say no more of this, Lady," answered the margrave. "He has so many warriors of Christian faith that you will not be unhappy at his court. And perhaps you can persuade him to be baptized. You need not hesitate on this account to become King Etzel's wife."

Then her brothers spoke again. "Give your promise, my sister, and abandon your sorrow."

They pleaded long with her until she sadly vowed before them all to become Etzel's wife. "I will obey you," she said, "wretched queen that I am, and go to the Huns as soon as I find friends who will take me to Etzel's land." To this Kriemhild pledged her hand in the presence of the warriors.

Then the margrave said, "Even if you find but two men, I have many more. We will see to it that you are escorted with honor across the Rhine. Lady, you need not remain in Burgundy any longer. I have five hundred vassals, and my kinsmen besides. They shall serve you here, Lady, and there at home they shall do as you command. I will do likewise whenever you remind me of today, and serve you so well that I'll have no cause to be ashamed. Now have your horses' equipment prepared—you will never regret Rudeger's counsel—and inform your maidens whom you wish to take with you. Many an excellent warrior will join us on the road."

Kriemhild still had richly decorated harnesses which they had used for riding in Siegfried's time, so that she could take many maidens with her in splendor whenever she was ready to depart. Oh, what fine saddles were brought for the ladies! Though in former times they had worn costly garments, many more were now prepared for the journey, for they had heard such marvels about the king. They opened the coffers, which till now had been tightly locked. For four and a half days they were very busy taking from their wrappings the many things inside. Kriemhild opened her treasure chamber, for she wanted to make all of Rudeger's men rich. Of the gold from the Nibelung land she still had so much that a hundred horses could not carry it, and this she intended to distribute among the Huns.

Hagen heard about what she was doing and said, "Since Lady Kriemhild will never be friends with me, Siegfried's gold must remain here. Why should I give up such great wealth to my enemies? I know very well what Kriemhild will do with this treasure. If she should take it with her, I'm sure it would be given away to stir up hatred against me. They don't even have enough horses to carry it. Hagen intends to keep it—tell Kriemhild so."

When she was informed of this, she was extremely angry. The three kings were also told, and they decided to prevent it.

But when nothing came of this, Rudeger said serenely, "Mighty Queen, why do you grieve for the gold? King Etzel's love for you is so great that when his eyes behold you, he will give you so much that you can never spend it all. This I swear to you, Lady."

"Noble Rudeger," said the queen, "never did a king's daughter acquire such riches as Hagen has robbed me of."

Gernot now went to her treasure chamber and by his kingly authority thrust the key into the door. Kriemhild's gold was brought out, thirty thousand marks or more, and he bade the guests take it. Gunther was glad at this.

Then Rudeger said, "Even if my lady Kriemhild could have all that was taken from the Nibelung land, neither my hand nor hers would ever touch it. Order it to be stored away, for I will have none of it. I brought from home so much wealth of my own that we can easily do without hers on the road. We have a great abundance for our expenses on the trip."

But in the meantime Kriemhild's maidens had already filled twelve chests with the best gold to be found anywhere. The fierce Hagen's power seemed to them too great. They took the gold with them and a great store of ladies' finery which they needed for the journey.

Of her gold for offerings Kriemhild still had a thousand marks, which she now dispensed for her dear husband's soul. Rudeger thought this a sign of great fidelity.

Then the mournful lady said, "Where are my friends who for love of me are willing to live in a foreign country? Let those who will ride with me to the Hunnish land take my treasure and buy horses and clothing."

Margrave Eckewart said to the queen, "Since I first became your vassal, I have served you faithfully, and will continue serving you till the end of my days. I will take with me five hundred of my men, and in true loyalty I place them at your disposal. Nothing shall part us but death."

For these words Kriemhild bowed her gratitude. The horses were now brought out, for they wanted to ride away. Then friends shed many tears. Ute and many a maid showed how very much they would miss Lady Kriemhild. She took with her a hundred maidens attired as was befitting. Tears poured down from their bright eyes, but later they enjoyed many pleasures at Etzel's court. Then came Giselher and Gernot with their following of a thousand men to escort their sister, as their courtesy bade them. Gere and Ortwin went with them too, and Rumolt, the master cook. They set up night quarters for the journey as far as the banks of the Danube. But Gunther rode no farther than a short distance from the town.

Before leaving the Rhine, the travelers had sent their messengers swiftly on ahead to the land of the Huns to announce to the king that Rudeger had won the queen for him as wife.

XXI

How Kriemhild Journeyed to the Huns

Let the messengers ride. We'll tell you how the queen journeyed through the lands and where Giselher and Gernot parted from her. They had served her as their loyalty bade them. They rode as far as Vergen on the Danube. Here they asked the queen's permission to leave, for they wished to ride back to the Rhine. The parting from faithful kinsmen was not without tears.

Brave Giselher said to his sister, "If you should ever need me, Lady, if any harm should come to you, let me know of it and I will ride to Etzel's land to serve you."

Those who were her kin she kissed on the mouth, and the Burgundians bade Rudeger's men a friendly farewell. The queen had with her many maidens, a hundred and four, wearing costly gowns of rich, gay-colored silks. Many broad shields were kept close by the ladies on the road. The warriors from Burgundy now turned and rode away from Kriemhild.

The travelers journeyed rapidly down through Bavaria. Here, where a cloister still stands today, and where the Inn flows into the Danube, the word spread that many strangers were approaching in great haste. In the town of Passau, where a bishop lived, the houses were emptied and the bishop's court as well, as everyone hurried up toward Bavaria to meet the strangers. There Bishop Pilgrim found the fair Kriemhild. The warriors of the land were not sorry to see so many lovely maids in her train and gazed at them with amorous eyes. Good lodgings were soon provided for the guests.

The bishop rode with his niece to Passau. When the townspeople were told that Kriemhild was coming, the daughter of the bishop's sister, the merchants greeted her warmly.

The bishop hoped they would remain there, but Lord Eckewart said, "It is impossible. We must journey down to Rudeger's land. Many knights know of our coming and are expecting us."

Gotelind had heard the news, and she and her daughter eagerly made themselves ready. Rudeger had sent her word that he thought it would be a good thing for her to cheer the queen's heart by riding up to the Ens with his vassals to meet her. When the preparations were complete, one could see the roads swarming all about, as they set out to meet the guests on horseback or on foot.

The queen had now arrived in Everdingen. If the Bavarians had practiced highway robbery, as was their custom, they might perhaps have done the guests harm, but the margrave had prevented this by taking with him a thousand knights or even more.

Gotelind had now also arrived, and with her many a warrior in splendid array. When they crossed the Trune to the plain by Ens, they saw tents and pavilions pitched, where the guests were to find quarters for the night. It was Rudeger who had provided accommodations and food. Gotelind left her tent. Handsome horses trotted along the roads with bridles jingling. The welcome was a fine one, and Rudeger was pleased. From either side many a warrior joined them on the way, riding skillfully. They practiced knightly sports as the maidens looked on. This service from the knights did not displease the queen. When Rudeger's men met the guests, spear splinters flew high from the warriors' hands in the knightly games. They rode admirably before the ladies.

But now the games ceased, and the knights greeted each other cordially. Then they led Gotelind to where she saw Kriemhild. Those who knew how to serve ladies had little rest. The lord of Bechelaren rode to his wife, who was not sorry to see that he had returned from the Rhine so fit. All her cares gave way to great joy. When she had greeted him, he bade her dismount to the grass with the ladies who were with her. Many a knight bestirred himself and served them with eager zeal. Now Lady Kriemhild saw the margravine standing with her train. Reining in her horse, she did not let it go nearer, but bade them lift her quickly from the saddle. The bishop, with Eckewart, was seen leading his sister's daughter to Gotelind, and everyone at once made way for them. Then the queen from foreign realms kissed Gotelind on the mouth.

Rudeger's wife said graciously, "How happy I am, dear Lady, that with my own eyes I have seen your fair self here in these lands! Nothing more pleasant could happen to me now."

"May God reward you, noble Gotelind," said Kriemhild. "If

Botelung's son and I remain alive and well, it may be of benefit to you to have seen me."

Neither knew what was later to happen.

Many maidens now went courteously to meet each other, and the warriors were quick to serve them. After the greeting they sat down on the clover and came to know many who had been strangers to them before. Orders were given to pour wine for the ladies, as it was now midday. The noble retinue remained there no longer, but rode to where they found spacious pavilions, and there bounteous service stood ready for them.

They rested through the night until the early morning. Meanwhile the men of Bechelaren were preparing accommodations for the guests. Rudeger had provided well, so that they lacked for nothing. The windows in the walls stood open, the castle gates swung wide. The welcome guests rode in, and the host bade that they be made comfortable. Courteously Rudeger's daughter went with her train to welcome the queen. Her mother, the margrave's wife, was present too, and many a maiden[1] received a warm greeting.

Knights and ladies now took each other by the hand and went to a beautiful and spacious hall, below which the Danube flowed past. They seated themselves near the breeze from the windows and passed the time in pleasant sociability. What more they did, I cannot say, but Kriemhild's men were heard to grumble that they were traveling so slowly. This annoyed them greatly. Oh, how many fine warriors went with her from Bechelaren![2]

Rudeger offered the guests many a friendly service. The queen gave Gotelind's daughter twelve red bracelets and a gown as fine as any she took to Etzel's land. Though the Nibelung gold had been taken from her, she won the hearts of all who saw her with the little wealth she still possessed. Handsome presents were given to the host's household. In turn Lady Gotelind did honor to the guests from the Rhine so graciously that there was not one of the strangers who did not wear her jewels or her splendid garments.

When they had eaten and it was time for them to depart, the lady of the house offered Etzel's wife her faithful service, and Kriemhild fondly embraced the margrave's lovely daughter.

---

1 Probably Kriemhild's.
2 I.e., Rudeger's men.

"If you agree," the maiden said to the queen, "I know my dear father will gladly send me to the Hunnish land to you."

Kriemhild saw clearly that the girl was devoted to her.

The horses had been saddled and led out before the castle, and the queen had taken leave of Rudeger's wife and daughter. Many a fair maid now parted with a greeting. They never saw each other again after that time.

From Medelick[3] the people carried out in their hands rich goblets of gold in which they brought wine for the strangers on the highway as a welcome to them. A castle lord lived there, called Astolt. He showed them the way to Austria, down the Danube toward Mutaren. There the queen was later well served.

The bishop parted fondly from his niece. He counseled her to conduct herself well and earn honor for herself, as Helca had done. And oh, what great honor she later won in the Hunnish land! Rudeger's men escorted the guests to the Treisem and tended them zealously until the Huns came riding across the land. The king of the Huns had a mighty fortress on the Treisem called Zeizenmure, which was known far and wide. Lady Helca had lived there once and practiced virtue so great that the like will probably never be done again unless by Kriemhild, who knew how to give so lavishly that after all her sorrow she had the joy of being granted the highest esteem of Etzel's vassals.

His sovereign power was so far-famed that at all times there could be found at his court the boldest warriors anyone ever heard of, whether Christian or heathen. They all went to him. Both Christian and heathen rites were always practiced at his court—a thing not likely to happen again. No matter to what faith a man belonged, the king's bounty bestowed abundance on all.

[3] The Burgundians do not stop at Medelick, but the castle lord sends them the wine as greeting.

XXII

How Kriemhild Was Received by Etzel

Kriemhild remained at Zeizenmure until the fourth day. During this time the dust on the highway never settled but whirled up as if fires were burning all around as Etzel's men rode through Austria. The king had been told in what splendor Kriemhild was journeying through the land. At the thought of this his sorrows vanished, and he hastened to meet her. Warriors of many tongues could be seen riding before Etzel on the road, great bands, both Christians and heathens. In magnificent array they went to meet the lady. Many a Russian and Greek rode there, and with might and main rode the Poles and the Walachs on their swiftly galloping horses. Each displayed the customs of his land. Many warriors from the land of Kiev rode there, and the wild Petchenegres, who shot the birds in flight with their arrows, tautening the bowstrings almost to the breaking point.

In Austria on the Danube is a city called Tulne. There Kriemhild became acquainted with foreign customs she had never seen before. Many who greeted her she later brought to grief. In front of King Etzel rode a stately retinue, courtly and joyful, four and twenty princes, distinguished and proud. They desired nothing but to see their lady. Duke Ramung from the land of the Walachs galloped up before her with seven hundred vassals. Like flying birds they rode. Then came Prince Gibeche with magnificent troops. The valiant Hornboge, with fully a thousand men, wheeled away from the king to approach his lady. Loudly they shouted, after the custom of their land. And the kinsmen of the Huns rode ardently too. Then came brave Hawart of Denmark and Iring the bold, free of guile, and Irnfried of Thuringia, a distinguished man. With twelve hundred vassals whom they had in their company, they greeted Kriemhild in a way that did them honor. Then came Lord Bloedel, Etzel's brother, from the Hunnish land, with three thousand men, and rode in state to where he found the queen. Now came King Etzel, and Lord Dietrich too, with all his following. Many noble knights were there, worthy and esteemed, and at this Lady Kriemhild's spirits rose.

Lord Rudeger said to the queen, "Lady, the king wishes to welcome you here. You must kiss whomever I bid you to. You cannot greet all of Etzel's vassals alike."

The queen was now lifted from her palfrey, and Etzel delayed no longer. Dismounting from his horse with his valiant men, he went joyfully to meet Kriemhild. Two mighty princes, we are told, escorted the lady, carrying her train, as King Etzel went toward her and as she greeted him graciously with a kiss. She pushed back her veiled headdress, and from out of the gold her fair coloring gleamed radiantly. Many a man there declared that Lady Helca could not have been lovelier than she.

Close by stood Bloedel, the king's brother, and Rudeger bade her kiss him and King Gibeche too. Dietrich was also there. Etzel's wife kissed twelve of the warriors and received many other knights with a greeting.

All the while that Etzel stood beside Kriemhild, the young knights did as people still do today. They rode fine jousts, the Christian warriors, and the heathens too, each according to his custom. With what true knightly art Dietrich's men sped the shafts from their hands so that the splinters flew high above the shields! Many a shield was riddled by the German[1] guests. Now a great crash of breaking spears was heard, for all the warriors from Etzel's land had come, as well as the king's guests.

The king and Lady Kriemhild withdrew. Nearby they saw a splendid pavilion, and round about the plain was filled with tents, where all were to rest after their exertions. Knights escorted the maidens to the tent where the queen was seated on a richly covered chair. The margrave had provided this seat for Kriemhild, and everyone thought it excellent. At this Etzel was pleased. What Etzel said there, I do not know. In his right lay her white hand. Thus they sat like lovers, but Rudeger would not permit the king to lie with Kriemhild.

[1] This is the only time the word *tiusch,* "German," is used in the *Nibelungenlied.* The reference may be specifically to Dietrich's Goths or, as de Boor suggests, it may include Kriemhild's Burgundians and Rudeger's vassals as well.

Orders were given for the bohourt to cease on all sides, and the great tumult came to a glorious end. Etzel's men went to the tents. The lodgings given them stretched out far away in all directions. The day was now ended, and they took their rest until the bright dawn shone again. Then they got to horse and oh, what games they began in honor of the king!

The king bade the Huns to provide everything his honor demanded, and they rode from Tulne to the city of Vienna. There they found a host of ladies finely adorned, who received Etzel's wife with great esteem. All that they needed was ready for them in profusion, and many a lusty warrior looked forward joyfully to the reveling.

The king's celebration commenced in gaiety. They began to lodge the guests, but they did not have quarters for all in the town. Rudeger asked those who were not guests to take lodgings in the country round about. Lord Dietrich was always to be seen with Lady Kriemhild, and many other warriors too. They had given up their rest for the effort of cheering the spirits of the guests. Rudeger and his friends passed the time pleasantly.

The festival fell on a Whitsuntide,[2] when King Etzel lay with Kriemhild in the city of Vienna. With her first husband, I am sure, she never gained so many men for her service. By presents she made herself known to those who had never seen her.

Many among them said to the guests, "We thought Lady Kriemhild had no wealth, but instead she has worked marvels with her gifts."

The festival lasted seventeen days. No one can tell of any king, I think, whose festival was more magnificent. If there was one, we have heard nothing about it. All who were there wore brand-new garments. In Netherland Kriemhild never lived, I am sure, surrounded by so many knights. Moreover, I believe that though Siegfried possessed great wealth, he never acquired so many warriors of noble rank as she saw standing before Etzel. Nor did anyone ever give at his own festival so many costly cloaks, wide and full, nor such fine clothing, of which Etzel and his princes all had great store and had given for Kriemhild's sake. Their friends, and the guests as well, were of one accord, that they should not be sparing with any of their wealth. Whatever anyone desired, they

[2] The first meeting between Kriemhild and Siegfried also occurred at Whitsuntide.

gave willingly, so that because of their generosity, many of the warriors stood there naked without any clothes.

Kriemhild thought of how she had lived on the Rhine with her noble husband, and her eyes grew moist, but she quickly concealed her tears, so that no one saw. After much suffering great honor had been done her.

Whatever generosity others showed was but a trifle compared with Dietrich's. What Botelung's son had given him was completely spent. Rudeger's lavish hand also did great marvels. Prince Bloedel of Hungary ordered many a traveling chest emptied of silver and gold; it was all given away. The king's minstrels, Werbel and Swemmel, each received at the festival fully a thousand marks or even more, when the fair Kriemhild sat beneath the crown at Etzel's side.

On the eighteenth morning they rode out of Vienna. In knightly games many shields were slashed by spears the warriors bore in their hands. Thus King Etzel came to the Hunnish land. In ancient Heimburg they spent the night. No one could know how great the throng, with what forces they rode across the land. At mighty Misenburg they boarded ship. The water was covered with horses and men as far as one could see, just as if it were solid earth. The way-worn ladies now had rest and comfort. Sturdy ships were lashed together, so that neither waves nor current could do them harm, and over them fine tents were spread as if they were still on land and plain.

From here the news of their coming was sent to Etzelnburg, where both men and women rejoiced. Helca's retinue, which she had once watched over, later spent many a happy day with Kriemhild. Many high-born maidens, who had known great grief as Helca's death, stood there expectantly. Among them Kriemhild found seven daughters of kings, the glory of Etzel's whole land. Herrat, daughter of Helca's sister and of the noble King Nantwin, still had charge of the retinue. She was Dietrich's betrothed, and possessed of many virtues. Great honor was later done her. Her heart rejoiced at the coming of the guests. Vast riches had been spent in preparation. Who could tell you truly how the king lived thereafter? Never did the Huns live better with any queen.

As the king rode away from the shore with his wife, each maiden was presented to her, and they greeted her courteously. With what power she ruled in Helca's place! Much loyal service was done her,

and the queen distributed gold and raiment, silver and precious
stones. Everything she had brought with her across the Rhine to
the Hunnish land was given away. Soon all the king's kinsmen and
vassals pledged allegiance and service to her. Lady Helca had
never reigned with such power as Kriemhild, whom they now had
to serve until her death. The court, and the land as well, enjoyed
such glory that everyone found there at all times whatever pleasures his heart desired, and knights flocked there for the sake of
the king and to win the queen's wealth.

XXIII

How Kriemhild Contrived to Have Her Brothers Invited to the Festival

In very great honor—and this is a fact—they lived with one another until the seventh year. In this time the queen had borne a
son, at which King Etzel could not have been happier. Kriemhild
urged and persisted in urging that the child be baptized according
to Christian rite. He was named Ortlieb. Now there was great rejoicing in all of Etzel's lands.

The same noble qualities Lady Helca had possessed, Lady
Kriemhild practiced for many a day. Herrat, the maiden far from
home, who in secret mourned bitterly for Helca, taught her the
customs of the court. Kriemhild was well known both to Etzel's
people and to those from foreign lands. They all declared that no
king's land had ever had a better or more generous mistress—of
this they were convinced. And so she enjoyed such repute among
the Huns until the thirteenth year.

Now when she had made sure that there was no one opposed to
her (as a king's warriors will sometimes do to their prince's wife),
and that she always had twelve kings at her service, she thought
of the many wrongs that had befallen her at home. She also recalled the many honors which had been hers in the Nibelung land
and which Hagen had robbed her of by Siegfried's death, and she
pondered whether she could still make him suffer for that. "It

might easily be done if I could get him to this land," she thought.

Again and again she dreamed of walking hand in hand with her brother Giselher, and often, in sweet sleep, she kissed him. Suffering was soon the lot of both. I think it was the wicked devil that counseled Kriemhild to break off friendship with Gunther, whom in token of forgiveness she had kissed in the Burgundian land. Now hot tears once more soiled her garments. Late and early she grieved in her heart that, without fault of hers, she had been forced to wed a heathen.[1] Hagen and Gunther had caused her this distress. The desire for revenge never left her, and she thought, "I am so powerful and have such great possessions that I may yet do my enemies harm. I would be very glad to make Hagen suffer. My heart often yearns for my loyal kin,[2] but if I could be near those who did me injury, my beloved would be well avenged. I can scarcely wait for this moment to come."

All the king's men, Kriemhild's warriors, were attached to her, as was fitting. Eckewart had charge of her treasure chamber, and by this won friends.[3] No one could thwart Kriemhild's will.

Constantly she thought, "I will ask the king if he will permit me to bring my kinsmen to the Hunnish land."

No one guessed the queen's evil intent. One night, as she lay with the king and he held her in his arms, fondling the lady as he always did, for she was as dear to him as his own life, she thought of her enemies and said to the king, "My dear Lord, I would like to ask you, by your grace, to show me—if I have deserved this— whether you are truly fond of my kinsmen."

Then the king said, and his heart was without guile, "I will prove it to you. I would rejoice at any good fortune that befalls these warriors, for I never won better friends from a woman's love."

The queen said, "You have undoubtedly been told that I have many well-born kinsmen. This is why it grieves me so that they never visit me. The people here call me an exile."

"My dear Lady," said King Etzel, "if they do not think it too far, I'll invite here to my lands anyone from across the Rhine that you would like to see."

---

[1] This passage is not consistent with the scene in XX, where the decision to marry Etzel is made by Kriemhild herself, nor is it consistent with her apparently happy marriage.

[2] I.e., Gernot and Giselher.

[3] He won friends for Kriemhild by generous gifts.

The lady rejoiced to hear that this was his desire and said, "If you would do me a kindness, my Lord, dispatch messengers to Worms. Then I can send word to my kinsmen as to what I wish, and many a knight will come here to our land."

"Whatever you command shall be done," he said. "You could not be happier than I to see your kin, the noble Ute's sons. It grieves me very much that they have been separated from us so long. If you like, my dear Lady, I'll gladly send my fiddlers to Burgundy."

He bade the good minstrels be fetched immediately, and quickly they hurried to where the king was seated beside the queen. He told the two that they were to be his messengers to the Burgundian land and ordered splendid attire to be prepared for them. For four and twenty warriors clothing was made ready. The king then gave the fiddlers his message, inviting Gunther and his men. Lady Kriemhild spoke to them privately.

"I will tell you what to say," said the king. "I wish my friends happiness and all good fortune and ask that they consent to ride here to my land. Such welcome guests I have never known. And if Kriemhild's kinsmen are inclined to fulfill my wish, tell them not to fail to come this summer to my festival, for much of my enjoyment will come from my wife's kin."

Then proud Swemmel, the fiddler, said, "When will your festival take place, so that we can tell your friends there?"

"In the days of next midsummer," King Etzel said.

"We shall do as you command," said Werbel.

The queen bade the messengers be led secretly to her chamber, where she spoke with them. Because of this, great misfortune was to befall many warriors.

"Now earn a generous reward," she said to the two, "by doing my will in all respects, and deliver the message that I send home to my native land. I shall make you rich in goods and give you fine clothing. You must not tell any of my kinsmen you see at Worms that you ever saw me sad at heart. Offer my service to the good and valiant heroes. Ask them to do what the king requests and thus deliver me from all my sorrow, or the Huns will think I am without any kin. If I were a knight, I would visit them myself on occasion. And say to my brother Gernot that no one in the world could be fonder of him. Ask him to bring our closest kinsmen with him to this land, that it may be to our honor. And tell Giselher to remember that I never knew grief through any fault of his, so my eyes would rejoice to see him. For his great loyalty I would like to have him here. Also tell my mother of the high repute I enjoy. And if Hagen of Troneg should decide to remain at home, ask who would then guide them through the lands. From childhood he has known the roads to the Huns." [4]

The messengers did not know why they were not to let Hagen stay on the Rhine. They suffered for this later. The move against Hagen meant violent death for him and many another man. Letters and messages had now been given them. Etzel and his wife dismissed them, and they departed, finely dressed and rich in goods, well able to live handsomely.

XXIV

How Werbel and Swemmel Delivered the Message

The news that Etzel had sent his envoys to the Rhine flew from land to land. With swift messengers he now invited and summoned guests to his festival, at which many a man was later to meet his death.

The envoys rode away from the land of the Huns to the Burgundians to bring three noble kings and their men to Etzel's court. Riding full speed, they arrived at Bechelaren, where they were gladly served and lacked for nothing. Rudeger and Gotelind and their daughter sent greetings by them to the Rhine. Nor did they allow them to depart without gifts, so that Etzel's men might travel all the better. To Ute and her sons Rudeger sent word that no other margrave was so devoted to them as he. To Brunhild also they tendered their devotion and good wishes, steadfast fidelity and readiness to serve her. After hearing the message, the envoys were ready to leave, and the margravine prayed God in heaven to protect them.

[4] This is another reference to the story of Walther of Aquitania.

Before they crossed through the Bavarian land, Werbel sought out the good Bishop Pilgrim. What word he sent to his kinsmen on the Rhine, I do not know. I know only that out of friendship he gave the messengers his red gold and let them ride, saying, "If I should see my sister's sons here, I would be very happy, for I can scarcely visit them."

I cannot report what roads they traveled to the Rhine, but no one robbed them of their silver and garments; their master was a powerful ruler, and his wrath was greatly feared. Within twelve days Werbel and Swemmel came to the Rhine, to the region of Worms.

The kings and their men were informed that strange messengers were arriving, and Gunther asked, "Who will tell us where these strangers are from that have ridden into this land?"

No one knew until Hagen saw them and said to Gunther, "Fresh news is coming to us, that I will vouch. I have just seen Etzel's fiddlers here. Your sister has sent them. For the sake of their lord we must give them a warm welcome."

Already they were riding up before the palace. Never did a prince's minstrels travel more splendidly. The king's retinue at once bade them welcome, lodging was provided, and their equipment put away. So rich and well fashioned were their traveling clothes that with all honor they could have appeared in them before the king, but they scorned to wear them longer there at court and inquired if anyone would like to have them. Accordingly, people were found who were eager for them, and to these the clothes were sent. The strangers put on far more elegant apparel, as becomes envoys from a king.

Etzel's men were now permitted to go to where the king was sitting, and the people rejoiced to see them. Courteously Hagen hastened toward them and welcomed them cordially, for which the squires thanked him. Wishing to hear their news, he asked how Etzel and his men were faring.

The fiddler answered, "I assure you the land was never more prosperous nor the people happier."

Then they proceeded toward the host. In the crowded hall people received them hospitably, as one should rightly greet guests in a strange land. Werbel saw many warriors there at Gunther's side.

The king greeted them politely. "I bid you both welcome, Hunnish minstrels, and your companions too. Did the mighty Etzel send you here to Burgundy?"

They bowed to the king, and Werbel said, "My dear lord and your sister Kriemhild convey to you their loyal devotion. They have sent us to you warriors, confident of your good faith."

"I am glad at this news," said Gunther. "How is Etzel faring, and my sister Kriemhild?"

"I will tell you," said the fiddler. "Be assured, things have never gone better for anyone than for those two and for all their followers, their kinsmen and their vassals. They were pleased about this journey when we left them."

"I am thankful for the greetings he and my sister have sent me, since it turns out that the king and his men live in happiness. It was with great anxiety that I questioned you."

The two young kings had now also arrived and had just heard the news. For love of his sister, Giselher rejoiced to see the envoys and said to them kindly, "You messengers are most welcome. If you rode here to the Rhine more often, you would find such friends as you would be glad to see. There would be no harm done you in this land."

"We are confident you will do us every honor," said Swemmel. "With all my powers I could not convey to you how affectionately Etzel and your sister greet you. They live in great glory. The king's wife bids you remember your affection and loyalty and that your heart always held her dear. But first and foremost we are sent here to the king to ask that you consent to ride to Etzel's land. The mighty Etzel enjoined us strictly to request this of you. And he bade us say to all of you that if you refused to visit your sister, he would like to know what he had done to you that you thus shun him and his lands. Even if the queen were a stranger to you, he would still deserve that you should be willing to see him. If you do so, he would be very pleased."

"When seven nights are past," said King Gunther, "I will tell you what my friends and I have decided. Meanwhile go to your lodgings, and may you have good rest."

But Werbel said, "Would it be possible for us to see Lady Ute before we go to our sleep?"

Giselher gave courteous answer, "No one will hinder you if you wish to go to her. Indeed, you will thus fulfill my mother's wish, for she will gladly see you and welcome you for the sake of my sister, Lady Kriemhild."

Giselher led them to the lady, and she rejoiced to see them. Gracious of spirit as she was, she greeted them kindly, and the good envoys delivered their message to her.

"My lady sends you her devotion and her love," said Swemmel. "If it were possible for her to see you frequently, believe me, nothing in the world would make her happier."

"That cannot be," said the queen. "However much I would like to see my dear daughter often, alas, she is too far from me. May she and Etzel always be happy! Let me know, before you depart, when you intend to go home. Not for a long time have I been so glad to see messengers."

Having promised her this, the squires repaired to their quarters. Meanwhile King Gunther sent for his friends and now asked them what they thought of the matter. Many a vassal, the very best among them, advised him to ride to Etzel's land. Only Hagen was violently opposed.

In private he said to the king, "You are planning your own ruin. You know very well what we did. We must always be on guard against Kriemhild, for I killed her husband with my own hand. How could we dare ride to Etzel's land?"

"My sister renounced her anger," said the king. "Before she left, she lovingly forgave us with a kiss for what we had done to her. Unless perhaps, Hagen, she is hostile to you alone."

"Now don't let yourself be deceived," said Hagen, "whatever the messengers from the Huns may say. If you decide to visit Kriemhild, you may well lose there your honor and your life. Revenge rankles long in King Etzel's wife."

Then Prince Gernot added his voice about the matter. "We would be doing a great wrong to give up visiting our sister just because you have good reason to fear death in the Hunnish realm."

And Prince Giselher said, "Friend Hagen, since you know you are guilty, stay here and keep yourself safe, and let those who dare, go with us to my sister."

The warrior of Troneg flew into a rage. "No one you take along will dare to ride to court with you more readily than I. And I'll prove that to you if you refuse to turn back."

Then Rumolt, the master cook, said, "You can quite well have strangers and friends entertained here to suit yourselves; you have abundant provisions. I don't think Hagen has ever made hostages of you.[1] If you won't follow him, listen to Rumolt's advice, for I am your true and faithful servant. Remain here for my sake and let King Etzel stay there with Kriemhild. Where in the world would you fare better? Here you are safe from your enemies. Adorn yourselves with rich clothes and drink the finest wine and pay court to lovely ladies. In addition, you will be served the best dishes any king ever ate. Even if this were not so, you ought to remain here for the sake of your beautiful wife rather than risk your life so foolishly. So I advise you to stay. Your lands are rich. Pawned goods can be redeemed for you more easily here than among the Huns.[2] Who knows how things are there? Stay here, my Lords. This is Rumolt's counsel."

"We don't want to stay," said Gernot. "Since my sister and Etzel have so kindly invited us, why should we refuse? Anyone who doesn't want to go can remain here at home."

To this Hagen answered, "Whatever may befall you, don't take my words amiss. But I counsel you in all sincerity, if you want to be safe, ride to the Huns well armed. If you won't turn back, send for your men, the best you have or can find anywhere. From them all I'll choose a thousand good knights. Then the wily Kriemhild cannot harm you."

"This counsel I'll gladly follow," said the king at once.

He bade messengers ride far and wide throughout his lands. Three thousand warriors were assembled, or even more. Little did they think to meet such grave peril. Joyously they rode to Gunther's land. To all who were to leave Burgundy horses and clothing were given, and the king gained many a willing man. Hagen now bade his brother Dankwart bring eighty of their warriors to the Rhine, and in knightly fashion, with armor and apparel, they arrived in Gunther's land. Then came the bold Volker, a noble minstrel, with thirty of his men, for the journey to the court. They had such garments as a king might wear. He sent word to Gunther that he too would go to the Huns. I will tell you who Volker was. He was a noble lord, and many good warriors in Burgundy were his vassals. Because he could play the fiddle, he was called the minstrel. Hagen chose a thousand men whom he knew well and

---

[1] I.e., Hagen has never given you treacherous counsel.

[2] I.e., it will be easier to get out of difficulties or dangers at home than abroad.

whose performance in stress of battle he had often observed and whatever else they had done. No one could deny their valor.

Kriemhild's messengers were uneasy at the delay, for their fear of their master was great. Every day they asked permission to leave, but Hagen craftily refused.

He said to his lord, "We must take care not to let them ride until we ourselves are ready to set out seven nights later for Etzel's land. If anyone bears us ill will, we shall find it out all the more easily, and yet Lady Kriemhild will not have time to prepare for harm to be done us through any plan of hers.[3] If this is her intention, things may go badly for her. We shall take with us so many picked men."

Shields and saddles and all the apparel they meant to take to Etzel's land were now made ready. Then Kriemhild's messengers were summoned before Gunther.

When they appeared, Gernot said, "The king will do as Etzel asked us. We will gladly go to his festival to see our sister. Of this you need have no doubt."

Then King Gunther said, "Can you tell us when the festival is to be or at what time we should arrive there?"

"It is to be next midsummer without fail," answered Swemmel.

The king gave them permission, as he had not yet done, to go with his consent to Lady Brunhild if they wished to see her. But Volker prevented this, with her approval.

"My lady Brunhild does not feel like seeing you now," he said. "Wait until tomorrow. Then you may visit her." But when they then thought to see her, they were not admitted.

Now the king, out of his own generosity and liking for the messengers, bade gold, of which he had great store, be brought out upon broad shields. Rich gifts were also given them by his kinsmen Giselher and Gernot, Gere and Ortwin. They gave ample proof that they too were generous, offering the envoys such rich gifts that for fear of their lord they dared not accept them.

Werbel said to the king, "Sir King, let your gifts remain here in this land. We cannot take them with us. My lord forbade us to accept any presents. Besides, we have no need of them."

[3] The interval of a week allows sufficient time for Kriemhild to begin preparations for hostility, which the Burgundians would notice on arrival, but not enough time for her to complete her preparations and thus have the advantage over the visitors.

The lord of the Rhine was very offended at their refusing the riches of a king so powerful as he, and at last they were forced to receive his gold and garments, which they then took to Etzel's land. Since the minstrels wished to see Ute before departing, Giselher led them to his mother. The queen sent word with them that she was happy at the honors Kriemhild enjoyed and bade them be given embroidered bands and gold for Kriemhild's sake, whom she loved, and for the sake of King Etzel. These gifts they accepted gladly, for she gave them in all sincerity.

Having now taken leave of women and of men, the envoys joyfully rode away to Swabia. Gernot had his men accompany them that far to see that no one did them harm. After their escort had parted from them, Etzel's sovereign power protected them on all the roads, so that no one robbed them of horses or clothing. Quickly they hurried toward his land, informing any friends they knew of on the way that in a very short time the Burgundians would come from the Rhine to the land of the Huns. Bishop Pilgrim also heard this news. As they rode down the highway past Bechelaren, they did not fail to tell Rudeger and Gotelind, who rejoiced that she was to see the guests. The minstrels now raced on with the tidings till they came to Etzel in his town of Gran. Greeting upon greeting they delivered, for many had been sent him, and the king turned red for very joy.

When the queen heard the news that her brothers were coming for certain, she was well content, and for the sake of her own honor rewarded the minstrels with goodly gifts.

"Now tell me, both of you, Werbel and Swemmel," she said, "which of my kinsmen will be at the festival. Will the closest kin we have invited come here to this land? Tell me, what did Hagen say when he heard the message?"

"He came early on a morning to the council," answered the minstrel, "and had little good to say. When they pledged the journey here to the Hunnish land, for the fierce Hagen that was pronouncement of death. Your brothers, the three kings, are coming in good spirits. I do not know exactly who else will be with them, but the minstrel Volker promised to ride along."

"I care very little whether I ever see Volker," said the queen. "But I feel friendly toward Hagen. He is a fine hero. I am very pleased that we shall see him here."

Then Lady Kriemhild went to the king, and with what affection she said, "How do you like the news, my dear Lord? What I have always desired shall now be brought to pass."

"Your will is my pleasure," he answered. "I would not be gladder if my own kin were to come here to my lands. The joy at seeing your kinsmen has dispelled all my cares."

The king's retainers gave orders for palace and hall to be provided with seats everywhere for the welcome guests who were to visit them. These guests were soon to deprive the king of great happiness.

XXV

How the Nibelungs Journeyed to the Huns

We shall tell no more now of the doings at Etzel's court. More high-spirited warriors never rode so proudly to any king's land. They had everything they desired, both weapons and apparel. The lord of the Rhine clad his men for the festival, a thousand and sixty, so I have heard, and nine thousand squires, and the harness for their horses was brought to the court at Worms. Those they left at home were soon to weep for them.

Now an aged bishop of Speyer said to Ute, "Our friends intend to journey to the festival. May God protect their honor there!"

And Ute said to her sons, "Stay here, good heroes. I dreamed last night of fearful peril, how all the birds in this land were dead."

"He who goes by dreams," said Hagen, "does not rightly know how to fulfill the demands of honor. I want my lord to go to court to take his leave of the ladies. We're eager to ride to Etzel's land. Stout warriors' hands can well serve kings when we are there at Kriemhild's festival."

Thus Hagen counseled the journey, though he regretted it afterward. He would have advised against it, had Gernot not abused him rudely. He reminded him of Siegfried and said, "That's why Hagen doesn't want to make the journey to the court."

"No, not out of fear," replied Hagen. "If you will have it so, heroes, go right ahead. I'll gladly ride with you to Etzel's land." He later slashed to pieces many a helmet and shield.

The ships were now ready, and their clothing was carried on board. The host of warriors gathered there had little leisure before evening, when in gay spirits they set out from home. On the grass across the Rhine tents and pavilions were set up. Once this was done, the king asked his lovely wife to linger a while, and that night she once more embraced his handsome body. Early in the morning blaring of trumpets and piping of flutes began, as signal for them to leave, and they made ready to start. Whoever held a loved one in her arms now caressed him tenderly. Many were soon to be parted in grief by King Etzel's wife.

Ute's sons had one vassal, brave and true. As they were about to depart, he spoke his mind privately to the king and said, "I cannot help but grieve that you make this journey to the court." His name was Rumolt, and he was a valiant hero. "To whose care will you entrust your people and your land?" he said. "Alas that no one can turn you warriors from your purpose! I never liked Kriemhild's message."

"I leave my land and child in your charge. And serve the ladies well. That is my will. Comfort any you see weeping. Be assured, King Etzel's wife will never do us harm."

The horses stood ready for the kings and their men, and many, still in high spirits, took farewell with fond kisses. Fair women later wept for them. As the warriors went to their horses, the host of ladies were seen standing there sorrowing. Their hearts must have told them it would be a long parting that would end in bitter grief. Such foreboding never soothes the heart.

The Burgundians prepared to set out, and there was great activity in the land. On either side of the mountains both men and women wept, yet no matter what their people did, the kings rode joyously away.

Nibelung's heroes[1] went with them, in a thousand coats of mail.

---

[1] From this point on the word "Nibelungs" or "Nibelung men" is used to refer to the Burgundians. Prior to this it meant King Nibelung's warriors, who then became Siegfried's vassals after the latter killed his two sons, Schilbung and Nibelung. Here the meaning has obviously changed, for in chapter XVIII it is clear that Siegfried's men went with Siegmund. Only Eckewart and his vassals, themselves Burgundians, remained with Kriemhild

They had left at home many ladies whom they never saw again. Siegfried's wounds tormented Kriemhild still.

Gunther's men now took their course toward the Main up through East Franconia. Hagen guided them, for he knew the way, and Dankwart was their marshal. As they rode from East Franconia toward Swalevelt, one could recognize the princes and their kinsmen by their proud bearing. On the twelfth morning the king came to the Danube. Ahead of them all rode Hagen of Troneg, the help and comfort of the Nibelungs. On the sandy shore the brave warrior dismounted and quickly tied his horse to a tree. The river was in flood, the ships beached and hidden, and the Nibelungs were greatly troubled as to how they should get across, for the water was far too wide. Many knights sprang to the ground.

"Ill fortune may well befall you here, Lord of the Rhine," said Hagen. "You can see for yourself, the river is flooded and its current very strong. I fear we shall lose many good warriors here today."

"Why do you reproach me, Hagen?" said the king. "For the sake of your own honor, dishearten us no more, but look for the ford over to the other bank, so that we can get both horses and equipment across."

"I am not so tired of life," said Hagen, "that I want to drown in these broad waves. Many a man in Etzel's lands shall first die at my hands. This is my firm intention. Stay by the river, proud Knights, and I'll look along the stream myself for ferrymen to take us across to Gelfrat's land."

Hagen picked up his good shield and took it with him. He was now fully armed; his bright helmet was bound upon his head, and over his coat of mail he wore a broad sword that cut savagely with both edges. Upstream and down he looked for ferrymen. Then he heard water splashing and began to listen. It came from wise women,[2] who to cool themselves were bathing in a lovely spring. Hagen saw them and crept up stealthily. When they became aware

---

in Burgundy. In any case, Siegfried's men would scarcely have joined the Burgundians for what was later to be a battle against Kriemhild. (See also Index of Names, below.)

[2] Mythological beings with supernatural powers, among them the power of prophecy, referred to as *wîsiu wîp*, "wise women," or as *merewîp*, "mermaids."

of this, they fled in haste, glad that they had escaped him. He took away their clothing, but did them no further harm.

Then the one mermaid said—Hadeburg was her name, "Noble Knight Hagen, if you will give us back our garments, we will tell you how you will fare on this journey to the court of the Huns."

They floated like birds before him on the waves. For this reason he thought their wisdom great and good and trusted all the more what they told him. Now they gave him the information he wished.

"You can safely ride to Etzel's land," said Hadeburg. "I pledge my faith as surety that never did heroes ride to any realm to win such great honors. Believe me, this is true."

At these words Hagen's heart rejoiced. Delaying no longer, he returned their clothing. When they had put on their strange attire,[3] they told him the truth about the journey to Etzel's land.

The other mermaid said—Siegelind was her name, "I want to warn you, Hagen, son of Aldrian. To get back our clothes my mother's sister lied to you. You are very foolish if you go to the Huns. Turn back while there is still time, for you brave heroes have been summoned that you may die in Etzel's land. Whoever rides there takes death by the hand."

"It is useless to try to deceive me," replied Hagen. "How could it happen that we should all die there because of one person's hatred?"

They explained the matter more precisely, and the first mermaid said, "It is your destiny that not one of you shall escape alive except the king's chaplain. We know this very well. He will return safely to Gunther's land."

His heart full of rage, the bold Hagen said, "It would not be pleasant to tell my lords that we should all lose our lives among the Huns. Now show us across the river, you wisest of all women."

"Since you will not give up the journey," she said, "up there by the river, where a house is standing, there is a ferryman, and elsewhere none."

He asked nothing more, but the mermaid called after the angry warrior, "Wait a bit, Lord Hagen. You are far too hasty. Listen first to how you get to the other bank. The ruler of this march is called Else. His brother is Gelfrat, a lord in the Bavarian land. It

[3] They are probably "swan maidens," able to assume either the form of a human or of a swan. A person who gains possession of their "strange attire," the plumage of a swan, has them in his power.

will go hard with you if you want to cross his territory. Watch out, and also deal cautiously with the ferryman. He is of so fierce a nature that he will not let you live unless you are friendly toward him. If you want him to ferry you over, pay him the fare.[4] He guards this land and is loyal to Gelfrat. If he doesn't come promptly, then call across the river and say your name is Amelrich. He was a fine hero, who left this land because of a feud. The ferryman will come to you as soon as he hears that name."

Hagen bowed his thanks to the women. He said no more, but kept silent. Then he went further up the bank of the river to where he found a house on the other side. Loudly he began to call across the water, "Come and get me, ferryman. As reward I'll give you an arm ring of red gold. I tell you, I *have* to make this crossing."

The ferryman was so wealthy that he did not relish giving service and seldom took pay from anyone.[5] His servants were also arrogant.

Hagen still stood alone, this side of the river. Then he shouted with such force that all the water echoed, for his strength was great, "Come and get me. I am Amelrich, Else's vassal, who fled this land because of a fierce feud."

Up high on the tip of his sword he swung an arm ring of red gold, shiny and handsome, offering it as payment for taking him over to Gelfrat's land. Now the haughty ferryman himself seized the oar. He was newly married and wanted to earn Hagen's red gold.[6] For this he suffered death from the warrior's savage sword. Greed for great wealth leads to an evil end.

Vigorously the ferryman rowed across to the shore. Finding no sign of the man whose name he had heard, he became very angry, and seeing Hagen, said furiously, "Your name may be Amelrich, but you are very unlike him I expected to find here. He was my brother, by my father and by my mother. Now that you have deceived me, you will have to stay on this side."

"No, by the Almighty God," said Hagen. "I am a warrior from foreign lands and have fighting men in my charge. Now be so good

---

[4] I.e., don't try to use force.

[5] This is no ordinary ferryman, but a vassal of the ruler of this part of Bavaria, and his post as guard of the ford across the Danube is a very important one.

[6] In the *Thidrekssaga* this episode is clearer. The ferryman wants the ring for his young wife.

as to accept my pay, and ferry me across, for I am truly your friend."

"That is impossible," replied the ferryman. "My dear lords have enemies, and for this reason I never ferry any stranger into the land. If your life is dear to you, step out at once onto the shore."

"Don't behave this way," said Hagen, "for my heart is troubled. Accept this good gold as a keepsake from me, and ferry us across, a thousand horses and as many men."

But the fierce ferryman answered, "I will never do it." And brandishing a sturdy oar, large and broad, he dealt Hagen such a blow that he staggered to his knees in the ship. Hagen was not pleased at this; so brutal a ferryman he had never met. Then to anger the arrogant stranger still more, the ferryman hit Hagen on the head with a punt-pole so savagely that it was completely shivered. Else's ferryman was a powerful man, but for this he reaped great injury.

In furious rage Hagen straightway reached for the sheath that held his sword, cut off his head, and cast it into the depths. This news soon reached the Burgundians. At the moment when he slew the boatman, the ship began drifting downstream. He was annoyed no little and was weary before he brought it round. He rowed with all his might, and with swift strokes he turned it until the stout oar snapped in his hand. He wanted to get to the shore and rejoin the warriors, but there was no other oar. Oh, how quickly he bound it with a shield thong, a narrow band, and steered downstream toward a wood, where he found his lord standing on the bank.

Many knights came to meet him and welcomed him with friendly greeting. Then they noticed the blood steaming in the ship from the savage wound he had dealt the ferryman, and the warriors plied him with questions enough.

When King Gunther saw the hot blood surging in the boat, he said at once, "Tell me, Lord Hagen, what has become of the ferryman? Your great strength, I think, has robbed him of his life."

Hagen denied it and said, "When I found the ship by a willow tree, I untied it. I haven't seen any ferryman here, and no harm has been done anyone through fault of mine."

Then Lord Gernot said, "I fear the death of dear friends today. Since we have no boatmen at hand, how can we get across? I am sad at this."

Loudly Hagen shouted, "You squires, lay the horses' harness

down on the grass. I still remember that I was once the very best ferryman to be found along the Rhine. You may be sure I'll take you safely across to Gelfrat's land."

They spurred the horses on with blows so that they would cross the river more rapidly. They swam well, and the mighty flood did not sweep away a single one, though some, being weary, drifted far downstream. The men then carried their gold and clothing on board, since there was nothing for it but to undertake the crossing. Hagen as skipper steered many a sturdy warrior to the sandy shore into the unknown land. First he took across a thousand knights, then his own men. And still there were more to come. Nine thousand squires he ferried to the land. Hagen's hand had little leisure that day.

When he had brought them safely across the river, he thought of the strange tale the wild mermaids had told him shortly before. This almost cost the king's chaplain his life. Hagen discovered the priest by the church baggage, leaning his hand on the reliquary. Little good *that* did him. As soon as Hagen spied him, it went hard with the unlucky priest. With all haste he flung him out of the boat.

"Catch hold of him, Lord Hagen, catch him!" many among them called out.

Giselher became angry, but Hagen did not want to give up until he had harmed the priest.

Then Lord Gernot said, "How can the chaplain's death help you, Hagen? If anyone else had done this, he would pay dearly for it. What do you have against the priest?"

The chaplain tried his best to swim. He hoped to save his life if someone would come to his aid. But that was not to be, for Hagen in a furious rage thrust him down to the bottom. No one approved of this. When the poor priest saw no help forthcoming, he turned back toward the shore. He was in sore distress, but though he could not swim, God's hand helped him and he came safely to land again. There he stood, and shook his clothes.

By this Hagen knew there was no escape from what the wild mermaids had foretold, and he thought to himself, "These warriors must all lose their lives."

After the three kings' men had unloaded the ship and carried away everything they had on board, Hagen hacked it to pieces and cast it into the water. The brave warriors were quite taken aback.

"Why do you do this, brother?" asked Dankwart. "How will we get across when we ride home to the Rhine?"

Later Hagen told him that that could never be, but now he answered, "I do it with the thought that if we have any coward with us on this journey who might run away out of timid fear, he would die a shameful death in these waves."

In their company was a valiant hero from Burgundy named Volker, who knew how to speak his mind adroitly. Whatever Hagen did the fiddler approved.

Their horses were now ready, and the pack horses well loaded. On their journey they had as yet suffered no injury that troubled them except the loss of the king's chaplain. He had to go back to the Rhine on foot.

XXVI

How Gelfrat Was Killed by Dankwart

When they had all reached the shore, the king asked, "Who will now show us the right roads through the land so that we shall not lose our way?"

"I shall," said Volker. "I alone will see to that."

"Keep silent now, knights and squires," said Hagen. "One ought to pay heed to friends. This is but right, I think. I have very bad news for you. We shall never return to the Burgundian land. Two mermaids told me this morning that we would not go back again. Now here is what I counsel. Arm yourselves, heroes, and guard yourselves well. We have powerful enemies here and must travel ready for combat. I hoped to find the wise mermaids were lying. They declared not one of us but the chaplain would return home safe and sound. That is why I would have liked to drown him today."

The news flew from group to group, and brave warriors turned pale for gloom at the fear of harsh death on this journey to Etzel's court. It was at Moeringen that they had crossed the river, and there Else's ferryman had lost his life.

"Since I have made enemies along our route," continued Hagen, "we shall certainly be attacked. I killed that ferryman this morning, and Gelfrat and Else must know about it. Now get ready quickly, so that it will go hard with them if they attack our forces here today. I know them to be so bold they will not fail to do it. Let the horses proceed slowly enough that no one will think we are running away."

"I will follow this counsel," said Giselher. "Who shall guide the troops across the land?"

"Let Volker do it," they said. "He knows the paths and roads here."

Even before the wish was fully spoken, the brave fiddler stood there well armed, his helmet bound on. His battle armor was brilliantly colored, and to his spearshaft he tied a red banner. Later he and the kings found themselves in grave peril.

Meanwhile trustworthy news of the ferryman's death had reached Gelfrat, and Else had heard it too. Angered, they both sent for their warriors, who speedily made themselves ready. In a very short time men who in fierce battles had inflicted injury and severe wounds were seen riding toward them. Seven hundred or more joined Gelfrat. Their lords took the lead as they now rode in pursuit of their savage enemies. They were all too hasty in following the bold strangers. They wanted to avenge their wrath, but in so doing a great number of their masters' friends were soon to be lost.

Hagen of Troneg had planned well—how could a warrior guard his kinsmen better? He had charge of the rear guard with his vassals and his brother Dankwart. This was wisely done. The day had passed away; nothing more of it was left. He feared injury and suffering for his friends as they rode beneath their shields through the Bavarian land. It was not long until they were attacked. On either side of the road and close behind they heard the beat of hoofs. The foe were in too great a hurry.

"They intend to attack us here," said Dankwart. "It would be a good thing to tie on your helmets now."

They reined in their horses, as was necessary. In the darkness they saw the glitter of bright shields. Hagen could keep silent no longer, "Who is chasing us on this road?"

Gelfrat, the margrave of Bavaria, said, "We are looking for our enemies and are in pursuit of them. I don't know who killed my ferryman today. He was a valorous hero, and I am very grieved."

"Was the ferryman yours?" said Hagen. "He refused to ferry us across. The responsibility is mine. I killed the warrior, but I was forced to it, for I almost died at his hands. I offered him gold and clothing as reward for ferrying us across to your land. This made him so angry that he struck me with a stout oar. At that I became furious. So I reached for my sword and warded off his wrath with a mighty wound. Thus the warrior died. I shall make reparation to you in any way you judge fit."

"I knew very well," said Gelfrat, "when Gunther and his following rode by, that Hagen of Troneg would do us injury. Now he shall not escape. He must answer for the ferryman's death."

Eager to charge each other, Gelfrat and Hagen couched their spears over the shields for the thrust. Else and Dankwart rode splendidly, pitting their strength against each other. The fighting was fierce indeed. How could warriors better put each other to the test? From a mighty thrust of Gelfrat's Hagen landed behind his horse. Its breast strap broke, and he learned what falling meant. From the followers the crash of spearshafts rang out. Now Hagen, who had fallen to the grass from the thrust, had gotten up again. He was not, I can tell you, kindly disposed toward Gelfrat. Who held their horses, I do not know. Both Hagen and Gelfrat, now on foot on the sandy ground, rushed at one another. Their companions, too, joined in combat, and all learned what fierce fighting was. Hagen sprang violently at Gelfrat, but the margrave struck off a big piece of his shield so that a whirl of sparks flew out. Gunther's vassal came near to losing his life.

Then he began to call Dankwart, "Help, dear brother, a mighty warrior has attacked me and he isn't going to let me get away alive."

"I'll be the umpire here," the brave Dankwart answered.

With that he sprang closer and dealt Gelfrat such a blow with his sharp sword that he fell dead. Else would have liked to avenge him, but he and his following came out of the struggle with heavy losses. His brother was dead, he himself wounded, and at least eighty of his warriors remained behind, struck down by a cruel death. There was nothing for it but to flee from Gunther's men.

When the Bavarians gave way, savage blows could be heard resounding in their wake, as the men of Troneg pursued their enemies. All who hoped to escape unharmed made off in great haste.

Then, as they fled, Dankwart said, "Let's turn back now on the road and let them go, for they are wet with blood. Let's hurry to join our friends. This is my counsel to you."

When they returned to the spot where the injury had been done them, Hagen said, "Warriors, look to see who is missing or whom we have lost here in this battle that we owe to Gelfrat's wrath."

They had a loss of only four to recover from, and these were well avenged. A hundred or more from the Bavarian land had been killed, and the shields of the men from Troneg were dulled and wet from their blood.

The gleam of the bright moon pierced in patches through the clouds.

Then Hagen spoke again, "No one is to tell my dear lords what we have done here. Let them remain free of care until the morning."

When those who had just been fighting caught up with the rest, weariness lay heavy on the whole company, and many a man asked, "How long must we keep on riding?"

"We can't make camp here," said Dankwart. "You must all ride until the day has come."

Volker, who had charge of the troops, sent word to the marshal to ask, "Where shall we stop tonight where our horses can rest and my dear lords too?"

"I can't tell you," answered Dankwart. "We cannot rest until it begins to dawn. Then wherever we find a place, we'll lie down on the grass."

How disappointed many of them were at hearing these words! No one discovered that they were red with hot blood until the sun sent its brilliant rays across the hills toward the dawn and the king noticed that they had been fighting.

"What now, friend Hagen?" he said angrily. "I see you scorned my help when your armor rings got wet with blood. Who did it?"

"Else," answered Hagen. "He attacked us in the night because of his ferryman. My brother killed Gelfrat, and Else was forced to flee. A hundred of them and four of ours died in the battle."

We cannot tell you where they camped. All the people from the surrounding country soon learned that the noble Ute's sons were on their way to court, and they were well received there in Passau.

Bishop Pilgrim, uncle of the kings, was very happy that his nephews had come to the land with such a host of warriors, and they soon became aware of how ready he was to serve them. They were warmly welcomed by friends along the way. Since it was impossible to lodge them in Passau, they crossed the river, where they found an open field and set up tents and pavilions. They were prevailed upon to remain there a whole day and a full night too. And how well they were cared for! Then they rode on to Rudeger's land, where the news of their coming was quickly made known.

When the way-weary men had rested and came closer to Rudeger's country, they found a man asleep on the border. Hagen took his stout sword from him. This good knight's name was Eckewart.[1] He was saddened at losing his sword because of the warriors' journey. They had found Rudeger's march poorly guarded.

"Alas for me at such disgrace!" said Eckewart. "How much I deplore this journey of the Burgundians! From the time I lost Siegfried my joy has vanished. Alas, Lord Rudeger, how I have behaved toward you!"

When Hagen heard the noble warrior's distress, he returned his sword to him and gave him six red armbands. "Keep these as a token that you are my friend. You are a brave warrior to be here at the border all alone."

"God reward you for your arm rings!" said Eckewart. "But I am very sorry that you take this journey to the Huns. You killed Siegfried, and you are hated here. I counsel you in all sincerity to guard yourselves well."

"As to that, God must guard us," answered Hagen. "These warriors, the kings and their men, now have no other care than concerning lodging, where we can find quarters in this land for the night. Our horses are spent from the long way, and our provisions have run out. We can find nothing for sale anywhere and need a host who out of courtesy would give us his bread tonight."

[1] He is apparently Margrave Eckewart, Kriemhild's devoted follower since the time of her marriage to Siegfried, but if so, it seems strange that he is so willing to warn the Burgundians against her. Various explanations of this curious scene have been attempted. Heusler and others believe it to be a vestige of older forms of the story where such a warning from Kriemhild, then on the side of her brothers (see Introduction), was appropriate. Panzer identifies this Eckewart with "the loyal Eckart" of German legend, whose

"I will show you a host," said Eckewart. "You have never been lodged so well in any land as you will be here if you go to Rudeger. He lives close by the highway and is the best host that ever owned a house. As sweet May bears grass and flowers, so his heart gives birth to virtues. He is always happy when he can serve good knights."

Then King Gunther said, "Will you be my messenger and ask whether for my sake my dear friend Rudeger will take us in, my kinsmen and our men? I will always show him my gratitude as best I can."

"I'll be glad to be the messenger," said Eckewart.

Eagerly he set out on the journey and reported to Rudeger the message he had heard. Such pleasant news had not reached him for many a long time.

The warrior was seen hastening toward Bechelaren. Rudeger himself recognized him and said, "There on the road comes Kriemhild's vassal Eckewart in a great hurry."

He thought enemies had done him harm and went out in front of the gate to meet the messenger. Eckewart ungirded his sword and laid it aside. Then the news he brought was not concealed from the host and his friends, but was quickly told them.

"Gunther, the lord of the Burgundian land," he said to the margrave, "and also his brother Giselher and Gernot have sent me to you. Each of these warriors tenders you his service, and likewise Hagen and Volker, in devoted loyalty. And I will tell you more— the king's marshal sends you through me the message that the good warriors have need of lodging from you."

With a smile Rudeger answered, "How glad I am at this news that the kings desire my service! It will not be denied them. I shall be very happy if they come to my home."

"Dankwart, the marshal, asked me to tell you whom you would receive in your house besides the kings—sixty brave warriors and a thousand good knights, with nine thousand squires."

Rudeger rejoiced and said, "How glad I am that these warriors, for whom I have never yet done any service, are coming to my

---

role as warner was well known. De Boor believes that this Eckewart is not the margrave, but another of Kriemhild's vassals, who gives the warning out of gratitude for Hagen's gift. (See de Boor's edition of the text.)

house as guests! Now ride out to meet them, kinsmen and vassals both."

Knights and squires hastened to their horses. What their lord had commanded they all thought proper, and so they sped to their service all the more urgently. Lady Gotelind, who was sitting in her chamber, as yet knew nothing of this.

XXVII

How They Came to Bechelaren

The margrave went to find the ladies, his wife and his daughter, and told them at once the good news he had heard, that their lady's brothers were soon to arrive at their home.

"Dear love," said Rudeger, "welcome the kings warmly when they come here to court with their following. And greet Hagen, Gunther's vassal, kindly. With them is one called Dankwart, and and another named Volker, well versed in courtesy. These six you and my daughter must greet with a kiss and graciously keep them company."

This the ladies promised willingly. They took from the coffers splendid gowns in which to go to meet the warriors. That day many a woman was busily at work. No false color was seen on their cheeks. On their heads they wore costly chaplets, bright circlets of gold, so that the wind should not dishevel their lovely hair.

Let us now leave the ladies thus occupied. Rudeger's friends dashed across the plain to where the princes were and gave them a cordial reception in the margrave's land.

When Rudeger saw them coming toward him, he said joyfully, "Welcome, my Lords, and your liegemen too. I am very glad to see you here in my land."

The warriors bowed their thanks to him in all sincerity without any hatred, and he showed them very plainly that he was devoted to them. To Hagen he gave a special greeting, for he had known him in earlier days,[1] and did likewise to Volker. He also welcomed Dankwart, who said, "You will provide for us, but who will take care of the followers we have brought along?"

"You shall have a good night," answered the margrave, "and all your following. I will provide such guard for everything you have brought with you, horses and apparel too, that no part of it shall be lost that would cause you harm, not even to the value of a single spear. Pitch the tents on the plain, you squires. I'll make good for whatever you lose here. Take off the bridles, and let the horses run free."

No host had ever done this for them before, and the guests were pleased. This accomplished, the lords rode away, and all about the squires lay down on the grass and took their ease. Never, I think, on the whole journey, were they treated so well.

The margravine had come out before the castle with her daughter. Beside her stood lovely ladies and fair maidens wearing sumptuous gowns and ever so many bracelets, and from their costly robes precious stones blazed afar.

The guests now arrived and dismounted immediately. Oh, what fine courtesy the Burgundians displayed! Six and thirty maidens and many matrons too, their persons shapely to perfection, went out to meet them with a host of valiant men. Graciously the ladies greeted them. The young margravine kissed the kings all three, and her mother did the same. Hagen was also standing close by. Rudeger bade his daughter to kiss him. She looked at Hagen, and he seemed to her so frightening that she would far rather have let it be. Yet she had to do what the master of the house demanded of her. Her color came and went, now pale, now red. Dankwart, too, she kissed, and then the minstrel. Because of his great valor this greeting was granted him.

The young margravine now took Giselher by the hand, and her mother did the same to Gunther. Joyfully they left with the warriors. The host walked at Gernot's side to a vast hall, where knights and ladies sat down. Orders were given at once to pour good wine for the guests. Never were heroes treated better. Rudeger's daughter was gazed at with tender glances—so very lovely she was. Indeed, many a knight caressed her in his thoughts, and this she well deserved, for her nobility of spirit. They thought whatever they

[1] Another reference to the young Hagen's stay at Etzel's court.

pleased, but it could not come to pass. Back and forth went the glances at the crowd of maidens and ladies seated there. The noble fiddler cherished great affection for his host.[2]

Then according to custom knights and ladies separated. Tables were set up in the wide hall, and the guests from abroad were magnificenlty served. In their honor the margravine went to table with them, but her daughter she left sitting with the maidens, as was proper. The guests were sorry not to see her any longer.

After they had all drunk and eaten, the fair maiden was once more brought into the hall. Now there was no lack of playful raillery, much of it from Volker, that brave and lusty warrior.

Then the minstrel spoke up for all to hear, "Mighty Margrave, God has dealt graciously with you, for he has given you a wife of great beauty and a life full of happiness. If I were a prince and wore a crown, I would wish to have your lovely daughter as my wife. This would be my heart's desire. She is fair to look upon, and noble and good as well."

"How would it be possible for any king to desire my daughter?" said the margrave. "We are exiles here,[3] both I and my wife. What good is great beauty to the maid?"

To this the courteous Gernot answered, "If I should have a bride after my own desire, I would always be glad of such a wife."

Hagen, too, replied graciously. "My lord Giselher ought to take a wife. The margravine is of such high lineage that we would gladly serve her, I and his men, if she should go crowned to the Burgundians."

This speech pleased Rudeger and Gotelind and gladdened their hearts. The warriors now arranged that Giselher should take her as his wife, a union well befitting a king. Who can hinder what is destined to be? She was summoned to court. Then they swore to give him the charming girl, and he vowed to marry her. The

[2] This sentence, the last line of a stanza, is a good example of the break in continuity which occurs when the poet "pads" the last line before going on to a new topic in the next stanza. See Introduction.

[3] The poet's references to Rudeger's past are casual and vague. Perhaps he assumed that his audience was familiar with the story. At any rate, he does not name Rudeger's homeland nor explain why he is in exile. The origin of the character is uncertain, though it is likely that this particular chapter is a reflection of the reception of Frederick Barbarossa in Gran by King Bela of Hungary in 1189.

maiden was allotted castles and land; the king pledged with oath and handclasp, and Lord Gernot too, that this should be done.

Then the margrave said, "I have no castles, but I shall always serve you loyally. I will give my daughter as much silver and gold as a hundred pack horses can scarcely carry, so that in all honor the hero's kinsmen may be well pleased."

Now, as was the custom, they bade them both step into a circle. Facing her stood many a youth happy at heart, thinking his own thoughts as young people still do today. The winsome maid was asked if she would have the warrior. She was a little disconcerted, though she had every intention of taking the handsome knight, for she was embarrassed at the question, as many a maid has been. Her father counseled her to say "Yes, she would gladly marry him." Instantly young Giselher was at her side, clasping her in his white hands. Little joy she was to have of him.

Then the margrave said, "Noble and mighty Kings, when you ride home again to Burgundy, I will give you my daughter to take with you."

To this they all agreed. Now the festive tumult ceased, and they sent the maiden to her chamber and bade the guests rest and sleep until the day.

In the morning food was prepared, and after eating, the visitors wanted to set out for the Hunnish land, but the host said, "I won't permit it. Stay here a while longer. I have never had such welcome guests."

"But that is not possible," replied Dankwart. "Where would you get the food, and the bread and the wine, that you would need for so many warriors for another night?"

When the host heard this, he said, "Don't say such a thing. My dear Lords, do not refuse me. I could give you, and all the followers who have come here with you, food for fourteen days. King Etzel has never yet dispossessed me of any of my wealth."

All protests were in vain, and they were obliged to remain there until the fourth morning. The generous host lavished such gifts upon his guests, both horses and clothing, that his bounty was talked about far and wide. Now they could delay no longer; they had to leave. In his generosity Rudeger spared nothing. No one was denied anything he desired; this could not but please them all. Their followers led the horses up in front of the gate, already saddled, and many of the stranger knights went out to them, bearing shields in their hands, ready to ride to Etzel's land.

Before they left the hall, the host distributed gifts to all the guests. He knew how to live open-handedly in great glory. His fair daughter he had given to Giselher, and he now gave Gunther a coat of mail which the king wore with honor, though as a rule he did not accept presents. And Gunther bowed,in thanks over Rudeger's hand. Then he gave a good sword to Gernot, who later wielded it splendidly in battle. The margrave's wife approved this gift unreservedly, but through it Rudeger was soon to lose his life. Since the king had accepted a present, Gotelind offered Hagen a token of friendship, as was fitting, so that he should not leave for the festival without a gift from her, but he refused it.

"Of all the things I have ever seen," he said, "I would like nothing better than to take with me that shield there on the wall. That I would gladly bear to Etzel's land."

Hagen's words reminded the margravine of her grief, and it was only natural that she wept. Sadly she thought of Nudung's[4] death, whom Witege had killed, and the memory brought her painful sorrow.

"I'll give you the shield," she said to the warrior. "Would to God in heaven that he who once bore it in his hand were still alive! He met his death in battle. I shall always weep for him, as I have every reason to, wretched woman that I am."

She rose from her seat, and with her white hands she grasped the shield and carried it to Hagen. He took it in his hand. The gift was worthily bestowed on this warrior. A cover of gleaming pfellel silk concealed its bright colors and the insets of precious stones. The day never shone upon a better shield. Had anyone wished to buy it—it was well worth a thousand marks. Hagen ordered it taken away.

At this moment Dankwart arrived at court, and the margrave's daughter gave him many rich garments, which he later wore proudly among the Huns. They would not have accepted any of the gifts except to please the host, who offered them so graciously.

---

[4] The poet does not explain the connection between Nudung and Gotelind. Nudung is a figure from the stories about Dietrich of Bern. In the Scandinavian saga, the *Thidrekssaga*, Nudung is Gotelind's brother; in the German tales (*Biterolf, Rosengarten*) he is her son.

Soon they became such foes of his that they were forced to kill him.

Taking his fiddle, Volker went courteously to stand before Gotelind. He fiddled sweet tones and sang his song to her.[5] This was his farewell before leaving Bechelaren. The margravine bade a chest be brought to her. Now listen as I tell you of the token of friendship. From the chest she took twelve arm rings and drew them over his hand.

"Take these to Etzel's land and wear them at court for my sake. When you return, I shall hear how you served me there at the festival."

What the lady asked he faithfully performed.

Then the host said to the guests, "You shall travel more comfortably, for I'll escort you myself and bid you be well protected so that no one can harm you on the road."

Quickly his pack horses were loaded, and the host was provided with horses and apparel for the five hundred men whom he took with him, gay at heart, to the festival. Not a one returned alive to Bechelaren. With tender kisses Rudeger took his leave, and likewise Giselher, as his courtesy bade him. They fondled lovely women clasped in their arms. Many a maiden was soon to weep for them.

Now on all sides the windows were opened wide, for the host and his men were about to mount. Many a lady and maiden wept. Their hearts told them, I think, of the bitter grief to come, and they yearned for their dear friends whom they never saw again. Yet the warriors rode joyfully along the shore down the Danube to the Hunnish land.

Then Rudeger said to the Burgundians, "The news that we are coming must not be concealed, for King Etzel has never heard anything so welcome."

So down through Austria the messenger sped, and everywhere the people were told that the heroes from Worms across the Rhine were approaching. Nothing could have pleased them more.

The messengers hurried on ahead with the news that the Nibe-

---

[5] This scene stands out in the poem as one completely in the tradition of courtly love. The minstrel knight sings a song he has composed himself to a lady above him in rank and receives from her a present which he then wears as a token that he is in her service, whether jousting, fighting, or composing new songs.

lungs had arrived in the Hunnish land. "Receive them well, Kriemhild, my Lady. Your dear brothers are coming to you in great state." [6]

Lady Kriemhild stood at a window watching for her kinsmen as one friend for another. Many a man she saw from her fatherland. The king also heard the news and laughed for sheer joy.

"How happy I am!" said Kriemhild. "My kinsmen are bringing with them many a new shield and shining coat of mail. Let him who wants gold remember my sorrows, and I'll always be his friend."

XXVIII

How the Burgundians Came to the Huns

When the Burgundians came into the land, the aged Hildebrand of Bern[1] heard of it and told his lord, who was very troubled. Dietrich bade him welcome the valiant knights well, and the doughty Wolfhart[2] gave orders to bring the horses. Then Dietrich, followed by a host of warriors, rode out to the plain to greet them. They had just loaded on pack horses the many splendid tents.

Seeing them from afar as they rode, Hagen said courteously to his lords, "Dismount now, brave warriors, and go to meet those who wish to welcome you. Here comes a company I know very well, the warriors from the Amelung land, led by the lord of Bern —high-spirited men they are. Do not scorn any service they do you."

Dismounting from their horses, as was proper, the many knights and squires now came with Dietrich to meet the strangers and greeted them warmly. Listen to what Lord Dietrich said to Ute's sons when he saw them approaching. He regretted their journey

---

[6] A messenger is speaking.

[1] He is Dietrich's teacher and armor-bearer and the hero of the *Hildebrandslied,* of which only a fragment, probably dating from the early years of the ninth century, has been preserved.

[2] Hildebrand's nephew and Dietrich's vassal.

and thought Rudeger knew the situation and had warned them.

"Welcome, my Lords, Gunther and Giselher, Gernot and Hagen, and also Lord Volker and the valiant Dankwart. Don't you know that Kriemhild is still weeping bitterly for the hero of the Nibelung land?"

"Let her weep," said Hagen. "He's been lying dead these many years. It's the king of the Huns she ought to love now. Siegfried won't come back. He was buried long ago."

"Siegfried's wounds aside—as long as Lady Kriemhild lives, harm may still be done." Thus spoke Lord Dietrich of Bern. "Protector of the Nibelungs, beware of this."

"Why should I beware?" asked the king. "Etzel sent us messengers asking us to ride to his land. Why should I question further? My sister Kriemhild also urged us to come."

"I would advise you," said Hagen, "to ask Lord Dietrich and his warriors to tell you more of this matter and let you know Lady Kriemhild's designs."

The three kings, Gunther and Gernot and Lord Dietrich, stepped aside to speak privately.

"Now tell us, noble Knight of Bern, what you know of the queen's intent."

"What more shall I tell you?" he said. "Every morning I hear Etzel's wife weeping and lamenting with grief-stricken heart to the Almighty God of heaven because of Siegfried's death."

"What we have heard from you cannot be changed," said brave Volker, the fiddler. "Let's ride to court and see what befalls us among the Huns."

The Burgundians now went to court, riding in splendor according to the custom of their land. Meanwhile many a Hun wondered what manner of man Hagen of Troneg might be. Enough tales had been told of how he had slain Siegfried of Netherland, Kriemhild's husband, strongest of all warriors, for many questions to be asked at court about him.

The hero was of sturdy build, broad of chest, his legs long. His hair was mixed with gray, and his glance was terrifying. He walked with proud step.

Orders were given to house the Burgundian men. At the queen's command, who bore Gunther great hate, his followers[3] were sepa-

---

[3] As is made clear by what follows, "the Burgundian men" are only the knights. The "followers" are the squires, who are later killed.

rated from the rest. So it came that these squires were afterwards slaughtered in their lodgings. Hagen's brother Dankwart was marshal. To him Gunther earnestly commended his men, that he should tend them well and provide plentifully for them, and Dankwart was very attentive to them all.

Kriemhild, accompanied by her retinue, went to meet the Nibelungs and greeted them with false heart. Giselher she kissed and took by the hand. This Hagen saw, and bound his helmet tighter.

"After such a greeting," said Hagen, "brave warriors may well watch out. The kings and their men are greeted differently. It's an unlucky trip we took to this festival."

"Let him who is glad to see you bid you welcome," said Kriemhild. "I have no greeting for you out of friendship. Tell me, what have you brought me from Worms across the Rhine that you should be so very welcome?"

"If I had known," said Hagen, "that warriors were expected to bring you gifts, I would certainly have been rich enough—had I thought of it—to bring you my presents here to this land."

"Now tell me, where did you put the Nibelung treasure? It was mine, and you know that very well. You should have brought me that to Etzel's land."

"On my word, my Lady Kriemhild, it has been many a day since I had charge of the Nibelung treasure. My masters ordered it sunk in the Rhine, and there it will have to stay till doomsday."

"I thought as much," said the queen. "You haven't brought me a bit of it, though it was my property and I used to have control of it. On this account I constantly suffer many a sorrowful day."

"The devil I'll bring you anything," answered Hagen. "I have enough to carry with my shield and breastplate. My helmet is shiny, my sword[4] is in my hand, and so I bring you nothing."

Then the queen spoke to all the warriors, "No weapons are to be brought into the hall. Deliver them to me, you heroes, and I will have them taken care of."

"Believe me," said Hagen, "we will never do that. I do not aspire to the honor, O bountiful Princess, of having you carry my shield and other weapons to the lodgings. You are a queen. This is not the way my father brought me up. I shall be my own chamberlain."

"Alas for my sorrows," said Lady Kriemhild then. "Why won't

---

[4] This was Siegfried's sword Balmung.

Hagen and my brother let their shields be put away? They have been warned. If I knew who had done it, he should certainly taste death."

At this Prince Dietrich answered her angrily, "I am the one who warned the kings and Hagen. Do your worst, you she-devil, you can't make me suffer for this."

Etzel's wife was greatly abashed, for she feared Dietrich sorely. She left him at once, without a word, but she cast furious glances at her enemies. Two warriors then clasped each other by the hand; the one was Lord Dietrich, the other Hagen.

Courteously Dietrich said, "I truly regret your coming to the Huns because of the way the queen spoke."

Hagen answered, "It will turn out all right."

Thus the two brave men talked together. King Etzel saw this and asked, "I would like to know who the warrior is that Lord Dietrich is greeting so warmly. He bears himself very proudly. Whoever his father may be, he is surely a fine hero."

One of Kriemhild's men answered the king, "By birth he is from Troneg, and his father's name was Aldrian. Though he may act friendly now, he is a ferocious man. I will prove to you that I'm telling no lie."

"How am I to find out that he is so fierce?" As yet he was ignorant of the many evil tricks the queen was later to practice on her kinsmen, letting none escape from the Huns alive.

"I knew Aldrian well. He was my vassal. Praise and great honor he won here at my court. I made him a knight and gave him of my gold. The faithful Helca loved him dearly. Since then I have known all about Hagen. Two handsome children became my hostages, he and Walther of Spain.[5] They grew to manhood here. Hagen I sent home again; Walther fled with Hildegund."

So he mused on things that had happened long ago. Observing him, he had recognized his friend from Troneg, who in his youth had given him staunch service. Now, in his ripe age, he was to send many of Etzel's dear friends to their death.

[5] This is Walther of Aquitania. Hildegund, also a hostage at Etzel's court, is the daughter of the Burgundian king Herrich and has been betrothed to Walther since childhood. The two escape, and after various adventures, succeed in reaching Spain.

XXIX

How Kriemhild Reproached Hagen and How He Would Not Rise for Her

Now the two warriors parted, Lord Dietrich and Hagen of Troneg. Gunther's man looked over his shoulder for a comrade-at-arms, whom he quickly found. He saw Volker standing with Giselher and asked the skillful fiddler to keep him company, for well he knew his grim courage. He was in all things a bold knight and good.

They left their lords still standing in the court. Only these two alone were seen walking away far across the courtyard to a spacious palace. They feared no one's enmity. They sat down on a bench before the house opposite a hall belonging to Kriemhild's apartments. Their rich apparel glistened. Plenty of those who saw them would have liked to know them. The Huns gaped at them as if they were wild beasts. Kriemhild, too, saw them through a window and again became downcast. She was reminded of her sorrow and began to weep. Etzel's men wondered greatly what had so suddenly saddened her heart.

"Brave warriors," she said, "it is Hagen who has done it."

"How did it happen?" they asked. "For we saw you happy just now. There is no one so bold but that if he has done you harm and you bid us avenge you, it shall cost him his life."

"If anyone would avenge my wrongs, I would always reward it. I would be ready to give him anything he desired. I kneel at your feet," said the queen. "Avenge me on Hagen, that he may lose his life."

Sixty brave men speedily armed themselves. For Kriemhild's sake they meant to go out and kill Hagen, and the fiddler too. This was treacherous behavior.[1]

When the queen saw such a small band of them, she said angrily,

---

[1] Treacherous because no challenge to battle has preceded.

"Give up any plans you have. With so few you can never withstand Hagen. And though Hagen of Troneg is strong and bold, the man who is sitting there beside him, Volker the fiddler, is stronger still by far. He is a dreadful man. You will not so easily conquer those heroes."

Hearing these words, more of them put on their armor, four hundred stalwart warriors, for the queen was bent on doing her enemies harm. Because of this the two heroes were soon in dire straits.

When she saw her followers well armed, she said to them, "Now stand still and wait a while. I will go out to my enemies wearing my crown. And listen to my reprimand for what Gunther's vassal Hagen did to me. I know he is too proud a man to deny it. After that I don't care what penalty he pays."

The fiddler noticed the queen coming down the steps from the house and said to his comrade, "Friend Hagen, look at her coming toward us, who faithlessly invited us to this land. I have never seen so many men escorting a queen and marching ready for battle, sword in hand. Do you know, friend Hagen, whether they are hostile to you? If so, I advise you to guard all the better your life and honor. I think it would be wise. As far as I can tell, they are in an angry mood. And some are so broad across the chest that he who wants to protect himself had better do it quickly. Under their robes of silk I am sure they are wearing bright coats of mail, but whom they intend to attack, I cannot say."

In a passion of anger Hagen said, "I know very well this is all aimed at me. That's why they bear their shining swords in their hands. But despite all of them, I can still ride back to Burgundy. Now tell me, friend Volker, will you stand by me if Kriemhild's men intend to fight me? Assure me of this if I am dear to you. I'll come to your aid ever after with devoted service."

"Certainly I'll help you," said the minstrel. "Even if I saw the king coming toward us here with all his warriors, no fear will make me yield one foot in aiding you, as long as I'm alive."

"May God in heaven reward you, noble Volker! What more do I need if they fight me? Since you are ready to help me, these warriors had better approach with caution."

"Let us rise now from our seats," said the minstrel, "till she passes by. She is a queen. Let us do her this honor, for she is a high-born lady. In so doing we honor ourselves."

"No," said Hagen, "not if you care about me. If I moved from here, these warriors would imagine I did it out of fear. I'll never get up from my seat for *any* of them. Besides, it becomes us both better to sit still. Why should I honor a person who hates me? I'll never do that as long as I live. And I don't care how much King Etzel's wife detests me."

The arrogant Hagen laid across his knees a gleaming sword, from whose pommel shone a sparkling jasper greener than grass. Its hilt was of gold, the sheath a red broidered band. Kriemhild knew well it was Siegfried's. When she recognized the sword, she could not but be sad. It revived her grief, and she began to weep. I think for this very reason the bold Hagen had done it. Volker drew closer to him on the bench a strong fiddle bow, large and long, like a sword,[2] very sharp and broad, and the two warriors sat there unafraid. These brave men had too high esteem for themselves to rise from their seats through fear of anyone. Hence the queen walked to their very feet, then gave them hostile greeting.

"Tell me, Lord Hagen," she said, "who sent for you, that you dared to ride here to this land, when you knew very well what you did to me. If you were in your right senses, you would better not have come."

"No one sent for me," said Hagen. "Three warriors were invited to this land. They are my lords, and I am their vassal. Never have I stayed behind on a journey to any court."

"Now tell me further," she said, "why did you do the deed that earned you my hatred? You killed Siegfried, my beloved husband. And I shall never cease to weep for him until my dying day."

"What is the use of more talk?" he said. "There has been enough of that. I am still the same Hagen who killed Siegfried. How dearly he paid for the insult Lady Kriemhild cast at the fair Brunhild! I won't deny it, mighty Queen. I am entirely to blame for the loss that caused you grief. Let him who will, avenge it, whether man or woman. Unless I were to lie—yes, I have done you great harm."

She said, "Now hear, you warriors, how he does not deny all the wrong he has done me. What happens to him for this, you men of Etzel's, I don't care in the least."

The warriors looked at one another. If anyone had then begun the fight, such exploits would have been performed that the honors

[2] This is a favorite joke in the *Nibelungenlied*. Volker's sword is often referred to as a fiddle bow, and his fighting is described as fiddling.

would have gone to the two comrades, for they had proved themselves in battle more than once. What the Huns had boldly undertaken, they were forced to abandon through fear.

Then one of the warriors said, "Why do you look at *me*? I don't
intend to do what I promised just now. I am not going to lose my
life for anyone's gifts. King Etzel's wife means to lead us to our
ruin."

And another, standing close by, spoke up, "I am of the same
opinion. Even if someone gave me towers full of good red gold, I
wouldn't want to encounter this fiddler, with such fierce glances as
I've seen him cast. Besides, I've known Hagen from the days of his
youth, and there's little you can tell me about *that* warrior. I saw
him in two and twenty battles that brought ladies heartfelt grief.
He and the warrior from Spain[3] trod many a war path together,
when here at Etzel's side they waged many battles for the honor of
the king. This happened very often, and so one must in justice concede Hagen's prowess. At that time he was in years a youth. How
gray they are now, those who were young then! Now he has come
to maturity and is a fearful man. And he carries Balmung, which
he won by foul means."

With that the matter was settled, so that no one fought, and the
queen grieved bitterly. Fearing death from the fiddler, and certainly with good reason, the warriors retreated.

Then the fiddler said, "We have seen quite clearly that we have
enemies here, as we were told before. Let's go to court to the kings;
then no one will dare attack our lords."

How often people abandon ventures out of fear, and if they are
sensible leave them undone when they see friend standing by
friend as a friend.[4] Prudence saves many a man from harm.

"I will go with you," said Hagen, and they went to where the
warriors stood in the courtyard, surrounded by welcoming knights.

Volker called loudly to his lords, "How long are you going to
stand there and let yourselves be jostled? You must go to court
and hear from the king how he is disposed toward us."

The knights now paired off. The prince of Bern took Gunther of
Burgundy by the hand, and Irnfried took Gernot, while Rudeger

---

[3] Another reference to Walther of Aquitania.

[4] This striking repetition is in the original and serves to stress the motif
of loyalty so important for this scene and for the whole relationship between
Hagen and Volker.

went to court with Giselher. However the others were coupled for the procession to court, Volker and Hagen never separated, save in one battle at the time of their end. It was not long till noble ladies wept bitterly for them. With the kings went a thousand men from their retinue and sixty warriors besides, who had come with them. These Hagen had brought from his land. Hawart and Iring, two peerless knights, were seen walking together near the kings. Dankwart and Wolfhart surpassed all others in courtly bearing.

As the lord of the Rhine entered the great hall, the mighty Etzel was not slow to spring up from his throne at sight of him. Never was so warm a greeting given by a king.

"Welcome, Lord Gunther, and Lord Gernot too, and your brother Giselher. In loyal friendship I sent you my greetings to Worms across the Rhine. I welcome also all your following. And to you two warriors, brave Volker and Lord Hagen, I bid a special welcome to this land, from me and from my wife. She sent many a messenger to the Rhine to you."

Then Hagen said, "I have heard their messages, and if I had not come to the Hunnish land for the sake of my lords, I would have ridden here in honor of you."

The host now took his guests by the hand and led them to the seat where he himself had sat before. And solicitously they poured wine, mead, and mulberry juice for the guests, in broad goblets of gold, and bade the strangers heartily welcome.

Then King Etzel said, "I assure you, nothing more pleasant could happen to me in all the world than that you have come to visit me. This will free the queen of much sadness. I have wondered greatly what I had done to you—since I have had so many noble guests—that you never cared to come to my land. It makes me very happy to see you here now."

To this Rudeger replied, "You may rightly be glad to see them. Their loyalty is true, and my lady's kinsmen know well how to practice it. They bring to your home many an excellent warrior."

It was Midsummer's Eve when the lords arrived at the mighty Etzel's court. No one has ever heard of a greeting so fine as that with which he welcomed them. Now it was time to dine, and the king went with them to table. No host ever sat more festively with his guests. Drink and food were given them in abundance. All they desired was readily provided, for many marvels had been told about these heroes.

XXX

How Hagen and Volker Stood Guard

The day was at an end, and the night drew near. The warriors, weary from the way, were concerned as to when they might go to their beds and rest. Hagen mentioned this, and they were informed at once.

Gunther said to the host, "God grant you good fortune! Permit us to leave, for we wish to go to our sleep. We shall come early tomorrow, whenever you command."

In good spirits Etzel parted from his guests.

From all sides the crowd pressed in on the strangers. Volker said to the Huns, "How dare you block the path of these warriors? If you don't stop, you will suffer for it. I'll deal some of you such a painful fiddle blow that your true friends, if you have any, will have cause to lament it. Make way for us. That's my advice. You *all* call yourselves warriors, but not all of you have the spirit for it."

As the fiddler spoke so angrily, Hagen looked over his shoulder and said, "The brave minstrel counsels you rightly. Get to your lodgings, you men of Kriemhild's. I don't think any of you will do what you have in mind, but if you want to start anything, come to us in the morning, and let us strangers have our rest tonight. As far as I know, no hero with such intentions as yours has ever acted otherwise." [1]

The guests were taken to a spacious hall, which they found furnished with costly beds, long and broad. Yet Lady Kriemhild was planning the very greatest wrongs against them. There were many fine quilts of bright pfellel silk from Arras and many a coverlet of Arabian silks, the best to be had, with borders that gleamed magnificently. There were bedspreads of ermine and of black sable, under which they could take their ease through the night until the

---

[1] I.e., true heroes, planning an attack, would naturally make it openly, in broad daylight, not under cover of night.

bright day. Never did a king and his retinue lie so sumptuously.

"Alas for these night quarters," said the youth Giselher, "and alas for my friends who have come with us! However well my sister has provided for us, I fear we shall soon lie dead because of her."

"Cast off your care for now," said Hagen. "I will stand watch tonight myself and undertake to guard us well until the day comes. So have no fear. After that let him who can, save himself."

They bowed to him and thanked him, then went to their beds, and it was not long until all the warriors were at rest. Bold Hagen began to arm himself.

Volker the fiddler said, "If you do not spurn my help, I would like to stand guard with you tonight until the dawn."

Hagen thanked him warmly, "May God in heaven reward you, dear Volker. In all my cares I would want no one else but you alone if I should be in danger. I will repay you for this, if death does not prevent me."

Both then donned their shining armor, each picked up his shield, and leaving the house, they took their stand before the door. Thus, faithfully, they kept watch over the guests. Volker leaned his good shield against the side of the hall, went back and fetched his fiddle and did his friends a service in a fashion worthy of this hero. He sat down on the stone sill beneath the door. There never was a bolder fiddler. When the tones of the strings sang out so sweetly, the warriors far from home gave Volker thanks. The strings rang till the whole palace resounded. Both his strength and his skill were great. Then he began to play more sweetly and softly and so lulled to sleep in their beds many a careworn man. When he saw that they were asleep, he again took his shield in his hand and left the hall to take up his stand before the door and guard the strangers in that land against Kriemhild's men.

About the middle of the night—or it may have been sooner, I do not know—Volker caught sight of a helmet glittering from afar through the darkness. It was Kriemhild's men, bent on doing harm to the guests.

"Lord Hagen, my friend," said the fiddler, "we must bear these cares together. I see armed men standing in front of the house, and so far as I can tell, they mean to attack us."

"Keep still," said Hagen, "and let them come nearer. Before they notice us, helmets will be pushed askew by the swords in our hands, and they'll be sent back to Kriemhild in a sorry state."

Suddenly one of the Hunnish warriors saw that the door was guarded and said quickly, "We can't do what we were planning. I see the fiddler standing watch. On his head he is wearing a shiny helmet, bright and hard, sturdy and undamaged. His armor rings glow like fire. And at his side stands Hagen. The strangers are well guarded."

They turned back at once. Seeing this, Volker said angrily to his comrade, "Let me leave the house and go to these warriors. I want to put some questions to Lady Kriemhild's men."

"No, don't, for my sake," said Hagen. "If you go away from the house, they might get you into such straits with their swords that I would have to help you even if it cost the death of all my kinsmen. If we both started fighting, in no time two of them, or four, would dash into the house and do the sleepers such injury as we would never get over."

"Let me at least give them notice that I've seen them," said Volker. "Then Kriemhild's men can't deny that they meant to act treacherously."

And at once he called out to them, "Why do you go armed in this way, brave warriors? Are you riding out to plunder, you men of Kriemhild's? If so, you ought to have me and my comrade to help you."

No one answered him. He was in a rage.

"Bah, you miserable cowards!" he said. "Did you plan to murder us in our sleep? Never before have brave warriors been treated in such a fashion."

The queen was told that her messengers had accomplished nothing. She was exasperated, and not without reason. Furious at heart, she devised another plan. It was soon to cause the death of good and valiant heroes.

X X X I

How the Burgundians Went to Church

"My armor rings are getting cold," said Volker. "The night will not last much longer, I think. By the air I can tell it will soon be day."

Then they wakened the many warriors who still lay sleeping. Bright dawn shone in on the guests in the hall. Hagen wakened all the knights to ask if they wished to go to the minster for mass. Bells were pealing loudly, according to Christian custom. Christians and heathens sang differently, so that it was plain to see they were not the same. Gunther's men had risen from their beds at once and now prepared to go to church. They were lacing themselves into magnificent garments; none better were ever brought to the land of any king.

This Hagen did not like, and he said, "You warriors must wear other clothing here. Plenty of you know how things stand. Instead of roses, carry swords in your hands, and instead of jeweled headbands, your bright and sturdy helmets, for we know very well the false Kriemhild's intention. I tell you we must fight today, so instead of silk shirts wear coats of mail, and instead of rich cloaks, your good broad shields. Then if anyone starts a fight with you, you will be fully armed. My dear Lords, and kinsmen and liegemen as well, go willingly to church, and lament to God Almighty your fear and your peril, for know beyond a doubt, death is drawing near. And do not forget to confess anything you have done, and stand there devoutly in God's presence. Of this I warn you, noble warriors, unless God in heaven wills it, you will never hear mass again."

So the princes and their vassals went to the minster. In the holy churchyard Hagen bade them halt so that they would not be separated.

"No one knows yet," he said, "what the Huns may do to us. Place your shields at your feet, my friends, and if anyone gives you hostile greeting, repay him with deep and deadly wounds. This is Hagen's counsel. May you acquit yourselves so as to do you honor."

The two of them, Volker and Hagen, now went and took their stand in front of the great cathedral. They did this, angry as they were, to force the queen to jostle against them in the crowd. Then the lord of the land and his wife appeared. Many warriors, adorned in costly garments, escorted Kriemhild, and one could see the dust whirling high as her troop approached.

When Etzel saw the kings and their followers thus armed, he said at once, "Why is it that I see my friends going helmeted? Upon my word, I shall be grieved if anyone has done them harm. I'll gladly make amends to them in any way they like, if someone has saddened their hearts and spirits. I'll show them clearly that I am extremely displeased. Whatever they command me, I am ready to do."

"No one has done us any harm," answered Hagen. "It is the custom of my lords to go armed at all festivals for full three days. If any harm had been done us here, we would tell Etzel."

Kriemhild heard very well what Hagen said, and with what hatred she looked him in the eye! Yet she would not reveal the custom of her land, though it had long been familiar to her in Burgundy. No matter how fiercely and violently she hated them, if anyone had told Etzel the truth, he would certainly have prevented what happened there later. But out of overweening pride not one of them said a word to the king.

With a great throng the queen advanced, but this pair, Hagen and Volker, would not yield even two handbreadths. The Huns were annoyed, for the queen was now forced to push her way through against them. This was not to the taste of Etzel's chamberlains, and they would have liked to provoke the two warriors but that they did not dare to in the presence of the king. So there was much jostling, but nothing more.

When they had worshiped God and were ready to leave, many a Hunnish warrior speedily sprang to horse. With Kriemhild were a host of lovely maidens, and seven thousand warriors rode as her escort. She and her ladies sat down at the windows near Etzel, which pleased him very much. They wanted to watch the lusty heroes joust. Oh, how many strange warriors rode in the courtyard before their eyes! Now Dankwart, the marshal, had arrived with the squires, bringing his lord's retainers from Burgundy and well-saddled horses for the Nibelungs. Once the kings and their men had mounted, Volker urged them to ride a bohourt according to the custom of their land, and they rode it brilliantly. This suggestion of his was not displeasing to them. The hurtling and the tumult grew loud as the crowd of men galloped into the broad court. Etzel and Kriemhild looked on.

Six hundred of Dietrich's warriors came to the bohourt, riding toward the guests. They meant to engage in knightly sports with the Burgundians and would have done this with a will if Dietrich had given them permission. Oh, what fine warriors rode in their train! But Lord Dietrich was told of it and forbade them the tourney with Gunther's men. He feared for his vassals—and well he might.

When the warriors from Bern had left, Rudeger's men from Bechelaren came riding out before the hall, five hundred, with their shields. The margrave would have liked it better if they had stayed away. Wisely he rode to them through the throng and said to his warriors that they could see for themselves how irritated Gunther's men were, adding that he would like them to leave the bohourt.

After these knights had departed, the men from Thuringia came, we are told, and a thousand warriors from Denmark. Now splinters flew thick from spear thrusts. Irnfried and Hawart rode into the tourney. Those from the Rhine awaited them proudly. Many a joust they offered the men of Thuringia, and many a fine shield was riddled by the thrusts.

Then Lord Bloedel arrived with three thousand men. Etzel and Kriemhild saw him plainly, for the knightly games took place before them. The queen looked on with pleasure, hoping the Burgundians would come to grief.

Schrutan[1] and Gibeche, Ramung and Hornboge, rode to the bohourt in Hunnish manner and stopped, facing the warriors from Burgundy. Spearshafts whirled high, up over the king's hall. Yet nothing came of all their jousting but a festive din. Palace and hall rang loudly with the clash of the shields of Gunther's men, who won great honor and fame. Their knightly sports were so brisk and strenuous that through the trappings the glistening sweat streamed

---

[1] Schrutan is not further identified and plays no role except as participant in this tourney.

from the fine horses they rode as they haughtily vied with the Huns.

Volker the minstrel said, "I think these warriors don't dare attack us. I've been told they hate us, and they could never have a better chance than now." And he continued, "Lead our horses to the stables, and let's ride again toward evening when the time for it has come. Who knows, perhaps the queen will give the Burgundians the prize."

Then they saw a man come riding along with a pompous air none of the Huns could equal. He must have had a sweetheart at that time, for he was as richly attired as the bride of a well-born knight.

Volker spoke again, "I can't pass this up. That ladies' man must have a few knocks. It will cost him his life, and no one is going to stop me. What do I care if King Etzel's wife gets angry?"

"No," said King Gunther, "for my sake, don't. The people will blame us if we start a fight. Let the Huns begin—that will be far better."

King Etzel was still sitting beside the queen.

"I will join the bohourt," said Hagen. "Let the ladies see, and the warriors too, how we can ride. That will be good, though they won't give the prize to King Gunther's men anyway."

Brave Volker rode into the lists again. This soon caused many ladies bitter grief. He stabbed the dapper Hun through the body with a spear. For this both maids and matrons were later seen to weep. Charging fast, Hagen and his sixty men followed Volker to where the joust was on. Etzel and Kriemhild saw it all distinctly. Nor did the three kings want to leave their minstrel unprotected amidst the foe, so a thousand warriors rode skillfully there and with haughty bearing did exactly as they pleased.[2]

When the wealthy Hun was killed, his kinsmen could be heard crying out and lamenting, and all their followers asked, "Who did it?"

"It was Volker, the bold fiddler."

At once the margrave's[3] kinsmen from the Hunnish land called for their swords and shields, intending to kill Volker. The host hastily left the window. On all sides a great uproar arose among the people. The Burgundian kings and their followers dismounted

[2] These knights engage the Huns in a mass tourney in order to prevent them from attacking Volker.

[3] The dapper Hun is here given his title for the first time.

before the hall and drove their horses to the rear. Then came King Etzel to settle the strife. Wrenching a sturdy sword from the hand of one of the Hun's kinsmen that stood near, he thrust them all back, for he was extremely angry.

"Am I to violate my obligation to these heroes?" he said. "It would be a disgrace if you killed this minstrel at my court. I saw quite clearly how he was riding when he stabbed the Hun. It was not his fault; his horse stumbled. You must leave my guests in peace."

Thus he protected them. The horses were led to the stables, for there were many servants eagerly ready to do them any service. The host went into the palace with his friends[4] and forbade further strife. Tables were set up and water brought in. The men from the Rhine had plenty of violent enemies there.

It was long before all the lords were seated, for Kriemhild was too greatly oppressed by fear and said, "Prince of Bern, I seek your counsel, help, and support. My affairs are in a perilous state."

To this Hildebrand answered, "Whoever attacks the Nibelungs for the sake of any treasure, will do it without my help. And he may well regret it, for they are still unconquered, these courageous knights."

Then Lord Dietrich added in his courteous way, "Forgo this request, mighty Queen. Your kin have done me no harm that I should want to engage in battle with them. The request does you little honor, noble Queen, in plotting against the lives of your kinsmen. They came here to this land trusting in your good will. Siegfried will not be avenged by Dietrich's hand."

Finding no faithlessness in the lord of Bern, she straightway promised Bloedel a large province that Nudung had owned before. Dankwart soon killed him, so that he quite forgot the gift.

"Help me, Lord Bloedel," she said. "My enemies are in this house, those who killed Siegfried, my dear husband. I shall always be at the service of him who helps me avenge that."

"Lady," answered Bloedel, "this you must know—I dare not attack them for fear of Etzel, since he is very glad to have your kinsmen here. The king would never forgive me if I did them any injury."

4 I.e., the Burgundians.

"No, no, Lord Bloedel, for I shall always be your friend. As reward I'll give you silver and gold, and a beautiful maiden, Nudung's bride, whose lovely body you can caress with pleasure. The land and castles too—all this I'll give you. Then you can live in happiness forever, noble Knight, if you get the province where Nudung lived. I will carry out faithfully what I promise you today."

When Lord Bloedel heard what the reward was and that the lady was very suitable for him because of her beauty, he thought to earn the lovely woman in battle. For this the warrior was to lose his life.

"Go back to the hall," he said to the queen. "Before anyone is aware of it, I'll provoke a fight, and Hagen shall pay for what he did to you. I'll deliver King Gunther's vassal to you, bound." And to his men he said, "Now arm yourselves, all of you. We must seek out the enemies in their lodgings. Etzel's wife will not release me from this, so we must all risk our lives."

Having left Bloedel resolved to do battle, the queen went to table with King Etzel and his men. She had devised wicked plots against the guests. Her ancient sorrow still lay buried in her heart, and since the strife could be started in no other way, she bade Etzel's son be brought to table. How could a woman, to avenge herself, ever do a more ghastly deed? Four of Etzel's men left immediately and brought Ortlieb, the young king, to the princes' table, where Hagen also sat. And because of his murderous hate the child then had to die.

When the king saw his son, he said genially to his wife's kinsmen, "Look, my friends, here is my only son, and your sister's too. This may benefit all of you, for if he takes after his kin, he will become a brave man, powerful and noble, stalwart and handsome. If I live a while longer, I'll give him twelve lands. Then young Ortlieb's hand can serve you well. Therefore I urge you, my dear friends, when you ride home again to the Rhine, take your sister's son with you, and treat the child kindly. And bring him up in honor until he has become a man.[5] If anyone in your lands has done you harm, he will help you avenge it when he is grown."

Kriemhild also heard his words.

[5] It was the custom for noblemen to send their young sons to the home of another nobleman to be educated to knighthood, and Etzel's request is thus a sign of his complete confidence in his wife's brothers.

"These warriors might well have confidence in him if he grew to be a man," said Hagen. "But he looks so ill-fated [6] that no one will ever see *me* going to Ortlieb's court."

The king looked at Hagen, troubled by his words, and though he said nothing, they saddened his heart and weighed upon his spirits. Nor had Hagen meant them as a joke. All the princes, as well as the king, were offended at what Hagen had said about the child, and annoyed that they had to endure it. Little did they know what this warrior was soon to do.

XXXII

How Dankwart Killed Bloedel

Bloedel's warriors were now fully armed, and a thousand hauberks strong, they set out to where Dankwart was sitting at table with the squires. Then there broke out among these heroes the most violent quarrel.

When Lord Bloedel strode up to the tables, Dankwart, the marshal, greeted him courteously: "Welcome here in this house, my Lord Bloedel. But I am surprised at your coming. Tell me, what does this mean?"

"You need not greet me," said Bloedel, "for my coming means your end, because of Hagen, your brother, who killed Siegfried. You must pay for this, and many another warrior too, here in the Hunnish land."

"No, Lord Bloedel, no," said Dankwart, "or else we might really regret this journey to your court. I was a small child when Siegfried lost his life.[1] I don't know what King Etzel's wife has against me."

[6] The Middle High German word *veiclîch* means "doomed to die," but it is related to the word *veige,* which means, among other things, "cowardly" or "timid." There is no English equivalent for Hagen's significant and insulting ambiguity.

[1] This is not consistent with the beginning of the epic, where Dankwart already holds the position of marshal. In an earlier version of the story these words were spoken by Giselher, for whom they would be more appropriate, and were only later transferred to Dankwart.

"I can tell you only this—your kinsmen, Gunther and Hagen, did the deed. Now defend yourselves, you strangers. You cannot escape, for your lives must be forfeit to Kriemhild."

"You won't turn back?" said Dankwart. "Then I regret my entreaty. I would better have spared my words."

The valiant warrior sprang up from the table, and drawing a sharp sword, broad and long, he struck Bloedel a sword blow so savage that in a trice the head lay at his feet.

"Let that be your marriage gift for Nudung's bride," said Dankwart, "whom you meant to love. They can betroth her tomorrow to another man. If he wants the dowry, he'll get the same treatment." [2]

A trusty Hun had told him what grievous wrongs the queen was plotting against them. When Bloedel's men saw that their lord lay dead, they could endure this from the guests no longer. With swords raised high they rushed grimly on the youths. More than one soon regretted it.

Loudly Dankwart called out to all the following, "Noble squires, you can see how things stand. Defend yourselves now, homeless lads. We have no other choice, even though Kriemhild did send us such a friendly message." [3]

Those who had no sword reached down in front of the benches and caught up from under their feet many a long footstool. The squires did not intend to suffer this without a struggle, and with the heavy stools they dented many a helmet. How fiercely these young strangers fought back! They drove the armed men out of the house, but five hundred of them, or better, remained behind dead. The Burgundian lads were red and wet with blood.

Etzel's warriors were then told the bad news that Bloedel and his men had been killed by Hagen's brother and the squires, and they were infuriated. Before the king had heard of it, the Huns in anger armed themselves, two thousand or even more. They went to the squires—for so it had to be—and of the company they left not one alive. The faithless Huns gathered a mighty host before the house, and though the stranger squires stood their ground well,

---

[2] Dankwart could not and should not have known about the promise Kriemhild had made to Bloedel. The explanation which the poet adds in the following lines spoils the point of the whole episode, namely, catching Dankwart and the squires off guard.

[3] This is irony, of course. The message is the attack.

what did their bold courage avail them? They were all to die. Soon a fearful struggle began. And now listen to a marvelous and monstrous thing. Nine thousand squires lay slain and twelve of Dankwart's knights besides. One could see him still standing there, all alone, among the enemies. The tumult was stilled, the din had died away.

Dankwart looked over his shoulder and said, "Alas for the friends I have lost! And alas that I now stand alone among my foes!"

The swords fell thick upon the solitary man. Many a hero's wife later wept for this. Raising his shield higher, he lowered the thong[4] and wetted many an armor ring with streaming blood.

"Alas for this misfortune!" said Aldrian's son. "Now give way, Hunnish warriors, and let me out into the wind, that the air may cool me, battle-weary man."

And proudly he came out. As he sprang from the house, how many fresh swords rang on his helmet! Those who had not seen what wonders his hand had done rushed at the warrior from Burgundy.

"Would to God," said Dankwart, "that I had a messenger who could let my brother Hagen know I am in such peril from these warriors! He would help me escape, or lie dead at my side."

"You must be your own messenger," said some Hunnish men, "when we bring your dead body to your brother. Then Gunther's vassal will see something that *really* grieves him. You have done King Etzel great injury."

"Stop your threats and stand further back," he said, "or I'll wet the armor of some more of you. I'll tell the news at court myself, and I'll also complain to my lords of my great distress."

He made himself so unpleasant to Etzel's men that they dared not oppose him with their swords, whereupon they shot so many javelins into his shield that it became too heavy and he had to drop it. Now that he bore no shield, they thought to vanquish him, but oh, what deep wounds he slashed through their helmets! Many a man staggered and fell before him, and for this bold Dankwart won great glory. From both sides they sprang upon him, but some of them joined the fray *too* hastily. Like a wild boar in the forest facing the hounds, he confronted his foes. How could he have been

---

[4] The shield strap must have been adjustable. In order to hold the shield higher, one needed only to lower the strap.

more courageous? His path was always wet with hot blood. Never did a warrior single-handed fight better against his enemies than he did there.

And now he could be seen, making his way proudly toward the court. Stewards and cup-bearers heard the clang of swords, and many of them flung away the drink or any food they were taking to the court. Strong foes aplenty met Dankwart at the stairs.

"What is the meaning of this, you stewards?" asked the tired warrior. "It's *your* duty to serve the guests courteously and carry good food to the lords. Now let me report to my masters."

Any who made so bold as to bar his way to the stairs he struck such a stout sword-swing[5] that they retreated up the steps in fear. His mighty strength had worked great marvels.

XXXIII

How the Burgundians Fought the Huns

As bold Dankwart stepped through the door, he bade Etzel's followers to stand aside. His armor was dripping with blood, and he bore a sturdy sword unsheathed in his hand.

Loudly he called out, "You have been sitting here all too long, brother Hagen. To you and to God in heaven I lament our distress. Knights and squires are dead in their lodgings."

"Who did that?" Hagen called back to him.

"Lord Bloedel and his men. But he paid dearly for it, I can tell you. With my own hands I struck off his head."

"It is small injury," said Hagen, "when one can say of a warrior that he lost his life at the hands of another warrior. Lovely ladies should mourn him all the less. Now tell me, brother Dankwart, why are you so red? You must be suffering great pain from wounds. If he who did this to you is anywhere in the land, unless the wicked devil saves him, it will cost him his life."

---

[5] The *s*-alliteration in this passage is even more frequent in the original.

"You see me unharmed. My armor is wet with blood from the wounds of other men. I have killed so many today that I couldn't swear to the number."

"Brother Dankwart," said Hagen, "guard the door for us and don't let a single Hun get out. I'll have a word with the warriors, as necessity compels. Innocent of all wrong, our followers lie dead before them."

"If I am to be chamberlain," said Dankwart, "I know well how to serve such mighty kings and I'll guard the stairs in a way that will do me honor."

Nothing could have dismayed Kriemhild's warriors more.

"I wonder," said Hagen, "what the Hunnish men are whispering about in here. I imagine they could easily dispense with him who stands at the door and who has just brought the Burgundians the news of the court. For a long time I have heard it said of Kriemhild that she could not forget her heart's grief. Now let's drink to the memory of the dead and repay the king for his wine.[1] The young lord of the Huns shall be the very first we toast."

With this Hagen struck the child Ortlieb so violently that the blood streamed down the sword toward his hand and the head flew into the queen's lap. Then a slaughter, grim and great, began among the warriors. Next, Hagen dealt the tutor who had reared the child such a fierce sword blow with both hands that in a trice the head lay on the floor by the table.[2] It was a wretched salary he

---

[1] This is a difficult phrase to interpret, as one can see from notes in various editions and from differences in various translations, and I have found no explanation which seems to me entirely plausible. Undoubtedly, as some scholars suggest, there is a play on words here, "wine" and "blood." Blood was often drunk in ancient rituals, as some commentators mention, but more important, perhaps, is Dietrich's remark a little later, when he says, "Hagen is pouring here the bitterest drink of all," where the drink is obviously blood. This does not, however, explain the idea of payment. For lack of a better interpretation, I offer my own. This whole speech of Hagen's is heavily ironic, and the word "repay" (*gelten*) clearly contains other levels of meaning than the literal. Just as the king, or rather, Kriemhild, has "paid" the guests in other coin than hospitality, with blood, if you like, so Hagen "pays" for the wine, the symbol of hospitality, by killing the king's son.

[2] Here there is no real motive for killing the tutor, but in earlier versions Kriemhild, wishing to provoke a quarrel and knowing what Hagen's response would be, instructed the child to slap Hagen in the face as he was eating. When the child obeyed, Hagen killed him and then, though he knew that Kriemhild was actually responsible, he also killed the tutor for not having taught the child better manners.

paid the tutor. Hagen then noticed a minstrel standing before Etzel's table. In his wrath he rushed at him and struck off his right hand as it rested on the fiddle.

"Take that for your message to the Burgundian land."

"Oh my hand—alas!" said the minstrel Werbel. "Lord Hagen, what have I done to you? I went in good faith to your masters' land. How can I play tunes, now that I have lost my hand?"

Little did Hagen care if he never fiddled again. He dealt out deadly fierce wounds to Etzel's warriors in the hall and killed a great number of them. Bold Volker now jumped up from the table, and his fiddle bow rang loud in his hands. The tunes he fiddled were harsh, and oh, how many enemies he made among the valiant Huns! The three kings, too, sprang up from the table. They would have liked to end the fray before greater harm was done, but for all their prudence they could not hinder it when Hagen and Volker were so beside themselves with rage. Seeing that the strife could not be settled, the lord of the Rhine himself dealt his foes many a gaping wound through the bright armor rings. He was a valorous hero, and of this he gave full proof. Then stout Gernot joined the battle and did many Huns to death with the sharp sword Rudeger had given him, dealing Etzel's warriors mighty wounds. Lady Ute's young son now rushed into the fray. Gloriously his sword clanged through the helmets of Etzel's men. The valiant Giselher performed great exploits there. Brave as the kings and their vassals were, Giselher surpassed them all in standing against the foe. At his hands many a man dropped in the blood from wounds.

Etzel's men defended themselves fiercely, but the guests could be seen hewing their way through the royal hall with their shining swords, and on all sides loud cries of pain were heard. Those outside tried to get in to their friends, but had small success at the doors. And those within would have liked to get outside the hall, but Dankwart let no one either up or down the steps. Thus there arose a mighty press before the doors and loud clang of helmets from the sword blows, so that brave Dankwart came in great peril.

His brother feared for him, as his loyalty bade him, and loudly Hagen called to Volker, "Comrade, do you see my brother standing over there facing the Hunnish warriors under a rain of blows? Friend, save my brother or we'll lose this warrior."

"I will, without fail," said the minstrel, and through the great hall he went fiddling, his stout sword ringing time and again in his hand. The warriors from the Rhine gave him fervent thanks.

"You have endured grave hardship today," Volker said to Dankwart, "and your brother asked me to come to your help. If you will go outside, I will stand within."

Dankwart stood outside the door, guarding the stairs against all who came, and swords could be heard resounding in the warriors' hands. And within, Volker did the same.

The bold fiddler called out over the crowd, "The hall is locked, Lord Hagen, my friend. Etzel's door is firmly barred. The hands of two heroes have made it fast with a thousand bolts." [3]

Seeing the door so well defended, Hagen slung his shield on his back and began to avenge in earnest what had been done him there. His foes now had not the slightest hope of remaining alive.

When the lord of Bern saw that the mighty Hagen was shattering so many helmets, he leaped on to a bench and said, "Hagen is pouring here the bitterest drink of all."

The host was in great fear, as was natural, for his own life was hardly safe from his enemies, and oh, how many dear friends were snatched away before his very eyes! Anxiously he sat there. What did it help him that he was king?

Kriemhild called to Dietrich, "Help me, noble Knight, to escape alive. If Hagen reaches me, it will mean certain death."

"How can I help you, noble Queen?" said Lord Dietrich. "I am even afraid for myself. Gunther's men are so wild with rage that I can't protect anyone *now*."

"No, no, Lord Dietrich, good and noble Knight. I beg you, give proof of your manly spirit, and help me to get away, or I shall die."

Kriemhild had serious cause for fear.

"I will attempt to help you, though it is long since I have seen so many knights in such a bitter fury. I see the blood spurting through the helmets from the swords."

The warrior began to shout so powerfully that his voice rang out like a trumpet of bison horn and the whole vast fortress resounded with the force. Dietrich's strength was immeasurably great. In the stress of battle Gunther heard him call.

He listened and said, "Dietrich's voice has reached my ears. I fear our warriors have robbed him of one of his men. I see him standing on the table, signaling with his hand. Friends and kins-

---

[3] These are the swords, which, in rapid swordplay (hence the "thousand"), are the equivalent of bolts.

men from the Burgundian land, stop fighting, and let us hear and see what my men have done to this warrior."

When King Gunther thus asked and commanded, in the heat of battle they lowered their swords. His authority was great indeed, that not one struck a blow. At once he questioned the lord of Bern.

"Noble Dietrich," he said, "what was done to you here by my friends? I am willing and ready to atone for it and make amends. If anything were done to you, I would be deeply grieved."

"Nothing has been done to me," said Lord Dietrich. "But I ask you to let me leave the house and this fierce strife under your safe-conduct, with my followers. For this I shall always be at your service."

"Why are you so quick to plead?" spoke up Wolfhart. "The fiddler hasn't barred the door so fast that we couldn't open it wide enough for us to go through."

"Hold your tongue," said Lord Dietrich. "*You* haven't done a thing."

Then King Gunther said, "I give you my permission. Take out of the hall few or many, but not my enemies. They are to stay here. Great harm has been done me here in the Hunnish land."

When Dietrich heard these words, he put one arm around the queen, for she was sore afraid, and taking Etzel on his other side, he went out, followed by six hundred warriors.

Now Rudeger said, "Tell us if others who serve you gladly are allowed to leave the hall. As good friends, we will be pleased to have inviolable peace."

To this Giselher replied, "Be assured of peace and good will from us, for you and your men are steadfast in loyalty. You and all your friends may leave without fear."

When Lord Rudeger quit the hall, five hundred or more followed him, his kinsmen and vassals from Bechelaren. From them King Gunther was soon to suffer grave injury. Then a Hunnish warrior noticed Etzel walking close beside Dietrich and tried to take advantage of this,[4] but the fiddler gave him such a blow that in a flash his head lay at Etzel's feet.

As the lord of the land went out of the house, he turned and looked at Volker. "Alas that I have such guests!" he said. "This is a grievous disaster, that all my warriors shall fall dead before them.

---

[4] By also escaping under Dietrich's protection.

And alas for such a festival! There is a man inside called Volker, a minstrel. He fights like a wild boar, and I thank my good fortune that I escaped this devil. His songs have an evil sound, and the strokes of his bow are red. His tones strike many a hero dead. I don't know what this minstrel has against us, but I have never had such a loathsome guest."

Those who were given permission had now left the hall, and a mighty uproar began inside. Furiously the guests avenged what had been done to them. Oh, how many helmets the bold Volker splintered!

King Gunther turned toward the noise. "Do you hear the tunes, Hagen, that Volker is fiddling there with the Huns when anyone approaches the doors? It's a red rosin he has on his fiddle bow."

"I regret exceedingly," said Hagen, "that I had a seat in the hall in precedence over this warrior. I have been his comrade, and he has been mine, and we shall still be so, in all loyalty, if we ever get home again. Noble King, just look how devoted Volker is to you. He is glad to serve for your silver and your gold. His fiddle bow cuts through the hard steel, and he crushes the ornaments sparkling brightly on the helmets. I never saw a fiddler stand his ground so magnificently as Volker has today. His songs resound through helmet and shield. He deserves to ride fine horses and wear a nobleman's garb."

Of all the kinsmen of the Huns within the hall, not a one remained alive. The tumult had died away, since there was no one to fight, and the brave warriors laid aside their swords.

XXXIV

How They Threw the Dead Out of the Hall

Wearied, the knights sat down. Volker and Hagen went out in front of the hall, and leaning upon their shields, they talked wisely and sensibly with each other.

Then Giselher said, "Dear friends, you can't take your rest yet.

You must carry the dead out of the house. We'll be attacked again —I can tell you that. They mustn't lie here any longer under our feet. Before the Huns vanquish us by storm, we'll yet hew such wounds as will do my heart good. This is my firm intention."

"How fortunate I am to have such a lord," said Hagen. "The advice my young master has given us just now could come only from a true warrior. For this you Burgundians can all be glad and confident."

Following his counsel, they carried seven thousand dead to the door and threw them outside. The bodies fell to the foot of the stairs, and from their kinsmen rose a piteous wail. There were some so little wounded that they would have recovered if they had been treated more gently, but dropped from that height, they had to die. This their friends had good cause to mourn.

Then Volker the fiddler said, "Now I see it is true, what was told me, that the Huns are cowardly. They wail like women when they ought to see to these badly wounded men."

A margrave thought he was saying this out of kindness, and seeing one of his kinsmen lying in his blood, he took him in his arms to carry him away, but as he bent over the body, the minstrel shot him dead. When the others saw this, a general flight began, and all fell to cursing the minstrel. He snatched up a spear, very sharp and hard, that one of the Huns had cast at him, and hurled it with great force clear across the courtyard, far over the heads of the folk. He thus compelled Etzel's men to seek refuge further from the hall, for all the people feared his mighty strength.

Many thousand men now stood before the house. Volker and Hagen began to speak their minds to King Etzel, and on this account the brave heroes soon found themselves in danger.

"The protector of a people would see his honor better served," said Hagen, "if the lords were to fight in the vanguard, as each of my masters does here. They slash through the helmets, so that blood gushes out in the wake of their swords."

Etzel seized his shield, for he was a valiant man.

"Be careful," said Lady Kriemhild. "Better offer your warriors the shield, filled to the rim with gold, for if Hagen reaches you, you'll be hand in hand with death."

The king was so courageous that he would not give up, a thing such a powerful prince seldom does today. They had to pull him away by his shield thong, and once more Hagen mocked him.

"It was a distant kinship," he said, "that bound Etzel and Siegfried. He loved Kriemhild before she ever saw you. Wicked King, why are you plotting against me?"

Kriemhild heard these words and was angry that Hagen dared insult her in the presence of Etzel's men. Because of this she again began to work against the guests.

"The man who kills Hagen of Troneg," she said, "and brings his head here to me, I'll give as reward Etzel's shield filled with red gold, and fine castles and lands besides."

"I can't imagine what they're waiting for," said the minstrel. "I never saw heroes stand so timidly when they heard such a high reward offered. Etzel should certainly never show them favor again. I see many standing here like cowards who so basely eat their prince's bread and now desert him in his greatest need—and yet they pretend to be brave. Shame on them for ever more!"

X X X V

How Iring Was Killed

Then Margrave Iring of Denmark called out, "I have long striven for honor and in the press of battle have been among the best. Now bring me my armor. I will withstand Hagen."

"I advise against it," said Hagen. "But if you insist, then order the Hunnish warriors to stand farther back. If two or three of you leap into the hall, I'll send you back down the steps in a sorry state."

"Your threats won't make me give up," answered Iring. "I've tried just as dangerous things before. I'll withstand you alone, with my sword, and arrogant words won't help you."

Iring armed himself speedily, and Irnfried of Thuringia too, and the stalwart Hawart, and a thousand men besides. Whatever Iring undertook, they were determined to give him aid. The fiddler saw a mighty host advancing armed with Iring, good helmets bound upon their heads, and he became furious.

"Friend Hagen, do you see Iring coming there, who vowed to

withstand you alone with his sword? How does lying become a hero? I call that a disgrace. A thousand warriors or more are coming with him, armed."

"Don't turn me into a liar," said Hawart's vassal.[1] "I'll gladly perform what I vowed, and I won't give it up out of fear. However terrible Hagen may be, I want to meet him alone."

On his knees Iring begged kinsmen and vassals to let him encounter the warrior in single combat. This they were reluctant to do, for they knew the proud Hagen well. But he pleaded with them so long that at last it came to pass. Seeing his determination to act according to the dictates of honor, his followers allowed him to go.

A furious struggle commenced between the two. Iring held his spear high and covered himself with his shield. Then he rushed at Hagen, up the steps and right to the door of the hall, and there began a loud clash of weapons. With all their strength they shot the spears from their hands through the sturdy shields to their shining armor, so that the shafts spiraled high into the air. Then the two fierce men reached for their swords. Hagen's strength was very great, but Iring struck him too, so that the whole palace rang. Hall and towers resounded from their blows.

Yet Iring was not able to achieve his purpose. He now left Hagen standing unwounded and sprang at the fiddler, thinking he could vanquish him with his mighty blows, but Volker knew how to guard himself well. The fiddler struck such a blow that the metal ribs on Iring's shield whirled up over the rim. He was a bad man to encounter, so Iring let him be and fell upon Gunther. Each of them was strong enough in battle, but the blows they dealt each other drew no blood flowing from wounds. This their good stout armor prevented. Iring now let Gunther be, and running at Gernot, he hewed sparks from his armor rings. Gernot came near to killing him, but he leaped nimbly away from the prince and speedily felled four Burgundians of the royal retinue. At this Giselher could not have been more enraged.

"By God, Lord Iring," he said, "you shall pay for those who have just now fallen dead before you."

Then he rushed at the Dane and struck him so hard that he could not stir. Under Giselher's blows he slumped down into the blood, and none of them thought he would ever deal another

---

[1] Iring is speaking here to his friends.

stroke in battle. Yet Iring lay there in front of Giselher unwounded. From the roaring of the helmet and the ringing of the sword his wits had given way, and the brave warrior was no longer conscious of life. This Giselher had done with his might.

When the roaring from the heavy blow began to leave his head, Iring thought to himself, "I am still alive and not wounded anywhere. Only now do I know Giselher's strength."

On both sides he could hear his enemies. Had they known the truth, worse injury would have been done him. He heard Giselher too, close by him, and he pondered how he could escape his foes. Wildly he sprang up out of the blood. His agility served him well. Out of the house he ran, to where he again found Hagen, and dealt him furious blows with his powerful hand.

Hagen thought to himself, "You are doomed to die. Unless the wicked devil protects you, you can't escape alive."

But Iring wounded Hagen through the helmet with Waske, an excellent sword. When Lord Hagen felt the wound, his sword jerked violently in his hand, and Hawart's vassal was forced to retreat, with Hagen pursuing him down the steps. Brave Iring swung his shield over his head, but even had the stairs been the length of three, Hagen would not have given him a chance in all that time to strike a single blow. Oh, what red sparks flew above his helmet!

Iring returned to his men unharmed. Then Kriemhild was told of what he had done to Hagen, and the queen thanked him warmly.

"May God reward you, Iring, far-famed hero. You have given comfort to my heart and mind. Now I see Hagen's armor red with blood."

For very joy Kriemhild herself took the shield from his hand.

"Don't be too lavish with your thanks," said Hagen. "It would well befit a warrior to try again. If he got away then, he would indeed be a valiant man. The wound I received from him will do you little good. You see the armor rings red from my wound, but this only goads me on to the death of many men. Now I am enraged in earnest at Iring. He has done me small injury as yet."

Meanwhile Iring stood in the breeze, unlaced his helmet, and cooled himself in his armor. All the people praised his courage, so that the margrave was in high spirits.

"My friends," said Iring, "bring me arms right away. I want to try again, to see if I can conquer that arrogant man."

His shield was slashed to pieces, and he got a finer one. He was soon armed, and better than before. In anger he chose a very solid spear with which to encounter Hagen again. Hostilely Hagen watched him, filled with murderous rage, until at last he could wait no longer and rushed to the very bottom of the steps to meet him with spear shots and sword blows. He was furiously angry, and Iring's strength availed him little. They beat through the shields till flames of fire-red sparks shot up. Through shield and breastplate Hagen's sword wounded Hawart's man so sorely that he never recovered. When Iring felt the wound, he raised his shield higher, over his helmet strap. The injury he had received seemed to him great enough, but King Gunther's vassal soon did him worse. Finding a spear lying at his feet, Hagen hurled it at Iring with such sure aim that the shaft projected from his head. Hagen had dealt him a cruel end.

Iring was forced to retreat to the Danish ranks. Before undoing his helmet, they pulled the spear from his head. Death now drew near to him, and his kinsmen wept. Then the queen came, and bending over Iring, began to mourn for him. She wept at his wounds, for she was desperately grieved.

Surrounded by his kinsmen, the brave warrior said, "Cease your lament, most royal Lady. Of what avail is your weeping? I must lose my life from the wounds I have received. Death refuses to let me serve you and Etzel any longer."

Then to the men of Denmark and Thuringia he said, "Let none of you take gifts from the queen, her shining red gold, for if you stand against Hagen, you will certainly face death."

His color had faded, and he bore the mark of death. They were all profoundly sad. Brave Iring could live no longer.

There was now no holding the Danish men from the fray. Irnfried and Hawart, with a thousand warriors, stormed up before the hall. All around one heard a tremendous uproar. Oh, what sharp spears were hurled at the Burgundians! Bold Irnfried rushed at the minstrel, but received great injury at his hands. The fiddler, fiercely angry, struck the landgrave through his sturdy helmet. Then Lord Irnfried dealt the fiddler such a blow that the links of his chain mail burst and his breastplate was showered with fire-red sparks. Nevertheless, the landgrave fell dead at the fiddler's feet.

Hawart and Hagen had come together. Anyone looking on

would have seen marvelous feats. The swords struck thick and fast in their hands. Thanks to the warrior from Burgundy, Hawart had to die.

When the Danes and the Thuringians saw their lords dead, a fearful struggle began in front of the hall, and before they won to the door with courageous hand, many a helmet and shield were hashed to bits.

"Give way," said Volker, "and let them in. Then they can't finish what they intend to do, for they'll die in here in a very short time. They will pay with their death for what the queen gives them."

As the warriors entered the hall, furious sword strokes bowed many a man's head so low that he had to die. Gernot fought well, as did Giselher too. A thousand and four had come into the hall, and swords were seen flashing in mighty whishing swings. Yet soon all the warriors within were slain. Great wonders could be told about the Burgundians.

Now there was silence as the clamor died away. Everywhere the blood of the dead streamed through the outlets into the gutters below. This the men from the Rhine had done with their great valor. The Burgundians now sat down to rest and laid aside their swords and shields. But still the valiant minstrel stood guard before the doors and watched to see if anyone intended to attack them again.

Bitterly the king lamented, and his wife likewise. Maids and ladies were racked with grief. Death, I think, had conspired against them, for many warriors were yet to die at the hands of the guests.

XXXVI

How the Queen Gave Orders to Burn Down the Hall

"Now unfasten your helmets," said Hagen. "My comrade and I will protect you. And if Etzel's men try to get at us again, I'll warn my lords as fast as I can."

Then many a knight bared his head. They sat down upon the wounded, who had met death at their hands and fallen at their feet in the blood. The guests were very poorly cared for.

Before evening of that same day the king and queen commanded the Hunnish warriors to make another attempt. At least twenty thousand men could be seen standing before them, who were now compelled to do battle. A savage assault on the guests commenced immediately. The valiant Dankwart dashed away from his masters to the enemies outside the door. One would have thought he would surely die, but he got outside unharmed. The furious struggle lasted till night put an end to it. All through the long summer day the guests, as became good heroes, defended themselves against Etzel's men. Oh, how many brave warriors lay dead before them!

It was on Midsummer's Day that the great slaughter took place, when Lady Kriemhild avenged her heart's grief on her nearest kin and many another man, and because of this King Etzel never knew joy again. The day had passed, but the Burgundians had good cause for fear and felt that a quick death would be better than lingering on in torment, awaiting sufferings beyond measure.

The proud knights requested a truce and asked that the king be brought to them there. Red with blood and blackened by their armor, the three kings stepped out of the hall. They did not know to whom to lament their grave distress. Both Etzel and Kriemhild arrived. Since this land was theirs, their troops were increasing in number.

Etzel said to the guests, "Tell me, what do you want of me? Are you hoping to get peace? That could hardly be, after such great injury as you have done me. You shall be punished for this if I remain alive. My child that you killed and so many of my kinsmen! Peace and reconciliation shall be denied you forever."

To this Gunther answered, "Dire need compelled us—because of your warriors, all my squires died in their lodgings. How did I deserve that? I came to you in trust. I thought you were friendly toward me."

Then the youth Giselher said, "You men of Etzel's who are still alive, what do you have against me? What have I done to you? I rode to this land as a friend."

"Due to your friendship," answered the Huns, "the whole castle is full of grief and the land as well. We wish you had never come across the Rhine from Worms. You and your brothers have filled this land with orphans."

Angrily Gunther said, "If you would end this violent hatred by making peace with us, it would be a good thing for both sides. We are completely blameless for what Etzel is doing to us."

Then the host said to the guests, "My wrongs and yours are very unlike. Because of this great calamity—the loss and the shame I have suffered—not a one of you shall ever leave here alive."

"Then may God grant that you deal mercifully with us," said Gernot to the king. "Kill us homeless warriors if you will, but let us out into the open to meet you. This will be to your honor. And whatever may befall us, let it be done quickly. You have so many men uninjured. They'll not hesitate to encounter us and will never let us battle-weary men escape alive. How long must we endure such trials?"

Etzel's warriors were on the point of allowing them to leave the palace when Kriemhild heard of it. She was extremely annoyed, and only too speedily the strangers were denied the truce.[1]

"No, no, Hunnish warriors, I advise you in true loyalty not to do what you intend. Don't let these vengeful murderers leave the hall, or your kinsmen will suffer a deadly fall. Even if none of them were alive but my brothers—if they get into the air and cool their coats of mail, you are all lost. Never in all the world were bolder warriors born."

Then young Giselher said, "Fair sister of mine, it was most unlucky for me that I trusted you when you invited me here to this land, and to this great peril. What have I done to deserve death from the Huns? I was always true to you and never did you harm. I rode here to court, confident that you were fond of me, noble sister of mine. Show us mercy, we have no other hope."

"I cannot show you mercy, for I have none. Hagen of Troneg caused me suffering so intense that it can never be atoned for as long as I live. You must all pay for it." Then she added, "If you will give me Hagen alone as hostage, I will not refuse to let you live, for you are my brothers, and we are children of one mother. Then I will speak with these warriors here about a reconciliation."

"God in heaven forbid," said Gernot. "Even if there were a

---

[1] I.e., the time necessary to leave the hall.

thousand of us, from the family of your kin, we would rather all die than give you as hostage one single man. That we will never do."

"We shall die in any case," said Giselher, "but no one can prevent us from defending ourselves like knights. We are still here, if anyone cares to fight us, for never have I failed a friend in loyalty."

Then the bold Dankwart said—it would not have been fitting for him to be silent—"My brother Hagen does not stand alone yet. Those who here deny us peace may be sorry for it. We'll teach you this, I assure you."

The queen said, "Valiant heroes, go closer to the stairs and avenge my sorrows. For this I will always reward you, as I rightly should. I'll pay Hagen well for his arrogance. Don't let one escape from the building, and I'll order the hall set on fire at the four corners. Then all my suffering will be fully avenged."

Quickly Etzel's warriors were ready. With blows and shots they drove into the hall those who still stood outside, and the din became tremendous. Yet the princes and their vassals would not part company. Out of loyalty they could never desert each other.

Etzel's wife now bade the hall be set on fire, and they tortured the warriors with the flames. Fanned by the wind, the whole building was soon ablaze. No troop, I am sure, ever suffered greater fear.

Many within cried out, "Alas at this plight! We would far rather die in battle. God have pity on us! We are all lost. The queen is taking a terrible vengeance on us for her anger."

And one among them said, "We shall have to die. What good is the welcome the king gave us? Thirst plagues me so from the intense heat that my life will soon ebb away, I think, in these torments."

"Noble Knights," said Hagen, "any who are overcome by the pangs of thirst, drink the blood here. In such heat it is even better than wine. Just now there is nothing better to be had."

One of the warriors went to a corpse, knelt down beside the wound, and unfastening his helmet, he began to drink the flowing blood. Unaccustomed though he was to such a beverage, he thought it very good.

"May God reward you, Lord Hagen," said the weary man, "that I have drunk so well at your advice. Better wine has never been poured for me. If I live a while longer, I'll always be your friend."

When the others heard that he found it good, many more of them also drank the blood. From this they all gained strength, and many women paid dearly for it later with the loss of dear friends. The fire fell thick and fast upon them in the hall, but with their shields they deflected it downward away from them. Both smoke and heat tormented them. Never again, I am sure, will heroes suffer such misery.

Then Hagen of Troneg said, "Stand by the wall, and don't let the firebrands fall on your helmet straps. Trample them down with your feet deeper into the blood. It's a devilish festival the queen is giving us."

Though they were in such distress, the night came to an end at last. Once more the bold minstrel and his comrade Hagen stood before the hall, leaning on their shields. They expected further injury from Etzel's warriors.

"Let's go into the hall," said the fiddler. "Then the Huns will think we are all dead from the torture that has been done us. They'll see us meet some of them in battle yet."

The youth Giselher said, "I think the dawn is almost here. A cool breeze is rising. May God in heaven let us live to see happier times. It's a wretched festival my sister Kriemhild has given us."

"I see the day now," said another. "Since we can't hope for better things, arm yourselves, heroes, and take thought to saving your lives. King Etzel's wife will soon visit us again."

The host would have expected the guests to be dead from their strain and the agony of the fire, but six hundred men were still alive within. Better warriors no king ever had. The Huns that were keeping watch over the strangers had seen that they still lived, in spite of the great injury and suffering that had befallen both the lords and their vassals. They could be seen standing in the hall quite unharmed.

Kriemhild was then told that many were still alive, but she replied that it was impossible for anyone to have survived the torment of the fire, adding, "I would think it more likely that they are all dead."

The princes and their men would still have liked to live if anyone had been ready to grant them mercy, but this they did not find among the Huns. So with willing hands they avenged their dying. Toward morning of this day they were greeted by a fierce onslaught, which put them in great peril. Many a stout spear was hurled at them, but they defended themselves like true knights.

Etzel's men were in fighting spirit, for they wished to earn Kriemhild's wealth and also perform what the king commanded. Because of this many of them soon saw death face to face. Of promises and of gifts marvels could be told. The queen bade red gold be brought on shields and gave it to all who wished it. Never were higher wages paid to win aid against enemies.

A great force of warriors in armor approached the hall, and bold Volker said, "We are still here. I never saw heroes come more willingly to fight than these who took the king's gold to accomplish our destruction."

And many of the Burgundians called out, "Nearer, heroes, nearer! Let us do quickly what we still have to finish. No one will fall here who is not already doomed to die."

Soon their shields were studded full with spears. What more can I tell you? At least twelve hundred men attacked again and again, thrusting forward, then falling back. The guests cooled their temper with the wounds they dealt. No one could check the struggle, and blood poured out of the many deadly wounds. Everyone could be heard lamenting the loss of friends. All King Etzel's ablest warriors died, and loving kinsmen mourned them grievously.

XXXVII

How Rudeger Was Killed

The strangers had fought well at dawn. Loyal Rudeger now came to court, and when he saw on both sides the terrible distress, he wept, touched to the heart.

"Alas for me," he said, "that I was ever born! And alas that no one can prevent this great misery! However much I would like to make peace, the king will not consent, for from hour to hour he sees the sufferings of his men increase."

Then the good Rudeger dispatched a message to Dietrich to ask if the two of them could not perhaps ward off disaster from the kings, but the lord of Bern sent answer, "Who could prevent it now? King Etzel will let no one intercede."

A Hunnish warrior, who saw Rudeger standing with weeping eyes—and he had shed many tears—said to the queen, "Just look at him standing there, the man who has the greatest power at Etzel's court. Both lands and people serve him. How many castles the king has given Rudeger in fief! Yet in all these battles he hasn't struck a single blow. In my opinion, he doesn't care how things go here, since he has all he desires in abundance. They say he is braver than anyone else, but in these perils he has given little proof of that."

Sad at heart, the faithful vassal looked at him as he heard these words and thought to himself, "You shall pay for this. You call me a coward. You have said your say at court too loudly."

Clenching his fist, he rushed at him and struck the Hun with such force that in an instant he lay dead at his feet. King Etzel's distress was increased anew.

"Away with you, you arrant coward!" said Rudeger. "I have enough sorrow and woe. Why do you reproach me for not fighting here? I would have good cause to hate the strangers and would have done all in my power against them, but that I brought them here myself. I was their escort to my lord's land, and for this reason I, unhappy man, cannot fight against them."

Then King Etzel said to the margrave, "What a help you have been to us, noble Rudeger! We already have so many dead in this land that we did not need any more. You have acted very badly."

"Oh, but he insulted me," answered the good knight, "and taunted me with the honors and wealth I have had from your hands in such plenty. This has cost the liar dear."

The queen had come up, too, and seen what Rudeger in his anger had done to the Hun. She lamented it bitterly, and her eyes grew moist as she said, "How have we deserved that you should add to my sorrow and the king's? Till now you have always said, noble Rudeger, that for our sakes you would risk both life and honor, and I have heard many warriors grant you the highest praise. Let me remind you of the help you promised me, peerless Knight, when you counseled me to take Etzel. You swore you would serve me until one of us should die. Never have I had such great need of this as now, wretched woman that I am."

"There is no denying that I swore to you, noble Lady, for your sake I would risk honor and life as well. But I swore no oath that I would lose my soul. It was I who escorted the princes to this festival."

"Remember, Rudeger," she said, "your great fidelity, your constancy, and your oaths that you would always avenge injury to me and all my sufferings."

"I have never denied you anything," answered the margrave.

Etzel also began to implore him, and both fell on their knees before their liegeman.

The faithful warrior was deeply troubled and said sorrowfully, "Alas for me, most miserable of men, that I have lived to see this. I must relinquish all honor, good faith, and knightliness that God has granted me. Alas, oh God in heaven, that death cannot turn this from me! Whichever side I take, whatever I do or leave undone, I shall act basely and dishonorably. But if I leave both undone, everyone will reproach me. Now may He who gave me life instruct me!"

Still the king and queen pleaded urgently, and due to this, warriors soon lost their lives at Rudeger's hands, and he also died. Listen now to what he did in his despair. He knew he would reap only ruin and immeasurable grief. He would have liked to refuse the king and queen, for he greatly feared that if he slew even one of the guests, the whole world would hate him for it.

"Sir King," he said, "take back again all that I have from you, my land and its castles. Nothing shall remain to me, and I will go on foot into exile."

"Who would help me then?" said King Etzel. "I'll give you the land and castles for your own, Rudeger, if you will avenge me on my enemies. You shall be a mighty king at Etzel's side."

"How can I do this?" replied Rudeger. "I invited them home to my house, as a friend I offered them drink and food and gave them my gifts. How can I plot their death? People may suppose I am a coward, but no service of mine have I ever refused the princes and their men. And I think with sadness of the bonds of kinship I have entered into with them. I gave my daughter to the warrior Giselher. She could not be better provided for anywhere in all that concerns courtesy and honor, loyalty and wealth. I never saw so young a king with such noble qualities."

Then Kriemhild spoke again. "Noble Rudeger, have pity on our grief, mine and the king's. Bear in mind that no host ever had such detestable guests."

The margrave answered, "Rudeger must pay today with his life for the kindness you and my lord have shown me. For this I shall have to die; it can be put off no longer. I know well that yet today my lands and castles will revert to you through some Burgundian's hand. I commend to your mercy my wife and children[1] and the many strangers[2] too, who are there at Bechelaren."

"May God reward you, Rudeger," said the king. He and the queen were both very happy. "Your people shall be well cared for. Besides, I have trust in my own good fortune and feel sure you yourself will come out unharmed."

Thus Rudeger risked soul and body. And Etzel's wife began to weep.

"I must do what I promised you. Alas for my friends—how I hate to fight them!"

Sadly he walked away from the king. Close at hand he found his warriors standing and said, "Arm yourselves, all my men. I regret to say, I must fight the brave Burgundians."

They bade the squires run quickly to where their weapons lay, and whether helmet or shield, they were all brought out to them. The proud warriors far from home were soon to hear ominous news. Rudeger was now armed, with five hundred men. And he obtained for his assistance twelve warriors besides, who wished to win renown in the stress of battle. They had no notion that death was so close to them. Rudeger could now be seen walking about with helmet on. His men carried sharp swords and held their bright, broad shields before them. This the fiddler noticed and was greatly dismayed. Young Giselher, too, saw his father-in-law walking with helmet fastened. How could he possibly have thought this portended anything but good? And the noble prince rejoiced.

"How happy I am that we have won such friends on this jour-

---

[1] This is the only mention of other children besides Rudeger's daughter.
[2] Presumably Rudeger's followers, who fled with him into exile and took refuge under Etzel's rule.

ney!" said Giselher. "We shall owe our safety to my wife. I am very glad indeed that this marriage[3] took place."

"I don't know where you find comfort," said the minstrel. "Where did you ever see such a host of warriors approach with helmets on and swords in hand in order to make peace? Rudeger intends to earn his lands and castles at our expense."

Before the fiddler had finished speaking, they saw Rudeger in front of the palace. He set his shield at his feet, and now he had no recourse but to tell his friends that he had renounced both service and friendship for them.

"Brave Nibelungs," he called into the hall, "arm yourselves, all of you. You were to have found a support in me, now through me you will come to grief. Until this day we were friends, but I now renounce my loyalty to you."

The hard-pressed men were aghast, for none of them took pleasure in the news that he for whom they all felt affection meant to fight with them. Already they had suffered grave hardship from their enemies.

"God in heaven forbid," said Gunther, "that you should renounce your love for us and the great loyalty we were relying on. I have faith enough in you to be sure that you will never do this."

"I cannot do otherwise," said Rudeger. "I have to fight you, for I gave my word. Now defend yourselves, brave heroes, if your lives are dear to you. King Etzel's wife would not release me from my promise."

"It is too late for you to break with us now," said the king. "May God recompense you, noble Rudeger, for the loyalty and love you have shown us if only you would let this affection end in a friendlier fashion. If you let us live, we would always be grateful to you, my kinsmen and I, for the rich gifts you gave us when you brought us faithfully into Etzel's land. Remember this, noble Rudeger."

"How glad I would be," said Rudeger, "to bestow my gifts on you in abundance, and with all my heart, as I had hoped. Then I would be free of reproach."

"Turn back, noble Rudeger," said Gernot, "for no host ever

[3] Words used here in this passage, "father-in-law," "wife," "marriage," imply that Giselher is already married to Rudeger's daughter. Yet the ceremony described in XXVII was only a betrothal ceremony.

offered guests such friendly hospitality as you did us. You shall benefit from this if we remain alive."

"I wish to God, noble Gernot," said Rudeger, "that you were on the Rhine and I were dead, with some measure of honor left —since I have no choice but to meet you in battle. Never were heroes treated worse by friends."

"May God reward you, Lord Rudeger," answered Gernot, "for your rich gift. Your death will grieve me, if such manly virtue is to be lost with you. I bear here the sword you gave me. In all this peril it has never failed me. Many a knight fell dead beneath its edges. It is excellent, bright, and solid. Never again, I am sure, will a warrior give so fine a gift. But if you refuse to give up your attack on us and if you kill any of the friends I still have here inside, with your own sword I'll take your life. I grieve for you, Rudeger, and for your noble wife."

"Would to God, Lord Gernot, that all might happen as you wish it and your friends remain unharmed. Both my daughter and my wife can well put their trust in you."

Then Giselher said, "Why do you act this way, Lord Rudeger? Those who have come with me are all your friends. You are taking a bad course. You want to make your lovely daughter a widow far too soon. If you and your warriors oppose me in battle, in what an unfriendly light you will show the qualities that make me trust you above all other men and that caused me to take your daughter as my wife."

"Remember your vow, noble King, if God sends you away from here," said Rudeger. "Don't make the maiden suffer for what I have done. For the credit of your own noble spirit, retain your affection for her."

"This would be only right," said the youth Giselher. "But if my kinsmen here within are to die at your hands, my steadfast friendship for you and for your daughter must come to an end."

"Now may God have mercy on us," said the valiant man.

Then they raised their shields as if about to attack the guests in Kriemhild's hall, but Hagen called loudly down the stairs, "Wait a moment, noble Rudeger. My lords and I would like to have further words with you, as necessity compels us. What good will the death of us strangers do Etzel? I am in sore straits. The shield Lady Gotelind gave me to carry has been hacked to pieces in my hand by the Huns. In friendly spirit I brought it to Etzel's land. If God in heaven would only grant that I might bear a shield as good as the one you hold in your hand, noble Rudeger! Then I'd no longer need a coat of mail in these battles."

"I would gladly help you with my shield if I dared offer it to you in Kriemhild's presence. But take it anyway, Hagen, and bear it in your hand. Oh, if you could only carry it back to the Burgundian land!"

Many eyes turned red with hot tears when he so willingly offered Hagen the shield as a gift. It was the last present Rudeger of Bechelaren ever gave to any warrior. Fierce and rough though Hagen was, he was moved by the gift which the good hero, so close to his last hour, had given him. And many a knight shared his sadness.

"God in heaven reward you, noble Rudeger. There will never be your like again for giving stranger warriors such magnificent gifts. God grant that such nobility as yours may live forever!" And Hagen continued, "What a cruel thing this is! We have had so many other troubles to bear. May God hear my protest if we must fight with friends!"

"It grieves me deeply too," said the margrave.

"I'll repay you for the gift, noble Rudeger. However these warriors treat you, my hand will never touch you in battle—even if you should kill all the men of Burgundy."

Rudeger bowed to him courteously in gratitude. Round about all the people wept and were greatly distressed that no one could end this heart-rending grief. In Rudeger would die the father of all knightly virtues.

Then from the palace Volker, the minstrel, spoke. "Since my comrade Hagen has made peace with you, you shall have just as firm a truce from me, for you earned it well when we came to this land. Noble Margrave, be my messenger. The margravine gave me these red arm rings to wear here at the festival. See them for yourself, so that you can testify afterward that I had them." [4]

"Would to God," said Rudeger, "that the margravine could give you even more! I'll gladly tell my dear love—have no doubt of that—if I live to see her."

When he had promised him this, Rudeger raised his shield. He waited no longer, but with raging heart he rushed upon the guests

[4] This is the final, ironic touch to the scene of pure romantic chivalry in XXVII

like a true warrior. Many a fierce blow the mighty margrave struck. Volker and Hagen stepped back, as they had vowed to him before. But Rudeger found such valiant men standing at the doors that he began the struggle with grave apprehension. Intent upon his death, Gunther and Gernot allowed him to enter; they had the spirit of heroes. Giselher drew back. This was not to his liking, to be sure, but he still hoped to live and so avoided Rudeger. Then the margrave's men sprang at their foes, boldly following their lord. In their hands they bore keen-edged swords, with which they split many a helmet and many a fine shield. The Burgundians, weary as they were, dealt the men of Bechelaren many a powerful blow that cut smooth and deep through the shining mail down to the very quick.

Rudeger's followers were now all inside. Quickly Volker and Hagen fell upon them, for they gave no quarter but to one man alone. At the hands of these two, blood streamed down through the helmets. How fiercely the swords rang out there in the hall! The shield plates sprang from their fastenings, and the precious stones, struck from the shields, fell into the blood. They fought with such a fury as one will never see again.

The lord of Bechelaren made his way up and down the hall like a man who knows well how to acquit himself in battle. That day Rudeger proved himself a bold and excellent warrior. Gunther and Gernot stood their ground and struck many heroes dead in the fray. Giselher and Dankwart, fearing nothing, sent many a man to his final hour. Rudeger showed clearly that he was powerful and bold and possessed of good weapons. Oh, what a host of warriors he slew!

This a Burgundian[5] noticed, and anger overwhelmed him. Thus Rudeger's death drew near.

Gernot called out to the margrave, "You don't intend to leave one of my men alive, noble Rudeger. This grieves me beyond measure. I can't bear the sight any longer. Now that you have robbed me of so many of my friends, your gift to me may well be your ruin. Turn around here to me. I'll earn your gift as dearly as I can."

Before the margrave could push through to him, bright mail grew dull with blood. Then, eager for fame, the two ran at each

[5] The poet does not name the Burgundian, but the following lines show that it is Gernot.

other. Each guarded himself with his shield against severe wounds, but so sharp were their swords that nothing could withstand them. Rudeger struck Gernot through his stone-hard helmet so that the blood poured down. In a flash the valiant knight retaliated. He swung Rudeger's gift high in his hand and though wounded to death, he dealt him a blow right through his good shield, down to his helmet strap. And thus fair Gotelind's husband lost his life. Never has so fine a gift been worse repaid. Both fell in the combat, Gernot and Rudeger, each slain by the other's hand.

When Hagen saw this grave loss, he became angry in earnest and said, "This is a great misfortune. In these two we have suffered such a loss that neither their people nor their lands will ever recover from it. Rudeger's warriors are now forfeit to us strangers."

"Alas for my brother,[6] here sent to his death! What sad tidings reach me with every hour! And for the noble Rudeger, too, I must always mourn. The bereavement and the grievous sorrow are felt on both sides."

When Lord Giselher saw his brother dead, those within the hall were made to endure great peril. Fiercely Death sought his own; of the men of Bechelaren not one remained alive.

Gunther and Giselher, and Hagen too, Dankwart and Volker, the good warriors, then went to where they found the two men lying, and they wept from grief.

"Death robs us with a vengeance," said Giselher. "But cease your weeping now, and let us go into the breeze so that we battle-weary men can cool our armor. I doubt that God will let us live much longer."

Many a warrior could now be seen, this one sitting, that one leaning, but all were again idle. Rudeger's men were dead. The din had died away. The stillness lasted so long that Etzel became annoyed.

"A plague upon such service!" said the queen. "It is not so dependable that our enemies will receive any punishment at Rudeger's hand. He means to take them back to the Burgundian land. What does it help, King Etzel, that we have shared with him whatever he wished? The knight has failed in his duty. He who was supposed to avenge us intends to make his peace."

---

[6] The speaker is not identified, but the tone of the speech and its content suggest Gunther.

To this Volker answered, "Unfortunately, this is not so, most noble Queen. If I dared call such a high-born person a liar, I would say you had lied fiendishly about Rudeger. He and his warriors were cheated in this peace. So willingly did he do what the king bade him that he and his followers lie here dead. Look about you, Kriemhild, to see whom you want to give orders to *now*. The hero Rudeger served you to the end. If you don't believe it, we'll let you see for yourself."

And to her heart's misery, this is what was done. They bore the mangled hero to where the king could see him. Never did sorrow so great befall Etzel's warriors. No scribe would know how to record or relate the frantic laments of men and women alike in their profound despair as they saw the margrave carried forth dead. Etzel's anguish grew so intense that like a roaring lion the mighty king cried out his grief of heart. And his wife did the same. They mourned beyond all measure the excellent Rudeger.

XXXVIII

How Lord Dietrich's Warrior's Were All Killed

On all sides were heard such sounds of grief that hall and towers resounded with the wailing. One of Dietrich's men heard it too, and how swiftly he hastened to deliver the fearful news!

"Listen, my Lord Dietrich," he said. "In all my life I have never heard such unrestrained laments as I did just now. I fear King Etzel himself has come to harm. Why else should they all be in such distress? The king or Kriemhild—one of the two has been killed by the strangers in their anger. Many a dignified warrior is weeping violently."

"My good men," said Dietrich, "do not be too hasty. Whatever the strangers have done here, grave necessity forced them to it. Let them profit from the peace I offered them."

Then the bold Wolfhart said, "I'll go and ask what they have done. And I'll tell you then, my dear Lord, all that I find out there as to what this lament means."

"Where one expects anger," answered Lord Dietrich, "and a rude question is then put, this can easily disturb warriors' good judgment. I don't want *you* to be the one to ask them the question, Wolfhart."

Then he bade Helfrich[1] go quickly and find out from Etzel's men or from the guests themselves what had happened there, since no one had ever seen people in such great sorrow.

The messenger asked, "What has happened here?"

One of Etzel's warriors answered, "All the joy we had in the land of the Huns has utterly vanished. Here lies Rudeger, slain by the Burgundians. Of those who went in with him, not one escaped alive."

Helfrich could not have been more grieved, and never did he report news with such reluctance. Weeping bitterly, the messenger returned to Dietrich.

"What have you discovered?" asked Dietrich. "Why are you weeping so, warrior Helfrich?"

"I have good cause to mourn," he answered. "The Burgundians have killed Rudeger."

"God forbid!" said Dietrich. "That would be a terrible vengeance and the devil's mockery. How did Rudeger deserve this from them? For I know very well, he is a friend of the strangers."

Wolfhart answered, "If they have done this, it shall cost all of them their lives. We would be disgraced if we let this pass. Good Rudeger's hand has often done us service."

The lord of the Amelungs ordered further inquiries to be made. Grief-stricken, he sat down at a window and bade Hildebrand go to the guests to find out from them what had happened. Master Hildebrand bore neither shield nor weapon in his hand. He wished to go to the guests in knightly courtesy.

His sister's son, the fierce Wolfhart, reproved him for this, saying, "If you go there unarmed, you'll never get off without insults, and you will return humiliated. But if you go there armed, they'll take good care not to offend you."

Then, following the youth's counsel, the wise old man armed

---

[1] One of Dietrich's vassals.

himself. Before he was aware of it, Dietrich's warriors were all in armor and had their swords in hand. Hildebrand was vexed at this and would have liked to turn them back. He asked where they were going.

"We're going there with you. Perhaps Hagen will then be less likely to dare address you with mockery, which he knows so well how to use."

On hearing this, the warrior permitted them to follow him. Now Volker saw Dietrich's men approaching well armed, girded with swords and bearing shields in their hands, and he reported this to his lords.

"I see Dietrich's men coming there like enemies," said the fiddler, "armed and helmeted. They intend to attack us. I fear it will go hard for us strangers."

Meanwhile Hildebrand had arrived. Setting his shield down at his feet, he began to question Gunther's men. "Alas, good heroes, what had Rudeger done to you? My lord Dietrich sent me here to say that if anyone among you had killed the noble margrave, as we have been told, we could never get over this great sorrow."

"The news is not a lie," said Hagen. "How much I wish, for Rudeger's sake, that the messenger had deceived you, and that he were still alive for whom both men and women will always have cause to weep!"

When they heard for certain that Rudeger was dead, Dietrich's warriors mourned him, as their fidelity bade them, and tears poured down over their beards and chins.

Siegstab,[2] the duke from Bern, then said, "Now the pleasant life Rudeger provided us after the days of our suffering has come to an end."

And Wolfwin[3] of the Amelungs said, "If I saw my own father dead today, I would not grieve more than at Rudeger's death. Alas, who shall now comfort the good margrave's wife?"

Beside himself with anger, Wolfhart said, "Who will now lead the warriors on so many a battle march, as the margrave often did? Alas, noble Rudeger, that we have lost you thus!"

[2] Dietrich's nephew. This speech refers to incidents in the stories about Dietrich. In the version given in the *Thidrekssaga*, Rudeger assists the exiled Dietrich and is more than once referred to as Dietrich's best friend.
[3] One of Dietrich's vassals.

Wolfbrand and Helfrich, Helmnot too,[4] and all their friends, wept at his death.

For sighing, Hildebrand was unable to question further. Then he said, "Now grant, you warriors, what my lord sent me for. Give us the dead Rudeger from out of the hall, in whom our joy lies turned to grief, and let us repay him for the great devotion he always showed to us and to many another man. We are exiles too, like Rudeger. Why do you make us wait? Let us bear him away, so that we may requite him in death. It would have been better done while he was still alive."

At this King Gunther said, "There is no service so fine as that which a friend does for a friend after his death. When anyone can do this, I call it steadfast loyalty. You are right to repay him, for he was very kind to you."

"How long are we to beg?" asked Wolfhart. "Since our staunchest helper has been killed by you, and alas we can have him with us no longer, let us carry him away that we may bury him."

"No one will give him to you," answered Volker. "Come and take the warrior from the hall where he lies, fallen in the blood, with deep and deadly wounds. Then the service you render Rudeger will be complete."

"God knows, Sir Minstrel, there is no need to provoke us," said bold Wolfhart. "You have already done us harm enough. Except that I dare not because of my lord, it would go hard with you. We must refrain from fighting here, for he has forbidden it."

"It is too much fear," said the fiddler, "if a man avoids everything that's forbidden him. I don't call that a true hero's spirit."

These words from his comrade-at-arms met with Hagen's approval.

"Don't wish for *that*," said Wolfhart, "or I'll jumble your fiddle strings so that you'll have something to talk about if you ride home to the Rhine. I can't, with honor, endure your insolence."

"If you spoil the fine tones of my strings," said the fiddler, "then I'll dull the shine of your helmet with my hand, whether or not I ride back to Burgundy."

Wolfhart was about to leap at him, but Hildebrand, his uncle, held him fast. "You must be out of your mind in your foolish anger. You would have lost my lord's favor forever."

---

[4] All three are Dietrich's vassals.

"Let the lion go, Master," said Volker. "He is in such a fierce mood. But if he gets into my hands, even if he had killed the whole world, I'll hit him so hard he'll never be able to tell the tale."

At this the men of Bern were furious. Wolfhart snatched up his shield and like a wild lion he dashed away ahead of the others, speedily followed by his friends. But however long the leaps he took toward the hall, old Hildebrand caught up with him at the foot of the stairs, not wanting to let him be first to the fray. They soon found with the strangers the strife they were seeking. Master Hildebrand sprang at Hagen, and the swords were heard clanging in the hands of both. They were very angry—this was plain to see—and from their two swords rose a gust of fire-red sparks. Then they were parted in the stress of battle. The men of Bern came between, as their strength bade them, and at once Hildebrand turned away from Hagen.

Then Wolfhart rushed at Volker and dealt the fiddler such a blow on his good helmet that the sword's edge pierced to the helmet bands. This the brave minstrel repaid with force. He struck Wolfhart so that his whole armor flared up in sparks. Fire aplenty they hewed from the rings of mail, for each bore hatred toward the other. Then Wolfwin of Bern intervened, a thing which only a true hero could have succeeded in doing.

With ready hand Gunther welcomed the famous heroes from the Amelung land. Lord Giselher made many a gleaming helmet red and wet with blood. Dankwart, Hagen's brother, was a fearsome man. What he had done to Etzel's warriors previously in combat was as nothing to the rage with which he fought now. Ritschart and Gerbart, Helfrich and Wichart[5] had never spared themselves in battles, and this they let Gunther's men feel. Wolfbrand, too, could be seen acquitting himself magnificently in the fray. Old Hildebrand fought like a madman, and at Wolfhart's hands many fine warriors, dying of sword blows, dropped into the blood. Thus these bold men avenged Rudeger.

Lord Siegstab fought as his valor urged him. Oh, how many of his enemies' stout helmets this son of Dietrich's sister hacked to pieces in the struggle! When Volker noticed how Siegstab was hewing a bloody stream from hard armor rings, he became angry and sprang toward him. Very quickly Siegstab lost his life at the

[5] All four are Dietrich's vassals.

hands of the fiddler, who gave him such a sample of his art that he fell dead under Volker's sword.

His fighting spirit roused, old Hildebrand avenged this. "Alas for my dear lord," [6] he said, "who lies here dead at Volker's hands. Now the fiddler shall escape no longer."

How could brave Hildebrand have been more ferocious? He struck Volker so hard that the straps of the minstrel's helmet and shield flew in all directions to the walls of the hall. Thus the mighty Volker met his death.

Now Dietrich's men pressed onward to the struggle. They struck so that armor rings spun far and wide, sword points flew high into the air, and from the helmets they drew hotly gushing streams.

Then Hagen saw Volker dead. This was the cruellest sorrow he had met with at the festival, for kinsman or for vassal. Oh, how fiercely Hagen avenged the hero!

"Old Hildebrand shall pay for this. My helpmate lies dead at his hand, the best comrade I ever had."

He raised his shield higher and strode forth, slashing as he went.

Stout Helfrich now struck Dankwart down. Gunther and Giselher were deeply grieved when they saw him fall in the thick of battle, yet with his own hands he had well avenged his death. Meanwhile Wolfhart paced back and forth, constantly mowing down Gunther's men. He had made the third round through the hall, and many a warrior had fallen at his hands.

Then Lord Giselher called out to Wolfhart, "Alas that I ever had such a ruthless enemy! Now turn in my direction, noble Knight, and I'll do my part in putting an end to this. It can't go on any longer."

Wolfhart threw himself into the fray to meet him, and both of them dealt many gaping wounds. So violently did Wolfhart press toward the king that the blood under his feet spurted up over his head. Ute's son greeted him with hard and furious blows, and strong as Wolfhart was, he could not save himself. No king so young was ever more courageous. He struck Wolfhart through his stout coat of mail so that blood poured down from the gash, and thus wounded him to death. No other warrior could have done it. When bold Wolfhart felt the wound, he dropped his shield, and

[6] As Dietrich's nephew, Siegstab belongs to the royal family and is thus one of Hildebrand's lords.

lifting higher in his hand his powerful, keen-edged sword, he struck Giselher right through helmet and hauberk. Each had dealt the other a cruel death.

Of Dietrich's men not one was now alive, and Gunther's men, too, had all perished. Old Hildebrand saw Wolfhart fall, and never, I think, till the day of his death, did a grief so great befall him. He went to where Wolfhart had sunk down into the blood and clasped the brave warrior in his arms. He meant to carry him out of the hall, but finding him much too heavy, he had to let him lie. Then the dying man looked up from out of the blood and saw that his uncle would have liked to help him.

"Dear uncle," he said, mortally wounded as he was, "you cannot help me now. Be on guard against Hagen. This is my advice. His heart is full of rage. And if my kinsmen want to mourn me after my death, tell those closest to me not to weep for me, for there is no need. I have met a glorious death at the hands of a king. Besides, I have so avenged myself here in this hall that many a good knight's wife will have cause to weep. If anyone asks you, you can say with assurance that a hundred men at least lie slain by my hand alone."

Meanwhile Hagen's thoughts turned to the minstrel, whom Hildebrand had killed, and he said to this warrior, "You shall pay for my grief. You have robbed us here of many a good fighter."

He gave Hildebrand such a blow that one could hear Balmung ringing loudly, Siegfried's sword, which Hagen had taken the day he killed him. But the old man stood his ground, for he had great courage. He brought his broad sharp-cutting sword down on the hero of Troneg, but was unable to wound him. Then once more Hagen struck him, right through his fine coat of mail. Old Hildebrand felt the wound, and fearing further injury, he slung his shield over his back, and though sorely wounded, the hero fled from Hagen.

Now of all the warriors none was alive but the two, Gunther and Hagen alone. Dripping with blood, old Hildebrand went to find Dietrich and bring the grievous news. He saw him sitting there sadly, but soon a much greater sorrow was to befall the prince.

He saw Hildebrand too, in his blood-red mail, and moved by fear, he asked, "Tell me, Master Hildebrand, why are you so wet with your lifeblood? Who did this to you? I fear you have fought with the guests in the hall. Yet I forbade you that so strictly, you would better have refrained."

"Hagen did it," he said to his lord. "He dealt me this wound in the hall as I was about to turn away from him. I barely escaped from that devil with my life."

Then the lord of Bern said, "It serves you right for breaking the peace I had sworn them, for you heard me promise the warriors friendship. If it weren't that I would be disgraced forever,[7] you should lose your life."

"Don't be so angry, my Lord Dietrich. The injury to me and my friends is all too great. We wanted to carry Rudeger away, but King Gunther's men would not allow it."

"Oh that such sorrow should come upon me! Is Rudeger really dead? This is a grief that surpasses all my trials. Gotelind is the child of my father's sister. Alas for the poor orphans[8] there in Bechelaren!"

Rudeger's death now reminded him of loyalty and of suffering,[9] and he began to weep bitterly, as he had cause to do. "Alas for the faithful helper I have lost! I shall never get over the loss of King Etzel's man. Can you give me a true report, Master Hildebrand, as to who it was that killed him?"

"It was the mighty Gernot," he answered, "but this hero, too, died at Rudeger's hands."

"Now tell my men," said Dietrich, "to arm themselves quickly, for I want to go there. And bid them bring me my shining battle armor. I intend to question the warriors from Burgundy myself."

"But who is there to join you?" said Master Hildebrand. "All the living men you have, you see standing beside you. I am the only one. The others are all dead."

Dietrich was shaken by this news, as well he might be, for never in his life had he had a grief so great.

"If all my men are dead," he said, "then God has forgotten me, wretched Dietrich. I was once a sovereign king, powerful and proud." And he went on, "How could it happen that they all died, these worthy heroes, at the hands of battle-weary men who had

[7] Because Hildebrand had been Dietrich's tutor and thus has a very special relationship with him.

[8] Dietrich is referring not merely to Rudeger's children, but to his whole family and his vassals.

[9] Dietrich remembers Rudeger's loyalty to him in his sufferings as an exile.

endured such stress? If it weren't for my ill luck, death would still be a stranger to them. Since my evil fate would not spare me this—tell me, are any of the guests still alive?"

"As God is my witness," said Master Hildebrand, "no one but Hagen and Gunther."

"Alas, dear Wolfhart, if I have lost you, I have good reason to regret that I was ever born! Siegstab and Wolfwin, and Wolfbrand too! Who will help me now to return to the Amelung land? Bold Helfrich—if he has been killed, and Gerbart and Wichart, how can I ever cease mourning for them? This day is the end of my joy. Alas that no one can die of grief!"

XXXIX

How Lord Dietrich Fought with
Gunther and Hagen

Now Lord Dietrich fetched his armor himself, and Master Hildebrand helped him put it on. All the while the warrior lamented so loudly that the whole house rang with his voice. But soon he recovered a true hero's spirit, and in wrath he armed himself and took a stout shield in his hand. Then they hastened away, he and Master Hildebrand.

Hagen said, "I see Lord Dietrich coming. He intends to attack us now after the great sorrow that has come to him here. Today we shall see who will be judged the best. Lord Dietrich may think himself strong and terrifying, but no matter—if he wants to take revenge on us for what was done to him, I'll venture to stand against him."

Dietrich and Hildebrand heard these words, and Dietrich went to where he found the two warriors standing outside the palace, leaning against the wall.

He set his shield down and said in profound sadness, "Gunther, mighty King, why have you acted so toward me, an exile? What had I done to you? I am bereft of all my consolation. You thought it not enough of sore distress when you killed Rudeger. Now you have robbed me of all my men. I would never have inflicted such a loss on you. Think of yourselves and of your suffering, the death of your friends and your own hardships. Doesn't this weigh heavy on your hearts, good warriors? Alas, how Rudeger's death pains me! Never in all the world has greater sorrow befallen any man. You gave no thought to my grief and yours. All the joy I had lies slain by you. I can never cease to mourn for my kinsmen."

"But we are not so guilty," said Hagen. "Your warriors came to this hall in a large band, and armed with care. I think the story wasn't told you correctly."

"What else am I to believe? Hildebrand told me that when my warriors asked you to give them Rudeger from out of the hall, you had nothing but mockery for them."

"They said they wanted to carry Rudeger away," replied Gunther, "and to annoy Etzel, not your men, I ordered that this be denied them. But then Wolfhart began to abuse us."

"Fate willed it thus," said Dietrich. "Gunther, noble King, by your courtesy compensate me for the wrongs you have done to me, and make such atonement, brave Knight, as I can attest to for you. Surrender yourself to me as hostage, you and your liegeman too. Then I will take care, as best I can, that no one here among the Huns does you any harm. In me you will find nothing but loyalty and kindness."

"God forbid," said Hagen, "that two warriors should surrender to you when they still face you so fully armed and still move about so freely in the presence of their enemies."

"Gunther and Hagen, don't refuse," said Dietrich. "You have both grieved me so deeply in heart and soul that it is only right for you to make amends. I give you my word, and my hand as pledge, that I will ride home with you to your land. I will escort you in all honor or die, and for your sakes I will forget my great distress."

"Do not urge this any more," answered Hagen. "It would scarcely be fitting for it to be said of us that two such bold men gave themselves up to you. And besides, there is no one with you but Hildebrand alone."

Then Master Hildebrand said, "God knows, Lord Hagen, the hour will still come when you would gladly accept peace if anyone offers it to you. You ought to be well content with the truce my lord offers you."

"I would certainly accept the truce," said Hagen, "before I'd flee from a hall so shamefully, Master Hildebrand, the way you did here. I thought you could stand your ground against enemies better than that."

"Why do you sneer at *me?*" answered Hildebrand. "Who was it that sat on his shield by the Waskenstein while Walther of Spain killed so many of his friends? [1] There is plenty that could be said against you."

Then Lord Dietrich said, "It is not becoming for heroes to quarrel like old women. I forbid you, Hildebrand, to say another word. Great sorrow torments me, homeless warrior that I am. Tell me, Hagen, what you were both saying when you saw me coming toward you armed. I'll venture you said you wanted to meet me in battle alone."

"No one will deny," said Hagen, "that I want to have a try at it, and with powerful blows, if Nibelung's sword doesn't break. I am angry that you demand the pair of us as hostages."

When Dietrich heard Hagen's intention, he hastily caught up his shield. How swiftly Hagen sprang down the stairs to meet him! And loudly Nibelung's good sword rang on Dietrich's armor. At this Dietrich realized how furious the bold man was, and he began to guard himself against the fearful blows, for he knew Hagen well. Moreover, he feared the stout sword Balmung. But from time to time he struck back cunningly till at last he vanquished Hagen in the struggle, dealing him a deep, long wound.

Then Lord Dietrich thought to himself, "You are exhausted from the battle. I'll derive little honor from killing you. I shall see if instead I can force you to become my hostage."

This he did, though not without danger. Dropping his shield, he seized Hagen in his arms and thus conquered him, for his strength was great. Gunther grieved at this. Dietrich bound Hagen and led him to the queen. Into her hand he delivered the bravest warrior that ever bore a sword. This made Kriemhild very happy after her bitter suffering.

Joyfully Etzel's wife bowed to the warrior in gratitude. "May good fortune ever be yours, in body and in soul. You have made

---

[1] This is another reference to the tale of Walther of Aquitania. In the incident referred to here, where Gunther and his men attack Walther, Hagen refrains from fighting out of friendship for Walther and looks on while the latter kills one after another of Hagen's comrades and even a nephew of his.

amends to me for all my distress. I shall always reward you for this unless death prevents me."

Then Lord Dietrich said, "Let him live, noble Queen. If this is possible, how well he will repay you for what he did to you! Do not make him suffer because he stands here before you in fetters."

She ordered that Hagen be led away to a dungeon, where he remained locked in and no one saw him.

Then King Gunther called out, "Where did the warrior from Bern go? He has done me injury."

At this Lord Dietrich went to meet him. Gunther's courage was admirable. Without delay he ran outside the hall, and from the swords of both a mighty clang arose. Though Dietrich had long since been widely renowned, Gunther was in such a frenzy of rage and so deadly hostile to him for the great injury he had suffered, that it is still considered a wonder Dietrich escaped alive. Both had great valor and strength, and palace and towers echoed with their blows as they beat on the sturdy helmets with their swords. King Gunther showed splendid spirit, but the lord of Bern overcame him, as had happened to Hagen before. His blood was seen streaming through the armor rings from the sharp sword Dietrich bore. Yet despite his weariness Lord Gunther had defended himself well.

Dietrich bound the king fast. Though sovereigns should not endure such fetters, yet Dietrich feared if he set the king and his vassal free, everyone they encountered would meet with death at their hands. He took Gunther by the hand and led him bound to Kriemhild. With his suffering many of her cares were ended.

She said, "Welcome, Gunther, from the Burgundian land."

"I would bow and thank you for your greeting, my dear sister," he answered, "if it were more gracious. But I know, Queen, you are so angry that you have only a cold greeting for me and Hagen."

"Noble Queen," said Dietrich, "never were such good knights made hostages as these I have given you, royal Lady. Now allow these men far from home to profit from my intercession."

She vowed she would gladly do it. With eyes full of tears, Lord Dietrich turned away. Soon Etzel's wife avenged herself fearfully by taking the lives of these peerless warriors. To make their confinement more painful, she kept them apart, so that neither saw the other again till she bore her brother's head to Hagen. Kriemhild took ample vengeance on both.

The queen now went to Hagen, and said maliciously, "If you give back what you took from me, you may still go home to Burgundy alive."

"Your words are wasted, noble Queen," answered the fierce Hagen. "I have sworn not to reveal the treasure nor give it to any person as long as one of my lords still lives."

"I'll put an end to this," said the queen. Then she gave orders for her brother to be killed. They struck off his head, and picking it up by the hair, she carried it to the hero from Troneg. He was overwhelmed with grief.

When the sorrowful man saw his master's head, he said to Kriemhild, "You have made an end according to your will, and things have come to pass just as I had thought. The noble king of Burgundy is dead, and young Giselher, and Lord Gernot too. Now no one knows where the treasure is except for God and myself, and it shall remain hidden from you forever, you devil."

"You have made me ill recompense," she said. "But at least I will keep Siegfried's sword. My dear love was wearing it when last I saw him, through whom, because of your doing, heart's grief became my lot."

Intending to kill the warrior, she drew it from the sheath. And he could do nothing to prevent her. She raised it with both hands and struck off his head. King Etzel saw this and sorrowed.

"Alas," said the king, "that the very best of warriors that ever went to battle or ever bore a shield now lies slain by a woman's hands! However much I was his enemy, I am deeply grieved."

Then old Hildebrand said, "She shall suffer for having dared to kill him, no matter what happens to me. Even though he put me in deadly peril, still I will avenge brave Troneg's death."

In a rage Hildebrand sprang at Kriemhild and dealt her a savage sword-swing. She was stricken with terror of him, but what could it help her to shriek so piercingly? Now all whom Fate had doomed were dead, the queen had been slashed to pieces. Dietrich and Etzel began to weep; sorely they mourned both kin and vassals. Their great glory had perished, and all the people lamented. The king's festival had come to a close in grief, for so it always is —joy turns to sorrow in the end.

I cannot tell you what happened afterward, save that knights and ladies, and noble squires too, were seen to weep for the death of their dear friends. Here my tale is ended. This is the fall of the Nibelungs.

Index of Names

(Names of well-known places, towns, or rivers, which correspond exactly or approximately to the modern names, are omitted from this list.)

Alberich, a dwarf, warden of the Nibelung treasure.
Aldrian, father of Hagen and Dankwart.
Alzei, a town northwest of Worms, Volker's home town.
Amelrich, brother of the ferryman on the Danube.
Amelung land, the name of Dietrich's country in northern Italy, from which he is exiled.
Araby, Arabia.
Arras, a city in northern France, famous for its fabrics and tapestries.
Astolt, lord of the castle in Medelick.
Austria, as described in chapters XXI and XXII, is the region between Mautern and Heimburg.
Azagouc, a fictitious land somewhere in the Orient, mentioned only here and in Wolfram's *Parzival.*

Balmung, Siegfried's sword.
Bechelaren, a town in Austria, now called Pöchlarn, at the junction of the Erlach river with the Danube.
Bern, Verona, Dietrich's residence, capital of the Amelung land.
Bloedel, Etzel's brother.
Botelung, Etzel's father.

Brunhild, queen of Isenland, Gunther's wife.
Burgundy, in the fourth century and approximately the first half of the fifth century, a region on the middle Rhine occupied by the Burgundians, with Worms as the capital.

Dankrat, Ute's husband, father of Kriemhild and the three Burgundian kings.
Dankwart, Hagen's brother.
Dietrich, king of the Amelung land, an exile living at.Etzel's court.

Eckewart, margrave of the Burgundian kings.
Else, ruler of the border province on the Danube in the Bavarian land, brother of the margrave Gelfrat.
Ens, a town in Austria on the river Ens, a tributary of the Danube.
Etzel, king of the Huns.
Etzelnburg, Etzel's capital. In chapter XXIV Etzel's court is located at Gran, a city in Hungary a few miles northwest of Budapest. Some scholars believe, however, that his court was at Ofen, the German name for the old part of Budapest.
Everdingen, now Eferding, a city in Austria on the Danube.

Gelfrat, a margrave in Bavaria, Else's brother.
Gerbart, one of Dietrich's vassals.
Gere, a margrave in Burgundy and a kinsman of the royal family.
Gernot, the second son of Ute and Dankrat, and one of the Burgundian kings.
Gibeche, a king at Etzel's court.
Giselher, the youngest of the three Burgundian kings.
Gotelind, the wife of Margrave Rudeger of Bechelaren.
Gran, a city in Hungary a few miles northwest of Budapest, mentioned in chapter XXIV as the location of Etzel's court.
Gunther 1. the oldest of the Burgundian kings, Brunhild's husband.
2. the son of Siegfried and Kriemhild.

Hadeburg, one of the two mermaids whom Hagen meets.
Hagen, son of Aldrian, vassal and kinsman of the Burgundian kings.
Hawart, a Danish prince living in exile at Etzel's court.
Heimburg, perhaps the modern Hainburg, in Austria near the Hungarian border.
Helca, Etzel's first wife.
Helfrich, one of Dietrich's vassals.
Helmnot, one of Dietrich's vassals.
Herrat, the daughter of Helca's sister and mistress of Etzel's court while he was a widower.
Hildebrand, Dietrich's teacher and armor bearer, uncle of Wolfhart.
Hildegund, fiancée of Walther of Spain, with whom she fled from Etzel's land.
Hornboge, one of Etzel's vassals.
Hunnish land, a territory only vaguely defined in the poem. In chapter XXII Etzel leaves Vienna on his way eastward in order to reach the Hunnish land, with Etzelnburg as its capital. Thus it may correspond approxi-

mately to Hungary. Yet Vienna itself and the region west of it clearly belong to Etzel, since Rudeger of Bechelaren (Pöchlarn) holds his land in fief from Etzel.

Hunolt, chamberlain of the Burgundian kings.

Iring, Hawart's vassal.
Irnfried, landgrave of Thuringia.
Isenland, Brunhild's land, an island across the sea, which can be reached by ship from Worms in twelve days.
Isenstein, Brunhild's castle in Isenland.

Kriemhild, daughter of Ute and Dankrat, sister of the Burgundian kings, Siegfried's wife, and later Etzel's.

Liudegast, king of Denmark.
Liudeger, king of the Saxons, brother of Liudegast.
Loche, perhaps the modern Lochheim not far from Worms.

Medelick, a town not far from Vienna, now called Melk.
Metz, a town in northeastern France on the Moselle river, Ortwin's home.
Misenburg, now Wieselburg, a town on the Danube in Hungary.
Moeringen, now Mehring, the town on the Danube west of Passau where the Burgundians crossed the river.
Mutaren, now Mautern, a town on the Danube not far from Vienna.

Nantwin, father of Herrat.
Netherland, the region of the lower Rhine, Siegmund's kingdom and Siegfried's home.
Nibelung 1. King Nibelung, father of Schilbung and Nibelung, during his life king of the Nibelung land and possessor of the Nibelung treasure.
2. one of King Nibelung's two sons.
Nibelungs, in the first part of the poem the original possessors of the Nibelung treasure and their vassals, who later became Siegfried's vassals, but from chapter XXV on, used to refer to the Burgundians. The origin and possible meaning of the name Nibelung have been much discussed. Some scholars base an interpretation on the etymological relationship between the first half of the name and Old High German *nebul* (modern German *Nebel,* "clouds" or "fog") and Old Norse *nifl,* "darkness," and believe it has some mythological significance as a description of the original owners of the treasure, who were giants or dwarfs. The name was then logically transferred to the Burgundians when they became the owners of the treasure. Other scholars explain it as a name found among the Franks from the eighth century on and point to the confusion in the epic *Waltharius,* where the Burgundians are thought to be Franks and are called *Franci Nebulones.* Old Norse sources also indicate that it is a name associated very early with the Burgundian kings of the Nibelung story.
Norway, here called the march of Norway. The reference is confusing. It is not clear whether the Scandinavian country is meant or whether the poet identifies the march of Norway with Siegfried's kingdom of Netherland.
Nudung, a kinsman of Gotelind.

Ortlieb, the son of Etzel and Kriemhild.
Ortwin, from Metz, the son of Hagen's sister, steward of the Burgundian kings.

Petchenegres, a nomadic Turkish tribe, in the ninth century located north of the Caspian Sea, in the tenth century in present-day Ukraine, later in Bulgaria. There is no trace of them after the thirteenth century.
Pilgrim, bishop of Passau, Ute's brother, uncle of Kriemhild and the Burgundian kings.

Ramung, a duke from the land of the Walachs.
Ritschart, one of Dietrich's vassals.
Rudeger, margrave of Bechelaren, Gotelind's husband.
Rumolt, master cook of the Burgundian kings.

Schilbung, one of King Nibelung's two sons.
Schrutan, one of the participants on the side of the Huns in the tourney described in chapter XXXI.
Siegelind 1. Siegmund's wife, mother of Siegfried.
        2. one of the two mermaids whom Hagen meets.
Siegfried 1. son of Siegmund and Siegelind, Kriemhild's husband.
        2. son of Gunther and Brunhild.
Siegmund, king of Netherland, Siegelind's husband, father of Siegfried.
Siegstab, duke from Bern, son of Dietrich's sister.
Sindolt, cupbearer of the Burgundian kings.
Spessart, hilly forest land east and northeast of Worms, mentioned by Hagen in chapter XVI. It is much too far away from Worms for a day's hunt, the nearest point being at least sixty miles distant.
Speyer, a town on the Rhine a few miles south of Worms.
Swalevelt, according to de Boor (*Das Nibelungenlied in Urtext und Übersetzung,* Bremen, n.d., p. 699), Schwalbenfeld, a province on the Schwalb river, a tributary of the Wörnitz, which joins the Danube at Donauwörth. De Boor points out that the description of this part of the Burgundians' journey shows that the author was not familiar with the territory, for Schwalbenfeld lies considerably south of the route as given in the poem.
Swemmel, one of King Etzel's minstrels.

Treisem, the Traisen, a tributary of the Danube in Lower Austria.
Troneg, Hagen's birthplace or residence, a name of uncertain origin which makes its first appearance in the *Nibelungenlied.* It has been variously explained. It may possibly be a corruption of the name of the Latin colony, *colonia Trajana,* on the lower Rhine, written as early as the fifth century as Troja and giving rise to the legend that the Franks were descended from the ancient Trojans. In the epic *Waltharius,* Hagen, a Frank, is described as being of Trojan descent.
Trune, the Traun river, a tributary of the Danube.
Tulne, now Tulln, a town on the Danube a few miles northwest of Vienna.

Ute, Dankrat's widow, mother of Kriemhild and the Burgundian kings, sister of Bishop Pilgrim of Passau.

Vergen, now Pföring, on the Danube below Ingolstadt.
Volker, from Alzei, a minstrel, vassal of the Burgundian kings.

Walachs, in modern German *Welsche,* now used as an indefinite reference to foreigners, usually of Romance origin, but in the poem apparently a reference to a Southeastern Slavic people.

Walther, from Spain, the hero of a well-known story, preserved in several versions, son of the king of Aquitania, for years a hostage of Etzel's, who reared him at his court.

Waske, Iring's sword.

Waskenstein, a narrow, rocky passage through the Vosges mountains where Walther of Aquitania fights Gunther and his men.

Wasken woods, the Vosges mountains, located here inaccurately on the eastern side of the Rhine.

Werbel, one of Etzel's minstrels.

Wichart, one of Dietrich's vassals.

Witege, not identified here except as the warrior who killed Nudung. In the *Thidrekssaga* he is the son of Wieland, the smith.

Wolfbrand, one of Dietrich's vassals.

Wolfhart, son of Hildebrand's sister and Dietrich's vassal.

Wolfwin, one of Dietrich's vassals.

Xanten, Capital of Netherland, in the poem located on the lower Rhine.

Zazamanc, a fictitious land somewhere in the Orient, also mentioned in Wolfram's *Parzival.*

Zeizenmure, probably a false reading in the chief manuscript and in most others. Two manuscripts have *Treysenmoure* and *treisem moure,* which correspond better to the modern Traismauer on the Traisen, approximately thirty-five miles west of Vienna.

THE POEM OF
THE CID

Translated, and with an introduction by,
W. S. Merwin

For Margot Pitt-Rivers

Introduction

The *Poem of The Cid* was written, as far as can be known, sometime around 1140. Its author, again as nearly as can be determined,
was a native of the Castilian frontier which faced the Moorish kingdom of Valencia; quite possibly he was from somewhere around
Medinaceli or San Esteban de Gormaz, both of which figure in the
poem. In the eleventh and early twelfth centuries Castilians and
Moors fought back and forth over this bit of border country; Medinaceli was taken from the Moors in 1104, then lost again, then re-
taken definitively in 1120, only twenty years or so before the
Poema was written. During the same period the border country
was also a center of poetic activity. The *Poema del Cid* was not the
only heroic poem of the period written in the vernacular, in a rough,
spare, sinewy, rapid verse, to be sung in market places. But it is almost the only one which did not vanish, leaving only a reference in
some chronicle, if that. The *Poema* itself has survived only in a
single manuscript copy (and even from this three pages are missing) made by one Per Abbat in 1307.

In 1140, or more or less, when the poet set out to write his epic, there must have been men still alive who remembered Rodrigo Díaz of Bivar, who had been called "the Cid." He had died in Valencia, only forty-odd years before, on Sunday, the 10th of July, 1099, at the age of fifty-six. His relatives and his many vassals and their families had shown the signs of mourning that at the time were customary at the passing of a lord: the men beat their breasts, ripped their clothes, stripped their heads bald; the women lacerated their cheeks with their nails and covered their faces with ashes; and both sexes wailed and shrieked their grief for days on end. But it was not only in Valencia, which he had taken from the Moors, that the Cid's death resounded. A contemporary French chronicle tells us that "his death caused grave sorrow in Christendom, and huge rejoicing among the Moorish enemies." To the two halves of the known world his passing was an event of great importance. Already in his lifetime he had been a legend.

Rodrigo Díaz had been born sometime around 1043—almost exactly a century before the poem was written—in Bivar, a village to the north of Burgos. His father's family was of highly honorable minor nobility; his father led a rather retired life in the ancestral home in Bivar. Rodrigo's mother's family was of a higher degree of nobility, with considerable influence at court. Rodrigo as a youth was brought up in the court of Prince Sancho, the eldest son of King Fernando, who at the time ruled León and Castile and held the title of Emperor, with hierarchical superiority over the Kings of Aragón and Navarre.

Feudal Spain of the mid-eleventh century was politically an extremely complicated place. By then the reconquest of the country from the Moors had made considerable progress. In the north of the peninsula were the Visigothic Christian kingdoms and states, most notably Castile, León, Aragón, Navarre, and the county of Barcelona. In the south were the Moorish kingdoms, chief among them Seville, Granada, Córdoba, and Valencia. To further complicate the division, the Christian states lived in rivalry with one another. Many of the Moorish states were dependencies of Christian kingdoms, paying them tribute in exchange for protection from other Moors or other Christians. These tributary kingdoms were a principal cause of the contentions and intermittent wars among the Christian states. Another was the Spanish kings' practice of dividing up their kingdoms among their heirs. Rodrigo, as a young man, was a witness to some of the tragic consequences of one of these partitions; they affected the whole course of his life.

By the spring of 1063, when Rodrigo was twenty, Prince Sancho had dubbed him a knight, and he accompanied the Prince on an expedition to lift the siege of Graus. This place occupied a strategic position at an entrance to the Moorish kingdom of Zaragoza, which was a tributary of Castile and hence under the protection of Sancho's father, King Fernando. Zaragoza was unique among the Moorish kingdoms in being entirely surrounded by Christian states; it had to have the protection of one of them, and inevitably it would choose the strongest. Ramiro I of Aragón, Prince Sancho's uncle, had designs on Zaragoza, and had begun by besieging Graus. On Thursday, May 8, 1063, Sancho, with Rodrigo among his knights, attacked Ramiro's besieging force, and in the battle Ramiro I was killed.

In December of the same year, King Ferdinand divided his kingdom, including the Moorish tributary states, among his three sons, Sancho, Alfonso, and García. Sancho was given Castile and Zaragoza; Alfonso was given León and the dependency of Toledo. García received Galicia and a bit of what is now Portugal, with the Moorish kingdoms of Seville and Badajoz. To his daughters, Urraca and Elvira, the King gave only certain monasteries, and these only on the condition that they should never marry; this condition, presumably, was designed to prevent claims to the succession from becoming still more complicated. According to poems of the period, Sancho was opposed to the partition of the kingdom, as well he might have been. He was not the only member of the family who was displeased. Several medieval accounts agree that Urraca carried on an incestuous affair with her brother Alfonso, and used it to acquire the town of Zamora from him; her attempts to redistribute the patrimony did not stop there.

The heirs kept the peace, and honored Fernando's division while their parents were alive. Fernando died in 1065 and the Queen in 1067. Then five years of civil war broke out.

Prince Sancho had been crowned Sancho II of Castile and had appointed Rodrigo Díaz chief marshal, or *alférez,* of his army, a title which also gave Rodrigo the highest post at Sancho's court. In his capacity as *alférez,* Rodrigo, aged twenty-eight, was a principal in a bizarre form of feudal diplomacy: a trial by combat to settle a boundary dispute between Navarre and Castile, involving several fortified places. Rodrigo was spectacularly victorious over the champion from Navarre, and the contest won him his first fame. Thereafter he was known as the "Campeador," meaning "the expert warrior."

There were other matters for Sancho to clear up. The Moorish King of Zaragoza, Moctádir, was not a prompt man with his tribute money. He had given the old King, Fernando, trouble on this account, and Fernando's final military campaign had been for the purpose of collecting from Zaragoza. Now Sancho was having the same difficulties. So in 1067, with Rodrigo Díaz (then twenty-four) as his general, he laid siege to Zaragoza. Moctádir capitulated. A contemporary Hebrew chronicle gives all the credit to "Cidi Ru Diaz"; Rodrigo must have been known already as "mio Cid"—"my lord."

Sancho wanted León. No doubt he felt that as the eldest son he had a good right to it. Furthermore there were family traditions and Christian traditions both behind him. León was the elder of the two kingdoms, the ancient imperial seat of Christian Spain, and it had formerly dominated the rest of the Christian states. But since the tenth century Castile had not been docile about this dominion, and by Sancho's time, Castile's political importance was greater than León's. Four generations of Sancho's ancestors had fought against León, including his father Fernando. In 1068—we do not know just how it happened—war broke out between Sancho's Castile and his brother Alfonso's León. The royal brothers arranged a time and place for a battle: on the border between the two kingdoms, on the plain of Llantada, on the banks of the Pisuerga, on July 19, 1068. There King Sancho, with the Cid at the head of his host, routed the army of León. The brothers had agreed that the victor should receive the kingdom of the vanquished without further fighting, but Alfonso fled to León and prepared to hold out there. The war decided nothing. In fact, the two brothers three years later found themselves on the same side, though only for a short time: Alfonso had fallen out with the third brother, García, and he and Sancho together, in 1071, attacked García, dethroned him, and split his kingdom between them.

A conscientious sensitivity about his rights and a respect for certain traditions may have been Sancho's guiding impulses; Alfonso, it is agreed, was plain covetous. In any case, in the beginning of

January 1072, León and Castile were again at war, and a battle was fought on the plain of Golpejera. According to one account, Sancho was captured during the battle and rescued by the Cid. All accounts agree that Rodrigo was largely responsible for the Castilians' victory over León.

Sancho took his brother Alfonso, in chains, to a number of castles and cities in the kingdom of León and received their submission; then he had himself anointed and crowned in León on January 12, 1072. After that he imprisoned Alfonso in the castle of Burgos, where the third brother, García, had been a prisoner not a year before.

The Princess Urraca, bound by ties of more than sisterly tenderness to Alfonso, could not endure this treatment of him without some complaint. She went to Burgos and interceded for him, begging Sancho to set him free and exile him to the Moorish kingdoms in the south. Sancho complied with her request: Alfonso was sent to Toledo, to the court of King Mamún, who was a friend and former tributary of Alfonso's.

Urraca also arranged that Alfonso should be accompanied by his former tutor, Pedro Ansúrez, and by Pedro's two brothers, Gonzalo and Fernando. These brothers were the chief members of the Beni-Gómez clan, a family of importance to the Cid's subsequent career and of prime importance in the *Poema:* they were the "Heirs of Carrion." The Beni-Gómez were a family of great fame, position, and influence; they were counts—a much higher degree of nobility than the Cid's. They enjoyed, under King Alfonso, roughly the same favor which the Cid enjoyed under King Sancho. The battle of Golpejera had taken place within three leagues of their capital of Carrión, and the Cid, in contributing to the overthrow and disgrace of King Alfonso, had also helped to effect theirs.

León did not submit passively to the Castilian conquest; from the outset there were signs of rebellion. In Toledo, Alfonso spent nine months in exile—and not in idleness. Pedro Ansúrez slipped back and forth between Toledo and Doña Urraca in Zamora. And finally news reached Castile that many of Alfonso's vassals, including those of the Beni-Gómez clan, had gathered in Zamora to raise a rebellion. Whereupon Sancho and the Cid laid siege to Zamora.

The siege was effective; unable to throw off the Castilians, the knights and populace in Zamora began to grow hungry. A bold stroke was conceived. On Sunday, October 7, 1072, a knight named Vellido Adolfo managed to enter the Castilian camp, mounted and unsuspected. There he sought out King Sancho and ran him through the breast with his lance, mortally wounding him. He then spurred his horse and escaped to Zamora, where the gates opened to receive him. King Sancho had been thirty-four years old, at the height of his power. The author of his death had been his sister, Princess Urraca.

While King Sancho's funeral procession was on its way to Oña, Urraca sent messengers to Alfonso, in Toledo, to inform him of the assassination. The news reached him before they did. Alfonso had some fears that King Mamún, if he heard the news, might hold him for ransom; but he had been treated so hospitably in Toledo, that he decided to act without duplicity, and when he told Mamún, the Moorish King sent him on his way with his blessing. Alfonso set out for Zamora and thence resumed his throne in León, giving Urraca the title of Queen. Shortly thereafter Alfonso, accompanied by Urraca and the Beni-Gómez clan, set out to receive the crown of Castile, in Burgos.

Naturally, a large number of Castilians, the Cid at their head, regarded Alfonso with anything but welcome. According to feudal law in Spain, in a case like this where assassination was suspected, the vassals had a right to demand as a condition of vowing allegiance to their new lord that he swear that he had had nothing to do with the death of the person to whose position he had been elevated. The Cid and an assembly of Castilian knights demanded that Alfonso should swear this in the Church of Santa Gadea in Burgos. There the King laid hands on the statues of the apostles on the altar and with twelve others swore at the Cid's dictation. The Cid then replied, as was his right, with a wish that "if what Alfonso spoke was a lie, it might please God that Alfonso might be killed by a treacherous vassal, as King Sancho had been by Vellido Adolfo." Alfonso and his co-swearers had to say "Amen," but the King turned pale. The Cid, still within his rights, repeated the oath and the wish and heard the replies three times. Then he kissed the King's hand, in token of vassalage. Whether to win him over, or for whatever reasons, the King began by favoring him highly at his court. Even so, the Cid was eclipsed by the Beni-Gómez clan (one of whom, García Ordóñez, assumed his post of *alférez*) and by many of Alfonso's other followers; his position in the Castilian court was far below what it had been under King Sancho, and far from secure at that.

The new *alférez* was not a great military success and was soon relieved of his post and given a county instead. Whether or not this had anything to do with the favor the King next bestowed on the Cid is not known. On July 19, 1074, when the Cid was thirty-one years old, the King married him to Doña Jimena Díaz, the King's own niece. It should be noted that her highly noble family was from León, not Castile. Children were born to the union, the first of them just a year later. And though he never regained the ascendancy he had enjoyed under King Sancho, the Cid continued to serve the King in important posts until toward the end of 1079, when he was sent to collect the tribute from the Moorish King of Seville, Motámid.

The Cid arrived to find Motámid menaced by his old enemy Abdállah, the Moorish King of Granada, who was also a tributary of Alfonso's. The situation was further complicated by the fact that four important vassals of Alfonso's, including García Ordóñez, the Cid's most important rival in the Beni-Gómez clan, were in Abdállah's court to collect the tribute there. The Cid felt it his duty to protect the King of Seville, and sent a letter to Abdállah, asking him to keep the peace, in the name of Alfonso the Emperor. Abdállah, backed up by the knights who were with García Ordóñez, replied by invading the territory of Seville and sacking it as far as Cabra. This, of course, is the situation with which the *Poema* originally opened, before the first three pages were lost and reconstructed in prose.

The Cid, acting for Alfonso as the protector of Seville, fell upon the invaders, who far outnumbered him, and after a hard battle defeated them with heavy losses, taking prisoner García Ordóñez, among others. He held them for three days to emphasize the situation and then released them, keeping only the loot his men had taken. By May 1080, both the Cid and García Ordóñez were back in Castile. The King was not pleased at the affair: García Ordóñez was his favorite. Suddenly the Cid's enemies at court were more numerous, and they had fresh matter for their art. They accused the Cid of having kept for himself the greater part of the tribute money from Seville. The King said nothing, but he listened.

In the following year Rodrigo, because of sickness, stayed behind in Castile while the King and his chief vassals laid siege to the city of Toledo, which had been split by a rebellion. While the King was away, a host of Moors made a serious incursion into Castile, plundering heavily and attacking the castle of Gormaz. The Cid quickly assembled his vassals, attacked the Moors, plundered and razed their lands, and returned with nearly seven thousand prisoners and vast spoils. This action merely increased the jealousy which Alfonso's vassals felt toward the Cid. They accused him of having antagonized the friendly Moors, whose territory bordered that of the attackers. Alfonso took the occasion to banish the Cid from Castile.

With the Cid went his own vassals, as was customary. Rodrigo first went to the Count of Barcelona, Ramón Berenguér, and offered his services to the Count. He and his vassals established themselves there.

But the arrangement was not successful. The Cid received neither the welcome nor the position he expected; something said or done by a nephew of Berenguér's roused his anger, and he left Barcelona and proceeded to offer his services to the Moorish King of Zaragoza, who welcomed him. It was as an ally of the King of Zaragoza that he shortly found himself in the field against the Count of Barcelona, whom he defeated and held prisoner for five days.

Alfonso's ambition was to make all Spain his empire. In 1085, after triumphs in other parts of the peninsula, he marched against Zaragoza. The Cid had either to fight against his former lord or to go elsewhere. He camped for a while at Tudela. He was forty-two, and at the nadir of his fortunes.

Alfonso's fortunes, at the same time, were approaching their summit. In the same year (1085), after six years of fighting, Toledo fell to him; a diplomatic maneuver and a stroke of luck gave him control of Valencia; Zaragoza was on the point of surrendering; his knights were virtually laying siege to Granada, Murcia, and Almería, and he was pressing claims against Córdoba. Success followed success until his sway extended over all the Moorish kingdoms of the peninsula, from Castile south to the straits of Gibraltar; and his influence over the other Christian princes of Spain had grown enormously. For the first time since the Moors had invaded Spain, a Christian ruler could claim with some reason to be King of all Spain.

Meanwhile, across the straits of Africa a still more ambitious imperial scheme was unfolding. By the eleventh century, in many parts of Islam, the original ferocity of that faith had given place to a graceful and in some cases effete civilization. This was true of many of the Moorish kingdoms in Spain, as well as those in Africa. In 1039, a tribe on the edge of the Sudan began to convert the desert tribesmen to the way of Mohammed; they preached a reformation of Islam, a return to the unadorned, primitive faith, to conversion by the sword, to the Holy War. In 1055 the converts of the Sahara began their conquest of the older and more decadent Moorish civilization in North Africa, and by 1075 they had swept westward across the top of the continent as far as Ceuta and Tangier. They were led by an ascetic chieftain of extraordinary gifts, one Yúsuf ben Texufín.

In 1075 the King of Seville had begged Yúsuf to cross the straits and help him against Alfonso; Yúsuf had answered that he would not leave Africa until he had taken the Mediterranean coastal cities of Morocco. In 1084 the last of these, Ceuta, fell to him. And the following year (when Alfonso's dominion over the Spanish peninsula was nearly complete) the Moorish Kings of Seville and Badajoz again invited Yúsuf to cross to Spain and help throw off the yoke of the Christians. This was a grave decision on the part of the Moorish monarchs. The court of Seville in particular was a flourishing center of the arts, learning, and pleasure, and King Motámid was a lavish patron of all three. The Moorish kings of Spain could hardly expect the fierce, ignorant, fundamentalist zealots who had overrun the rich culture of North Africa to play a subservient or a gentle role in their kingdoms. Almost certainly they could expect worse treatment from Yúsuf than from Alfonso. Motámid's son opposed the invitation to Yúsuf. But Motámid, in the name of his religion, persisted.

Yúsuf sent a large force to occupy Algeciras and then crossed the straits himself with an enormous army. He had not reached Seville before the Kings of Granada, Málaga, and Almería were in league with him. Alfonso, hearing the news, raised the siege of Zaragoza and began to assemble an army to repel the new invasion. The King of Aragón and several other Christian princes sent him reinforcements; in his hosts there were even knights from Italy and France. But he did not choose to ask the Cid to accompany him.

The two armies came in sight of each other at a place called

Sagrajas, near Badajoz. The Moors were encamped there, and Alfonso made camp, facing them across a small stream. For three days, while messengers came and went between the camps, both armies drank from the same waters. The battle took place on Friday, October 23, 1085.

The vanguard of the Christians, led by Alvar Fáñez, attacked the Moorish vanguard, composed of Spanish Moors, routed them, and set off in pursuit of them. The rest of the Castilians attacked, carried the field as far as the moat around Yúsuf's tents, only to find that the Moors had circled around and attacked them from the rear and had entered the Christian camp, slaughtering and burning. The Castilians fell back to reorganize, whereupon Yúsuf, with his main force, charged them. As he did, there was a sound which had never before been heard in the armies of Europe: drums. The drummers of Africa built up a thunderous roar, and the sound was not without effect on the Christians; some of them thought the earth was shaking. At the same time they had to face other military phenomena which they had never encountered before: disciplined bodies of fighters, moving in formation and maneuvering to orders; parallel lines of Turkish archers firing on command. They were heavily outnumbered, besides. They were disastrously defeated, and King Alfonso himself barely escaped. That same night Yúsuf had all the Christian corpses beheaded and the heads piled up into hills, from whose tops at dawn his muezzins summoned the troops to prayer.

At once Yúsuf was recalled to Africa by the death of his son, so his Spanish campaign, for the moment, went no further. But he was securely established on the peninsula; and Alfonso, at one blow, had lost all hope of control of most of the Moorish states in what, only a short time before, had been his empire. He had also, of course, sustained great losses in men and in prestige, and if Yúsuf should return, his own kingdom was in danger. He effected a reconciliation with the Cid; apart from needing every knight he could muster, he no doubt remembered that no body of knights ever led by the Cid had been defeated, though numbers and circumstances had often been heavily against them. In any case, the Cid returned to Castile and was showered with honors, lands, and castles.

It was as Alfonso's vassal that the Cid began to take an active part in the politics of the eastern coast of Spain. Chaos had resulted from Yúsuf's triumph and subsequent absence; loyalties were broken everywhere, alliances among the Moorish states shifted and dissolved; in some cases the Moors refused tribute and taxes not only to the Christians but to their own kings. The Moorish King of Valencia, Alcádir, threatened on all hands, sent out pleas for help to Alfonso and to the Moorish King of Zaragoza. The Cid, at the time, was in Zaragoza, and he arrived soon after in Valencia with three thousand knights.

In Valencia the Cid acted as Alfonso's lieutenant; he studied the country and sent back reports to Castile. Ramón Berenguér of Barcelona and Mostaín of Zaragoza combined against him; he conducted a skillful campaign that drove them from the region, and he subdued the country and restored order for the King of Valencia, all in the name of Alfonso. Alcádir, in Valencia, was enormously grateful; he became the Cid's tributary, offering him a large weekly sum; and the Cid forced tribute from a large number of lesser rulers throughout the territory. He had restored a large piece of Alfonso's empire.

From the castle of Aledo, in the Murcia region, García Jiménez, one of the Cid's lieutenants, was carrying the campaign into the territories of Almería, to the grave discomfort of Motámid, the King of Seville. Motámid took a force against Aledo but was routed by a much smaller number of Christians. He decided that there was nothing to do but to call Yúsuf over again, and in June 1089 Yúsuf landed for the second time in Algeciras. He and the combined Kings of Seville, Granada, Málaga, Almería, and Murcia laid siege to the castle of Aledo.

By the end of four months the besieging armies were hungry, and the Kings had fallen to squabbling among themselves. They asked Yúsuf to arbitrate. His decision went against the King of Murcia, whereupon all the Murcians packed up and went home. At this point they learned that Alfonso was coming against them with a large army.

Alfonso had written to the Cid to join him, and the Cid had gone to meet him: but the armies missed each other by accident, and Alfonso arrived first at Aledo. Yúsuf, not trusting his allies, retired at once to Lorca, and the whole thing was not only over, but Alfonso and his army had started back, by the time the Cid arrived on the scene. The incident was a boon to the Cid's old enemies in Castile. Alfonso's latent jealousy, suspicion, and resentment of the Cid broke out afresh. He exiled him a second time; he took from him all the castles and privileges he had recently accorded him and all the gold and silver in the Cid's own house and lands, and he imprisoned Doña Jimena and her three children. The Cid was accused of having conspired against the King's life, and Alfonso would not entertain any messages from Rodrigo; but he did, after a short time, relent so far as to release Doña Jimena and the Cid's children and allow them to join him.

Yúsuf departed from Spain again, leaving behind him a large army to be used against the Cid. Alcádir of Valencia now refused tribute to the Cid (and all the other lords of the region were supposed to pay their tribute to the Cid through Alcádir). The Cid had no allies and many enemies. He conducted a raiding campaign, in the spring of 1089, in the Levant to the south of Valencia, and when the rulers there sued for peace, Alcádir in Valencia hastened to do the same.

Once again the Cid found himself ranged against the Count of Barcelona; Berenguér had raised a coalition to drive the Cid from the region and enjoy the tributes in his stead. The Cid met Berenguér's army, and though heavily outnumbered he managed to divide and defeat it, take enormous spoils and many prisoners, including Berenguér himself—for the second time. He released all the prisoners after exacting considerable ransoms, including, from the Count, the sword Colada. This is the battle with Berenguér that is described in the *Poema*.

Meanwhile the army which Yúsuf had left on the peninsula had not been winning hearts among the Spanish Moors. It was not long before the Moorish kings came to regard the Africans with a mixture of dislike and dread; and a number of Moorish kings, those of Granada and Seville among them, began secret negotiations with Alfonso.

But in 1090, Yúsuf landed in Spain for the third time. Without any help from the Spanish Moors, he laid siege to Toledo; and when this proved futile he visited his annoyance on the Moorish kings, sending the Kings of Granada and Málaga to Africa in chains. His next move was to attack the King of Seville. Again the peninsula's complex system of interreligious alliances shifted. The King of Seville called on Alfonso to help him against Yúsuf, and Alfonso, in March 1091, struck south and seized Granada. Here, through the efforts of his Queen, Constanza, he was met by the Cid, who had abandoned the siege of Liria to come and support him; once again the King and the Cid were reconciled, and once again the reconciliation did not last long. Only a slight and accidental pretext was necessary, the King's disfavor erupted once more, and the Cid and his vassals turned back toward Valencia.

Yúsuf's army took Córdoba, and Yúsuf's general decapitated the Moorish governor of that city. Then he marched on against Seville. Alfonso sent a force against him, under Alvar Fáñez, but this army was badly beaten and many of its knights taken prisoner. On September 7, 1091, Yúsuf's Africans took Seville. King Motámid was thrown into prison, and thence sent to a dungeon in Morocco. Almería and Murcia quickly went the way of Seville, and Alfonso seemed powerless to do anything against Yúsuf in the southern part of the peninsula. By the end of 1091, the only Christian outside Christian Spain who still opposed Yúsuf was the Cid.

The Cid drew back his line of outposts and fortified Peña Cadiella, which commanded the pass between the south, where Yúsuf's army was, and the plain of Valencia. At this point the King of Aragón, and Mostaín, the Moorish King of Zaragoza, offered him help. The Cid went to Zaragoza to sign a treaty of peace with Mostaín. While he was there, King Alfonso, with a large army, descended on Valencia. He had arranged to join forces with the fleets of Genoa and Pisa, to take the city. The Cid sent a letter to Alfonso expressing his astonishment, and at the same time his continued loyalty to the King. Alfonso's expedition proved a failure; the fleets arrived too late, the siege was ill-provided and had to be lifted.

The Cid, assuming with good reason that the Beni-Gómez clan were among the instigators of this expedition, decided at last to strike back: from Zaragoza he invaded their ancestral domains, sacking, burning, and leaving ruin everywhere behind him. García Ordóñez, in reply, sent a message to the Cid, challenging him to meet him for a battle. On the day appointed, the Cid arrived at the place that had been fixed, but there was no sign of García Ordóñez or his vassals. The Cid waited there for seven days, but the Beni-Gómez never appeared.

He remained in Zaragoza until the end of 1092. While he was there, a conspiracy led by one Ben Jehhaf had taken root within Valencia. The conspirators planned to turn the city to Ben Ayixa, Yúsuf's son, who was encamped in Murcia, to the south. Letters were sent to Ben Ayixa, who proceeded against Valencia and took possession of Alcira, a short distance from the city. Inside Valencia, open rebellion broke out. The old weak-hearted King, Alcádir, the Cid's ally and tributary, locked himself in the palace and was there besieged by the partisans, aided by a handful of Ben Ayixa's Africans. Alcádir dressed himself as a woman, filled a box with a collection of jewels which he prized as highly as his own life, and fastened around himself a jewel-studded girdle famous throughout the Arab world, which had been worn by Zobeida, the wife of Haroun Al-Raschid, and had brought disaster to owner after owner. Then, surrounded by women, he fled the palace and hid in a little house in another part of the city. The partisans stormed into the palace, killing and smashing everywhere. Ben Jehhaf controlled Valencia. He knew that Alcádir had not escaped from the city, and he wanted the jewels and especially the famous girdle of Zobeida. A hireling of his managed to locate Alcádir and at night seized him, cut off his head, and returned to Ben Jehhaf with the head and the jewels. The head was paraded around the streets on a pike; the body, next day, was flung into a manure heap where dead camels were buried. It was forbidden to mourn for him.

Too late, the Cid arrived in the territory of Valencia; the city was already lost. He laid siege to the castle of Juballa, on a hill in the neighborhood of Valencia, and from his camp there he began at once to send out raiding parties all around the city. He demanded provisions from all the local Moorish chieftains. His depredations had their effect: after a few months Ben Jehhaf sent to the Cid to try, without success, to bargain with him. After eight months of siege, in July 1093, the castle of Juballa fell to the Cid; in a few weeks be built around the fortress an entire walled city. In the same month he seized Villanueva and Alcudia, the two suburbs to the north of Valencia, and Valencia decided to yield. The conditions of the surrender were: first, that Yúsuf's soldiers should leave the city; next, that Ben Jehhaf should pay the Cid the same tribute that Alcádir had paid, and retroactively since the beginning of the rebellion; and last, that the Cid and his host should continue to occupy Juballa.

Yúsuf had already sent threatening letters to the Cid, warning him not to remain in the territory of Valencia. Rodrigo had answered with a scornful note, and at the same time had sent letters to all the Moorish chieftains of southern Spain, declaring that

Yúsuf, then in Africa, did not dare to cross the straits to attack him. Yúsuf, on hearing that Valencia had fallen to the Cid, crossed to Spain and prepared to attack the Campeador himself. The Cid sent a new proposal to Valencia, a kind of ultimatum which was customary in the wars of the period. He offered the Valencians thirty days in which to hope for succor from Yúsuf: if the African should arrive before that time, the Valencians then were to be released from their treaty with the Cid, and might side with Yúsuf; but if at the end of that time Yúsuf had not come to their aid, they were to side with the Cid against him. The Valencians accepted.

For a month the Cid prepared his fortifications. At the end of August 1093, when the term of the ultimatum was up, Yúsuf was nowhere in sight. The Cid had September and October, too, in which to continue his preparations for the defense. Then, with Yúsuf's army already in Lorca, to the south, the Cid camped in Villamediana, to the north of Valencia. Ben Jehhaf, he knew, was not to be trusted, and he had decided that it would be best to surround the city.

News came that Yúsuf's army, commanded by Abú Béker, was moving north from Lorca to Murcia. And news came from within Valencia that the pro-Yúsuf faction, led by the Beni-Uéjib clan, had seized power; that Ben Jehhaf had abdicated; and that the new rulers had abjured the July treaty with the Cid and planned to defend the city against him.

The Cid consolidated his position as well as he could, and waited for the Africans. They advanced closer; news of their approach came day after day, until they were within nine miles of Valencia. The Castilians, and the pro-Yúsuf Valencians who planned to despoil the Cid's camp, expected an encounter the next day. That night a cloudburst and thunderstorm of unprecedented violence struck the region, and in the middle of the night the Africans took panic and fled.

The Cid tightened the siege of the city. Inside Valencia, as conditions and morale grew worse, Ben Jehhaf regained power; in January 1094 he agreed to sign a treaty with the Cid, then changed his mind. The inhabitants began to suffer the extremes of hunger. In June the city surrendered unconditionally. The Cid was magnanimous and considerate to the inhabitants. But though he allowed Ben Jehhaf to remain the titular governor of the city, he required him to swear that he was not hiding the treasures of the Cid's old ally, Alcádir. Ben Jehhaf, in public, solemnly swore that he was not.

Two months later, news arrived that the Africans were assembling in Murcia for an attack on Valencia. Yúsuf's forces continued to grow; he landed more troops from Africa, and in September a vast army, commanded by Yúsuf's nephew, moved to the plain of Valencia and camped there. Certain of victory, for ten days their raiding parties pillaged the vicinity of the city and of the Cid's camp. The Campeador decided not to wait for reinforcements which were said to be coming to him; on the night of October 25, his force left camp. Parties of his knights managed to conceal themselves in the ravines around Yúsuf's camp. At daybreak the Cid's main host was drawn up facing the Africans. When Yúsuf's army charged, the Cid retreated, whereupon the rest of the Castilians, from the ravines, attacked the African camp. Yúsuf's army thought the Castilian reinforcements had arrived; they broke and fled, pursued by the Cid's knights, to be cut down or captured. The rout was complete, and immense quantities of booty were gathered up from the field.

King Alfonso was on his way to help the Cid when he heard of the victory. He changed his direction to take advantage of the situation, and attacked Guadix, further south, laying waste that part of the African empire.

In Valencia, new evidence indicated that Ben Jehhaf had been responsible for the death of Alcádir, the old King; the Cid had Ben Jehhaf seized and thrown into prison, where Ben Jehhaf shortly confessed and, upon some considerable prompting, told also where Alcádir's jewels were hidden. He was then tried before a court of Christians and Moors, and condemned, as a regicide, to be buried up to the waist and then burned alive. The sentence was carried out in May 1095.

The Cid spent the next year or so consolidating his position in Valencia. The new King of Aragón, Pedro, was now his firm ally and sent a force of knights to help him. The Cid, late in the year 1096, took an expedition to secure the outer fortresses of the territory, particularly Peña Cadiella, which he had fortified five years before. On this campaign he encountered an African army numbering thirty thousand knights, many times the Christian force. By brilliant maneuvering, the Cid caught them in a narrow place, and there was a repetition of his battle with the Africans before Valencia: a rout, great slaughter, and enormous spoils. In the same year, Alfonso was again defeated by Yúsuf at Consuegra (the Cid's son, serving with Alfonso, was killed in this battle) and another Christian army, under Alvar Fáñez, was routed by Ben Ayixa in the vicinity of Cuenca.

Ben Ayixa, on the heels of that victory, turned toward Valencia, met a detachment of the Cid's army at Alcira, and cut it to pieces. Notwithstanding intense grief at the death of his son, and at the disaster to his vassals at Alcira, the Cid laid siege to the two cities of Almenara and Murviedro, which were known to be sympathetic to the Africans. By the late summer of 1098 he had taken them both, Murviedro after a siege of some months. The capture of these two cities left the Cid in secure control of the whole province of Valencia.

A year later he died, aged fifty-six.

Two years after his death, Mazdalí, a new African general, laid siege to Valencia. Jimena successfully defended the city until King Alfonso arrived from Castile with his army, whereupon the Africans retired. Alfonso, after a reconnaissance of the territory and a few brushes with some of Mazdalí's forces, decided that it would be impossible for him to hold the city now that the Campeador was dead. He and his army, and Jimena and the Cid's army, taking with them Rodrigo's body, evacuated the city and set out for Toledo. Upon leaving, in order to prevent the Africans from taking it intact, they burned Valencia to the ground.

The Poem of the Cid is the best evidence we have of how far the legend of the Cid had developed forty years after Rodrigo's death. The author celebrates in the Cid not only the hero who defeated Yúsuf and stemmed the second African invasion of the peninsula; with considerable historical justification he presents the Campeador as the type of most of the virtues which in that era most impressed the people of feudal Spain. The Cid is seen not only as the unconquerable defender of Christendom, but as the champion of the Christian feudal order itself; proof of this is his loyalty to King Alfonso, even when according to feudal law all his obligations toward the King had been dissolved. His moderation, self-control, magnanimity, dignity, piety, and of course honor are emphasized by the poet. And it is important to notice that the Cid is presented as a hero of relatively humble origins, that the real villains of the piece are arrogant members of the upper courtly nobility, and that the Cid triumphs over them in the two ways that mattered to the Christians of feudal Spain: by force and by law. The same cast of sympathy is apparent in the account of the Cid's battle with Ramón Berenguér, where a band of "ill-shod outcasts" defeats and humiliates a highborn braggart.

A nation's character is projected more or less directly into the figure it idealizes as its national hero, and it was ultimately the Spanish character, at least of the period between the twelfth century and the Renaissance, that made the legend of the Campeador and continued to see Rodrigo as the national hero long after the order that he defended had changed.

The body of literature which, in the five hundred years after his death, grew around the figure of the Cid is unique in that it comprises a complete cycle. First, there are the historic facts—such as remain. Then the anonymous epics of the twelfth century; the *Poema* was not even the only poem of its period about the Cid. Then, for several hundred years, the ballads of the Cid. Even the verse form of the ballads is a direct continuation of the verse form of the popular epics. As an example, here is a translation of one of the most dramatic of the Cid ballads, describing a completely legendary episode. The ballad begins just after the death of the Cid; Valencia is threatened by a great army under the command of King Búcar.

> ### The Cid's vassals, mounting his body
> ### upon Babieca, defeat Búcar

> Dead lies that good Cid
> Rodrigo of Bivar.
> Gil Díaz, his good servant,
> Will do as he was bidden.
> He will embalm his body,
> And rigid and stiff it was left;
> Its face is beautiful,
> Of great beauty and well colored,
> Its two eyes equally open,
> Its beard dressed with great care;
> It does not appear to be dead,
> But seems to be still alive,
> And to make it stay upright

Gil Díaz used this cunning:
He set it in a saddle
With a board between its shoulders
And at its breast another,
And at the sides these joined together:
They went under the arms
And covered the back of the head.
This was behind, and another
Came up as far as the beard,
Holding the body upright,
So that it leaned to no side.
Twelve days have passed
Since the Cid's life ended.
His followers armed themselves
To ride out to battle
Against that Moorish king Búcar
And the rabble he led.
When it was midnight
The body, thus as it was,
They placed upon Babieca
And onto the horse tied it.
Erect and upright it sits,
It looked as though it were living,
With breeches on its legs
Embroidered black and white,
Resembling the hose he had worn
When he was alive.
They dressed it in garments
Displaying needlework,
And his shield, at the neck,
Swung with its device.
A helmet on its head
Of painted parchment
Looks as though it were iron,
So well it was fashioned.
In the right hand the sword Tizona
Was cunningly tied,
It was a wonder to watch it
Go forward in the raised hand.
On one side rode the bishop,

The famous Don Jerome,
On the other Gil Díaz,
Who guided Babieca.
Don Pedro Bermúdez rode forth
With the Cid's banner raised,
With four hundred nobles
In his company:
Then went forth the main file
With as many again for escort;
The Cid's corpse rode forth
With a brave company.
One hundred are the guardians
Who rode with the honored corpse,
Behind it goes Doña Jimena
With all her company,
With six hundred knights
There to be her guard:
They go in silence, and so softly
You would say they were less than twenty.
Now they have left Valencia,
The clear day has dawned;
Alvar Fáñez was the first
Who charged with fury
Upon the great force of the Moors
Assembled with Búcar.
He found before him
A beautiful Mooress,
Skilled at shooting
Arrows from a quiver
With a Turkish bow;
Star was what they called her
Because of her excellence
At striking with the javelin.
She was the first
Who took horse and rode forward
With a hundred others like her,
Valiant and daring.
With fury the Cid's vassals charged them
And left them dead on the ground.
King Búcar has seen them,

And the other kings who are with him.
They are filled with wonder
At the sight of the Christian host.
To them it looks as though
There are seventy thousand knights
All white as snow,
And one who fills them with dread,
Grown now more huge than ever,
Who rides on a white horse,
A crimson cross on his breast,
In his hand a white signal;
The sword looks like a flame
To torment the Moors;
Great slaughter it wields among them,
They flee, they do not wait.
King Búcar and his kings
Abandon the field;
They make straight for the sea
Where the ships were left;
The Cid's knights charge after them.
Not one of them escaped,
All gasped and sank in the sea;
More than ten thousand drowned,
All rushing there together,
Not one of them embarked.
Of the kings, twenty were killed;
Búcar escaped, fleeing;
The Cid's vassals seize the tents
And much gold and much silver.
The poorest was made rich
With what they took there.
They set out for Castile,
As the good Cid had commanded;
They have arrived at San Pedro,
San Pedro of Cerdeña;
There they left the body of the Cid
To whom all Spain has paid honor.

Finally, as the last phase of the cycle, in the great age of the Spanish drama there is Guillén de Castro's two-part play *Las Mocedades*

del Cid (The Youth of the Cid). The connection between popular and cultivated poetry, which was one of the great strengths of Spanish literature in its great age, could scarcely be better exemplified: the basic verse form of Spanish classical drama grew directly out of the ballad form, and Guillén de Castro, like many other dramatists, based his story on incidents in the ballads. It was Guillén de Castro's plays which served as a model for Corneille's *Le Cid*.

In the whole cycle, the most magnificent single work is the oldest, the *Poema del Cid* itself. The author's governing design is simple: the *Poema* as a whole celebrates the rise of Rodrigo from his exile in disgrace from Castile to a position which represented, to twelfth-century feudal Spain, very nearly as complete a triumph as a human being not born to royalty could conceivably achieve this side of the grave. The poet simplifies history, but where he describes historical events he does so with considerable accuracy.

The poem is divided into three parts, or *cantares*. The first relates the cause of the Cid's disgrace and banishment, and his early triumphs in exile, culminating in his defeat of the Count of Barcelona. The second *cantar* describes his conquest of Valencia, his reconciliation with the King, and the marriage of his daughters to the two Heirs of Carrión, of the Beni-Gómez Clan. The third *cantar* tells how his two sons-in-law beat and abandoned the girls to insult the Campeador; how he was avenged on them, both in the royal court with the King sitting in judgment and in a trial-by-combat; and finally, how the Cid's daughters were remarried to the Princes of Navarre and Aragón.

Numerous incidents in the poem—such as the story of the coffers of sand in the first *cantar* and several episodes in the third *cantar*—are fictitious. On the other hand, most of the battles, sieges, and other military encounters in the poem actually took place, and a list of the characters who have been identified as historical personages would include very nearly all the names mentioned by the poet.

The vocabulary of the *Poema* is small; the language is simple; there is little ornament of any kind. The versification relies on two things chiefly: rhythm and the use of assonance. I have felt that of these two, the rhythm was the more important, and I have tried to render the poem into an English line which would give some sense of the strength and sweep of the original.

Within the *cantares,* the poem is subdivided into groups of lines, known as *laisses,* all ending on the same vowel sound. I have not duplicated this scheme in the English version, since I was certain that too much would have to be sacrificed to the demands of making all the lines, in passages running in some cases to a hundred and twenty-five lines and more, end on the same assonance. Occasionally, where it seemed important, I have tried to indicate the effect of the assonance in the original; and in general I have tried to use a certain amount of assonance within the lines to suggest some of the effects which the original gets in other ways.

Apart from that, I have tried to put the poem into English that would be neither deathly archaic nor pointlessly and jarringly colloquial. In doing so I have kept as close to the literal meaning of the original as I have known how to. In most places I have also kept the use of present and past tenses as they are in the original. It appears that the poet, following the traditions of the kind of poetry he was writing, used the historic present, in general, to bring details into the foreground, and the past tenses to hold them at a remove. (I am indebted to Professor Stephen Gilman of the Modern Languages Department of Harvard University for pointing this out to me). I have not wanted to try to improve upon the poet's system of shading for the sake of a minor degree of clarity.

I wish to thank Douglas Cleverdon, first, for commissioning this translation for the Third Programme of the British Broadcasting Corporation, on which it was broadcast. I cannot adequately express my gratitude to Professor Gilman, who found time and patience to go through the translation with me and to correct blunders which I would rather not remember—though I must say at once that he is not responsible for any that may still remain.

Anyone who has any pleasure or profit from the *Poema* is obligated to the great modern Spanish scholar, Ramón Menéndez Pidal; I should like just to indicate the extent of my debt. I have used his reconstructed text, in the Clásicos Castellanos edition, for my translation, and his reproduction of the original text (*Cantar de Mio Cid*) for reference. Without his notes to both texts, and his glossary, I would often have been at a loss. His *La España del Cid* is an indispensable guide to the background of the poem. Anyone familiar with his *El Cid Campeador* will realize how closely I have relied on that book for the biographical and historical matter in this preface. Finally, scattered essays of his on such subjects as the formation of the Spanish language and his book on the popular epics and the bards that sang them (*Poesía Juglaresca y Juglares*) have provided me, in the course of the work, not only with relevant information, but with excitement.

W. S. MERWIN

THE POEM OF
THE CID

THE FIRST CANTAR

The Exile

[Since the opening pages of the poem are lost, the beginning of the story must be supplied from the *Chronicle of Twenty Kings;* the part of that chronicle relating to the Cid had, in the first place, been translated from the poem into Latin prose. The passage immediately preceding the beginning of Per Abbat's manuscript has been reconstructed in verse from the chronicle.]

King Alfonso sends the Cid to collect tribute from the Moorish King of Seville. The King of Seville is attacked by Count García Ordóñez of Castile. The Cid, defending the Castilian King's Moorish vassal, defeats García Ordóñez at Cabra and imprisons and humiliates him. The Cid returns to Castile with the tribute, but his enemies make mischief between him and the King. The King banishes the Cid.

King Alfonso sent Ruy Díaz, My Cid, to collect the annual tribute from the Kings of Córdova and Seville. Almutamiz, King of Seville, and Almudafar, King of Granada, at that time were bitter enemies and wished each other's death. And there were then with Almudafar, King of Granada, these noblemen who supported him: the Count Don García Ordóñez, and Fortún Sánchez, the son-in-law of King García of Navarre, and Lope Sánchez; and each of these noblemen with all his power supported Almudafar, and went against Almutamiz, King of Seville.

Ruy Díaz Cid, when he heard that they were coming against the King of Seville, who was a vassal and tributary of his lord King Alfonso, took it ill and was much grieved; and he sent letters to all of them begging them not to come against the King of Seville nor destroy his land, because of the allegiance they owed to King Alfonso; for they might know if they continued to do so, King Alfonso could not do otherwise than to come to the aid of his vassal, who was his tributary. The King of Granada and the noblemen took no note of the Cid's letters, but using violence they destroyed all the land of the King of Seville as far as the castle of Cabra.

When Ruy Díaz Cid saw this, he took all the force of Christians and Moors that he could muster, and went against the King of Granada to expel him from the land of the King of Seville. And the King of Granada and the noblemen who were with him, when they knew that he was coming thus, sent to tell him that they would not leave the land on his account. Ruy Díaz Cid, when he heard this, could not rest until he had set upon them, and he went against them and fought with them in the field, and the battle lasted from nine o'clock until midday, and the Moors and Christians on the side of the King of Granada suffered great slaughter, and the Cid overcame them and forced them to flee from the field. And in this battle the Cid took prisoner the Count Don García Ordóñez and pulled out part of his beard, and took prisoner many other gentlemen and so many of the ordinaries that they lost count; and the Cid held them three days and then released them all. While he held them prisoner he sent his men to gather together the belongings and things of value which remained on the field; afterwards the Cid with all his company and all his gains returned to Almutamiz, King of Seville, and gave to him and to all his Moors whatever they knew to be theirs, and whatever they wished to take besides. And always after that, both Moors and Christians called this same Ruy Díaz of Bivar the Cid Campeador, which is to say, the warrior, the winner of battles.

Then Almutamiz gave him many fine presents and the tribute for which he had come, and the Cid with all the tribute went back to King Alfonso, his lord. The King received him very well and was highly pleased with him and most satisfied with all he had done there. Because of this, many were envious and sought to do him evil, and spoke against him to the King.

The King, who already nursed an ancient rancor against him, came to believe them, and sent letters to the Cid telling him that he must leave the kingdom. The Cid, when he had read the letters, was much grieved, and yet he did not wish to disobey, although he was allowed only nine days' grace in which to leave the kingdom.

1

The Cid calls his vassals together. They will go with him into exile. The Cid's farewell to Bivar

[*He sent for his family and his vassals and told them of the King's ordering him to leave his lands, and that he was given no more than nine days in which to go, and that he wished to know from them which of them would go with him and which would stay.*]

[*Here Per Abbat's manuscript begins*]

"and those who come with me   God's good mercy sustain,
and those who remain here   I shall be content with them."
    Then spoke Alvar Fáñez,   his first cousin:
"We shall go with you, Cid,   through deserts, through towns,
and never fail you   while we are whole in limb;
with you we shall wear out   horses and beasts of burden
and our goods and our garments
and serve you always   as faithful liege men."
Then to what Don Alvaro had said   all gave their consent;
My Cid thanked them deeply   for all they had there spoken.
    My Cid went out from Bivar,   toward Burgos riding,
and left his palaces   disinherited and barren.

His eyes,   grievously weeping,
he turned his head   and looked back upon them.
He saw doors standing open   and gates without fastenings,
the porches empty   without cloaks or coverings
and without falcons   and without molted hawks.
He sighed, My Cid,   for he felt great affliction.

He spoke, My Cid,   well, and with great moderation.
"Thanks be to Thee, our Father   Who art in Heaven!
My evil enemies   have wrought this upon me."

2

Omens on the road to Burgos

There they set spur   there they released the reins.
At the gate of Bivar   on their right hand the crow flew;
as they rode into Burgos   it flew on their left.
My Cid raised his head   and shrugged his shoulders:
"Rejoice, Alvar Fáñez,   though this exile is ours!
We shall come back to Castile   laden with honor."

3

The Cid enters Burgos

My Cid Ruy Díaz   rode into Burgos,
in his company   sixty pennons.
They crowded to see him,   women and men;
townsmen and their wives   sat at the windows
weeping from their eyes,   so great was their sorrow.
And one sentence only   was on every tongue:
"Were his lord but worthy,   God, how fine a vassal!"

4

*No one gives lodging to the Cid. Only one little girl speaks
to him to tell him he must leave. The Cid finds he must camp outside
the town, on the shingle of the river bed*

They would have asked him in gladly,   but did not dare,
for King Alfonso   cherished such anger.
His letter had come   to Burgos the night before
with all formality   and sealed with a great seal:
that to My Cid Ruy Díaz   no one must give shelter,
that who should do so,   let him learn the truth of the matter,
he would lose all that he had   and the eyes out of his face
and, what is more, they would lose   their bodies and their souls.
Those Christian people,   great sorrow they had

hiding from My Cid,   for none dared say a word.
  The Campeador   rode up to the inn;
when he reached the portal   he found it closed against him.
For fear of King Alfonso   they had concluded thus:
unless he break the door   on no account admit him.
Those with My Cid   shouted out for them to open,
those within   would not answer them.
My Cid spurred forward,   to the door he came,
drew his foot from the stirrup,   kicked a gash in the wood;
the door was well secured   and did not open.
  A little girl of nine appeared in sight:
"Ah, Campeador, in a good hour   you first girded on sword!
The King forbids us this;   last night his letter came here,
with all formality   and sealed with a great seal.
We dare not let you in   nor lodge you for any reason,
or we shall lose   our goods and our houses,
and besides these   the eyes out of our faces.
Cid, you will gain nothing   by our miseries;
but the Creator bless you   with all his holy virtues."
The child spoke this   and then turned back to her house.
Now the Cid can see that he finds   no grace in the King's eyes.
He went from the doorway   and spurred through Burgos;
at the Church of Santa Maria,   there he stepped from his horse;
there he knelt down,   from his heart he prayed.
The prayer ended,   once more he mounted,
rode out of the gate,   passed over the Arlanzón.
Outside the town of Burgos   at the river bed he stayed,
set his tent   and there dismounted.
My Cid Ruy Díaz,   who in good hour girded on sword,
when no house would have him   pitched camp on the shingle,
and a goodly company   encamped around him.
There he camped, My Cid   as in a wilderness.
In the town of Burgos   the law forbade
that he should so much as buy   anything that was food;
no one dared sell him   a pennyworth of bread.

5

Martín Antolínez comes from Burgos to bring food to the Cid

Martín Antolínez,   the accomplished man of Burgos,
to My Cid and his men   brought bread and wine
which was not bought   because it was his own;
of all manner of food   they had ample provision.
He was pleased, My Cid   the accomplished Campeador,
and all the others   who were in his train.
Martín Antolínez spoke,   you will hear what he said:
"Ah, Campeador,   in a good hour you were born!
We stay here tonight,   we must be gone by morning,
for I shall be accused   of this service I have done;
in King Alfonso's anger   I shall be included.
If I escape with you   alive and sound of limb,
sooner or later the King   will love me as a friend;
if not, all that I leave,   I value at nothing."

6

The Cid, impoverished, resorts to Martín Antolínez's cunning.
The coffers filled with sand

My Cid spoke,   who in good hour girded on sword:
"Martín Antolínez,   you are a hardy lance!
If I live,   I will double your pay.
Gone is my gold   and all my silver;
you can see plainly   that I carry nothing
and I need money   for all my followers;
I am forced to this   since freely I can have nothing.
With your aid   I will build two coffers;
we shall stuff them with sand   to make them heavier,
stud them with nails   and cover them with worked leather,
the leather crimson   and the nails well gilded.

7

The coffers destined to obtain money from the two Jews of Burgos

Go in haste and find me   Raquel and Vidas, and say:
'Since in Burgos I may not buy, and the King's disfavor pursues
    me,
I cannot carry this wealth   for it is too heavy.
I must put it in pawn   for whatever is reasonable.
So that no Christians may see it,   come and fetch it in by night.'
Let the Creator see it   and all His saints besides;
I cannot do otherwise   and for this have little heart."

8

Martín Antolínez goes back into Burgos

    Martín Antolínez   without delay
went into Burgos,   into the castle.
For Raquel and Vidas   he asked immediately.

9

*Martín Antolínez's negotiations with the Jews. They go to
the Cid's tent. They carry away the coffers of sand*

    Raquel and Vidas   were both in the same place
counting over the goods   that they had gained.
Martín Antolínez approached   with all shrewdness.
"Are you there, Raquel and Vidas,   my dear friends?
I would speak with you both   in secret confidence."
They did not keep him waiting;   all three withdrew together.
"Raquel and Vidas,   give me your hands,
swear you will not betray me   to Moors or Christians;
I shall make you rich forever,   you will lack for nothing.
The Campeador   was sent for the tribute;
he seized much wealth   and great possessions.
He kept for himself   a considerable portion,
whence he has come to this,   for he was accused.
He has two coffers   full of pure gold.
You know full well   the King's disfavor pursues him.

He has left houses and palaces,   all his inheritance.
He cannot take these   for they would be discovered.
The Campeador   will leave the coffers in your hands;
lend him, in money,   whatever is reasonable.
Take the coffers   into your safekeeping,
but you must both pledge your faiths,   with a great oath,
for the rest of this year   not to look inside them."
    Raquel and Vidas   conferred together:
"In any business   we must gain something.
Of course we know   that he gained something;
in the lands of the Moors   he seized much booty.
His sleep is uneasy   who has money with him.
As for the coffers,   let us take both of them
and put them in a place   where no one will sniff them.
"But tell us, concerning the Cid,   what sum will content him,
what interest will he give us   for the whole of this year?"
Martín Antolínez answered   with all shrewdness:
"My Cid desires   whatever is reasonable;
he asks little of you   for leaving his wealth in safety.
Needy men from all sides   are gathering around him;
he requires   six hundred marks."
Raquel and Vidas said,   "We will gladly give that many."
"You see, night is falling   the Cid has no time,
we have need   that you give us the marks."
Raquel and Vidas said,   "Business is not done that way,
but by first taking   and giving afterwards."
Martín Antolínez said,   "I am content with that.
Come, both of you,   to the famous Campeador,
and we will help you,   as is only just,
to carry away the coffers   to where you can keep them safely
so that neither Moors nor Christians   may know where they lie."
Raquel and Vidas said,   "That will content us.
When the coffers are here,   you may take the six hundred marks."
    Martín Antolínez   rode off at once
with Raquel and Vidas   willingly and gladly.
He did not go by the bridge,   but through the water,
so that no man in Burgos   should get wind of it.
    They have come to the tent   of the famous Campeador;
they kiss the hands of the Cid   when they enter.
My Cid smiled   and spoke with them:

"Greetings, Don Raquel and Vidas,   had you forgotten me?
I must depart into exile   for the King's disfavor pursues me.
From the look of things   you will have something of mine;
as long as you live   you will not be paupers."
Raquel and Vidas   kissed My Cid's hands.
Martín Antolínez   sealed the bargain.
Six hundred marks   they would give for those coffers
and would guard them well   till the end of the year,
and to this they vowed their consent   and to this swore:
that should they break their promise   and open them before,
the Cid should not give so much   as one wretched farthing for
        their profit.
Martín Antolínez said,   "Carry them off at once.
Take them, Raquel and Vidas,   put them in your safe place;
I shall go with you   to bring back the money,
for My Cid must depart   before the cock sings."
When they went to load the coffers   you could see how great was
        their pleasure.
They could not lift them   although they were strong.
They rejoiced, Raquel and Vidas,   to have so much treasure;
they should be rich   as long as they lived.

10

The Jews leave the Cid. Martín Antolínez goes back
to Burgos with the Jews

Raquel has kissed   the hand of My Cid:
"Ah, Campeador,   in good hour you girded on sword!
You go from Castile   forth among strangers.
Such is your fortune   and great are your gains;
I kiss your hand   begging you to bring me
a skin of crimson leather,   Moorish and highly prized."
My Cid said, "Gladly,   from this moment it is ordered.
I will send it to you from there.   If not, count it against the
        coffers."
Raquel and Vidas   took up the coffers.
With Martín Antolínez   they went back to Burgos;
with all caution   they came to their house.
In the middle of the dwelling   a carpet was spread,
a sheet over it   pure white, of fine cloth.

At the first fling there fell   three hundred marks of silver.
Don Martino counted   and without weighing took them;
the other three hundred   in gold they paid him.
Don Martino has five squires.   He loaded them all.
You will hear what he said   when this was done:
"Raquel and Vidas,   in your hands are the coffers;
I who gained them for you   have well deserved my commission."

11

The Cid, provided with money by Martín Antolínez,
makes ready to march

    Raquel and Vidas   walked to one side:
"Let us make him a fine gift   since he found this for us.
Martín Antolínez,   renowned man of Burgos,
we will make you a fine gift.   You have deserved your commission;
we will give you enough to make trousers,   a good cloak and rich
       tunic.
We will make you a present   of thirty marks,
as is only proper   and what you have deserved,
since you shall testify   to this that we have agreed."
Don Martino thanked them   and took the money;
he was glad to go from the house   and leave them both.
    He has gone out of Burgos,   passed over the Arlanzón
and come to the tent of him   who in good hour was born.
    The Cid received him   with his arms open:
"Welcome, Martín Antolínez,   my faithful vassal!
May I see the day   when you will receive something from me!"
"I come, Campeador,   with all care and prudence;
you have gained six hundred   and I thirty.
Bid them strike the tent   and let us leave at once;
in San Pedro of Cardeña   let the cock sing to us.
We shall see your wife   of gentle birth and good report,
rest for a little   then quit the kingdom,
as we must, for the term   of the sentence draws near."

12

The Cid mounts and bids farewell to the Cathedral of Burgos,
promising a thousand Masses at the altar of the Virgin

These words said,   the tent is struck.
My Cid and his followers   mount at once.
He turned his horse   toward Santa María,
raised his right hand,   crossed himself:
"Praise be to Thee, O God,   Who guide earth and sky;
thy grace be with me,   glorious Santa María!
Now I depart Castile   since the King's wrath pursues me,
and know not if I shall return   in all my days.
Thy favor be with me,   thou Glorious, on my going;
aid and sustain me   by night and by day;
Grant thou as I beg,   and if fortune bear with me,
fine gifts on thy altar,   rich offerings I shall lay,
and a thousand Masses   have sung in thy chantry."

13

Martín Antolínez returns to the city

He the excellent one   bade hearty farewell.
They release the reins   and set spur to their horses.
Martín Antolínez,   the loyal man of Burgos,
said, "I shall see my wife,   who is all my solace,
and leave instructions   as to what must be done.
I care not if the King   should seize my possessions.
I shall be with you   before the sun shines."

14

The Cid goes to Cardeña to say good-by to his family

Don Martino turned toward Burgos,   and My Cid spurred on
with all speed   toward San Pedro of Cardeña
with those knights   who do his pleasure.
The cocks quicken their song   and dawn is breaking
when the good Campeador   rode up to San Pedro;
the abbot Don Sancho,   a servant of the Lord,
was saying his matins   in the gray morning.
And there Doña Jimena   with five gentlewomen
was praying to Saint Peter   and to the Creator praying:
"Thou Who guidest all creatures,   bless My Cid the Campeador."

15

The monks of Cardeña receive the Cid. Jimena and her
daughters come to greet the outcast

They called at the door,   the message was taken;
the abbot Don Sancho,   God, how great was his rejoicing!
There was running in the courtyard   with candles and torches
to receive with gladness   him who in good hour was born.
"Thanks be to God, My Cid,"   said the abbot Don Sancho,
"that I see you before me   to share my dwelling."
My Cid answered,   who in good hour was born:
"My thanks, abbot,   I am well pleased with you;
I would have a meal made ready   for myself and my followers,
and since I must leave this land   I give you fifty marks;
if I live,   you shall have two for each of these.
I would not occasion this abbey   a farthing of loss;
take these hundred marks   for Doña Jimena,
wait on her this full year   and on her daughters and ladies.
My two small daughters,   clasp them safe in your arms;
they and my wife,   care for them closely.
I commend them to you,   to you, abbot Don Sancho.
If this money runs out   or you need anything,
yet provide for them well;   I shall pay accordingly,
for each mark you spend,   four to the abbey."
The abbot agreed   to all of this gladly.
Behold where Doña Jimena   is coming with her daughters,
each carried and brought   in the arms of a nurse.
And Doña Jimena knelt down   on both knees before him.
She kissed his hands,   weeping from her eyes:
"Grace, Campeador,   who in good hour was born!
Because of evil meddlers   you are sent into exile."

16

Doña Jimena laments the helplessness in which her daughters
will be left. The Cid hopes to be able to see them
honorably married

"Grace, Campeador   of the excellent beard!
Here before you   are your daughters and I,

and they in their infancy,   and their days are tender,
with these my ladies   who wait upon me.
I know well   that you pause here merely,
and in this life   must part from us.
In the name of Santa María,   give us counsel!"
    He stretched out his hands,   he of the splendid beard;
his two daughters   in his arms he took,
drew them to his heart   for he loved them dearly.
He weeps from his eyes   and sighs deeply:
"Ah, Doña Jimena,   my perfect wife,
I love you   as I do my own soul.
You know well   we must part in this life;
I shall go from here   and you will stay behind.
May it please God   and Santa María
one day with my own hands   I may give my daughters in
              marriage,
and may good fortune attend me   and few days be left me
that you, my honored wife,   may receive once more my homage."

17

A hundred Castilians gather in Burgos to join the Cid

    They laid a great banquet   for the good Campeador.
They clanged and pealed   the bells of San Pedro.
Through all Castile   the cry goes:
"He is leaving the land,   My Cid the Campeador."
Some leave houses   and others honors.
On that day   at the bridge on the Arlanzón
a hundred fifteen horsemen   are come together,
all of them asking   for My Cid the Campeador.
Martín Antolínez   rode up where they were.
They set off for San Pedro   to him who was born in good hour.

18

*The hundred Castilians arrive at Cardeña and make themselves
vassals of the Cid. He makes ready to continue his march in
the morning. The matins at Cardeña. Jimena's prayer.
The Cid's farewell to his family. His last instructions to
the abbot of Cardeña. The Cid sets out on his exile; night
falls after he has crossed the Duero*

When My Cid of Bivar   heard the news
that his band was growing,   that his strength was increasing,
he mounted in haste   and rode out to receive them;
he broke into smiles   as soon as he saw them.
Each of them came up   and kissed his hand.
My Cid spoke   with all his heart:
"I pray to God   our Father in heaven
that you who for me have left   home and possessions,
before I die,   may receive from me some gain;
that all you lose now   twofold may be returned."
My Cid rejoiced   that his company had grown.
All rejoiced   who were there with him.
    Six days of the sentence   already have run;
three remain   and afterwards none.
The King has sent   to keep watch on My Cid,
so that if when the time was up   they could take him in the land,
not for silver nor gold   might he escape.
The day went   and night came in.
He called together   all his horsemen:
"Hear me, my knights,   let no heart be heavy.
I own little;   I would give you your portion.
Listen and learn   what must be done:
In the morning   when the cocks sing,
have the horses saddled   without delay;
in San Pedro   the good abbot will ring matins
and sing us the Mass   of the Holy Trinity.
We shall set out   when Mass has been sung,
for time runs out   and we have far to go."
All will do   as the Cid has commanded.
The night passes   and morning comes;
at the second cock   they saddle their horses.
    With all dispatch   the matins are rung;
My Cid and his wife   into the church have gone.
On the steps before the altar   Doña Jimena knelt down
praying to the Creator   with all her heart
that God might keep from harm   My Cid the Campeador:
"Glorious Lord, Father   Who art in heaven,
Who made heaven and earth   and the sea the third day,
Who made stars and moon   and the sun to warm us,
Who became incarnate   in Santa María Thy mother,

Who, as was Thy will,   appeared in Bethlehem;
shepherds praised Thee   and glorified Thee.
Three kings of Arabia   came to adore Thee,
Melchior   and Gaspar and Balthasar,
gold and frankincense and myrrh   with glad hearts they offered
          Thee;
Thou didst save Jonas   when he fell into the sea,
Thou savedst Daniel   from the evil den of lions,
Thou in Rome savedst   lord Saint Sebastian,
Thou didst save Saint Susannah   from the lying criminal;
Father in heaven, Thou didst walk   thirty-two years on earth
showing miracles   of which we must tell:
Thou didst from water make wine   and bread from stones,
Thou didst raise Lazarus   as was Thy intention,
Thou didst let the Jews take Thee;   on Mount Calvary
where it is called Golgotha   on a cross they hanged Thee
and, one on each side,   two thieves with Thee.
One is in paradise,   the other did not go there.
Much grace didst Thou work   on the cross hanging:
Longinus was blind   and had never seen anything;
he thrust his spear in Thy side,   from which blood came,
which down the shaft ran   and anointed his hands,
which covered his arm   and to his face came;
he opened his eyes   and looked in all directions
and believed in Thee then,   from whence came his salvation.
Thou from the sepulchre   didst rise again,
descended into hell,   as was Thy will,
burst open the doors   and saved the holy fathers.
Thou art King of Kings   and of the whole world Father.
I adore Thee and believe   with all my will,
and I pray to Saint Peter   that he may aid my prayer
that God may keep from harm   My Cid the Campeador.
Though we part now,   in this life may we come together."
     When the prayer was ended,   Mass was said.
They went out from the church   and made ready to ride.
My Cid went   and embraced Doña Jimena;
Doña Jimena   kissed My Cid's hand,
weeping;   she could not hold back the tears.
He turned and looked   upon his daughters.
"To God I commend you   and to the heavenly Father;

now we part. God knows   when we shall come together."
Weeping from his eyes,   you have never seen such grief,
thus parted the one from the others   as the nail from the Flesh.
    My Cid and his vassals   set off riding,
he looking behind him   delaying them all.
Minaya Alvar Fáñez   spoke with great wisdom:
"Cid, who in good hour were born   of mother, where is your
      strength?
We must be on our way;   this is idleness.
All these sorrows   will yet turn to joy:
God who gave us souls   will give us guidance."
    They turned and bade   the abbot Don Sancho
to serve Doña Jimena   and her two daughters
and all the ladies   who were with them there;
the abbot knew well   that he would be recompensed.
Don Sancho has turned   and Alvar Fáñez spoke:
"Abbot, if you meet with any   who would come with us,
tell them to take up our trail   and ride after us,
so that in wasteland or town   they may overtake us."
    They slackened the reins   and rode forward;
the time draws near   when they must quit the kingdom.
The Cid pitched camp   by Espinazo de Can;
that night from all hands   men flocked to go with him.
Next day in the morning   they rode on again.
He is leaving the land,   the loyal Campeador.
By the left of San Esteban,   a goodly city;
he passed through Alcubilla   on the edge of Castile;
to the path of Quinea   they came, and passed over;
at Navapalos   crossed over the Duero;
at the Figueruela   My Cid paused for the night.
Still from all hands   men gathered to go with him.

19

The last night in which the Cid sleeps in Castile.
An angel consoles the exile

There lay down, My Cid,   after night had come;
he slept so deeply   a dream seized him sweetly.
The angel Gabriel   came to him in a vision:
"Ride forward, Cid,   good Campeador,

for no man ever rode forth   at so propitious a moment;
as long as you live   that which is yours will prosper."
He crossed himself, My Cid,   when he awoke.

20

The Cid camps on the Castilian frontier

He made the sign of the cross,   and commended himself to
    God.
He was deeply glad   because of the dream he had dreamed.
Next day in the morning   they ride onward;
the last day of their time has come.   Know, after that there is no
    more.
By the mountains of Miedes   they were going to halt,
on the right the towers of Atienza,   which the Moors hold.

21

The tally of the Cid's followers

It was still day,   the sun not down,
When My Cid the Campeador   assembled his men.
Not counting the foot soldiers,   and brave men they were,
he counted three hundred lances,   each with its pennon.

22

*The Cid enters the Moorish kingdom of Toledo,
a tributary of King Alfonso's*

"Let the horses be fed early   and may the Creator keep you!
Let those who desire to, eat,   and those who do not, ride on.
We shall cross over that range,   high and forbidding;
this same night   we shall leave Alfonso's kingdom.
He who comes looking for us   may find us then."
    They crossed the range in the night,   and morning came,
and on the downward ridge   they began riding.
Halfway down a mountain   which was marvelous and high,
My Cid halted   and fed the horses their barley.
He told them all that he wished   to ride on all that night;
all were stout hearted   and good liege men

who for their lord   would do anything.
Before night fell   they set off again;
My Cid pressed on   so that none might discover them.
They rode forward by night   without resting.
Where it is called Castejón,   on the bank of the Henares,
My Cid lay in ambush   with those who were with him.

23

The plan of the campaign. Castejón falls into the
Cid's power by surprise. The vanguard goes against Alcalá

All that night   My Cid lies in ambush.
Alvar Fáñez Minaya   thus advised them:
"Ah, Cid, in good hour   you girded on sword!
With one hundred   of our company,
after we have surprised   and taken Castejón,
do you remain there   and be our fixed base.
Give me two hundred   to go on a raid;
with God and good fortune   we shall take rich spoils."
The Campeador said,   "You speak well, Minaya.
You with two hundred   ride out raiding;
take Alvar Alvarez   and Alvar Salvadórez
and Galindo García,   who is a hardy lance,
all of them brave knights;   let them go with Minaya.
Ride forward boldly,   let no fear detain you.
Ride down along the Fita   and along the Guadalajara,
take your raiders   as far as Alcalá
and let them carry off   all that is of value,
leaving nothing behind   out of fear of the Moors.
I with the hundred   shall stay here behind
and hold Castejón,   where we will be secure.
If on your raiding foray   any trouble befalls you,
send word at once   to me here behind;
all Spain will talk   of the aid I shall bring."
    They have been named   who will ride out on the raid,
and they who will remain   with My Cid in the fixed base.
The dawn goes gray   and the morning comes,
the sun came forth.   God, how fair was the dawn!
All began to stir   in Castejón;
they opened the gates   and went out of the town

to see to their tasks   and all their property.
All have gone out   and left the gates open,
few there are   who remain in Castejón;
all who have gone out   are scattered abroad.
The Campeador   came out of hiding;
he rode around Castejón   all the way.
He has seized   the Moors and their women
and those cattle   that were about there.
My Cid Don Rodrigo   rode up to the gate;
those there to defend it,   when they saw the attack,
were taken with fear,   and the gate was unguarded.
My Cid Ruy Díaz   rode in at the gate;
in his hand he carried   a naked sword.
Fifteen Moors he killed   who came in his way,
took Castejón   and its gold and its silver.
His knights arrive   with the spoils;
they give it to My Cid;   all this, to them, is nothing.
    Behold now the two hundred and three   in the raiding party;
they ride on without pausing   and plunder all the land.
As far as Alcalá,   went the banner of Minaya,
and from there with the spoils   they return again,
up along the Henares   and along the Guadalajara.
Such great spoils   they bring back with them:
many flocks   of sheep and of cattle,
and clothing   and great quantities of other riches.
Forward comes   the banner of Minaya;
no one dares   attack the band of raiders.
That company returns   with its plunder;
see, they are in Castejón,   where the Campeador was.
Leaving the castle secure,   the Campeador rode out,
rode out to receive them   with his company.
He greeted Minaya   with his arms open:
"Have you returned, Alvar Fáñez,   hardy lance!
Wherever I send you   I may well be hopeful.
Your booty and mine together,   of all we have gained
a fifth is yours   if you will take it, Minaya."

24

*Minaya will take no part of the booty, and makes a
solemn vow*

"I thank you from my heart,   famous Campeador,
for this fifth part   which you offer me;
it would please   Alfonso the Castilian.
I give it up   and return it to you.
I make a vow   to God Who is in heaven:
Until I have satisfied myself   on my good horse
with joining battle   in the field with the Moors,
with handling the lance   and taking up the sword,
with the blood running   to above my elbow,
before Ruy Díaz   the famous warrior,
I shall not take from you   a wretched farthing.
Until by my hand you have won   something truly of value,
behold, I leave everything   in your hands."

25

*The Cid sells his fifth to the Moors. He does not wish
to fight with King Alfonso*

All they had taken   was gathered together.
My Cid, who girded on sword   in a good hour, considered
that King Alfonso   would send forces to follow him
and would seek to work him evil   with all his armies.
He bade them divide   all they had taken;
he bade his partitioners   parcel it out.
There good fortune   befell his knights:
a hundred marks of silver   went to each of them,
and to the foot soldiers   half as much without stint;
all the fifth part   remained to My Cid.
He could not sell it there   nor give it as a present,
nor did he wish to have men or women   as slaves in his train.
He spoke with those of Castejón,   he sent to Hita and
        Guadalajara,
to learn how much   they would give him for his fifth;
even with what they gave   their gain would be great.
The Moors offered   three thousand marks of silver.

My Cid was content   with this offering.
On the third day   they paid it all.

   My Cid was of the opinion,   with all his company,
that in the castle   there would not be room for them
and that it might be held,   but there would be no water.
"Let us leave these Moors in peace   for their treaty is written;
King Alfonso will seek us out   with all his host.
Hear me, my men and Minaya,   I would quit Castejón!"

26

*The Cid proceeds to the lands of Zaragoza, which are dependencies
of the Moorish King of Valencia*

   "Let no one take amiss   what I have to say:
We cannot remain   in Castejón;
King Alfonso is near   and will come seeking us.
But as for the castle,   I would not lay it waste;
I wish to set free   a hundred Moors and a hundred Moorish
          women,
that they may speak no evil of me   since I took it from them.
You have full share, every one,   and no one is still unrewarded.
Tomorrow in the morning   we must ride on;
I do not wish to fight   with Alfonso my lord."
All are contented   with what My Cid spoke.
All went away rich   from the castle they had taken;
the Moors and their women   are giving them their blessings.
   They go up the Henares   as far as they can,
passed through Alcarria   and went on from there;
by the Caves of Anguita   they are going,
crossed over the waters   into the Plain of Taranz
and through those lands below there   as far as they extend.
Between Ariza and Cetina   My Cid pitched his tent.
Great spoils he takes   in the lands through which he goes;
the Moors do not know   what their intention is.
My Cid of Bivar   the next day moved on;
beyond Alhama,   beyond La Hoz he rode on,
beyond Bubierca   to Ateca farther on.
Close to Alcocer   My Cid came to camp
on a round hill   that stood high and strong.

The stream Jalón around them,   none could cut off their water.
My Cid Don Rodrigo   thinks to take Alcocer.

27

The Cid encamps close to Alcocer

He mans the hill strongly,   makes strong the encampments,
some along the hillside,   some near the water.
The good Campeador,   who in good hour girded on sword,
set all his men   to digging a moat
on all sides of the hill   down near the water,
so that by day or night   they might not be surprised
and that the Moors might know that My Cid   meant to remain
        there.

28

The Moors' fear

Through all those lands   the news had gone
that My Cid the Campeador   had built an encampment there.
He has gone out from the Christians   and come among the Moors;
all about their encampment   none dares work the land.
My Cid and all his vassals   begin to rejoice:
the castle of Alcocer   is beginning to pay tribute.

29

The Campeador takes Alcocer by a stratagem

Those of Alcocer   now send tribute to My Cid,
and those of Ateca   and of the village of Terrer
and of Calatayud,   you may know, though it weighed heavy on
        them.
Fully fifteen weeks   My Cid remained there.
When My Cid saw that Alcocer   would not yield to him,
he thought of a stratagem   and wasted no time:
He left one tent standing,   he carried off the rest;
he went down the Jalón   with his banner raised,
his men in their armor   with their swords girded,
shrewdly   to take them by ambush.

God, how those of Alcocer   rejoiced to see it!
"My Cid has no more provisions   of bread and barley.
He can hardly bear off the tents,   he has left one standing.
He makes off, My Cid,   like one fleeing from a rout.
Let us fall upon him   and we shall seize great gains
before he is taken   by those of the town of Terrer,
for if those of Terrer take him   they will give us nothing.
He shall return twofold   the tribute we sent him."
They went out from Alcocer,   their haste was unseemly.
When My Cid saw them   he rode on as from a rout.
    He went down the stream Jalón   with his men.
Those of Alcocer said,   "Our plunder is escaping!"
They ran out of the town,   all, big and little,
thirsting to take him;   beyond that, not thinking.
They left the gates open   with none to guard them.
The Campeador   turned his face round;
he judged the distance   between the Moors and their castle,
bade them turn with the banner.   With all speed they rode
        forward.
"Charge them, knights,   let none lag behind.
With the Creator's blessing   ours is the gain!"
Halfway across the meadow   they came together.
God, their hearts were glad   upon that morning!
My Cid and Alvar Fáñez   rode on ahead;
they had good horses,   you may know, that went at their pleasure;
they rode clear between   the Moors and the castle.
My Cid's vassals   attacked without mercy;
they kill three hundred Moors   in a short time.
Those who are in the ambush,   giving great shouts,
leaving those who are in the van,   charged upon the castle,
halted at the door   bare swords in their hands.
Then their own men rode up,   for they had routed them.
Know, in this manner   My Cid took Alcocer.

30

The Cid's banner floats over Alcocer

    Pedro Bermúdez came   with the banner in his hand;
he flew it from the peak,   from the highest point of all.

My Cid spoke, Ruy Díaz,   who in good hour was born:
"Thanks be to God in heaven   and to all His saints,
both horses and riders   now shall have better lodging."

31

The Cid's mercy toward the Moors

"Hear me, Alvar Fáñez   and all my men!
In this castle   we have taken great gains;
the Moors lie dead,   I see few living.
We cannot sell   the Moors and their women;
it would gain us nothing   to cut off their heads.
Let us take them in   for we are the lords here;
we shall live in their houses   and they shall wait upon us."

32

The King of Valencia, wishing to recover Alcocer,
sends an army against the Cid

My Cid is in Alcocer   with all he has taken;
he has sent back for the tent   which he left standing.
They are grieved in Ateca,   and those of Terrer are not merry,
and those of Calatayud,   you may know, are heavy hearted.
They have sent a message   to the King of Valencia,
telling how one who is called   My Cid Ruy Díaz of Bivar,
"whom King Alfonso   has banished from his kingdom,
came to camp near Alcocer   in a strong place,
drew us out into ambush   and has taken the castle.
If you send us no help   you will lose Ateca, lose Terrer,
lose Calatayud,   which cannot escape;
all will go ill   here on the bank of the Jalón
as well as in Jiloca   on the other side."
When King Tamín heard this   his heart was heavy.
"Three Kings of the Moors   are here with me;
let two without delay   proceed to the place,
take three thousand Moors   armed for battle.
Muster from the frontier   all who will come to your aid,
take him alive   and fetch him before me;
since he entered my lands   I will mete him his due."

Three thousand Moors   mount and ride off;
they came at night   to camp in Segorbe.
Next day in the morning   they ride on again;
they came at night   to camp at Celfa.
From there to the frontier   they send letters ahead;
none lag behind,   from all sides they gather.
They went out from Celfa,   which is called the Canal.
All that day   without rest they went forward
and came that night   to camp in Calatayud.
Through all those lands   the cry goes
and many have come;   great crowds have assembled
with those two Kings   called Fáriz and Galve
to surround My good Cid   in Alcocer.

33

Fáriz and Galve surround the Cid in Alcocer

They set up their tents   and built an encampment;
their host is great already   and still it grows stronger.
The sentinels   whom the Moors post
go armed   by day and by night;
many are the sentinels   and great is the host.
They cut off the water   from My Cid's men.
Those who were with My Cid   wished to give battle;
he who was born in good hour   strictly forbade it.
Fully three weeks   the Moors lay camped around them.

34

The Cid's council with his followers. Secret preparations.
The Cid rides out to pitched battle with Fáriz and Galve. Pedro
Bermúdez draws first blood

At the end of three weeks,   as the fourth was beginning,
My Cid called   his men to council.
"They have cut off our water,   our bread will soon be gone;
if we tried to leave by night   they would not let us;
if we should give battle   their strength is great;
tell me, my knights,   what you think were best done."
Minaya spoke first,   that worthy knight:

"From sweet Castile   we have come to this place;
unless we fight with the Moors   they will give us no bread.
We are six hundred   and something over;
in the name of the Creator   we can do no other
than attack them   when this next day dawns."
The Campeador said,   "You speak to my liking;
your speech does you honor, Minaya,   as will your action."

     All the Moors and their women   he sent from the castle,
so that no one might know   what was planned in secret.
That day and that night   they made themselves ready.
Next day in the morning   as the sun rose
My Cid was armed,   and all his men.
He spoke, My Cid,   you will hear what he said:
"Let us all go out,   let no one remain behind
except two foot soldiers   who will guard the gate.
If we die in the field   they will possess the castle;
if we beat them in battle   we may add to our wealth.
And you, Pedro Bermúdez,   take my banner;
you are a good vassal,   you will bear it faithfully;
but do not charge with it   until I send you word."
He kisses My Cid's hand   and goes to take the banner.

     They open the gates   and ride out onto the field;
the Moors' sentinels see them   and turn back to their army.
What haste among the Moors!   They set to arm;
it seemed the earth would split   with the noise of drums.
You could see the Moors arm   and rush into ranks.
On the side of the Moors   there were two kingly banners,
and as for the colored pennons,   who could number them?
The files of the Moors   are moving forward
to meet, hand to hand,   My Cid and his men.

     "Stay, knights, where you are,   here in this place;
let no one break ranks   till I give the word."
That same Pedro Bermúdez   could not abide it,
took the banner in hand   and spurred forward.
"The Creator bless you,   loyal Cid Campeador!
I shall set your standard   in the main rank there;
those who owe it allegiance,   let us see how they aid it."
The Campeador said,   "No, in charity's name!"
Pedro Bermúdez answered,   "Nothing can keep it here!"
He spurred his horse   into their main rank;

Moors rush upon him   to gain the banner,
give him great blows   but can break no armor.
The Campeador said,   "To his aid, for charity's sake!"

35

Those with My Cid attack to rescue Pedro Bermúdez

They clasp their shields   over their hearts,
they lower the lances   swathed in their pennons,
they bowed their faces   over their saddletrees,
with strong hearts   they charged to attack them.
He who in good hour was born   cried with a great voice:
"Attack them, knights,   for the love of the Creator!
I am Ruy Díaz, the Cid,   the Campeador of Bivar!"
All rushed at the rank   where Pedro Bermúdez was.
They were three hundred spears,   each with its pennon;
all struck blows   and killed as many Moors;
on the second charge   they killed three hundred more.

36

They destroy the enemy ranks

You would have seen so many lances   rise and go under,
so many bucklers   pierced and split asunder,
so many coats of mail   break and darken,
so many white pennons   drawn out red with blood,
so many good horses   run without their riders.
The Moors call on Mohammed   and the Christians on Saint
          James.
A thousand three hundred   of the Moors fell dead
upon the field   in a little space.

37

Mention of the principal Christian knights

How well they fight   above their gilded saddletrees:
My Cid Ruy Díaz,   the good warrior,
Minaya Alvar Fáñez,   who commanded at Zorita,
Martín Antolínez,   the excellent man of Burgos,

Muño Gustioz,   who was his vassal,
Martín Muñoz,   from Monte Mayor,
Alvar Alvarez   and Alvar Salvadórez,
Galindo García,   excellent knight from Aragón,
Félix Muñoz,   the nephew of the Campeador!
These and the rest,   as many as are there,
support the banner   and My Cid the Campeador.

38

Minaya in danger. The Cid wounds Fáriz

They have killed the horse from under   Minaya Alvar Fáñez;
hosts of Christians   charge to his aid.
His lance is broken,   his sword in his hand;
even afoot   he deals great blows.
Ruy Díaz the Castilian,   My Cid, saw him,
rode up to a Moorish lord   who had a good horse,
struck so with his sword,   with his right arm,
he cut him through at the belt;   half the body fell to the field.
He took the horse   to Minaya Alvar Fáñez.
"Mount, Minaya,   you who are my right arm!
This very day   I shall have need of you;
the Moors stand firm,   they have not yet fled the field.
We must fall upon them   relentlessly."
Minaya mounted,   his sword in his hand,
fighting bravely   through all that host,
delivering of their souls   all who came near him.
My Cid Ruy Díaz,   who in good hour was born,
has aimed three blows   at King Fáriz;
two of them missed   and the third struck home;
the blood ran down   over the tunic of chain mail;
he turned his horse   to flee from the field.
With that blow   the army was beaten.

39

Galve wounded and the Moors routed

Martín Antolínez   struck Galve a blow.
He broke in pieces   the rubies of his helmet;

he split the helmet,   cut into the flesh;
the other dared not wait,   you may know, for another.
King Fáriz and King Galve   and their armies are routed.
It is a great day   for Christendom,
for the Moors flee   on either hand.
My Cid's vassals   ride in pursuit.
King Fáriz   has gone into Terrer;
as for Galve,   they would not receive him.
Toward Calatayud   he rode on at full speed.
The Campeador   rode in pursuit;
they continued the chase   as far as Calatayud.

40

Minaya's vow is fulfilled. The loot from the battle.
The Cid puts aside a present for the King

The horse ran well   under Minaya Alvar Fáñez;
he killed thirty-four   of those Moors.
His sword cut deep,   his arm was crimson,
the blood ran   above his elbow.
Minaya said,   "My vow is fulfilled,
the news will travel   into Castile
that My Cid Ruy Díaz   has won in pitched battle."
So many Moors lie dead,   few are left living.
Pursuing without pause,   they struck them down.
Already his men turn back,   his who in good hour was born.
He rode, My Cid,   on his fine horse,
his skullcap pushed back—   God, how splendid his beard!—
his mailed hood on his shoulders,   his sword in his hand.
He saw his men   as they were returning:
"Thanks be to God   Who is in heaven
that we have triumphed   in such a battle."
My Cid's men   have sacked the Moors' encampment,
seized shields and arms   and much else of value;
when they had brought them in,   they found they had taken
five hundred and ten   Moorish horses.
There was great joy   among those Christians;
not more than fifteen   of their men were missing.
They took so much gold and silver,   none knew where to put it
        down;

all those Christians   were made rich
with the spoils   that had fallen to them.
They have called back the Moors   who lived in the castle;
My Cid ordered   that even they should be given something.
My Cid rejoiced greatly,   and all his men.
He bade them divide the money   and those great spoils;
in the Cid's fifth   there were a hundred horses.
God, they were well content,   all his vassals,
both the foot soldiers   and they who rode horses!
He who in good hour was born   deals with them justly;
all who came with him   are well content.
    "Hear me, Minaya,   who are my right arm!
Take from this treasure,   which the Creator has given,
as much as may please you;   take it with your own hand.
I wish to send you   to Castile with the news
of this battle   which we have won.
I would send   a gift of thirty horses
to King Alfonso,   whose anger is turned against me,
each with its saddle   and lavishly bridled,
each with a sword   slung from the saddletree."
Minaya Alvar Fáñez   said, "I will do that gladly."

41

The Cid pays what he had offered to the Cathedral of Burgos

    "Here I have   gold and fine silver,
a bootful,   and the boot brimming over.
In Santa María of Burgos   pay for a thousand Masses;
give what is left over   to my wife and daughters,
ask them to pray for me   by night and by day;
they will command riches   if I live."

42

Minaya leaves for Castile

    Minaya Alvar Fáñez   is well pleased with this;
the men are named   who will go with him.
Now they give the beasts barley,   already the night has come;
My Cid Ruy Díaz   confers with his men.

43

The Farewell

"Are you off, Minaya,   for Castile the noble?
When you meet our friends   you may say to them:
'God gave us aid   and we won the battle.'
When you come back,   if we are not here,
when you learn where we are   follow us there.
Lances and swords   must be our shelter
or else on this meager earth   we cannot live,
and for that same reason   I think we must move on."

44

The Cid sells Alcocer to the Moors

All is made ready;   Minaya will depart in the morning
and the Campeador   stayed there with his men.
The land is poor,   gaunt and barren.
Every day   Moors from the frontier
and some from beyond   kept watch on My Cid;
they plotted with King Fáriz,   whose wounds have healed.
Among those of Ateca   and those of the town of Terrer
and those of Calatayud,   which is a place of more note,
as the bargain was driven   and set down on paper,
My Cid sold them Alcocer   for three thousand marks of silver.

45

Sales of Alcocer (*Repetition*)

My Cid Ruy Díaz   has sold Alcocer;
how well he rewarded   each of his vassals!
He has made his knights rich   and his foot soldiers;
in all his company   you would not find a needy man.
Who serves a good lord   lives always in luxury.

46

*They abandon Alcocer. Good omens. The Cid encamps on
the stone ledge at El Poyo near Monreal*

When My Cid came   to leave the castle,
the Moors and their women   fell to lamenting.
"Are you leaving us, My Cid?   Our prayers go before you,
We are well content, sire,   with what you have done."
When My Cid of Bivar   left Alcocer,
the Moors and their women   fell to weeping.
He raised the banner,   the Campeador departed,
rode down the Jalón,   spurred forward.
As they left the Jalón   there were many birds of good omen.
The departure pleased those of Terrer   and still more those of
          Calatayud;
it grieved those of Alcocer,   for he had done much for them.
My Cid spurred his horse   and rode on
and halted on a stone ledge   at El Poyo near Monreal;
high is that ledge   great and wonderful;
it fears no attack,   you may know, from any side.
From Daroca onwards   he forced them to pay tribute
as far as Molina,   on the other side,
and a third town, Teruel,   which is farther on;
he brought under his hand   Celfa of the Canal.

47

*Minaya arrives before the King. The King pardons Minaya,
but not the Cid*

My Cid Ruy Díaz,   God give him grace!
Alvar Fáñez Minaya   has gone to Castile.
Thirty horses   he gave to the King;
the King smiled with pleasure   when he saw them.
"Who gave you these,   as God may save you, Minaya?"
"My Cid Ruy Díaz,   who in good hour girded on sword.
When you had banished him,   he took Alcocer by a ruse;
the King of Valencia   sent a message
bidding them surround him,   and they cut off his water.
My Cid went out of the castle   and fought in the field

and overcame two Kings of the Moors   in that battle.
Enormous, sire,   are the spoils he has taken.
He sends this gift   to you, honored King;
he kisses your feet   and both your hands
and begs mercy of you   in the name of the Creator."
The King said,   "It is early in the day
to receive into one's favor   at the end of three weeks
one who was banished   having lost his lord's love.
But I shall take this gift   since it comes from the Moors;
I am pleased that the Cid   has taken such spoils.
Above all,   I forgive you, Minaya.
I return to you freely   your lands and honors.
Come and go   henceforth in my favor;
but of the Cid Campeador   I will say nothing.

48

The King allows the Castilians to go with the Cid

    "And furthermore, Alvar Fáñez,   concerning this,
in all my kingdom   those good and valiant
who wish to go   to aid My Cid,
I shall not forbid them   nor seize their possessions."
Minaya Alvar Fáñez   kissed his hands.
"Thanks, thanks, my King   and natural lord;
you concede this now,   later you will grant more;
with God's aid we shall do   such things as will persuade you."
The King said, "Minaya,   enough has been said.
Go through Castile   unmolested,
return at your liberty   to My Cid."

49

*The Cid's raids from El Poyo. Minaya, with two hundred
Castilians, returns to the Cid*

    I would tell you of him   who in good hour girded on sword:
By the stone ledge of El Poyo   he set up his camp;
as long as there are Moors   and Christian people
it will be called: The Chair of My Cid.
While he was there   he pillaged much of the country.

All the Martín valley   he forced to pay tribute.
The news of him went   to Zaragoza
and did not please the Moors   but weighed heavy on them.
Fully fifteen weeks   My Cid stayed there.
When it was clear to My Cid   that Minaya delayed,
he took all his men   and marched by night;
he left El Poyo,   abandoned the place.
Beyond Teruel   Don Rodrigo passed;
in the pine grove of Tévar   Ruy Díaz pitched his camp.
He overran   all the country around there
and made them pay tribute   as far as Zaragoza.

At the end of three weeks   when this was done,
Minaya came   out of Castile
and two hundred with him,   all with swords girded,
and of foot soldiers, you may know,   there were great numbers.
When My Cid   sets eyes on Minaya
he spurs his horse,   rides forward to embrace him;
he kissed his mouth   and the eyes in his face.
All was told to him,   nothing left hidden.
The Campeador   smiled with pleasure.
"Thanks be to God   and His holy virtues,
as long as you live   I shall prosper, Minaya!"

50

The joy of the exiles at receiving news from Castile

God, how they rejoiced,   all that company,
that Minaya Alvar Fáñez   had returned thus,
bringing them greetings   from cousins and brothers
and from the families   they had left behind!

51

The joy of the Cid. (Parallel passage)

God, how he rejoices,   he, bearded handsomely,
because Alvar Fáñez   had paid the thousand Masses
and had given greetings   to his wife and his daughters!
God, the Cid was pleased   and rejoiced!
"Ah, Alvar Fáñez,   may you live many days!

You are worth more than us all,   you have done your mission so
    well!"

52

The Cid raids the countryside of Alcañiz

He who in good hour was born   did not delay;
he took two hundred knights,   chose them with his own hand;
he went on a raid,   riding all night.
He leaves black behind him   the lands of Alcañiz;
he goes pillaging   the lands round about.
On the third day   he has come back again.

53

The chastisement of the Moors

The news has gone   through all the country around there;
it grieves the people of Monzón   and of Huesca;
it pleases those of Zaragoza   to give tribute
that they may fear no affront   from My Cid Ruy Díaz.

54

*The Cid abandons El Poyo. He raids lands which are under
the protection of the Count of Barcelona*

With what he had taken   he came back to the encampment.
All rejoice,   they bear with them great spoils;
My Cid was pleased,   and Alvar Fáñez also.
My Cid, the perfect one,   could not help smiling.
"Ah, knights,   I must tell you the truth:
One would grow poor   staying in one place always;
tomorrow in the morning   let us move on,
let us leave the encampment   and go forward."
My Cid moved next   to the Pass of Olocau;
from there he overran   as far as Huesa and Montalbán;
he was away ten days   on that foray.
The news went out   in all directions
that the exile from Castile   was using them ill.

55

Threats from the Count of Barcelona

The tidings have gone out   in all directions;
the news has come   to the Count of Barcelona
that My Cid Ruy Díaz   overruns all his land!
It weighed on him heavily,   he took it as an affront.

56

The Cid tries in vain to calm the Count

The Count is a great braggart   and spoke foolishly:
"My Cid of Bivar   inflicts great losses on me.
He offended me once   in my own court:
he struck my nephew   and gave no reparation;
now he sacks the lands   under my protection.
I have never affronted him   nor withdrawn my friendship,
but since he seeks me out   I shall force him to a reckoning."
Great are his armies,   they assemble with speed.
Moors and Christians   all gather about him
and ride forward   toward My good Cid of Bivar;
three days and two nights,   still they rode on
and came to My Cid   in the pine grove of Tévar;
they come in such numbers   they think to take him in their hands.
My Cid Don Rodrigo,   bringing great spoils,
came down from a mountain   into a valley.
The message arrives   from Count Ramón;
when My Cid heard it   he sent back an answer:
"Tell the Count   not to take it amiss.
I have nothing of his.   Tell him to let me alone."
The Count answered,   "That is not true!
Now he shall pay me all   from now and from before;
he shall learn, this outcast,   whom he has dishonored."
The messenger returned   at full speed.
Thereupon My Cid   of Bivar understood
that he could not leave that place   without a battle.

57

The Cid's speech to his men

"Now, knights,   set the spoils to one side.
Arm yourselves quickly,   put on your armor;
Count Ramón   seeks a great battle;
he has with him multitudes   of Moors and Christians,
Without a battle,   on no account will he let us go.
If we go on, they will follow us;   let the battle be here.
Cinch tight the saddles   and arm yourselves.
They are coming downhill,   all of them in breeches;
their saddles are flat   and the girths loose.
We shall ride with Galician saddles,   with boots over our hose;
with a hundred knights   we should overcome their host.
Before they reach the plain   let us greet them with lances;
for every one that you strike,   three saddles will be emptied.
Ramón Berenguer will see   whom he has come seeking
in the pine grove of Tévar,   to take back the spoils from me."

58

The Cid wins the battle and the sword Colada

When My Cid had spoken,   all made ready;
they have taken up their arms   and mounted their horses.
They saw the Catalans   descending the slope;
when they came near the foot of the hill,   where it joins the plain,
My Cid, who in good hour was born,   called to his men to
        attack.
His knights charged forward   with a will,
skillfully handling   their pennons and lances,
wounding some   and unhorsing the rest.
He who was born in good hour   has won the battle.
He has taken prisoner   the Count Ramón;
he has taken the sword Colada,   worth more than a thousand
        marks.

59

*The Count of Barcelona prisoner. He would rather
die of hunger*

Thus he won the battle,   honor to his beard,
took the Count prisoner   and brought him to his tent
and ordered his servants   to mount guard upon him.
He went at once   out of the tent again;
from all sides   his men came together.
My Cid was pleased   with the great spoils they had taken.
For My Cid Don Rodrigo   they prepared a great banquet.
The Count Don Ramón   takes no interest in this;
they bear him food,   they bring it before him.
He will not eat it.   He rebuffed them all:
"I will not eat a mouthful   for all the wealth in Spain;
I will abandon my body first   and give up the ghost,
since such ill-shod outcasts   have beaten me in battle."

60

The Cid promises the Count his freedom

As for My Cid Ruy Díaz,   you will hear what he said:
"Count, eat this bread   and drink this wine.
If you do as I say,   I shall set you free;
if not, for the rest of your days   you will never see Christendom."

61

The Count refuses

"Eat if you please, Don Rodrigo,   and lie down and rest.
I would rather die;   I will eat nothing."
They could not persuade him   until the third day.
They continued to make division   of the great spoils they had
        taken,
but they could not make him eat   a morsel of bread.

62

The Cid repeats his promise to the Count. He sets the
Count free and bids him farewell

My Cid said,   "Count, eat something,
for unless you eat   you will see no Christian soul;
if you eat   to satisfy me,
I shall set free,   out of my hand,
You, Count,   and two of your knights."
When the Count heard this   he felt more joyful.
"Cid, if you do   as you have promised,
as long as I live   I will marvel at it."
    "Then eat, Count,   and when you have eaten
I shall set you at liberty,   and the two knights besides.
But of all that which you lost   and I won on the field,
you may know, I will not give you   so much as one wretched
        farthing.
I need it for my men,   who share my pauperdom.
We keep alive   by taking from you and from others.
And while it pleases our heavenly Father,   we shall continue thus,
as one must who is out of favor   and exiled from his country."
    The Count was joyful;   he asked for water for his hands
and they brought it before him   at once, and gave it to him.
And with the two knights   whom the Cid had promised him,
the Count began to eat.   God, he ate with a will!
He who was born in good hour   sat beside him.
"Unless you eat well, Count,   and to my full satisfaction,
you will remain here;   we shall not part from each other."
The Count said, "I will eat,   I will eat with a will."
With those two knights   he eats quickly.
My Cid, sitting there watching,   is well pleased
because the Count Don Ramón   moved his hands so expertly.
    "If it please you, My Cid,   we are ready to go;
tell them to give us our beasts   and we shall ride at once.
I have not eaten so heartily   since I was made a Count;
the pleasure of that meal   will not be forgotten."
    They were given three palfreys,   all with fine saddles,
and rich garments,   fur tunics and cloaks.
The Count Don Ramón   entered between his two knights;

the Castilian rode with them   to the end of the encampment.
"Now depart from us, Count,   a free Catalan.
I extend you my thanks   for what you have left me.
If it should occur to you   to wish vengeance
and come seeking me,   let me know beforehand,
and either you will leave something of yours   or bear off
        something of mine."
"Be at peace, My Cid,   on that account.
I have paid you tribute   for all this year;
I have no intention   of coming to seek you."

63

The Count mistrustfully departs. The wealth of the exiles

The Count spurred his horse   and rode forward,
turning his head   and looking behind him
for fear that the Cid   might change his mind,
which that perfect one would not have done   for the world's
        wealth,
for in all his life he had done no treachery.
    The Count is gone;   he of Bivar turned back,
returned to his vassals.   God, how great was their rejoicing,
for great and wonderful   was the booty they had won.
His men are so rich   they cannot count all they have.

THE SECOND CANTAR

The Wedding

64

The Cid proceeds against the domain of Valencia

Here begins the story   of My Cid of Bivar.
My Cid has made his camp   by the Pass of Olocau;
he has left Zaragoza   and the country there;
he has left Huesa   and the lands of Montalbán.
He has carried his war   toward the salt sea;
the sun comes from the east,   he turned to that direction.
My Cid took Jérica   and Onda and Almenara,
and he has overrun   all the lands of Burriana.

65

The taking of Murviedro

The Creator aided him,   the Lord in heaven,
and by that means,   he took Murviedro;
My Cid knew well   that God was his strength.
There was great fear   in the city of Valencia.

66

The Moors of Valencia surround the Cid. He assembles
his men. His speech

It grieves those of Valencia.   Know, they are not pleased.
They took counsel   and came to besiege him.
They rode all night;   next day at dawn
around Murviedro   they set up their tents.
My Cid saw them   and exclaimed:
"Thanks be to Thee,   Father Who art in heaven!
We ride through their lands   and do them mischief,
we drink their wine   and eat their bread;
if they come to besiege us   they are within their rights.
We shall not leave here   without a battle;
send out the messages   to those who should aid us,
some in Jérica   and others in Olocau,
from there to Onda   and to Almenara,
and to those of Burriana,   bid them come here.
We shall begin   this pitched battle;
I trust in God   Who will favor us."
On the third day   all have come together.
He who was born in good hour   began to address them:
"Hear me, my vassals,   as the Creator may save you!
Ever since we came   out of clean Christendom—
not at our own choice,   for we could not do otherwise—
God be thanked,   we have met no reverses.
Now those of Valencia   have encircled us;
if we are to remain   in these lands,
we must defeat them   most severely.

67

End of the Cid's speech

"When the night has passed   and morning has come,
I would have the horses saddled   and the arms ready;
we shall go and see   that army of theirs.
We are exiles   from a foreign country;
there we shall see   who is worth his wages."

68

*Minaya gives the plan of battle. The Cid wins another
pitched battle. The taking of Cebolla*

Hear Minaya Alvar Fáñez,   what he had to say:
"Campeador,   let us do as you will.
Give me a hundred knights,   I ask for no more.
You with the rest   ride to the attack.
You will strike them hard,   I have no doubt.
I with the hundred   will charge from another side.
As I trust in God,   the field will be ours."
The Campeador was much pleased   with what he had said.
It was morning   and they set to arm;
each of them knows well   what he must do.
    When the dawn came,   My Cid rode to attack them.
"In the name of the Creator   and of Saint James the apostle,
attack them, knights,   heartily, with a will.
I am Ruy Díaz,   My Cid of Bivar!"
    You would have seen   so many tent cords snapped,
the poles wrenched out, the canvas collapsing.
The Moors are many   and begin to recover.
Alvar Fáñez   rode in from another side;
hard against their wills   they were forced to flee
on foot or on horse,   those who could escape.
In that chase they killed   two Kings of the Moors;
they continued the pursuit   as far as Valencia.
My Cid   has taken great spoils;
they despoil the camp   and start to return;
they enter Murviedro   with those spoils they bear;
great is the rejoicing   in that town.
"They have taken Cebolla   and all that lies beyond it;
they are frightened in Valencia,   they do not know what to do.
Know, the fame of My Cid   has gone everywhere."

69

The Cid's raids to the south of Valencia

His fame goes re-echoing   even beyond the sea;
My Cid rejoiced,   and all his company,
because God had given him aid   and he had routed them there.
He sent out raiders,   all night they rode;
they came to Cullera   and to Játiva
and below there   to the town of Denia.
They destroyed the lands of the Moors   as far as the seashore.
They took Benicadell,   its exits and entrances.

70

The Cid in Benicadell

When the Cid Campeador   had taken Benicadell,
they are grieved in Játiva,   and in Cullera.
As for Valencia,   its dismay is boundless.

71

The conquest of the entire region of Valencia

Seizing and despoiling,   riding at night,
sleeping in the daytime,   taking those towns,
My Cid spent three years   in the lands of the Moors.

72

*The Cid lays siege to Valencia. He sends heralds
among the Christians announcing the war*

And he has chastised severely   those of Valencia.
They do not dare leave the city   or meet him in battle;
he has laid waste their farmlands   and brought havoc among
       them;
every year of those three,   My Cid deprived them of bread.
They grieve in Valencia,   not knowing what to do.
They cannot obtain   bread from anywhere;
the father cannot help his son   nor the son his father,

friend and friend　cannot console each other.
Great hardship it is, sirs,　to be without bread,
to see children and women　dying of hunger.
And they see their affliction growing,　that there is no remedy,
and they have sent word　to the King of Morocco;
he was so deep in war　with the King of the Atlas,
that he neither sent to advise them　nor came to their rescue.

　　My Cid learned of this;　it gladdened his heart.
He went out from Murviedro　one night, and rode all night;
he appeared at daybreak　in the lands of Monreal.
He sent forth a herald　to Aragón and Navarre;
he sent his messages　to the lands of Castile:
"Whoever would leave　his toil and grow rich,
let him come to My Cid,　whose taste is for battle.
He would now lay siege to Valencia　to give it to the Christians."

73

Repetition of the announcement (*Parallel passage*)

　　"Whoever will come with me　to besiege Valencia—
let all come freely　and no one against his will—
I shall wait three days for him　by the Canal of Celfa."

74

*Those who responded to the herald. The siege and
entry of Valencia*

　　This he spoke, My Cid,　the loyal Campeador.
He returned to Murviedro,　which he had already taken.
The cries went out,　you may know, in all directions;
at the odor of riches　they do not wish to delay;
great numbers gather to him　from good Christendom.
The fame of him resounds　in every direction;
more flock to My Cid,　you may know, than go from him
and his wealth increases,　My Cid's of Bivar.
When he saw so many assembled　he rejoiced.
My Cid Don Rodrigo　did not wish to delay;
he set out for Valencia　and will attack them.
My Cid besieges it closely;　there was no escape.

He permits no one   to enter or depart.
He gave them a term of grace   if any would come and save them.
Nine full months   his tents surrounded them;
when the tenth began   they were forced to surrender.
Great is the rejoicing   in that place
when My Cid took Valencia   and entered the city.
Those who had gone on foot   became knights on horses,
and who could count   the gold and the silver?
All were rich,   as many as were there.
My Cid Don Rodrigo   sent for his fifth of the spoils;
in coined money alone   thirty thousand marks fell to him;
and the other riches,   who could count them?

My Cid rejoiced,   and all who were with him,
when his flag flew from the top   of the Moorish palace.

75

The King of Seville tries to retake Valencia

Then my Cid rested,   and all his men.
The news came   to the King of Seville
that Valencia was taken,   there had been no help for it;
he set out to attack it   with thirty thousand armed men.
Beyond the farmlands   they joined battle.
My Cid of the long beard   routed them there;
as far as Játiva   the pursuit went on.
Crossing the Júcar,   you would have seen them struck down;
Moors caught in the current,   forced to drink water.
That King of Seville   escaped with three wounds.
My Cid returned   with all his gains.
Great were the spoils of Valencia   when they took that city;
those from this victory,   you may know, were still richer;
to the least among them   fell a hundred marks of silver.
You can see how the fame   of this warrior has grown.

76

The Cid leaves his beard untrimmed. The wealth of the Cid's men

There is great rejoicing   among all those Christians
with My Cid Ruy Díaz,   who in good hour was born.

His beard grows on him,   it grows longer upon him;
these words My Cid   spoke of it with his mouth:
"For love of King Alfonso,   who sent me into exile."
No scissors would touch it   nor one hair be cut,
and let Moors and Christians   all tell of this.

    My Cid Don Rodrigo   is resting in Valencia;
Minaya Alvar Fáñez   does not leave his side.
Those who came with him into exile   have all grown rich.
The renowned Campeador   gave them all, in Valencia,
houses and fiefs   with which they are satisfied;
they all have tasted   of the Cid's generosity.
Those who joined him later   are content also;
My Cid knows   that with the gains they have taken,
if they might depart now,   they would go gladly.
My Cid commanded,   as Minaya had advised him,
that no man among them   who with him had gained anything
should leave without bidding farewell   and kissing his hand,
or else he would seize him again   wherever he might be hidden
and take from him everything   and hang him on a gallows.
Behold, all this   was put in good order;
he is talking things over   with Minaya Alvar Fáñez:
"If you please, Minaya,   I should like to know
how many are with me here   and have received of the spoils.
I would have them all counted   and set down in writing
so that if anyone hide,   or anyone is missing,
his possessions may be returned to me   by those vassals of mine
who guard Valencia,   keeping watch around it."
Then Minaya said,   "That is well advised."

77

*The numbering of the Cid's followers. He arranges to
send a new present to the King*

    He bade them all come to the court   and gather together.
When they had come   he numbered them all:
three thousand six hundred   were under My Cid of Bivar;
his heart was pleased   and he began to smile.
"God be praised, Minaya,   and Santa María His mother!
With less than these we rode out   from the gate at Bivar,
and now riches are ours   and more shall be ours hereafter.

"If you please, Minaya,   and it would not burden you,
I would send you to Castile,   where our lands are,
to King Alfonso,   my natural lord.
Out of these my gains   which we have taken here
I would give him a hundred horses,   I would have you take them,
kiss his hand for me   and urgently beg him
that he, of his grace, may allow me   to bring from there
Doña Jimena, my wife,   and my daughters.
I shall send for them;   know, this is the message:
'My Cid's wife   and his daughters
in such wise will be sent for   that with great honor they will come
to these foreign lands   which we have taken.' "
Then Minaya said,   "I will do it gladly."
When they had spoken this   they began to make ready.
My Cid gave a hundred men   to Alvar Fáñez
to serve him on his way   and do his will,
and he sent a thousand marks   of silver to San Pedro,
five hundred of them to be given   to the abbot Don Sancho.

78

Don Jerome arrives in Valencia

While they were rejoicing   at this news,
out of the east   came a cleric,
the Bishop Don Jerome   is his name.
Learned in letters   and with much wisdom
and a ready warrior   on foot or on horse,
he came inquiring   of the Cid's brave deeds,
sighing to see himself   with the Moors in the field,
saying if he should weary   of fighting them with his hands,
let no Christian mourn him   all the days of this world.
When My Cid heard this   he was well pleased.
"Hear, Minaya Alvar Fáñez,   by Him Who is in heaven,
when God would give us aid   let us heartily thank Him for it:
I would ordain a bishopric   in the lands of Valencia;
I would give it   to this good Christian.
Take the good news   when you go to Castile."

79

Don Jerome ordained Bishop

Alvar Fáñez was pleased   with what Don Rodrigo said.
That same Don Jerome   they ordained Bishop;
they arranged that he might live   richly in Valencia.
God, how great was the rejoicing   of all those Christians
for in the lands of Valencia   there was a lord Bishop!
Minaya was joyful   and bade farewell and set out.

80

Minaya goes to Carrión

Leaving the lands of Valencia   lying in peace,
Minaya Alvar Fáñez   rode toward Castile.
I do not wish to recount   all the places where he paused.
He asked for King Alfonso,   asked where he might find him.
The King had gone to Sahagún   only shortly before
and thence to Carrión,   and there he might find him.
Minaya Alvar Fáñez   was pleased to hear this;
he rode toward that place   with the gifts he had brought.

81

Minaya greets the King

Just as King Alfonso   had come out from Mass,
behold where Minaya Alvar Fáñez   arrives most opportunely.
He knelt down on his knees   before all the people;
he fell down in great sorrow   at the feet of King Alfonso;
he kissed the King's hands   and spoke with all eloquence.

82

Minaya's speech to the King. The envy of García Ordóñez.
The King pardons the Cid's family. The Heirs of
Carrión covet the Cid's riches

"Grace, lord Alfonso,   for the love of the Creator!
My Cid the warrior   kisses your hands,

kisses your feet and your hands   as his duty to so good a lord,
and may you grant him grace   as the Creator may bless you!
You sent him from your lands,   he is without your favor;
nevertheless, in foreign lands   he manages well:
he has taken Jérica   and the place called Onda
and seized Almenara,   and Murviedro, which is larger;
likewise he took Cebolla   and Castejón farther on,
and Benicadell,   which is a strong hill,
and besides all these   he is lord of Valencia.
The good Campeador   a Bishop has ordained with his own hands,
fought five pitched battles   and triumphed in them all.
Great are the gains   the Creator has given him.
Here are the proofs   that it is the truth I tell you:
a hundred horses,   strong-limbed and swift,
each one provided   with saddle and bridle.
He kisses your hands   and begs you to accept them;
he calls himself your vassal   and regards you as his lord."
    The King raised his right hand   and crossed himself.
"Saint Isidore bless me,   my heart is pleased
with the vast spoils   the Cid has taken!
And I am pleased with the deeds   the Campeador has done;
I accept these horses   which he sends as a gift."
    Though it pleased the King,   it grieved García Ordóñez:
"It seems that in the lands of the Moors   there is no man living
since the Cid Campeador   thus does as he pleases."
The King said to the Count,   "Leave off such talk;
in whatever he does   he serves me better than you do."
    Then manfully   Minaya spoke:
"The Cid begs of your grace,   if it meet your pleasure,
that his wife Doña Jimena   and both his daughters
may leave the monastery   where he left them
and go to Valencia   to the good Campeador."
Then the King said,   "It pleases my heart;
I shall provide them with escort   while they go through my lands
and keep them from harm and grievance   and from dishonor,
and when these ladies have come   to the end of my lands,
then you and the Campeador   take care to guard them.
Hear me, my vassals   and all my court!
I would not have the Campeador   lose anything,
and as for all those vassals   who call him lord,

whom I disinherited,   I return to them all that they had;
let them keep their inheritances   while they serve the Campeador,
and I free their bodies   from threat of injury;
all this I do   that they may serve their lord."
Minaya Alvar Fáñez   kissed him on the hands.
The King smiled   and spoke thus sweetly:
"Those who wish to go   to serve the Campeador
have my leave,   and may the Creator bless them.
We shall gain more by this   than by disaffection."
    Then the Heirs of Carrión   spoke between themselves:
"Great grows the fame   of My Cid the Campeador;
it would serve our advantage   to marry his daughters.
Yet we would not dare   propose such a plan.
My Cid is from Bivar   and we, of the Counts of Carrión."
They spoke of it to no one   and there the scheme rested.
    Minaya Alvar Fáñez   bade the good King farewell.
"Are you leaving us now, Minaya?   May the Creator bless you.
Take with you a royal herald,   who will serve your needs;
if you go with the ladies,   care for their comfort
as far as Medinaceli;   in my name demand all they require.
From that point forward   they concern the Campeador."
Minaya bade farewell   and went from the court.

83

*Minaya goes to Cardeña for Doña Jimena. More Castilians
offer to go to Valencia. Minaya in Burgos. He promises
the Jews full payment for the Cid's debt. Minaya returns
to Cardeña and leaves with Jimena. Pedro Bermúdez sets out
from Valencia to receive Jimena. In Molina they are met by
Abengalbón. They meet Minaya in Medinaceli*

    The Heirs of Carrión   have made their decision;
they went out a little way   with Minaya Alvar Fáñez.
"We have been your friends in all things,   now be friend to us:
give our greetings   to My Cid of Bivar,
we shall serve him in all things   as well as we may;
we wish the Cid to lose nothing   by the friendship he bears us."
Minaya answered, "Your message   will not overburden me."
    Minaya has ridden on   and the Heirs turn back.
He rode toward San Pedro,   where the ladies are;

great was their joy   when he appeared.
Minaya has dismounted   and prays to San Pedro.
When the prayer ended   he turned to the ladies.
"I humble myself before you, Doña Jimena;
may God keep you   and both your daughters from evil.
My Cid sends you greetings   from where he is;
I left him in health   and with great riches.
The King, in his grace,   has set you free
so that you may come to Valencia   which is ours for inheritance.
If the Cid might see you   well and without harm,
all would be joy   and he would grieve no longer."
Doña Jimena said,   "May the Creator will it so!"
Minaya Alvar Fáñez   chose three knights
and sent them to My Cid   in Valencia where he was:
"Say to the Campeador   —whom may God keep from harm—
that the King has set free   his wife and daughters;
while we are in his lands   he will provide us with escort.
Within fifteen days   if God keep us from harm
we shall be with him,   I and his wife and his daughters
and all their good ladies with them,   as many as are here."
The knights have set out   and will take care to do this.
Minaya Alvar Fáñez   remained in San Pedro.

You would have seen knights   ride in from all directions
wishing to go to Valencia   to My Cid of Bivar,
asking Alvar Fáñez   to aid them in this,
Minaya saying,   "I shall do so gladly."
Sixty-five warriors   have assembled with him there
besides the hundred   whom he had brought with him;
they made a fine escort   to go with those ladies.

Minaya gave the abbot   the five hundred marks;
I must tell what he did   with the other five hundred.
The good Minaya   took thought to provide
Doña Jimena   and her daughters there,
and the other ladies   who served them and went before them,
with the finest garments   to be found in Burgos
and with palfreys and mules,   that their appearance might be
        seemly.
When he had thus   decked out these ladies
the good Minaya   made ready to ride,
when behold Raquel and Vidas   fall at his feet.

"Grace, Minaya,   worthy knight!
The Cid has undone us,   you may know, if he will not aid us;
we shall ignore the interest   if he give back the capital."
"I shall speak of it with the Cid   if God will take me there.
You will be well rewarded   for all you have done."
Raquel and Vidas said,   "May the Creator will it so!
If not, we shall leave Burgos   and go to seek him in Valencia."

Minaya Alvar Fáñez   has gone to San Pedro;
many gathered about him,   he made ready to ride.
Their sorrow is great   at the parting from the abbot.
"The Creator keep you,   Minaya Alvar Fáñez!
In my name kiss the hands   of the Campeador,
let him not forget   this monastery;
all the days of the world   as he may give it aid,
the Cid Campeador   will increase in honor."
Minaya answered,   "I shall tell him gladly."

They bid farewell   and ride forward,
the King's herald with them   to be at their service;
through the lands of the King   they were well escorted.
They go in five days   from San Pedro to Medinaceli;
behold them in Medinaceli,   the ladies and Alvar Fáñez.

I shall tell you of the knights   who took the message.
When My Cid of Bivar   heard the news
it pleased his heart   and he rejoiced,
and in these words   he began to speak:
"He who sends a good messenger   may expect good news.
You, Muño Gustioz   and Pedro Bermúdez
and Martín Antolínez,   loyal man of Burgos,
and you, Bishop Don Jerome,   honored cleric,
ride with a hundred   armed as though for battle,
ride forward   through Santa María
to Molina,   which is farther on;
Abengalbón is lord there,   my friend, at peace with me.
He is certain to join you   with another hundred knights;
ride toward Medinaceli   at your best speed;
my wife and my daughters   with Minaya Alvar Fáñez
you will find there,   as I have been told;
conduct them here before me   with great honor.
And I shall stay in Valencia,   whose conquest was costly.
It would be great folly   to abandon it now;

I shall stay in Valencia,   which is my inheritance."
    When this was said   they make ready to ride,
and as far as they can   they ride on without resting.
They passed Santa María   and lodged at Bonchales,
then another day's riding   and they slept in Molina.
When the Moor Abengalbón   knew of the message
he rode out to receive them   with great rejoicing:
"Have you come, vassals   of my dear friend?
It does not sadden me,   believe me, it fills me with joy!"
Muño Gustioz spoke,   he waited for no one:
"My Cid sent you greetings   and asked you to provide us
with a hundred knights   to ride with us at once;
his wife and his daughters   are in Medinaceli;
he would have you go   and escort them here
and not go from them   as far as Valencia."
Abengalbón said,   "I will do it gladly."
That night he served them   a great banquet.
In the morning   they made ready to ride.
They had asked for a hundred,   but he came with two hundred.
They ride into the mountains   which are wild there and high,
and they pass   the Plain of Taranz
riding in such manner   that none feels fear;
by the Valley of Arbujuelo   they begin to descend.
    Close guard is mounted   in Medinaceli;
Minaya Alvar Fáñez,   seeing them come armed,
was alarmed, and sent two knights   to find out the truth;
at this they did not take long   for they were eager to know;
the one stayed and the other   turned back to Alvar Fáñez:
"Forces of the Campeador   have come to find us;
behold, there at their head   is Pedro Bermúdez,
and Muño Gustioz,   your unfailing friend,
and Martín Antolínez,   who was born in Burgos,
and the Bishop Don Jerome,   the loyal cleric,
and the chief Abengalbón,   and his warriors with him;
for the love of My Cid   and to do him honor
they are all riding together;   now they are about to arrive."
Then Minaya said,   "Let us mount and ride."
They did so at once   without delay.
All the hundred rode out;   the sight of them was splendid,
mounted on good horses   caparisoned with sendal,

bells on their breast leathers,   shields from their necks hanging,
the knights bearing lances,   from each its pennon hanging,
that all might know   with what prudence came Alvar Fáñez
and how he would leave Castile   with these ladies he was bringing.

    Those who rode as scouts   and arrived first
grasped their weapons   and jousted for the sport;
not far from Jalón   there was great rejoicing.
When the others came up   they made obeisance to Minaya.
When Abengalbón came up   and set eyes on him,
smiling with his mouth   he went to embrace him;
he kisses him on the shoulder   as is the Moors' custom.
"It is a glad day in which I meet you,   Minaya Alvar Fáñez!
You bring with you these ladies   whose presence does us honor,
the wife and the daughters   of the Cid, the warrior;
we must all do them honor   for such is his fortune
that though we should wish him evil   we could not perform it;
in peace or in war   he will have what is ours;
who does not know the truth   I hold stupid."

84

The travelers rest in Medinaceli. They leave Medinaceli
for Molina. They arrive near Valencia

    Alvar Fáñez Minaya   smiles at these words.
"Greetings, Abengalbón,   unfailing friend!
If God allow me to reach the Cid   and this soul may see him,
you will lose nothing   for this that you have done.
Come rest for the night with us   for a banquet is spread."
Abengalbón said,   "This courtesy delights me;
before three days have passed   I shall return it to you twofold."
They entered Medinaceli;   Minaya saw to their comfort.
All were well pleased   with the care that was shown them.
The King's herald   bade farewell and left them;
far off in Valencia   the Cid was honored
by such pomp and celebration   as were seen in Medinaceli;
the King paid for it all   and Minaya owed no one.

    The night has passed   and morning come
and Mass heard,   and then they mounted.
They rode out of Medinaceli   and passed Jalón;
up the river by Arbujuelo   they spurred without pausing,

then they passed by   the Plain of Taranz;
they came to Molina   where Abengalbón was lord.
The Bishop Don Jerome,   a good Christian without fault,
guarded the ladies   day and night
with a good war horse on his right   which rode ahead of his
        weapons.
He and Alvar Fáñez   rode together.
They have entered Molina,   a rich and goodly town.
The Moor Abengalbón   without fail serves them well;
there was no lack   of all they might desire.
Even their horses   he shod newly.
And Minaya and the ladies,   God, how he honored them!
Another day in the morning   they mounted again;
as far as Valencia   without fail he served them.
The Moor spent his own   and would take nothing from them.
Amid such rejoicings   and tidings of honor
they came within three leagues   of Valencia.
The news came   into Valencia
to My Cid,   who in good hour girded sword.

85

The Cid sends people to meet the travelers

Never greater joy,   nor as great, as My Cid's then,
for the news had come   from that which he most loved.
He sent two hundred knights   to ride with all speed
to receive Minaya   and the noble ladies;
he himself remained in Valencia   keeping watch and guard
for he trusts Alvar Fáñez   to take every care.

86

Don Jerome rides ahead to Valencia to prepare a procession.
The Cid rides out to meet Jimena.
All enter the city

Behold, how all these   receive Minaya
and the ladies and the girls   and the rest of their companions.
My Cid ordered   those who were with him
to guard the castle   and the other high towers

and all the gates   and the exits and entrances,
and to lead him his horse Babieca,   which he had taken lately
from that King of Seville   when he had defeated him.
My Cid, who in good hour girded sword,   had not yet ridden him
nor learned whether he were swift   and answered the reins well;
at the gate of Valencia,   where it was safe,
he wished to bear arms   before his wife and daughters.

    The ladies were received   with great honor;
the Bishop Don Jerome   entered ahead of them
and dismounted   and went to the chapel;
with as many as he might muster   who were ready in time,
dressed in surplices   and with crosses of silver,
he went out to receive the ladies   and the good Minaya.

    He who was born in good hour   did not delay:
he put on his silk tunic,   his long beard hung down;
they saddled for him Babieca and fastened the caparisons.
My Cid rode out upon him   bearing wooden arms.
On the horse they called   Babieca he rode,
rode at a gallop;   it was a wonder to watch.
When he had ridden one round   everyone marveled;
from that day Babieca   was famous through all Spain.
When he had ridden,   My Cid dismounted.
He went up to his wife   and his two daughters;
when Doña Jimena saw him   she fell at his feet:
"Grace, Campeador,   who in good hour girded sword!
You have delivered me   from much vile shame.
Here am I, sire,   I and both your daughters;
with God's help and yours   they are good and well brought up."
He took his wife in his arms   and then his daughters;
such was his joy   the tears flowed from his eyes.
All his vassals   were filled with jubilation;
they jousted with arms   and rode at targets.
Hear what he said,   who in good hour girded sword:
"You, Doña Jimena,   my honored and dear wife,
and both my daughters,   my heart and my soul,
enter with me   the town of Valencia,
the inheritance   which I have won for you."
Mother and daughters   kissed his hands.
They entered Valencia   with great celebration.

87

The ladies see Valencia from the castle

My Cid and they   went to the castle;
there he led them up   to the highest place.
Then fair eyes   gaze out on every side;
They see Valencia,   the city, as it lies,
and turning the other way   their eyes behold the sea.
They look on the farmlands,   wide and thick with green,
and all the other things   which gave delight;
they raised their hands   to give thanks to God
for all that bounty   so vast and so splendid.
    My Cid and his vassals   lived in great content.
The winter has gone   and March begun.
I would tell you news   from across the sea,
from that King Yusuf,   who is in Morocco.

88

The King of Morocco comes to lay siege to Valencia

The King of Morocco was troubled   because of My Cid
    Don Rodrigo:
"For in lands that are mine   he has trespassed gravely
and gives thanks for it to no one   save Jesus Christ."
That King of Morocco   assembled his nobles.
Fifty times a thousand armed men   gathered under him;
they have embarked on the sea,   they have entered into the ships,
they leave for Valencia   to find My Cid Don Rodrigo.
The ships have entered harbor,   the men have come forth on land.

89

They arrived at Valencia,   which My Cid conquered.
The unbelievers have made camp,   they have pitched their tents.
The news of this   has come to My Cid.

90

The Cid's joy at seeing the Moroccan hosts.
Jimena's fear

"Thanks be to the Creator   and to the heavenly Father!
All that I own   is here before me;
with toil I took Valencia   for my inheritance;
as long as I live   I will not leave it.
Thanks be to the Creator   and Santa María Mother,
that I have here with me   my wife and my daughters.
Delight has come to me   from the lands beyond the sea;
I shall arm myself,   I cannot evade it;
my wife and my daughters   will see me in battle,
in these foreign lands they will see   how houses are made,
they will see clearly   how we earn our bread."
He led his wife and daughters   up into the castle;
they raised their eyes   and saw the tents pitched.
"What is this, Cid,   in the name of the Creator?"
"My honored wife,   let it not trouble you!
This is great and marvelous wealth   to be added unto us;
you have barely arrived here   and they send you gifts,
they bring the marriage portion   for the wedding of your
    daughters."
"I give thanks to you, Cid,   and to our heavenly Father."
"Wife, stay here in the palace,   here in the castle;
have no fear   when you see me fighting;
by the grace of God   and Santa María Mother,
my heart grows within me   because you will be watching;
with God's help I shall triumph   in this battle."

91

The Cid reassures his wife and daughters. The Moors invade
the farmlands of Valencia

The tents are pitched   and the dawn comes;
with a quickening stroke   the Moors beat on the drums.
My Cid rejoiced and said,   "A day of delight is this!"
His wife is frightened,   thinks her heart must shatter;
the ladies are frightened also   and both the daughters;

they had not known such terror   since the day they were born.
He stroked his beard,   the good Cid Campeador.
"Have no fear, for all this   is to your favor;
before these two weeks have gone,   if it please the Creator,
we will have wrenched from them   those same drums;
they shall be fetched before you   and you shall see what they are,
then they shall be given   to the Bishop Don Jerome
and hung in the Church   of Santa María, mother of God."
This is the vow   the Cid Campeador made.
The ladies are reassured   and their fear goes from them.
The Moors of Morocco   ride out boldly;
without fear   they have entered the farmlands.

92

The Christians attack

The sentinel saw them   and rang the bell;
the vassals are ready,   the men of Ruy Díaz;
they arm themselves with a will   and ride from the city.
Where they met the Moors   they charged them at once,
drove them from the farmlands   with much harsh treatment.
They killed five hundred of them   on that day.

93

The plan of battle

As far as the tents   they pursued them;
they have accomplished much   and they turn back.
Alvar Salvadórez   remained captive there.
Those who eat the Cid's bread   have returned to his side;
he saw it with his own eyes   yet they retell it;
My Cid is pleased   with what they have done.
"Hear me, knights, it must be   thus, and not otherwise;
today has been a good day,   tomorrow will be better.
Be armed all of you   by the time day breaks;
the Bishop Don Jerome   will give us absolution;
he will sing us Mass   and then we shall ride.
In the name of the Creator   and of Saint James the apostle
we shall attack them;   thus it must be.

It is better that we should beat them   than that they should take
      our bread."
Then all said, "Willingly   and with all our hearts."
Minaya spoke,   he waited no longer:
"Since you wish it so, Cid,   send me another way;
give me for the battle   a hundred and thirty knights;
when you fall upon them. I shall attack from the other side.
On both sides, or one only,   God will aid us."
Then the Cid answered,   "I will do it gladly."

94

The Cid grants the Bishop the right of striking the first blows

The day has gone   and the night come.
That Christian host   was not slow in making ready.
By the second cock crow,   before morning came,
the Bishop Don Jerome   sang them the Mass.
When the Mass was said   he gave them full absolution:
"He who may die here   fighting face to face
I absolve of his sins,   and God will receive his soul.

    "Cid Don Rodrigo,   who in good hour girded sword,
I sang Mass   for you this morning;
I crave a boon of you,   I beg you to grant it:
I would have you let me strike   the first blows in the fight."
The Campeador said,   "From this moment it is granted."

95

The Christians sally to battle. The rout of Yusuf. The
enormous spoils. The Cid greets his wife and daughters.
He settles dowries on Jimena's ladies. The division of the spoils

    All have ridden out armed   from the towers of Cuarto,
My Cid giving full instructions   to his vassals.
They leave at the gates   men they can count on.
My Cid sprang   onto his horse, Babieca,
that is splendidly caparisoned   with all manner of ornaments.
They ride out with the banner,   they ride out from Valencia;
four thousand less thirty   ride with My Cid;
gladly they go   to attack the fifty thousand.
Alvar Alvarez and Minaya   rode in from the other side.

As pleased the Creator,   they overcame them.

    My Cid used his lance   and then drew his sword;
he killed so many Moors   that the count was lost;
above his elbow   the blood ran.
He has struck King Yusuf   three blows;
Yusuf escaped from his sword   for hard he rode his horse
and sheltered in Cullera,   a noble castle;
My Cid of Bivar   arrived there in pursuit
with those of his good vassals   who stay by his side.
And there he turned back,   he who in good hour was born.
Great was his joy   at what they had taken,
and there he knew the worth of Babieca   from head to tail.
All those spoils   remain in his hands.
A count was made: of the fifty thousand Moors,
only a hundred and four   had escaped.
My Cid's vassals   have despoiled the field;
they found three thousand marks   of mixed gold and silver;
the other spoils   were beyond numbering.
My Cid was joyful,   and all his vassals,
because God of His grace   had given them triumph.
When they had thus routed   the King of Morocco
My Cid left Alvar Fáñez   to attend to the rest;
with a hundred knights   he returned to Valencia.
He had his helmet off   and his hood drawn back;
thus he rode in on Babieca,   his sword in his hand.

    There he received the ladies,   who were waiting for him;
My Cid reined in his horse   and stopped before them.
"I bow before you, ladies,   great spoils I have won for you;
you kept Valencia for me   and I have won in the field;
this was the will of God   and of all His saints;
upon your arrival   they have sent us great treasure.
You see the sword bloody   and the horse sweating:
thus it is   that one conquers Moors in the field.
Pray to the Creator   to grant me a few years' life;
you will grow in honor   and vassals will kiss your hands."
This My Cid spoke,   dismounting from his horse.
When they saw him on foot   when he had dismounted,
the ladies and the daughters   and the noble wife
all kneeled   before the Campeador.
"By your grace we are all that we are;   may you live long!"

Then with him   they entered the palace
and sat with him   on the elaborate benches.
"My wife, Doña Jimena,   have you not begged this of me?
These ladies you bring with you   who so well serve you,
I wish to marry them   with those vassals of mine;
to each of them   I give two hundred marks.
Let it be known in Castile   who it is they have served so well.
For your daughters, we shall come   to decide that more slowly."
All rose   and kissed his hands;
great was the rejoicing   in the palace.
And the Cid had spoken,   so it was done.
    Minaya Alvar Fáñez   was abroad in the field
with all those men   counting and writing down;
as for tents and arms   and garments of value,
it passed belief   what they found.
I will tell you   what was most important:
there was no counting   all the horses
who went without riders   and none to take them.
Even the Moors in the farmlands   captured some,
and despite this there fell   to the famous Campeador
a thousand horses   of the best and best broken,
and when My Cid   received so many,
surely the others   were well requited.
So many precious tents   and jeweled tent poles
My Cid has taken   with all his vassals!
The tent of the King of Morocco,   which surpassed all the others,
hangs on two tent poles   wrought with gold;
My Cid commanded,   the famous Campeador,
that no Christian touch it,   that it be left standing.
"Such a tent as this,   which has come from Morocco,
I wish to send to Alfonso the Castilian
that he may believe the news   that My Cid has possessions."
    With all these riches   they have returned to Valencia.
The Bishop Don Jerome,   the mitered man of great merit,
when he has finished fighting   with both his hands
has lost count   of the Moors he has killed.
The spoils that fell to him   also were enormous;
My Cid Don Rodrigo,   who was born in good hour,
has sent him a tithe   out of his own fifth.

96

*The rejoicing of the Christians. The Cid sends a new
present to the King*

These Christian people   in Valencia rejoice
at their great wealth,   at so many horses and weapons;
Doña Jimena is pleased,   and her daughters,
and all the other ladies,   who count themselves already married.
My good Cid   delayed for nothing.
"Where are you, worthy knight?   Come here, Minaya.
For that which has fallen to you   you owe me no thanks;
I mean what I say;   out of this fifth that is mine
take what you wish   and leave the rest for me.
And when tomorrow dawns   you must go without fail
with horses from this fifth   which I have taken,
with saddles and bridles   and each with its sword;
for my wife's sake   and that of my daughters,
since he sent them here   where they are content,
these two hundred horses   will go to him as a gift,
that King Alfonso may speak no ill   of him who rules in Valencia."
He commanded Pedro Bermúdez   to go with Minaya.
The next day in the morning   they rode off early
to kiss the King's hands   with the Cid's greetings,
and two hundred men   rode as their retinue.
My Cid sent as a gift   two hundred horses
from this battle   in which he had triumphed.
"And I shall serve him always   while my soul is with me."

97

Minaya takes the gift to Castile

They have left Valencia   and begin their journey;
they bear such riches with them   they must guard them closely.
They ride two days and nights   without pausing to rest,
and they have passed the mountains   that cut off the other
          country.
They begin to inquire   for King Alfonso.

98

Minaya arrives in Valladolid

They have passed the ranges,   the mountains and the waters;
they arrive in Valladolid   where King Alfonso is.
Pedro Bermúdez and Minaya   sent a message
requesting him to prepare   to receive this company,
for My Cid of Valencia   was sending him a gift.

99

*The King rides out to receive the Cid's men. The envy
of García Ordóñez*

The King rejoiced;   you have not seen him so pleased.
He commanded all his nobles   to mount at once,
and the King rode out   among the first
to see those messengers   from him who was born in good hour.
The Heirs of Carrión,   you may know, murmured at this,
and the Count Don García,   the Cid's sworn enemy.
What pleases some   weighs heavy upon others.
Those sent by My Cid   came into sight;
one would have thought them an army,   not mere messengers;
King Alfonso   crosses himself.
Minaya and Pedro Bermúdez   have arrived before him;
they set foot on the earth,   they get down from their horses,
they kneel down   before King Alfonso,
they kiss the ground   and both his feet.
"Grace, King Alfonso,   greatly honored!
We kiss your feet   for My Cid the Campeador;
he calls you his lord   and remains your vassal
and prizes greatly   the honor you have given him.
A few days since, King,   he triumphed in a battle
over that King of Morocco   whose name is Yusuf
and fifty thousand besides;   he beat them from the field.
The spoils that he took   are very great;
all of his vassals   have become rich men,
and he sends you two hundred horses   and kisses your hands."
King Alfonso said,   "I receive them with pleasure.

I send thanks to My Cid   for this gift he has sent me;
he will yet see the hour   I shall do as much for him."
This pleased many   and they kissed his hands.
It weighed heavy on Count Don García; it enraged him
    deeply.
With ten of his kinsmen   he rode to one side.
"What a marvel, this Cid,   how his honor grows.
And in his honor   we are dishonored.   ´
For killing Kings in the field   as casually
as though he had found them dead   and seized their horses,
for his deeds of this sort   we shall suffer."

100

The King shows himself benevolent toward the Cid

    King Alfonso spoke,   hear what he said:
"I thank the Creator   and lord Saint Isidore
for these two hundred horses   which My Cid has sent me.
In the coming days of my kingdom   I shall expect still greater
    things.
You, Minaya Alvar Fáñez,   and Pedro Bermúdez there,
I command   that you be given rich garments,
and choose arms for yourselves   at your pleasure
so that you may appear well   before Ruy Díaz, My Cid.
I give you three horses;   take them now.
Thus it seems to me,   and I am convinced
that from these new things   good must follow."

101

*The Heirs of Carrión think of marrying the
Cid's daughters*

They kissed his hands   and went in to rest;
he commanded that they should be served   with whatever they
    needed.
    I would tell you   of the Heirs of Carrión
taking counsel together,   plotting in secret:
"The Cid's affairs   prosper greatly;
let us ask   for his daughters in marriage;

our honor will grow   and we shall prosper."
They come to King Alfonso   with this secret.

102

The Heirs persuade the King to arrange the marriage
for them. The King asks to see the Cid.
Minaya returns to Valencia and informs the Cid of everything.
The Cid fixes the place of meeting

"We beg your grace   as our King and lord,
by your leave   we would have you ask for us
for the hands of the daughters   of the Campeador;
we would marry them,   to his honor and our advantage."
A long while   the King thought and meditated:
"I sent the good Campeador   into exile
and wrought him harm,   and he has returned me much good.
I cannot tell   if he will favor this marriage,
but since you wish it   I shall discuss it with him."
Then King Alfonso   called to himself
Minaya Alvar Fáñez   and Pedro Bermúdez
and took them aside   into another room.
"Hear me, Minaya,   and you, Pedro Bermúdez.
Ruy Díaz, Campeador,   My Cid, serves me well.
He shall receive my pardon   as he deserves;
let him come and appear before me   if it meet his pleasure.
There are further tidings   from here in my court:
Diego and Fernando,   the Heirs of Carrión,
wish to marry   his two daughters.
Be good messengers,   I beg of you,
and tell all this   to the good Campeador:
his name will be ennobled   and his honor increase
by thus contracting marriage   with the Heirs of Carrión."
Minaya spoke,   in agreement with Pedro Bermúdez:
"We shall ask him   as you have told it to us,
then the Cid may do   what meets his pleasure."
"Say to Ruy Díaz,   who in good hour was born,
that I shall come to meet him   wherever he prefers;
wherever he says,   let us meet each other.
I wish to help My Cid   however I may."
They said farewell to the King   and turned away;

they depart for Valencia   with all who are with them.
  When the good Campeador   heard they were coming
he mounted in haste   and rode out to receive them.
He smiled, My Cid,   and warmly embraced them:
"Have you come, Minaya,   and you, Pedro Bermúdez!
In few lands   are there two such knights.
What greeting   from Alfonso my lord?
Is he satisfied?   Did he receive the gift?"
Minaya said,   "With heart and soul
he is satisfied   and returns you to his favor."
My Cid replied,   "The Creator be thanked!"
And when this was said   they began to tell
what Alfonso of León   had asked of them,
of giving the Cid's daughters   to the Heirs of Carrión
that his name might be ennobled   and he increase in honor,
that the King approved this   with heart and soul.
When he heard this, My Cid,   the good Campeador,
a long while   he thought and meditated:
"I give thanks   to Christ, to my lord.
I was sent into exile   my honors were taken away;
with toil and pain I have taken   what is now mine.
I give thanks to God   that I have regained the King's love
and that he asks for my daughters   for the Heirs of Carrión.
Tell me, Minaya,   and you, Pedro Bermúdez,
what do you think   of this marriage?"
"Whatever would please you   seems best to us."
    The Cid spoke: "They have a great name,   these Heirs of
        Carrión;
they are swollen with pride   and have a place in the court,
and this marriage   would not be to my liking.
But since he wishes it   who is worth more than we,
let us talk of the matter   but do it in secret,
and may God in heaven   turn it to the best."
    "And besides this,   Alfonso sends to tell you
that he will meet you   wherever you please;
he wishes to see you   and make manifest his favor,
after which you may decide   what you think best."
Then the Cid said,   "It pleases my heart."
    And Minaya said,   "As for this meeting,
you are to decide   where it is to be."

"It would be no marvel   if King Alfonso had bid me
come where he was,   and we should have gone
to do him honor   as befits a King and lord.
But what he wishes   we must wish also.
By the Tagus,   the great river,
let us meet   when my lord pleases."
They wrote letters   and sealed them straitly,
and they sent them   in the hands of two horsemen;
the Campeador will do   what the King desires.

103

*The King fixes the time of the meeting. He prepares his
retinue to go there*

The letters have come   to the honored King;
he rejoiced   when he saw them.
"My greetings to My Cid,   who in good hour girded on sword,
let the meeting be   three weeks from now;
if I live   I shall be there without fail."
They returned to My Cid   without delay.
On this side and that   they made ready for the meeting;
who had ever seen   so many fine mules in Castile,
and so many palfreys   of graceful gait,
heavy chargers   and swift horses,
so many fair pennons   flown from good lances,
shields braced at the center   with gold and with silver,
cloaks and furs,   fine cloth from Alexandria?
The King has them send   ample provisions
to the banks of the Tagus   where the meeting will be.
A splendid company   goes with the King.
In high spirits   go the Heirs of Carrión;
here they make new debts   and there pay the old,
as though their fortunes   had so much increased already
and they had gold and silver   as much as they could wish for.
The King Don Alfonso   mounts without delay;
counts and nobles ride with him   and a host of vassals.
And a goodly company goes   with the Heirs of Carrión.
With the King go men of León   and of Galicia,
and Castilians,   you may know, without number;
they release the reins,   they ride to the meeting.

104

The Cid and his men make ready to go to the meeting. The departure
from Valencia. The King and the Cid meet on the banks of the Tagus.
The King solemnly pardons the Cid. Invitations. The King asks the
Cid for the hands of his daughters for the Heirs of Carrión.
The Cid gives his daughters to the King, who marries them. The end
of the meeting. The Cid's gifts to those who depart.
The King commends the Heirs to the Cid

In Valencia   My Cid the Campeador
does not delay,   but makes ready for the meeting.
So many fat mules   and fine palfreys,
so many splendid weapons   and so many swift horses,
so many fine capes   and cloaks and furs;
everyone, young and old,   all dressed in colors.
Minaya Alvar Fáñez   and that same Pedro Bermúdez,
Martín Muñoz,   lord of Monte Mayor,
and Martín Antolínez,   the loyal citizen of Burgos,
the Bishop Don Jerome,   the worthy cleric,
Alvar Alvarez   and Alvar Salvadórez,
Muño Gustioz, that excellent knight,
Galindo García,   who came from Aragón,
these make ready   to go with the Campeador,
and all the others,   as many as there were.
       Alvar Salvadórez   and Galindo García of Aragón,
the Campeador commanded these two
to guard Valencia   with heart and soul,
and he commanded all who should remain there   to obey these
       two.
My Cid ordered   that they should not open
the gates of the palace   by day or by night;
his wife and both his daughters   are within,
in whom his heart is   and his soul,
and there also are the other ladies   who wait upon their pleasure.
My Cid in his prudence   has commanded
that none may come forth   out of the castle
until he himself returns   who in good hour was born.
       They went out from Valencia and spurred forward,
so many fine horses,   sleek, and swift runners;
My Cid had won them,   they had not been given as gifts.

And they rode on toward the meeting   arranged with the King.
    The King arrived   one day before him,
and when he saw   the Campeador coming
he rode out to meet him   to do him honor.
When he who was born in good hour   saw the King coming
he commanded those who were with him   to come to a halt,
all except a few knights   nearest to his heart.
Then as he had thought to do   who in good hour was born,
he and fifteen knights   got down from their horses
and on his knees and hands   he knelt down on the ground;
he took the grass of the field   between his teeth
and wept from his eyes   so great was his joy,
and thus he rendered homage   to Alfonso his lord
and in this manner   fell at his feet.
The King Don Alfonso   was grieved at this sight:
"Rise, rise,   Cid Campeador,
kiss my hands   but not my feet;
if you humble yourself further   you will lose my love."
The Campeador   remained on his knees:
"I beg grace of you,   my natural lord,
thus on my knees I beg you   to extend to me your favor
so that all may hear it,   as many as are here."
The King said, "I will do it   with all my heart and soul;
I hereby pardon you   and grant you my favor;
be welcome from this hour   in all my kingdom."
My Cid spoke,   here is what he said:
"My thanks. I accept the pardon,   Alfonso, my lord;
I thank God in heaven   and afterwards you
and these vassals   here about us."
Still on his knees   he kissed the King's hand
then rose to his feet   and kissed him on the mouth.
And all who were there   rejoiced to see it,
but it grieved Alvar Díaz   and García Ordóñez.
    My Cid spoke,   here is what he said:
"I give thanks   to our Father the Creator
for this grace I have received   from Alfonso my lord;
now God will be with me   by day and by night.
If it please you, my lord,   be my guest."
The King said,   "That would not be right.
You arrive only now   and we came here last night;

you must be my guest,   Cid Campeador,
and tomorrow we shall do   what meets your pleasure."
My Cid kissed his hand   and agreed to this.
Then the Heirs of Carrión   came and made him obeisance.
"We bow before you,   Cid, who in good hour were born!
We shall serve your fortune   as far as we are able."
The Cid answered,   "God grant that it may be so."
My Cid Ruy Díaz,   who in good hour was born,
on that same day   was the guest of the King,
who so loved him   he could not have enough of his company
and looked a long while at his beard,   which had grown so long.
All who beheld the Cid   marveled at the sight of him.
    The day has passed   and the night has come.
Next day in the morning   the sun rose bright;
the Campeador   called together his men,
bade them prepare a meal   for all who were there.
My Cid the Campeador   so well contented them,
all were merry   and of one mind;
they had not eaten better,   not for three years.
    The next day in the morning   as the sun was rising
the Bishop Don Jerome   sang Mass for them.
When they came from Mass,   all assembled together;
the King did not delay,   but began to speak.
"Hear me, my vassals,   counts and barons:
I would express a wish   to My Cid the Campeador,
and may Christ grant   that it be for the best.
I ask you for your daughters,   Doña Elvira and Doña Sol;
I ask you to give them as wives   to the Heirs of Carrión.
The marriage, to my eyes,   is honorable and to your advantage;
the Heirs request it   and I commend it to you.
And on this and on that side   as many as are here,
your vassals and mine,   may they second what I ask for;
give us your daughters, My Cid,   and may the Creator bless you."
"I have no daughters ready for marriage,"   the Campeador
       answered,
"for their age is slight   and their days are few.
I fathered them both   and you brought them up;
they and I   wait upon your mercy.
The fame is great   of the Heirs of Carrión,

enough for my daughters   and for others of higher station.
Doña Elvira and Doña Sol   I give into your charge;
give them to whom you think best   and I shall be content."
"My thanks," said the King,   "to you and to all this court."
The Heirs of Carrión   then got to their feet,
went and kissed the hands   of him who was born in good hour,
and they exchanged swords   before Alfonso the King.
The King Don Alfonso spoke   as a worthy lord:
"My thanks, Cid, for your goodness,   you, favored of the Creator,
who have given me your daughters   for the Heirs of Carrión.
Here I take into my charge   Doña Elvira and Doña Sol
and give them as wives   to the Heirs of Carrión.
By your leave   I marry your daughters;
may it please the Creator   that good may come of it.
Here I give into your hands   the Heirs of Carrión;
they will go with you now   for I must return.
Three hundred marks of silver   I give to help them,
to be spent on the wedding   or whatever you please;
let them remain under you   in Valencia, that great city.
Sons-in-law and daughters,   all four are your children:
do with them   as seems best to you, Campeador."
My Cid kissed his hands   and received the Heirs.
"My deep thanks,   my King and lord.
It is you, not I,   who have married my daughters."
    The words are said,   the promises given.
The next day in the morning   when the sun rose
each one would return   to the place from which he had come.
Then My Cid the Campeador   did a thing they would tell about:
So many fat mules   and so many fine palfreys,
so many precious garments   of great value
My Cid gave   to whomever would receive gifts,
and he denied no one   whatever he asked for.
My Cid gave as gifts   sixty of his horses.
All went from the meeting contented,   as many as there were;
it was time to part   for the night had come.
    The King took   the Heirs' hands
and put them in the hands   of My Cid the Campeador.
"These now are your sons,   since they are your sons-in-law.
Know, from today forward   they are yours, Campeador;

let them serve you as their father　and honor you as their lord."
"My thanks, King,　and I accept your gift.
May God Who is in heaven　give you reward."

105

The Cid refuses to give his daughters in marriage himself.
Minaya will be the King's representative

"I beg grace of you,　my natural King:
Since you marry my daughters　as suits your will,
name someone to give them in marriage　in your name.
I will not give them with my hand;　none shall boast of that."
The King answered,　"Here is Alvar Fáñez;
let him take them by the hand　and give them to the Heirs.
Let him act at the wedding　as though he were myself;
at the ceremony　let him be as the godfather
and let him tell me of it　when next we come together."
Alvar Fáñez said,　"With all my heart, sire."

106

*The Cid bids farewell to the King. **Gifts***

You may know, all this was done　with great care.
"Ah, King Alfonso,　my honored lord,
take something of mine　to commemorate our meeting;
I have brought you thirty palfreys　with all their trappings
and thirty swift horses　with their saddles;
take these　and I kiss your hands."
King Alfonso said,　"You fill me with confusion.
I accept this gift　which you have brought me;
may it please the Creator　and all His saints besides
that this pleasure you give me　may be well rewarded.
My Cid Ruy Díaz,　you have done me great honor;
you have served me well　and I am contented;
if I live　I shall reward you somehow.
I commend you to God;　now I must leave.
May God Who is in heaven　turn all to the best."

107

Many of the King's men go with the Cid to Valencia.
The Heirs accompanied by Pedro Bermúdez

My Cid mounted   his horse Babieca.
"Here I say   before Alfonso my lord:
Whoever will come to the wedding   and receive gifts from me,
let him come with me   and he shall not regret it."
The Cid has said good-by   to Alfonso his lord;
he would not have the King escort him   on his way, but parted
    there.
You would have seen knights   of excellent bearing
saying farewell to King Alfonso,   kissing his hands:
"Grant us your grace   and give us your pardon;
we go as the Cid's vassals   to Valencia, that great city;
we shall be at the wedding   of the Heirs of Carrión
and the daughters of My Cid,   Doña Elvira and Doña Sol."
This pleased the King,   he gave them all his consent;
the Cid's company grows   and that of the King dwindles.
There are many   who go with the Campeador.
They ride for Valencia,   which in a blessed hour he had taken.
He sent Pedro Bermúdez   and Muño Gustioz—
there were not two better knights   among all the Cid's vassals—
to ride as companions   with Fernando and Diego
that they might learn the ways   of the Heirs of Carrión.
And with them went Asur González,   who was a noisy person,
more ready of tongue   than of other things.
They paid much honor   to the Heirs of Carrión.
They have arrived in Valencia,   which My Cid had taken;
the closer they come   the greater is their rejoicing.
My Cid said to Don Pedro   and to Muño Gustioz:
"See to the lodging   of the Heirs of Carrión
and stay with them   for I command it.
When the morning comes   and the sun rises
they will see their wives,   Doña Elvira and Doña Sol."

108

The Cid announces the marriage to Doña Jimena

That night everyone   went to his lodging.
My Cid the Campeador   entered the palace;
Doña Jimena received him   and both his daughters.
"Have you returned, Campeador,   who girded sword in good
     hour?
Many days may we look upon you   with these eyes of ours."
"The Creator be thanked,   honored wife, that I have returned;
I bring you two sons-in-law   in whom we have much honor;
give me thanks, my daughters,   for I have married you well."

109

Doña Jimena and the daughters are pleased

His wife and his daughters   kissed his hand,
as did all the ladies   who wait upon them.
"The Creator be thanked,   and you, Cid of the splendid beard.
All you have done   has been done well.
They will lack for nothing   as long as you live."
"When you give us in marriage,   father, we shall be rich."

110

The Cid's misgivings concerning the marriage

"Doña Jimena, my wife,   I give thanks to the Creator.
And I say to you, my daughters,   Doña Elvira and Doña Sol,
that by your marriage   we shall increase in honor.
But you may know   that none of this was my doing:
my lord Alfonso   asked me for your hands,
and that so urgently   with all his heart,
that I in no way   could have denied him.
I gave you into his hands,   both of you, my daughters;
believe this that I say: he will marry you, not I."

111

Preparations for the wedding. The presentation of the Heirs.
Minaya gives the wives to the Heirs. Benedictions and Masses.
The two-week festivities. The end of the wedding festivities;
the gifts given to the guests. The poet bids his audience farewell

Then they began   to get the palace ready:
┼hey covered the floor   and the walls with carpets,
with bolts of silk and purple   and many precious fabrics.
You would have been well pleased   to sit and eat in the palace.
All the Cid's knights   have gathered together.
Then they sent   for the Heirs of Carrión,
and the Heirs took horse   and rode to the palace
covered in finery   and splendid garments;
on foot and in seemly fashion   God, how meekly they entered!
My Cid received them   with all his vassals;
they humbled themselves   before him and his wife
then went and sat down   on a bench of precious work.
All My Cid's vassals,   quiet and prudent,
sit watching his face   who in good hour was born.
The Campeador   rose to his feet:
"Since it must be done,   why should we delay?
Come here, Alvar Fáñez,   beloved knight.
Both my daughters   I hereby give into your hands;
you know that the King   has commanded that it be so
and I would in every way   satisfy the agreement.
With your hand give them   to the Heirs of Carrión,
let them receive the benediction   and let it be properly done."
Then Minaya said,   "I will do it gladly."
The girls stood up   and he took them by the hands.
Minaya speaks   to the Heirs of Carrión:
"Now both you brothers   stand before Minaya.
By the hand of King Alfonso,   who has commanded me thus,
I give you these ladies,   both of gentle birth;
take them for wives   for the honor and good of all."
Both received them   with love and joy
and went to kiss the hands   of My Cid and his wife.
When they had done this   they went out from the palace
and without delay   rode to Santa María;

the Bishop Don Jerome   put on his vestments;
at the door of the church   he waited for them,
gave them his benedictions   and sang them Mass.
     When they came from the church   all mounted in haste
and rode out   to the arena of Valencia.
God, how well they jousted,   My Cid and his vassals!
Three times he changed horses,   he who was born in good hour.
My Cid was well content   with what he saw there:
the Heirs of Carrión   proved themselves good horsemen.
They returned to the ladies   and re-entered Valencia;
there were rich wedding feasts   in the gorgeous palace,
and the next day   My Cid set up seven tablets:
all must be ridden at and broken   before they went in to eat.
     Two full weeks   the wedding feasts went on;
at the end of that time   the noble guests went home.
My Cid Don Rodrigo,   who in good hour was born,
gave at least a hundred   of all sorts of beasts,
palfreys and mules   and swift running horses,
besides cloaks and furs   and many other garments,
and there was no counting   the gifts of money.
My Cid's vassals   also gave presents;
each one gave something   to the guests who were there.
Whatever the guests might wish for   their hands were filled;
all who had come to the wedding   returned rich to Castile.
Then those guests   made ready to leave,
took leave of Ruy Díaz,   who in good hour was born,
and of all those ladies   and the knights who were there;
they parted contented   from My Cid and his vassals.
They spoke well   of the way they had been treated.
And Diego and Fernando   were highly pleased,
they, the sons   of the Count Don Gonzalo.
     The guests have departed   for Castile;
My Cid and his sons-in-law   remain in Valencia.
And there the Heirs dwell   nearly two years,
and all in Valencia   showered them with their favor.
My Cid was joyful,   and all his vassals.
May it please Santa María   and the heavenly Father
to bless My Cid   and him who proposed this marriage.
     Herewith are ended   the verses of this cantar.
The Creator be with you   and all His saints besides.

THE THIRD CANTAR

The Outrage at Corpes

112

The Cid's lion gets loose. The fear of the Heirs of
Carrión. The Cid tames the lion. The shame of the Heirs

My Cid is in Valencia   with all his vassals,
and with him his sons-in-law,   the Heirs of Carrión.
The Campeador was asleep,   lying on a bench,
when, you may know, there occurred   an unlooked-for misfortune:
the lion broke from his cage   and stalked abroad.
Great terror ran   through the court;
the Campeador's men   seize their cloaks
and stand over the bench   to protect their lord.
Fernando González,   Heir of Carrión,
could find nowhere to hide,   no room nor tower was open;
he hid under the bench,   so great was his terror.
Diego González   went out the door
crying, "I shall never   see Carrión again."
Behind a beam of the wine press   he hid in his fear;
there his cloak and his tunic   were covered with filth.

At this point he wakened   who in good hour was born;
he saw the bench surrounded   by his brave vassals.
"What is this, knights,   what do you wish?"
"Ah, honored lord,   we are frightened of the lion."
My Cid rose to his elbow,   got to his feet,
with his cloak on his shoulders   walked toward the lion;
the lion, when he saw him,   was so filled with shame,
before My Cid he bowed his head   and put his face down.
My Cid Don Rodrigo   took him by the neck,
led him as with a halter   and put him in his cage.
And all marveled,   as many as were there,
and the knights returned   from the palace to the court.
    My Cid asked for his sons-in-law   and could not find them;
though he calls out   no one answers.
When at last they were found,   their faces were without color;
you have not seen such mockery   as rippled through the court;
My Cid the Campeador   commanded silence.
And the Heirs of Carrión   were covered with shame
and bitterly mortified   at this occurrence.

113

King Búcar of Morocco attacks Valencia

    While they were still sore   with the smart of this,
hosts from Morocco   came to surround Valencia;
they pitched their camp   in the field of Cuarto;
they set up their tents,   fifty thousand of the largest:
this was King Búcar,   of whom you have heard tell.

114

The Heirs are afraid of battle. The Cid reprimands them

    The Cid rejoiced,   and all his knights;
they thanked the Creator,   for the spoils would enrich them.
But, you may know, it grieved   the Heirs of Carrión;
so many Moorish tents   were not to their taste.
Both brothers   walked to one side:
"We thought only of the wealth   and not of the dangers;

for we have no choice   but to go into this battle.
This could keep us from ever again   seeing Carrión,
and the daughters of the Campeador   will be left widows."
Muño Gustioz   overheard them talking in secret
and brought what he had heard   to My Cid the Campeador.
"These sons-in-law of yours   are so filled with daring
that now at the hour of battle   they yearn for Carrión.
Go and console them,   as God is your grace,
let them sit in peace   and not enter the battle;
with you we shall conquer   and the Creator will give us aid."
My Cid Don Rodrigo   went up to them smiling:
"God save you, sons-in-law,   Heirs of Carrión,
you have in your arms my daughters   white as the sun.
I look forward to battle   and you to Carrión;
remain in Valencia   at your pleasure,
for I am seasoned   at managing the Moors
and shall make bold to rout them   with the help of the Creator."

115

*Búcar's message. The charge of the Christians. The
cowardice of the Heir Fernando. (Lacuna in the
manuscript; fifty verses supplied out of the Chronicle of
Twenty Kings.) The generosity of Pedro Bermúdez.*

As they were speaking of this, King Búcar sent to tell the Cid to leave
Valencia, and he, Búcar, would let him go in peace; but if he would not go,
then Búcar would make the Cid pay for everything he had done. The Cid
said to the messenger: "Go and tell Búcar, that son of my enemies, that
within three days I shall give him what he asks for." The next day My Cid
bade them all arm, and they rode out against the Moors. The Heirs of Carrión then begged of him the honor of striking the first blows; and when the
Cid had formed his ranks, Don Fernando, one of the Heirs, rode forward to
attack a Moor named Aladraf. When the Moor saw him he spurred toward
him, and the Heir, overcome with terror, turned his horse and fled, not daring to wait.

Pedro Bermúdez, who was near him, when he saw this, attacked the
Moor and fought with him and killed him. Then he took the Moor's horse
and went after the Heir, where he was still fleeing, and said: "Don Fernando, take this horse and tell everyone that you killed the Moor who was
its master, and I will affirm it."

The Heir said to him: "Don Pedro Bermúdez, I thank you deeply,

and may the hour come   when I can doubly repay you."
Then they returned   riding together.

And Don Pedro affirmed the deed   of which Don Fernando
    boasted.
It pleased My Cid   and all his vassals.
"If it please God,   our Father Who is in heaven,
both my sons-in-law   will prove brave in the battle."
    As they speak thus,   the armies draw together.
The drums are sounding   through the ranks of the Moors,
and many of these Christians   marveled much at the sound,
for they had come lately to the war   and never heard drums.
Don Diego and Don Fernando   marveled more than any;
they would not have been there   if the choice had been theirs.
Hear what he said,   he who was born in good hour:
"Ho, Pedro Bermúdez,   my dear nephew,
watch over Don Diego   and watch over Don Fernando,
my sons-in-law,   for whom I have much love,
and with God's help   the Moors will not keep the field."

116

*Pedro Bermúdez declines to guard the Heirs. Minaya and the
Bishop Don Jerome ask for the foremost position in the battle*

"I say to you, Cid,   in the name of charity,
that today the Heirs   will not have me for protector;
let who likes watch over them   for I care little for them.
I wish to attack in the van   with my men,
and you with yours   might guard the rear;
and if I have need,   you can come to my aid."
    Minaya Alvar Fáñez   then rode up.
"Hear me, Cid,   loyal Campeador.
This battle   the Creator will decide
and you, of so great worth,   who have His favor.
Send us to attack   where you think best,
let each one of us   look to his obligation.
With God and your good fortune   we shall attack them."
My Cid said,   "Let us proceed calmly."
    Then came Don Jerome   the Bishop, heavily armed.
He stopped before the Campeador   of unfailing fortune.
"Today I have said you the Mass   of the Holy Trinity;
I left my own country   and came to find you
because of the hunger I had   for killing Moors;

I wish to gain honor   for my hands and for my order,
and I wish to go in the van   and strike the first blows.
I bear pennon and arms   blazoned with crosiers;
if it please God   I wish to display them,
and thus my heart   will be at peace,
and you, My Cid,   will be further pleased with me.
Unless you do me this favor   I shall leave you."
Then My Cid answered,   "I am pleased with your request.
Now the Moors are in sight;   go try yourself against them.
Now we shall see   how the monk does battle."

117

The Bishop begins the battle. The Cid attacks.
He invades the Moorish camp

　　The Bishop Don Jerome   began
and charged against them   at the end of the camp.
By his good fortune   and the grace of God Who loved him,
with the first blows   he killed two Moors.
His lance splintered   and he drew his sword.
God, how hard he fought,   the Bishop, how well he did battle!
He killed two with his lance   and five with the sword.
And many Moors came   and surrounded him
and dealt him great blows   but could not break through his armor.
　　He who was born in good hour   kept his eyes upon him,
clasped his shield   and lowered his lance,
set spur to Babieca,   his swift horse,
and rode to attack them   with heart and soul.
In the first ranks   which he entered, the Campeador
unhorsed seven   and killed four.
There the rout began,   as it pleased God.
My Cid and his knights   rode in pursuit;
you would have seen so many tent cords   snapped, and the poles
　　　　down,
and so many embroidered tents   lying on the ground;
My Cid's vassals   drove Búcar's men from their camp.

118

*The Christians pursue the enemy. The Cid overtakes and
kills Búcar. The capture of the sword Tizón*

They drove them from the camp   and pursued them closely;
you would have seen fall   so many arms with their bucklers,
and so many heads in their helmets   fall in the field,
and horses without riders   running in all directions.
Seven full miles   the pursuit went on.
My Cid overtook   Búcar the King:
"Turn, Búcar,   who have come from beyond the sea!
Now you must face the Cid,   he of the long beard;
we must greet each other   and swear friendship."
Búcar answered the Cid,   "God confound such friendship:
you have a sword in your hand,   you ride at full speed,
and it would seem that you wish   to prove your sword upon me.
But if my horse does not stumble   or fall under me,
you will not overtake me   though you follow me into the sea."
Then My Cid answered,   "That cannot be true."
Búcar had a good horse,   he rode in great bounds,
but the Cid's Babieca   gained steadily on him.
The Cid overtook Búcar   three fathoms from the sea,
raised Colada   and struck him a great blow,
and there he cut away   the jewels of his helmet,
split the helmet   and, driving through all below,
as far as the waist   his sword sank.
He killed Búcar,   the King from beyond the sea,
and captured the sword Tizón,   worth a thousand marks of gold.
My Cid has won   that marvelous great battle;
here all who are with him   have gained honor.

119

*The Cid's men return from the pursuit. The Cid is content
with his sons-in-law; their shame. The spoils of the victory*

They turned back from the chase   with the spoils they had
     taken;
you may know, before they went   they stripped the field.

They have come to the tents   with him who was born in good
    hour,
My Cid Ruy Díaz,   the famous Campeador;
he came with two swords   which were worth much to him,
at full speed came riding   over the field of slaughter,
his face bare,   hood and helmet off,
and the cowl loose   over his hair.
From all directions   his knights regather;
My Cid saw a thing   which pleased him greatly;
he lifted his eyes   and looked before him
and saw approaching him   Diego and Fernando,
both the sons   of the Count Don Gonzalo.
My Cid rejoiced,   fair was his smiling:
"Greetings, my sons-in-law,   both of you are my sons!
I know you are well contented   with the fighting you have done;
the good news of your deeds   will go to Carrión,
and the tidings of our conquest   of Búcar the King.
I trust in God   and in all His saints
that we shall be satisfied   with the results of this victory."
Minaya Alvar Fáñez   rode up at this moment,
his shield at his neck   marked with sword dents
and with blows of lances   beyond number;
and those who had aimed them   had not profited by it.
Down from his elbow   the blood is dripping;
he had killed more than twenty   of the Moors.
"Thanks be to God   and to our heavenly Father
and to you, Cid,   who in good hour were born!
You have killed Búcar   and we have won the field.
All these spoils   are for you and your vassals.
And your sons-in-law   here have proved themselves
and sated themselves with fighting   with Moors in the field."
My Cid said,   "I am pleased with this;
they have been brave today   and in time to come they will be
    braver."
My Cid intended it kindly   but they took it as a jeer.
    All the spoils   have been brought to Valencia;
My Cid rejoices,   and all his vassals;
to each one there falls   six hundred marks of silver.
    My Cid's sons-in-law,   when they had taken this portion

which was theirs from the victory   and had put it safely away,
were sure that in all their days   they should not lack for money.
Those in Valencia   were lavishly provided
with excellent food,   fine furs and rich cloaks.
And My Cid and his vassals   all rejoiced.

120

The Cid pleased with the victory and with his sons-in-law. (Repetition)

It was a great day   in the court of the Campeador
after they had won that battle   and King Búcar had been killed;
the Cid raised his hand   and grasped his beard.
"I give thanks to Christ   Who is lord of the world,
that now I have seen   what I have wished to see:
both my sons-in-law   have fought beside me in the field;
good news concerning them   will go to Carrión;
they have been much help to us   and won themselves honor."

121

The division of the spoils

All have received   enormous spoils;
much was theirs already,   now these new gains are stored away.
My Cid, who was born   in a good hour, commanded
that from this battle   which they had won
each one should take   what fell by rights to him,
and the fifth which went to My Cid   was not forgotten.
This they all do   without disagreements.
In the fifth which fell to My Cid   were six hundred horses,
and other beasts of burden   and large camels;
there were so many   they could not be counted.

122

The Cid at the height of his glory meditates the capture of Morocco.
The Heirs live rich and honored in the Cid's court

All these spoils   the Campeador has taken.
"Thanks be to God   Who is lord of the world!
In the old days I was poor,   now I am rich,

for I have wealth and domains   and gold and honor,
and my sons-in-law   are the Heirs of Carrión;
I win battles,   as pleases the Creator;
Moors and Christians   go in fear of me.
There in Morocco,   where the mosques are,
they tremble   lest perhaps some night
I should take them by surprise,   but I plan no such thing.
I shall not go seeking them,   but stay in Valencia,
and they will send me tribute,   as the Creator aids me;
they will send money to me   or to whomever I please."
    Great were the rejoicings   in Valencia, that great city,
among all the company   of My Cid the Campeador
at this rout   in which heartily they had fought;
and great was the joy   of both the sons-in-law;
five thousand marks   was the portion which fell to them.
These Heirs of Carrión   considered themselves rich.
    They with the others   came to the court;
there with My Cid   was the Bishop Don Jerome,
the good Alvar Fáñez,   knight and warrior,
and many others   whom the Campeador had reared.
When the Heirs of Carrión   entered there
Minaya received them   for My Cid the Campeador:
"Come here, my kinsmen,   we profit by your company."
As they approached,   the Campeador grew more pleased:
"Here, my sons-in-law,   are my excellent wife
and both my daughters,   Doña Elvira and Doña Sol,
to embrace you closely   and serve you with all their hearts.
I thank Santa María,   mother of the lord our God,
that from this marriage   you shall have gained honor.
Good news will go   to the lands of Carrión."

123

The Heirs' vanity. The jibes of which they are the butt

    At these words   the Heir Fernando spoke:
"I thank the Creator   and you, honored Cid,
that so much wealth,   that riches beyond measure are ours.
From you we receive our honor   and for you we fought;
we conquered the Moors   in the field and killed

that King Búcar,   a proved traitor.
Think of other things,   for our affairs are in good order."
The vassals of My Cid   smiled to hear this;
some had battled bravely   and some ridden in pursuit,
but they had not seen   Diego nor Fernando there.
Because the mockeries   made at their expense,
day and night, always,   so tormented them,
both the Heirs   conceived of an evil plan.
They walked aside.   Indeed, they were brothers;
let us have no part   in what they said:
"Let us go to Carrión;   we have stayed here too long.
The wealth we have   is great and immeasurable;
we could not spend it all   in the rest of our lives.

124

*The Heirs decide to do injury to the Cid's daughters. They ask
the Cid for permission to take their wives to Carrión. The Cid consents.
The bridal clothing he gives to his daughters. The Heirs make
ready to travel. The daughters say good-by to their father*

Let us ask for our wives   from the Cid Campeador;
let us say we will take them   to the lands of Carrión,
for we must show them   the lands that are theirs.
We shall take them from Valencia,   from the power of the
          Campeador;
afterwards, on the journey,   we shall do as we please with them
before they reproach us   with the story of the lion.
For we are descended   from the Counts of Carrión!
We shall take much wealth with us,   riches of great value;
we shall work our punishment   on the daughters of the
          Campeador."
"With the wealth we have now,   we shall be rich forever;
we can marry the daughters   of kings or emperors,
for we are descended   from the Counts of Carrión.
Therefore we shall punish   the daughters of the Campeador
before they throw in our faces   what happened with the lion."
      When they had made up their minds   they turned back again.
Fernando González spoke,   requesting silence in the court:
"As the Creator may bless you,   Cid Campeador,

may it please Doña Jimena   and before all others, you,
and Minaya Alvar Fáñez   and as many as are here,
to give us our wives,   who have been blessed to us;
we would take them with us   to our lands of Carrión
so that they may possess the lands   we have given them for their
        honor;
your daughters will see   what belongs to us,
in which our children   will have a share."
        My Cid the Campeador   suspected no harm:
"I will give you my daughters   and more things that are mine;
you have given them as wedding gifts   villages in Carrión;
I would give them for their betrothal   three thousand marks,
and I give you mules and palfreys   sleek and fine limbed,
and war horses   strong, and swift runners,
and many garments of cloth   and of cloth-of-gold,
and I will give you two swords,   Colada and Tizón;
you know well that I gained them   as befits a man.
Both of you are my sons   since I give you my daughters;
you bear away with you   the threads of my heart.
Let them know in Galicia   and in Castile and in León
how richly I send from me   my two sons-in-law.
Cherish my daughters,   who are your wives;
if you treat them well   I shall reward you handsomely."
The Heirs of Carrión   have agreed to everything.
They receive the daughters   of the Campeador,
and now they take   the Cid's gifts.
        When they are sated   with receiving presents
the Heirs of Carrión bade them   load up the beasts of burden.
There is much bustle   in Valencia, that great city;
all seize their arms   and mount in haste;
they are sending off the Cid's daughters   to the lands of Carrión.
        They are ready to ride,   they are saying good-by.
Both the sisters,   Doña Elvira and Doña Sol,
knelt down   before the Cid Campeador:
"We beg your blessing, father,   and may the Creator be with you;
you sired us,   our mother brought us forth;
here we are before you both,   our lady and our lord.
Now you send us   to the lands of Carrión;
we owe it to you to obey you   in whatever you demand.

And thus we beg   your blessing on us both.
Send messages to us   in the lands of Carrión."
My Cid embraced them   and kissed them both

125

Jimena says good-by to her daughters. The Cid mounts
to see the travelers off. Bad omens

Their mother embraces them   twice over:
"Now go hence, daughters,   and the Creator bless you,
and take with you   your father's blessing and mine.
Go to Carrión,   where you are heirs;
in my eyes it seems   that you were well married."
They kissed the hands   of their father and mother,
who both blessed them   and gave them their grace.
    My Cid and the others   began to ride;
there were great provisions   and horses and arms.
The Heirs have ridden out   from Valencia the Shining;
they have said good-by to the ladies   and all their companions.
Through the farmlands of Valencia   they ride, playing at arms;
My Cid goes merrily   among all his companions.
    But he who in good hour was born   looked upon the omens
and saw that this marriage   will not be without stain.
But now he may not repent   for both of them are wedded.

126

The Cid sends Félix Muñoz with his daughters. The last
good-by. The Cid returns to Valencia. The travelers
arrive at Molina. Abengalbón accompanies them to Medinaceli.
The Heirs consider killing Abengalbón
    "Oh, where are you, my nephew,   you, Félix Muñoz:
you are cousin to my daughters   and love them with heart and
        soul.
I command you to go with them   all the way to Carrión;
you will see the inheritances   which have been given to my
        daughters
and with news of these things   return to the Campeador."
Félix Muñoz said,   "It pleases my heart and soul."
    Minaya Alvar Fáñez   stopped before My Cid:

"Let us go back, Cid,   to Valencia, the great city,
and if it please God   and our Father the Creator,
one day we shall go to see them   in the lands of Carrión."
"To God I commend you,   Doña Elvira and Doña Sol;
behave in such manner   as shall give us cause for pleasure."
The sons-in-law answered,   "May God send that it be so."
Great were their sorrows   when they came to part.
The father and the daughters   wept from their hearts,
as did also the knights   of the Campeador.

"Hear me, my nephew,   you, Félix Muñoz;
go to Molina   and spend the night there;
in my name greet my friend,   the Moor Abengalbón;
let him receive my sons-in-law   with his fairest welcome;
tell him I am sending my daughters   to the lands of Carrión;
let him serve their pleasure   in whatever they need
and, for love of me, bid him escort them   as far as Medinaceli.
For all he does for them   I shall reward him well."
They parted, one from the other,   as nail from flesh.

He has turned back to Valencia   who in good hour was born.
The Heirs of Carrión   ride forward;
at Santa María of Albarracín   the camp was made;
from there the Heirs of Carrión   spur forward at all speed;
they have come to Molina   and the Moor Abengalbón.
When the Moor knew they were there   it pleased his heart;
with great rejoicing   he rode out to receive them.
God, how well he served them   in whatever they pleased!
The next day in the morning   he rode on with them
with two hundred knights   whom he sent to escort them;
they have passed the mountains   called the range of Luzón,
crossed the valley of Arbujuelo   and come to Jalón;
where it is called Ansarera   they made their camp.
The Moor gave presents   to the Cid's daughters
and fine horses for each   of the Heirs of Carrión;
all this the Moor did for love   of the Cid Campeador.

When they saw the riches   which the Moor had brought
both brothers   began to plot to betray him:
"Now that we plan to desert   the Campeador's daughters,
if we could murder   the Moor Abengalbón
all his wealth   would be ours.
We could keep it as safely   as what is ours in Carrión,

and the Cid Campeador   could enforce no claim against us."
While they of Carrión   were speaking of this deceit,
a Moor who knew Castilian   heard what they said
and did not keep it secret   but told Abengalbón:
"My lord, my master,   have a care of these,
for I have heard them plotting your death,   these Heirs of
    Carrión."

127

Abengalbón departs, threatening the Heirs

    The Moor Abengalbón   was tough and stouthearted;
with the two hundred who were with him   he came riding;
all of them were armed;   they halted before the Heirs.
What the Moor said to the Heirs   gave them no pleasure:
"If it were not for respect   for My Cid of Bivar
I would wreak such deeds on you   as the whole world would
    hear of
and I would return his daughters   to the loyal Campeador;
and as for Carrión,   you would never see it again.

128

*The Moor returns to Molina, with premonitions of the disgrace of the
Cid's daughters. The travelers enter the kingdom of Castile.
They sleep in the grove of Corpes. In the morning the Heirs
are alone with their wives and prepare to do them injury. Doña Sol
calls out vainly. The Heirs' cruelty*

    "Tell me what harm have I done you,   Heirs of Carrión!
I serve you without malice   and you plot my death.
Here I leave you,   vile men and traitors.
By your leave I go,   Doña Elvira and Doña Sol;
I scorn the fame   of the Heirs of Carrión.
May God Who is lord of the world   will and command
that the Campeador may remain   contented with this marriage."
When he had said this   the Moor turned away
and they went with their arms at ready   till they had crossed the
    stream Jalón.
As a man of prudence   he went back to Molina.
    The Heirs of Carrión   have left Ansarera.

They march without rest   all day and all night;
on their left they leave Atienza,   that is a strong hill;
the mountains of Miedes   fall behind them;
upon Montes Claros   they spur forward,
and on their left leave Griza,   which Alamos peopled,
and there are the caves   where he encircled Elpha;
further on, on their right   was San Esteban de Gormaz.
The Heirs have entered   the oak wood of Corpes;
the mountains are high,   the branches touch the clouds
and there are savage beasts   which walk about there.
They found a glade   with a clear spring.
The Heirs of Carrión   bade their men set up the tent;
there they spend the night   with as many as are with them,
with their wives in their arms,   showing them love;
yet they meant to do them evil   when the sun rose!
    They had the beasts of burden   loaded with their riches,
and they have taken down the tent   where they spent the night,
and those who waited on them   have all ridden ahead
as they were orderd to do   by the Heirs of Carrión,
so that none remained behind,   neither man nor woman,
except both their wives,   Doña Elvira and Doña Sol.
They wished to amuse themselves with these   to the height of
        their pleasure.
    All had gone ahead,   only these four remained;
the Heirs of Carrión   had conceived great villainy:
"Know this for a certainty,   Doña Elvira and Doña Sol,
you will be tormented here   in these savage mountains.
Today we shall desert you   and go on from this place;
you will have no share   in the lands of Carrión.
The news of this will go   to the Cid Campeador,
and we shall be avenged   for the story of the lion."
    Then they stripped them   of their cloaks and furs;
they left nothing on their bodies   but their shirts and silk
        undergarments.
The wicked traitors   have spurs on their boots;
they take in their hands   the strong hard saddle girths.
When the ladies saw this,   Doña Sol said:
"You have two swords,   strong and keen edged,
one that is called Colada   and the other Tizón.
For God's sake, we beg you,   Don Diego and Don Fernando,

cut off our heads   and we shall be martyrs.
Moors and Christians   will speak harshly of this,
for such treatment   we have not deserved.
Do not visit upon us   so vile an ensample;
if you whip us   the shame will be yours;
you will be called to account   at assemblies or courts."
    The ladies' pleadings   availed them nothing.
Then the Heirs of Carrión   began to lash them;
they beat them without mercy   with the flying cinches,
gored them with the sharp spurs,   dealing them great pain.
They tore their shirts   and the flesh of both of them,
and over the silken cloth   the clean blood ran,
and they felt the pain   in their very hearts.
Oh, it would be such good fortune   if it should please the
        Creator
that the Cid Campeador   might appear now!
    They beat them so cruelly,   they left them senseless;
the shirts and the silk skirts   were covered with blood.
They beat them   until their arms were tired,
each of them trying   to strike harder than the other.
Doña Elvira and Doña Sol   could no longer speak;
they left them for dead   in the oak grove of Corpes.

129

The Heirs abandon the women. (Parallel passage)

    They took away their cloaks   and their furs of ermine,
and left them fainting   in their shifts and silk tunics,
left them to the birds of the mountain   and to the wild beasts.
They left them for dead,   you may know, with no life left in them.
What good fortune it would be   if the Cid Ruy Díaz should
        appear now!

130

The Heirs congratulate themselves on their cowardice

    The Heirs of Carrión   left them there for dead,
so that neither   might give aid to the other.
Through the mountains where they went   they praised themselves·

"Now we have avenged ourselves   for our marriage.
We would not have them for concubines   even if they begged us.
As legitimate wives   they were unworthy of us;
the dishonor of the lion   thus will be avenged."

131

*Félix Muñoz is suspicious of the Heirs. He turns back
looking for the Cid's daughters. He revives them and carries
them on his horse to San Esteban de Gormaz. The Cid hears of
this dishonor. Minaya goes to San Esteban to fetch the ladies.
The meeting between Minaya and his cousins*

The Heirs of Carrión   rode on, praising themselves.
But I shall tell you   of that same Félix Muñoz —
he was a nephew   of the Cid Campeador —
they had bidden him ride forward   but this was not to his liking.
On the road as he went   his heart was heavy;
he slipped to one side   apart from the others;
he hid himself   in a thick wood,
waiting for his cousins   to come by
or to see what they had done,   those Heirs of Carrión.
He saw them come   and heard something of their talk;
they did not see him there   nor suspect that he heard them;
he knew well that if they saw him   they would not leave him alive.
        The Heirs set spur   and ride on.
Félix Muñoz   turned back the way they had come;
he found his cousins   both lying senseless.
He called, "Cousins, cousins!" Then he dismounted,
tied his horse   and went up to them.
"Cousins, my cousins,   Doña Elvira and Doña Sol,
they have vilely proved themselves,   the Heirs of Carrión!
May it please God   that their punishment find them!"
He stayed there   endeavoring to revive them.
Their senses had gone far from them;   they could not speak at all.
The fabrics of his heart   tear as he calls:
"Cousins, my cousins,   Doña Elvira and Doña Sol,
come awake, cousins,   for the love of the Creator!
Wake now while the day lasts   before the night comes
and the wild beasts   devour us on this mountain!"
Doña Elvira and Doña Sol   come back to themselves;

they opened their eyes   and saw Félix Muñoz.
"Quickly, cousins,   for the love of the Creator!
the Heirs of Carrión   when they miss me
will come looking for me   at full speed;
if God does not aid us   we shall die here."
Then with great pain   Doña Sol spoke:
"If our father the Campeador   deserves it of you, my cousin,
give us a little water,   for the love of the Creator."
Then with his hat,   which was new, with its sheen still on it,
which he had brought from Valencia,   Féliz Muñoz
took up water   and gave it to his cousins;
they were gravely hurt   and both had need of it.
    He urged them a long while   till they sat upright.
He gave them comfort   and made them take heart again
till they recovered somewhat,   and he took them both up
and with all haste   put them on his horse;
he covered them both   with his own mantle,
took his horse by the reins   and went off with them both.
They three alone   through the forest of Corpes
between night and day   went out from among the mountains;
they have arrived   at the waters of the Duero;
at the tower of Doña Urraca   he left those two.
Félix Muñoz came   to San Esteban
and found Diego Téllez,   who was Alvar Fáñez's vassal;
he was grieved in his heart   when he heard the story,
and he took beasts   and fine garments
and went to receive   Doña Elvira and Doña Sol;
he brought them   into San Esteban;
he did them honor   as well as he could.
Those of San Esteban   are always sensible folk;
when they knew of this deed   it grieved their hearts;
they brought tribute from their farms   to the Cid's daughters.
There the girls remained   until they were healed.
    And the Heirs of Carrión   continued to praise themselves.
Through all those lands   the tidings are made known;
the good King Alfonso   was grieved deeply.
word of it goes   to Valencia, the great city;
when they tell it   to My Cid the Campeador,
for more than an hour   he thought and pondered;
he raised his hand   and grasped his beard:

"I give thanks to Christ Who is lord of the world;
this is the honor they have done me, these Heirs of Carrión;
I swear by this beard, which no one ever has torn,
these Heirs of Carrión shall not go free with this;
as for my daughters I shall yet marry them well!"
My Cid was grieved with all his heart and soul,
as were Alvar Fáñez and all the court.
   Minaya mounted with Pedro Bermúdez
and Martín Antolínez, the worthy man of Burgos,
with two hundred knights whom My Cid sent;
he commanded them strictly to ride day and night
and bring his daughters to Valencia, the great city.
They do not delay to fulfill their lord's command;
they ride with all speed, they travel day and night;
they came to Gormaz, a strong castle,
and there in truth they paused for one night.
The news has arrived at San Esteban
that Minaya is coming for his two cousins.
The men of San Esteban, like the worthy folk that they are,
receive Minaya and all his men;
that night they presented Minaya with great tribute;
he did not wish to take it but thanked them deeply:
"Thanks, people of San Esteban, you conduct yourselves well.
For this honor you do us in this misfortune
My Cid the Campeador thanks you from where he is,
and here where I am I do the same.
By God Who is in heaven you will be well rewarded!"
All thank him for what he said and are content;
they go each to his place for the night's rest.
Minaya goes to see his cousins where they are.
Doña Elvira and Doña Sol, fix their eyes upon him:
"We are as glad to behold you as though you were the Creator,
and give thanks to Him that we are still alive.
When there is more leisure in Valencia, the great city,
we shall be able to recount all our grievance."

132

*Minaya and his cousins leave San Esteban. The Cid rides out
to receive them*

      Alvar Fáñez and the ladies   could not keep back the tears,
and Pedro Bermúdez   spoke to them thus:
"Doña Elvira and Doña Sol,   forget your cares now,
since now you are healed   and alive, and without other harm.
You have lost a good marriage,   you may yet have a better.
And we shall yet see the day   when you will be avenged!"
They spent that night there   amid great rejoicings.
The next day in the morning   they mounted their horses.
The people of San Esteban   went with them on their way
as far as the River Amor,   keeping them company;
there they said good-by   and turned back again,
and Minaya and the ladies   rode on ahead.
They crossed over Alcoceba,   on their right they left Gormaz;
where it is called Vadorrey   they came and went by;
in the village of Berlanga   they paused to rest.
Next day in the morning   they rode on again
as far as the place called Medinaceli   where they took shelter,
and from Medinaceli to Molina   they came in one day.
The Moor Abengalbón   was pleased in his heart;
he rode out to receive them   with good will;
he gave them a rich dinner   for the love of My Cid.
Then straightway they rode on   toward Valencia.
      The message came   to him who in good hour was born;
he mounts in haste   and rides out to receive them;
he went brandishing his weapons   and showing great joy.
My Cid rode up   to embrace his daughters;
he kissed them both   and began to smile:
"You are here, my daughters!   God heal you from harm!
I permitted your marriage   for I could not refuse it.
May it please the Creator   Who is in heaven
that I shall see you   better married hereafter.
God give me vengeance   on my sons-in-law of Carrión!"
Then the daughters   kissed their father's hands.
All rode into the city   brandishing their weapons;
Doña Jimena, their mother,   rejoiced at the sight of them.

He who was born in good hour   wished no delay;
he spoke in secret   with his own men.
He prepared to send a message   to King Alfonso in Castile.

133

The Cid sends Muño Gustioz to beg justice of the King. Muño finds the King in Sahagún and delivers his message. The King promises reparation

"Oh, stand before me, Muño Gustioz,   my loyal vassal.
In a good hour I brought you up   and placed you in my court!
Carry my message   to Castile, to King Alfonso;
kiss his hand for me   with all my heart and soul,
since I am his vassal   and he is my lord;
this dishonor they have done me,   these Heirs of Carrión,
I would have it grieve the King   in his heart and soul.
He married my daughters;   it was not I who gave them.
Since they have been deserted   and gravely dishonored,
whatever in this   may redound to our dishonor,
in small things or in great,   redounds to my lord's.
They have taken away wealth   beyond measure;
this should be reckoned in   with the other dishonor.
Let them be called to a meeting,   to a court or assembly,
and give me my due,   these Heirs of Carrión,
for I bear much rancor   within my heart."
Muño Gustioz   mounted quickly,
and two knights with him   to wait upon his will,
and with him squires   of the Cid's household.
They rode out of Valencia   and with all speed go forward;
they take no rest   by day or night.
In Sahagún   they found King Alfonso.
He is King of Castile   and King of León
and of Asturias   and the city of Oviedo;
as far as Santiago   he is the lord,
and the Counts of Galicia   serve him as their lord.
There Muño Gustioz,   as soon as he dismounts,
knelt to the saints   and prayed to the Creator;
he went up to the palace   where the court was,
and two knights with him   who serve him as their lord.
When they entered   into the midst of the court

the King saw them   and knew Muño Gustioz;
the King rose   and received them well.
Before King Alfonso   Muño Gustioz
went down on his knees   and kissed the King's feet.
"Grace, King of great kingdoms   that call you lord!
The Campeador   kisses your hands and feet;
he is your vassal   and you are his lord.
You married his daughters   with the Heirs of Carrión;
the match was exalted   because you wished it so.
You know already what honor   that marriage has brought us:
how the Heirs of Carrión   have affronted us,
how they beat and abused the daughters   of the Cid Campeador,
stripped them naked, lashed them with whips   and deeply
        dishonored them
and abandoned them   in the oak forest of Corpes,
left them to the wild beasts   and the birds of the mountain.
Behold, now his daughters   are once more in Valencia.
For this the Cid kisses your hands   as a vassal to his lord;
he asks you to call these Heirs   to a court or assembly;
the Cid has been dishonored   but you still more deeply;
he asks you to share his grief, King,   as you are wise,
and to help My Cid to receive reparation   from these Heirs of
        Carrión.
For more than an hour the King   thought, and said nothing.
"I tell you, in truth   this grieves my heart,
and in this I speak truth   to you, Muño Gustioz.
I married the daughters   to the Heirs of Carrión;
I did it for the best,   for his advantage.
Oh, that such marriage   never had been made!
As for myself and the Cid,   our hearts are heavy.
I must see he receives justice,   so may the Creator keep me!
I never expected   such a thing as this.
My heralds shall go   through all my kingdom
and call my court   to assemble in Toledo;
let all gather there,   counts and nobles;
and the Heirs of Carrión,   I shall bid them come there
and give just reparation   to My Cid the Campeador;
he shall not be left with a grievance   if I can prevent it.

134

The King convokes court in Toledo

"Say to the Campeador,   he who was born in good hour,
to be ready with his vassals   seven weeks from now
and come to Toledo;   that is the term I set for him.
Out of love for My Cid   I call this court together.
Give my greetings to all   and bid them take comfort;
this which has befallen them   shall yet redound to their honor."
Muño Gustioz took his leave   and returned to My Cid.
Alfonso the Castilian,   as he had promised,
took it upon himself.   He brooks no delays,
he sends his letters   to León and Santiago,
to the Portuguese   and the Galicians
and to those of Carrión   and the nobles of Castile,
proclaiming that their honored King   called court in Toledo,
that they should gather there   at the end of seven weeks;
and whoever should not come to the court,   he would hold no
          longer his vassal.
Through all his lands   thus the message ran,
and none thought of refusing   what the King had commanded.

135

Those of Carrión beg in vain that the King should not hold court.
The court convenes. The Cid arrives last. The King rides out
to receive him

And the Heirs of Carrión   are gravely concerned
because the King holds court   in Toledo;
they are afraid of meeting   My Cid the Campeador.
They ask aid and advice   of their relatives;
they beg the King   to excuse them from this court.
The King replied, "In God's name,   I shall not grant you this!
For My Cid the Campeador   will come there
and receive reparation,   for he has a grievance against you.
Whoever does not wish to obey   and come to my court,
let him quit my kingdom,   for he has incurred my displeasure."
The Heirs of Carrión   see that it must be done;

they ask aid and advice   from their relatives.
The Count Don García   took part in all this;
he was an enemy of My Cid   and sought always to do him harm,
and he gave counsel   to the Heirs of Carrión.
The appointed time came;   they must go to the court.
The good King Don Alfonso   arrived there first,
the Count Don Enrique   and the Count Don Ramón—
he was the father   of the good emperor—
the Count Don Fruela   and the Count Don Birbón.
And many others learned in law   came from all parts of the
      kingdom,
and the best came   from ali Castile.
The Count Don García,   Twisted-Mouth of Grañón,
and Alvar Díaz,   who governed Oca,
and Asur González   and Gonzalo Ansúrez
and Pedro Ansúrez,   you may know, arrived there,
and Diego and Fernando,   both of them came,
and a great crowd with them   came to the court
hoping to abuse   My Cid the Campeador.
   From all sides   they have gathered there.
He who in good hour was born   has not yet arrived,
and the King is not pleased,   for he is late.
On the fifth day   My Cid the Campeador came;
Alvar Fáñez   he sent on before him
to kiss the hands   of the King his lord
and tell him that the Cid   would arrive that evening.
When the King heard this   his heart was pleased;
with many knights   the King mounted
and went to receive   him who in good hour was born.
Well prepared,   the Cid comes with his men,
an imposing company   worthy of such a lord.
When he set eyes   on the good King Alfonso
My Cid the Campeador   flung himself to the ground,
wishing to humble himself   and do honor to his lord.
When the King saw this   in all haste he went forward:
"By Saint Isidore,   this shall not be so today!
Remain mounted, Cid,   or I shall be displeased;
we must greet each other   with heart and soul.
That which has befallen you   grieves my heart;
God grant you will honor the court   today with your presence!"

"Amen," said My Cid,   the good Campeador;
he kissed the King's hand   and then embraced him.
"I give thanks to God   for the sight of you, my lord.
I humble myself before you   and before the Count Ramón
and the Count Don Enrique   and all who are here with you;
God save your friends   and above all, you, my lord!
My wife, Doña Jimena,   that worthy lady,
kisses your hands,   as do my daughters,
and beg you to partake   of our grief in this, my lord."
The King answered,   "I do so, in God's name!"

136

The Cid does not enter Toledo. He keeps vigil in San Servando

The King has turned   and started toward Toledo;
My Cid did not wish   to cross the Tagus that night:
"Grace, my King,   may the Creator bless you!
Return as you will, my lord,   into the city,
and I with my men   shall lodge in San Serván;
the rest of my vassals   will arrive tonight.
I shall hold vigil   in that holy place;
tomorrow in the morning   I shall enter the city
and come to the court   before I have broken my fast."
The King said,   "I am pleased it should be so."
The King Don Alfonso   returns to Toledo;
My Cid Ruy Díaz   goes to stay in San Serván.
He sent for candles   to set on the altar;
he wishes to keep vigil   in this holy place,
praying to the Creator,   speaking with Him in secret.
Minaya and the other   good vassals who were there
were ready and waiting   when the morning came.

137

*The Cid's preparations, in San Servando, to go to the court.
The Cid goes to Toledo and enters the court. The King offers
him a place on his bench. The Cid refuses. The King opens
the session. He proclaims peace between the litigants.
The Cid makes his demands. He reclaims Colada and Tizón.
The Heirs of Carrión give up the swords. The Cid gives them
to Pedro Bermúdez and Martín Antolínez. The Cid's second*

demand: the dowry of his daughters. The Heirs find it
difficult to repay

As dawn drew near   they said matins and primes,
and Mass was finished   before the sun rose.
All My Cid's men   made precious offerings.
"You, Minaya Alvar Fáñez,   my sword arm,
come with me   and you, Bishop Don Jerome
and Pedro Bermúdez   and Muño Gustioz
and Martín Antolínez,   the worthy man of Burgos,
and Alvar Alvarez   and Alvar Salvadórez
and Martín Muñoz,   born under a good star,
and my cousin,   Félix Muñoz,
and let Mal Anda come with me,   who is learned in law,
and Galindo García,   the good warrior from Aragón;
and others to make up a hundred   from among my good vassals.
Put on your armor   over padded tunics;
put on your breastplates,   white as the sun,
furs and ermines   over your breastplates,
and draw the strings tight   that your weapons be not seen;
under your cloaks   gird the sweet keen swords.
In this manner   I would go to the court.
to demand justice   and say what I must say.
If the Heirs of Carrión   come seeking a quarrel,
if such a hundred are with me   it will not concern me."
All answered,   "Let it be so, lord."
All made ready   as he had commanded.
     He who in good hour was born   made no delay:
he covered his legs   in stockings of fine cloth
and over them he put shoes   of elaborate work.
He put on a woven shirt   as white as the sun,
and all the fastenings   were of silver and gold;
the cuffs fitted neatly   for he had ordered it thus.
Over this he put a tunic   of fine brocade
worked with gold   shining in every place.
Over these a crimson skin   with buckles of gold,
which My Cid the Campeador   wears on all occasions.
Over the furs he put   a hood of fine cloth
worked with gold   and set there
so that none might tear the hair   of My Cid the Campeador;
his beard was long   and tied with a cord,

for he wished to guard all his person   against insult.
On top of it all he wore   a cloak of great value;
all admired it,   as many as were there to see.
   With that hundred   whom he had bidden make ready
he mounted in haste   and rode out of San Serván;
thus prepared,   My Cid went to the court.
   At the outer door   they dismounted;
My Cid and his men   entered with due circumspection:
he goes in the middle   with his hundred around him.
When they saw enter   him who in good hour was born,
the good King Alfonso   rose to his feet,
and the Count Don Enrique   and the Count Don Ramón,
and all the others,   you may know, who were in the court.
With great honor they receive him   who in good hour was born.
Twisted-Mouth of Grañón   did not wish to stand,
nor all the rest of the band   of the Heirs of Carrión.
   The King took   My Cid by the hands:
"Come, sit down here   with me, Campeador,
on this bench   which was a gift from you;
though it annoy some,   you are of more worth than we."
Then he who had taken Valencia   thanked him much:
"Sit on your bench   as King and lord;
here I shall stay   among my men."
What the Cid said   pleased the King's heart.
Then My Cid sat down   on a bench of lathwork,
and the hundred who guard him   stand around him.
All who are in the court   are watching My Cid
and his long beard   tied with a cord;
his appearance   was in every way manly.
The Heirs of Carrión   can not look up for shame.
   Then the good King Alfonso   rose to his feet.
"Hear me, my vassals,   and the Creator bless you!
Since I have been King   I have not held more than two courts:
one was in Burgos   and the other in Carrión,
and this third   I open today in Toledo
for the love of My Cid,   who in good hour was born,
so that he may receive reparation   from the Heirs of Carrión.
They have done him great wrong,   as all of us know;
now let Counts Don Enrique and Don Ramón   be the judges,
and these other counts   who are not of the Heirs' company.

You who are learned in law,   fix well your attentions
and find out what is just,   for I would command no injustice.
Let us have peace today   on one side and the other.
I swear by Saint Isidore   that whoever disturbs my court
will be banished from my kingdom   and lose my favor.
I am of that side   on which justice is.
Now let My Cid the Campeador   make his demand,
and let us hear what they answer,   these Heirs of Carrión."
     My Cid kissed the King's hand   and rose to his feet.
"I thank you deeply,   as my King and lord,
for having held this court   for my sake.
Here is what I demand   of the Heirs of Carrión:
I am not dishonored   because they abandoned my daughters,
for since you, King, married them,   you will know what to do
          now;
but when they took my daughters   from Valencia, the great city,
from my heart and soul   I showed them much love.
I gave them two swords,   Colada and Tizón—
these I had taken   fighting like a man in the field—
that with them they might do themselves honor,   and you service;
when they abandoned my daughters   in the oak grove of Corpes
they wanted nothing more of me   and they lost my love;
let them give me my swords,   since they are no longer my
          sons-in-law."
     The judges granted,   "He is right in this."
The Count Don García said,   "We must speak of this."
Then the Heirs of Carrión   walked to one side
with all their kinsmen   and the company who were with them;
they discuss it quickly   and decide what to say:
"The Cid Campeador   does us a great favor
in not calling to account today   the dishonor of his daughters;
we can easily come to an arrangement   with King Alfonso.
Let us give him the swords,   since that will end his demand,
and when he has them   the court will adjourn;
and the Cid Campeador   will have no more claims upon us."
Having decided this,   they returned to the court.
"Grace, King Alfonso,   you who are our lord!
We cannot deny   he gave us two swords;
now that he claims them   and wants them back again,
we wish to return them   here before you."

They took out the swords,   Colada and Tizón;
they put them in the hands   of the King their lord.
The swords are drawn   and shine through all the court;
the hilts and guards   were all of gold.
All in the court   marveled to see them.
The King called My Cid   and gave him the swords;
he received the swords   and kissed the King's hands;
he returned to the bench   from which he had risen.
He held them in his hands   and looked on them both;
they could not have been false ones,   for he knew them well.
All his body was glad   and he smiled from his heart,
he raised his hand   and stroked his beard.
"By this beard,   which none has ever torn,
thus proceeds the avenging   of Doña Elvira and Doña Sol."
He summoned his nephew, Don Pedro,   called him by name.
He stretched out his arm   and gave him the sword Tizón:
"Take it, nephew,   it has found a better master."
To Martín Antolínez,   worthy man of Burgos,
he stretched out his arm   and gave him Colada:
"Martín Antolínez,   my worthy vassal,
take Colada;   I won it from a good lord,
from Ramón Berenguer   of Barcelona, the great city.
Therefore I give it to you   that you may care for it well.
I know that if the time   or the occasion should find you,
with it you will gain   honor and glory."
Martín Antolínez kissed his hand   and took the sword.
    Then My Cid the Campeador   got to his feet.
"I give thanks to the Creator   and to you, King and lord!
I am satisfied as to my swords,   Colada and Tizón.
I bear another grievance   toward the Heirs of Carrión:
When they took my daughters   from Valencia
I gave them three thousand marks   in gold and silver;
thus I did,   and they carried out their own business;
let them return me my riches,   since they are not my sons-in-law."
    God, they groaned then,   those Heirs of Carrión!
The Count Don Ramón said,   "Answer him, yes or no."
Then the Heirs of Carrión   answered thus:
"For this reason we gave his swords   to the Cid Campeador,
so that he should ask us no more   and end his demands."
Then the Count Don Ramón   answered them thus:

"If it please the King,   the court speaks thus:
You must render to the Cid   what he demands."
The good King said,   "I wish it to be so."
My Cid the Campeador   rose again to his feet.
"As for all the riches   which I gave you,
either return them to me   or give me an account."
    Then the Heirs of Carrión   walked to one side
but could reach no agreement,   for the riches were great
and the Heirs of Carrión   had spent them.
They returned to the court   and spoke their wish:
"He who took Valencia   presses us close;
since he sets such store   by what is ours
we shall pay him in lands   from the country of Carrión."
When they had made this plea   the judges said:
"If such pleases the Cid   we shall not refuse,
but to our judgment   it would appear better
that the money itself be repaid   here in the court."
    At these words   the King Don Alfonso spoke:
"This affair is plain   for us all to see,
and My Cid the Campeador   has a just claim.
I have two hundred   of those three thousand marks;
they were given me   by the Heirs of Carrión.
I wish to return them,   since the Heirs are ruined,
so that they may give them to My Cid,   who in good hour was
        born;
since they must pay them   I do not wish to keep them."
Fernando González spoke,   hear what he said:
"We do not have   any wealth in coin."
Then the Count Don Ramón   answered him:
"You have spent   the gold and the silver;
here is the judgment we give   before the King Don Alfonso:
You must pay in kind   and the Campeador accept it."
    The Heirs of Carrión   know what they must do.
You would have seen them lead in   so many swift horses,
so many fat mules,   so many palfreys of good breed,
so many good swords   with all their trappings,
and My Cid took them   at the court's evaluation.
All but the two hundred marks   which were King Alfonso's
the Heirs paid   to him who was born in good hour;

they had to borrow from elsewhere,   their own goods were not
    enough.
You may know, this time   they are sorely mocked.

138

His civil claim ended, the Cid proposes a challenge

These valued goods   My Cid has taken;
his men receive them   and take them in charge.
But when this was done   there was something still to do.
   "Grace, King and lord,   for the love of charity!
The greatest grievance   I cannot forget.
Let all the court hear me   and share in my injury;
the Heirs of Carrión   have so gravely dishonored me,
I cannot leave this case   without challenging them.

139

The Heirs are accused of infamy

   "Tell me, what did I deserve of you,   Heirs of Carrión,
in jest or in truth   or in any fashion?
Here before the court's judgment   this must be repaired.
Why have you torn   the webs of my heart?
When you went from Valencia   I gave you my daughters
with much honor   and countless riches;
if you did not want them,   treacherous dogs,
why did you take them   and their honors from Valencia?
Why did you wound them   with whips and spurs?
You left them alone   in the oak grove of Corpes
to the wild beasts   and the birds of the mountain.
For all you have done   you are infamous.
Let the court judge   if you must not give satisfaction."

140

Altercation between García Ordóñez and the Cid

The Count Don García   rose to his feet.
"Grace, King,   the best in all Spain!

My Cid has rehearsed himself   for this solemn court;
he has let his beard grow   and wears it long;
he strikes fear into some   and dread into others.
The Heirs of Carrión   are of such high birth
they should not want his daughters   even as concubines,
and who would command them to take them   as their lawful
    wives?
They did what was just in leaving them.
All that the Cid says   we value at nothing."
    Then the Campeador   laid his hand on his beard:
"Thanks be to God   Who rules heaven and earth,
my beard is long   because it grew at its own pleasure.
    "What have you, Count,   to throw in my beard?
It has grown at its own pleasure   since it began;
no son of woman   ever dared touch it,
no son of Moor or Christian   ever has torn it
as I tore yours, Count,   at the castle of Cabra.
When I seized Cabra   and you by your beard,
there was not a boy there   who did not tear out his wisp;
that which I tore out   has not yet grown again,
and I carry it here   in this closed pouch."

141

Fernando denies the accusation of infamy

    Fernando González   rose to his feet.
Hear what he said   in a loud voice:
"Cid, let your claim   here have an end;
all your goods   have been returned to you.
Let this suit   go no further between us.
We are by birth descended   from the Counts of Carrión:
we should marry the daughters   of kings or emperors;
we are worthy of more than the daughters   of petty squires.
We did what was just   when we abandoned your daughters;
our honor is greater than before,   you may know, and not less."

142

The Cid incites Pedro Bermúdez to make a challenge

My Cid Ruy Díaz   looked at Pedro Bermúdez.
"Speak, Mute Pedro,   knight who are so much silent!
They are my daughters,   but they are your first cousins;
when they say this to me   they pull your ears also.
If I answer,   you will have no chance to fight."

143

Pedro Bermúdez challenges Fernando

Then Pedro Bermúdez   started to speak,
but his tongue stumbles   and he cannot begin;
yet once he has begun,   know, he does not hesitate:
"I will tell you, Cid,   that is a custom of yours:
always in the courts   you call me Pedro the Mute!
But you know well   that I can do no better,
yet of what I can do   there shall be no lack.
    "You lie, Fernando,   in all you have said,
you gained great honor   through the Campeador.
Now I shall tell   of your ways:
Remember when we fought   near Valencia the great?
You begged the Campeador   to grant you the first blows.
You saw a Moor   and you went toward him,
but before he came upon you   you fled from there.
Had I not been there   the Moor would have used you roughly;
I passed you by   and encountered the Moor;
with the first blows   I overcame him.
I gave you his horse   and have kept all this secret
and told it to no one   until today.
Before My Cid and before all   you were heard to boast
that you killed the Moor   and had done a knightly deed,
and all believed you,   not knowing the truth.
Oh, you are pretty   and a vile coward!
Tongue without hands,   how do you dare to speak?

144

Pedro Bermúdez's challenge continues

"Speak, Fernando,   admit to this:
Do you not recall   the lion in Valencia,
the time when My Cid slept   and the lion got loose?
And you, Fernando,   what did you do in your terror?
You hid behind the bench   of My Cid the Campeador!
You hid there, Fernando,   and for that I now defame you.
We all stood around the bench   to shield our lord,
until My Cid woke,   who had taken Valencia;
he rose from the bench   and went toward the lion;
the lion bowed his head   and waited for My Cid,
let himself be taken by the neck   and went back into his cage.
And when the good Campeador   returned again
he saw his vassals   all around him;
he asked for his sons-in-law.   No one could find them!
I defy your body,   villain and traitor.
I will fight it out here   before King Alfonso
for the daughters of the Cid,   Doña Elvira and Doña Sol;
because you abandoned them   I now defame you.
They are women   and you are men;
in every way   they are worth more than you.
When the fight takes place,   if it please the Creator,
I will make you admit   that you are a traitor,
and all I have said here   I will prove true."
And between those two   the dispute thus ended.

145

Diego rejects the accusation of infamy

As for Diego González,   hear what he said:
"We are by birth   of the purest lineage of counts.
Oh, that this marriage   had never been made
that made us kin   of My Cid Don Rodrigo!
We still do not repent   that we abandoned his daughters;
let them sigh   as long as they live,
and what we have done to them   will be thrown in their faces
    always.

This I will maintain   against the bravest,
for in abandoning them   we have gained in honor."

146

Martín Antolínez challenges Diego González

Martín Antolínez   rose to his feet.
"Be silent, traitor,   mouth without truth!
You should not have forgotten   the episode of the lion;
you went out the door   into the courtyard
and hid yourself   behind the beam of the winepress;
since then you have not worn   that cloak and silk shirt again.
I shall maintain this by combat,   it shall not be otherwise,
because you abandoned   the Cid's daughters.
You may know, their honor   in every way exceeds yours.
When the fight is over,   with your own mouth you will admit
that you are a traitor   and have lied in all you have said."

147

Asur González enters the court

The talk was ended   between these two.
Asur González   entered the palace
with an ermine cloak   and his tunic trailing;
his face was red   for he had just eaten.
There was little prudence   in what he said:

148

Asur insults the Cid

"Ah, knights,   whoever has seen such evil?
Since when might we receive honor   from My Cid of Bivar!
Let him go now to the river Ubierna   and look after his mills
and be paid in corn   as he used to do!
Whoever suggested he marry   with those of Carrión?"

149

*Muño Gustioz challenges Asur González. Messengers from Navarre
and Aragón come to ask for the Cid's daughters for the sons of their
Kings. Alfonso consents to the new marriage. Minaya challenges
those of Carrión. Gómez Peláez accepts the challenge, but the King
fixes time and place only for those who had challenged before.
The King will help the Cid's three champions. The Cid offers parting
gifts to everyone.* (Lacuna. Prose of the Chronicle of Twenty Kings)
*The King leaves Toledo with the Cid. He asks the Cid to put his
horse through its paces*

Then Muño Gustioz   rose to his feet.
"Be silent, traitor,   evil and full of deceit!
First you have breakfast   and then you say your prayers
and all whom you kiss   in greeting smell your belches.
You speak no truth   to friend or lord;
you are false to all   and still more false to the Creator.
I want no portion in your friendship,
and I shall make you confess   that you are all that I say."
King Alfonso said,   "Let this case rest now.
Those who have made challenges   shall fight, as God may
        save me!"
    Thus they bring   this case to an end,
and behold, two knights   came into the court:
one was called Ojarra   and the other Iñigo Jiménez;
one is the herald of the Prince of Navarre
and the other the herald   of the Prince of Aragón.
They kiss the hands   of King Alfonso
and ask for the daughters   of My Cid the Campeador
to make them Queens   of Navarre and Aragón
as honored wives   blessed in marriage.
At this all the court   was hushed and listened.
My Cid the Campeador   rose to his feet.
"Grace, King Alfonso,   you are my lord!
I give thanks   to the Creator
for what Navarre and Aragón   have asked of me.
You married my daughters before   and not I;
here once again I say   my daughters are in your hands:
without your bidding   I shall do nothing."
The King rose   and bade the court be silent.

"Cid, perfect Campeador,   I ask that it meet your pleasure
that I should consent   to this marriage.
Let it be arranged   here and now in this court,
and thus may you increase   in fiefs, in estates and honor."
My Cid rose   and kissed the King's hands:
"As it pleases you,   I grant it, lord."
Then the King said,   "God reward you well!
And you, Ojarra,   and you, Iñigo Jiménez,
I consent   to this marriage
of the daughters of My Cid,   Doña Elvira and Doña Sol,
with the Princes   of Navarre and Aragón,
that the girls may be given to them   as their honored wives."
Ojarra and Iñigo Jiménez   rose to their feet;
they kissed the hands of King Alfonso
and afterwards those   of My Cid the Campeador;
they gave pledges   and swore the oaths,
that all might be   as had been said, or better.
This pleases many   there in the court
but gives no pleasure   to the Heirs of Carrión.
   Minaya Alvar Fáñez   rose to his feet.
"I beg grace of you,   as my King and lord,
and hope it may not displease   the Cid Campeador:
I have heard all speak their minds   here in the court,
and now I would say   something of my own."
The King said,   "Granted gladly.
Speak, Minaya,   say what you wish."
"I beg all the court   to hear what I say,
for I have great grievance against   the Heirs of Carrión.
I gave them my cousins   by the hand of King Alfonso;
they took them in the honor   and blessing of marriage;
My Cid the Campeador   gave them much wealth,
and then they left them   to our sorrow.
I challenge their bodies   as villains and traitors.
You are of the family   of the Beni-Gómez,
in which there have been counts   of worth and courage,
but now we know well   what your ways are.
I give thanks   to the Creator
that the Princes   of Navarre and Aragón
have asked for my cousins,   Doña Elvira and Doña Sol;
before, you had them for wives,   both, between your arms;

now you will kiss their hands   and call them 'My Lady,'
and do them service,   however it pains you.
I give thanks to God in heaven   and to this King Alfonso
that thus grows the honor   of My Cid the Campeador!
In every way   you are as I described you;
if there is any among you   to deny it and say no,
I am Alvar Fáñez,   a better man than any of you."
   Gómez Peláez   rose to his feet.
"To what end, Minaya, is all this talk?
There are many in this court   as brave as you,
and whoever should wish to deny this,   it would be to his harm.
If God wills   that we should come well out of this
you will have cause   to look to what you have said."
   The King said,   "Let this talk end;
let no one add a further claim   to this dispute.
Let the fight be tomorrow   when the sun rises,
the three against three   who challenged here in the court."
   The Heirs of Carrión   answered then:
"Give us more time, King   for we cannot do it tomorrow.
We have given our arms and horses   to the Campeador;
first we must go   to the lands of Carrión."
   The King said   to the Campeador:
"This battle shall take place   wherever you wish."
   Then My Cid said,   "I will not do as they say.
I would rather return to Valencia   than go to Carrión."
   Then the King said,   "It is well, Campeador.
Give me your knights   all well armed;
let them come with me,   I shall stand surety for them
and see to their safety   as a lord does for his good vassal,
and they will come to no harm   from count or noble.
Here in my court   I set the term:
Three weeks from now   in the plain of Carrión
let this battle take place,   and I there to see;
whoever is not there   forfeits the fight
and will be declared beaten   and called traitor."
   The Heirs of Carrión   accepted the decision.
   My Cid kissed   the King's hands:
"My three knights   are in your hands;
here I commend them to you   as my King and lord.

They are well prepared   to fulfill what they go for;
send them with honor to Valencia,   for the love of the Creator!"
Then the King answered,   "May God grant it be so."
    Then the Cid Campeador   drew back his hood,
his coif of fine cloth,   white as the sun,
and freed his beard   and undid the cord.
All who are in the court   cannot keep from staring at him.
He went to the Count Don Enrique   and the Count Don Ramón;
he embraced them closely   and asked them from his heart
to take of what he owned   whatever they wished.
These and the others   who had sided with him,
he begged them all   to take what they wished;
and some of them take   and others not.
He bade the King keep   the two hundred marks
and to take from him besides   as much as he wished.
    "I beg grace of you, King,   for the love of the Creator!
Now that all these things   have been provided for,
I kiss your hands   and with your grace, my lord,
would return to Valencia,   for painfully I took it."
    Then My Cid commanded that mounts and whatever they
needed should be given to the messengers from the Princes of
Navarre and Aragón, and he sent them on their way.
    Then King Alfonso mounted, with all the nobles of his court, to
ride out with My Cid as he left the town. And when they came to
Zocodover, the King said to My Cid, who was riding on his horse,
which was called Babieca. "Don Rodrigo, I should like to see you
urge your horse to his full speed, for I have heard much of him."
The Cid began to smile, and said, "Lord, here in your court are
many nobles and men who would be most pleased to do this; ask
them to race their horses." The King said to him, "Cid, I am contented with what you say, but nevertheless I wish you to race your
horse, to please me."

150

The King admires Babieca, but will not accept him as a gift.
The Cid's final orders to his three champions. The Cid returns to
Valencia. The King in Carrión. The time for the fight arrives.
Those of Carrión try to ban Colada and Tizón from the fight.
Those on the side of My Cid ask the King's help and ride out onto the

battlefield. The King names the judges for the combat and admonishes
those of Carrión. The judges prepare for the fight. The first
encounter. Pedro Bermúdez overcomes Fernando

Then the Cid set spur to his horse, who ran so swiftly that
all who were there marveled at his speed.
The King raised his hand   and crossed himself:
"I swear by Saint Isidore   of León
that in all our lands   there is not such another knight."
My Cid has ridden forward   on his horse
and come to kiss the hand   of his lord Alfonso:
"You have bidden me race   Babieca, my swift horse;
neither among Moors nor among Christians   is there such
          another;
I offer him to you as a gift.   Take him, my lord."
Then the King said,   "I do not wish it so;
if I take your horse from you   he will not have so fine a master.
Such a horse as this   needs such a rider as you
for routing Moors in the field   and pursuing them after the battle.
May the Creator not bless   whoever would take your horse from
          you,
since by means of your horse and you   we have all received
          honor."
Then they parted   and the court rode on.
The Campeador gave counsel   to those who were to fight:
"Martín Antolínez,   and you, Pedro Bermúdez
and Muño Gustioz,   my worthy vassal,
maintain the field   like brave men;
send me good news   to Valencia."
Martín Antolínez said,   "Why do you say this, lord?
We have accepted the charge,   it is for us to carry it out;
you may hear of dead men   but not of vanquished."
He who in good hour was born   was pleased at this;
he said good-by to them all   for they were his friends.
My Cid rode toward Valencia   and the King toward Carrión.
The three weeks of the delay   have all run out.
Behold, the Campeador's men   have come on the appointed day;
they wish to accomplish   what their lord had required of them.
They are protected   by Alfonso of León;
two days they waited   for the Heirs of Carrión.
The Heirs come well provided   with horses and arms,

and all their kin with them   and they had plotted
that if they might draw   the Campeador's men to one side
they should kill them in the field   for the dishonor of their lord,
They were bent on evil   had they not been prevented,
for great is their fear   of Alfonso of León.
    My Cid's men held vigil by their arms   and prayed to the
      Creator.
The night has passed   and the dawn breaks;
many of the nobles   have gathered together
to see this battle,   which will give them pleasure,
and above them all   is the King Don Alfonso,
to see that justice is done   and prevent any wrong.
The Campeador's men   have armed themselves;
all are of one mind,   since they serve the same lord.
In another place   the Heirs of Carrión arm,
the Count García Ordoñez   giving them advice.
They raised a complaint   and begged King Alfonso
that Colada and Tizón   should be banned from the combat
and that the Campeador's men   should not use them in the fight;
the Heirs deeply regretted   having given them back.
They begged this of the King,   but he would not consent:
"There in the court   you objected to none.
If you have good swords   they will serve you,
and the Campeador's men will be served   by theirs in the same
      way.
Rise and ride out on the field,   Heirs of Carrión;
you have no choice,   you must fight like men,
for the Campeador's men   will not lack for anything.
If you win on the field   you will have great honor,
and if you are beaten   put no blame on us,
for everyone knows   you have brought this on yourselves."
The Heirs of Carrión   now repent
of what they had done,   they regret it deeply;
they would have given all Carrión   not to have done it.
    The Campeador's men,   all three, are armed;
they have gone to see   the King Don Alfonso.
Then the Campeador's men   said to him:
"We kiss your hands,   as our King and lord;
be a faithful judge   today, between them and us;
aid us with justice   and allow no wrong.

The Heirs of Carrión   have all their kin with them;
we cannot tell   what they may or may not have plotted.
Our lord commended us   into your hands;
see that justice is done us,   for the love of the Creator!"
Then the King said,   "with my heart and soul."
   They bring out   their fine swift horses;
they blessed the saddles   and mounted briskly;
the shields with gilded bucklers   are at their necks;
they take up the lances   tipped with sharp steel,
each of the lances   with its pennon,
and all around them   many worthy men.
They rode out on the field,   where the markers were set.
The Campeador's men   are all in agreement
how each of them   would attack his man.
On the other side   are the Heirs of Carrión,
well accompanied,   for they have many kinsmen.
The King appointed judges   to decide what was just and what not,
and commanded that none should dispute   their yes or their no.
When they were in the field   King Alfonso spoke:
"Hear what I have to tell you,   Heirs of Carrión.
This fight should have been in Toledo   but you did not wish it so.
These three knights   of My Cid the Campeador
I have brought in my safekeeping   to the lands of Carrión.
Now fight justly   and try no trickery,
for if anyone attempts treachery   I am here to prevent it,
and he who tries it shall not be welcome   in all my kingdom."
The Heirs of Carrión   were much cast down at this.
   The judges and the King pointed out the markers,
then all the spectators went from the field   and stood around it.
They explained carefully   to all six of them
that he will be judged conquered   who leaves the field's borders.
All who stood about there   then drew back
the length of three lances   beyond the markers.
They drew lots for the ends of the field   —the sunlight in each
         half was the same—
and the judges went from the center   and they stood face to face,
the Cid's men facing   the Heirs of Carrión
and the Heirs of Carrión   facing the Campeador's men;
each of them   faced his own opponent;
they hugged their shields   over their hearts,

lowered the lances   wrapped in their pennons,
bent their faces   over their saddletrees,
dug their spurs   into their horses,
and the earth shook   as they leapt forward.
Each of them is bent   on his own opponent;
three against three   they have come together.
All who stand about   fear they will fall dead.
   Pedro Bermúdez,   who had made the first challenge,
came face to face   with Fernando González,
and fearlessly   they struck each other's shields.
Fernando González   pierced Don Pedro's shield
but drove through upon nothing   and touched no flesh,
and in two places   the shaft of his spear snapped.
Pedro Bermúdez remained firm,   he was not shaken by this;
he received one blow,   he struck another,
burst the shield's buckler   and broke it apart,
cut through it all,   nothing withstood him,
drove his lance through to the breast   close to the heart.
Fernando was wearing three suits of chain mail   and this saved
       him;
two folds were pierced   and the third held firm,
but the mail and the tunic   with its binding
were driven a hand's breadth   into the flesh,
so that the blood ran   from Fernando's mouth,
and the girth broke,   nothing held it;
Fernando was flung to the ground   over the horse's crupper.
It seemed to those who stood there   that he must be dead.
With that Pedro Bermúdez left his lance   and laid hand on his
       sword.
When Fernando González saw him   and knew Tizón,
he said, "I am beaten"   without waiting for the blow.
The judges agreed   and Pedro Bermúdez left him.

151

Martín Antolínez defeats Diego

   Don Martín and Diego González   struck with their spears;
such were the blows   that both were broken.
Martín Antolínez   set hand on his sword;

it is so bright and clean   that it shines over all the field.
It struck a blow   which caught him from the side;
it split apart   the top of the helmet
and it broke all   the helmet buckles;
it sheared the head mail   and to the coif came;
head mail and coif   it cut through them,
razed the hair of the head   and came to the flesh;
part fell to the field,   the rest remained.

When the precious Colada   had struck this blow
Diego González saw   that he should not escape with his soul;
he drew on the reins of his horse   to turn away;
he had a sword in his hand   but did not use it.
Then Martín Antolínez   struck him with his sword,
a blow with the flat of his sword,   not with the edge.
Then the Heir   shouted aloud:
"Bless me, glorious God,   lord, save me from this sword!"
Reining his horse,   keeping his distance from the sword,
he went beyond the marker;   Don Martín stayed on the field.

Then the King said,   "Come to my side;
with what you have done   you have won the fight."
The judges agree   that what he says is true.

152

*Muño Gustioz defeats Asur González. The father of the
Heirs declares the combat won. The Cid's men return
cautiously to Valencia. The Cid's joy. The second
marriage of the daughters. The bard ends his poem*

Two have been defeated;   I shall tell you of Muño Gustioz
and how his fight went   with Asur González.
They struck great blows   on each other's shields.
Asur González   was vigorous and brave;
he struck Muño Gustioz   on the shield,
drove through the shield   and to the armor,
then his lance cut through on nothing,   touching no flesh.
When this blow was struck,   Muño Gustioz returned another:
he split his shield   at the middle of the buckler,
nothing withstood his stroke,   he broke the armor;
he sheared it apart   and, though not close to the heart,
drove the lance and pennon   into the flesh

so it came out an arm's length   on the other side,
then he pulled on the lance   and twisted González from his saddle.
When he pulled out the lance   González fell to the ground,
and the spear shaft was red,   and the lance and the pennon.
All fear that González   is mortally wounded.
Muño Gustioz again seized his spear   and stood over him.
Gonzalo Ansúrez said,   "For the love of God, do not strike him!
The field is won   and the combat is finished!"
The judges said,   "We agree to this."
    The good King Don Alfonso   sent to despoil the field;
he took for himself   the arms that remained there.
The Campeador's men   departed in great honor;
with the aid of the Creator   they had won this fight.
Hearts were heavy   in the lands of Carrión.
    The King warned My Cid's men   to leave at night
so that none might attack them   and they have no cause for fear.
They, prudently,   ride night and day.
Behold, they have come to Valencia,   to My Cid the Campeador.
They had left in shame   the Heirs of Carrión
and fulfilled the duty   they owed to their lord;
My Cid the Campeador   was pleased at this.
The Heirs of Carrión   are in deep disgrace.
May whoever injures a good woman   and abandons her afterwards
suffer as great harm as this   and worse, besides.
    Let us leave this matter   of the Heirs of Carrión;
they take no pleasure   in what has befallen them.
Let us speak of him   who in good hour was born.
Great are the celebrations   in Valencia the great
because the Campeador's men   have won great honor.
Ruy Díaz their lord   stroked his beard:
"Praised be the King of Heaven,   my daughters are avenged!
Now freed of all debts   is their heritage in Carrión!
I shall marry them now without shame,   let it weigh on whom it
    will."
    The Princes of Navarre and Aragón   continued their suits,
and all met together   with Alfonso of León;
The wedding is performed   of Doña Elvira and Doña Sol;
the first marriage was noble   but this much more so;
to greater honor he weds them   than was theirs before.
See how he grows in honor   who in good hour was born;

his daughters are wives of the Kings   of Navarre and Aragón.
Now the Kings of Spain   are his kinsmen,
and all advance in honor   through My Cid the Campeador.
My Cid, the lord of Valencia,   passed from this world
on the Day of Pentecost,   may Christ give him pardon!
And may He pardon us all,   both the just and the sinners!
These were the deeds   of My Cid the Campeador,
and in this place   the song is ended.